Opening the Heavens

Accounts of Divine Manifestations, 1820–1844

Edited by John W. Welch with Erick B. Carlson

Brigham Young University Press
Provo, Utah

and

Deseret Book
Salt Lake City, Utah

This volume is part of the Joseph Fielding Smith Institute for Latter-day Saint History and BYU Studies series
Documents in Latter-day Saint History

Also included in this series:
Exemplary Elder: The Life and Missionary Diaries of Perrigrine Sessions, 1814–1893
The Personal Writings of Joseph Smith, rev. ed.

Cover and jacket design by Bjorn W. Pendleton.
Photographs in the text are courtesy John W. Welch, except where noted otherwise.

Opinions expressed in this publication are the opinions of the authors and their views should not necessarily be attributed to The Church of Jesus Christ of Latter-day Saints, Brigham Young University, BYU Studies, the Joseph Fielding Smith Institute for Latter-day Saint History, or Deseret Book Company. All revenues from this book will help fund future publications.

 To contact BYU Studies, write to 403 CB, Brigham Young University, PO Box 24098, Provo, Utah 84602, or visit http://byustudies.byu.edu. To contact the Joseph Fielding Smith Institute for Latter-day Saint History, write to 121 KMB, Brigham Young University, Provo, Utah 84602. To contact Deseret Book Company, write to P. O. Box 30178, Salt Lake City, Utah, 84130. This volume was prepared for publication by BYU Studies, with particular assistance from Jennifer Hurlbut, Heather M. Seferovich, Marny K. Parkin, and Jed Woodworth.

Library of Congress Cataloging-in-Publication Data

Opening the heavens : accounts of divine manifestations, 1820–1844 / edited by John W. Welch with Erick B. Carlson.
p. cm. — (Documents in Latter-day Saint history)
Includes bibliographical references and index.
ISBN 0-8425-2607-2 (hardcover : alk. paper)
1. Church of Jesus Christ of Latter-day Saints—History—19th century—Sources. 2. Church of Jesus Christ of Latter day Saints—Doctrines—History—19th century. I. Welch, John W. (John Woodland) II. Title. III. Series.

BX8611.O64 2005
289.3—dc22

2004030859

Printed in the United States of America
10 9 8 7 6 5 4 3 2 1

Contents

Introduction

This volume strives to bring together, for the first time, all the known contemporaneous documents relevant to the key events of the Restoration of the gospel of Jesus Christ that were accompanied by divine manifestations: Joseph Smith's First Vision; the coming forth of the Book of Mormon; the restoration of priesthood authority; the heavenly visions received by Joseph Smith and his companions; the bestowal of keys and the outpouring of holy gifts in the Kirtland Temple; and the mantle of the Prophet Joseph Smith passing to Brigham Young. These events are the backbone of The Church of Jesus Christ of Latter-day Saints.[1] If these visions, revelations, miracles, and powers were, in fact, received as claimed, nothing surpasses the importance of knowing so.

The plan of this book is to allow the documents, as much as possible, to stand for themselves. Contemporaneous documents are critical in getting close to these key events. Firsthand accounts uniquely convey the spirit of these important occasions. Eyewitness reports provide precious details that help modern readers construct a vivid image of what transpired. Although only a verbal shadow of greater realities, and although inevitably some reporters were more observant, better informed, or more articulate than others, the words of close participants offer us the feeling of almost being there.

Each document in this collection is presented, unvarnished, according to the established standards of documentary editing. Since 1959, *BYU Studies* has been a premiere voice of the Latter-day Saint academic community. This quarterly journal has placed great emphasis on the technical editing and groundbreaking publication of scores of newly discovered documents from the founding years of the Restoration. These scholarly treatments of primary sources have earned acclaim for their accuracy, reliability, and objectivity. Four of the chapters in this book appeared initially in *BYU Studies*. They have been brought up to date in this new anthology, particularly with assistance by Erick B. Carlson and Jed Woodworth. Several documents are published here for the first time.

The impact of these documents is cumulative. As one reads account after account, the truth becomes clearer. Together these accounts reliably reveal the inside story of the rise, progress, and faith of the Latter-day Saints in the 1820s, 1830s, and 1840s. As an author and editor, I have enjoyed reading these documents over and over, word by word. As these accounts become more and more familiar to me, I notice especially their honesty, integrity, consistency, and forthrightness. In transcribing, proofreading, and typesetting these powerful declarations, all who have worked on this volume have come closer to hearing the individual voices of these original writers. I recommend reading these crucial accounts slowly, thoughtfully, and at times even out loud. Listen as these numerous witnesses offer their own testimonies.

The value of these documents is immeasurable. In the history of world religions, no other body of foundational documentation rivals it for its immediacy and size. Think, for example, how few documents have survived from the time of Mohammed. And what would New Testament scholars give for a single letter from Mary about the raising of Lazarus? Or a diary entry by someone who was present when Jesus was baptized by John in the Jordan River? Or a brief report from Peter to the Twelve about what he had just seen and heard on the Mount of Transfiguration? In the case of Joseph Smith and the key events of the Restoration, we enjoy, by comparison, an overwhelming abundance.

The function of this book is inviting. Each of these historical documents beckons to be understood. In a literal sense, documents do not speak for themselves, for they have no tongues, lips, or vocal chords that cry from their fragile paper and faded ink. Instead, readers supply the determinative factors of seeing (or not seeing), of catching (or missing), of emphasizing (or ignoring). Readers are invited to evaluate these primary documents themselves, to know what they say (or do not say).

We start with Joseph Smith's First Vision. Dean Jessee presents an up-to-date collection of all the known accounts that come from the lifetime of Joseph Smith: ten accounts in thirteen documents, including his journal entries, his letters to newspapermen, and the recordings of others who heard Joseph Smith relate his experience. As James Allen and I then show, these accounts are coherent, credible, and more consistent than some people have surmised. With the full record in view, one sees that Joseph Smith shared his Vision experience with intimate groups, the general public, enquiring visitors, and newspapermen, and he did so spontaneously at their request. The details supplied by each of these accounts add to our understanding and enhance the credibility of the Prophet's story, as he addressed the particular interests and needs of various audiences.

The second key event in the Restoration, the coming forth of the Book of Mormon, stands as a monumental miracle. One biblical scholar under whom I studied once compared the dictation of the Book of Mormon by Joseph Smith to Moses' parting of the Red Sea. And rightly so. Dictating to his scribes, Joseph Smith translated the Book of Mormon in less than two and a half months, from April 7 to the end of June 1829. The historical documents corroborate this feat. The data they contain are organized here into an annotated chronology. Over two hundred accounts from participants and observers reveal that many people immediately sensed the importance of the work that was taking place. More than any other Restoration event, the story of the golden plates piqued the public's interest. Years later, all Joseph Smith's closest associates, especially his wife Emma and the three Book of Mormon witnesses Oliver Cowdery, Martin Harris, and David Whitmer, continued to tell remarkably consistent stories and never wavered in their testimonies of the Book of Mormon.

A surprisingly large number of early Church documents record crucial details about the restoration of both the Aaronic and Melchizedek Priesthoods. Brian Cannon and the *BYU Studies* staff introduce the seventy extant documents that deal directly with priesthood restoration. Half of these documents come from Joseph Smith and Oliver Cowdery, the key participants. Nearly thirty other people voiced their understanding of what they had heard, often from Joseph or Oliver themselves. While May 15, 1829, the date of the Aaronic Priesthood restoration, is well known, the timing of the restoration of the Melchizedek Priesthood is less clear. Though Cannon acknowledges that the documentary record has a few gaps, the available sources support the traditional dating of the Melchizedek Priesthood restoration—June 1829. The sources further reveal that early Church members realized the necessity of priesthood authority and understood that it had been restored from heaven.

During his prophetic ministry, Joseph Smith enjoyed the gift of seeing visions and receiving visitations. From the time he was fourteen, he garnered strength and knowledge from his communions with the heavens, which allowed him to establish the Church. He enjoyed numerous visions, and each was unique. Students of LDS Church history will readily recognize Joseph Smith's most famous visions. But Alexander Baugh goes well beyond those well-known few and places them against the expansive backdrop of many additional heavenly manifestations, some of which were simultaneously shared by multiple recipients. The impressive total truly evinces the opening of the heavens.

Several Church members experienced some of these heavenly manifestations with Joseph Smith at the time of the dedication of the Kirtland Temple in early 1836. If only one isolated account existed of the great pentecostal outpouring that accompanied this spiritual season, one might wonder about that account's accuracy or credibility. As Steven Harper shows, however, several people went home and independently recorded what they had just seen, heard, felt, and experienced. The keys that were restored on April 3, 1836, by Moses,

Elias, and Elijah, constitute the basis of divinely authorized temple building, temple sealings, and temple work for the dead among the Latter-day Saints. This set of six contemporaneous documents brings attentive readers into the sacred spheres of the temple.

Fortunately, one more divinely manifested key event in the Restoration assures that these priesthood powers were not lost when Joseph Smith died. Many Church members reported that they received a strong spiritual witness that convinced them that Joseph Smith's mantle of authority had fallen on Brigham Young. Long an integral part of Mormon history, the story of Brigham Young appearing and speaking as Joseph Smith at a public meeting on August 8, 1844, had not been fully documented until the late 1990s. Lynne Jorgensen has exhaustively chronicled all known written testimonies of this singular event. These statements, now numbering 121, come from a great variety of individuals and document the mantle experience as an extraordinary collective spiritual experience. Men and women, old and young, attest to it in greater numbers than ever was previously suspected. Some wrote as early as fall 1844; others wrote of this indelible experience much later. Several witnesses bore their testimony orally to their descendants, who then recorded their words.

Finally, this book ends with a bibliography of additional documentary articles, covering other important events in early Church history, that have also been published in *BYU Studies*. Many of these publications have been prepared for publication in collaboration with the Church Archives of The Church of Jesus Christ of Latter-day Saints. These studies deal with the organization of the Church in 1830, the commencement of missionary work, and many other steps in the Restoration. Further documentary publications will soon be forthcoming from BYU Studies and the Joseph Fielding Smith Institute for Latter-day Saint History, including the *Joseph Smith Papers* and a volume of the Relief Society's organizational documents.

Here are the documentary exhibits of the Restoration. They are open for the world to read. They may be judged without hesitation.

The outlook for this book of documents is enduring. It may be one of the most important LDS Church history books you will ever read, for these original, eyewitness accounts will outlive us all.

They will endure. A generation from now, few people will care how various historians in our day have interpreted the past. Academic reputations are short-lived, and popular memories are even shorter. Voguish theories come and go; they offer their flash of light on certain corners and fade out of fashion. But the original documents convey testimonies that will always be of utmost interest.

In submitting his Wentworth letter to the publisher of the *Chicago Democrat*, Joseph Smith made only one request: "All that I shall ask at his hands, is, that he publish the account entire, ungarnished, and without misrepresentation."[2] In this book, we hope to have complied with this request. Here are six major collections of key Restoration documents, in their fullness, authenticity, and veracity.

Notes

1. "We declare without equivocation that God the Father and His Son, the Lord Jesus Christ, appeared in person to the boy Joseph Smith. . . . Our whole strength rests on the validity of that vision. It either occurred or it did not occur. If it did not, then this work is a fraud. If it did, then it is the most important and wonderful work under the heavens. . . . But this glorious vision was but the beginning of a series of manifestations that constitute the early history of this work. . . . [T]here followed the coming forth of the Book of Mormon. . . . There followed the restoration of the priesthood—first, of the Aaronic under the hands of John the Baptist, who had baptized Jesus in Jordan. Then came Peter, James, and John, Apostles of the Lord, who conferred in this age that which they had received under the hands of the Master with whom they walked, even 'the keys of the kingdom of heaven,' with authority to bind in the heavens that which they bound on earth (see Matt. 16:19). Subsequently came the bestowal of further priesthood keys under the hands of Moses, Elias, and Elijah." Gordon B. Hinckley, "The Marvelous Foundation of Our Faith," *Ensign* 31 (November 2002): 78.

2. Dean C. Jesse, ed. and comp., *The Personal Writings of Joseph Smith*, rev. ed. (Salt Lake City: Deseret Book; Provo, Utah: Brigham Young University Press, 2002), 242.

The Earliest Documented Accounts of Joseph Smith's First Vision

Dean C. Jessee

The direct, primary historical sources pertaining to Joseph Smith's First Vision now known total ten accounts in thirteen documents—eight produced or reported in the first person by or from the Prophet himself, and five contemporary reports by others who heard him relate his experience and recorded what he said in the third person. The purpose of this essay is to identify and present these accounts and to consider the context in which each was created.

First Vision Accounts in Context

From the beginning of his public ministry, Joseph Smith struggled to record the events of his life. The conditions in which he was raised did not facilitate a literary course—indigent circumstances, which required the labor of the entire Smith family to meet their daily needs, limited Joseph's schooling. He later wrote that he had been "deprived of the bennefit of an education suffice it to say I was mearly instructid in reading writing and the ground rules of Arithmatic which const[it]uted my whole literary acquirements."[1]

In light of Joseph's background it is not surprising that the boy Joseph did not record his experience that spring morning in 1820 after returning from the grove. Years later, still harboring misgivings about his inability to communicate with the pen, he yearned for deliverance from what he called "the little narrow prison . . . of paper pen and ink and a crooked broken scattered and imperfect language."[2] And his writings contain occasional apologies for his lack of writing skill. Even had his literary preparations been ideal, the at times violent forces that dogged him continually were persisently present to disrupt his record-keeping ventures. Large gaps in his record coincide with periods of unrest and disorder in his life, and many important portions of his life's story were either lost or never recorded.

Another factor that shaped the historiography of the First Vision grew out of the process of developing a record-keeping plan in the early years of the Church. Problems of defining the nature, scope, and format of a historical record limited the resultant archive, as did difficulties in finding and retaining capable clerical help to assist in the creation and care of the records. Following the 1830 revelation that initiated Joseph Smith's record keeping,[3] procedures for creating pertinent records were slow to develop. It took several years marked by false starts before a format was settled on and the enduring work began on Joseph Smith's History of the Church. As evidence of the challenges he faced, by October 29, 1839, when Joseph left Nauvoo for Washington, D.C., to present the Missouri grievances of his people before the federal government, only fifty-nine pages of his history had been written; and six days after his departure, his scribe, James Mulholland, died.[4] After returning to Nauvoo in March 1840, Joseph lamented the passing of his "faithful scribe" and expressed disappointment that an adequate record of his Washington trip had not been kept: "I depended on Dr. Foster to keep my daily journal during this journey, but he has failed me."[5] Robert B. Thompson, who was appointed General Church Clerk on October 3, 1840, continued writing the history where Mulholland left off. Nevertheless, only sixteen pages were added to the manuscript before he too met an untimely death on August 27, 1841.[6]

By the time Willard Richards was appointed General Church Clerk and private secretary to the Prophet in December 1841, a mere 157 pages had been written of a history that would eventually number more than two thousand pages. The History would not be finished during his lifetime.[7] Shortly before his death, Joseph Smith summarized the problems that had beset his record keeping:

> Since I have been engaged in laying the foundation of the Church of Jesus Christ of Latter Day Saints I have been prevented in various ways from continuing my Journal and the History, in a manner satisfactory to myself, or in justice to the cause. Long imprisonments, vexatious and long continued Law Suits – The treachery of some of my Clerks; the death of others; and the poverty of myself and Brethren from continued plunder and driving, have prevented my handing down to posterity a connected memorandum of events desirable to all lovers of truth.

He added, "I have continued to keep up a Journal in the best manner my circumstances would allow, and dictate for my history from time to time, as I have had opportunity, so that the labors and sufferings of the first Elders and Saints of this last kingdom might not wholly be lost to the world."[8] The historical records of Joseph Smith's life, including those pertaining to the First Vision, are best seen in this context.

First Vision Accounts Produced by the Prophet

The Church records created during these turbulent years include eight documents in which Joseph Smith recorded details of his initial vision experience. Three of these, with minor differences, are duplications of a previous one.

1. Joseph Smith History Account (1832)

The first of these was a six-page autobiographical narrative intended to be a history of his life and "an account of the rise of the Church," but it was abruptly discontinued evidently when a new plan for the history was conceived. It was written most probably between February and November 1832 on three leaves that were later cut from the ledger book that contained them.[9] This 1832 narrative contains the earliest known account of Joseph's First Vision and the only account in his own handwriting. In the transcription that follows, the boldfaced type indicates the portions of the document written in the

Prophet's handwriting. The remainder is in the handwriting of his secretary, Frederick G. Williams. Underlining is reproduced from the original document. Editorial marks include angle brackets < > to indicate above-the-line insertions. Strikeouts are shown by ~~strike-outs~~. Brackets [ ] indicate editorial comments.

> A History of the life of Joseph Smith Jr. an account of his marvilous experience and of all the mighty acts which he doeth in the name of Jesus Ch[r]ist the son of the living God of whom he beareth record and also an account of the rise of the church of Christ in the eve of time according as the Lord brough<t> forth and established by his hand <firstly> he receiving the testamony from on high seccondly the ministering of Angels thirdly the reception of the holy Priesthood by the ministring of Aangels to adminster the letter of the Gospel – < – the Law and Commandments as they were given unto him – > and the ordinencs, forthly a confirmation and reception of the high Priesthood after the holy order of the son of the living God power and ordinence from on high to preach the Gospel in the administration and demonstration of the spirit **the Kees of the Kingdom of God confered upon him and the continuation of the blessings of God to him &c – I was born in the town of Charon [Sharon] in the <State> of Vermont North America on the twenty third day of December AD 1805 of goodly Parents who spared no pains to instruct<ing> me in <the> christian religion at the age of about ten years my Father Joseph Smith Siegnior moved to Palmyra Ontario [now Wayne] County in the State of New York and being in indigent circumstances were obliged to labour hard for the support of a large Family having nine chilldren and as it required the exertions of all that were able to render any assistance for the support of the Family therefore we were deprived of the bennifit of an education suffice it to say I was mearly instructtid in reading ~~and~~ writing and the ground <rules> of Arithmatic which constuted my whole literary acquirements. At about the age of twelve years my mind become seriously imprest [p. 1] with regard to the all importent concerns for the wellfare of my immortal Soul which led me to searching the scriptures believeing as I was taught, that they contained the word of God thus applying myself to them and my intimate acquaintance with those of differant denominations led me to marvel excedingly for I discovered that <they did**

not ~~adorn~~> ~~instead~~ of adorn~~ing~~ their profession by a holy walk and Godly conversation agreeable to what I found contained in that sacred depository this was a grief to my Soul thus from the age of twelve years to fifteen I pondered many things in my heart concerning the sittuation of the world of mankind the contentions and divi[si]ons the wicke[d]ness and abominations and the darkness which pervaded the ~~of the~~ minds of mankind my mind become excedingly distressed for I become convicted of my sins and by searching the scriptures I found that ~~mand~~ <mankind> did not come unto the Lord but that they had apostatised from the true and liveing faith and there was no society or denomination that built upon the gospel of Jesus Christ as recorded in the new testament and I felt to mourn for my own sins and for the sins of the world for I learned in the scriptures that God was the same yesterday to day and forever that he was no respecter to persons for he was God for I looked upon the sun the glorious luminary of the earth and also the moon rolling in their magesty through the heavens and also the stars shining in their courses and the earth also upon which I stood and the beast of the field and the fowls of heaven and the fish of the waters and also man walking forth upon the face of the earth in magesty and in the strength of beauty whose power and intiligence in governing the things which are so exceding great and [p. 2] marvilous even in the likeness of him who created ~~him~~ <them> and when I considired upon these things my heart exclaimed well hath the wise man said ~~the~~ <it is a> fool <that> saith in his heart there is no God my heart exclaimed all all these bear testimony and bespeak an omnipotant and omnipreasant power a being who makith Laws and decreeeth and bindeth all things in their bounds who filleth Eternity who was and is and will be from all Eternity to Eternity and when I, considered all these things and that <that> being seeketh such to worship him as worship him in spirit and in truth therefore I cried unto the Lord for mercy for there was none else to whom I could go and ~~to~~ obtain mercy and the Lord heard my cry in the wilderness and while in <the> attitude of calling upon the Lord <in the 16th year of my age> a piller of ~~fire~~ light above the brightness of the sun at noon day come down from above and rested upon me and I was filled with the spirit of god and the <Lord> opened the heavens upon me and I saw the Lord and he spake unto me saying Joseph <my son> thy sins

marvilous even in the likeness of him who created ~~him~~ them
and when I considered upon these things my heart exclai
-med well hath the wise man said ~~the~~ it is a fool that saith in
his heart there is no God my ~~heart~~ heart exclaimed all all
these bear testimony and bespeak an omnipotent
and omnipreasant power a being who makith Laws and
decreeth and bindeth all things in their bounds who
filleth Eternity who was and is and will be from all
Eternity to Eternity and when I considered all these things
and that that being seeketh such to worship him as wors
-hip him in spirit and in truth therefore I cried unto
the Lord for mercy for there was none else to whom I could go and
to obtain mercy and the Lord heard my cry in the wilderne
ss and while in the attitude of calling upon the Lord in the 16th year of my age a piller of
~~fire~~ light above the brightness of the sun at noon day
come down from above and rested upon me and I was filled
with the spirit of god and the Lord opened the heavens upon
me and I saw the Lord and he spake unto me saying
Joseph my son thy sins are forgiven thee. go thy way walk in my
statutes and keep my commandments behold I am the
Lord of glory I was crucifyed for the world that all those
who believe on my name may have Eternal life behold the world
lieth in sin ~~and~~ at this time and none doeth good no
not one they have turned asside from the gospel and
keep not my commandments they draw near to me with their
lips while their hearts are far from me and mine anger
is kindling against the inhabitants of the earth to visit
them acording to thier ungodliness and to bring to pass
that which hath been spoken by the mouth of the prophe
-ts and apostles behold and lo I come quickly as it was
written of me in the cloud clothed in the glory of my Father
and my soul was filled with love and for many days I
could rejoice with great Joy and the Lord was with me
but could find none that would believe the hevenly
vision nevertheless I pondered these things in my heart
~~about that time my mother and~~ but after many days

Courtesy Church Archives, The Church of Jesus Christ of Latter-day Saints

Joseph Smith's first written account of the First Vision in his own handwriting, History, 1832, Joseph Smith Letterbook 1, p. 3.

are forgiven thee. go thy <way> walk in my statutes and keep my commandments behold I am the Lord of glory I was crucifyed for the world that all those who believe on my name may have Eternal life <behold> the world lieth in sin ~~and~~ at this time and none doeth good no not one they have turned asside from the gospel and keep not <my> commandments they draw near to me with their lips while their hearts are far from me and mine anger is kindling against the inhabitants of the earth to visit them acording to th[e]ir ungodliness and to bring to pass that which <hath> been spoken by the mouth of the prophets and Ap[o]stles behold and lo I come quickly as it [is] written of me in the cloud <clothed> in the glory of my Father and my soul was filled with love and for many days I could rejoice with great Joy and the Lord was with me but [I] could find none that would believe the hevnly vision nevertheless I pondered these things in my heart.[10]

2 and 3. Joseph Smith Journal Account (November 9, 1835) and History (1834–1836)

On November 27, 1832, Joseph began keeping a journal, a practice which he continued to the end of his life. Although the beginning pages were in his own handwriting, much of the journal was dictated to scribes and was eventually written entirely from their own observations. Extensive gaps in the journal must be bridged so far as possible, by reference to outside sources. Under the date of November 9, 1835, Joseph dictated to his clerk Warren Parrish the visit of a religious eccentric by the name of Robert Matthias who claimed to be Joshua, a Jewish minister. During the ensuing conversation Joseph Smith related his early vision experience:

> After I had made some remarks concerning the bible I commenced giving him a relation of the circumstances connected with the coming forth of the book of Mormon, as follows – being wrought up in my mind, respecting the subject of religion and looking at the different systems taught the children of men, I knew not who was right or who was wrong and I considered it of the first importance that I should be right, in matters that involve eternal consequ[e]nces; being thus perplexed in mind I retired to the silent

> grove and bow[e]d down before the Lord, under a realising sense that he had said (if the bible be true) ask and you shall receive knock and it shall be opened seek and you shall find and again, if any man lack wisdom let him ask of God who giveth to all men libarally and upbradeth not; information was what I most desired at this time, and with a fixed determination to obtain it, I called upon the Lord for the first time, in the place above stated or in other words I made a fruitless attempt to p[r]ay, my toung seemed to be swolen in my mouth, so that I could not utter, I heard a noise behind me like some person walking towards me, I strove again to pray, but could not, the noise of walking seemed to draw nearer, I sprung up on my feet, ~~and~~ [p. 23] and looked around, but saw no person or thing that was calculated to produce the noise of walking, I kneeled again my mouth was opened and my toung liberated, and I called on the Lord in mighty prayer, a pillar of fire appeared above my head, it presently rested down upon me ~~head~~, and filled me with Joy unspeakable, a personage appeard in the midst of this pillar of flame which was spread all around, and yet nothing consumed, another personage soon appeard like unto the first, he said unto me thy sins are forgiven thee, he testifyed unto me that Jesus Christ is the Son of God; <and I saw many angels in this vision> I was about 14 years old when I received this first communication.[11]

This journal entry soon found its way into another historical document, Joseph Smith's History 1834–1836. This particular effort to compile materials toward the publication of a history of the Church had commenced in October 1834 when Oliver Cowdery, the editor of the Church's magazine, the *Messenger and Advocate*, began publishing the history in Kirtland, Ohio. The work appeared serially, initially in the form of correspondence between Cowdery and William W. Phelps, and was anticipated to become a "full history of the rise of the church of the Latter Day Saints, and the most interesting parts of its progress, to the present time." It was announced at the outset by the editor that "our brother J. Smith Jr. has offered to assist us. Indeed, there are many items connected with the fore part of this subject that render his labor indispensible. With his labor and with authentic documents now in our possession, we hope to render this a pleasing and agreeable narrative."[12] In the series of eight letters that followed, Cowdery presented various historical events, beginning in the October 1834 issue with an account of the priesthood restoration, and concluding in the October 1835 issue with the visit of Joseph Smith to Harmony, Pennsylvania, shortly after receiving the Book of Mormon plates in 1827.

Toward the end of 1835, Frederick G. Williams and Warren Parrish, two of Joseph Smith's clerks, then copied the eight Cowdery-Phelps letters into a large record book that was designated to become "a history" of Joseph's life. Following the transcription of the eight published letters, the format of the anticipated "history" was changed when another clerk, Warren Cowdery, began copying Joseph Smith's journal into the record, commencing with the September 22, 1835, entry. Warren prefaced his addition with this statement: "Here the reader will observe that the narrative assumes a different form. The subject of it becoming daily more and more noted, the writer deemed it proper to give a plain, simple, yet faithful narration of every important item in his every-day-occurrences."[13] There then follows 142 pages of Joseph Smith's journal entries covering the period from September 22, 1835, to January 18, 1836, when the record was abruptly discontinued, evidently as a different approach to organizing the history again became desirable. Except for a few grammatical alterations to the text, including introductory sentences changed from first to third person, the entry included by Warren Cowdery for November 9, 1835, in which Joseph related his 1820 Vision experience to Matthias, is a duplication of the Joseph Smith journal entry for the same date (document 2 above); and thus these two accounts are listed together.

> The conversation soon turned upon the subject of Religion, and after the subject of this narrative [Joseph] had made some remarks concerning the bible, he commenced giving him [Matthias] a relation of the circumstances, connected with the coming forth of the Book of Mormon, which were nearly as follows. ["]Being wrought up in my mind respecting the subject of Religion, and looking at the different systems taught the children of men, I knew not who was right or who was wrong, but considered it of the first importance to me that I should be right, in matters of so much moment,

> matter[s] involving eternal consequences. Being thus perplexed in mind I retired to the silent grove and there bowed down before the Lord, under a realizing sense, (if the bible be true) ask and you shall receive, knock and it shall be opened, seek and you shall find, and again, if any man lack wisdom, let [him ask] of God who giveth to all men liberally & upbraideth not. Information was what I most desired [p. 120] at this time, and with a fixed determination to obtain it, I called on the Lord for the first time in the place above stated, or in other words, I made a fruitless attempt to pray My tongue seemed to be swoolen in my mouth, so that I could not utter. I heard a noise behind me like some one walking towards me: I strove again to pray, but could not; the noise of walking seemed to draw nearer; I sprang upon my feet and looked round, but saw no person, or thing that was calculated to produce the noise of walking. I kneeled again, my mouth was opened and my tongue loosed; I called on the Lord in mighty prayer. A pillar of fire appeared above my head; which presently rested down upon me, and filled me with unspeakable joy. A personage appeared in the midst of this pillar of flame, which was spread all around and yet nothing consumed. Another personage soon appeared like unto the first: he said unto me thy sins are forgiven thee. He testified also unto me that Jesus Christ is the son of God. I saw many angels in this vision. I was about 14 years old when I received this first communication.["][14]

4 and 5. Joseph Smith Journal Account (November 14, 1835) and History (1834–1836)

On November 14, 1835, five days after the Robert Matthias visit, Joseph Smith related his vision to Erastus Holmes, from Newberry, Clermont County, Ohio, who had called "to make inquiry about the establishment of the church of Latter-day Saints and to be instructed more perfectly in our doctrine." Joseph dictated a summary of his conversation with Holmes that his clerk Warren Parrish recorded in the Prophet's journal.

> I commenced and gave him a brief relation of my experience while in my [p. 36] juvenile years, say from 6 years old up to the time I received the first visitation of Angels which was when I was about 14. years old and also the visitations that I received afterward,

> concerning the book of Mormon, and a short account of the rise and progress of the church.[15]

In a fashion similar to the inclusion of the November 9 journal entry explained above, the November 14 entry was also incorporated into the 1834–1836 History as follows:

> He (Smith) commenced and gave him a brief relation of his experience while in his youthful days, say from the age of six years up to the time he received the first visitation of Angels which was when he was about 14 years old. He also gave him an account of the revelations he ~~had~~ afterward received concerning the coming forth of the Book of Mormon, and a succinct account of the rise and progress of the church up to this date.[16]

6. Joseph Smith History Account (1838)

In March 1838, Joseph Smith moved his family and the center of the Church from Kirtland, Ohio, to Far West, Missouri. Only a month later, on April 27, 1838, while engaged in establishing a new gathering place for the Latter-day Saints in Caldwell County, Missouri, he again began writing a history of the Church "from the earliest period of its existance,"[17] this time with the help of his counselor Sidney Rigdon and his secretary George W. Robinson. Only a few pages of the history were written before the project was suspended, no doubt due to the conditions that forced the removal of the Latter-day Saints from the state later that year and resulted in the imprisonment of the Prophet. Not until June 1839, shortly after his arrival in Illinois from his six-month confinement in Missouri, and again only one month after moving his family into a small log house near Commerce (later Nauvoo), Illinois, to begin anew the process of community building, did Joseph Smith turn his attention back to writing the History. Dictating to James Mulholland,[18] Joseph continued the work he had commenced the previous year—a work that some sixty years later would be edited by the Church historian Brigham H. Roberts and published in six volumes as the *History of the Church of Jesus Christ of Latter-day Saints, Period I, History of Joseph Smith, the Prophet, by Himself.* The beginning pages of this history were in time canonized as scripture in the Pearl of Great Price and contain the best-known account of the First Vision.[19]

> Owing to the many reports which have been put in circulation by evil disposed and designing persons in relation to the rise and progress of the Church of <Jesus Christ of> Latter day Saints, all of which have been designed by the authors thereof to militate against its character as a church, and its progress in the world; I have been induced to write this history so as to disabuse the publick mind, and put all enquirers after truth into possession of the facts as they have transpired in relation both to myself and the Church as far as I have such facts in possession.
>
> In this history I will present the various events in relation to this Church in truth and righteousness as they have transpired, or as they at present exist, being now the eighth year since the organization of said Church. I was born in the year of our Lord One thousand Eight hundred and five, on the twenty third day of December, in the town of Sharon, Windsor County, State of Vermont. <see page Note A 131>[20] My father Joseph Smith Senior[21] left the State of Vermont and moved to Palmyra, Ontario, (now Wayne) County, in the State of New York when I was in my tenth year. <or thereabout.>
>
> In about four years after my father's arrival at Palmyra, he moved with his family into Manchester in the same County of Ontario. His family consisting of eleven souls, namely, My Father Joseph Smith, My Mother Lucy Smith whose name previous to her marriage was Mack, daughter of Solomon Mack, My brothers Alvin (who <died Nov. 19th: 1823 in the 25 year of his age.> ~~is now dead~~) Hyrum, Myself, Samuel – Harrison, William, Don Carloss, and my Sisters Soph[r]onia, Cathrine and Lucy. Sometime in the second year after our removal to Manchester, there was in the place where we lived an unusual excitement on the subject of religion. It commenced with the Methodists, but soon became general among all the sects in that region of country, indeed the whole district of Country seemed affected by it and great [p. 1] multitudes united themselves to the different religious parties, which created no small stir and division among the people, Some crying, "Lo here" and some Lo there. Some were contending for the Methodist faith, Some for the Presbyterian, and some for the Baptist; for notwithstanding the great love which the converts to these different

faiths expressed at the time of their conversion, and the great Zeal manifested by the respective Clergy who were active in getting up and promoting this extraordinary scene of religious feeling in order to have everybody converted as they were pleased to call it, let them join what sect they pleased yet when the Converts began to file off some to one party and some to another, it was seen that the seemingly good feelings of both the Priests and the Converts were ~~mere pretence~~ more pretended than real, for a scene of great confusion and bad feeling ensued; Priest contending against priest, and convert against convert so that all their good feelings one for another (if they ever had any) were entirely lost in a strife of words and a contest about opinions.

I was at this time in my fifteenth year. My Fathers family w~~as~~<ere> proselyted to the Presbyterian faith and four of them joined that Church, Namely, My Mother Lucy, My Brothers Hyrum, Samuel Harrison, and my Sister Soph[r]onia.

During this time of great excitement my mind was called up to serious reflection and great uneasiness, but though my feelings were deep and often pungent, still I kept myself aloof from all these parties though I attended their several meetings <as often> as occasion would permit. But in process of time my mind became somewhat partial to the Methodist sect, and I felt some desire to be united with them, but so great was the confusion and strife amongst the different denominations that it was impossible for a person young as I was and so unacquainted with men and things to come to any certain conclusion who was right and who was wrong. My mind at different times was greatly excited ~~for~~ the cry and tumult were so great and incessant. The Presbyterians were most decided against the Baptists and Methodists, and used all their powers of either reason or sophistry to prove their errors, or at least to make the people think they were in error. On the other hand the Baptists and Methodists in their turn were equally Zealous in endeavoring to establish their own tenets and disprove all others.

In the midst of this war of words, and tumult of opinions, I often said to myself, what is to be done? Who of all these parties are right? Or are they all wrong together? And if any one of them be right which is it? And how shall I know it?

While I was laboring under the extreme difficulties caused by the contests of these parties of religionists, I was one day reading the Epistle of James, First Chapter and fifth verse which reads, "If any of you lack wisdom, let him ask of God, that giveth to all men liberally and upbraideth not, and it shall be given him." Never did any passage of scripture come with more power to the heart of man [than] this did at this time to mine. It seemed to enter with great force into every feeling of my heart. I reflected on it again and again, knowing that if any person needed wisdom from God, I did, for how to act I did not know and unless I could get more wisdom than I then had would never know, for the teachers of religion of the different sects understood the same [p. 2] passage of Scripture so differently as <to> destroy all confidence in settling the question by an appeal to the Bible. At length I came to the Conclusion that I must either remain in darkness and confusion or else I must do as James directs, that is, Ask of God. I at last came to the determination to ask of God, concluding that if he gave wisdom to them that lacked wisdom, and would give liberally and not upbraid, I might venture. So, in accordance with this, my determination to ask of God, I retired to the woods to make the attempt. It was on the morning of a beautiful clear day early in the spring of Eightteen hundred and twenty. It was the first time in my life that I had <made> such an attempt, for amidst all <my> anxieties I had never as yet made the attempt to pray vocally.

After I had retired into the place where I had previously designed to go, having looked around me and finding myself alone, I kneeled down and began to offer up the desires of my heart to God, I had scarcely done so, when immediately I was <siezed> upon by some power which entirely overcame me and <had> such astonishing influence over me as to bind my tongue so that I could not speak. Thick darkness gathered around me and it seemed to me for a time as if I were doomed to sudden destruction. But exerting all my powers to call upon God to deliver me out of the power of this enemy which had siezed upon me, and at the very moment when I was ready to sink into despair and abandon myself to destruction, not to an imaginary ruin but to the power of some actual being from the unseen world who had such a marvelous power as I had never before felt in any being. Just at this moment of great alarm I saw a pillar <of> light exactly over my head above the brightness of the sun, which descended ~~gracefully~~ gradually untill it fell upon me. It no sooner appeared than I found myself delivered from the enemy which held me bound. When the light rested upon me I saw two personages (whose brightness and glory defy all description) standing above me in the air. One of <them> spake unto me calling me by name and said (pointing to the other) "This is my beloved Son, Hear him." My object in going to enquire of the Lord was to know which of all the sects was right, that I might know which to join. No sooner therefore did I get possession of myself so as to be able to speak, than I asked the personages who stood above me in the light, which of all the sects was right, (for at this time it had never entered into my heart that all were wrong) and which I should join. I was answered that I must join none of them, for they were all wrong, and the Personage who addressed me said that all their Creeds were an abomination in his sight, that those professors were all Corrupt, that "they draw near to me with their lips but their hearts are far from me, They teach for doctrines the commandments of men, having a form of Godliness but they deny the power thereof." He again forbade me to join with any of them and many other things did he say unto me which I cannot write at this time. When I came to myself again I found myself lying on <my> back looking up into Heaven. <B See Note P 132 {When the light had departed I had no strength, but soon recovering in some degree. I went home. – & as I leaned up to the fire piece. Mother Enquired what the matter was. I replied never mind all is well. – I am well enough off. I then told my mother I have learned for myself that Presbyterianism is not true. – It seems as though the adversary was aware at a very early period of my life that I was destined to prove a disturber & [p. 132] annoyer of his kingdom, or else why should the powers of Darkness combine against me, why the oppression & persecution that arose against me, almost in my infancy?}>[22] Some few days after I had this vision I happened to be in company with one of the Methodist Preachers who was very active in the before mentioned religious excitement and conversing with him on the subject of religion I took occasion to give him an account of the vision which I had had. I was greatly surprised at his behaviour, he treated my communication not only lightly but with great contempt, saying it was all of the Devil, that there was no such thing as visions or revelations in these days, that all such things had ceased with the [p. 3] apostles and that there never would be any more of them. I soon found however that my telling the story had excited a great deal of prejudice against me among professors of religion and was the cause of great persecution which continued to increase and though I was an obscure boy only between fourteen and fifteen years of age <or thereabouts,> and my circumstances in life such as to make a boy of no consequence in the world, yet men of high standing would take notice sufficient~~ly~~ to excite the public mind against me and create a hot persecution, and this was common <among> all the sects: all united to persecute me. It has often caused me ~~m~~ serious reflection both then and since, how very strange it was that an obscure boy of a little over fourteen years of age and one too who was doomed to the necessity of obtaining a scanty maintainance by his daily labor should be thought a character of sufficient importance to attract the attention of the great ones of the most popular sects of the day so as to create in them a spirit of the bitterest persecution and reviling. But strange or not, so it was, and was often cause of great sorrow to myself. However it was nevertheless a fact, that I had had a vision. I have thought since that I felt much like ~~as~~ Paul ~~did~~ when he made his defence before King Aggrippa and related the account of the vision he had when he saw a light and heard a voice, but still there were but few who believed him, some said he was dishonest, others said he was mad, and he was ridiculed and reviled, But all this did not destroy the reality of his vision. He had seen a vision he knew he had, and <all> the persecution under Heaven could not make it otherwise, and though they should persecute him unto death yet he knew and would know to his latest breath that he had both seen a light and heard a voice speaking unto him and all the world could not make him think or believe otherwise. So it was with me, I had actualy seen a light and in the midst of that light I saw two personages, and they did in reality speak <un>to me, or one of them did, And though I was hated and persecuted for saying that I had seen a vision, yet it was true and while they were persecuting me reviling me and speaking all manner of evil against me falsely for so saying, I was led to say in my heart, why persecute <me> for telling the truth? I have actually seen a vision, "and who am I that I can withstand God" or why does the world think to make me deny what I have actually seen, for I had seen a vision, I knew it, and I knew that God knew it, and I could not deny it, neither dare I do it, at least I knew that by so doing <I> would offend God and come under condemnation. I had now got my mind satisfied so far as the sectarian world was concerned, that it was not my duty to join with any of them, but continue as I was untill further directed, ~~for~~ I had found the testimony of James to be true.[23]

7 and 8. Joseph Smith Account for Barstow History (1842) and for Rupp History (1843)

In 1842, John Wentworth, the twenty-six-year-old editor of the Chicago *Democrat*, requested from Joseph Smith a "sketch of the rise, progress, persecution and faith of the Latter-day Saints" for a friend of his, George Barstow, who was writing a history of New Hampshire. Joseph Smith responded to his request, and even included a short account of his First Vision with the response. The historical sketch supplied to Wentworth was apparently not used by Barstow, but it was published in the March 1, 1842, issue of the Nauvoo paper *Times and Seasons*, the first published account of the Vision in the United States.

> I was born in the town of Sharon Windsor co., Vermont, on the 23d of December, A.D. 1805. When ten years old my parents removed to Palmyra New York, where we resided about four years, and from thence we removed to the town of Manchester.
>
> My father was a farmer and taught me the art of husbandry. When about fourteen years of age I began to reflect upon the importance of being prepared for a future state, and upon enquiring the plan of salvation I found that there was a great clash in religious sentiment; if I went to one society they referred me to one plan, and another to another; each one pointing to his own particular creed as the summum bonum of perfection: considering that all could not be right, and that God could not be the author of so much confusion I determined to investigate the subject more fully, believing that if God had a church it would not be split up into factions, and that if he taught one society to worship one way, and administer in one set of ordinances, he would not teach another principles which were diametrically opposed. Believing the word of God I had confidence in the declaration of James; "If any man lack wisdom let him ask of God who giveth to all men liberally and upbraideth not and it shall be given him," I retired to a secret place in a grove and began to call upon the Lord, while fervently engaged in supplication my mind was taken away from

> the objects with which I was surrounded, and I was enwrapped in a [p. 706] heavenly vision and saw two glorious personages who exactly resembled each other in features, and likeness, surrounded with a brilliant light which eclipsed the sun at noon-day. They told me that all religious denominations were believing in incorrect doctrines, and that none of them was acknowledged of God as his church and kingdom. And I was expressly commanded to "go not after them," at the same time receiving a promise that the fulness of the gospel should at some future time be made known unto me.[24]

In 1843, Israel Daniel Rupp, a Pennsylvania historian, planned to publish a work containing the history and doctrine of religious organizations in the United States as written by representatives of each church. In July 1843, Rupp requested from Joseph Smith a chapter on the Mormons. The book containing the Prophet's response was published the following year under the title *An Original History of the Religious Denominations at Present Existing in the United States.* The portion of the chapter dealing with the First Vision was essentially a reprint of the statement sent to John Wentworth the previous year with very slight changes.

> When about fourteen years of age, I began to reflect upon the importance of being prepared for a future state; and upon inquiring the place of salvation, I found that there was a great clash in religious sentiment; if I went to one society they referred me to one place, and another to another; each one pointing to his own particular creed as the "summum bonum" of perfection. Considering that all could not be right, and that God could not be the author of so much confusion, I determined to investigate the subject more fully, believing that if God had a church, it would not be split up into factions, and that if he taught one society to worship one way, and administer in one set of ordinances, he would not teach another principles which were diametrically opposed. Believing the word of God, I had confidence in the declaration of James, "If any man lack wisdom let him ask of God, who giveth to all men liberally and upbraideth not, and it shall be given him."
>
> I retired to a secret place in a grove, and began to call upon the [p. 404] Lord. While fervently engaged in supplication, my mind was taken away from the objects with which I was surrounded, and

> I was enrapt in a heavenly vision, and saw two glorious personages, who exactly resembled each other in features and likeness, surrounded with a brilliant light, which eclipsed the sun at noonday. They told me that all the religious denominations were believing in incorrect doctrines, and that none of them was acknowledged of God as his church and kingdom. And I was expressly commanded to "go not after them," at the same time receiving a promise that the fulness of the gospel should at some future time be made known unto me.[25]

Contemporaneous First Vision Accounts by Others

In addition to the seven accounts of Joseph Smith's Vision directly formulated by him, five others were written by witnesses who heard him relate the experience and reported what he said during his lifetime.

1. Orson Pratt Report (1840)

As one of the members of the Quorum of the Twelve Apostles who assisted in introducing Mormonism in the British Isles in 1840–41, Orson Pratt arrived in Edinburgh, Scotland, in May 1840. To arouse interest in his message, Pratt published in September 1840 a pamphlet titled *A[n] Interesting Account of Several Remarkable Visions, and of the Late Discovery of Ancient American Records* in which he drew from his personal acquaintance with Joseph Smith for details of the Prophet's First Vision. The significance of the Pratt pamphlet is that it was the first time an account of the Vision had been published. The Pratt pamphlet shows some evidence that it was used by the Prophet to formulate the letter he sent to John Wentworth in 1842.

> When somewhere about fourteen or fifteen years old, he [Joseph Smith] began seriously to reflect upon the necessity of being prepared for a future state of existence: but how, or in what way, to prepare himself, was a question, as yet, undetermined in his own mind: he perceived that it was a question of infinite importance, and that the salvation of his soul depended upon a correct understanding of the same. He saw, that if he understood not the [p. 3] way, it would be impossible to walk in it, except by chance; and the thought of resting his hopes of eternal life upon chance, or

uncertainties, was more than he could endure. If he went to the religious denominations to seek information, each one pointed to its particular tenets, saying – "This is the way, walk ye in it;" while, at the same time, the doctrines of each were, in many respects, in direct opposition to one another. It, also, occurred to his mind, that God was not the author of but one doctrine, and therefore could not acknowledge but one denomination as his church; and that such denomination must be a people, who believe, and teach, that one doctrine, (whatever it may be,) and build upon the same. He then reflected upon the immense number of doctrines, now, in the world, which had given rise to many hundreds of different denominations. The great question to be decided in his mind, was – if any one of these denominations be the Church of Christ, which one is it? Until he could become satisfied, in relation to this question, he could not rest contented. To trust to the decisions of fallible man, and build his hopes upon the same, without any certainty, and knowledge, of his own, would not satisfy the anxious desires that pervaded his breast. To decide, without any positive and definite evidence, on which he could rely, upon a subject involving the future welfare of his soul, was revolting to his feelings. The only alternative, that seemed to be left him, was to read the Scriptures, and endeavour to follow their directions. He, accordingly, commenced perusing the sacred pages of the Bible, with sincerity, believing the things that he read. His mind soon caught hold of the following passage: – "If any of you lack wisdom, let him ask of God, that giveth to all *men* liberally, and upbraideth not; and it shall be given him." – James i.5. From this promise he learned, that it was the privilege of all men to ask God for wisdom, with the sure and certain expectation of receiving, liberally; without being upbraided for so doing. This was cheering information to him: tidings that gave him great joy. It was like a light shining forth in a dark place, to guide him to the path in which he should walk. He, now, saw that if he inquired of God, there was, not only, a possibility, but a probability; yea, more, a certainty, that he should [p. 4] obtain a knowledge, which, of all the doctrines, was the doctrine of Christ; and, which, of all the churches, was the church of Christ. He, therefore, retired to a secret place, in a grove, but a short distance from his father's house, and knelt down, and began to call upon the Lord. At first, he was severely tempted by the powers of darkness, which endeavoured to overcome him; but he continued to seek for deliverance, until darkness gave way from his mind; and he was enabled to pray, in fervency of the spirit, and in faith. And, while thus pouring out his soul, anxiously desiring an answer from God, he, at length, saw a very bright and glorious light in the heavens above; which, at first, seemed to be at a considerable distance. He continued praying, while the light appeared to be gradually descending towards him; and, as it drew nearer, it increased in brightness, and magnitude, so that, by the time that it reached the tops of the trees, the whole wilderness, for some distance around, was illuminated in a most glorious and brilliant manner. He expected to have seen the leaves and boughs of the trees consumed, as soon as the light came in contact with them; but, perceiving that it did not produce that effect, he was encouraged with the hopes of being able to endure its presence. It continued descending, slowly, until it rested upon the earth, and he was enveloped in the midst of it. When it first came upon him, it produced a peculiar sensation throughout his whole system; and, immediately, his mind was caught away, from the natural objects with which he was surrounded; and he was enwrapped in a heavenly vision, and saw two glorious personages, who exactly resembled each other in their features or likeness. He was informed, that his sins were forgiven. He was also informed upon the subjects, which had for some time previously agitated his mind, viz. – that all the religious denominations were believing in incorrect doctrines; and, consequently, that none of them was acknowledged of God, as his church and kingdom. And he was expressly commanded, to go not after them; and he received a promise that the true doctrine – the fullness of the gospel, should, at some future time, be made known to him; after which the vision withdrew, leaving his mind in a state of calmness and peace, indescribable.[26]

2. 1842 Orson Hyde Report (1842)

At the 1840 April conference in Nauvoo, Elder Orson Hyde spoke of a prophecy calling him to "a great work" among the Jews, a work that would "prepare the way" for the gathering of that people. He felt the time had come to fulfill that prophecy by visiting the Jews of Europe and the Holy Land, whereupon the conference authorized him to proceed on his mission. After arriving in London, he wrote, with Joseph Smith's sanction, a treatise on the faith, doctrine, and history of the Church. Continuing this journey, he stopped in Germany where he studied German, then proceeded on to the Middle East, where he dedicated the Holy Land for the return of the Jews. Returning to Germany in 1842, he translated his book into German and published it in Frankfurt before returning to the United States. Written "in something the manner" of Orson Pratt's 1840 pamphlet, Hyde's work was titled *Ein Ruf aus der Wüste*, the first time an account of the First Vision was published in a foreign language.[27]

> When he had reached his fifteenth year, he began to think seriously about the importance of preparing for a future [existence]; but it was very difficult for him to decide how he should go about such an important undertaking. He recognized clearly that it would be impossible for him to walk the proper path without being acquainted with it beforehand; and to base his hopes for eternal life on chance or blind uncertainty would have been more than he had ever been inclined to do.
>
> He discovered the world of religion working under a flood of errors which by virtue of their contradictory opinions and principles laid the foundation for the rise of such different sects and denominations whose feelings toward each other all too often were poisoned by hate, contention, resentment and anger. He felt that there was only one truth and that those who understood it correctly, all understood it in the same way. Nature had endowed him with a keen critical intellect and so he looked through the lens of reason and common sense and with pity and contempt upon those systems of religion, which were so opposed to each other and yet were all obviously based on the scriptures.
>
> After he had sufficiently convinced himself to his own satisfaction that darkness covered the earth and gross darkness [covered] the nations, the hope of ever finding a sect or denomination that was in possession of unadulterated truth left him.
>
> Consequently he began in an attitude of faith his own investigation of the word of God [feeling that it was] the best way to arrive at a knowledge of the truth. He had not proceeded very far

in this laudable endeavor when his eyes fell upon the following verse of St. James [1:5]: "If any of you lack wisdom, let him ask of God, that giveth to all men liberally, and upbraideth not; and it shall be given him." He considered this scripture an authorization for him to solemnly call upon his creator to present his needs before him with the certain expectation of some success. And so he began to pour out to the Lord with fervent determination the earnest desires of his soul. On one occasion, he went to a small grove of trees near his father's home and knelt down before God in solemn prayer. The adversary then made several strenuous efforts to cool his ardent soul. He filled his mind with doubts [p. 15] and brought to mind all manner of inappropriate images to prevent him from obtaining the object of his endeavors; but the overflowing mercy of God came to buoy him up and gave new impetus to his failing strength. However, the dark cloud soon parted and light and peace filled his frightened heart. Once again he called upon the Lord with faith and fervency of spirit.

At this sacred moment, the natural world around him was excluded from his view, so that he would be open to the presentation of heavenly and spiritual things. Two glorious heavenly personages stood before him, resembling each other exactly in features and stature. They told him that his prayers had been answered and that the Lord had decided to grant him a special blessing. He was also told that he should not join any of the religious sects or denominations, because all of them erred in doctrine and none was recognized by God as his church and kingdom. He was further commanded, to wait patiently until some future time, when the true doctrine of Christ and the complete truth of the gospel would be revealed to him. The vision closed and peace and calm filled his mind.[28]

3. Levi Richards Report (1843)

A native of Massachusetts, Levi Richards was the older brother of Willard Richards, Church historian and Joseph Smith's secretary, and a cousin of Brigham Young. Levi was a skilled Thompsonian physician. Shortly after his conversion to Mormonism in 1835, he moved to Kirtland, Ohio. He was present during the difficulties that beset the Church in Ohio and Missouri and assisted in the evacuation of the Saints when they were forced out of Missouri in 1838–39. After resettling with the Church at Nauvoo, Illinois, he continued his medical practice, served as surgeon general of the Nauvoo Legion, and was elected a member of the city council. On Sunday June 11, 1843, after Joseph Smith had spoken to the Saints gathered near the temple, he announced that George J. Adams would lecture that evening on the Book of Mormon. Levi Richards attended the lecture and reported the following:

> At 6 PM. heard Eld. G J Adams upon the book of Mormon proved from the 24th, 28th & 29 of Isaiah that the everlasting covenant which was set up by Christ & the apostles had been broken . . . – Pres. J. Smith bore testimony to the same – saying that when he was a youth he began to think about these things but could not find out which of all the sects were right – he went into the grove &, enquired of the Lord which of all the sects were right – he received for answer that none of them were right, that they were all wrong, & that the Everlasting covenant was broken – he said he understood the fulness of the Gospel from beginning to end – & could Teach it & also the order of the priesthood in all its ramifications – Earth & hell had opposed him & tryed to destroy him – but they had not done it & they <never would.>[29]

4. David Nye White Report (1843)

A visitor to Nauvoo who heard Joseph Smith speak of his Vision was David Nye White, the senior editor of the *Pittsburgh Weekly Gazette*. On August 28, 1843, while traveling through the western frontier of America, White stopped in Illinois to visit the Prophet. Two days later he wrote his perceptions of the "far-famed kingdom of the 'Latter-day Saints,'" which were published in the September 15 issue of the *Gazette*. Included in the article was his report of what the Prophet told him about his 1820 Vision. Joseph said,

> The Lord does reveal himself to me. I know it. He revealed himself first to me when I was about fourteen years old, a mere boy. I will tell you about it. There was a reformation among the different religious denominations in the neighborhood where I lived, and I became serious, and was desirous to know what Church to join.

> While thinking of this matter, I opened the [New] Testament promiscuously on these words, in James, "Ask of the Lord who giveth to all men liberally and upbraideth not." I just determined I'd ask him. I immediately went out into the woods where my father had a clearing, and went to the stump where I had stuck my axe when I had quit work, and I kneeled down, and prayed, saying, "O Lord, what Church shall I join?" Directly I saw a light, and then a glorious personage in the light, and then another personage, and the first personage said to the second, "Behold my beloved Son, hear him." I then, addressed this second person, saying, "O Lord, what Church shall I join." He replied, "don't join any of them, they are all corrupt." The vision then vanished, and when I come to myself, I was sprawling on my back; and it was some time before my strength returned. When I went home and told the people that I had a revelation, and that all the churches were corrupt, they persecuted me, and they have persecuted me ever since. They thought to put me down, but they hav'nt succeeded, and they can't do it.[30]

5. Alexander Neibaur Report (1844)

Another Latter-day Saint who heard Joseph Smith relate his First Vision experience and recorded what he heard was Alexander Neibaur, a convert originally from Germany. After studying dentistry in his native land, Neibaur moved to England, where he set up his practice in Preston. When Latter-day Saint missionaries arrived in England in 1837, Neibaur was among the first converts to the Church. Four years later he and his family migrated to Nauvoo, Illinois, where he continued his dental practice, and as a linguist, taught German and Hebrew to Joseph Smith. On May 24, 1844, Neibaur, still struggling to master the English language, recorded in his diary what the Prophet had said that day while Neibaur visited in Joseph's home.

> Br Joseph tolt us the first call he had a Revival meeting his mother & Br & Sist got Religion, he wanted to get Religion too wanted to feel & ~~sho~~ shout like the Rest but could feel nothing, opened his Bible ~~f~~ the first Passage that struck him was if any man lack wisdom let him ask of God who giveth to all men liberallity & upbraidat[h] not went into the Wood to pray kneelt himself down his tongue was closet cleavet to his roof – could utter not a word,

> felt easier after a while = saw a fire towards heaven came near & nearer saw a personage in the fire light complexion blue eyes a piece of white cloth drawn over his shoulders his right arm bear after a wile a other person came to the side of the first Mr Smith then asked must I join the Methodist Church = No = they are not my People, ~~all~~ have gone astray there is none that doeth good no not one, but this is my Beloved son harken ye him, the fire drew nigher Rested upon the tree enveloped him [*page torn*] comforted Indeavoured to arise but felt uncomen feeble = got into the house told the Methodist priest, [who] said this was not a age for God to Reveal himself in Vision Revelation has ceased with the New Testament.[31]

Other Likely Contemporaneous First Vision Accounts

Should the foregoing historical sources pertaining to Joseph Smith's First Vision seem sparse in some respects, those gaps are primarily the result of inadequate record keeping of his many conversations and discourses on the subject or related topics. If record keeping in the harsh literary environment of the early years of the Church had commenced at the level of efficiency that it later achieved, no doubt other contemporary reports of the Vision would be available. This conclusion is strongly suggested by occasions when Joseph is known to have talked about the experience, but no official report was made.

For example, William Phelps, writing to his wife, Sally, in Missouri in June 1835, noted that "President Smith preached last Sabbath, and I gave him the text: 'This is my belovd Son; hear ye him!' He preached one of the greatest sermons I ever heard – it was about 3½ hours long – and unfolded more mysteries than I can write at this time."[32]

A year later, in November 1836, Parley P. Pratt informed the Saints in Canada that one of the most interesting meetings he ever attended had been held recently in the Kirtland Temple:

> One week before word was publicly given that Br. J. Smith Jr. would give a relation of the coming forth of the records and also of the rise of the church and of his experience. Accordingly a vast concourse assembled at an early hour. Every seat was crowded and

> 4 or 5 hundred People stood up in the Aisles. Br. S[mith] gave the history of these things relating many Particulars of the manner of his first visions &c. the Spirit and Powr of God was upon him in Bearing testimony insomuch that many if not most of the congregation were in tears—as for my self I can say that all the reasonings in uncertainty and all the conclusions drawn from the writings of others . . . however great in themselves dwindle into insignificance when compared with the living testimony when your Eyes sea and your Ears hear from the living oracles of God.[33]

Aside from the Pratt letter, there are no known additional reports of this discourse, which gave many details of Joseph's first visions; the date on which it was given coincides with a large gap in the Prophet's journal.

Subsequent Recollections of First Vision Accounts

After the death of Joseph Smith, other witnesses wrote of occa sions on which they had heard him speak about his First Vision. For example, on the "special request of a few particular friends," Mary Isabella Hales Horne recalled the time when she had heard Joseph "relate his first vision when the Father and Son appeared to him: also his receiving the Gold Plates from the Angel Moroni. . . . While he was relating the circumstances, the Prophet's countenance lighted up, and so wonderful a power accompanied his words that everybody who heard them felt his influence and power."[34]

Similiarly, Joseph Curtis recalled a visit of Joseph Smith to Pontiac, Michigan, in spring 1835, where the Prophet, in a meeting there, "stated the reason" for the doctrines he taught:

> As a revival of some of the sec[t]s was going on some of his fathers family joined in with the revival himself being quite young[.] he feeling an anxiety to be religious his mind some what troubled this scriptures came to his mind which sayes if a man lack wisdon let him ask of god who giveth liberaly and upbradeth not[.] believeing it he went with a determinati[on] to obtain to enquire of the lord himself after some strugle the Lord minifested to him that the different sects were rong also that the Lord had a great work for him to do.[35]

The devoted record keeper Edward Stevenson, while also living in Pontiac, heard Joseph speak to the branch of the Church there:

> A great stir was made in this settlement at so distinguished visitors the meetings held were crowded to see and hear the testamonies given which were very powerful I will here relate my own experience on the ocaision of a meeting in our old log school House The Prophet stood at a table for the pulpit whare he began relateing his vision and before he got through he was in the midst of the congregation with uplifted hand. I do believe that there was not one person presant who did at the time being or who was not convicted of the truth of his vision, of an Angle to him his countanance seemed to me to assume a heavenly whiteness and his voice was so peirseing and forcible for my part it so impressed me as to become indellibly imprinted in my mind.[36]

A secondhand report of Joseph Smith relating his Vision, remembered many years later, comes from the pen of the diligent southern Utah diarist Charles Walker. In 1893 he attended a testimony meeting one Sunday at which one of the local elders, John Alger, said that when he was a small boy he heard Joseph Smith "relate his vision of seeing the Father and the Son, That God touched his eyes with his finger and said, 'Joseph this is my beloved Son hear him.' As soon as the Lord had touched his eyes with his finger he immediately saw the Savior." At the close of the meeting Walker and others questioned the speaker:

> He told us at the bottom of the meeting house steps that he was in the House of Father Smith in Kirtland when Joseph made this declaration, and that Joseph while speaking of it put his finger to his right eye, suiting the action with the words so as to illustrate and at the same time impress the occurrence on the minds of those unto whom He was speaking.[37]

Conclusion

The primary historical sources of Joseph Smith's First Vision are best understood in the broad record-keeping setting in which they were created. In 1830 a revelation commanded that records be kept in the Church, and the Prophet entered upon the stage of record keeping without the benefit of a well-defined tradition of doing so. He first farmed out the task to others, but when he saw their effort did not adequately chronicle his personal experience, he belatedly commenced his autobiography. For years he struggled with a format for his personal history as indicated by the haphazard nature of his earliest attempts to create a record of his life. Another factor that had an impact upon the historical record was the inability of those who heard Joseph speak to make a verbatim report of what he said.

Furthermore, since public knowledge of his religious claims and intentions had been the source of much of the persecution against him and his people, this fact also affected the writing and dissemination of his history. A little more than a year before his death he told the Saints, "The History is going out by little & little in the papers & cutting its way, so that when it is completed it will not raise a persecution against us."[38] The extraordinary opposition and hardships he faced in his role as religious reformer, and the problems associated with the development of a historical record had a significant impact upon the timing and nature of the records he produced. This context is the lens through which the collection of the pieces of the historical record of Joseph Smith's First Vision is best seen and appreciated.

Dean C. Jessee is a Senior Research Fellow at the Joseph Fielding Smith Institute for Latter-day Saint History and General Editor of the Joseph Smith Papers series.

An earlier version of this article appeared in BYU Studies *9, no. 3 (1969): 275–94.*

Notes

1. Joseph Smith History, 1832, in Joseph Smith Letterbook 1, MS, 1, Joseph Smith Collection, Church Archives, The Church of Jesus Christ of Latter-day Saints, Salt Lake City.

2. Joseph Smith to William Phelps, November 27, 1832, in Joseph Smith Letterbook 1, 4; Dean C. Jessee, ed. and comp., *The Personal Writings of Joseph*

Smith, rev. ed. (Salt Lake City: Deseret Book; Provo, Utah: Brigham Young University Press, 2002), 287.

3. The opening words of the revelation presented by Joseph Smith at the organization of the Church on April 6, 1830, were, "Behold, there shall be a record kept among you" (D&C 21:1).

4. Joseph Smith Jr., "History of the Church," MS, C-1, 1023, Church Archives; Joseph Smith Jr., *History of the Church of Jesus Christ of Latter-day Saints*, ed. B. H. Roberts, 2d ed., rev., 7 vols. (Salt Lake City: Deseret Book, 1971): 4:88–89 (hereafter cited as *History of the Church*).

5. Smith, "History," C-1, 1023; *History of the Church*, 4:89.

6. Smith, "History," C-1, 1223; *History of the Church*, 4:89.

7. The manuscript of the History shows that the first fifty-nine pages were written by James Mulholland, that Robert B. Thompson wrote at least part of the next sixteen, and that William W. Phelps had written eighty-two pages before Willard Richards began writing. It was not until after Richards's appointment in December 1841 that any significant progress was made on writing the History. Dean C. Jessee, "The Writing of Joseph Smith's History," *BYU Studies* 11, no. 4 (1971): 429–73.

8. Smith, "History of the Church," C-1, 1260. See *History of the Church*, 4:470. Speaking to the newly appointed Twelve in February 1835, Joseph remarked:

> If I now had in my possession every decision which has been had upon important items of doctrine and duties, since the commencement of this work, I would not part with them for any sum of money; but we have neglected to take minutes of such things, thinking perhaps that they would never benefit us afterwards. . . . [A]nd now we cannot bear record to the church and to the world of the great and glorious manifestations which have been made to us, with that degree of power and authority we otherwise could, if we now had these things to publish abroad ("A Record of the Transactions of the Twelve Apostles . . . ," MS, 1–2, Church Archives; compare *History of the Church*, 2:198–99).

9. Joseph Smith Letterbook 1, 1; Jessee, *Personal Writings of Joseph Smith*, 9–10.

Evidence for the 1832 date comes from handwriting identification and inspection of the ledger book that contained the severed pages. The handwriting reveals that the document was alternately penned by Joseph and Frederick G. Williams, Joseph's scribe and counselor in the First Presidency. Williams converted to the Church in fall 1830 and immediately left for Missouri. His handwriting in the beginning pages of the Kirtland Revelation Book shows that by February 1832 Williams was writing for Joseph Smith, after returning to Ohio. And according to his own statement, he was officially appointed on July 20 as the Prophet's scribe. (F. G. Williams, Statement, n.d., MS, Frederick G. Williams Papers, Church Archives.) From this it is evident that the writing of the History could have occurred as early as February 1832.

Nor is it likely that the History was written after November 27, 1832, since on that date the ledger book in which it was written was converted to a letterbook for recording important historical Church documents. The evidence for this is two-fold. First, although they were later cut from the volume, the three leaves containing the History match the cut edges still protruding from the binding of the ledger book. The terminal letters of words severed when the pages were removed also match. The cut page stubs immediately precede the November 27, 1832, letter entry, the first item in the letterbook. Second, the page numbering indicates this arrangement. The pages of the History were numbered one through six, and the November 27 letter begins on page 1a. Both the last page of the History and the pages of the letter were written by Frederick Williams. He would not have started numbering the pages containing the letter with "1a" had there not been a preceding page 1.

10. Joseph Smith Letterbook 1, 1–3. For the entire text of this narrative, see Jessee, *Personal Writings of Joseph Smith*, 9–14.

11. Joseph Smith Journal, 1835–36, MS, 23–24, Church Archives; Jessee, *Personal Writings of Joseph Smith*, 104–5.

12. *Messenger and Advocate*, October 1834, 13.

13. Joseph Smith, "History, 1834–1836," MS, A-1, 105 (numbering from the back of the book), Church Archives; Dean C. Jessee, ed., *The Papers of Joseph Smith*, 2 vols. (Salt Lake City: Deseret Book, 1989–92), 1:97.

14. Smith, "History, 1834–1836," A-1, 120–22; Jessee, *Papers of Joseph Smith*, 1:125–27.

15. Joseph Smith Journal, November 14, 1835; Jessee, *Personal Writings of Joseph Smith*, 112–13.

16. Smith, "History, 1834–1836," A-1, 129; Jessee, *Papers of Joseph Smith*, 1:136–37.

17. Joseph Smith Journal, 1838, MS, 34, Church Archives; Jessee, *Papers of Joseph Smith*, 2:233.

18. Joseph Smith, "History of the Church," C-1, 954. See also *History of the Church*, 3:375.

19. See Joseph Smith—History; *History of the Church*, 1:1–20, 32–33, 39–44; and Jessee, *Papers of Joseph Smith*, 1:267–86, 288, 290–92.

When Joseph began dictating this history to James Mulholland on June 11, 1839, the Prophet's large record book containing the above 1835 History account was turned over and re-titled as book "A-1" of the ensuing multivolume history. Dates in the opening pages of the narrative indicate that the Prophet was dictating from a text that had been written the previous year. On p. 1, reference is made to the "eighth year since the organization of said Church," and on p. 8, "this day, being the Second day of May, One thousand Eight hundred and thirty eight" (*History of the Church*, 1:2, 18–19). Joseph Smith's journal for April 27, 1838, in the hand of George W. Robinson, notes that he spent the day "writing a history of th<i>s Church from the earliest perion [period] of its existance up to this date." During the first four days of May the journal adds, "the First Presidency were engaged in writing church History" (Joseph Smith Journal, April 27 and May 1–4, 1838; Jessee, *Papers of Joseph Smith*, 2:233, 237; *History of the Church*, 3:25–26). The statement on p. 8 of the History confirms this was the narrative being written on May 2, 1838.

Further evidence that the beginning pages of the History manuscript volume A-1 were copied in 1839 from the Prophet's dictation beginning with the account written the previous year is that the first fifty-nine pages of the manuscript are in the handwriting of Mulholland, who did not begin writing for Joseph Smith until September 3, 1838; a short time later he discontinued writing during the Missouri imprisonment of the Prophet (October 1838–March 1839) and did not recommence until April 22, 1839 (James Mulholland, Journal, MS, Church Archives). Mulholland's journal entry for June 11, 1839, notes that he was "writing &c for Church history." In addition, the Prophet's History for that date states, "I commenced dictating my history for my Clerk—James Mulholland to write," and on June 12 and 13, Joseph's History reads, "I continued to dictate my history" (Smith, "History of the Church," C-1, 954; *History of the Church*, 3:375–76).

20. This insertion added by Willard Richards in 1842 contains the Prophet's account of his 1813 leg operation. See Jessee, *Papers of Joseph Smith*, 1:268–69; Lucy Mack Smith, *Biographical Sketches of Joseph Smith, the Prophet, and His Progenitors for Many Generations* (London: Published for Orson Pratt by S. W. Richards, 1853), 62–66; see also LeRoy S. Wirthlin, "Joseph Smith's Boyhood Operation: An 1813 Surgical Success," *BYU Studies* 21, no. 2 (1981): 131–54.

21. An insertion here to "Addendum, note E, page 2" gives birth dates and places of Joseph Smith's paternal ancestors.

22. This insertion is in the handwriting of Willard Richards on pages 132–33 of the History manuscript.

According to Richards's diary, this note was written on December 2, 1842, which explains why it does not appear in the History in the *Times and Seasons* that began publication in March of that year (Willard Richards, Diary, December 2, 1842, MS, Church Archives).

23. Smith, "History of the Church," A-1, 1–4; Jessee, *Personal Writings of Joseph Smith*, 226–32.

24. Joseph Smith, "Church History," *Times and Seasons* 3 (March 1, 1842): 706–10 (Jessee, *Personal Writings of Joseph Smith*, 242). Appended to this account was the statement of belief later canonized as the Articles of Faith.

25. Joseph Smith, "Latter Day Saints," in I. Daniel Rupp, comp., *An Original History of the Religious Denominations at Present Existing in the United States* (Philadelphia: J. Y. Humphreys, 1844), 404–10; Jessee, *Papers of Joseph Smith*, 1:448–49.

26. Orson Pratt, *Interesting Account of Several Remarkable Visions, and The Late Discovery of Ancient American Records* (Edinburgh: Ballantyne and Hughes, 1840), 3–5; Jessee, *Papers of Joseph Smith*, 1:389–91.

27. Joseph Smith Letterbook 2, 201–6; Orson Hyde and John E. Page to Joseph Smith, May 1, 1840, in Joseph Smith Letterbook 2, 144–45; Joseph Smith to Orson Hyde and John E. Page, May 14, 1840, in Joseph Smith Letterbook 2, 146–47; Orson Hyde to Joseph Smith, June 15, 1841, *Times and Seasons* 2 (October 1, 1841): 551–55. See also *History of the Church*, 4:105–6, 123–24, 129, 386; and Jessee, *Papers of Joseph Smith*, 1:402–4.

28. Orson Hyde, *Ein Ruf aus der Wüste, eine Stimme aus dem Schoose der Erde* (A Cry from the Wilderness, a Voice from the Dust of the Earth) (Frankfurt: n.p., 1842), 14–16. The text here is a literal translation from the German by Marvin Folsom, professor emeritus of German, Brigham Young University. The text is also reprinted with a translation in Jessee, *Papers of Joseph Smith*, 1:402–25.

29. Levi Richards, Journal, June 11, 1843, MS, Church Archives. See also Andrew F. Ehat and Lyndon W. Cook, eds., *The Words of Joseph Smith: The Contemporary Accounts of the Nauvoo Discourses of the Prophet Joseph*, Religious Studies Monograph Series, no. 6 (Provo, Utah: Religious Studies Center, Brigham Young University, 1980), 215.

30. "The Prairies, Nauvoo, Joe Smith, the Temple, the Mormons, &c.," *Pittsburgh Weekly Gazette* 58 (September 15, 1843): 3; Jessee, *Papers of Joseph Smith*, 1:438–44.

31. Alexander Neibaur, Journal, May 24, 1844, MS, Church Archives.

32. William W. Phelps to Sally Phelps, June 2, 1835, MS, Church Archives.

33. Parley P. Pratt to the Elders and Brethren of the Church of Latter-day Saints in Canada, November 27, 1836, MS, Church Archives.

34. *Woman's Exponent* 39 (June 1910): 6.

35. Joseph Curtis, Reminiscences and Journal, MS, 5, Church Archives.

36. Edward Stevenson, "The Life and History of Elder Edward Stevenson," MS, 21, Church Archives. See also Edward Stevenson, *Reminiscences of Joseph the Prophet and the Coming Forth of the Book of Mormon* (Salt Lake City: By the author, 1893), 4–5; and Edward Stevenson, *Juvenile Instructor* 29 (July 15, 1894): 444–45.

37. Charles Walker, Diary, February 2, 1893, published as A. Karl Larsen and Katharine Miles Larsen, eds., *Diary of Charles Lowell Walker* (Logan, Utah: Utah State University Press, 1980), 755–56.

38. Willard Richards report of Joseph Smith discourse, in Joseph Smith Journal, April 19, 1843; *History of the Church*, 5:367.

Fence running from the reconstructed Joseph Smith log cabin down to the Sacred Grove, between Manchester and Palmyra, New York.

The Appearance of the Father and the Son to Joseph Smith in 1820

James B. Allen and John W. Welch

The Restoration of the gospel of Jesus Christ and the history of The Church of Jesus Christ of Latter-day Saints began when God the Father and his Son Jesus Christ appeared to the youthful Joseph Smith in spring 1820. In the brilliant light of this key event, almost everything else in Church history pales by comparison.

Fortunately, Joseph Smith spoke and wrote on several occasions about this sublime and formative experience, now known as the First Vision. In addition to numerous circumstantial and secondary evidences that have expanded and supported our historical knowledge of this all-important event, ten accounts in thirteen documents have come down to modern readers from the hand or voice or time of Joseph Smith himself. Few events so central to the foundations of any of the world's religions are so informatively documented.

What do these ten accounts say? What can we learn from them? Who wrote them, and when and why were they written? Why are they not all the same? Are they historically accurate and credible? How well documented is the historical record concerning the First Vision? This overview gives answers to such questions as it analyzes and synthesizes these various accounts, the texts of which are presented in full in the proceeding chapter, "The Earliest Documented Accounts of Joseph Smith's First Vision," by Dean C. Jessee.

Serious historical interest in gathering and studying the First Vision accounts began in 1965 when Paul Cheesman, a graduate student at Brigham Young University, presented a gentle surprise to scholars who study Mormonism by including in his master's thesis an account of Joseph Smith's First Vision that was largely unknown at that time.[1] What made the new discovery significant was the fact that most people had supposed that the Manuscript History of Joseph Smith, formally begun in 1838, was the first place where the Prophet had committed his remarkable experience to writing. Cheesman's master's thesis demonstrated that an account of the First Vision had, in fact, been recorded in 1832.

In the wake of that find, historians both inside and outside the Church took new interest in Joseph Smith's testimony. Shortly after the 1832 narrative was discovered, another account from 1835, also predating the 1838 Manuscript History, came to light; it was published in 1966.[2] Three years later, Dean Jessee's first article detailing four texts of First Vision accounts (1832, printed versions of the 1835 journal entries, and the 1838 manuscript) appeared in *BYU Studies.*[3] In addition, other scholars in the late 1960s began to examine the setting of the vision, seeking to determine the extent to which the events described by Joseph Smith could be verified by other contemporary sources.[4] Mormon historiography thus entered a new era of documentary research as more historical sources needed to be examined and as many outstanding scholars published insightful results from their research.[5] To promote popular awareness and understanding, open treatments of these multiple accounts appeared in the *Improvement Era* and the *Ensign* in 1970, 1985, and 1996.[6] The wave of interest in these important historical documents continues today, with a tide of studies raising a number of questions and expressing various opinions on several issues.[7] But as interesting as the perspectives of these commentators may be, long after the scholars' personal conclusions have become obscure, the ten basic accounts will rightfully remain the focus of attention among serious investigators and diligent enquirers.

Understanding the Differences in the Accounts

Whenever new historical information is published, a host of questions demand answers, and the disclosure that Joseph Smith told his story more than once was no exception. Scholars asked whether the Prophet's description of his experience squares with other known historical events, to what degree the various accounts are consistent with each other, and how one might explain the differences.

Several factors undoubtedly affected the nature of each of Joseph Smith's accounts: (1) the timing of his narrations, including his age and recent experiences at the time a particular account was given; (2) the circumstances under which he gave each account, including any special purposes he may have had in mind for each particular audience; (3) the possible literary influences of those who wrote for him as his scribes or who reported his words (namely Levi Richards, David Nye White, and Alexander Neibaur); and (4) the extent to which versions written by others (namely Orson Pratt and Orson Hyde) may have emphasized points that most impressed them personally, thus making each version slightly different.

One would hardly expect to find every account to be precisely alike. Obviously people answer a simple question, such as "what happened at the soccer game?" differently, depending on who has asked the question. If a man's teenage son, who happened to be a soccer fanatic, were to ask his father this question, the father would know that the son wanted to know about who scored which goals and how many players were red-carded. If the man's wife, who had no interest in soccer, were to ask such a question, however, he might know to tell her about who he met on the sidelines and if he had yelled too much. Only after such a question has been asked by a number of people and answered with each inquisitor's interests in mind does a full picture of the event begin to emerge.

So it is with the First Vision accounts. It is fortunate that these ten reports come from a wide variety of circumstances, for no single account tells the whole story. At the same time, all the details in each of the accounts add significantly to the entire picture. The purpose of the following study is to identify the nature of each of these accounts and to examine the details they each provide in order to explain the differences and accentuate the consistency that exists among them.

Actually, the differences in the accounts may be grossly overemphasized, for the truth is that there is wide and credible agreement in detail among them all. Another impressive fact is that the 1832 version, which was the first to be recorded, is very comprehensive. This early narrative includes the essential elements of the more carefully prepared Manuscript History and contains more additional details than any other source. When all the accounts are combined, only a couple of details call for explanation, as given below.

Joseph Smith's Initial Audiences

One of the first steps in reading and understanding these ten historical accounts is to appreciate the various audiences that Joseph Smith had in mind as he wrote or spoke of this overwhelming experience. Processing the meanings and appreciating the implications of that life-changing event cannot have been a short or simple task for him. The vision served as a guiding star throughout his life, a star on which he often took his bearings, no matter his surroundings or circumstances.

Apparently Joseph Smith did not speak often of the First Vision in his teenage years. As he himself understandably said, he kept most of these things to himself and pondered them in his heart. His first audience was his mother, Lucy Mack Smith. Returning to the family log home shortly after his experience in the Sacred Grove, he told his mother, perhaps among other things, that he had learned "that Presbyterianism is not true" (Joseph Smith—History 1:20), as he noted in an addition to the manuscript of his history in 1842.[8] This was an understandable, yet courageous, thing for a young boy to emphasize to his mother, who had recently converted to Presbyterianism.

How much he told in those early years is unknown. Apparently he was judicious and cautious about telling all. Indeed, the hostile reactions of clergy and the violent opposition from neighbors would have been enough to deter any boy in his mid-teens. As Joseph stated in his 1838 account, dictated about eighteen or nineteen years after the following reactions occurred, one Methodist preacher responded "with great contempt" when Joseph gave him "an account of the vision" which he had had (JS–H 1:21). Joseph soon found that whenever he told his story, it "excited a great deal of prejudice . . . and was the cause of great persecution, which continued to increase. . . . [I continued] to attract the attention of the great ones of the most popular sects of the day, and in a manner to create in them a spirit of the most bitter persecution and reviling" (JS–H 1:22–23).

Indeed, there is no contemporary evidence (that is, documents from the 1820s) to show that Joseph Smith told his story very widely in 1820; and it is not clear, even from his own accounts, how long he continued to tell it. With the reception he apparently received, it was probably not very long. The lack of evidence is not surprising, however, for even if certain ministers warned people not to believe young Joseph, they were also preoccupied with many other things that to them were more important. Since this was a time when many were claiming spiritual experiences, the claims of a fourteen-year-old boy were hardly something the ministers would record. Nor would such a youth have much likelihood of finding his way into the newspapers or diaries of the time, even though he later said that all the "great ones" were against him. To a young boy, the rejection of such an experience by those whom he respected would have been most frustrating, and he would tend to emphasize this frustration as he told of the experience in later years.

In the hostile environment during the fledgling years of the Restoration, even after the Church was first organized, Joseph apparently did not relate the account of his First Vision very widely, for neither the earliest Latter-day Saint nor regional publications of the 1830s carried accounts of it.[9] Although early Church literature included several clear allusions to the First Vision,[10] none of these brief references gave specific details. However, the *Reflector*, a contemporary newspaper published in Palmyra, New York, confirms that at least by 1831 those in the community had heard allusions to Joseph Smith's vision (and an indication of the criticism he continued to receive). On February 14, 1831, the clearly anti-Mormon publisher reported on news of the Mormons in Ohio. Joseph Smith, he said, claimed to have received a "commission from God" to establish a religion, and those who would not submit to his authority "would speedily be destroyed." Further, the publisher reported, Joseph Smith's followers affirmed that he "had seen God frequently and personally."[11] While this report did not refer specifically to the First Vision, it is significant that members of the community had at least heard of the Latter-day Saint belief that God had appeared to their leader and that this belief was used as part of the continuing denunciation of the Church.

Because of the scant evidence of the vision in early publications, one writer prematurely suggested in 1945 that Joseph Smith did not even "make up" the story until 1835 or later.[12] That view clearly may be dismissed, for we now know that the Prophet wrote his first account of this vision in 1832. Beginning at least as early as spring 1835, and continuing until his death in 1844, he felt more confident in openly describing his experience to friends, converts, inquisitive visitors, faithful congregations, the public at large, dignitaries, and publishers.

The Audiences for Joseph Smith's Surviving Accounts

With this background in mind, it becomes all the more evident that each document that preserves a contemporary account of the Prophet's First Vision was directed toward a particular audience. Striving to understand the objective that Joseph Smith had in mind as he communicated with each audience helps today's readers appreciate the particular details uniquely conveyed in each of these statements. Underlining is reproduced from the original document. Editorial marks include angle brackets < > to indicate insertions made by the author of the document. Strikeouts are shown by ~~strike-outs~~. Brackets [ ] indicate editorial comments.

The 1832 Account

This important account was written in the second half of 1832, a time when the Church was very small, still only a few hundred members. It is an intimate, personal statement, preserved in the handwriting of Joseph Smith and composed when he was only twenty-six years old.

Significantly, LDS scholars have noted that the language of this first effort to write the story of the First Vision is somewhat reflective of the revivalistic language of the time.[13] This seems only natural, given Joseph Smith's likely memory of attending revivalistic meetings in his youth and probably hearing intensive revival-type preaching that vividly reminded listeners of their sinful nature. In this context it is not surprising that the 1832 account should strongly emphasize his private feelings, his mourning for his own sins, his exclamation of awe before God, and the individual forgiveness and personal guidance that he received from the Savior as part of the First Vision experience. Having been commanded repeatedly to "say nothing but repentance unto this generation" (D&C 6:9; 11:9; see also 14:8; 19:21), he strongly emphasized his own experience in seeking and obtaining forgiveness.

Joseph also told how a pillar of light came down upon him, how he was filled with the Spirit of God, how the heavens were opened before him, and how he saw and conversed with the Lord, who said to him in the first person, "I was crucifyed for the world that all those who believe on my name may have Eternal life." Precise identifying details or descriptions of externalities are infrequent amidst the rapture of this very personal account. Indeed, Joseph uniquely introduced the vision here by affirming that God "seeketh such to worship him as worship him in spirit and in truth," echoing the New Testament text that "true worshippers shall worship the Father in spirit and in truth" (John 4:23); and, in direct fulfillment of this personal requirement, Joseph said that, as the pillar of light came to rest upon him, "I was filled with the spirit of God."

It is doubtful that the 1832 manuscript was planned for straight publication, at least not in the unpolished form in which it survives. It seems, rather, to have been an early and fervent effort to express, for the benefit of already faithful members of the Church, the Prophet's youthful religious feelings and the powerful spiritual impact that the First Vision had upon him personally. The Church was hardly over two years old at this time, and Joseph had already acted upon the commandment that the Church should begin keeping such historical records.[14] He was successfully gathering faithful followers such as Sidney Rigdon, Frederick G. Williams, Newell K. Whitney, Brigham Young, Parley P. Pratt, William E. McLellin, and Charles C. Rich. As Joseph Smith sat down to write at this time, he could look back on the amazing publication of the Book of Mormon, the restoration of the priesthood, the successful relocation of the Church from New York to Ohio, and other profound events in the promising rise of the Church. His mind reflected on the truly "marvilous experience" and "mighty acts" that his own remarkable life had already enjoyed, and this early account is a powerful expression of how it all began.

In many, but not all respects, the year 1832 was good for Joseph Smith, and the 1832 account reflects the positive prospects of this time. Work on the translation of the Bible was progressing smoothly. Eighteen revelations would be received that year, including the major sections 76, 84, and 88 of the Doctrine and Covenants. Missionary work was successfully going forth as several of the brethren had answered calls to serve. Joseph had survived a painful tarring and feathering in March in Hiram, Ohio, but he had traveled successfully to Missouri, the second center of gathering, returning the end of July. In October he would travel to Manhattan; and in November, to Albany, New York, and Boston, Massachusetts, returning on November 6, the joyous day on which his son Joseph Smith III was born. Sometime between the end of July and November, the Prophet found time to begin writing his history. His pages exude an optimistic tone, making no mention of the dark struggles or persecutions that he had experienced during and after the First Vision.

The 1835 Accounts

The entry in Joseph Smith's Journal for November 9, 1835, tells how he explained his early experiences to Robert Matthias, a curious visitor in Kirtland, Ohio, who claimed to be a Jewish minister called Joshua. His appearance was "some thing singular." He had a grey beard; was about 50–55 years old; was slender; wore a green coat, pantaloons, and a black fur hat; and frequently shut his eyes "with a scowl" when he spoke. Warren Parrish, the Prophet's scribe, recorded the interview as part of the Prophet's daily record. Parrish was necessarily selective in remembering and choosing the points that he included.

Speaking to a total stranger, Joseph's conversation on this occasion tended to deal with objective details, rather than intimate feelings. This account is plain, bold, and to the point. We are told that the Prophet remarked "upon the subject of Religion" and spoke "concerning the Bible" (laying a broad foundation for belief); that he then spoke about "the circumstances connected with the coming forth of the book of Mormon" (apparently not saying much about the specific details); and that he focused on his concern about "matters that involve eternal consequ[e]nces" (formulating his anxiety about salvation in generic terms, with which a person of any religious persuasion, Jewish or Christian or other, could identify). This account only briefly alludes to the contention that had arisen among the Protestant sects, simply indicating that Joseph did not know "who was right or who was wrong." Squabbles between Christian ministers would have been of little interest to a Jew. Instead, Joseph turned directly in this narration to the supernatural opposition that soon impeded his petition: his swollen tongue and the alarming sound like some person walking toward him. A Jewish minister would have related to powers of religious opposition such as these. (Ironically, two days later Joseph would invite Joshua to leave Kirtland, as his doctrines were of the devil.)

Joseph then went on to say in this 1835 narrative that "a personage appeard" in the midst of the pillar of fire that rested above his head, and that "another personage soon appeard like unto the first." He (the second personage?) said, "Thy sins are forgiven," and one of them testified that "Jesus Christ is the Son of God." Terms such as "pillar of fire" (as with Moses and Israel in the wilderness, Exodus 13:21) and "like unto" (compare Deuteronomy 18:18) would have resonated with Jewish expectations concerning divine manifestations; and the withholding of any mention of a divine name in connection with the Supreme One, together with the mention of "many angels in this vision," would have comported with Jewish sensitivities. Yet, the clear assertion of the presence of two divine beings and the unambiguous

23

I should think he is about 50 or 55 years old. tall and
strait slender built of thin visage blue eyes, and fair com-
plexion, he wore a sea-green frock coat, & pantaloons of
the same, black fur hat with narrow brim, and while
speaking frequently shuts his eyes with a scowl on his
countinance: I made some enquiry after his name
but received no definite answer; we soon comm-
enced talking upon the subject of religion and af-
ter I had made some remarks concerning the bible
I commenced giving him a relation of the circum-
stances connected with the coming forth of the book
of Mormon, as follows— being wrought up in my
mind, respecting the subject of religion and looking
at the different systems taught the children of
men, I knew not who was right or who was wrong
and I considered it of the first importance that
I should be right, in matters that involve
eternal consequences; being thus perplexed in mind
I retired to the silent grove and bowed down before
the Lord, under a realizing sense that he had said
(if the bible be true) ask and you shall receive
knock and it shall be opened seek and you shall
find and again, if any man lack wisdom let
him ask of God who giveth to all men liber-
ally and upbraideth not; information was what
I most desired at this time, and with a fixed
determination to obtain it, I called upon the Lord
for the first time, in the place above stated or in
other words I made a fruitless attempt to pray, my
toung seemed to be swolen in my mouth, so that
I could not utter, I heard a noise behind me
like some person walking towards me, I strove again
to pray, but could not, the noise of walking seem-
ed to draw nearer, I sprung up on my feet, and

Two pages from Joseph Smith's Journal (November 9, 1835), in the handwriting of his clerk Warren Parrish, in Kirtland, Ohio.

24 and looked around, but saw no person or thing
that was calculated to produce the noise of wal-
king, I kneeled again my mouth was opened and
my tongue liberated, and I called on the Lord in
mighty prayer, a pillar of fire appeared above
my head, it presently rested down upon me
head, and filled me with joy unspeakable, a
personage appeard in the midst of this pillar
of flame which was spread all around, and yet
nothing consumed, another personage soon appeard
like unto the first, he said unto me thy sins are
forgiven thee, he testifyed unto me that Jesus Christ
is the Son of God; and I saw many angels in this vision I was about 14 years old
when I received this first communication; When
I was about 17 years old I saw another vision of
angels in the night season after I had retired to
bed I had not been a sleep, when but was me-
ditating upon my past life and experience,
I was verry concious that I had not kept the
commandments, and I repented hartily for
all my sins and transgression, and humbled
myself before Him; whose eyes are upon all things, all at once the room was
iluminated above the brightness of the sun
an angel appeared before me, his hands and
feet were naked pure and white, and he
stood between the floors of the room, clothed with
purity inexpressible, he said unto me I
am a messenger sent from God, be faithful
and keep his commandments in all things,
he told me of a sacred record which was
written on plates of gold, I saw in the vision
the place where they were deposited, he said the
Indians were the literal descendants of Abraham
he explained many things of the prophesies to

On this page Joseph tells how he "called on the Lord in mighty prayer," saw two divine personages, and was told "thy sins are forgiven thee."

testimony that Jesus Christ is the Son of God were bold declarations for the relatively young (not yet thirty years old) Church leader to deliver to a listener whom he thought was Jewish.

Three days after dismissing Joshua, on November 14, Joseph told his story to yet another visitor, Erastus Holmes, who wanted to learn about the establishment of the Church and "to be instructed more perfectly in [its] doctrine." The brief journal entry shows that Joseph spoke openly about "the first visitation of Angels which was when I was about 14. years old," other visitations, the Book of Mormon, and the progress of the Church. These were the subjects about which Erastus had asked. Exactly what Joseph said is not reported, but the reference to the visitation of angels suggests that he most likely told Holmes much the same thing that he told Robert Matthias.

This was an opportune time in the Prophet's life for him to be speaking openly about his experiences. For a change, people were coming to him and inquiring about the Church. The Quorum of the Twelve Apostles had been organized in February and had gone together on a mission to New England, returning in September. New revelation was coming forth in the form of the Book of Abraham, which Joseph began translating in July and worked on through the fall. The first edition of the Doctrine and Covenants had been published to the world in October, with twelve witnesses resolutely attesting to its divine inspiration. Joseph was meeting regularly with the School of the Prophets. The Kirtland Temple was nearing completion, its dedication only a few months away. In this context, Joseph spoke confidently about the First Vision throughout the year. He also allowed his personal journal with its account of the vision to be copied into the historical record of the Church.

The 1838–39 Account

This account is from Joseph Smith's Manuscript History and is the source for the version of the First Vision published in the *Times and Seasons* in 1842 and later in the Pearl of Great Price.[15] The Prophet began working on this history on April 27, 1838, and his journal records that the First Presidency was engaged in this official work May 1–4. On September 3, James Mulholland began working for Joseph as a scribe, but their efforts were soon interrupted by the onset of the Missouri War, convoluted courtroom appearances, and Joseph's incarceration. After his release, Joseph recommenced work on the history on June 11, 1839, with Mulholland serving again as scribe and taking down the Prophet's testimony verbatim, as would a court reporter.

It is unknown whether the pages covering the First Vision were written in April–May 1838, in September 1838, or in June 1839; whenever the writing occurred, it is evident that the Prophet intended this narrative to become the basic source for Church literature and that he had a special purpose in mind that does not seem as clear in the earlier renditions. Long the object of almost merciless public abuse, he now told his story in order to correct erroneous reports "put in circulation by evil disposed and designing persons" and "to disabuse the publick mind, and put all enquirers after truth into possession of the facts." With such a purpose in mind, to set the record straight once and for all, it is likely that Joseph would more carefully consider this account than he had the earlier versions.

Public abuse and persecution continued to plague Joseph Smith during this period of his life. Apostasy and the excommunication of several prominent Church leaders also took place. Serious opposition in Kirtland grew to the point that on January 12, 1838, in the dead of winter, the Prophet and a large company of followers left Kirtland for Missouri, arriving at Far West on March 12. By October, troubles had erupted into violence, and in November, Joseph Smith was imprisoned in Liberty Jail. He finally arrived at Quincy, Illinois, on April 22, 1839, and only a few weeks later resumed work on his history where he had left off. In this context, it is no wonder that persecution, contention, competition, religious excitement, bad feelings, strife, contempt, bitterness, hatred, and rejection were recalled so vividly and stated so graphically in this 1838 account.

Vindicating the Saints also may have been on the Church leader's mind. If so, a full and detailed account was needed in order to be convincing—one that gave dates (1820), descriptions of the weather ("a beautiful clear day"), the time of day ("morning"), and precise quotations of conversations as well as the words of the Lord.

A compelling and persuasive narrative was needed to hold and win the attention of a prejudiced public. Like Paul before Agrippa some twenty-five years after the appearance of the resurrected Lord on the road to Damascus, Joseph Smith testified unshakably of what he had seen some eighteen or nineteen years previous. "'Who am I that I can withstand God,' or why does the world think to make me deny what I have actually seen?" he asked. By denying, he would "offend God and come under condemnation." But just as God had delivered Joseph from the unseen powers when he seemed "doomed to sudden destruction," God would sustain and deliver his Saints in their darkest hours of despair and affliction.

The 1842 Account

The beginning of the year 1842 was the heart of Nauvoo's boom time. Property was selling; buildings were being constructed; immigrants were arriving; the Nauvoo Temple was under construction; a third printing of the Book of Mormon was underway; tithing was being collected; and political and religious difficulties were imperceptibly over the horizon. On February 15, 1842, Joseph became the editor of the *Times and Seasons*, involving him directly in the newspaper business.

An account of the First Vision written by the Prophet in 1842 was tied to the newspaper world in several ways. In the same year that his Manuscript History began to be published in the *Times and Seasons*, he was invited to prepare a brief history of the Church for publication by John Wentworth in the *Chicago Democrat*. The resulting letter containing this account was published in the *Times and Seasons* on March 1, 1842. In 1843, Joseph Smith provided Israel Daniel Rupp, a historian who planned to publish a compendium about religious denominations in the United States, with a history of the Church at Rupp's request. The First Vision account submitted to that publication is nearly identical to the account in the letter sent to Wentworth. Rupp published his work in 1844.

From its inception as part of the Wentworth letter, this account was meant for publication by the non-Mormon press. It has the characteristics that one would expect to find in a public relations statement: it is concise, straightforward, unadorned, informative, and matter-of-fact. Its content is reported in a strong, first person voice: "I began," "I found," "I went," "I determined," "I had confidence," "I retired," "I was enwrapped," "I was expressly commanded." Of particular interest in the public sphere is the unique element in this account that none of the churches "was acknowledged of God as his church and kingdom." Concluding this brief release was an enticing "promise that the fulness of the gospel should at some future time be made known." The tone of this account of the First Vision is confident and self-assured, in keeping with the concluding prediction of the Wentworth letter that the restored gospel will visit every clime and sound in every ear.

The 1843 Levi Richards Report

Levi Richards was a prominent citizen of Nauvoo who attended a lecture on June 11, 1843, and heard Joseph Smith tell about his First Vision. Richards's diary entry for that day contains a very brief summary of the Prophet's experience. Joseph's comments came after the lecture of Elder G. J. Adams, who told how "the everlasting covenant which was set up by Christ & the apostles had been broken." The Prophet then testified that, in the grove, he learned "that the Everlasting covenant was broken," and that he understood "the fulness of the Gospel from beginning to end," including "the order of the priesthood in all its ramifications" (the ordinances of baptism for the dead and the endowment had only recently been introduced). Richards was impressed by the confident testimony that "Earth & hell had opposed him & tryed to destroy him—but they had not done it & they <never would.>" This reference to opposition may have included the forces of evil in the grove as well as many other persecutions.

The 1843 David Nye White Report

In summer 1843, David Nye White, the editor of the *Pittsburgh Weekly Gazette*, visited Joseph Smith in Nauvoo. White's report, which included an account of the First Vision as related to him by the Prophet, appeared in the *Gazette* on September 15 and was later reprinted in the *New York Spectator* on September 23. It reads as if

Joseph Smith's words have been rephrased and paraphrased, making the account seem a bit odd, although obviously consistent with his authentic first-person narratives.[16]

The 1844 Alexander Neibaur Report

An entry in the personal diary of Alexander Neibaur illustrates that the Prophet sometimes told the story to small, rather intimate groups. Born in Germany of Jewish parents, Neibaur was converted to the Church in England, where he practiced dentistry. He immigrated to Nauvoo in 1841, where he set up a dental practice and soon became an intimate friend of the Prophet and also taught German and Hebrew to Joseph and others. On May 24, 1844, Joseph told his sacred experience to Neibaur, who recorded it in his diary in the sincere, unpolished style that one would expect from a humble devotee not used to writing in English. A few unique, intimate details contained in this account, such as the description of God the Father ("light complexion blue eyes a piece of white cloth drawn over his shoulders his right arm bear") bespeak the intimate setting of this narration by Joseph, in the privacy of his home, to his tutor.

The Audiences of Orson Pratt and Orson Hyde

Two additional accounts of the First Vision, published during Joseph Smith's lifetime, were prepared by members of the Quorum of the Twelve Apostles for inclusion in missionary pamphlets. As close associates of the Prophet, Orson Pratt and Orson Hyde undoubtedly heard the story directly from him and likely had early access to the official 1838–39 version. Their reports are close in style and content to that account, though both also adapted the basic story in ways that were suitable for and reflected their particular audiences, their interests, and their own literary proclivities.

The 1840 Orson Pratt Report

In 1840, Orson Pratt of the Quorum of the Twelve published in Scotland a missionary tract entitled *A[n] Interesting Account of Several Remarkable Visions, and of the Late Discovery of Ancient*

American Records. His narrative was similar to Joseph's 1838 account, except that it elaborated upon several details. Whether these were given to him by Joseph or whether he was using literary license is not known, but some of his additions find corroboration in other accounts as well.

As a person interested in science, Orson Pratt featured how Joseph was concerned about leaving matters of eternal consequence to "chance, or uncertainties," how problems "occurred to his mind," how he sought "certainty, and knowledge, of his own," and how the Epistle of James had brought him to see that "there was, not only, a possibility, but a probability; yea, more, a certainty, that he should obtain a knowledge." Pratt's detailed description of the light, its brightness and magnitude, its effect on the surrounding trees and "the whole wilderness, for some distance around," and Joseph's mind being "caught away, from the natural objects with which he was surrounded," provides the kinds of empirical data that a scientist would relish and that Scottish empiricism would appreciate.

The 1842 Orson Hyde Report

Another member of the Twelve, Orson Hyde, published a missionary tract in Germany in 1842 entitled *Ein Ruf aus der Wüste, eine Stimme aus dem Schoose der Erde* (A Cry from the Wilderness, a Voice from the Dust of the Earth). This tract contained an account of the vision similar to Orson Pratt's account, much of it, in fact, having been translated directly from the earlier publication. To the rationalistic Germans, Hyde emphasized Joseph Smith's concern about basing his hopes not just on uncertainty, but on "blind uncertainty," and Hyde averred that the Prophet had been endowed by nature "with a keen critical intellect and so he looked through the lens of reason and common sense and with pity and contempt" on the various "systems of religion." When the forces of evil beset the prayerful youth, the opposition came in the form of "doubts" and "inappropriate images" that filled his "mind," and in the end Joseph was promised "the complete truth of the gospel." Germans also being known for their authoritarianism, Hyde added that the scripture gave "an authorization for him to solemnly call upon his creator."

Consolidating the Ten Accounts

Mindful of such factors as why, when, where, and to whom the ten First Vision accounts were given, we turn to an examination of what these accounts actually say. Latter-day Saints believe that Joseph Smith was telling the truth each time he related his experience, and that the scribes recorded his ideas as accurately and suitably as possible. Thus, a study of the combined accounts presents some fascinating new insights into the experience and personal development of the young prophet. Not only do we discover in each account more details about what happened both before and after he entered the Sacred Grove, but we also gain valuable insight into how these events affected him personally and helped him in his spiritual growth. What follows is an attempt to weave these accounts into a composite story of Joseph's sacred experience in order to show their collective value and consistency. In the tables and explanations that follow, nine of these accounts are considered. The 1835 account of the Prophet's comments to Erastus Holmes is not listed or discussed because of its brevity; it is reproduced in the previous chapter by Dean Jessee. The two 1835 journal entries, together with their published versions, are lumped together in column two; and the 1842 Wentworth letter and its virtually identical 1843 reprint are combined in column five. The 1838–39 account will be referred to simply as the 1838 account, even though it is uncertain whether Joseph dictated this part of the Manuscript History of the Church in 1838 in Missouri or in 1839 in Nauvoo.

Situating the Vision

In 1819 young Joseph Smith and his parents, brothers, and sisters lived in what is now Manchester township in western New York. This region has been dubbed the "Burned-over District," because of the intense outpouring of religious enthusiasm that characterized it in the early nineteenth century.[17] While the 1843 White report simply states that Joseph Smith spoke of "a reformation among the different religious denominations in the neighborhood," and while the Neibaur diary briefly mentions "a Revival meeting," only the 1838 narrative gives any detail about the religious excitement that stirred young Joseph's interest. In this light, the question has arisen as to whether a general religious movement of the proportions described by the Prophet in the 1838 account actually took place around 1820 in his area, and, if so, whether his description agrees with the known facts. It has even been argued, for example, that no such movement took place in the town of Palmyra in spring 1820, and therefore Joseph's account is seriously flawed.[18]

The Prophet's words, however, do not present such a problem. The 1838 account merely says that the excitement began "sometime in the second year after our removal to Manchester," which could mean almost any time in 1819 or 1820. Further, his narrative does not specifically state that such a movement centered or even began in Palmyra. The Smith family, by 1819, lived outside the village of Palmyra, on a farm that was actually in the township (not village) of Manchester.[19] The phrase "in the place where we lived" could easily refer, in context, not to a specific town but, rather, to the general area.

In addition, this 1838 account referred to the "whole district of Country" being affected by the awakening, and this can be interpreted very broadly. Professor Milton Backman has demonstrated conclusively that there was considerable religious excitement in the general area of the Burned-over District of western New York in 1819 and 1820 and that "spiritual quickenings" were particularly intense in 1819, as mentioned in Joseph's 1838 account. Indeed, itinerant preachers, camp meetings, intense spiritual experiences, and conversions all were common in the area, and in 1819–20 some sort of revival activity took place in at least ten towns within a twenty-mile radius of the Smith home.[20] Thus, Joseph had ample opportunity to know of and become involved in camp meetings and other religious activities in the vicinity of his home during 1817, 1818, or 1819, and none of the accounts of his vision are inconsistent with these facts.

Whether he actually attended very many of these camp meetings is less clear. His 1838 narrative reports that his mind "at different times was greatly excited," because "the cry and tumult were so great and incessant," but the confusion and strife that troubled him so deeply probably extended into general religious discussions and was not limited to camp meetings as such. The Neibaur diary affirms that "the first call he had [came at (?)] a Revival meeting." Joseph's mother and brother and sister "got Religion" on that occasion, and Joseph "wanted to feel & ~~sho~~ shout like the Rest but could feel nothing." The observation that general confusion rather than revival meetings alone caused his agitation would explain why most of the First Vision accounts make little mention of revivalist excitement.

Dating the Vision

Joseph Smith reached his fourteenth birthday on December 23, 1819. In the familiar 1838 First Vision account, he said that he was "at this time in my fifteenth year," and the Orson Hyde account uses these same words (meaning Joseph was fourteen years old). A few paragraphs later in the 1838 account, Joseph said, "I was an obscure boy only between fourteen and fifteen years of age <or thereabouts,>"[21] the last two words being inserted in the manuscript above the line, possibly at his direction, but deleted before it was published in the *Times and Seasons* in 1841. The words "or thereabouts" should not be taken necessarily to contradict the previous statement of his age when the vision occurred, but, rather, simply as part of a very careful approach to writing history. As edited and then published in 1841, the account reflected what Joseph Smith intended the public to understand.

In three other accounts, Joseph simply said (or was reported to have said) that he was "about fourteen years old" when the First Vision was received, when God first revealed himself to him, "a mere boy" (White 1843; see also Nov. 9 and 14, 1835); and the 1842 Wentworth letter account says that Joseph was "about fourteen years of age" when he began to reflect upon the importance of his soul's future state. These uses of the word "about" remind us that the validity of his experience does not hinge on knowing the precise day, month, or year on which that vision occurred, and in light of this slight uncertainty it is interesting to note that the scientifically minded Orson Pratt allowed in 1840 that Joseph Smith was "somewhere about fourteen or fifteen" when his spiritual awakening began.

The only account that cannot be squared exactly with his having been fourteen when the First Vision was received is the earliest draft, the 1832 narrative. There, Joseph Smith wrote that "at about the age of twelve years" his mind became concerned "with regard to the all importent concerns" of his immortal soul. He then became aggrieved that the various denominations did not "adorn their profession by a holy walk" as required by the Bible, and he pondered in his heart many things concerning the darkness of the world for three years, "from the age of twelve years to fifteen," culminating with the vision in that year, as he says, when he was "in the 16th year of my age" (that is, fifteen years old). Here we learn that Joseph's personal spiritual concerns began earlier (at the age of twelve) than we might otherwise have supposed, and that his discontent over the contentions, divisions, wickedness, and abominations around him grew over a period of two to three years. That, in preparing his 1832 draft, he might have thought of those intense struggles as having lasted a year longer than they actually had is readily understandable. After more careful reflection he would consistently report that the answer came in his fifteenth year.

In sum, this examination leads to the conclusion that the First Vision, in all probability, occurred in spring 1820, when Joseph was fourteen years old. The preponderance of the evidence supports that conclusion.

Joseph Smith's Concerns

Joseph Smith's personal spiritual awakenings began at the age of twelve and grew over a period of about two or three years. Several issues, not just a single problem, concerned and perplexed him.

At first, his thoughts turned inward. He was concerned about the eternal welfare of his own soul, as he had become "convicted of [his] sins" (1832). He became almost overwhelmed with the awesomeness of the eternities (1832), and

> he began seriously to reflect upon the necessity of being prepared for a future state of existence: but how, or in what way, to prepare himself, was a question, as yet, undetermined in his own mind: he

Table 1: Background Conditions Mentioned in the First Vision Accounts

	1832 Smith	1835 Documents	1838 Smith	1840 Pratt	1842 and 1843 Smith	1842 Hyde	1843 Richards	1843 White	1844 Neibaur
Joseph's age 14 or about 14		✓	✓	✓	✓	✓		✓	
Joseph's age 15 or about 15	✓			✓					
Religious excitement of the period			✓					✓	✓
Wanted to get religion									✓
Joseph's concern for his soul (or future state)	✓	✓		✓	✓	✓			
His quest for forgiveness of sin	✓								
Joseph's concern for mankind in general	✓								
Confusion or strife among denominations	✓	✓	✓	✓	✓	✓			
Insincerity and bad feelings among religionists			✓			✓			
No church built or set up as in New Testament	✓						✓		
His quest to know which church (if any) was right	✓	✓	✓	✓	✓	✓	✓	✓	
Convinced of God's goodness and greatness	✓					✓			
Reason told him there was only one truth				✓	✓	✓			
All could not be right, God not author of confusion					✓				
Not to rely on chance but positive evidence				✓		✓			
His searching the scriptures, James 1:5	*	✓	✓	✓	✓	✓		✓	✓

*Includes the phrase "no respecter to persons."

> perceived that it was a question of infinite importance, and that the salvation of his soul depended upon a correct understanding of the same. (Pratt 1840)

With so much religious activity going on around him, young Joseph Smith found himself influenced in many ways as he sought answers. He saw four members of his family join the Presbyterian Church, while his own "mind became somewhat partial toward the Methodist sect" (1838). It would not be inconsistent with any of these accounts to conclude that Joseph then became involved in the religious excitement known to have occurred in his area during summer or fall 1819, while he was thirteen years old. At first he desired but could not find the emotional experience he had witnessed in others, as he told Alexander Neibaur, but he continued his quest.

As Joseph struggled, more questions came to his mind. According to his earliest statement, this led to an intensive searching of the scriptures. For a period of time, he tried to evaluate the different denominations and found that they did not agree with what he saw in the scriptures. He determined that various churches had "apostatised from the true and liveing faith" (1832). He was shocked by the confusion, strife, insincerity, and bad feelings he found among those who professed to be religious. Such apprehensions about the world worked within him for several months. He became concerned with the "wicke[d]ness and abominations" of the world, and came to mourn "for the sins of the world" as much as for his own sins (1832).

These concerns caused him to consider joining one of the various denominations. Here, however, as recorded in practically all the accounts,[22] he became disillusioned, especially with the fact that the ministers would contend so bitterly for converts. It became so bad, he wrote in 1838, that "great confusion and bad feeling ensued—priest contending against priest, and convert against convert; so that all their good feelings one for another, if they ever had any, were entirely lost in a strife of words and a contest about opinions" (JS–H 1:6).

At this point the youth became even more confused. He still wanted to join a church. When he finally decided to make it a matter of prayer, he had in mind specifically that he wanted to "know what Church to join" (White 1843). In looking at all the churches, he said, "I knew not who was right or who was wrong, but considered it of the first importance to me that I should be right" (History 1835). This burning question is, in fact, mentioned in all the accounts, excepting only Neibaur's short diary entry.

At the same time, young Joseph began to suspect that perhaps none of the churches were right. The first time he recorded the vision he declared that in searching the scriptures he "found that ~~mand~~ <mankind> did not come unto the Lord but that they had apostatised from the true and liveing faith and there was no society or denomination that built upon the gospel of Jesus Christ as recorded in the new testament" (1832). Later he explained his feelings this way: "I often said to myself, what is to be done? Who of all these parties are right? Or are they all wrong together?" (1838).[23] His youthful mind apparently still clung to the hope that one of the contending sects was "right," but at the same time he could not ignore the disturbing possibility that "the true and liveing faith" no longer existed (1832). Orson Hyde went so far as to write that "the hope of ever finding a sect or denomination that was in possession of unadulterated truth left him."[24]

Amid this war of words and feelings, the Prophet's mind was drawn especially to James 1:5. "If any of you lack wisdom," he read, "let him ask of God, that giveth to all men liberally, and upbraideth not; and it shall be given him." Joseph Smith said,

> Never did any passage of scripture come with more power to the heart of man than this did at this time to mine. It seemed to enter with great force into every feeling of my heart. I reflected on it again and again, knowing that if any person needed wisdom from God, I did; . . . At length I came to the conclusion that I must either remain in darkness and confusion, or else I must do as James directs, that is, ask of God. (JS–H 1:12–13)

The influence of this passage is mentioned explicitly in eight of the accounts, and it probably stands behind the 1832 account's affirmation that God is "no respecter to persons" as well.[25]

Joseph Smith's Quest and Struggle in the Grove

Taking this provocative scripture deeply to heart, being convinced by the scriptures of God's power and goodness (1832), having been emboldened by "the lens of reason and common sense" that told him "that there was only one truth" (Hyde 1842), and not wanting to rely on chance but to decide in the light of "positive and definite evidence" (Pratt 1840), the youthful Joseph decided then, for the first time in his life, to pray vocally about the matter (1835, 1838). After months of struggle, he finally knew the course he must follow, and sometime in spring 1820 he went "immediately" to a familiar spot in the woods near his home to make the attempt (White 1843).

The months of anguish had resulted in obvious spiritual maturity, and he had at least three serious questions on his mind as he bowed in fervent prayer: (1) he was concerned for his own salvation and sought forgiveness of his sins (1832); (2) he was concerned for the welfare of mankind in general, for, he said, "I felt to mourn for my own sins and for the sins of the world" (1832); and (3) he wanted to know which, if any, of the churches was right, and which he should join.

No one knows how long young Joseph remained in the grove, but it is clear that before the object of his prayer was accomplished he had a long, desperate, and perhaps almost fatal struggle with the forces of evil from the unseen world. His first effort to pray was fruitless, for, he said, "immediately I was <siezed> upon by some power which entirely overcame me and <had> such astonishing influence over me as to bind my tongue so that I could not speak" (1838). He later told his friends that his tongue seemed swollen in his mouth, so much so that he could not utter a word (1835, 1844).

As he struggled to pray, several strange things happened. Unwanted and distracting thoughts ran through his mind: "The adversary then made several strenuous efforts to cool his ardent soul. He filled his mind with doubts and brought to mind all manner of inappropriate images to prevent him from obtaining the object of his endeavors" (Hyde 1842).

At one point, Joseph said, "I heard a noise behind me like some one walking towards me: I strove again to pray, but could not; the

Table 2: Joseph Smith's Quest and Struggle

	1832 Smith	1835 Documents	1838 Smith	1840 Pratt	1842 and 1843 Smith	1842 Hyde	1843 Richards	1843 White	1844 Neibaur
He prayed	✓		✓				✓	✓	✓
He prayed mightily or fervently		✓		✓	✓	✓			
Cried for mercy	✓								
Called on God for the first time		✓	✓						
Realized no church was built on scriptural gospel	✓					✓			
Wanted to know which church was right		✓	✓	✓	✓		✓	✓	
Heard footsteps		✓							
Inability to speak, tongue swollen or bound		✓	✓						✓
Beset by doubts and strange images						✓			
Tempted or beset by dark powers			✓	✓					
Thick darkness or cloud			✓			✓			
Exerted all powers			✓						
Prayed again		✓	✓	✓		✓			
Felt easier									✓

noise of walking seemed to draw nearer; I sprang upon my feet and looked round, but saw no person, or thing that was calculated to produce the noise of walking" (History 1835).

During the struggle, "thick darkness" (1838) or a "dark cloud" (Hyde 1842) seemed to gather around him. He was "severely tempted by the powers of darkness" (Pratt 1840), and he felt that he was "doomed to sudden destruction" and must abandon himself "to the power of some actual being from the unseen world" (1838). It was more of a struggle, more of an agony, than readers usually stop to think about. This experience left a deep, indelible impression on Joseph Smith.

What Joseph Smith Saw

Despite this alarm, Joseph was able to gather enough inner strength to continue his fervent supplication and to call upon God for deliverance. It was then that he saw overhead "a piller of ~~fire~~ light" (1832). Every account, except for Richards, mentions "light," two calling it "fire." Three accounts use the word "pillar" (1832, 1835, 1838), and three state that it shone "above the brightness of the sun" (1832, 1838; see also Wentworth Letter 1842). Pratt simply called it "glorious."

It seemed to begin far way, in the heavens (1840), gradually descending (1838, 1840, 1844) above his head (1835, 1838), even increasing in brightness so that

> by the time that it reached the tops of the trees, the whole wilderness, for some distance around, was illuminated in a most glorious and brilliant manner. He expected to have seen the leaves and boughs of the trees consumed, as soon as the light came in contact with them. . . . It continued descending, slowly, until it rested upon the earth, and he was enveloped in the midst of it. (1840)

The light first rested upon the trees (1840, 1844), then it seemed that flames spread all around but nothing was consumed (1835); when the light "rested upon the earth" (1840), it rested upon Joseph, surrounding or enveloping him in light, as five accounts state (1832, 1835, 1838, 1840, 1844).

As soon as the light had come to rest, Joseph felt himself freed from his spiritual enemy, and as the light rested upon him he was "filled

Table 3: What Joseph Smith Saw and Asked

	1832 Smith	1835 Documents	1838 Smith	1840 Pratt	1842 and 1843 Smith	1842 Hyde	1843 Richards	1843 White	1844 Neibaur
Appearance of light or pillar of light	✓		✓	✓	✓			✓	
Appearance of fire or pillar of fire		✓							✓
Light brighter than the sun	✓		✓		✓				
Above my head		✓	✓						
Light desended from above	✓		✓	✓					✓
Gradually			✓	✓					✓
Flame rested on trees				✓					✓
Light rested on Joseph	✓	✓	✓	✓					✓
Light all around		✓		✓	✓				
First one personage in pillar, then another	*	✓						✓	✓
Two personages			✓	✓	✓	✓			
Exactly like each other		✓		✓	✓	✓			
Glory, defies description			✓	✓	✓	✓		✓	
Appearance of many angels		✓							
Joseph asks which church to join or which is right			✓					✓	✓

*Possibly implied; see discussion on p. 63–64.

with the spirit of god and the <Lord> opened the heavens upon me" (1832). As Elder Pratt described later, "When it first came upon him, it produced a peculiar sensation throughout his whole system; and, immediately, his mind was caught away, from the natural objects with which he was surrounded; and he was enwrapped in a heavenly vision" (1840), and Elder Hyde explained that the natural world was excluded so that he would be open to heavenly things (Hyde 1842). Joseph Smith simply described it as a "heavenly vision" (Wentworth Letter 1842).

According to three of the First Vision accounts, Joseph then saw within the light a single personage, who was soon joined by a second personage (1835, White 1843, 1844). Four of the accounts (1838, 1840, Wentworth Letter 1842, Hyde 1842) simply report that Joseph beheld two personages, without saying whether they both appeared at the same time or one and then the other. Four accounts make the additional point that the two beings were like each other or "exactly resembled each other in features, and likeness" (Wentworth Letter 1842; see also 1835, 1840, Hyde 1842). They seemed to stand above him in the air and their own "brightness and glory" defied all description (1838). There is no doubt that the Prophet intended to convey the message that they were the Father and the Son.

Because the 1832 account does not say that two beings were present in the vision, some people have wondered, Did Joseph Smith see two personages or one? Did he alter his story as time went on?[26] With a little explanation, these questions can be answered. First, it is clear that the consensus of the First Vision accounts is that two personages appeared. While the brief 1843 Richards report leaves out many details, including any specific mention of God's appearance, all of the other eight accounts speak clearly of two divine beings. Second, the remaining account, the 1832 narrative, actually suggests that the vision progressed in two stages: first, Joseph "was filled with the spirit of god and the <Lord> opened the heavens upon me," and second he "saw the Lord and he spake unto me." The second stage clearly refers to Jesus Christ, who identifies himself as the one who was crucified. Though not explicitly stated, the initial mention of the Spirit of God and the Lord may have reference to the presence of

God the Father and his opening of this vision, since it is clear in all the other accounts that the vision was opened by God who then introduced his Son.[27] To be sure, the main point of emphasis, especially in the official 1838 account, was that "I had actualy seen a light and in the midst of that light I saw two personages, and they did in reality speak <un>to me, or one of them did." Finally, remembering that the 1832 manuscript was an unpolished effort to record the spiritual impact of the vision on him, and that the main content of the heavenly message was delivered by the Son, it is understandable that the Prophet simply emphasized the Lord in the 1832 account. Thus, nothing precludes the possibility that two beings were present.

The various versions of the event do not contradict each other regarding the number of personages, even though they emphasize different ideas and details. Similarly, in two of his accounts, Joseph mentions that he saw "Angels" or "many angels in this vision" (Nov. 9 and 14, 1835), a point that does not contradict but rather supplements the other accounts and confirms that multiple beings were involved.

What Joseph Smith Heard

The messages and information received by Joseph as the vision progressed were all that a person with his concerns could ask for, and more. As he listened, he was told several things. Exactly how many things were said, we do not know; but the cumulative information from all these accounts presents a clear and consistent collection that could have taken several minutes to deliver.

First in importance, Joseph received an unmistakable knowledge of the reality of Christ, as one of the two personages pointed to the other and said, "This is my beloved Son, Hear him" (1838; see also White 1843 and 1844). Later in the vision, the Savior himself declared, "Behold I am the Lord of glory I was crucifyed for the world that all those who believe on my name may have Eternal life" (1832). From this Joseph learned that eternal life was possible for all who truly believe on the name of Jesus Christ.

Second, he learned that the Father and the Son knew him personally, for one of them (seemingly the Son) called him intimately by name, “Joseph <my son>,” and told him, “thy sins are forgiven thee” (1832; see also Nov. 9, 1835). Thus purified and filled with the spirit of God, Joseph Smith was able to stand in the presence of God and behold his glory.

Third, young Joseph was encouraged to go his way and to keep the commandments.

Fourth, undoubtedly astonished at all that was happening, Joseph gained possession of himself and asked the main questions that were on his mind: “which of all the sects was right” and which he should join (1838). Neibaur recalled that Joseph asked, “Must I join the Methodist Church[?]” In response, he was informed that he should join none of them, for all were wrong and none was doing good.

Fifth, he learned something more about the current state of Christianity as the Lord confirmed Joseph’s personal conclusion, reached through study of the scriptures, about the great Apostasy, namely that all churches had gone astray. Even before going into the grove, he understood that the gospel had been preached originally in truth and purity, but that the world had strayed from it. The 1832 account adds to that understanding with these words spoken by the Lord: “the world lieth in sin ~~and~~ at this time and none doeth good no not one they have turned asside from the gospel and keep not <my> commandments they draw near to me with their lips while their hearts are far from me.” Levi Richards (1843) reported Joseph Smith as saying he was told “that none of them were right, that they were all wrong, & that the Everlasting covenant was broken.” Alexander Neibaur emphasized this same point: “they are not my People, ~~all~~ have gone astray there is none that doeth good no not one, but this is my Beloved son harken ye him.”

Sixth, he was instructed that the causes and manifestations of the Apostasy were to be found in sin, corruption, and the teaching of false doctrine. Joseph was told “that all the religious denominations were believing in incorrect doctrines; and, consequently, that none of them was acknowledged of God, as his church and kingdom” (1840), and he was expressly commanded a second time not to join with them (1838). The personage who was speaking pointedly warned young Joseph that the churches “were all wrong, and . . . all their

Table 4: What Joseph Smith Heard

	1832 Smith	1835 Documents	1838 Smith	1840 Pratt	1842 and 1843 Smith	1842 Hyde	1843 Richards	1843 White	1844 Neibaur
Father introduced or testified of the Son		✓	✓					✓	✓
Joseph called by name	✓		✓						
Your prayers are answered, special blessing to be given						✓			
Thy sins are forgiven	✓	✓		✓					
Go thy way, keep the commandments	✓								
Jesus described himself	✓								
Join no church			✓			✓		✓	
Do not join Methodists									✓
All wrong, none right	✓		✓						✓
None do good	✓								✓
All in sin, gone astray, broken everlasting covenant	✓						✓		✓
All professors of religion corrupt			✓					✓	
Creeds are an abomination			✓						
All churches teach false doctrine				✓	✓	✓			
Draw near with lips only	✓		✓						
Form of godliness but deny the power thereof			✓						
Forbidden again to join any church			✓	✓					
None acknowledged as his church, kingdom, people				✓	✓	✓			✓
Lord angry, comes quickly	✓								
Gospel fullness promised				✓	✓	✓			

Creeds were an abomination in his sight," explaining further that the professors of religion "were all Corrupt, that 'they draw near to me with their lips but their hearts are far from me, They teach for doctrines the commandments of men, having a form of Godliness but they deny the power thereof'" (1838). While the 1838 account is the only one that mentions the "Creeds" explicitly, most of the accounts contain equally unambiguous words to the effect that the churches of his day had "erred in doctrine" (Hyde 1842). The word "abomination" also appears exclusively in the 1838 account as one of the words used by the Savior.[28] This biblical term has a range of meanings, all pointing to any impure practices that take people away from God.[29]

Seventh, the Prophet learned that God was not the author of the confusion and contention in the lives of those who professed to be followers of Christ. It was one thing for people to disagree with civility and kindness while pondering various inscrutable mysteries of divine truth. It was another thing for chaos and conflict to reign. At the age of twelve, Joseph was pierced to the soul by "the contentions and divi[si]ons the wicke[d]ness and abominations and the darkness which pervaded the ~~of the~~ minds of mankind" (1832). In the 1835 history he similarly spoke of "being wrought up in my mind respecting the subject of Religion, and looking at the different systems taught the children of men." Being torn by the "tumult . . . so great and incessant," as various professors of religion "used all their powers of either reason or sophistry to prove their errors, or at least to make the people think they were in error" (1838), Joseph turned to the Lord for mercy and help.

Eighth, he learned that God was not pleased with the situation in the world. In fact, the Lord said: "mine anger is kindling against the inhabitants of the earth" (1832).

Ninth, Joseph learned that the Second Coming of the Lord was close at hand. "And lo I come quickly as it [is] written of me in the cloud <clothed> in the glory of my Father" (1832).

Finally, Joseph received a promise that "the fulness of the gospel should at some future time be made known unto me" (Wentworth Letter 1842). Elder Hyde stated, "He was further commanded, to wait patiently until some future time, when the true doctrine of Christ

Table 5: Aftermaths of the Vision

	1832 Smith	1835 Documents	1838 Smith	1840 Pratt	1842 and 1843 Smith	1842 Hyde	1843 Richards	1843 White	1844 Neibaur
Lying on his back			✓						
Uncommonly feeble									✓
Joseph filled with love	✓								
Joseph filled with joy	✓	✓							
Joseph filled with calmness, comfort, peace				✓		✓			✓
Ponder in heart	✓								
Lord was with Joseph	✓								
Tried to get others to believe the story	✓		✓					✓	✓
Many tried to oppose Joseph unsuccessfully			✓				✓	✓	

and the complete truth of the gospel would be revealed to him" (Hyde 1842). This promise of further revelation would seem to indicate Joseph Smith's initial calling as a prophet of God.

In addition, Joseph was told "many other things" that he was unable to write (1838).

Aftermaths of the Vision

According to scripture, it is impossible for any person to behold Deity with natural eyes.[30] Joseph Smith made it clear that this profound experience transcended his physical senses (Wentworth Letter 1842; see also Pratt 1840, Hyde 1842) and that it had an exhausting effect upon him. "When I came to myself again," he wrote in 1838, "I found myself lying on <my> back looking up into Heaven," and he told Alexander Neibaur that he endeavored to rise but felt uncommonly feeble.

The effect of this vision on the mind of the youthful prophet was great. After all his earlier confusion, he now felt comforted, and his mind was left "in a state of calmness and peace, indescribable" (Pratt 1840; see also Hyde 1842). Joseph said in his earliest account, "My soul was filled with love and for many days I could rejoice with great Joy and the Lord was with me" (1832). Having been commanded to be patient, he pondered these things in his heart, and he felt that the Lord was with him (1832).

This early account best expresses the tender feelings that must have overwhelmed young Joseph. It is little wonder that he should wish to tell his experience to friends and acquaintances, and one can sense his profound disappointment when, as he stated in the same account, he "could find none that would believe the hevnly vision" (1832). Later he described in detail the immediate unfriendly reception he received upon telling of the vision. He was particularly disappointed at the surprising reaction of a Methodist preacher who "treated my communication not only lightly but with great contempt, saying it was all of the Devil, that there was no such thing as visions or revelations in these days, that all such things had ceased with the apostles and that there never would be any more of them" (1838).

It seemed to young Joseph that he was being attacked from all sides:

> I soon found however that my telling the story had excited a great deal of prejudice against me among professors of religion and was the cause of great persecution which continued to increase and though I was an obscure boy only between fourteen and fifteen years of age <or thereabouts,> and my circumstances in life such as to make a boy of no consequence in the world, yet men of high standing would take notice sufficient~~ly~~ to excite the public mind against me and create a hot persecution, and this was common <among> all the sects: all united to persecute me. (1838)

Conclusion

This chapter does not presume, of course, to provide all the details of what happened at the time of Joseph Smith's First Vision. Joseph himself testified that "many other things did he say unto me, which I cannot write at this time" (JS–H 1:20). Nor does this discussion presume to answer all the questions that may be raised about the meaning and implications of the vision. It has simply demonstrated that the account was repeated several times and on several different occasions, even by the Prophet, and that although each narrative emphasizes different ideas and events, none is incompatible with other accounts. There is, in fact, striking consistency throughout the narratives; they combine impressively to give a consistent and coherent picture. A high percentage of the elements shown in tables 1–5 sporadically appear in multiple accounts, showing a high degree of independent, cumulative corroboration among these accounts.

We offer this information in hopes that it will correct misinformation that has been put in circulation about the authorship, variations, historicity, publications, awareness, and reception of Joseph Smith's First Vision. Despite the impossibility of providing all the details and answering all conceivable questions,[31] we believe that the documentary evidence amply shows that the First Vision can in truth become meaningful in a personal way when one seeks, as Joseph Smith sought, to reach God through earnest and sincere supplication, seeking to worship him in spirit, righteousness, and truth.

James B. Allen is a Senior Research Fellow at the Joseph Fielding Smith Institute for Latter-day Saint History at Brigham Young University. John W. Welch is the Robert K. Thomas Professor of Law at BYU and editor of BYU Studies.

A preliminary version of this article by James Allen appeared in Improvement Era *73 (April 1970): 4–13. Since that time we have learned much more about the documentary evidence of the First Vision, due largely to the painstaking efforts of Dean C. Jessee.*

Notes

1. Paul R. Cheesman, "An Analysis of the Accounts Relating to Joseph Smith's Early Visions" (master's thesis, Brigham Young University, 1965), app. D, 126–32.

2. This document, located by Dean Jessee in the Church Archives, The Church of Jesus Christ of Latter-day Saints, Salt Lake City, was first printed in James B. Allen, "The Significance of Joseph Smith's 'First Vision' in Mormon Thought," *Dialogue: A Journal of Mormon Thought* 1 (Autumn 1966): 40–41.

3. Dean C. Jessee, "The Early Accounts of Joseph Smith's First Vision," *BYU Studies* 9, no. 3 (1969): 275–94.

4. For example, Wesley P. Walters, "New Light on Mormon Origins from Palmyra (N.Y.) Revival," *Bulletin of the Evangelical Theological Society* 10 (Fall 1967): 227–44; Milton V. Backman Jr., "Awakenings in the Burned-over District: New Light on the Historical Setting of the First Vision," *BYU Studies* 9 (Spring 1969): 301–20; Wesley P. Walters, "New Light on Mormon Origins from the Palmyra Revival," *Dialogue* 4 (Spring 1969): 60–81; Richard L. Bushman, "The First Vision Story Revived," *Dialogue* 4 (Spring 1969): 82–93.

5. One of the most significant publications of that era was the Spring 1969 issue of *BYU Studies*, in which nine Mormon writers presented the results of research on "Mormon Origins in New York."

6. James B. Allen, "Eight Contemporary Accounts of Joseph Smith's First Vision—What Do We Learn from Them?" *Improvement Era* 73 (April 1970): 4–13; Milton V. Backman Jr., "Joseph Smith's Recitals of the First Vision," *Ensign* 15 (January 1985): 8–17; Richard L. Anderson, "Joseph Smith's Testimony of the First Vision," *Ensign* 26 (April 1996): 10–21.

7. See, for example, the studies discussed in Dean C. Jessee, "Sources for the Study of Joseph Smith," in *Mormon Americana*, ed. David J. Whittaker (Provo,

Utah: BYU Studies, 1995), 7–28; Grant H. Palmer, *An Insider's View of Mormon Origins* (Salt Lake City: Signature Books, 2002), 235–58, reviewed by Davis Bitton, "The Charge of a Man with a Broken Lance (but Look What He Doesn't Tell Us)," Steven C. Harper, "Trustworthy History?" Mark Ashurst-McGee, "A One-sided View of Mormon Origins," and Louis Midgley, "Prying into Palmer," in the *FARMS Review* 15, no. 2 (2003), 257–410, and by James B. Allen in *BYU Studies* 43, no. 2 (2004): 175–89. For dozens of other publications about the First Vision, consult the bibliography by James B. Allen, Ronald W. Walker, and David J. Whittaker, *Studies in Mormon History, 1830–1997* (Urbana: University of Illinois Press, 2000), s.v. "Smith, Joseph, Jr., First Vision," 933.

8. See note 24 below.

9. Allen, "Significance of Joseph Smith's 'First Vision,'" 30–32.

10. As early as June 1830, a revelation alluded to the remission of sins that probably occurred during the First Vision: "For, after that it truly was manifested unto this first elder, that he had received a remission of his sins, he was entangled again in the vanities of the world." Book of Commandments (Independence, Mo., 1833), 24:6, also published in "Revelations. The Articles and Covenants of the Church of Christ," *Evening and the Morning Star*, June 1832, 1, and Doctrine and Covenants 20:5. There are some slight variations in the latter references, including the dating of the revelation as April instead of June. This revelation, known as the Articles and Covenants of the Church, was widely used as the foundational document in the organization of the Church. In 1831 another early revelation read, "Wherefore, I the Lord, knowing the calamity which should come upon the inhabitants of the earth, called upon my servant Joseph, and spake unto him from heaven, and gave him commandments." Book of Commandments 1:4, also published in Doctrine and Covenants 1:17.

11. *Palmyra (N.Y.) Reflector,* February 14, 1831, 102. Joseph's own testimony on this subject is corroborated by his mother's testimony, as well as by accounts of those in the community who knew him as a young man. Richard L. Anderson's incisive article in the Spring 1969 issue of *BYU Studies* carefully analyzes some of these writers, including Mother Smith, and presents convincing verification for Joseph's claims with regard to what was happening both before and after his experience in the Sacred Grove. See Richard Lloyd Anderson, "Circumstantial Confirmation of the First Vision through Reminiscences," *BYU Studies* 9 (Spring 1969): 373–404.

12. Fawn M. Brodie, *No Man Knows My History: The Life of Joseph Smith, the Mormon Prophet* (New York: A. A. Knopf, 1945), 25.

13. Neal E. Lambert and Richard H. Cracroft, "Literary Form and Historical Understanding: Joseph Smith's First Vision," *Journal of Mormon History* 7 (1980): 31–42; Richard L. Bushman, "The Visionary World of Joseph Smith," *BYU Studies* 37, no. 1 (1997–98): 183–204.

14. In April 1830, a revelation (D&C 21) required that a record be kept in the Church. In March 1831, John Whitmer was appointed to keep a history (see D&C 47:1; 69:2–3).

15. There were a few minor changes between the original Manuscript History and the publication in the *Times and Seasons*. There have been a few additional changes in the account found in the Pearl of Great Price. The reason for these changes is not always clear, although in some cases it was probably simply a matter of improving grammatical style. In any case, the essential details and meaning of the account have not been changed, and the changes are not significant enough to discuss in the text above.

16. In James Allen's original 1970 article on the First Vision, Allen indicated that this report had been published in the *New York Spectator* on September 23, 1843. Allen, "Eight Contemporary Accounts," 6. This is correct, but Allen did not realize at the time that it had appeared first in White's own newspaper, as indicated above, on September 15.

17. For a full account of the period, see Whitney R. Cross, "The Prophet," in *The Burned-over District: The Social and Intellectual History of Enthusiastic Religion in Western New York, 1800–1850* (Ithaca: Cornell University Press, 1950), 138–50.

18. See both Walters articles referenced above.

19. Actually, Professor Milton Backman has found that this area was called Farmington township when the Smiths moved there, but the name was changed to Manchester township a few years later. Horatio Gates Spafford, *A Gazetteer of the State of New-York* (Albany, N.Y.: B. D. Packard, 1824), 302–3; and Hamilton Child, *Gazetteer and Business Directory of Ontario County, N.Y., for 1867–8* (Syracuse, N.Y.: By the author, 1867), 49; quoted in Backman, "Awakenings in the Burned-over District," 303n5.

20. Backman, "Awakenings in the Burned-over District," 312–13.

21. The words "or thereabouts" were not included in the *Times and Seasons* account, 3 (April 1, 1842): 748, nor are they in the 1981 Pearl of Great Price. It is significant, however, that the Prophet should add them to his manuscript as he was preparing it.

22. Except Neibaur, and this account clearly implies the same thing.

23. By way of comparison, Joseph wrote in the 1842 Wentworth Letter: "I determined to investigate the subject more fully, believing that if God had a church it would not be split up into factions," and Orson Pratt wrote: "The great question to be decided in his mind, was—if any one of these denominations be the Church of Christ, which one is it?" The common point in all these accounts is the possibility that none of the churches could be correct.

24. At this point an interesting problem occurs with respect to the 1838 account. After telling of his asking the heavenly visitors which of all the sects

was right, Joseph added, in parenthesis, "(for at this time it had never entered into my heart that all were wrong)." While this seems somewhat inconsistent, it may actually reflect the real confusion of the fourteen-year-old Joseph, who did not want to believe, deep in his heart, that there was no "true" church, even though his mind already asked the obvious questions: "Who of all these parties are right? Or are they all wrong together?" (1838). The confusion within the account, then, might reflect the actual experience of a young man who had thought the unthinkable and yet had not let it sink into his soul (or heart), because it was not what he wanted to believe. Certainly the deep, personal emotions described in nearly all the accounts could lead to a desire to join some church, and hence Joseph's hesitancy to believe that all were wrong. Compare "History of Joseph Smith," *Times and Seasons* 3 (April 1, 1842): 748, and Joseph Smith—History 1:18. The words in parentheses were published in the *Times and Seasons* as well as in all editions of the Pearl of Great Price down to 1902. In the 1902 edition, the words were deleted and remained so until the 1981 printing, which reintroduced the phrase into the text.

25. We do not know what guided or prompted Joseph, but fortuitously he came to this passage in James.

26. For the best treatment of Joseph Smith's concept of God, showing that the assumption is overrated that the Prophet's ideas about God, the Godhead, and divine embodiment migrated over time, see David L. Paulsen, "The Doctrine of Divine Embodiment: Restoration, Judeo-Christian, and Philosophical Perspectives," *BYU Studies* 35, no. 4 (1995–96): 6–94.

27. As Joseph wrote this line in the 1832 manuscript, he originally wrote "with the spirit of god and *the* opened the heavens" (emphasis added). Perhaps he had intended to write "and he opened the heavens." Later, Joseph inserted the word "Lord," the simplest correction of the error, although one that created an ambiguity. But if David could use the word "Lord" in Psalm 110:1, "The Lord said unto my Lord," to refer first to the Father and then to the Son (see Mark 12:36), so could Joseph.

28. This word also appears in the 1832 account but in the context of Joseph having determined through his own searching of the scriptures and observation of the situation around him that "abominations" and "darkness . . . pervaded the ~~of the~~ minds of mankind."

29. The term *abomination*, of course, is offensive and jarring to our friends of other faiths. And indeed, it was a very strong word in the vocabulary of Joseph Smith's America. Webster's 1828 *Dictionary of the American Language* defines "abomination" as "1. extreme hatred; detestation. 2. The object of detestation, . . . 3. Hence, defilement, pollution, in a physical sense, or evil doctrines and practices, which are moral defilements." Nevertheless, an "abomination" in the biblical sense can include anything that takes a person away from God or

his righteousness. The Bible uses the word "abomination" in connection with a wide range of sin or transgression, including idolatry (Deut. 27:15), sexual transgression (Lev. 18:22; 20:13), human sacrifice (Deut. 12:31), eating ritually unclean animals (Lev. 11:10–12; Deut. 14:3–8), witchcraft and divination (Deut. 18:9–14), and dishonest business dealings (Deut. 25:13–16). Proverbs 6:16–19 gives a list of seven things, some more serious than others, that are counted as an abomination unto God: "A proud look, a lying tongue, and hands that shed innocent blood, An heart that deviseth wicked imaginations, feet that be swift in running to mischief, A false witness that speaketh lies, and he that soweth discord among brethren." Thus, seeing the creeds as an abomination may be understood in a number of ways, mainly as a shorthand way of referring to the very problems that they had caused, as identified in the First Vision accounts, namely turning people aside from the gospel, teaching incorrect doctrines of men, professing errors and corruptions, and inciting tumult.

30. See John 1:18; D&C 67:10–13; Moses 1:2.

31. For further discussions of these and other questions, see Allen, review of Palmer, *Insider's View of Mormon Origins*, 175–89.

THE TESTIMONY OF THREE WITNESSES.

Be it known unto all nations, kindreds, tongues, and people, unto whom this work shall come, that we, through the grace of God the Father, and our Lord Jesus Christ, have seen the plates which contain this record, which is a record of the people of Nephi, and also of the Lamanites, his brethren, and also of the people of Jared, which came from the tower of which hath been spoken; and we also know that they have been translated by the gift and power of God, for his voice hath declared it unto us; wherefore we know of a surety, that the work is true. And we also testify that we have seen the engravings which are upon the plates; and they have been shewn unto us by the power of God, and not of man. And we declare with words of soberness, that an Angel of God came down from heaven, and he brought and laid before our eyes, that we beheld and saw the plates, and the engravings thereon; and we know that it is by the grace of God the Father, and our Lord Jesus Christ, that we beheld and bear record that these things are true; and it is marvellous in our eyes: Nevertheless, the voice of the Lord commanded us that we should bear record of it; wherefore, to be obedient unto the commandments of God, we bear testimony of these things.—And we know that if we are faithful in Christ, we shall rid our garments of the blood of all men, and be found spotless before the judgement seat of Christ, and shall dwell with him eternally in the heavens. And the honor be to the Father, and to the Son, and to the Holy Ghost, which is one God. Amen.

OLIVER COWDERY,
DAVID WHITMER,
MARTIN HARRIS.

Courtesy Foundation for Ancient Research and Mormon Studies

The Testimony of the Three Witnesses, which appeared at the end of the 1830 first edition of the Book of Mormon.

The Miraculous Translation of the Book of Mormon

John W. Welch

The translation of the Book of Mormon, completed by Joseph Smith in June 1829, was an amazing feat. By any standard, this 588-page holy book is extraordinary. Isaiah's words, "a marvelous work and a wonder" (Isa. 29:14), which can be translated from the Hebrew more literally as "a miraculous work and a miracle," readily describe the coming forth of this key restoration text.

Divine manifestations of several kinds directed the rapid course of the translation. Through angelic ministrations, the gift of powers to translate, the guidance of visions, and in many other ways, the hand of God was evident in the truly astounding work of bringing forth the ancient Nephite record. Through the Book of Mormon came many crucial revelations opening the heavens for all to receive: vital testimonies of the divinity of Jesus Christ, abundant declarations of God's plan of salvation, heavenly dispensations of ethical teachings, and prophetic patterns for religious rites and ordinances. It is impossible to imagine Mormonism without the Book of Mormon. Its translation was a key event that unlocked a treasury of God's dealings with mankind in the past and, in so doing, opened the way for his work to go forward in the present and on into the future.

While the embedding had occurred centuries earlier, the unfolding process commenced in September 1823, when Joseph Smith Jr.

was visited several times by the angel Moroni, who informed him that God "had a work for [him] to do" (Joseph Smith—History 1:33). The angel went on to state that a book written upon gold plates containing the fullness of the gospel was deposited in a stone box in a nearby hill, and that in due time he, Joseph Smith, would be given stewardship over that book. This extensive record had been complied mainly by the final Nephite leader, Mormon, who lived in the fourth century AD. Painstakingly, he had engraved onto the final set of plates carefully quoted, purposefully abridged, and paraphrased materials that he drew from a much larger collection of historical and religious records that had been written by his predecessors over the previous centuries. Most prominently, Mormon's account featured numerous instances of angelic and divine manifestations, including appearances of Jesus Christ during the year after his resurrection. In about AD 385, Mormon, after adding his own concluding narrative, gave the plates to his son Moroni (who died about AD 421). After appending his abridgement of the Jaredite records, a few ecclesiastical documents, and his own farewell, Moroni finally deposited the plates in the Hill Cumorah in modern-day western New York. On September 22, 1827, Moroni released those plates to Joseph, thus inaugurating one of the most important stages in the Restoration of the gospel.

Numerous approaches can and should be taken in approaching the Book of Mormon. This complex book has been read and scrutinized in many ways: textually, doctrinally, historically, comparatively, literarily, legally, statistically, geographically, philosophically, practically, biographically, intellectually, prayerfully, and spiritually—to name some of the most obvious. The richness of this book inevitably invites several questions: How was this book written? Where did it come from? Joseph Smith testified that he translated the Book of Mormon miraculously, by the gift and power of God. Is that testimony credible?

The following set of over two hundred documents assembles data pertinent to that ultimate question. In particular, from these contemporaneous historical records, this study seeks to determine, as precisely as possible, when the Book of Mormon was translated and how long it took to complete this impressive task. The overwhelming accumulation of the consistent historical details provided by eyewitness participants and local observers leads to the solid conclusion that the Book of Mormon was translated in a very short period of time. Inside of three astonishingly compressed months, Joseph Smith produced the Book of Mormon. Its text simply emerged as it fell from his lips, line after line, recorded by his attentive scribe. The rapidity of the translation left no time for steps normally taken in producing translations.

The historical records corroborating the translation of the Book of Mormon are indeed copious and quite detailed. In addition to several contemporaneous references in the Doctrine and Covenants to the translation as it was underway (documents 1–9 below), accounts were left by many of the participants, eyewitnesses, or observant people who were closely associated with the unfolding translation. These people include Joseph Smith (documents 10–37) and Emma Smith (documents 38–43). Next come the Three Witnesses of the Book of Mormon—Martin Harris (documents 44–68), Oliver Cowdery (documents 69–77), David Whitmer (documents 78–98)—followed by one of the Eight Witnesses, John Whitmer (documents 99–101). The testimonies of these eleven witnesses are found in every printed edition of the Book of Mormon. The thirty-seven accounts given by Joseph Smith and Oliver Cowdery, who were most directly involved in the translation process, are notably specific and powerfully consistent. Further statements by members of the Joseph Smith Sr. family come from Joseph Smith Sr., Lucy Mack Smith, William Smith, and Katharine Smith Salisbury (documents 102–10), and additional testimonies were left by other people who were close to those involved with the translation: Sarah Conrad, Elizabeth Ann Whitmer, Alva Hale, Isaac Hale, Joseph Knight Sr., and Joseph Knight Jr. (documents 111–16).[1]

Many other accounts listed chronologically by publication date (documents 117–202) have survived from people who were not personally involved with or close to the work of translating the Book of Mormon but who may have had contact with some who were;

some of these contemporaneous reports or rumors were circulated by people who were farther removed from these events. Even though their words are patently less useful in reconstructing the historical sequence of events regarding the translation of the Book of Mormon, all such identifiable accounts, including the hostile statements, are interesting to compare and analyze.

Consisting of 202 documents, the entire collection is presented in the document section following this article. Underlining is reproduced from the original document. Editorial marks include angle brackets < > to indicate insertions made by the author of the document. Strikeouts are shown by ~~strikeouts~~. Brackets [ ] indicate editorial comments.

By way of introducing these documents, an annotated chronology is first given, detailing the main events and heavenly manifestations that transpired during the translation and publication of the Book of Mormon from 1827 through 1830. Despite a few minor uncertainties in this historical data, most of the information falls clearly into a single logical sequence of events. The historical record abundantly sustains the basic narrative concerning the coming forth of the Book of Mormon. The sheer number of witnesses, friendly or otherwise, who were aware of this work as it progressed and who sensed its importance enough to speak or write to others about it, renders alternative accounts of fabrication or deception unlikely. At least, perpetrating such a ruse would have necessarily involved the willing collusion of many others who do not appear prone to have been willing coconspirators.

In sum, it is shown that nearly all the 590 pages printed in the 1830 edition of the Book of Mormon were translated, dictated, and written all within an extremely short and intensely busy period of time, from April 7 to the last week of June 1829. Virtually no excess time existed during those three months for Joseph Smith to plan, to ponder about, to research around, to hunt for sources, to organize data, to draft, to revise, or to polish the pages of the original manuscript of this book. Although Joseph became aware of and began contemplating this assignment in September 1823, and while he translated the

116 pages containing the book of Lehi from April 12, 1828, to June 14, 1828, which were sadly lost that summer, once Joseph and Oliver set to work on April 7, 1829, the pages of the Book of Mormon flowed forth in rapid succession. The text of the Book of Mormon was dictated one time through, essentially in final form. This was done despite significant interruptions and distractions. Such a feat, in and of itself, constitutes a considerable achievement, given the length, quality, and complexity of the Book of Mormon alone.

Further details concerning the description of the plates, complex structure of the Book of Mormon, and what can be gathered concerning Joseph Smith's means and methods of translating the Book of Mormon can be found conveniently at the beginning of published editions of the book, in standard histories of the Church,[2] in the *Encyclopedia of Mormonism*, or in other surveys of scholarship about the Book of Mormon.[3] More than this brief mention of these additional topics, however, goes beyond the limited purpose of this documentary presentation.

I am grateful to several people who have assisted over the years in gathering and editing these documents and processing this information for this publication, in particular Erick Carlson, Heather Seferovich, and Jed Woodworth. While everyone involved has attempted to be as thorough as possible, I recognize that further research may yet discover additional information to clarify various individual points. If there are faults, they are ours alone. Dates listed in the chronology are, for the most part, historically verifiable, but some have been approximated. Taken together these details coalesce into a clear picture of the miraculous time of translation of the Book of Mormon.

Events Surrounding the Translation of the Book of Mormon

1827	Sep	Joseph obtains the plates from the angel Moroni.
1828	Jan	Joseph and Emma move to Harmony, Pennsylvania.
	Feb	Martin Harris visits Professor Charles Anthon in New York City.
	Apr 12 ↓ June 14	The 116 pages are translated.
	June 15	Joseph and Emma's first child is born and dies.
		Martin Harris loses the 116 pages.
	July	Joseph travels to Manchester, New York.
	Sep 22	Joseph again obtains interpreters and plates.
	Dec	David Whitmer makes a business trip to Palmyra, New York, where he meets Oliver Cowdery.
1829	Feb	Joseph's parents come from Manchester to Harmony.
		Joseph receives Doctrine and Covenants 4.
		The Lord first appears to Oliver Cowdery.
	Mar	A few pages are translated.
		Martin Harris visits Joseph from Palmyra.
	Apr 5	Oliver Cowdery arrives in Harmony.
	Apr 7 ↓ Late June	The Book of Mormon is translated (see p. 92).
	July	E. B. Grandin and T. Weed decline to print.
	Aug	E. B. Grandin agrees to print.
		Martin Harris mortgages his farm for the printing.
		Typesetting commences.
	Nov	Oliver Cowdery's preparation of the Printer's Manuscript reaches Alma 36.
1830	Mar 26	Publication of the Book of Mormon completed.

Chronology of Events from September 1827 to April 1830 relating to the Translation and Publication of the Book of Mormon

September 21–22, 1827. This was the appointed time when Joseph Smith received the plates from Moroni (documents 105, 106, 116, 146). In 1831, Joseph described the box, the plates (which "resembled gold"), the interpreters (which "resembled spectales"), and explained that by looking into them "he could read a writing engraven upon the plates" (document 14) by the gift and power of God (documents 16, 20, 21, 22, 32, 33, 34, 37, and several others). Moroni charged Joseph that he "should be responsible for them" and that he would be "cut off" if he should let them go carelessly (JS–H 1:59), that is, by "tattling the secrets of the work among his neighbors" (document 93). This charge was strict, for there were reasons to know that "strenuous exertions" would soon be made to try to get the plates from Joseph (JS–H 1:60). Some time before 1847, but possibly as early as 1835, Joseph Knight wrote that he was in Palmyra for several days at this time and that "Joseph [Smith] was some affraid of him [Samuel Lawrence] that he mite be a trouble to him" (document 116). Joseph sent his father to watch Lawrence's house that evening, but no trouble materialized.[4] Joseph (leaving Emma[5] with Joseph Knight's carriage) then went after midnight to the site on the hill, which was two to three miles southeast of the Smith home, and received the plates from Moroni.[6] Joseph then hid the plates "in an old black oak tree top which was hollow"[7] according to Martin Harris, or in "a birch log" according to Lucy Mack Smith. Shortly thereafter, he retrieved the plates and brought them home wrapped in a linen smock.[8]

A few days later a mob (consisting of Samuel Lawrence, Luman Walters, Willard Chase, and others) attempted to get the plates from Joseph. According to Lucy Mack Smith's preliminary manuscript (transcribed from Lucy's dictation by Martha Jane Coray around 1845–47) and according to Brigham Young in 1855, during this time the conjuror Luman Walters (of Sodus, Pultneyville, New York), and others, attempted to get the plates from Joseph, which were hidden at his father's home in Manchester Township.[9]

October 1827. Joseph "commenced working with his father and brothers on the farm."[10] Several attempts were made to get the plates from Joseph, such as the one by Willard Chase's sister, Sally, who used a green glass to see the precise place where Joseph had hidden the plates,[11] and another attempt by a mob of fifty.[12]

Joseph began to "take some measures to accomplish the translation of the record into English but he was instructed to take off a facsimile of characters" (document 106).[13]

November 1827. "[The Smiths] had to garde the house until some time in November. He [Joseph] obtaind fifty Dollars in money and hired a man to move him and his wife to Pennsylvany to hir Fathers,"[14] namely Isaac Hale.

December 1827. Joseph moved from his parents' frame house in the Manchester township, New York, to Emma's parents' house in Harmony, Pennsylvania, while hiding the plates in a barrel of beans.[15] The money for this move was provided by Martin Harris (document 67). Isaac Hale recalled Joseph's arrival at this time as follows: "In a short time they returned, . . . and subsequently came to the conclusion they would move out and reside upon a place near my residence."[16] Immediately after arriving in Harmony, Joseph with Emma "Drew of[f] the Caricters exactley like the ancient"[17] (document 116; see also 25). Before his departure from Manchester Township, Joseph had made arrangements with Martin Harris to join him in Harmony for a specific purpose:

> When Joseph had had a sufficient time to accomplish the journey [to Harmony], and transcribe some of the Egyptian characters, it was agreed that Martin Harris should follow him—and that he (Martin) should take the characters to the East, and, on his way, he was to call on all the professed linguists, in order to give them an opportunity to display their talents in giving a translation of the characters.[18]

December 1827–February 1828. Joseph translated some characters.[19] According to one description of this process given by Joseph, he would put his finger "on one of the characters and imploring divine aid, then looking through the Urim and Thummin, he would see the import written in plain English on a screen placed before him" (document 23). Emma and Reuben Hale acted as scribes: "Now when he Began to translate he was poor and was put to it for provisions and had no one to write for him But his wife, and his wifes Brother would sometimes write a little for him through the winter"[20] (document 116). David Hale substantiated the idea that his brother played some role when he said that Reuben "assisted Joe Smith to fix up some characters such as Smith pretended were engraven on his book of plates"[21] (document 174). Also, Joseph McKune boarded in the neighborhood and attended school at Hickory Grove during the time Joseph Smith was translating at Harmony. He was "quite often in Smith's house," and stated that "Reuben Hale acted as scribe a part of the time"[22] (document 196). At this time, Joseph and those working with him were "thretned By a Mob" and Joseph Knight "came Down" from Colesville on one occasion (document 36).

Apparently during this time, when the book of Lehi was being translated and Emma was acting as scribe, Joseph translated a passage describing Jerusalem as a walled city (compare 1 Ne. 4:4) and stopped to ask Emma if Jerusalem indeed had walls. In 1856, Emma Smith described how she wrote down part of the translation as Joseph

> dictated each sentence, word for word, and when he came to proper names he could not pronounce, or long words, he spelled them out, and while I was writing them, if I made a mistake in spelling, he would stop me and correct my spelling, although it was impossible for him to see how I was writing them down at the time. Even the word *Sarah* he could not pronounce at first, but had to spell it, and I would pronounce it for him.
>
> When he stopped for any purpose at any time he would, when he commenced again, begin where he left off without any hesitation, and one time while he was translating he stopped suddenly, pale as a sheet, and said, "Emma, did Jerusalem have walls around it?" When I answered, "Yes," he replied "Oh! I was afraid I had been deceived." He had such a limited knowledge of history at that time that he did not even know that Jerusalem was surrounded by walls.[23] (document 38; details corroborated in documents 40, 54, 88, 93, 95, and others)

Several further accounts similarly focus on the point that Joseph Smith was poorly equipped educationally to produce the Book of Mormon. David Whitmer stated that "Joseph Smith was a man of limited education" who was "ignorant of the Bible"[24] (document 95). In 1875, David Whitmer expressed a similar view:

> So illiterate was Joseph at the time, said Mr. Whitmer, that he didn't even know that Jerusalem was a walled city and he was utterly unable to pronounce many of the names which the magic power of the Urim and Thummim revealed, and therefore spelled them out in syllables and the more erudite scribe put them together.[25]

February 1828. Martin Harris arrived in Harmony as Joseph and Martin had planned (document 13). Martin then left for Palmyra, Utica, Albany, New York City, and Philadelphia, visiting with Professor Dr. Samuel Latham Mitchill (the vice president of Rutgers Medical School, located in New York City) (documents 119, 132, 148), and with Professor Charles Anthon (documents 51, 66, 86, 132, 148, 158, 165) at Columbia College and others concerning the characters copied from some part of the unsealed plates of Mormon, perhaps even calling upon Lt. Governor Luther Bradish for consultation.[26] Joseph wrote in 1832 that the Lord appeared to Martin in a vision, instructing him to go to New York City "with some of the c[h]aracters so we proceeded to coppy some of them"[27] (document 13). Martin took with him the transcript of the characters and a translation.[28] That Philadephia was possibly among the "Eastern Cittys" mentioned by Joseph is contained in Joseph Knight Sr.'s recollection that Emma and Joseph drew off some of the characters exactly like the ancient and sent Harris to Albany, Philadelphia, and New York City to get them translated.[29]

April 12, 1828. Martin Harris returned from New York to Joseph's home in Harmony and consulted with Joseph (document 25). Apparently during this time, Harris stated in 1859, "did I not at one time hold the plates on my knee an hour-and-a-half, whilst in conversation with Joseph, when we went to bury them in the woods" (document 46). Harris then returned to his farm in Palmyra township where he "arranged his affairs" for an extended absence.[30] On this date, he and his wife, Lucy, returned to Pennsylvania where Martin joined Joseph as his scribe for the translation of the plates of the Book of Mormon (documents 45, 49) beginning with the book of Lehi[31] (document 84). Lucy Harris wanted to see the plates:

> As soon as she [Lucy Harris] arrived there, she informed him [Joseph] that her object in coming, was to see the plates, and that she would never leave until she had accomplished it. Accordingly, without delay, she commenced ransacking every nook and corner about the house—chests, trunks, cupboards, &c; consequently, Joseph was under the necessity of removing both the breast-plate and the Record from the house, and secreting them elsewhere. Not finding them in the house, she concluded that Joseph had buried them, and the next day she commenced searching out of doors, which she continued to do until about two o'clock P.M. The woman was so perplexed and disappointed in all her undertakings that she left the house and took lodgings during her stay in Pennsylvania with a near neighbor.[32]

Issac Hale also wrote of this time: "About this time, Martin Harris made his appearance upon the stage; and Smith began to interpret the characters or hieroglyphics which he said were engraven upon the plates, while Harris wrote down the interpretation. It was said, that Harris wrote down one hundred sixteen pages"[33] (document 114; see also 49, 84, 93, 116). Although usually in the Hale house, the plates were apparently placed in a box and sometimes secreted in the woods or "in the Mountin" (according to Joseph Knight, document 116; see also 103), or elsewhere, when they were not being employed.[34]

April 12–June 14, 1828. The book of Lehi was translated (document 10). According to Martin Harris's account, "The Prophet possessed a seer stone, by which he was enabled to translate as well as from the Urim and Thummim, and for convenience he then used the seer stone"[35] (documents 52, 56; see also 92, 93, 94, 98, 106, 108, 109, 110). Harris once tested Joseph with the seer stone by replacing the stone with one of a similar shape and color, but Joseph immediately apprehended the difference, thus satisfying Martin (document 55).[36]

June 15, 1828. Joseph and Emma's first child, Alvin (Alva?), was born but died shortly thereafter.[37]

Late June or Early July 1828. The 116 pages of the book of Lehi, which Martin Harris had borrowed from Joseph around June 14 and taken to Palmyra to show to his wife and family, were lost. Lucy Smith and others suspected that Martin Harris' wife, Lucy, stole the 116 pages.[38] Joseph tried with "utmost exertions" to recover these pages (document 10).

July 1, 1828. Joseph remained with Emma for two weeks after the death of their child.[39] He then left for his father's farm in Manchester, New York, and asked Martin to come to his father's house to tell him what happened to the 116 pages. The 116 pages were lost. The interpreters and the plates were then taken from Joseph by an angel[40] (documents 85, 92, 93, 94, 102, 116).

July 1828. Joseph returned to Harmony and stayed "for nearly two months."[41] There the spectacles were returned to him long enough to receive a revelation from the Lord chastising him for allowing "the counsel of thy director to be trampled upon," and assuring him that "nevertheless, my work shall go forth" (D&C 3:15, 16).[42] The spectacles were taken again.[43] Portions of Doctrine and Covenants 10 may have been received around this time (document 2), although it took its final form essentially in 1829, as discussed below, May 15–May 25, 1829.

September 22, 1828. It was promised that Moroni would return the plates to Joseph on this familiar date.[44] David Whitmer said of this time that "the plates, however, were not returned, but instead Smith was given by the angel a Urim and Thummim of another pattern" (document 93; see also 94, 97, 106).

1828–1829 in general. A February 1879 interview with Emma Smith detailed information about the translation during this time period:

> Q. Who were scribes for father when translating the Book of Mormon?
>
> A. Myself [Emma Smith], Oliver Cowdery, Martin Harris, and my brother, Reuben Hale. . . .
>
> Q. What is the truth of Mormonism?
>
> A. I know Mormonism to be the truth; and believe the Church to have been established by divine direction. I have complete faith

in it. In writing for your father I frequently wrote day after day, often sitting at the table close by him, he sitting with his face buried in his hat, with the stone in it, and dictating hour after hour with nothing between us. . . .

Q. Are you sure that he had the plates at the time you were writing for him?

A. The plates often lay on the table without any attempt at concealment, wrapped in a small linen table cloth, which I had given him to fold them in. I once felt of the plates, as they thus lay on the table, tracing their outline and shape. They seemed to be pliable like thick paper, and would rustle with a metalic sound when the edges were moved by the thumb, as one does sometimes thumb the edges of a book. . . .

Q. Could not father have dictated the Book of Mormon to you, Oliver Cowdery and the others who wrote for him, after having first written it, or having first read it out of some book?

A. Joseph Smith [and for the first time she used his name direct, having usually used the words "your father" or "my husband"] could neither write nor dictate a coherent and well-worded letter; let alone dictating a book like the Book of Mormon. And, though I was an active participant in the scenes that transpired, . . . it is marvelous to me, "a marvel and a wonder," as much so as to any one else.[45] (document 41)

A generally reliable non-Mormon journalist stated that "the little low chamber in Smith's house was used as a translating-room," naming the scribes as Martin Harris, Oliver Cowdery, and Reuben Hale.[46] Later, Harris stated that he "wrote for him about one third of the first part of the translation" of the 116 pages (document 53).

Winter 1828. Joseph and Emma visited Joseph Knight: "He and his wife Came up to see me [Joseph Knight] the first of the winter 1828 and told me his Case."[47] Probably during this season, David Whitmer made a business trip to Palmyra, where he met Oliver Cowdery for the first time and learned of Joseph and the golden plates (document 86).[48]

February 1829. Joseph's parents came from New York and visited him in Harmony.[49] Joseph received Doctrine and Covenants 4 for his father. Joseph Sr. and Lucy return to Manchester. Oliver, who was boarding with Joseph Sr. and Lucy at this time, began to "importune Mr. Smith" for information concerning the plates and after "a considerable length of time" succeeded in receiving information.[50] About this time, Joseph Smith wrote in 1832, "[the] Lord appeared unto a young man by the name of Oliver Cowdry and shewed unto him the plates in a vision and also the truth of the work and what the Lord was about to do through me his unworthy servant therefore he was desirous to come and write for me to translate"[51] (document 12).

March 1829. A few pages were translated. Emma acted "some" as scribe (documents 78, 79, 86),[52] as did Samuel Smith also (documents 12, 38, 43, 106). During this month, Martin Harris visited Joseph from Palmyra, "seemingly for the prime purpose of being permitted to see the plates. According to other testimonies Martin had not seen the plates during the time he was writing for the Prophet, and he wanted to know of their existence."[53] This visit was the catalyst for Doctrine and Covenants 5. Joseph was told to translate "a few more pages" and then to "stop for a season" (D&C 5:30; document 3).

April 5, 1829. Oliver Cowdery arrived in Harmony to assist Joseph with the translation of the Book of Mormon.[54] Joseph told Oliver "his entire history as far as it was necessary for his information in those things which concerned him" (document 106). Oliver was given assurances that "the words or the work which thou hast been writing are true" (D&C 6:17, 1833 ed.; document 4), and he was offered "a gift, if you desire of me, to translate, even as my servant Joseph" (document 4; see also 5). Joseph and Oliver probably started writing at or shortly after Mosiah 1.[55] Oliver and Joseph met for the first time in person on April 5, 1829. Joseph Knight reports this event: "Next Spring Oliver Cowdry a young man from palmyra Came to see old Mr Smith, Josephs father, about this work and he sent him Down to pensylveny to see Joseph and satisfy him self. So he Came Down and was soon Convinced of the truth of the work"[56] (document 116). A few paragraphs later, Knight expressly places this event in "the spring of 1829"[57] (document 116). Lucy Smith's published reminiscences indicate that Oliver had only second-hand information about Joseph before April 1829, stating that after Oliver "had been in the school but a short time, when he began to hear from all quarters concerning the plates, and as soon began to importune Mr. Smith upon the subject, but for a considerable length of time did not succeed in eliciting any information."[58] David Whitmer, who was first to hear of Joseph Jr. among the Whitmers, recalled speaking with Oliver about the matter in 1828.[59] Oliver was then a teacher in Palmyra, and boarded with the Joseph Smith Sr. family for a time until the school term ended in March 1829.[60] During this time, Joseph Jr. was in Harmony.

Oliver explicitly dates his first meeting with Joseph Smith Jr. as April 5, 1829: "Near the time of the setting of the Sun, Sabbath evening, April 5th, 1829, my natural eyes, for the first time beheld this brother"[61] (document 70; see also 116). On the same page printed in 1834, Oliver said he had endured many "fateagues and privations . . . for the gospel's sake, since 1828, with this brother." Apparently Oliver had begun suffering criticism as early as 1828 for his interest in Joseph and the plates. In 1835 he said he had known Joseph intimately for "almost seven years."[62] From 1829 to 1835 is seven years inclusive. Clear evidence supports April 5, 1829, as the date for the first meeting of Oliver Cowdery and Joseph Smith.

April 6, 1829. Oliver recorded: "On Monday the 6th, I assisted [Joseph] in arranging some business of a temporal nature"[63] (document 70).

April 7, 1829. Oliver began writing as scribe to Joseph Smith, as he remained for the greater part of the translation. He said he transcribed it all "with the exception of a few pages" (document 75). Joseph remembered that Oliver wrote "with little cessation" (document 25). Oliver later recalled, "These were days never to be forgotten—to sit under the sound of a voice dictated by the *inspiration* of heaven, awakened the utmost gratitude of this bosom! Day after day I continued, uninterrupted, to write from his mouth, as he translated . . . 'The book of Mormon'"[64] (document 70; see also 72). Sometime during April 1829, Doctrine and Covenants 6 (document 4), 7, 8 (document 5), and 9 (document 6) were received, and Joseph made a trip to Colesville (document 31). Oliver unsuccessfully attempts to translate (document 6).

Mid to Late April. Oliver wrote two letters to David Whitmer, telling him that "he was convinced that Smith had the records" and

Events Transpiring during the Translation of the Book of Mormon, April to June 1829

Apr	5	Oliver Cowdery arrives in Harmony, Pennsylvania.
	7	Joseph and Oliver begin work.
		Doctrine and Covenants 6, 7, 8, and 9 received.
May	10	Joseph and Oliver go to Colesville, New York.
	15	Aaronic Priesthood restored.
		Doctrine and Covenants 10 received.
		About this time Joseph and Oliver may have gone to Colesville again.
	25	Samuel Smith baptized.
		Doctrine and Covenants 11 received.
June	1	Joseph, Emma, and Oliver begin their move from Harmony, Pennsylvania, to Fayette, New York.
	11	Copyright application filed.
		Doctrine and Covenants 14, 15, 16, and 18 received.
	15	Hyrum Smith, David Whitmer, and Peter Whitmer Jr. are baptized around this date.
	20	Three Witnesses see the plates around this date.
	25	Eight Witnesses handle the plates around this date.
	30	Translation finished by this date.

giving "a few lines of what they had translated" and assuring David "that he knew of a certainty that [Joseph] had a record of a people that inhabited this continent, and that the plates they were translating gave a complete history of these people" (document 84).

About May 10, 1829. Around this time, Joseph and Oliver ran out of provisions (document 25). They went to Colesville (Coleville) to see if Joseph Knight would help them with some provisions, but he was in "Cattskill"[65] (document 116). An account attributed to Joseph Smith might relate to this same trip to Colesville, although an occasion in 1830 is possible:

> When I first commenced this work, and had got two or three individuals to believe, I went about thirty miles with Oliver Cowdery, to see them. We had only one horse between us. When we arrived, a mob of about one hundred men came upon us before we had time to eat, and chased us all night; and we arrived back again [in Harmony] a little after daylight, having traveled about sixty miles in all, and without food.[66]

Joseph and Oliver returned to Harmony and looked to see "if they Could find a place to work for provisions, But found none. They returned home and found me [Joseph Knight] there with provisions, and they ware glad for they ware out"[67] (document 116). Joseph Knight brought writing paper (foolscap) and other provisions for the translation and visited "several times" during May, traveling the distance of at least thirty miles each way (from his farm in Broome County).[68] Joseph was admonished by the Lord to "be patient until you shall accomplish it" (document 7).

May 10–15, 1829. The work progressed steadily until Joseph and Oliver reached the account of the ministry of the resurrected Christ to the inhabitants of ancient America in 3 Nephi. "After writing the account given of the Savior's ministry to the remnant of the seed of Jacob, upon this continent,"[69] the question arose in the minds of the Prophet and his scribe concerning the mode and authority of baptism (document 106).

May 15, 1829. The Aaronic Priesthood was restored to Joseph Smith and Oliver Cowdery by John the Baptist. Oliver and Joseph baptized each other as commanded by God.[70] (See D&C 13.)

May 15–May 25, 1829. Apparently after the completion of 3 Nephi, the final form of Doctrine and Covenants 10 (particularly 10:38–70) was essentially dictated.[71] Doctrine and Covenants 10:41 appears to instruct Joseph to translate the Small Plates of Nephi at a time when he had already translated the account of the reign of King Benjamin: "You shall translate the engravings which are on the plates of Nephi, down even till you come to the reign of king Benjamin, or until you come to that which you have translated." Katharine Smith Salisbury confirmed in 1895 that Joseph had "fasted and prayed several days" and the angel told him "to begin where he had left off" (document 102). This would eventually bring him to the portion he still "retained" from his translation apparently of the first pages of the book of Mosiah, which he had not given to Martin Harris (D&C 10:41; document 2).[72]

May 25, 1829. Oliver Cowdery baptized Samuel Smith,[73] both having possibly arrived in Harmony in April.[74] The translation continued after Samuel's baptism.[75] Hyrum visited a few days later.[76] Doctrine and Covenants 11 was then received; Doctrine and Covenants 11:19 told Hyrum to be patient: "You may assist in bringing to light those things of which has been spoken—yea, the translation of my work" (document 7).

May 15–May 31, 1829. During this time, Joseph and Oliver may have gone to Colesville again.[77] This may have been the time when the Melchizedek Priesthood was restored as Joseph and Oliver were returning from Colesville, but the dating of that event is uncertain.[78] It would take about a day to travel from Harmony to Colesville. At this time Oliver wrote a third letter to David Whitmer telling him "to come down into Pennsylvania and bring him and Joseph to my father's house, giving as a reason therefor that they had received a commandment from God to that effect" (document 84) through the Urim and Thummim. David came, met Joseph Smith for the first time (documents 86 and 106), and remained in Harmony "long enough to satisfy himself of the divine inspiration of Smith" (document 97).

June 1–3, 1829. Joseph and Oliver moved with David Whitmer from Harmony to Fayette, Seneca County, New York, to the home of Peter Whitmer. The journey from Harmony to Fayette (ninety-eight miles direct) would have taken about three days.[79] Emma came a short time afterward (document 89).

June 4–end of June 1829. The translation of the Book of Mormon commenced the day after their arrival (document 85) and was finished in the upstairs room of Peter Whitmer's home by July 1, "about one month" later (document 84). Some of the Whitmers helped as scribes (document 80): "They continued so, boarded and lodged us according to arrangements; and John Whitmer, in particular, assisted us very much in writing during the remainder of the work" (document 25, see also 79, 80).[80] Christian Whitmer is also mentioned as a scribe (documents 78 and 86). Oliver B. Huntington records in his journal a conversation in 1897 with Sarah (Sally) Heller Conrad, who may have been a cousin of the Whitmers and who was at the Whitmer home during these days. She recalled seeing the men "come down from translating room several times when they looked so exceedingly white and strange that she inquired of Mrs. Whitmer the cause of their unusual appearance" (document 111). She soon embraced the gospel.[81] An affidavit of Elizabeth Ann Whitmer Cowdery also pertains to this period: "I often sat by and saw and heard them translate and write for hours together. Joseph never had a curtain drawn between him and his scribe while he was translating"[82] (document 112). Concerning the translation in Fayette, David Whitmer reported a time when Joseph was "put out about . . . something that Emma, his wife, had done." As a result, "he could not translate a single syllable. He went downstairs, out into the orchard and made supplication to the Lord; was gone about an hour—came back to the house, and asked Emma's forgiveness and then came upstairs where we were and the translation went on all right"[83] (document 87, also 94, 96).

June 11, 1829. Before this date, Joseph and Oliver had translated all the Plates of Mormon and the title page inscribed by Moroni. On this day, the copyright for the Book of Mormon was secured at the office of the Federal District Court Clerk, Richard R. Lansing. The application contains the title page of the forthcoming book.[84]

June 5–14, 1829. Doctrine and Covenants 14, 15, 16 (revelations for David Whitmer, John Whitmer, and Peter Whitmer Jr.) were received around this time; Doctrine and Covenants 18 was then also received by Joseph Smith, Oliver Cowdery, and David Whitmer.[85]

June 14, 1829. Oliver wrote a letter to Hyrum from Fayette, stating, among other things: "Remember the worth of souls is great in the sight of God" (compare D&C 18:10); "behold the Lord your god . . . suffered the pains of all men that all men might repent and come unto him. . . . behold he commandeth all men . . . every where to repent" (compare 2 Ne. 9:21–23); "that there they may be willing to take upon them the name of Christ for that is the name by which they shall be called at the Last day and if we know not the name by which we are called I fear" (compare Mosiah 5:9–10); and instructing Hyrum to baptize all men, women, and children over the age of accountability (compare Moro. 8).[86]

Library of Congress

Engraving of Hyrum and Joseph Smith (ca. 1840s) by Sutcliffe Maudsley. The Nauvoo Temple appears in the background.

Mid-June 1829. The translation continued. John Whitmer "assisted us very much in writing during the remainder of the work" (document 25), and previous to that David Whitmer had offered "his own assistance when convenient."[87] Finishing was "slow work, and they could write only a few pages a day" (document 88). Hyrum Smith, David Whitmer, and Peter Whitmer Jr. were baptized sometime in the middle of June 1829 in Seneca Lake, Fayette township, Seneca County, New York.[88] Discussions were also held in mid-June "with many from time to time who were willing to hear us, and who desired to find out the truth as it is in Christ Jesus, and apparently willing to obey the Gospel, when once fairly convinced and satisfied in their own minds. . . . From this time forth many became believers, and some were baptized whilst we continued to instruct and persuade as many as applied for information."[89] A document entitled "Articles of the Church of Christ" was prepared by Oliver Cowdery around this time or later in 1829.[90]

Around June 20, 1829. In Fayette, the Three Witnesses were shown the plates (D&C 17:1–4; documents 46, 51, 61, 62, 63, 64, 65, 72, 74, 136, 155). It appears that this manifestation was prompted by the translation of 2 Nephi 27:12,[91] which reads, "the eyes of none shall behold it save it be that three witnesses shall behold it, by the power of God, besides him to whom the book shall be delivered; and they shall testify to the truth of the book and the things therein." At this time the translation was finished (D&C 17:6; document 8), and the plates were returned to the angel (document 17). A few days later in Manchester, New York, near the Smith log home, the Eight Witnesses were allowed to see and handle the plates (documents 99, 100). Lucy Mack Smith said that she also, at one point, saw and handled the plates (document 105).

AND ALSO THE TESTIMONY OF EIGHT WITNESSES.

Be it known unto all nations, kindreds, tongues, and people, unto whom this work shall come, that Joseph Smith, Jr. the Author and Proprietor of this work, has shewn unto us the plates of which hath been spoken, which have the appearance of gold; and as many of the leaves as the said Smith has translated, we did handle with our hands; and we also saw the engravings thereon, all of which has the appearance of ancient work, and of curious workmanship. And this we bear record, with words of soberness, that the said Smith has shewn unto us, for we have seen and hefted, and know of a surety, that the said Smith has got the plates of which we have spoken. And we give our names unto the world, to witness unto the world that which we have seen: and we lie not, God bearing witness of it.

CHRISTIAN WHITMER,
JACOB WHITMER,
PETER WHITMER, Jr.
JOHN WHITMER,
HIRAM PAGE,
JOSEPH SMITH, Sen.
HYRUM SMITH,
SAMUEL H. SMITH.

Courtesy Foundation for Ancient Research and Mormon Studies

The Testimony of the Eight Witnesses, which appeared at the end of the 1830 first edition of the Book of Mormon.

June 26, 1829. The *Wayne Sentinel* published the Book of Mormon title page, perhaps obtaining the text from the federal copyright application. Probably around this time, Martin Harris approached E. B. Grandin to see if he would publish the book, but Grandin declined, considering it financially a "losing speculation."[92]

July 1, 1829. The translation was completed. David Whitmer later stated that "the translation at my father's occupied about one month, that is from June 1st to July 1st, 1829"[93] (document 84).

July 1829. Thurlow Weed, owner-editor of the *Rochester Telegraph*, was approached twice, but he likewise declined to print the book[94] (document 194). Sometime during July 1829, the printer's manuscript of the Book of Mormon was begun by Oliver Cowdery.

August 25, 1829. Harris mortgaged his farm.[95] Around this same time the contract with Grandin for the printing of the Book of Mormon was possibly signed.[96] It was agreed that five thousand copies would be printed, which was an unusually large press run for that day.[97] Harris promised to deliver the sum of $3,000 to Grandin within eighteen months. If Harris defaulted, his land was to be "sold at public auction to satisfy the demand."[98] Hyrum deliverd the first manuscript installment, and typesetting commenced "in August."[99]

Fall 1829. The original typesetter was John H. Gilbert and proofs were printed by J. H. Bortles until December. Grandin then hired Thomas McAuley, a "journeyman pressman." McAuley and Bortles did the "balance of the press-work" until March 1830.[100] Martin Harris, Hyrum Smith, and Oliver Cowdery visited Grandin's office frequently during this period; Joseph, returning to Harmony on October 4, came only once for a short visit to Grandin's office.[101] Manuscript pages were hand delivered and retrieved frequently. Oliver "held and looked over the manuscript when most of the proofs were read."[102]

November 6, 1829. Oliver wrote a letter to Joseph in Harmony: "The printing goes rather Slow yet as the type founder has been sick but we expect that the type will be in and Mr. Granden still think[s] ~~we~~ <he> will finish printing by the first of feb[r]uary." In a postscript Cowdery noted his progress in preparing the Printer Manuscript: "P S I have Just got to alma['s] commandment to his son in coppying the manuscrip," that is, to Alma 36.[103]

Restoration of the Grandin print shop, where the Book of Mormon was printed.

January 1830. Abner Cole (alias Obediah Dogberry), in his *Palmyra Reflector*, January 2, 13, and 22, printed several extracts of the Book of Mormon from sheets he pilfered at Grandin's printing office (where his own newspaper was printed).[104] This made it necessary for Joseph to return to Palmyra from Harmony and to assert his copyright privileges in order to stop this unauthorized publication of sections of the Book of Mormon.[105] During that winter,[106] Joseph apparently sent Oliver Cowdery and Hiram Page to Kingston, Ontario, Canada, to try to sell the Book of Mormon copyright.[107]

January 16, 1830. Joseph Smith Jr. entered into an agreement with Martin Harris which reads:

> I hereby agree that Martin Harris shall have an equal privilege with me & my friends of selling the Book of Mormon of the Edition now printing by Egbert B Grandin until enough of them shall be

> sold to pay for the printing of the same or until such times as the said Grandin shall be paid for the printing the aforesaid Books or copies[.]
>
> Manchester January the 16th 1830— /s/ Joseph Smith Jr
>
> Witness /s/ Oliver H P Cowdery.[108]

February 12, 1830. Lucius Fenn of Covert, Seneca County, New York, wrote to Birdseye Bronson in Winchester, Connecticut, that the publication of the Book of Mormon was widely awaited; it was expected to tell when "the Millenniam day . . . is a goeing to take place" (document 121). About this time, according to David Whitmer, Joseph gave the seer-stone to Oliver Cowdery (document 96).

March 26, 1830. The printing and binding were finished and the book was offered for sale to the public on March 26, 1830. After printing the complete title page of the Book of Mormon, the newspaper notice continued: "The above work, containing about 600 pages, large Duodecimos, is now for sale, wholesale and retail, at the Palmyra Book Store, by Howard & Grandin."[109] Prices at Grandin's Bookstore seem to have ranged from $1.25 to $1.75 per book.[110]

April 6, 1830. The Church of Christ was organized. Affirmations were given that the Book of Mormon was translated by the power of God, that by repenting, humbling himself, and having faith, Joseph received the power to translate (documents 9 and 10). In the ensuing years, Joseph described and bore testimony of the translation process on several occasions (see documents 16, 17, 18, 19, 20, 21, 22, 23, 24, 25, 26, 28, 29, 30, 32, 33, 34, 35, 37).

In conclusion, the question can now be answered, How long did it take for Joseph Smith to translate the Book of Mormon as it was published in 1830? Assuming that he resumed translating on April 7, 1829, "where he had left off" at the begining of King Benjamin's reign,[111] the translation of Mosiah 1 to Moroni 10 (about 390 pages in the 1981 edition, with the exception of "a few pages" translated in March) took place from April 7 to the end of May. Subtracting time to eat, to sleep, to seek employment to earn money for supplies, to restore the Aaronic and Melchizedek Priesthoods, to make at least one (and possibly two) trips to Colesville, to baptize Hyrum and Samuel, to write three letters to David Whitmer, to receive Doctrine and Covenants sections 6 through 13, and to worry about rising persecution, there would seem to be about forty-five possible translating days in this window of time. This would mean that Joseph translated and Oliver wrote down on average eight present Book of Mormon pages per day, working "from morning till night" (document 89).

The translation of 1 Nephi to 2 Nephi 27 (about 100 pages) appears to have taken about 12 days in June, since one must allow most of the first week of June for the move from Harmony to Fayette, some time to acquire the copyright on June 11, several days for preaching and baptizing near Fayette, and one must get at least to 2 Nephi 11:3 and probably to 27:12 before the Three Witnesses see the plates around June 20. This again would be about 8 pages per day. During this time, Doctrine and Covenants sections 14 through 18 were also received and written.

The last block of translation (about 33 pages) would have taken about 4 days if Joseph and Oliver continued working at their regular translating pace, or it is possible that the translation of these last few pages was spread out over the last 10 days of June. Assuming the last 33 pages took about 6 days time, whenever in the end of June those days may have been finished, the total approximate maximum time involved in translating the entire text can be estimated at 63 days (45 plus 12 plus 6), averaging about 8 pages per day overall.

Alternatively, it is possible that 1 Nephi 1 through the account of Jesus' ministry among the Nephites in 3 Nephi (with the exception of the "few pages" translated in March before Oliver Cowdery's arrival) was translated in about 33 working days (from April 7 to May 15, subtracting a few days for the activities already mentioned). This is some 460 pages in about 33 days, or an average of almost 14 pages per day. The last 71 pages from the later part of 3 Nephi to the end of the book would then have been translated from the middle of May and the end of June, in which there would have been about 30 translating days. Here they would have been averaging only 2⅓ pages per day. This alternative puts about 85 percent of the translation into a relatively even shorter time (33 working days, from April 7 to May 15).

Either way and in any event, the pace was blistering. Either sequence has the entire work as it now stands completed within around 63 working days. Consider producing all King Benjamin's Speech—final copy, from start to finish (some 13 pages long, Mosiah 1–6)—in less than a day and a half. This rate alone is staggering.[112] As Terryl Givens concludes, "Joseph and Oliver managed a truly prodigious rate of translation during the months of April and May—over 3,500 original words a day essentially set down indelibly as they went."[113] On top of all else that was going on during these weeks, this must have been quite a time. As Oliver Cowdery said: "These were days never to be forgotten—to sit under the sound of a voice dictated by the *inspiration* of heaven, awakened the utmost gratitude of this bosom! Day after day I continued, uninterrupted, to write from his mouth, as he translated . . . 'The book of Mormon'"[114] (document 70).

John W. Welch is the Robert K. Thomas Professor of Law at the J. Reuben Clark Law School at Brigham Young University, Editor in Chief of BYU Studies, *and Director of Publications for the Joseph Fielding Smith Institute for Latter-day Saint History at Brigham Young University. FARMS circulated a preliminary version of this chronology.*

Notes

1. See generally, Richard Lloyd Anderson, *Investigating the Book of Mormon Witnesses* (Salt Lake City: Deseret Book, 1981); Milton V. Backman Jr., *Eyewitness Accounts of the Restoration* (Orem, Utah: Grandin Book, 1983; reprint Salt Lake City: Deseret Book, 1986).

2. See Joseph Smith—History in the Pearl of Great Price; Joseph Smith Jr., *History of The Church of Jesus Christ of Latter-day Saints*, ed. B. H. Roberts, 2d ed., rev., 7 vols. (Salt Lake City: Deseret Book, 1971) (hereafter cited as *History of the Church*); Richard L. Bushman, *Joseph Smith and the Beginnings of Mormonism* (Urbana: University of Illinois Press, 1984); B. H. Roberts, *A Comprehensive History of The Church of Jesus Christ of Latter-day Saints, Century One*, 6 vols. (Provo, Utah: Corporation of the President, The Church of Jesus Christ of Latter-day Saints, 1965).

3. For example, Monte S. Nyman and Lisa Bolin Hawkins, "Book of Mormon: Overview," 1:139–43; Royal Skousen, "Book of Mormon Manuscripts," 1:185–86; Grant R. Hardy and Robert E. Parsons, "Book of Mormon Plates and Records," 1:195–201; John W. Welch and Tim Rathbone, "Book of Mormon Translation by Joseph Smith," 1:210–13, in *Encyclopedia of Mormonism,* ed. Daniel H. Ludlow, 4 vols. (New York: Macmillan, 1992). For a thorough discussion of the coming forth of the Book of Mormon, its structure, and the various religious and scholarly receptions or reactions it evoked, see Terryl L. Givens, *By the Hand of Mormon: The American Scripture that Launched a New World Religion* (Oxford: Oxford University Press, 2002).

4. Dean Jessee, "Joseph Knight's Recollection of Early Mormon History," *BYU Studies* 17, no. 1 (1976): 32–33 (document 116; brackets in original). Samuel Lawrence is presented as a friend by Willard Chase in document 147.

5. Joseph had married Emma Hale on January 18, 1827. Joseph Smith—History 1:57.

6. Midnight marked the beginning of the 22nd. Joseph Smith—History 1:59, *History of the Church*, 1:18; Dean C. Jessee, ed. and comp., *The Personal Writings of Joseph Smith*, rev. ed. (Salt Lake City: Deseret Book; Provo, Utah: Brigham Young University Press, 2002), 13; Oliver Cowdery, "Letter VII," *Messenger and Advocate*, July 1835, 158–59. Along with the plates, Joseph also received spectacles, a rod, and a breastplate; Jessee, "Joseph Knight's Recollection," 33 (see also document 116); William Smith, according to J. W. Peterson, "The Urim and Thummim," *Rod of Iron* 1 (February 1924): 6–7 (see also documeents 108, 109, 110); Lucy Mack Smith, Preliminary Manuscript 1, dictated to Martha Jane Coray around 1845–47, Church Archives, The Church of Jesus Christ of Latter-day Saints, Salt Lake City, published in Lavina Fielding Anderson, ed., *Lucy's Book* (Salt Lake City: Signature Books, 2001), 376–79, 384, 388–92; see also documents 104, 105. (Manuscript 1 underwent further editing by Howard Coray [MS 2] and was finally published in 1853 as *Biographical Sketches of Joseph Smith the Prophet.*)

7. As reported by Martin Harris to Joel Tiffany in "Mormonism—No. II," *Tiffany's Monthly* 5 (August 1859): 165. In "a birch log" according to Lucy Mack Smith, Prelim. MS 1, cited in Anderson, *Lucy's Book*, 385. Roberts, *Comprehensive History*, 1:86.

8. Joseph Smith's sister Katharine was at home

> when he came in running and burst through the door carrying the plates; and that his hand was injured from striking one of the villains [who had chased him]. He told her that he had jumped over a rail fence; when one of the villains grabbed for the plates, he knocked him down with his right fist while carrying the plates under his left arm

> clasped to his body. Then he ran the guantlet with several more, and when he came in the house she said he was completely out of breath. She took the plates from him and laid them on the table temporarily, and helped revive him until he got breathing properly and also examined his hand, and treated it for the bruises on his knuckles, where he had struck the villain and thus defended himself and the plates. (H. S. Salisbury [grandson of Katharine Smith Salisbury], "The Prophet's Sister Testifies She Lifted the Book of Mormon Plates," Interview, August 31, 1954, by Isaac B. Ball, 2, Church Archives)

See also Lucy Mack Smith, Prelim. MS 1, cited in Anderson, *Lucy's Book*, 386–88; and Roberts, *Comprehensive History*, 1:90–91. On the weight of the plates, see Robert F. Smith, "The 'Golden' Plates," in *Reexploring the Book of Mormon*, ed. John W. Welch (Salt Lake City: FARMS, 1992), 275–77.

9. Jessee, "Joseph Knight's Recollection," 33–34; History of the Church, 1:18–19; Lucy Mack Smith, Prelim. MS 1, cited in Anderson, Lucy's Book, 380–82; Lucy Mack Smith, *Biographical Sketches of Joseph Smith, the Prophet, and His Progenitors for Many Generations* (London: Published for Orson Pratt by S. W. Richards, 1853), 102–9; Brigham Young, in *Journal of Discourses*, 26 vols. (Liverpool: F. D. Richards, 1855–86), 2:180–81, February 18, 1855, and 5:55, July 19, 1857 (cited in Jessee, "Joseph Knight's Recollection," 33n12); see also documents 124, 134, 138.

10. Lucy Mack Smith, *Biographical Sketches*, 107; Lucy Mack Smith, Prelim. MS 1, cited in Anderson, *Lucy's Book*, 389.

11. Lucy Mack Smith, *Biographical Sketches*, 109; Lucy Mack Smith, Prelim. MS 1, cited in Anderson, *Lucy's Book*, 393; see also document 198.

12. Lucy Mack Smith, *Biographical Sketches*, 113; Lucy Mack Smith, Prelim. MS 1, cited in Anderson, *Lucy's Book*, 401. Note also the Joseph Bates Noble reminiscence of Joseph Smith and the plates:

> My first introduction to this young Mormon [Mary A. Beman] was at McMillens my place of boarding, She was teaching School in the neighbor hood. her ~~parents~~ Father Alvah Beman lived a bout [*sic*] two 1/2 miles distance a man well off as to houses and land and goods of this world and verry highly esteemed amoung men for his word this man was well acquainted with the Smith family before the coming forth of the book of Mormon. and was with Joseph at one time assisted him in hiding the Plates, from a mob he was permited to handle the Plates with a thin cloth covering over them. This Mary A. Beman Brought the Book of Mormon into the Neighbour, the first I had ever heard of. (Joseph B. Noble, Autobiographical Sketch, 1810–1836, Church Archives)

Likewise Mary A. [Beman] Noble speaks of her father, Alvah Beman, the mob, and the plates:

> Father sold his place in Livonia and removed with his family to Avon Livingston County some years previous my Father became acquainted with Father Joseph Smith the Father of the Prophet he frequently would go to Palmira to see Father Smiths and his family during this time Brother Joseph Smith come in possession of the plates that contained the Book of Mormon as soon as it was noised around that there was a golden Bible found (for that was what it was called at that time) the minds of the people become so excited and it arose at such a pitch that a mob collected together to search the house of Father Joseph Smith to find the records my Father was there at the time and assisted in concealing the plates in a box in a secluded place where no one could find them although he did not see them my Father soon returned. (Mary Adeline Beman Noble, Autobiography, 1810–34, Church Archives)

13. Lucy Mack Smith, *Biographical Sketches*, 109 (Lucy Mack Smith, Prelim. MS 1, cited in Anderson, *Lucy's Book*, 393), gives the impression that this was done at the Smith home. Joseph and Emma may have begun this work, however, after arriving in Pennsylvania. Jessee, "Joseph Knight's Recollection," 34.

14. Jessee, "Joseph Knight's Recollection," 34; see also documents 115, 116, 147, 154.

15. Lucy Mack Smith, *Biographical Sketches*, 112–13; Lucy Mack Smith, Prelim. MS 1, cited in Anderson, *Lucy's Book*, 401. Alvah Hale, Emma's brother, assisted the Smiths in their move from Manchester to Harmony. Larry C. Porter, "A Study of the Origins of the Church of Jesus Christ of Latter-day Saints in the States of New York and Pennsylvania, 1816–1831" (Ph.D. diss., Brigham Young University, 1971; BYU Studies, 2000), 83, 130.

16. Francis W. Kirkham, *A New Witness for Christ in America*, 2 vols. (Independence, Mo.: Zion's Printing and Publishing, 1942), 1:135, noting that a copy of the 1833 deed for that land is in the Church Archives. Joseph and Emma may have moved into a nearby house that Joseph purchased from Jesse Hale, one of Isaac's sons. Porter, "Origins of the Church," 133.

17. Jessee, "Joseph Knight's Recollection," 34. "I commenced copying the characters off the plates. I copied a considerable number of them." Joseph Smith—History 1:62. Reuben Hale may have helped prepare a transcript of the characters; see note 21.

18. Lucy Mack Smith, *Biographical Sketches*, 113–14; Lucy Mack Smith, Prelim. MS 1, cited in Anderson, *Lucy's Book*, 402. Lucy Harris obtained a copy of the transcript surreptitiously through the services of her prospective son-

in-law, a Mr. Dikes. Lucy Mack Smith, Prelim. MS 1, cited in Anderson, *Lucy's Book*, 404; see also documents 13, 49, 67, 96, 103, 106, 116, 119, 164.

19. Joseph Smith—History 1:62; *History of the Church*, 1:19.

20. Jessee, "Joseph Knight's Recollection," 35.

21. Statement of David Hale, cited in Emily C. Blackman, *History of Susquehanna County, Pennsylvania* (Philadelphia: Claxton, Remsen, and Haffelfinger, 1873), 104.

22. Statement of Joseph Fowler McKune, cited in Rhamanthus M. Stocker, *Centennial History of Susquehanna County, Pennsylvania* (Philadelphia: R. T. Peck, 1887), 556. Michael Morse, brother-in-law of Emma, recalled seeing Joseph translate in Harmony, with Emma and others acting as scribes, W. W. Blair, "Letter of W. W. Blair about Mr. Michael Morse," *Saints' Herald* 26 (June 15, 1879): 190–91; recollection may also be of events in 1829.

23. Edmund C. Briggs, "A Visit to Nauvoo in 1856," *Journal of History* 9 (October 1916): 454. See also Edmund C. Briggs, "Interview with David Whitmer," *Saints' Herald* 31 (June 21, 1884): 396–97:

> This brings to my mind a statement of the Elect Lady, Emma, in the winter of 1856. She said to me, "When you see David Whitmer you will see an honest man." And in the same conversation, she remarked of her husband Joseph's limited education while he was translating the Book of Mormon, and she was scribe at the time, "He could not pronounce the word Sariah." And one time while translating, where it speaks of the walls of Jerusalem, he stopped and said, "Emma, did Jerusalem have walls surrounding it." When I informed him it had, he replied, "O, I thought I was deceived."

24. M. J. Hubble, Interview, November 13, 1886, located at Missouri State Historical Society, Columbia, Mo.; cited in Lyndon W. Cook, ed., *David Whitmer Interviews: A Restoration Witness* (Orem, Utah: Grandin Book, 1991), 210–11.

25. "The Golden Tables," *Chicago Times*, August 7, 1875, 1. See also Blair, "Letter of W. W. Blair about Mr. Michael Morse," 190–91.

26. See *History of the Church*, 1:19–20; FARMS Staff, *Martin Harris' Visit with Charles Anthon: Collected Documents on the Anthon Transcript and Short-Hand Egyptian*, FARMS Preliminary Report 85a; *FARMS Update*, "What Did Charles Anthon Really Say?" (May 1985); and Stanley B. Kimball, "The Anthon Transcript: People, Primary Sources, and Problems," *BYU Studies* 10, no. 3 (1970), 328–30. Wayne C. Gunnell, "Martin Harris—Witness and Benefactor to the Book of Mormon" (master's thesis, Brigham Young University, 1955), 114, and Rhett Stephens James, *The Man Who Knew: The Early Years. A Play about Martin Harris, 1824–1830* (Cache Valley, Utah: Martin Harris Pageant Committee, 1983), 56–62, note that Martin left Palmyra by wagon with Hyrum,

since the Erie Canal was closed for the winter; Lucy Mack Smith, Prelim. MS 1, cited in Anderson, *Lucy's Book*, 402–3. For more information on Mitchill, see Alan David Aberbach, *In Search of an American Identity: Samuel Latham Mitchill, Jeffersonian Nationalist*, American University Studies, Series IX, History, vol. 46 (New York: Peter Lang, 1988). On Bradish, see Allen Johnson, ed., *Dictionary of American Biography*, 10 vols. (New York: Charles Scribner's Sons, 1927), 1:567–68.

27. Joseph Smith Letterbook 1, 5, Joseph Smith Collection, Church Archives; Jessee, *Personal Writings of Joseph Smith*, 13.

28. Joseph Smith—History 1:64.

29. Jessee, "Joseph Knight's Recollection," 34. See above at December 1827 for this and related statements.

30. *History of the Church*, 1:20.

31. Lucy Mack Smith, *Biographical Sketches*, 115; Lucy Mack Smith, Prelim. MS 1, cited in Anderson, *Lucy's Book*, 404–5.

32. Lucy Mack Smith, *Biographical Sketches*, 115–16; Lucy Mack Smith, Prelim. MS 1, cited in Anderson, *Lucy's Book*, 405–6.

33. Isaac Hale, "Statement of Mr. Hale," *Montrose Susquehanna Register*, May 1, 1834.

34. Lucy Mack Smith, *Biographical Sketches*, 115–16; Jessee, "Joseph Knight's Recollection," 34.

35. "One of the Three Witnesses," *Millennial Star* 44 (February 6, 1882): 86, from lecture of Martin Harris recorded by Edward Stevenson, September 4, 1870, Salt Lake City, printed in "One of the Three Witnesses," *Deseret News*, December 28, 1881, 762–63, reprinted with slight differences in Andrew Jenson, ed., "The Three Witnesses," *Historical Record* 6 (May 1887), 216–17.

36. "One of the Three Witnesses," 87.

37. Dates and the words "infant son," but no name, appear on the tombstone in Harmony; see Porter, "Origins of the Church," 146. Richard L. Anderson reports that the Smith family Bible clearly reads "Alvin."

38. Lucy Mack Smith, *Biographical Sketches*, 118, 120–23; Lucy Mack Smith, Prelim. MS 1, cited in Anderson, *Lucy's Book*, 411, 417–22; Porter, "Origins of the Church," 146.

39. Lucy Mack Smith, *Biographical Sketches*, 118; Lucy Mack Smith, Prelim. MS 1, cited in Anderson, *Lucy's Book*, 412, 416.

40. *History of the Church*, 1:21–23. William E. McLellin mentions this period in a letter to Joseph Smith III, Independence, Missouri, July and September 8, 1872:

> When Joseph delivered the 116 pages of the translation to Martin Harris, his plates, his Interpreters, and his gift were taken from him for some two months. The Plates and gift of translation was restored to him, but not the Interpreters. He translated the entire book of Mormon

> by the use of a little stone he had in his possession before he obtained the plates. (Library-Archives, Community of Christ, Independence, Missouri [hereafter cited as Community of Christ Library-Archives])

Elsewhere in his letter, McLellan cites certificates he has from Elizabeth Ann Whitmer Cowdery (Oliver's widow), Martin Harris, and Emma [Smith] Bidamon, as well as testimony from John and David Whitmer, and refers to "The Directors, or Interpreters," and differentiates them from the Urim and Thummim (the so-called spectacles). For discussions of the possible meanings of such terminology, see Richard Van Wagoner and Steven C. Walker, "Joseph Smith: 'The Gift of Seeing,'" *Dialogue: A Journal of Mormon Thought* 15 (1982): 48–68; Robert F. Smith, "'Translation of Languages' (*hermeneia glosson*, 1 Corinthians 12:10)," unpublished paper, Independence, Missouri, 1980, Community of Christ Library-Archives; and Lyndon W. Cook, *The Revelations of the Prophet Joseph Smith* (Provo, Utah: Seventy's Mission Bookstore, 1981), 122–23.

41. See Lucy Mack Smith, *Biographical Sketches*, 124, and Lucy Mack Smith, Prelim. MS 1, cited in Anderson, *Lucy's Book*, 423.

42. Document 1. See also Lucy Mack Smith, *Biographical Sketches*, 125–26, and Lucy Mack Smith, Prelim. MS 1, cited in Anderson, *Lucy's Book*, 425–27.

43. Whitmer interviews: "The Golden Tables," *Chicago Times*, August 7, 1875, 1; "The Book of Mormon," *Chicago Tribune*, December 17, 1885, 3; "An Old Mormon's Closing Hours," *Chicago Tribune*, January 24, 1888, 5; "David Whitmer's Death," *Chicago Times*, January 26, 1888, 8. All these interviews are reproduced in Cook, *David Whitmer Interviews*.

44. Lucy Mack Smith, Prelim. MS 1, cited in Anderson, *Lucy's Book*, 425, 428, speaks only of the "plates" or "record," with "Urim and Thummim" added above the line later in a different handwritting on p. [96]; compare Lucy Mack Smith, *Biographical Sketches*, 125. Joseph did not use the spectacles for translation after this time according to Emma Hale Smith, Emma Smith Bidamon to Emma Pilgrim, March 27, 1870, Emma Smith Papers, Community of Christ Library-Archives; cited in John T. Clark, "Translation of Nephite Records," *The Return* 4 (July 15, 1895): 2.

45. Joseph Smith III, "Last Testimony of Sister Emma" (dated February 1879), *The Saints' Advocate* 2 (October 1879): 50–51, reprinted in *Saints' Herald* 26 (October 1, 1879): 289–90.

46. Frederic G. Mather, "The Early Days of Mormonism," *Lippincott's Magazine* 26 (August 1880): 198–211, esp. 201.

47. Jessee, "Joseph Knight's Recollection," 35.

48. In "Mormonism," *Kansas City Daily Journal*, June 5, 1881, 1, reprinted in "Mormonism," *Millennial Star* 43 (July 4, 1881): 421–23 and (July 11, 1881): 437–39, cited in Cook, *David Whitmer Interviews*, 58–71. David Whitmer states that he made this trip "in the year 1828." The trip was probably late in 1828,

because Oliver probably first arrived at the district school in Palmyra in fall 1828. Lucy says Oliver was there "a short time" before March 1829 (see Lucy Mack Smith, *Biographical Sketches*, 128), and David Whitmer says in his June 5, 1881, statement that it was only a matter of "several months" after this visit that Oliver went to Harmony in April 1829 to "see [Joseph] about the matter." It also appears that David would have been in Palmyra at a time when Joseph Smith Sr. and Lucy were away (as they were in the first part of winter 1828) or else David would likely have met them at the same time he met Oliver. Lucy Mack Smith, Prelim. MS 1, cited in Anderson, *Lucy's Book*, 431–34, seems to indicate that Oliver taught the full term of fall and winter at school while boarding with the Smiths and was able to leave Palmyra at the close of school.

49. Lucy Mack Smith, *Biographical Sketches*, 124; Lucy Mack Smith, Prelim. MS 1, cited in Anderson, *Lucy's Book*, 423–24; *History of the Church*, 1:28.

50. Lucy Mack Smith, *Biographical Sketches*, 128.

51. Joseph Smith Letterbook 1, part 1, p. 6; Jessee, *Personal Writings of Joseph Smith*, 14.

52. Joseph Smith Letterbook 1, part 1, p. 6; Jessee, *Personal Writings of Joseph Smith*, 14. The text adds "also my Brother Samuel H Smith."

53. Gunnell, "Martin Harris," 29–30.

54. *History of the Church*, 1:32; Oliver Cowdery, "Letter I," *Messenger and Advocate*, October 1834, 14; Lucy Mack Smith, *Biographical Sketches*, 128–31. Lucy Mack Smith, Prelim. MS 1, cited in Anderson, *Lucy's Book*, 438, states that Joseph had been praying for assistance and had been assured by the angel of the Lord that a scribe "should be forthcoming in a few days." Document 106.

55. See footnote 111 below.

56. Jessee, "Joseph Knight's Recollection," 35.

57. Jessee, "Joseph Knight's Recollection," 36.

58. Lucy Mack Smith, *Biographical Sketches*, 128; Lucy Mack Smith, Prelim. MS 1, cited in Anderson, *Lucy's Book*, 432, says "He had not been in the place long till he began to hear about the plates from all quarters and immediately he commenced importuneing Mr. Smith upon the subject but he did not succeed in eliciting any information from him for a long time."

59. See above at Winter 1828.

60. Oliver apparently began boarding with Joseph Sr. in 1828. Larry C. Porter, "The Prophet's New York Years: Restoration, Publication, and Organization, 1829–1830," lecture, October 18, 1984, Brigham Young University, Provo, Utah. See note 48 above.

61. Cowdery, "Letter I," 14. Oliver apparently mentions his "natural eyes" because he had seen the plates and perhaps Joseph before in a vision; see above at February 1829.

62. Oliver Cowdery to W. W. Phelps, "Letter VIII," *Messenger and Advocate*, October 1835, 196.

63. Cowdery, "Letter I," 14.

64. Cowdery, "Letter I," 14.

65. Jessee, "Joseph Knight's Recollection," 36.

66. *History of the Church*, 5:219, taken from Willard Richards's Journal. It is possible, however, that this trip to Colesville occurred after May 25, but this would allow little time for Joseph Knight to have made "several" visits (*History of the Church*, 1:47) before Joseph and Oliver left for Fayette on June 1. The account in *History of the Church*, 1:97, contains most of the same elements, making an 1830 date equally likely, although then the reference to only "two or three" believers seems odd; see below at May 15–May 31, 1829.

67. Jessee, "Joseph Knight's Recollection," 36.

68. *History of the Church*, 1:47.

69. Cowdery, "Letter I," 15.

70. "One morning however they sat down to their usual work when the first thing that presented itself to Joseph was a commandment from God that he and Oliver should repair to the water each of them be baptized they immediately went down to the susquehana river and obeyed the mandate given them through the urim and Thumim." Lucy Mack Smith, Prelim. MS 1, cited in Anderson, *Lucy's Book*, 439. Document 106.

71. The dating of Doctrine and Covenants 10 has been discussed on several occasions. Stanley R. Larson, "A Study of Some Textual Variations in the Book of Mormon comparing the Original and the Printer's Manuscripts and the 1830, the 1837, and the 1840 Editions" (master's thesis, Brigham Young University, 1974), 17–18n15, stated:

> The date of section 10 has become a problem. When the original manuscript of the "History of Joseph Smith" was written, the discussion about this section was accidentally omitted. This omission was soon noticed and two additional sheets with the text of the revelation and the correct date of May 1829 were inserted into the history; but unfortunately it was placed in the wrong context. This incongruity caused later editors to attempt to rectify the situation by altering the date of the revelation to "the summer of 1828." During the lifetime of Joseph Smith the date was consistently reported as May 1829. *The Book of Commandments* in 1833 first printed this revelation in its proper chronological order and with the correct date.

See also Stephen Snow, "Queries," *Mormon History Association Newsletter* 44 (June 1980): 15; Max H. Parkin, "Queries," *Mormon History Association Newsletter* 45 (November 1980): 2–4; Max H. Parkin, "A Preliminary Analysis of the Dating of Section 10," in *Sidney B. Sperry Symposium, January 27, 1979* (Provo, Utah: Brigham Young University, 1979), 68–84; Cook, *Revelations of the Prophet*,

17, 122; Woodford, "Historical Development," 1:200–205. Lyndon Cook and Max Parkin argue for an 1828 date for the first part of Doctrine and Covenants 10, with additional material being added in 1829. For example, Parkin points out several clear similarities between Doctrine and Covenants 10:49–70 and 3 Nephi that support their concurrent dating. If references to receiving the "gospel" in Doctrine and Covenants 10:62 and 11:16, 19 refer to the impending translation of "which was ministered unto" the Nephites in 3 Nephi, and if, similarly, the statement in 18:17 was made at a time after Joseph, Oliver, and David had received 3 Nephi, then those sections bracket the translation of 3 Nephi, as Monte Nyman points out. On the other hand, it is possible that 10:62, which speaks of "that which you have received," is already speaking of the account of the ministry of Christ among the Nephites in 3 Nephi.

72. See Dean C. Jessee, "The Original Book of Mormon Manuscript," *BYU Studies* 10, no. 3 (1970): 260, 277–78, citing also Doctrine and Covenants 5:30. See further, note 111 below.

73. *History of the Church*, 1:44. Lucy Mack Smith, Prelim. MS 1, cited in Anderson, *Lucy's Book*, 439, however, gives the impression that Samuel was baptized on the same day as were Joseph and Oliver.

74. Lucy Mack Smith, *Biographical Sketches*, 130. *History of the Church*, 1:44, however, reports that Samuel did not come to visit until a few days after May 15.

75. Lucy Mack Smith, *Biographical Sketches*, 131.

76. *History of the Church*, 1:44–45.

77. It is possible, but not likely, that Joseph had to appear in court in Colesville at this time, as remembered by Addison Everett in his letter of February 17, 1881, St. George, Utah, to Oliver B. Huntington, recorded in Oliver Boardman Huntington, Journal no. 14, January 31, 1881, L. Tom Perry Special Collections, Harold B. Lee Library, Brigham Young University, Provo, Utah, and discussed in Larry C. Porter, "The Restoration of the Aaronic and Melchizedek Priesthoods," *Ensign* 26 (December 1996): 43–44. See also Lucy Mack Smith, *Biographical Sketches*, 135, but the reference is vague ("After Samuel left them, they still continued the work as before, until about the time of the trial that took place in New York"). No records for such a trial are presently known. The sources seem to be confusing various events with an inconclusive hearing in Lyons, Wayne County, N.Y. (Lucy Mack Smith, Prelim. MS 1, cited in Anderson, *Lucy's Book*, 441–45), or with a Bainbridge, N.Y., trial in 1830.

78. See sources discussed in Porter, "Aaronic and Melchizedek Priesthoods," 33–44. See also Roberts, *Comprehensive History*, 1:183. Richard L. Bushman discusses the date of this event in *Beginnings of Mormonism,* 163, esp. n55. Discussed further below in Brian Q. Cannon and *BYU Studies* staff, "Seventy Contemporaneous Priesthood Restoration Documents."

79. As reported by Joseph F. Smith, David Whitmer told him and Orson Pratt that Joseph prophesied to Oliver "a perfect description of what David did on the way" before David arrived. Joseph F. Smith, Statement, written April 25, 1918, 2, Church Archives. They traveled on "an ordinary wagon with two long poles in it at each end across the end gates of the wagon box, and then two boards laid across that for seats on those hickory poles. Joseph and Emma were on the hind seat and Oliver and David on the front seat." Joseph F. Smith, Statement, 2. The plates were carried to Fayette by Moroni in a bundle on his back. Joseph F. Smith, Statement, 3. Lucy Mack Smith, Prelim. MS 1, cited in Anderson, *Lucy's Book*, 450, does not include Emma on this trip to Fayette (Waterloo). See also Cook, *David Whitmer Interviews*, 114–15, 197.

80. *History of the Church*, 1:49. John Whitmer later said that he wrote "sixty pages" (document 101). John Whitmer, interview by Zenas H. Gurley, in "Synopsis of a Discourse Delivered at Lamoni, Iowa," reported by S. F. Walker, *Saints' Herald* 26 (December 15, 1879): 370b. At this time, Joseph translated with some aid from a seer-stone (documents 82, 85, 92) or the Urim and Thummim (documents 83, 84, 86, 91, 97), though these instruments were not essential (document 98). He used "no manuscript notes or other means" (document 86, see also 41).

81. She married David Edwin Bunnell in the Peter Whitmer home on April 15, 1830, and was the mother of Stephen Bunnell of Provo, Utah. See Oliver B. Huntington, "History of the Life of Oliver B. Huntington," typescript, 49–50, Perry Special Collections; Pearl Bunnell Newell, interview by Carma DeJong Anderson, January 1970, 3–4, Perry Special Collections, provides a similar reminiscence of Sally Conrad; marriage date of Sally Conrad courtesy of Helen Bunnell Weeks of Orem, Utah. See article by Richard L. Anderson, "The House Where the Church Was Organized," *Improvement Era* 73 (April 1970): 16–25, for full discussion of the one-and-a-half story log house with attic and of the Whitmers and their relatives.

82. Copy contained on obverse of William E. McLellin to "My Dear Friends," February 1870, Community of Christ Library-Archives; cited in Cook, *David Whitmer Interviews*, 233–34.

83. David Whitmer, Statement of September 15, 1882, to William Kelley and G. A. Blakeslee, in Braden and Kelley Debate February 12 to March 8, 1884 (St. Louis: Christian Publ., c. 1884), 186; also cited in Roberts, *Comprehensive History*, 1:131; see also document 87.

84. Copies of the two originals prepared by Lansing are found in the Church Archives and in the Library of Congress in Washington, D.C., respectively.

85. *History of the Church*, 1:48–51.

86. Original no longer extant. Copy found in Joseph Smith Letterbook 1, part 1, pp. 5–6.

87. *History of the Church*, 1:49. Zenas Gurley's interview with John Whitmer, reported by Gurley in "Synopsis of a Discourse," 370b; John stated "that he had written [as scribe] sixty pages" of the Book of Mormon [about thirty pages of manuscript?]. See also documents 92, 101.

88. *History of the Church*, 1:51; Doctrine and Covenants 27:12. On January 14, 1885, David Whitmer stated: "Sometime in June 1829 Joseph ordained Oliver Cowdery to be an Elder, and Oliver ordained Joseph to be an Elder in the church of Christ. And during that year Joseph both baptized and ordained me an elder in the church of Christ." Z. H. Gurley, "Questions asked of David Whitmer at His Home in Richmond, Ray County, Missouri, 1885," 4, Church Archives. Brigham Young later stated that the first Apostles of this dispensation were Joseph Smith Jr., Oliver Cowdery, and David Whitmer. See discussion of Porter, "Prophet's New York Years," citing a Smith family prayer and B. Young. David Whitmer later maintained that he continued to hold that apostleship. "The Book of Mormon," *Chicago Tribune*, December 17, 1885, 3, col. 5; cited in Cook, *David Whitmer Interviews*, 179.

89. *History of the Church*, 1:51.

90. An early "copy" of the Articles of the Church of Christ initialed by O. C., bearing the date 1829 and discussed by Robert J. Woodford, "The Historical Development of the Doctrine and Covenants," 3 vols. (Ph.D. diss., Brigham Young University, 1974), 1:287–91, is held in Church Archives. It is unclear of what, if anything, it is a copy, or when the copy or its original was written. It quotes the sacrament prayers in Moroni 4–5 and the sacramental instructions in 3 Nephi 18:28–32 that were translated late in May 1829, and in some other ways the document resembles Doctrine and Covenants 20, but the two documents are not directly connected. Doctrine and Covenants 20 took its basic present form in June 1830. For a full discussion, see Scott H. Faulring, "An Examination of the 1829 'Articles of the Church of Christ' in Relation to Section 20 of the Doctrine and Covenants," *BYU Studies* 43, no. 4 (2004): 57–91.

91. The other possibility is Ether 5:2–4. Ether 5, however, only expressly states that "unto three," that is, a total of three, "shall they be shown." 2 Nephi 27, on the other hand, provides that "three witnesses shall behold it, by the power of God, *besides* him to whom the book shall be delivered" (italics added), and 27:13–14 refers to the eight witnesses. Since 2 Nephi 27 authorizes more precisely what in fact eventually happened regarding the witnesses, it appears that it was not until that passage was translated that the manifestations to the witnesses ensued. This comports further with the earliest notes on the manuscript history of the Church, discussed further in note 111. See also p. 76 above.

92. Pomeroy Tucker, *Origin, Rise, and Progress of Mormonism* (New York: D. Appleton, 1867), 4, quoted in Kirkham, *New Witness for Christ*, 1:109. John H. Gilbert, "Memorandum made by John H. Gilbert Esq., Sep 8, 1892 Palmyra,

N.Y.," Palmyra King's Daughters Free Library, Palymyra, N.Y. (document 172), later remembered that Martin Harris approached Grandin twice "in the fore-part of June, 1829," although this seems a little too early. See generally *History of the Church*, 1:71; see also documents 171, 172, 199.

93. "Mormonism," *Kansas City Daily Journal*, June 5, 1881, 1, reprinted in "Mormonism," *Millennial Star* 43 (July 4, 1881): 421–23 and (July 11, 1881): 437–39; cited in Cook, *David Whitmer Interviews*, 58–71.

94. Porter, "Origins of the Church," 86–87, citing Thurlow Weed, *Life of Thurlow Weed, Including His Autobiography and a Memoir*, 2 vols., ed. Harriet A. Weed (Boston: Houghton Mifflin, 1884), 1:358–59. One Rochester publisher did agree to print it. See Bushman, *Beginnings of Mormonism*, 107, citing Tucker, *Origin*, 51–53.

95. The mortgage is dated August 25, 1829, signed August 26, 1829, and was recorded on September 11, 1829 (see documents 123, 199). See Miner T. Patton, "The Gold That Paid for the Printing of the First Book of Mormon," unpublished manuscript with copies of documents, August 1983, Sun City, Arizona; with appreciation to Ken Godfrey for this item.

96. Peter Crawley, "A Bibliography of The Church of Jesus Christ of Latter-day Saints in New York, Ohio, and Missouri," *BYU Studies* 12, no. 4 (1972): 471. The nature of the contract, however, is uncertain.

97. Gayle G. Ord, "From Golden Plates to Printing Press," 1972, 11, Church Archives: "A cross sampling of 'first editions for 138 books published between 1880 and 1882 [still show that] only 28 per cent of these exceeded 1,500 copies. About 15 per cent were 2,500 or more, and the maximum printing' . . . 6,000 copies—was reserved for one particularly successful book," quoting Donald Sheehan, *This Was Publishing* (Bloomington, Ind.: Indiana University Press, 1952), 30.

98. Mortgages, book 3, p. 325, Wayne County Courthouse, Lyons, New York, cited in Porter, "Origins of the Church," 88.

99. Gilbert, "Memorandum," 3. John H. Gilbert to F. M. Lyman, October 23, 1887, cited in Kirkham, *New Witness for Christ*, 225; Porter, "Origins of the Church," 88–89.

100. Gilbert, "Memorandum," 3; see Ord, "Golden Plates to Printing Press," 24–43; Richard Lloyd Anderson, "Gold Plates and Printer's Ink," *Ensign* 6 (September 1976): 71–76; Wilford C. Wood, comp., *Joseph Smith Begins His Work*, 2 vols. (Salt Lake City: Deseret News Press, 1958–62), 1:introductory pages.

101. Joseph Smith Jr. to Oliver Cowdery, October 22, 1829, in Jessee, *Personal Writings of Joseph Smith*, 251. Gilbert, "Memorandum," 2–3, 4.

102. Gilbert, "Memorandum," 3.

103. Oliver to Joseph, November 6, 1829, Joseph Smith Letterbook, part 1, p. 8. Original letter not extant—copy is in Joseph's handwriting and follows his own spelling and punctuation.

104. 1 Nephi 1:1–2:3, 2:4–15, and Alma 43:22–40, respectively.

105. Russell Rich, "The Dogberry Papers and the Book of Mormon," *BYU Studies* 10, no. 3 (1970), 319–20; Kirkham, *New Witness for Christ*, 271, confuses the dates and contents.

106. They went "over on the ice." Mr. J. L. Traughber, letter, in Wilhelm (von Wymetal) Wyl, *Mormon Portraits*, vol. 1, *Joseph Smith the Prophet* (Salt Lake City: Tribune, 1886), 311.

107. Wyl, *Mormon Portraits*, 311. See generally, Roberts, *Comprehensive History*, 1:162–66.

108. "Note on the sale of the book of Mormon, now printed," January 16, 1830, Simon Gratz Collection, Historical Society of Pennsylvania, Philadelphia.

109. "The Book of Mormon," *Palmyra, N.Y., Wayne Sentinel*, March 26, 1830.

110. Porter, "Prophet's New York Years." Hyrum sold copies to missionaries for $1.25, who sold them for about $2.50. Hyrum Smith, Diaries [and Account Book] 1831–1844, 35, 37–38, Church Archives.

111. See note 72 above. Two theories exist about the order in which the Book of Mormon was translated in 1829. The book of Lehi was translated and lost in 1828. In March 1829, the translation resumed with both Samuel Smith and Emma acting as scribe for a few pages (document 12). In April 1829, Oliver Cowdery arrived and the pace of the work accelerated. Where in the text did Joseph begin at this time? Did he pick up where the 116 pages had left off (around the time of King Benjamin near Mosiah 1), or did he start at the beginning of the Small Plates (with 1 Nephi 1)? A few considerations make the "Mosiah-first" theory more plausible than the "Nephi-first" theory:

First, which scripture triggered the experience of the Three Witnesses in June 1829, toward the end of the translation? Was it Ether 5:2–4 or 2 Nephi 27:12, 22? If they were translating 2 Nephi in June, this would strongly indicate that they had begun with Mosiah in April and had returned after finishing Moroni in May to translate the Small Plates of Nephi in June. On the other hand, if they were translating the Book of Ether in June, this would support the Nephi-first theory, since in the few days remaining in June after the experience of the Three Witnesses there would have been only enough time left to finish Ether and Moroni.

The *History of the Church* first appeared in print as a serial in the *Times and Seasons* in 1842. "History of Joseph Smith," *Times and Seasons* 3 (March 15, 1842): beginning on p. 726. A blank was left in the sentence that was to tell which passage in the Book of Mormon inspired the manifestation to the Three Witnesses. "History of Joseph Smith," *Times and Seasons* 3 (September 1, 1842): 897a. Joseph Smith, "History of the Church," A-1, MS 23, Joseph Smith Collection, Church Archives, likewise has a blank at this point. Page 25 of one of the manuscripts of the *History of the Church*, however, contains a note that the relevant scripture was found "in the 1st ed. . . . page 110 [2 Nephi 27]." This information was added to the manuscript some time after 1852, as is evident since that scribe also refers to a European edition of the Doctrine and Covenants of that date. Smith, "History of the Church," A-2, 25. Therefore, the earliest recorded understanding saw 2 Nephi 27 as the scripture involved. B. H. Roberts chose to refer principally to Ether 5 in the published edition of *History of the Church* 1:52, but he also mentioned 2 Nephi 11:3 in this context. Significantly, the scripture in 2 Nephi 27 authorizes more precisely what in fact transpired with the witnesses (as discussed above under the date "Around June 20, 1829"), all making it more likely that 2 Nephi 27 was the relevant scripture authorizing the manifestation to the Witnesses than Ether 5.

Second, the Mosiah-first theory allows five weeks (from April 7 to May 15) for the translation of Mosiah 1 through the account of the ministry of Christ among the Nephites in 3 Nephi. The book was then finished at about the same rate in June. Under the Nephi-first theory, however, all the material from 1 Nephi 1 through the account in 3 Nephi would have to have been translated within that time, requiring a faster rate. Correlatively, the Mosiah-first theory leaves a significant amount of material to be translated after May 15, which accommodates the fact that the translation continued at Harmony for two more weeks and that "many pages" were translated at the Whitmer house in Fayette. One report indicates that John Whitmer acted as scribe for as many as "sixty pages." Gurley, "Synopsis of a Discourse," 370b.

Third, the title page of the Book of Mormon was translated before June 11, 1829, the date on which this text appears on the copyright application. Since the title page was written by Moroni and was found at the end of the Plates of Mormon ("I wish to mention here that the title-page of the Book of Mormon is a literal translation taken from the very last leaf, on the left hand side of the collection or book of plates, which contained the record which has been translated," *History of the Church*, 1:71), it would appear that books up to and including the title page, namely 4 Nephi, Mormon, Ether, Moroni, and the title page itself, were translated after May 15 but before June 11. This supports the Mosiah-first theory.

Fourth, the handwriting on the original manuscript for 1 Nephi is neither Oliver Cowdery's nor Emma Smith's. It may be Reuben Hale's, which would support the Nephi-first theory, but it is also possible that it is one of the Whitmers', which would favor the Mosiah-first theory.

In light of the foregoing, the Mosiah-first theory seems more likely than the Nephi-first theory. Accepting this view, see George Reynolds, "History of the Book of Mormon," *Contributor* 5 (November 1883): 41–47; (February 1884): 161–68; (June 1884): 321–27; (July 1884): 361–67; Stanley R. Larson, "A Most Sacred Possession: The Original Manuscript of the Book of Mormon,"

Ensign 7 (September 1977): 87–88; Parkin, "Dating of Section 10," 76; Bushman, *Beginnings of Mormonism*, 105; Welch, *Reexploring the Book of Mormon*, 1–8. Royal Skousen, *The Original Manuscript of the Book of Mormon* (Provo, Utah: FARMS, 2001), 33, notes that "there is some evidence that Joseph Smith translated the small plates of Nephi at the very end of the process," but defers further discussion for a future publication. Ruminating about the implications and idologies of some discussions of the Mosiah-first theory, see Alan Goff, "Positivism and the Priority of Ideology in Mosiah-First Theories of Book of Mormon Production," *FARMS Review* 16, no. 1 (2004): 11–36, arguing that the Mosiah-first theory need not pose any compositional difficulty.

112. Discussed further in John W. Welch, "How Long Did It Take Joseph Smith to Translate the Book of Mormon?" *Ensign* 18 (Jaunary 1988): 46–47; Neal A. Maxwell, "By the Gift and Power of God," *Ensign* 27 (January 1997): 36–41, reprinted in Donald W. Parry and others, eds., *Echoes and Evidences of the Book of Mormon* (Provo, Utah: FARMS, 2002), 1–15. It is also significant that the original manuscript of the Book of Mormon "gives no aid or comfort" to those who have sought alternative explanations to account for the existence of the Book of Mormon; the manuscript "shows no evidence" of developmental research, of revision and rethinking, or rewriting or reformulation. John W. Welch, "What the Original Book of Mormon Manuscript Is Not," in John W. Welch, ed., *Pressing Forward with the Book of Mormon* (Provo, Utah: FARMS, 1999), 293–95.

113. Givens, *By the Hand of Mormon*, 37.

114. Cowdery, "Letter I," 14.

Documenting the Translation Chronology

1. Doctrine and Covenants 3:9, 12, 14 (1828)

Behold, thou art Joseph, and thou wast chosen to do the work of the Lord, but because of transgression, if thou art not aware thou wilt fall. . . .

And when thou deliveredst up that which God had given thee sight and power to translate, thou deliveredst up that which was sacred into the hands of a wicked man. . . .

And this is the reason that thou hast lost thy privileges for a season.[1]

2. Doctrine and Covenants 10:1–3, 8, 10–11, 30, 34; 40–41, 45 (1828; 1829)

Now, behold, I say unto you [Joseph Smith], that because you delivered up those writings which you had power given unto you to translate by the means of the Urim and Thummim, into the hands of a wicked man, you have lost them.

And you also lost your gift at the same time, and your mind became darkened.

Nevertheless, it is now restored unto you again; therefore see that you are faithful and continue on unto the finishing of the remainder of the work of translation as you have begun. . . .

And because you have delivered the writings into his hands, behold, wicked men have taken them from you. . . .

And, behold, Satan hath put it into their hearts to alter the words which you have caused to be written, or which you have translated, which have gone out of your hands.

And behold, I say unto you, that because they have altered the words, they read contrary from that which you translated and caused to be written; . . .

Behold, I say unto you, that you shall not translate again those words which have gone forth out of your hands. . . .

But behold, here is wisdom, and because I show unto you wisdom, and give you commandments concerning these things, what you shall do, show it not unto the world until you have accomplished the work of translation. . . .

And now, because the account which is engraven upon the plates of Nephi is more particular concerning the things which, in my wisdom, I would bring to the knowledge of the people in this account—

Therefore, you shall translate the engravings which are on the plates of Nephi, down even till you come to the reign of king Benjamin, or until you come to that which you have translated, which you have retained. . . .

Behold, there are many things engraven upon the plates of Nephi which do throw greater views upon my gospel; therefore, it is wisdom in me that you should translate this first part of the engravings of Nephi, and send forth in this work.[2]

3. Doctrine and Covenants 5:4, 30–31 (1829)

And you [Joseph Smith] have a gift to translate the plates; and this is the first gift that I bestowed upon you; and I have commanded that you should pretend to no other gift until my purpose is fulfilled in this; for I will grant unto you no other gift until it is finished.

And if this be the case, behold, I say unto thee Joseph, when thou hast translated a few more pages thou shalt stop for a season, even until I command thee again; then thou mayest translate again.

And except thou do this, behold, thou shalt have no more gift, and I will take away the things which I have entrusted with thee.[3]

4. Doctrine and Covenants 6:17, 25 (1829)

I tell thee these things as a witness unto thee [Oliver Cowdery]—that the words or the work which thou hast been writing are true.

And, behold, I grant unto you [Oliver Cowdery] a gift, if you desire of me, to translate, even as my servant Joseph.[4]

5. Doctrine and Covenants 8:11 (1829)

Ask that you [Oliver Cowdery] may know the mysteries of God, and that you may translate and receive knowledge from all those ancient records which have been hid up, that are sacred; and according to your faith shall it be done unto you.[5]

6. Doctrine and Covenants 9:1–5, 8–10 (1829)

Behold, I say unto you [Oliver Cowdery], my son, that because you did not translate according to that which you desired of me, and did commence again to write for my servant, Joseph Smith, Jun., even so I would that ye should continue until you have finished this record, which I have entrusted unto him.

And then, behold, other records have I, that I will give unto you power that you may assist to translate.

Be patient, my son, for it is wisdom in me, and it is not expedient that you should translate at this present time.

Behold, the work which you are called to do is to write for my servant Joseph.

And, behold, it is because that you did not continue as you commenced, when you began to translate, that I have taken away this privilege from you. . . .

But, behold, I say unto you, that you must study it out in your mind; then you must ask me if it be right, and if it is right I will cause that your bosom shall burn within you; therefore, you shall feel that it is right.

But if it be not right you shall have no such feelings, but you shall have a stupor of thought that shall cause you to forget the thing which is wrong; therefore, you cannot write that which is sacred save it be given you from me.

Now, if you had known this you could have translated; nevertheless, it is not expedient that you should translate now.[6]

7. Doctrine and Covenants 11:19 (1829)

Yea, cleave unto me with all your heart, that you may assist in bringing to light those things of which has been spoken—yea, the translation of my work; be patient until you shall accomplish it.[7]

8. Doctrine and Covenants 17:6 (1829)

And he [Joseph Smith] has translated the book, even that part which I have commanded him, and as your Lord and your God liveth it is true.[8]

9. Doctrine and Covenants 20:6–9 (1830)

But after repenting, and humbling himself sincerely, through faith, God ministered unto [Joseph Smith] by an holy angel. . . .

And gave unto him commandments which inspired him;

And gave him power from on high, by the means which were before prepared, to translate the Book of Mormon;

Which contains a record of a fallen people, and the fulness of the gospel of Jesus Christ to the Gentiles.[9]

10. Joseph Smith (1830)

I would inform you that I translated, by the gift and power of God, and caused to be written, one hundred and sixteen pages, the which I took from the Book of Lehi, which was an account abridged from the plates of Lehi, by the hand of Mormon; which said account, some person or persons have stolen and kept from me, notwithstanding my utmost exertions to recover it again.[10]

11. Joseph Smith, as recorded by Oliver Cowdery (1831)

Br. Hyrum Smith said that he thought best that the information of the coming forth of the book of Mormon be related by Joseph himself to the Elders present that all might know for themselves.

Br. Joseph Smith jr. said that it was not intended to tell the world all the particulars of the coming forth of the book of Mormon, & also said that it was not expedient for him to relate these things &c.[11]

12. Joseph Smith (1832)

[The] Lord appeared unto a young man by the name of Oliver Cowdry and shewed unto him the plates in a vision and also the truth of the work and what the Lord was about to do through me his unworthy servant therefore he was desirous to come and write for me to translate now my wife had writen some for me to translate and also my Brother Samuel H Smith but we had be come reduced in property and my wives father was about to turn me out of doors & I had not where to go and I cried unto the Lord that he would provide for me to accomplish the work whereunto he had commanded me.[12]

13. Joseph Smith (1832)

[Martin Harris] imediately came to Su[s]quehanna and said the Lord had shown him that he must go to new York City with some of the c[h]aracters so we proceeded to coppy some of them and he took his Journy to the Eastern Cittys and to the Learned <saying> read this I pray thee and the learned said I cannot but if he would bring the blates [plates] they would read it but the Lord had fo<r>bid it and he returned to me and gave them to <me to> translate and I said [I] cannot for I am not learned but the Lord had prepared spectacles for to read the Book therefore I commenced translating the characters and thus the Prop[h]icy of Is<ia>ah was fulfilled.[13]

14. Joseph Smith, as recorded by Nancy Towle (1832)

He accordingly went; and was directed by the angel to a certain spot of ground, where was deposited a "Box"—and in that box contained "Plates," which resembled gold; also, a pair of "interpreters," (as he called them,) that resembled spectacles; by looking into which, he could *read* a writing engraven upon the plates, though to himself, in a tongue unknown.[14]

15. Joseph Smith, as recorded by Lydia Bailey Knight (1833)

The Prophet commenced by relating the scenes of his early life. He told how the angel visited him, of his finding the plates, the translation of them.[15]

16. Joseph Smith to N. E. Seaton (1833)

The Book of Mormon is a record of the forefathers of our western tribes of Indians; having been found through the ministration of an holy angel, and translated into our own language by the gift and power of God.[16]

17. Joseph Smith, as interviewed by Peter Bauder (1834)

[Joseph Smith] went, and after the third or fourth time, which was repeated once a year, he obtained a parcel of plate resembling gold, on which were engraved what he did not understand, only by the aid of a glass which he also obtained with the plate, by which means he was enabled to translate the characters on the plate into English. . . . and after he had a part translated, the angel conmanded him to carry the plate into a certain piece of woods, which he did:—the angel took them and carried them to parts unknown to him.[17]

18. Joseph Smith (1834)

Bro. Joseph Smith Jun. . . . then gave a relation of obtaining and translating the Book of Mormon, the revelation of the priesthood of Aaron. . . . Take away the book of Mormon, and the revelations, and where is our religion? We have none.[18]

19. Joseph Smith, as recorded by Oliver Cowdery (1835)

[The messenger] said this history was written and deposited not far from that place, and that it was our brother's privilege, if obedient to the commandments of the Lord, to obtain, and translate the same by the means of the Urim and Thummim, which were deposited for that purpose with the record.[19]

20. Joseph Smith, as recorded by Oliver Cowdery (1835)

[Joseph Smith] was ministered unto by the angel, and by his direction he obtained the Records of the Nephites, and translated by the gift and power of God.[20]

21. Joseph Smith, as recorded by Oliver Cowdery (1835)

The angel said, ". . . they cannot be interpreted by the learning of this generation; consequently, they would be considered of no worth, only as precious metal. Therefore, remember, that they are to be translated by the gift and power of God. By them will the Lord work a great and a marvelous work."[21]

22. Joseph Smith, as recorded by Warren Parrish (1835)

I called on God. The Angel told me, that the reason why I could not obtain the plates at this time [1823], was because I was under transgression, but to come again in one year from that time. I did so but did not obtain them, also the third and the fourth year the last of which time I obtained them, and translated them into <the> english language by the gift and power of God and have been preaching it ever since.[22]

23. Joseph Smith, as recorded by Truman Coe (1836)

The manner of translation was as wonderful as the discovery. By putting his finger on one of the characters and imploring divine aid, then looking through the Urim and Thummin, he would see the import written in plain English on a screen placed before him. After delivering this to his emanuensi, he would again proceed in the same manner and obtain the meaning of the next character, and so on till he came to a part of the plates which were sealed up, and there was commanded to desist: and he says he has a promise from God that in due time he will enable him to translate the remainder.[23]

24. Joseph Smith (1838)

I obtained them, and the Urim and Thummim with them; by the means of which, I translated the plates; and thus came the book of Mormon.[24]

25. Joseph Smith (1839)

He [the angel] said there was a book deposited written upon gold plates, giving an account of the former inhabitants of this continent and the source from whence they sprang. He also said that the fullness of the everlasting Gospel was contained in it as delivered by the Saviour to the ancient inhabitants.

Also that there were two stones in silver bows and these (put <stones fastened> in to a breast plate) which constituted what is called the Urim & Thummin deposited with the plates, and <the possession and use of these

stones> that was what constituted seers in ancient or former times and that God <had> prepared them for the purpose of translating the book. . . .

. . . Immediately after my arrival there [Pennsylvania] I commenced copying the characters of all the plates. I copyed a considerable number of them and by means of the Urim and Thummin I translated some of them which I did between the time I arrived at the house of my wife's father in the month of December [1827], and the February following.

Mr [Martin] Harris . . . returned again to my house about the twelfth of April, Eighteen hundred and twenty eight, and commenced writing for me while I translated from the plates, which we continued untill the fourteenth of June following, by which time he had written one hundred and sixteen <pages> of manuscript on foolscap paper. . . .

I did not however go immediately to translating [in the winter of 1828], but went to laboring with my hands . . . in order to provide for my family.

Two days after the arrival of Mr Cowdery (being the seventh of April [1829]) I commenced to translate the book of Mormon and he commenced to write for me. . . .

. . . During the month of April I continued to translate, and he to write with little cessation, during which time we received several revelations. . . .

Whilst continuing the work of translation during this month of April; Oliver Cowdery became exceedingly anxious to have the power to translate bestowed upon him and in relation to this desire the following revelations were obtained [D&C 8, 9; see excerpts above]. . . .

We still continued the <work of> translation, when in the ensuing month (May, Eighteen hundred and twenty nine) we on a certain day went into the woods to pray and inquire of the Lord respecting baptism for the remission of sins as we found mentioned in the translation of the plates. . . .

. . . my wife's father's family . . . were willing that I should be allowed to continue the work of translation without interruption: And therefore offered and promised us protection from all unlawful proceedings as far as in them lay.

. . . we also showed him [Samuel Smith] that part of the work which we had translated, and labored to persuade him concerning the Gospel of Jesus Christ. . . .

. . . Mr Joseph Knight Senr. . . . very kindly and considerately brought us, a quantity of provisions, in order that we might not be interrupted in the work of translation . . . which enabled us to continue the work. . . .

. . . we accepted the invitation and accompanied Mr [David] Whitmer to his father's house, and there resided untill the translation was finished, . . . and John Whitmer, in particular, assisted us very much in writing during the remainder of the work. . . .

In the course of the work of translation, we ascertained that three special witnesses were to be provided by the Lord, to whom he would grant, that they should see the plates from which this work (the Book of Mormon) should be translated, and that these witnesses should bear record of the same. . . .

. . . when immediately afterwards we heard a voice from out of the bright light above us, saying "These plates have been revealed by the power of God, and they have been translated by the power of God; the translation of them which you have seen is correct, and I command you to bear record of what you now see and hear." . . .

Mean time we continued to translate, at intervals, when not necessitated to attend to the numerous enquirers, that now began to visit us. . . .

I wish also to mention here, that the Title Page of the Book of Mormon is a literal translation, taken from the very last leaf, on the left hand side of the collection or book of plates, which contained the record which has been translated.[25]

26. Joseph Smith, as recorded by Mathew L. Davis (1840)

Throughout his [Joseph Smith's] whole address, he displayed strongly a spirit of charity and forbearance. The Mormon Bible, he said, was communicated to him, *direct from heaven*. If there was such a thing on earth, as the author of it, then he (Smith) was the author; but the idea that he wished to impress was, that he had penned it as dictated by God.[26]

27. Joseph Smith, as recorded by George Moore (1842)

Called on the "Prophet Jo Smith." His carriage was at the door, and he was about going away, but he received me very kindly, and asked me into his house. I remained about 10 minutes. He was very communicative. We conversed about the golden plates, which he professes to have dug up and translated into the Book of Mormon. "Those plates are not now in this country," he said—"they were exhibited to a few at first for the sake of obtainng their testimony—no others have ever seen them—and they will never again be exhibited." He showed me some specimens of the heiroglyphics, such as, he says, were on the gold plates. He asked me if I was a Clergyman—and of what denomination—and what were the fundamental doctrines of our faith. . . . Our interview was short, but pleasant.[27]

28. Joseph Smith (1842)

With the records was found a curious instrument which the ancients called "Urim and Thummim," which consisted of two transparent stones set in the rim of a bow fastened to a breastplate.

Through the medium of the Urim and Thummim I translated the record by the gift, and power of God.[28]

29. Joseph Smith to the *Times and Seasons* (1843)

SIR:—Through the medium of your paper, I wish to correct an error. . . . The error I speak of, is the definition of the word "MORMON." It has been stated that this word was derived from the Greek word *mormo*. This is not the case. There was no Greek or Latin upon the plates from which I, through the grace of God, translated the Book of Mormon. . . .

Here then the subject is put to silence, for "*none other people knoweth our language*," [Morm. 9:34] therefore the Lord, and not man, had to interpret, after the people were all dead.[29]

30. Joseph Smith to James Arlington Bennett (1843)

The fact is, that by the power of God I translated the Book of Mormon from hieroglyphics; the knowledge of which was lost to the world: in which wonderful event I stood alone, an unlearned youth, to combat the worldly wisdom, and multiplied ignorance of eighteen centuries.[30]

31. Joseph Smith (1843)

During this month of April, I (Joseph Smith) went on a visit to the residence of Mr. Joseph Knight, of Colesville, Broom county, N.Y., with whom and his family I had been previously acquainted, and of whose name I have above mentioned as having been so kind and thoughtful towards us while translating the Book of Mormon.[31]

32. Joseph Smith, as published by Daniel Rupp (1844)

With the records was found a curious instrument which the ancients called "Urim and Thummim," which consisted of two transparent stones set in the rim on a bow fastened to a breastplate.

Through the medium of the Urim and Thummim I translated the record, by the gift and power of God.[32]

33. Joseph Smith, as recorded by Parley P. Pratt (1874)

[Smith] spoke in great power, bearing testimony of the visions he had seen, the ministering of angels which he had enjoyed; and how he had found the plates of the Book of Mormon, and translated them by the gift and power of God.[33]

34. Joseph Smith, as recorded by Joseph Curtis (1881)

[Joseph Smith] saw an angel with a view of the hill Cumorah & the plates of gold had certain instructions got the plates & by the assistance of the Urim & Thumin translated them by the gift & power of God.[34]

35. Joseph Smith, as recorded by Emily M. Austin (1882)

He [Joseph Smith] also affirmed that he had seen the angel, and had talked with him face to face; and the angel told him at a certain time he would conduct him to the place where the plates could be obtained; also that he was a chosen vessel in the hands of God, to translate them, and bring them to the world.[35]

36. Joseph Smith, as recorded by Addison Everett (1882)

And then [Joseph Smith] said as they Ware Tranlating the Book of Mormon at His Father In Laws in Susquhanah County[,] penny [Pennsylvania]. T[h]ey ware thretned By a Mob and in the same time Father Kn<i>ghts came Down from Colevill [Colesville] Broom[e] County[,] New York.[36]

37. Joseph Smith, as recorded by James Palmer (not dated)

Said he [Joseph Smith], I did translate the book of Mormon by the gift and power of God, and it is before the world, and all the powers of earth and hell can never rob me of the honour of it.[37]

38. Emma Smith Bidamon, as interviewed by Edmund C. Briggs (1856)

When my husband was translating the Book of Mormon, I wrote a part of it, as he dictated each sentence, word for word, and when he came to proper names he could not pronounce, or long words, he spelled them out, and while I was writing them, if I made any mistake in spelling, he would stop me and correct my spelling, although it was impossible for him to see how I was writing them down at the time. Even the word *Sarah* he could not pronounce at first, but had to spell it, and I would pronounce it for him.

When he stopped for any purpose at any time he would, when he commenced again, begin where he left off without any hesitation, and one time while he was translating he stopped suddenly, pale as a sheet, and said, "Emma, did Jerusalem have walls around it?" When I answered "Yes," he replied "Oh! I was afraid I had been deceived." He had such a limited knowledge of history at that time that he did not even know that Jerusalem was surrounded by walls.[38]

39. Emma Smith Bidamon to Emma Pilgrim (1870)

Now, the first part my husband translated, was translated by the use of Urim and Thummim, and that was the part that Martin Harris lost *After that he used a small stone*, not exactly black, but was rather a dark color.[39]

40. Emma Smith Bidamon, as interviewed by Nels Madsen and Parley P. Pratt Jr. (1877)

Q. Did he receive the plates from which he claimed to have translated the Book of Mormon?

A. Yes, They lay in a box under our bed for months but I never felt at liberty to look at them.

In regard to the Book of Mormon Mrs. Bidemon stated emphatically that he husband, Joseph Smith could not have written such a book without inspiration. He had not read the Bible enough to know that there were walls around Jerusalem and he came and asked me if there were walls around the city of Jerusalem.[40]

41. Emma Smith Bidamon, as interviewed by Joseph Smith III (1879)

Q. Who were scribes for father when translating the Book of Mormon?

A. Myself, Oliver Cowdery, Martin Harris, and my brother, Reuben Hale.

Q. Was Alva Hale one?

A. I think not. He may have written some; but if he did, I do not remember it. . . .

Q. What of the truth of Mormonism?

A. I know Mormonism to be the truth; and believe the Church to have been established by divine direction. I have complete faith in it. In writing for your father I frequently wrote day after day, often sitting at the table close by him, he sitting with his face buried in his hat, with the stone in it, and dictating hour after hour with nothing between us.

Q. Had he not a book or manuscript from which he read, or dictated to you?

A. He had neither manuscript nor book to read from.

Q. Could he not have had, and you not know it?

A. If he had had anything of the kind he could not have concealed it from me.

Q. Are you sure that he had the plates at the time you were writing for him?

A. The plates often lay on the table without any attempt at concealment, wrapped in a small linen table cloth, which I had given him to fold them in. I once felt of the plates, as they thus lay on the table, tracing their outline and shape. They seemed to be pliable like thick paper, and would rustle with a metalic sound when the edges were moved by the thumb, as one does sometimes thumb the edges of a book.

Q. Where did father and Oliver Cowdery write?

A. Oliver Cowdery and your father wrote in the room where I was at work.

Q. Could not father have dictated the Book of Mormon to you, Oliver Cowdery and the others who wrote for him, after having first written it, or having first read it out of some book?

A. Joseph Smith [and for the first time she used his name direct, having usually used the words, "your father," or "my husband"] could neither write nor dictate a coherent and well-worded letter; let alone dictating a book like the Book of Mormon. And, though I was an active participant in the scenes that transpired, and was present during the translation of the plates, and had cognizance of things as they transpired, it is marvelous to me, "a marvel and a wonder," as much so as to any one else.

Q. I should suppose that you would have uncovered the plates and examined them?

A. I did not attempt to handle the plates, other than I have told you, nor uncover them to look at them. I was satisfied that it was the work of God, and therefore did not feel it to be necessary to do so.

Major Bidamon here suggested: Did Mr. Smith forbid your examining the plates?

A. I do not think he did. I knew that he had them, and was not specially curious about them. I moved them from place to place on the table, as it was necessary in doing my work.

Q. Mother, what is your belief about the authenticity, or origin of the Book of Mormon?

A. My belief is that the Book of Mormon is of divine authenticity—I have not the slightest doubt of it. I am satisfied that no man could have dictated the writing of the manuscripts unless he was inspired; for, when acting as his scribe, your father would dictate to me hour after hour; and when returning after meals, or after interruptions, he would at once begin where he had left off, without either seeing the manuscript or having any portion of it read to him. This was a usual thing for him to do. It would have been improbable that a learned man could do this; and, for one so ignorant and unlearned as he was, it was simply impossible.[41]

42. Emma Smith Bidamon, as recorded by Joseph Smith III (1879)

She wrote for Joseph Smith during the work of translation, as did also Reuben Hale, her brother, and O[liver]. Cowdery; that the larger part of this labor was done in her presence, and where she could see and know what was being done; that during no part of it ~~was~~ did Joseph Smith have any Mss. [manuscripts] or Book of any kind from which to read, or dictate, except the metalic plates, which she knew he had.[42]

43. Emma Smith Bidamon, as recorded by Joseph Smith III (1900)

My mother [Emma Smith] told me that she saw the plates in the sack; for they lay on a small table in their living room in their cabin on her father's farm, and she would lift and move them when she swept and dusted the room and furniture. She even thumbed the leaves as one does the leaves of a book, and they rustled with a metalic sound. Yes, mother did some of the writing for father while he was translating[.] She testified that father found and had the plates, and translated them as the history states; that she had no doubt as to the truth of it.[43]

44. Martin Harris (1834)

The case of Bro. Martin Harris, against whom certain charges were preferred by bro. Sidney Rigdon, [was presented]. One was that he told Esqr. A. C. Russel that Joseph [Smith] drank too much liquor when he was translating the Book of Mormon and that he wrestled with many men and threw them &c. Another charge was that he exalted himself above bro. Joseph, in that he said bro. Joseph knew not the contents of the Book of Mormon until it was translated. Bro. Martin said he did not tell Edqr Russell that bro. Joseph drank too much liquor while translating the Book of Mormon, but this thing took place before the Book of Mormon was translated. He confessed that his mind was darkened and that he had said many things, inadvertently calculating to wound the feelings of his brother and promised to do better. The council forgave him and gave him much good advice.[44]

45. Martin Harris, as interviewed by John A. Clark (1840)

[T]hat there had been a revelation made to [Joseph Smith] by which he had discovered this sacred deposit, and two transparent stones, through which, as a sort of spectacles, he could read the Bible, although the box or ark that contained it, had not yet been opened; and that by looking through those mysterious stones, he had transcribed from one of the leaves of this book, the characters which Harris had so carefully wrapped in the package which he was drawing from his pocket. . . .

. . . He was already in possession of the two transparent stones laid up with the GOLDEN BIBLE, by looking through which he was enabled to read the golden letters on the plates in the box. How he obtained theses spectacles without opening the chest, Harris could not tell. But still he had them; and by means of them he could read all the book contained. . . .

. . . The way that Smith made his transcripts and transcriptions for Harris was the following. Although in the same room, a thick curtain or blanket was suspended between them, and Smith concealed behind the blanket, pretended to look through his spectacles, or transparent stones, and would then write down or repeat what he saw, which, when repeated aloud, was written down by Harris, who sat on the other side of the suspended blanket. Harris was told that it would arouse the most terrible divine displeasure, if he should attempt to draw near the sacred chest, or look at Smith while engaged in the work of decyphering the mysterious characters. This was Harris's own account of the matter to me.[45]

46. MARTIN HARRIS, AS INTERVIEWED BY DAVID B. DILLE (1859)

"I know that the plates have been translated by the gift and power of God, for his voice declared it unto us; therefore I know of a surety that the work is true. For," continued Mr. Harris, "did I not at one time hold the plates on my knee an hour-and-a-half, whilst in conversation with Joseph, when we went to bury them in the woods, that the enemy might not obtain them? Yes, I did. And as many of the plates as Joseph Smith translated I handled with my hands, plate after plate.["][46]

47. MARTIN HARRIS, AS INTERVIEWED BY *TIFFANY'S MONTHLY* (1859)

The following narration we took down from the lips of Martin Harris, and read the same to him after it was written, that we might be certain of giving his statement to the world. . . .

"The two stones set in a bow of silver were about two inches in diameter, perfectly round, and about five-eighths of an inch thick at the centre; but not so thick at the edges where they came into the bow. They were joined by a round bar of silver, about three-eighths of an inch in diameter, and about four inches long, which, with the two stones, would make eight inches."

"The stones were white, like polished marble, with a few gray streaks. I never dared to look into them by placing them in the hat, because Moses said that 'no man could see God and live,' and we could see anything we wished by looking into them; and I could not keep the desire to see God out of my mind. And beside, we had a command to let no man look into them, except by the command of God, lest he should 'look aught and perish.'"[47]

48. Martin Harris, as interviewed by David H. Cannon (1861)

He testified to me in all solemnity, although not a member of the Church at that time, that the angel did appear with the plates from which the Book of Mormon was translated, and testified that they contained a history of the ancient inhabitants of this continent, and that they had been translated by the gift and power of God. There was a feeling accompanied his testimony, when he bore it, that I have never experienced either before or since in any man that I ever heard bear testimony.[48]

49. Martin Harris, as interviewed by the *Iowa State Register* (1870)

There was also found in the chest, the urim and thummim, by means of which the writing upon the plates was translated, but not until after the most learned men had exhausted their knowledge of letters in the vain effort to decipher the characters.

It had been revealed to Joseph Smith that the writing upon the tablets contained a history of the aborigines of this country down to the time of Columbus' discovery, and after, all human means had failed to secure a translation, Smith was commissioned to undertake the task. By means of the urim and thummim "a pair of large spectacles," as Mr. Harris termed them, the translation was made, and Mr. Harris claims to have written, of the translations as they were given by Smith, "116 solid pages of cap [fools-cap]." The remainder was written by others.[49]

50. Martin Harris, as interviewed by Thomas Godfrey and four others (1874)

"The angel showed me the plates and I heard the voice of God declare they were translated correctly." He was very earnest and sincere in his testimony.[50]

51. Martin Harris to H. B. Emerson (1875)

I do say that the angel did show to me the plates containing the Book of Mormon. Further, the translation that I carried to Prof. Anthon was copied from these same plates; also, that the Professor did testify to it being a correct translation. I do firmly believe and do know that Joseph Smith was a prophet of God; for without I know he [Joseph Smith] could not had that gift; neither could he have translated the same.[51]

52. Martin Harris, as recorded by Edward Stevenson (1881)

Martin Harris related an instance that occurred during the time that he wrote that portion of the translation of the Book of Mormon, which he was favored to write direct from the mouth of the Prophet Joseph Smith. He said that the Prophet possessed a seer stone, by which he was enabled to translate as well as from the Urim and Thummim, and for convenience he then used the seer stone. Martin explained the translating as follows: By aid of the seer stone, sentences would appear and were read by the Prophet and written by Martin, and when finished he would say, "Written," and if correctly written, that sentence would disappear and another appear in its place, but if not written correctly it remained until corrected, so that the translation was just as it was engraven on the plates, precisely in the language then used. . . .

Martin said further that the seer stone differed in appearance entirely from the Urim and Thummim that was obtained with the plates, which were two clear stones set in two rims, very much resembled spectacles, only they were larger. Martin said there were not many pages translated while he wrote; after which Oliver Cowdery and others did the writing.[52]

53. Martin Harris, as interviewed by Simon Smith (1884)

He [Martin Harris] also said, "I was Joseph Smith's scribe, and wrote for him a great deal; for he was such a poor writer, and could not even draw up a note of hand as his education was so limited. I also wrote for him about one third of the first part of the translation of the plates as he interpreted them by the Urim and Thummim. And I paid the printer about three thousand dollars for the first edition of the Book of Mormon."[53]

54. Martin Harris, as recalled by Reuben P. Harmon (ca. 1885)

I was well acquainted with Martin Harris, who was often at my house for days at a time. I have questioned him much about the plates from which the "Book of Mormon" purports to have been translated. He never claimed to have seen them with his natural eyes, only spiritual vision. He said it was impossible for the prophet Joseph to get up the "Book of Mormon," for he could not spell the word Sarah. He had him repeat the letters of the word. He was a very illiterate man.[54]

55. Martin Harris, as interviewed by Edward Stevenson (1886)

Brother Harris gave Joseph $50 (£10) on one occasion to help translate the Book of Mormon. . . . [Martin Harris] also stated that the Prophet translated a portion of the Book of Mormon, with the seer stone in his possession. The stone was placed in a hat that was used for that purpose, and with the aid of this seer stone the Prophet would read sentence by sentence as Martin wrote, and if he made any mistake the sentence would remain before the Prophet until corrected, when another sentence would appear. When they became weary, as it was confining work to translate from the plates of gold, they would go down to the river and throw stones into the water for exercise. Martin on one occasion picked up a stone resembling the one with which they were translating, and on resuming their work Martin placed the false stone in the hat. He said that the Prophet looked quietly for a long time, when he raised his head and said: "Martin, what on earth is the matter, all is dark as Egypt." Martin smiled and the seer discovered that the wrong stone was placed in the hat. When he asked Martin why he had done so he replied, to stop the mouths of fools who had declared that the Prophet knew by heart all that he told him to write, and did not see by the seer stone; when the true stone was placed in the hat, the translation was resumed, as usual.[55]

56. Martin Harris, as published by Andrew Jenson (1887)

On Sunday, Sept. 4, 1870, Martin Harris addressed a congregation of Saints in Salt Lake City. He related an incident which occurred during the time that he wrote that portion of the translation of the Book of Mormon which he was favored to write direct from the mouth of the Prophet Joseph Smith, and said that the Prophet possessed a seer stone, by which he was enabled to translate as well as from the Urim and Thummim, and for convenience he then used the seer stone. Martin explained the translation as follows: By aid of the seer stone, sentences would appear and were read by the Prophet and written by Martin, and when finished he would say, "Written," and if correctly written, that sentence would disappear and another appear in its place; but if not written correctly it remained until corrected, so that the translation was just as it was engraven on the plates, precisely in the language then used. Martin said that after continued translation they would become weary, and would go down to the river and exercise by throwing stones out on the river, etc. While so doing, on one occasion, Martin Harris found a stone very much resembling the one used for translating, and on resuming their labor of translation, he put in place the stone that he had found. He said that the Prophet remained silent, unusually and intently gazing in darkness, no traces of the usual sentences appearing. Much surprised, Joseph excla[i]med, "Martin! What is the matter! All is as dark as Egypt!" Martin's countenance betrayed him, and the Prophet asked Martin why he had done so. Martin said, to stop the mouths of fools, who had told him that the Prophet had learned those sentences and was merely repeating them, etc.

Martin said further that the seer stones differed in appearance entirely from the Urim and Thummim obtained with the plates, which were two clear stones set in two rims, very much resembling spectacles, only they were larger. Martin said, there were not many pages translated while he wrote, after which Oliver Cowdery and others did the writing.[56]

57. Martin Harris, as interviewed by R. W. Alderman (1888)

In February, 1852, I was snowbound in a hotel in Mentor, Ohio, all day. Martin Harris was there, and in conversation told me he saw Jo Smith translate the "Book of Mormon," with his peep-stone in his hat. Oliver Cowdery, who had been a school-teacher, wrote it down. Sidney Rigdon, a renegade preacher, was let in during the translation. Rigdon had stolen a manuscript from a printing office in Pittsburgh, Pa., which [Solomon] Spaulding, who had written it in the early part of the century, had left there to be printed, but the printers refused to publish it, but Jo and Rigdon did, as the "Book of Mormon."[57]

58. Martin Harris, as recorded by George Mantle (1888)

When he [Martin Harris] was asked if Joseph Smith was a true prophet of God, he answered yes; and when asked if the Book of Mormon was true, this was his answer: "Do you know that is the sun shining on us? Because as sure as you know that, I know that Joseph Smith was a true prophet of God, and that he translated that book by the power of God."[58]

59. Martin Harris, as interviewed by Anthony Metcalf (1888)

He told me all about the translating of the Book of Mormon, and said he had given $5,000 towards its publication. He said: "I never saw the golden plates, only in a visionary or entranced state. I wrote a great deal of the Book of Mormon myself, as Joseph Smith translated or spelled the words out in English. Sometimes the plates would be on a table in the room in which Smith did the translating, covered over with a cloth. I was told by Joseph Smith that God would strike him dead if he attempted to look at them, and I believed it."[59]

60. Martin Harris, as interviewed by Ole A. Jensen (1918)

[A]nd we did kneel down and pray Imediately the angle [angel] stood before me and said: "Look["] and when I glanced at the angel, I fell but I stood on my feet and seen the angle turn the leaves of gold and I said "It is enough my Lord and my God.["] I then heard the voice of God say "The book is true and is translated correctly."[60]

61. Martin Harris, as interviewed by William Harrison Homer (1922)

For I saw the angel, I heard <his> voice, I saw and handled the plates upon which the Book of Mormon was written; and by the power and influence of the Holy Ghost, the translation was made by the Prophet Joseph Smith, whom I know by the power and gift of the Holy Ghost, was a true Prophet of God.[61]

62. Martin Harris, as interviewed by William Waddoups (1923)

"[W]ith these ears," pointing to his ears, "I heard the voice of the angel, and with these hands," holding out his hands, "I handled the plates containing the record of the Book of Mormon, and I assisted the Prophet in the translation thereof. I bear witness that this testimony is true."[62]

63. Martin Harris, as interviewed by William Harrison Homer (1925)

Just as surely as the sun is shining on us by day, just as surely as the breath of life sustains us, so surely do I know that Joseph Smith was a true prophet of God; so surely do I know that the Book of Mormon was divinely translated. I saw the plates, I saw the angel. I heard the voice of God. I know that the Book of Mormon is true.[63]

64. Martin Harris, as interviewed by John E. Godfrey (1933)

And I saw with these two eyes the angel stand with the gold plates in his hands, and I saw him turn leaf by leaf the plates of gold, and I also heard the voice of the Lord saying that these words were true and translated correctly.[64]

65. Martin Harris, as interviewed by Thomas Godfrey (1933)

"I saw the angel and saw the plates from which the Book of Mormon was translated and heard the voice of God declare it was translated correctly." He said this so that all present could hear.[65]

66. Martin Harris, as interviewed by William Pilkington (1934)

[Martin Harris] related Experiences in connection with the Translation of the Book of Mormon. he told me it was he who took some of the copied Characters along with the Interpretation "which Joseph Smith had made through the gift and Power of God" to Proffessor Charles Anthon. . . .

. . . I offered my services as a scribe for the Prophet in the work of Translating. Joseph gladly accepted my Offer, it was the 12th day of April 1828, when I commenced to write for the Prophet from this time on until the 14th day of June 1828 Joseph dictated to me from the Plates of Gold as the characters thereon assumed through the Urim and Thummim the forms of Equivelent modern words, which were familiar to the understanding of the Prophet and Seer, from the 12th day of April until the 14th day of June he said he had written One Hundred and Sixteen pages Foolscap of the translation he said at this period of the Translation a circumstance happened that he was the cause of the One Hundred and Sixteen pages that he had written being lost, and never was found. . . .

. . . Joseph was told in a Revelation to retranslate from the Small Plates of Nephi, and thereby thawart [thwart] the plans of wicked men, but I was never permitted to write for the Prophet anymore. Oliver Cowdery did all the rest of the writing. . . .

. . . The Heavens were then opened and I heard the voice of God declare, that every thing the Angel had told us was True, and that the Book of Mormon was Translated correct. . . .

. . . I was the first scribe for Joseph in the Translating of the Book of Mormon.[66]

67. Martin Harris, as interviewed by William Pilkington (1939)

Joseph Smith had just received the plates from the Angel Moroni, "but I promised them that I would begin translating, but I can not do it, because wicked men haunt me, day and night. And I can not begin the translation, and it hurts. Mr. Harris, I am a poor boy; my parents and family are poor, but we are honest. I have a letter in my possession, recently received from my father-in-law [Isaac Hale], stating that if I will come to his house, with my wife, Emma, he will let me have a room where I will be secluded—but I am poor, and have not the money to go there with." Then it was that Martin Harris put his hand in his pocket. He said, "Take that." "No, No. I am not giving it to you, I am giving it to the Lord, for His Servant to do his bidding." . . . [In Harmony, Pennsylvania], through the help of his wife, Emma, and what faith he could muster up, he tried to translate and failed. And he found he had put all his trust in the Lord. It was to be through the Power of God—not through the power of man—through the Power of God. They did some little translating, his wife Emma as Scribe; and the following February, in the winter time, when the snow was deep on the ground, Martin Harris wanted to know more about the Boy Prophet, and he walked all the way through the snow from Palmyra to Harmony. And he found out what he had done. He had quite a long talk with the Prophet, and he finally asked if he would be kind enough to join him in his work, and asked the Prophet if he would let him take what he had written to some learned man, to some linguist.[67]

68. Martin Harris, as recorded by Theodore Farley (1940)

[A]fter the angel had shown him the plates and disappeared, he [Martin Harris] heard a voice from Heaven that thrilled every fiber of his body, stating that the book had been translated by the gift and power of God, and not of man, and he was commanded by the Lord to so make that statement to the world. And he did.[68]

69. Oliver Cowdery, as recorded by Ashbel Kitchell (1830)

Oliver Lowdree . . . stated that he had been one who had been an assistant in the translation of the golden Bible, and had also seen the Angel, and had been commissioned by him to go out and bear testimony, that God would destroy this generation.[69]

70. Oliver Cowdery to W. W. Phelps (1834)

Near the time of the setting of the Sun, Sabbath evening, April 5th, 1829, my natural eyes, for the first time beheld this brother. He then resided in Harmony, Susquehanna county Penn. On Monday the 6th, I assisted him in arranging some business of a temporal nature, and on Tuesday the 7th, commenced to write the book of Mormon. These were days never to be forgotten—to sit under the sound of a voice dictated by the *inspiration* of heaven, awakened the utmost gratitude of this bosom! Day after day I continued, uninterrupted, to write from his mouth, as he translated, with the *Urim* and *Thummim*, or, as the Nephites whould have said, "Interpreters," the history, or record, called the "The book of Mormon."[70]

71. Oliver Cowdery, as interviewed by Josiah Jones (1841)

In the last part of October, 1830, four men appeared here by the names of [Oliver] Cowdery, [Parley P.] Pratt, [Peter] Whitmar and [Ziba] Peterson; they stated they were from Palmyra, Ontario county, N.Y. with a book, which they said contained what was engraven on gold plates found in a stone box, in the ground . . . and was found about three years ago by a man named Joseph Smith Jr. who had translated it by looking into a stone or two stones, when put into a dark place, which stones he said were found in the box with the plates. They affirmed while he looked through the stone spectacles another sat by and wrote what he told them, and thus the book was all written. . . .

He [Cowdery] stated that Smith looked into or through the transparent stones to translate what was on the plates. I then asked him if he had ever looked through the stones to see what he could see in them; his reply was that he was not permitted to look into them. I asked him who debarred him from looking into them; he remained sometime in silence; then said that he had so much confidence in his friend Smith, who told him that he must not look into them, that he did not presume to do so lest he should tempt God and be struck dead.[71]

72. Oliver Cowdery, as recorded by Reuben Miller (1848)

Friends and brethren my name is Cowdrey, Oliver Cowdrey, In the early history of this church I stood Identified with her. And [was] one in her councils. . . .

I wrote with my own pen the intire book of mormon (Save a few pages) as it fell from the Lips of the prophet [Joseph Smith]. As he translated <it> by the gift and power of god, By [the] means of the urum and thummim, or as it is called by that book holy Interperters. I beheld with my eyes. And handled with my hands the gold plates from which it was translated. I also beheld the Interperters. That book is true. Sidney Rigdon did not write it. Mr [Solomon] Spaulding did not write it. I wrote it myself as it fell from the Lips of the prophet.[72]

73. Oliver Cowdery, as recounted by George Q. Cannon (1881)

When I was a boy I heard it stated concerning Oliver Cowdery, that after he left the Church he practised law, and . . . in a court in Ohio, the opposing counsel thought he would say something that would overwhelm Oliver Cowdery, and . . . alluded to him as the man that had testified and had written that he had beheld an angel of God, and that the angel had shown unto him the plates from which the Book of Mormon was translated. He supposed, of course, that it would cover him with confusion . . . but . . . he [Oliver Cowdery] arose in the court, and in his reply stated that, whatever his faults and weaknesses might be, the testimony which he had written, and which he had given to the world, was literally true.[73]

74. Oliver Cowdery, as recorded by Edward Stevenson (1886)

He testified that he beheld the plates, the leaves being turned over by the angel, whose voice he heard, and that they were commanded as witnesses to bear a faithful testimony to the world of the vision that they were favored to behold, and that the translation from the plates in the Book of Mormon was accepted of the Lord, and that it should go forth to the world and no power on earth should stop its progress.[74]

75. Oliver Cowdery, as recorded by William M. Frampton (1901)

Brother Cowdery looked up[on] the people for a short time without speaking, his manner caused deep attention then in a distinct and very impressive voice, said "My name is Cowdery, Oliver Cowdery, in an early day I was identified with this Church in her councils, I wrote the Book Of Mormon, Spaulding did not write it, Sidney Rigdon did not write it, I wrote it (with the exception of a few pages) with this right hand, (extending his hand) as the inspired words fell from the lips of Joseph Smith.[75]

76. Oliver Cowdery, as interviewed by Samuel Whitney Richards (1907)

He [Oliver Cowdery] represents Joseph as sitting by a table with the plates before him. and he reading the record with the Urim & Thummim. Oliver, his scribe, sits close beside to hear and write every word as translated. This is done by holding the translators over the words of the written record, and the translation appears distinctly in the instrument, which had been touched by the finger of God and dedicated and consecated for the express purpose of translating languages. This instrument now used fully performed its Mission. Every word was made distinctly visible even to every letter, and if Oliver did not in writing spell the word correctly it remained in the translator until it was written correctly. This was the Mystery to Oliver, how Joseph being compar[a]tively ignorant could correct him in spelling, without seeing the word written, and he would not be satisfied until he should be permitted or have the gift to translate as well as Joseph.[76]

77. Oliver Cowdery, as interviewed by Jacob F. Gates (1912)

I am a dying man, and what would it profit me to tell you a lie? I know . . . that this Book of Mormon was translated by the gift and power of God. My eyes saw, my ears heard, and my understanding was touched, and I know that whereof I testified is true. It was no dream, no vain imagination of the mind,—it was real.[77]

78. David Whitmer (1878)

David Whitmer brought out the manuscripts of the Book of Mormon. We examined them closely and those who knew the handwriting pronounced the whole of them, excepting comparatively a few pages, to be in the handwriting of Oliver Cowdery. It was thought that these few pages were in the handwriting of Emma Smith and John and Christian Whitmer.[78]

79. David Whitmer, as interviewed by P. Wilhelm Poulson (1878)

I–How did you know Joseph to be at that time?

He–As a very humble and meek man, and very simple minded indeed. He did the will of the Lord, and an arduous task it was to translate the Book of Mormon.

I–Did Joseph use the Urim and Thummim when he translated?

He–The Urim and Thummim were two white stones, each of them cased in as spectacles are, in a kind of silver casing, but the bow between the stones was more heavy, and longer apart between the stones, than we usually find it in spectacles. Martin Harris, Oliver Cowdery, Emma and my brother John each at different times wrote for Joseph as he translated.[79]

80. David Whitmer, as interviewed by Thomas Wood Smith (1879)

I personally heard him state, in Jan. 1876 in his own house in Richmond, Ray Co. Mo. . . . that he saw Joseph translate, by the aid of the Urim and Thummim, time and again, and he [David] then produced a large pile of foolscap paper closely written in a very fair hand, which he declared was the manuscript written mainly by Oliver Cowdery and Martin Harris, as the translation was being read by the aid of the Urim and Thummim of the characters on the plates by Joseph Smith, which work of translation and transcription he frequently saw.[80]

81. David Whitmer, as interviewed by J. L. Traughber Jr. (1879)

I, too, have seen the "manuscripts" and examined them. I, too, have heard Father [David] Whitmer say that he was present many times while

Joseph was translating; but I never heard him say that the translation was made by aid of Urim and Thummim; but in every case, and his testimony is always the same, he declared that Joseph first offered prayer, then took a dark colored, opaque stone, called a "seer-stone," and placed it in the crown of his hat, then put his face into the hat, and read the translation as it appeared before him. This was the daily method of procedure, as I have often heard Father Whitmer declare; and, as it is generally agreed to by parties who know the facts, that a considerable portion of the work of translation was performed in a room of his father's house, where he then resided, there can be no doubt but what Father David Whitmer is a competent witness of the manner of translating. . . .

With the sanction of David Whitmer, and by his authority, I now state that he does not say that Joseph Smith ever translated in his presence by aid of Urim and Thummim; but by means of one dark colored, opaque stone, called a "Seer Stone," which was placed in the crown of a hat, into which Joseph put his face, so as to exclude the external light. Then, a spiritual light would shine forth, and parchment would appear before Joseph, upon which was a line of characters from the plates, and under it, the translation in English; at least, so Joseph said.[81]

82. David Whitmer, as interviewed by Thomas Wood Smith (1880)

[U]nless my interview with David Whitmer in January, 1876, was only a dream, or that I failed to understand plain English, I believed then, and since, and now, that he said that Joseph possessed, and used the Urim and Thummim in the translation of the inscriptions referred to, and I remember of being much pleased with that statement, as I had heard of the "Seer stone" being used. And unless I dreamed the interview, or very soon after failed to recollect the occasion, he described the form and size of the said Urim and Thummim. The nearest approach to a retraction of my testimony as given in the Fall River *Herald* and that given publicly in many places from the stand from January, 1876, till now, is, that unless I altogether misunderstood "Father Whitmer" on this point, he said the translation was done by the aid of the Urim and Thummim. If he says he did not intend to convey such an impression to my mind, then I say I regret that I misunderstood him, and unintentionally have misrepresented him. But that I understood him as represented by me frequently I still affirm. If Father

Whitmer will say over his own signature, that he never said, or at least never intended to say, that Joseph possessed or used in translating the Book of Mormon, the Urim and Thummim, I will agree to not repeat my testimony as seen in the Fall River *Herald* on that point.[82]

83. David Whitmer, as interviewed by Eri B. Mullin (1880)

Mr. D. Whitmer told me in the year 1874, that Joseph Smith used the Urim and Thummim when he was translating. . . .

I for my part know he said that Joseph had the instrument Urim and Thummim. I asked him how they looked. He said they looked like spectacles, and he (Joseph) would put them on and look in a hat, or put his face in the hat and read. Says I, "Did he have the plates in there." "No, the words would appear, and if he failed to spell the word right, it would stay till it was spelled right, then pass away; another come, and so on."[83]

84. David Whitmer, as interviewed by the *Kansas City Journal* (1881)

After several months Cowdery told me he was going to Harmony, Pa.—whither Joseph Smith had gone with the plates on account of persecutions of his neighbors—and see him about the matter. He did go and on his way stopped at my father's house and told me that as soon as he found out anything either

TRUTH OR UNTRUTH

he would let me know. After he got there he became acquainted with Joseph Smith, and shortly after, wrote to me telling me that he was convinced that Smith had the records and that he (Smith) had told him that it was the will of heaven that he (Cowdery) should be his scribe to assist in the translation of the plates. He went on and Joseph translated from the plates and he wrote it down. Shortly after this Cowdery wrote me another letter in which he gave me a few lines of what they had translated, and he assured me that he knew of a certainty that he had a record of a people that inhabited this continent, and that the plates they were translating gave a complete history of these people. When Cowdery wrote me these things and told me that he had revealed knowledge concerning the truth of them, I showed these letters to my parents, and brothers and sisters. Soon after I received another letter from Cowdery, telling me to come down into Pennsylvania and bring him and Joseph to my father's house, giving as a reason therefor that they had received a commandment from God to that effect. I went down to Harmony, and found everything just as they had written me. The next day after I got there they packed up the plates and we proceeded on our journey to my father's house where we arrived in due time, and the day after we commenced upon the translation of the remainder of the plates. I, as well as all of my father's family, Smith's wife, Oliver Cowdery, and Martin Harris were present during the translation. The translation was by Smith and

THE MANNER AS FOLLOWS:

"He had two small stones of a chocolate color, nearly egg shaped and perfectly smooth, but not transparent, called interpreters, which were given him with the plates. He did not use the plates in the translation, but would hold the interpreters to his eyes and cover his face with a hat, excluding all light, and before his eyes would appear what seemed to be parchment, on which would appear the characters of the plates in a line at the top, and immediately below would appear the translation in English, which Smith would read to his scribe, who wrote it down exactly as it fell from his lips. The scribe would then read the sentence written, and if any mistake had been made the characters would remain visible to Smith until corrected, when they faded from sight to be replaced by another line. The translation at my father's occupied about one month, that is from June 1 to July 1, 1829."

"Were the plates under the immediate control of Smith all the time?"

"No, they were not. I will explain how that was. When Joseph first received the plates he translated 116 pages of the book of 'Lehi,' with Martin Harris as scribe. When this had been completed they rested for a time, and Harris wanted to take the manuscript home with him to show to his family and friends. To this Joseph demurred, but finally

ASKED THE LORD

if Harris might be allowed to take it. The answer was 'no.' Harris teased Joseph for a long time and finally persuaded him to ask the Lord a second time, pledging himself to be responsible for its safe keeping. . . . [T]hrough some carelessness [Martin Harris] allowed it to be stolen from him. This incurred the Lord's displeasure, and he sent an angel to Joseph demanding the plates, and until Joseph had thoroughly repented of his transgressions would not allow him to have the use of them again. When Joseph was again allowed to resume the translation the plates were taken care of by a messenger of God, and when Joseph wanted to see the plates this messenger was always at hand. The 116 pages of the book of 'Lehi' which were stolen were never recovered, nor would the Lord permit Joseph to make a second translation of it.

"A few months after the translation was completed, that is in the spring of 1830, Joseph had the book published and this (showing a well worn volume) is a copy of the first edition which I have had in my possession ever since it was printed."[84]

85. David Whitmer (1881)

To the Editor of the [Kansas City] Journal.

RICHMOND, Mo., June 13 [1881].—I notice several errors in the interview had with me by one of your reporters as published in the *Daily Journal* of June 5th, '81, and wish to correct them.

. . . In regard to my going to Harmony, my statement was that "I found everything as Cowdery had written me, and that they packed up next day and went to my father's, (did not say 'packed up the plates') and that he, Smith, (not 'we') then commenced the translation of the remainder of the plates." I did not wish to be understood as saying that those referred to as being present were all of the time in the immediate presence of the translator, but were at the place and saw how the translation was conducted. I did not say that Smith used "two small stones," as stated nor did I call the stone "interpreters." I stated that "he used one stone (not two) and called it a sun stone." The "interpreters" were as I understood taken from Smith and were not used by him after losing the first 116 pages as stated. It is my understanding that the stone referred to was furnished him when he commenced translating again after losing the 116 pages.

My statement was and now is that in translating he put the stone in his hat and putting his face in his hat so as to excluded the light and that then the light and characters appeared in the hat together with the interpretation which he uttered and was written by the scribe and which was tested at the time as stated.[85]

86. David Whitmer, as interviewed by the *Chicago Times* (1881)

It was not until June, 1829, that he met the future prophet who visited his fathers house, and while there completed the translation of the "Book of

Mormon;" and thus he became conversant with its history, having witnessed Smith dictate to Oliver Cowdery the translation of the characters that were inscribed on the plates, said by Mr. Anthon, our Egyptian scholar, to resemble the characters of that ancient people. Christian Whitmer, his brother, occasionally assisted Cowdery in writing, as did Mrs. Joseph Smith, who was a Miss Hale before she was married. . . .

After the plates had been translated, which process required about six months, the same heavenly visitant appeared and reclaimed the gold tablets of the ancient people, informing Smith that he would replace them with other records of the lost tribes that had been brought with them during their wanderings from the Asia, which would be forthcoming when the world was ready to receive them. . . .

The tablets or plates were translated by Smith, who used a small oval kidney-shaped stone, called Urim and Thummim, that seemed endowed with the marvelous power of converting the characters on the plates, when used by Smith, into English, who would then dictate to Cowdery what to write. Frequently, one character would make two lines of manuscript, while others made but a word or two words. Mr. Whitmer emphatically asserts as did Harris and Cowdery, that while Smith was dictating the translation he had no manuscript notes or other means of knowledge save the seer stone and the characters as shown on the plates, he being present and cognizant how it was done.[86]

87. David Whitmer, as interviewed by William H. Kelley and G. A. Blakeslee (1882)

I know Joseph Smith was a prophet of God, and he translated the Book of Mormon by the inspiration of God from the plates of the Nephites. . . .

. . . He [Joseph Smith] *had* to trust in God. He could not translate unless he was humble and possessed the right feelings towards every one. To illustrate, so you can see. One morning when he was getting ready to continue the translation, something went wrong about the house and he was put out about it. Something that Emma, his wife, had done. Oliver and I went up stairs, and Joseph came up soon after to continue the translation, but he could not do anything. He could not translate a single syllable. He went down stairs, out into the orchard and made supplication to the Lord; was gone about an hour—came back to the house, asked Emma's forgiveness and then came up stairs where we were and the translation went on all right. He could do nothing save he was humble and faithful.[87]

88. David Whitmer, as interviewed by E. C. Briggs (1884)

"The boys, Joseph and Oliver, worked hard, early and late, while translating the plates. It was slow work, and they could write only a few pages a day."

Of Joseph he continued:

"He could not do a thing except he was humble, and just right before the Lord."

I said, "Why not?"

He replied:

"The Urim and Thummim would look dark; he could not see a thing in them."

"How did it appear in them?" we asked.

His answer was:

"The letters appeared on them in light, and would not go off until they were written correctly by Oliver. When Joseph could not pronounce the words he spelled them out letter by letter."[88]

89. David Whitmer, as interviewed by James H. Hart (1884)

"In regard to the translation," said Mr. Whitmer, "it was a laborious work for the weather was very warm, and the days were long and they worked from morning till night. But they were both young and strong and were soon able to complete the work.

"The way it was done was thus: Joseph would place the seer-stone in a deep hat, and placing his face close to it, would see, not the stone, but what appeared like an oblong piece of parchment, on which the hieroglyphics would appear, and also the translation in the English language, all appearing in bright luminous letters. Joseph would then read it to Oliver, who would write it down as spoken. Sometimes Joseph could not pronounce the words correctly, having had but little education; and if by any means a mistake was made in the copy, the luminous writing would remain until it was corrected. It sometimes took Oliver several trials to get the right letters to spell correctly some of the more difficult words, but when he had written them correctly, the characters and the interpretation would disappear, and be replaced by other characters and their interpretation.

"When the seer-stone was not placed in the hat, no characters or writing could be seen therein, but when so placed then the hieroglyphics would appear as before described. Some represented but one word, or name, some represented several, and some from one to two lines.

"Emma, Joseph' s wife, came to my father's house a short time after Joseph and Oliver came, and she wrote a little of the translation, my brother Christian wrote some, but Oliver wrote the greater portion of it."[89]

90. David Whitmer, as interviewed by George Q. Cannon (1884)

In speaking of the translating he [David Whitmer] said that Joseph had the stone in a hat from which all light was excluded. In the stone the characters appeared and under that the translation in English and they remained until the scribe had copied it correctly. If he had made a mistake the words still remained and were not replaced by any other.[90]

91. David Whitmer, as interviewed by the *St. Louis Republican* (1884)

"Yes," said Mr. Whitmer, "I have no objections to giving the particulars of my early life. . . . The translation was done in my father's house; at least two months of the time, was thus taken up with it there. Oliver Cowdery was the principal amanuensis. . . .

"Joseph Smith dictated every word in the book. The understanding we have about it was that when the book was discovered an angel was present and pointed the place out. In translating from the plates, Joseph Smith looked through the Urim and Thummim, consisting of two transparent pebbles set in the rim of a bow, fastened to a breastplate. He dictated by looking through them to his scribes."[91]

92. David Whitmer, as interviewed by Zenas H. Gurley (1885)

Questions asked of David Whitmer at his home in Richmond Ray County Mo. Jan 14 1885. relating to Book of Mormon, and the history of the Church of Jesus Christ of L. D. S. by Elder Z. H. Gurley. . . .

19. Were the plates from which the Book of Mormon was translated in Joseph Smiths possession while translating and seen and handled by several different persons, if not, where were they?

Ans—I do not know.

20. Q—Did Joseph use his "peep stone" to finish up the translation? if so why?

Ans—He used a stone called a "Seers stone," the "Interpreters" having been taken away from him because of transgression. . . .

25: Q. Were you present during any of the time of translation, if so, state how it was done.

Ans—The "Interpreters" were taken from Joseph after he allowed Martin Harris to carry away the 116 pages of Ms of the Book of Mormon as a punishment, but he was allowed to go on and translate by the use of a "Seers stone" which he had, and which he placed in a hat into which he buried his face, stating to me and others that the original Character appeared upon parchment and under it the translation in english which [enabled him?] to read it readily.[92]

93. David Whitmer, as interviewed by the *Chicago Tribune* (1885)

In order to give privacy to the proceeding a blanket, which served as a portière, was stretched across the family living room to shelter the translators and the plates from the eyes of any who might call at the house while the work was in progress. This, Mr. Whitmer says, was the only use made of the blanket, and it was not for the purpose of concealing the plates or the translator from the eyes of the amanuensis. In fact, Smith was at no time hidden from his collaborators, and the translation was performed in the presence of not only the persons mentioned, but of the entire Whitmer household and several of Smith's relatives besides.

The work of translating the tablets consumed about eight months, Smith acting as the seer and Oliver Cowdery, Smith's wife, and Christian Whitmer, brother of David, performing the duties of amanuenses, in whose handwriting the original manuscript now is. Each time before resuming the work all present would kneel in prayer and invoke the Divine blessing on the proceeding. After prayer Smith would sit on one side of a table and the amanuenses, in turn as they became tired, on the other. Those present and not actively engaged in the work seated themselves around the room and then the work began. After affixing the magical spectacles to his eyes, Smith would take the plates and translate the characters one at a time. The graven characters would appear in succession to the seer, and directly under the character, when viewed through the glasses, would be the translation in English.

Sometimes the character would be a single word, and frequently an entire sentence. In translating the characters Smith, who was illiterate and but little versed in Biblical lore, was ofttimes compelled to spell the words out, not knowing the correct pronunciation, and Mr. Whitmer recalls the fact that at that time Smith did not even know that Jerusalem was a walled city. Cowdery, however, being a school-teacher, rendered invaluable aid in pronouncing hard words and giving their proper definition.

. . . It seems that Smith, who was puffed up with his great importance as a confidential secretary to the Lord, displeased the Master by entering into some carnal confab in relation to the work. For this offense he was punished by having the celestial visitant, who first commissioned him to inaugurate the work, suddenly appear and carry off the plates and spectacles. . . .

. . . Smith's offense of tattling the secrets of the work among his neighbors was less readily condoned [than Harris losing the 116 pages], and for a long time the work was suspended, the angel being in possession of the plates and spectacles. Finally, when Smith had fully repented of his rash conduct, he was forgiven. The plates, however, were not returned, but instead Smith was given by the angel a Urim and Thummim of another pattern, it being shaped in oval or kidney form. This seer's stone he was instructed to place in his hat, and on covering his face with the hat the character and translation would appear on the stone.

This worked just as satisfactorily as the old method, but at no time thereafter was the backsliding Joseph intrusted with the precious plates. However, the entire portion of the golden volume, which the angel said might be translated, was reduced by the nimble amanuenses to readable manuscript.[93]

94. David Whitmer, as interviewed by the *Omaha Herald* (1886)

Much of the translation of the plates was accomplished at the house of Peter Whitmer, the father of David, and the latter witnessed demonstrations, on more occasion than one, of the prophet's manipulation of the stone spectacles. He [David] states that the work of translation occupied fully eight months, and that at times this peculiar instrument would refuse to perform its functions. On such occasions the prophet would resort to prayer, and after a short season he would return to his work to find that the urim and thummum reflected the words of the translation with its wonted power. This rigorous exactment required him to be humble and spotless in his deportment in order that the work might progress. On one occasion the prophet had indulged in a stormy quarrel with his wife. Without pacifying her or making any reparation for his brutal treatment, he returned to the room in the Whitmer residence to resume the work with the plates. The surface of the magic stone remained blank, and all his persistent efforts to bring out the coveted words proved abortive. He went into the woods again to pray, and this time was gone fully an hour. His friends became positively concerned, and were about to institute a search, when Joseph entered the room, pale and haggard, having suffered a vigorous chastisement at the hands of the Lord. He went straight in humiliation to his wife, entreated and received her forgiveness, returned to his work, and, much to the joy of himself and his anxious friends surrounding him, the stone again glared forth its letters of fire. The urim and thummum, in this strange process of translation, would reflect a number of words in pure English, which would remain on its face until the party acting as scribe had got it correctly written, and the occasional disposition of the characters to remain long after they had been so written was always an infallible evidence that there was something wrong in the translation of the record, and a close comparison would invariably reveal this fact. When the necessary corrections ha[d] been made the words would instantly disappear from the urim and thummum and new ones take their place. . . . [After the loss of the 116 pages, the Lord] took from the prophet the urim and thummum and otherwise expressed his condemnation. By fervent prayer and by otherwise humbling himself, the prophet, however, again found favor, and was presented with a strange oval-shaped, chocolate-colored stone about the size of an egg, only more flat, which, it was promised, should serve the same purpose as the missing urim and thummim. . . . With this stone all of the present Book of Mormon was translated.[94]

95. David Whitmer, as interviewed by M. J. Hubble (1886)

A part of the book of Lehigh [Lehi] had been translated, about 150 pages & taken to Philadelphia by one of the parties, who put it in a bureau drawer at night, the next morning it was gone and has never yet been found. Joseph Smith was informed that for his transgressing the command, to keep it always under his care, he would be punished and the "gift" of reading through the spectacles was taken from him for about 3 months & never was allowed to see the "plates" again but at the end of his punishment, he was told that he might translate the book of Mormon, instead of the book of Lehigh but would not be permitted to see the "plates" that the "Characters" would appear before him & when he translated them correctly they would disappear & new ones come in their place if not translated correctly the first time they would remain until they were which in several instances he knew to be true because he said Joseph Smith was a man of limited education and could hardly write legibly. . . .

He said the Brass or Gold Plates were bound together at the back by having 3 rings run through & when a page was translated it turned back on the ring.

He said Smith translated by means of a pair of large bound Spectacles ie the "Book of Mormon", that the Characters would appear in the air & stay until correctly translated and then disappear that Smith was ignorant of the Bible that when translating he first came to where Jerusalem was spoken of as a "Walled City" he stopped until they got a Bible & showed him where the fact was recorded—Smith not believing it was a walled city.[95]

96. David Whitmer (1887)

The people cannot understand why the Lord would bring forth his word from *"a book* (plates) *that is sealed"* and was buried in the ground by his ancient prophets on this land: and why He should have the words of the book delivered *"to one that is learned,"* telling him to read it, etc.; (see Isa. xxix) but the learned and wise men of the world could not read it; God gave to an unlearned boy, Joseph Smith, the gift to translate it by the means of a STONE. . . .

. . . I will say that all who desire to investigate the Spaulding manuscript story will not be obliged to go very far before they will see the entire falsity of that claim. I testify to the world that I am an eye-witness to the translation of the greater part of the Book of Mormon. Part of it was translated in my father's house in Fayette, Seneca County, N. Y. . . .

I will now give you a description of the manner in which the Book of Mormon was translated. Joseph Smith would put the seer stone into a hat, and put his face in the hat, drawing it closely around his face to exclude the light; and in the darkness the spiritual light would shine. A piece of something resembling parchment would appear and on that appeared the writing. One character at a time would appear, and under it was the interpretation in English. Brother Joseph would read off the English to Oliver Cowdery, who was his principal scribe, and when it was written down and repeated to Brother Joseph to see if it was correct, then it would disappear, and another character with the interpretation would appear. Thus the Book of Mormon was translated by the gift and power of God, and not by any power of man. . . .

At times when Brother Joseph would attempt to translate, he would look into the hat in which the stone was placed, he found he was spiritually blind and could not translate. He told us that his mind dwelt too much on earthly things, and various causes would make him incapable of proceeding with the translation. When in this condition he would go out and pray, and when he became sufficiently humble before God, he could then proceed with the translation. Now we see how very strict the Lord is; and how he requires the heart of man to be just right in His sight, before he can receive revelation from him. . . .

After the translation of the Book of Mormon was finished, early in the spring of 1830, before April 6th, Joseph gave the stone to Oliver Cowdery and told me as well as the rest that he was through with it, and he did not use the stone any more. . . .

Now, bear in mind that these revelations were given through the "stone," while the Book of Mormon was being translated. The revelations in June, 1829, were given about the time the translation of the book was finished. As I have stated before, Brother Joseph gave up the stone a few months after translating the Book of Mormon.[96]

97. David Whitmer, as recorded by the *Richmond Democrat* (1888)

When he [David Whitmer] was twenty-four years of age . . . Oliver Cowdery . . . mentioned the matter [the discovery of the gold plates] to him and announced his determination to visit Smith. . . . A few days later he [Whitmer] received a letter from Cowdery, urging him to join him, which he did. . . . After remaining long enough to satisfy himself of the divine inspiration of Smith, the three returned to Whitmer's home, where it was agreed that the work of translation should be prosecuted. . . .

. . . The "urim and thummim," mentioned in the account of the vision were a pair of transparent stone spectacles. Smith would put on the spectacles, when a few words of the text of the Book of Mormon would appear on the lenses. When these were correctly transcribed by Cowdery, who acted as his amanuensis, these words would disappear and others take their place. . . . [After the loss of the 116 pages, Smith] again found favor with the Lord, and was presented with a strange oval-shaped, chocolate colored stone, about the size of an egg but more flat, which it was promised should answer the same purpose. With this stone all the present book was translated. The prophet would place the stone in a hat, then put his face in the hat and read the words that appeared thereon.[97]

98. David Whitmer, as interviewed by Nathan A. Tanner Jr. (1909)

He [David Whitmer] said that Joseph was separated from the scribe by a blanket, as I remember; that he had the Urim and Thummim, and a chocolate colored stone, which he used alternately, as suited his convenience, and he said he believed Joseph could as well accomplish the translation by looking into a hat, or any other stone, as by the use of the Urim and Thummim or the chocolate colored stone. David expressed absolute faith in the Prophet's power to get any information he desired, and by any means he should adopt for the purpose. I mean he appeared to have absolute faith in the Prophet's power with God, to get any information he wished for. And he did not think that either the Urim and Thummim or the stone he had were essential, or absolutely essential, to the obtaining of the information.

He said that Joseph would—as I remember—place the manuscript beneath the stone or Urim and Thummim, and the characters would appear in English, which he would spell out, and they would remain there until the word was fully written and corrected, when it would disappear and another word appear, etc.[98]

99. John Whitmer (1836)

I desire to testify to all that will come to the knowledge of this address; that I have most assuredly seen the plates from whence the book of Mormon is translated, and that I have handled these plates, and know of a surety that Joseph Smith, jr. has translated the book of Mormon by the gift and power of God, and in this thing the wisdom of the wise most assuredly has perished.[99]

100. John Whitmer (1839)

[Theodore] Turley said, "Gentlemen, I presume there are men here who have heard Corrill say, that 'Mormonism' was true, that Joseph Smith was a prophet, and inspired of God. I now call upon you, John Whitmer: you say Corrill is a moral and a good man; do you believe him when he says the Book of Mormon is true, or when he says it is not true? There are many things published that they say are true, and again turn around and say they are false?" Whitmer asked, "Do you hint at me?" Turley replied, "If the cap fits you, wear it; all I know is that you have published to the world that an angel did present those plates to Joseph Smith." Whitmer replied: "I now say, I handled those plates; there were fine engravings on both sides. I handled them;" and he described how they were hung, and "they were shown to me by a supernatural power;" he acknowledged all.

Turley asked him, "Why is not the translation now true?" He said, "I could not read it [in the original] and I do not know whether it [i.e., the translation] is true or not." Whitmer testified all this in the presence of eight men.[100]

101. John Whitmer, as interviewed by Zenas H. Gurley (1879)

He had seen the plates; and it was his especial pride and joy that he had written sixty pages of the Book of Mormon. . . . When the work of translation was going on he sat at one table with his writing material and Joseph at another with the breast-plate and Urim and Thummim. The latter were attached to the breast-plate and were two crystals or glasses, into which he looked and saw the words of the book. The words remained in sight till correctly written, and mistakes of the scribe in spelling the names were corrected by the seer without diverting his gaze from the Urim and Thummim.[101]

102. Katharine Smith Salisbury (1895)

And when he went to Pennsylvania he commenced translating the book of Mormon, and translated some one hundred and sixteen pages that Martin Harris took home and lost, and when my brother found they were lost, he was very much troubled and said:

"I am afraid I have broken the commandments and will not be allowed to translate the record."

The angel came and took the Urim and Thummim from him. He fasted and prayed several days, and the angel returned them again, and told him that his sins were forgiven, and for him to go ahead and translate, but not to translate that that was lost, but to begin where he had left off. He commenced, and when he had got the record partly translated, persecution rose there, and he wrote for David Whitmer to come and take him to his house. David came, and he asked how he should carry the plates and he was told that they would be there when he got there, in the garden.

When he got to Father Whitmer's he found the records, as he had been told he would, and there he finished tra[n]slating the Book of Mormon.[102]

103. Joseph Smith Sr., as interviewed by Fayette Lapham ([1830]/1870)

Under the first plate, or lid, he found a pair of spectacles, about one and a half inches longer than those used at the present day, the eyes not of glass, but of diamond. On the next page were representations of all the masonic implements, as used by masons at the present day. The remaining pages were closely written over in characters of some unknown tongue, the last containing the alphabet of this unknown language. Joseph, not being able to read the characters, made a copy of some of them, which he showed to some of the most learned men of the vicinity. . . . Returning home, he one day tried the spectacles, and found that, by looking through them, he could see everything—past, present, and future—and could also read and understand the characters written on the plates. Before proceeding to translate the characters, Joseph was directed to choose twelve Apostles, who must be men who believed in the supernatural. . . . Joseph succeeded in finding the requisite number of believers, among them Martin Harris, who was chosen Scribe. . . . [H]e and Martin went to Harmony, in Pennsylvania, where they would be less persecuted, and where Joseph, with spectacles on, translated the characters on the gold plates, and Harris recorded the result.

After thus translating a number of plates, Harris wanted to return to Palmyra, taking a part of the writings with him; but the Lord objected, for fear that Harris would show them to unbelievers, who would make sport and derision of them. But Harris finally obtained leave to take them, on condition that he should let no one see them, except those who believed in them: in this he was indiscreet, and showed them to some one that he ought not to. When he next went to his drawer to get them, behold! they were not there; the Lord had taken them away.

Joseph and Harris returned to Harmony, and found the plates missing—the Lord had taken them also. Then Joseph put on the spectacles, and saw where the Lord had hid them, among the rocks, in the mountains. Though not allowed to get them, he could, by the help of the spectacles, read them where they were, as well as if they were before him. They were directed not to re-translate the part already gone over, for fear the new work would not correspond, in every particular, with the old; their enemies might take advantage of that circumstance, and condemn the whole. But they could begin where they left off, and translate until they were directed to stop; for, in consequence of their indiscretion, they would not be allowed to translate the whole, at present. At some future time, they would be allowed to translate the whole; and then their translation, the gold plates, the gold hilt, ball and pointers could all be circulated together, each a witness of the others.[103]

104. Lucy Mack Smith to Solomon Mack Jr. (1831)

Joseph after repenting of his sins and humbling himself before God was visited by an holy Angel whose countenance was as lightning and whose garments were white above all whiteness and gave unto him commandments which inspired him from on high. and gave unto him by the means of which was before prepared that he should translate this this book, and by <reading> this this our eyes are opened that we can see the situation in which the world now stands that the eyes of the whole world are blinded, that the churches have all become corrupted, yea every church upon face of the earth that the Gospel of Christ is no where preached. this is the situation which the world is now in, and you can judge for yourselves if we did not need something more than the wisdom of men for to show us the right way.[104]

105. Lucy Mack Smith, as interviewed by Henry Caswall (1842)

The angel of the Lord appeared to him fifteen years since, and shewed him the cave where the original golden plates of the book of Mormon were deposited. He shewed him also the Urim and Thummim, by which he might understand the meaning of the inscriptions on the plates, and he shewed him the golden breastplate of the high priesthood. My son received these precious gifts, he interpreted the holy record, and now the believers in that revelation are more than a hundred thousand in number. I have myself seen and handled the golden plates; they are about eight inches long, and six wide; some of them are sealed together and are not to be opened, and some of them are loose. They are all connected by a ring which passes through a hole at the end of each plate, and are covered with letters beautifully engraved. I have seen and felt also the Urim and Thummim. They resemble two large bright diamonds set in a bow like a pair of spectacles. My son puts these over his eyes when he reads unknown languages, and they enable him to interpret them in English. I have likewise carried in my hands the sacred breastplate. It is composed of pure gold, and is made to fit the breast very exactly.[105]

106. Lucy Mack Smith (1845)

It soon became necessary to take some measures to accomplish the translation of the record into English but he was instructed to take off a fac simile of the ~~alphabet Egyptian~~ characters <composing the alphabet which were called reformed egyptian> Alphabetically and send them to all the learned men that he could find and ask them for the translation of the same. Joseph was very solicitous about the work but as yet no means had come into his hands of accomplishing ~~the same~~ it. . . .

. . . when she [Lucy Harris] returned home which was ~~in~~ about 2 weeks from the time she arrived ~~there~~ in Harmony she endeavored to disuade Mr H[arris] from having any thing farther to do with writing or translating the record but ~~Martin~~ he paid but little attention to her and as he agreed to go back and write for a season at least he did so— . . .

I ~~then~~ continued[,] <said> Joseph[,] my suplications to God without cessation this his mercy might again be exercised towards me and on the 22 of september I had the joy and satisfaction of again receiving the ~~record~~ <urim and Thummin> into my possession and I have commenced translating and Emma writes for me now but the angel said that ~~if I got the plates again~~ that the Lord woul[d] send some one to write for me and I trust that it will be so—he also said that ~~the ange<l>~~ <he> ~~seemed~~ <was> rejoiced when he gave ~~him~~ <me> back The ~~plates~~ <urim and Thummin> and ~~said~~ that ~~he~~ <God> was pleased with ~~his~~ <my> faithfulness and humility ~~also that the Lord was pleased with him~~ and loved ~~him~~ <me> for ~~his~~ <my> penitence and dilligence in prayer in the which ~~he~~ <I> had performed his duty so well as to receive the ~~record~~ <urim and Thummin> and ~~he~~ <was> able to enter upon the work of translation again. . . .

. . . Emma had so much of her time taken up with her work that she could not write but little for him[.] accordingly 2 or 3 days before the arrival of Oliver and Samuel he feeling it his priviledge to lay hold of the promise of the angel that the Lord would send him a scribe he called upon ~~the~~ His Heavenly Father for the promised assistance and was informed that the same should be forthcoming in a few days as soon <after> Oliver was introduced to him he ~~said Mr Smi<th> I have come for the purpose of writing for you. This was not at all unexpected to Joseph for although he had never seen Mr Cowdray before he knew that the Lord was able to perform and that he had been faithful to fulfull all his promises~~ <informed Joseph what his business was> They ~~then~~ sat down and conversed togather untill late bed time and Joseph told Oliver his entire history as far as it was necessary for his information in those things which concerned him. They <were> soon deeply engaged in the work of writing and translation and pr[o]gressed rapidly. one morning however they sat down to their usual work when the first thing that presented itself to Joseph was a commandment from God that he and Oliver should repair to the water each of them be baptized they immediately went down to the susquehana<h> river and obeyed the mandate given them through the urim and Thumim. . . .

In the mean time Joseph was 150 miles distant and knew naught of the matter except an intimation that was given through the urim and thumim for as he one morning applied the latter to his eyes to look upon the record instead of the words of the book being given him he was commanded to write a letter to one David Whitmore[.] this man Joseph had never seen but he was instructed to say [to] him that he must come with his team immediately in order to convey Josep<h> and his ~~family~~ <Oliver> back to his house which was 135 miles that they might remain with him there untill the translation should be completed for that an evil designing people were seeking to take away Joseph's life in order to prevent the work of God from going forth among the worl<d>. . . .

The Trio viz Joseph, Oliver, and David whitmore started for Waterloo where they arived after a short and plasant Journey in health and fine spirits for commencing anew on their labors[.] here they continued translating untill the whole work was completed.[106]

107. William Smith, as interviewed by James Murdock (1841)

After this Joseph Smith was supernaturally assisted to read and to understand the inscription; and he was directed to translate a great part of it. The pages which he was not to translate were found to be sealed together, so that he did not even read them and learn their contents. With an assistant to correct his English, he translated so much of the inscription as now makes the book of Mormon.[107]

108. William Smith (1883)

In consequence of his vision, and his having the golden plates and refusing to show them, a great persecution arose against the whole family, and he was compelled to remove into Pennsylvania with the plates, where he translated them by means of the Urim and Thummim, (which he obtained with the plates), and the power of God. The manner in which this was done was by looking into the Urim and Thummim, which was placed in a hat to exclude the light, (the plates lying near by covered up), and reading off the translation, which appeared in the stone by the power of God.[108]

109. William Smith (1884)

When Joseph received the plates he a[l]so received the Urim and Thummim, which he would place in a hat to exclude all light, and with the plates by his side he translated the characters, which were cut into the plates with some sharp instrument, into English. And thus, letter by letter, word by word, sentence by sentence, the whole book was translated.[109]

110. William Smith, as interviewed by J. W. Peterson and W. S. Pender (1921)

Explaining the expression as to the stones in the Urim and thummim being set in two rims of a bow he said: A silver bow ran over one stone, under the other, arround over that one and under the first in the shape of a horizontal figure 8 much like a pair of spectacles. That they were much too large for Joseph and he could only see through one at a time using sometimes one and sometimes the other. By putting his head in a hat or some dark object it was not necessary to close one eye while looking through the stone with the other. In that way sometimes when his eyes grew tires [tired] he releaved them of the strain.[110]

111. Sarah (Sally) Heller Conrad, as recorded by Oliver B. Huntington (1897)

I conversed with one old lady 88 years old who lived with David Whitmer when Joseph Smith and Oliver Cowdery were translating the Book of Mormon in the upper room of the house, and she, only a girl, saw them come down from translating room several times when they looked so exceedingly white and strange that she inquired of Mrs. Whitmer the cause of their unusual appearance, but Mr. Whitmer was unwilling to tell the hired girl, the true cause as it was a sacred holy event connected with a holy sacred work which was opposed and persecuted by nearly every one who heard of it. The girl felt so strangely at seeing so strange and unusual appearance, she finally told Mrs. Whitmer that she would not stay with her until she knew the cause of the strange looks of these men. Sister Whitmer then told her what the men were doing in the room above and that the power of God was so great in the room that they could hardly endure it; at times angels were in the room in their glory which nearly consumed them.[111]

112. Elizabeth Whitmer Cowdery, as recorded by William E. McLellin (1870)

I staid in Richmond two days and nights. I had a great deal of talk with widow Cowdry, and her amiable daughter. She is married to a Dr Johnson, but has no children. She gave me a certificate, And this is the copy. "Richmond, Ray Co., Mo. Feb 15, 1870——I cheerfully certify that I was familiar with the manner of Joseph Smith's translating the book of Mormon. He translated the most of it at my Father's house. And I often sat by and saw and heard them translate and write for hours together. Joseph never had a curtain drawn between him and his scribe while he was translating. He would place the director in his hat, and then place his face in his hat, so as to exclude the light, and then [read the words?] as they appeared before him."[112]

113. Alva Hale (1834)

Alva Hale, son of Isaac Hale, states, that Joseph Smith Jr. told him that his (Smith's) gift in seeing with a stone and hat, was a gift from God," but also states "that Smith told him at another time that this *"peeping"* was all d—d nonsense. He (Smith) was deceived himself but did not intend to deceive others;—that he intended to quit the business, (of peeping) and labor for his livelihood." That afterwards, Smith told him, he should see the Plates from which he translated the book of Mormon," and accordingly at the time specified by Smith, he (Hale) "called to see the plates, but Smith did not show them, but appeared angry." He further states, that he knows Joseph Smith Jr. to be an impostor, and a liar, and knows Martin Harris to be a liar likewise.[113]

114. Isaac Hale (1841)

About this time, Martin Harris made his appearance upon the stage; and Smith began to interpret the characters or hieroglyphics which he said were engraven upon the plates, while Harris wrote down the interpretation. It was said, that Harris wrote down one hundred and sixteen pages, and lost them. . . .

. . . I went to the house where Joseph Smith Jr., lived, and where he and Harris were engaged in their translation of the Book. Each of them had a written piece of paper which they were comparing, and some of the words were *"my servant seeketh a greater witness, but no greater witness can be given him."* There was also something said about *"three that were to see the thing"*—meaning I supposed, the Book of Plates, and that *"if the three did not go exactly according to the orders, the thing would be taken from them."* I enquired whose words they were, and was informed by Joseph or Emma, (I rather think it was the former) that they were the words of Jesus Christ. I told them, that I considered the whole of it a delusion, and advised them to abandon it. The manner in which he pretended to read and interpret, was the same as when he looked for the money-diggers, with the stone in his hat, and his hat over his face, while the Book of Plates were at the same time hid in the woods!

After this, Martin Harris went away, and Oliver Cowdery came and wrote for Smith, while he interpreted as above described. This is the same Oliver Cowdery, whose name may be found in the Book of Mormon. Cowdery continued a scribe for Smith until the Book of Mormon was completed as I supposed and understood.[114]

115. Joseph Knight Jr. (ca. 1844)

[A]t last he [Joseph Smith] got the plates, and rode in my Father's wagon and carried them home. I left my Father, purchased a building spot adjoining my Father's and began to work for myself, and nearly ready to build a large house. Joseph had commenced to translate the plates, he told my Father he wanted fifty dollars; my Father could not raise it; he then came to me, the same day I sold my house lot and sent him a one horse wagon. Father and I often went to see him and carry him something to live upon: at last Oliver Cowdery came to write for him, then he got along faster, after many trials and troubles he got it wrote off.[115]

116. Joseph Knight Sr. (ca. 1847)

Nothing material took place untill toard fall the forepart of September. I went to Rochester on Buisness and returnd By Palmyra to be there about the 22nt of September. I was there several Days. I will say there [was] a man near By By the name Samuel Lawrance. He was a Seear [Seer] and he had Bin to the hill and knew about the things in the hill and he was trying to obtain them. He [Joseph Smith] had talked with me and told me the Conversation he had with the personage which told him if he would Do right according to the will of God he mite obtain [the plates] the 22nt Day of Septemer Next and if not he never would have them. Now Joseph was some affraid of him [Samuel Lawrence] that he mite be a trouble to him. He therefore sint his father up to Sams as he Called him near night to see if there was any signs of his going away that night. He told his father to stay till near Dark and if he saw any signs of his going you till him if I find him there I will thrash the stumps with him. So the old man came a way and saw no thing like it. This is to shoe [show] the troubles he had from time to time to obtain the plates.

So that night we all went to Bed and in the morning I got up and my Horse and Carriage was gone. But after a while he Came home and he turned out the Horse. All Come into the house to Brackfirst [breakfast]. But no thing said about where they had Bin. After Brackfirst Joseph Cald me into the other Room and he set his foot on the Bed and leaned his head on his hand and says, "Well I am Dissopinted. "Well," says I, "I am sorrey." "Well," says he, "I am grateley Dissopinted; it is ten times Better then I expected." Then he went on to tell the length and width and thickness of the plates, and said he, "they appear to be Gold." But he seamed to think more of the glasses or the urim and thummem then [than] he Did of the Plates, for, says he, "I can see any thing; they are Marvelus. Now they are writen in Caracters and I want them translated."

Now he was Commanded not to let no [any] one see those things But a few for witness at a givin time. Now it soon got about that Joseph Smith had found the plates and peopel Come in to see them But he told them that they Could not for he must not shoe [show] them. But many insisted and oferd money and Property to see them. But, for keeping them from the Peopel they persecuted and abused them [him] and they [the Smiths] ware obliged to hide them [the plates], and they hid them under a Brick harth in the west Room. About this time Came this Samuel Lawrance and one Beeman a grate Rodsman and wanted to talk with him. And he went into the west Room and they Proposed to go shares with him and tried every way to Bargain with him But Could not. Then Beeman took out his Rods and hild [held] them up and they pointed Dow[n] to the harth whare they ware hid. "There," says Beeman, "it is under that harth." So they had to garde the house until some time in November. He obtained fifty Dollars in money and hired a man to move him and his wife to Pensylvany to hir Fathers, his wife Being onwell and wanted to go to her Fathers. He Bout [bought] a piece of Land of hir Father with a house and Barn on it. Here the People Began to tease him to see the Book and to offer him money and property and they Crouded so harde that he had to hide it in the Mountin.

He now Began to be anxious to git them translated. He therefore with his wife Drew of[f] the Caricters exactley like the ancient and sent Martin Harris to see if he Could git them Translated. . . . Now he [Joseph Smith] Bing [being] an unlearned man did not know what to Do. Then the Lord gave him Power to Translate himself. Then ware the Larned men Confounded, for he, By the means he found with the plates, he Could translate those Caricters Better than the Larned.

Now the way he translated was he put the urim and thummim into his hat and Darkned his Eyes then he would take a sentance and it would apper in Brite Roman Letters. Then he would tell the writer and he would write it. Then that would go away the next sentance would Come and so on. But if it was not Spelt rite it would not go away till it was rite, so we see it was marvelous. Thus was the hol [whole] translated.

Now when he Began to translate he was poor and was put to it for provisions and had no one to write for him But his wife, and his wifes Brother would sometimes write a little for him through the winter. The Next Spring

Oliver Cowdry a young man from palmyra Came to see old Mr Smith, Josephs father, about this work and he sent him Down to pensylveny to see Joseph and satisfy him self. So he Came Down and was soon Convinced of the truth of the work. The next Spring Came Martin Harris Down to pennsylvany to write for him and he wrote 116 pages of the first part of the Book of Mormon. . . . [Following the loss of the 116 pages] There fore Joseph Lost his privilige for a while. But after Repenting he again received the privelage of translating again, as in Book of Covenants page 163.

Now he Could not translate But little Being poor and nobody to write for him But his wife and she Could not do much and take Care of her house and he Being poor and no means to live But work. . . . In January his father and Samuel [Smith] came from Manchester to my house when I was Buisey a Drawing Lumber. I told him they had traviled far enough. I would go with my sley and take them down to morrow. I went Down and found them well and the[y] were glad to see us. We conversed about many things. In the morning I gave the old man a half a Dollar and Joseph a little money to Buoy paper to translate, I having But little with me. The old gentlemen told me to Come and see him once in a while as I Could I went home followed teaming till the last of March the slaying [sleighing] Being good. I told my wife I must go Dow[n] and see Joseph again. "Why Do you go soon, for," said she. Says I, "Come go and see." And she went with me. Next morning we went Down and found them well and ware glad to see us. Joseph talked with us about his translating and some revelations he had Received and from that time my wife Began to Beleve and Continuwed a full Believer untill she Died and that was the 7 Day of August 1831.

In the spring of 1829 Oliver Cowdry a young man from Palmry went to see old Mr. Smith about the Book that Joseph had found. And he told him about it and advised him to go Down to Pensylvany and see for him self and to write for Joseph. He went Down and Received a Revelation Concerning the work and he was Convinced of the truth of the work and he agreed to write for him till it was Done. Now Joseph and Oliver Came up to see me if I Could help him to some provisons, [they] having no way to Buy any. But I was to Cattskill. But when I Came home my folks told me what Joseph wanted. But I had ingaged to go to Catskill again the next Day and I went again and I Bought a Barral of Mackrel and some lined paper for writing. And when I came home I Bought some nine or ten Bushels of grain and five or six Bushels taters [potatoes] and a pound of tea, and I went Down to see him and they ware in want. Joseph and Oliver ware gone to see if they Could find a place to work for provisions, But found none. They returned home and found me there with provisions, and they ware glad for they ware out. Their familey Consisted of four, Joseph and wife, Oliver and his [Joseph's] Brother Samuel. Then they went to work and had provisions enough to Last till the translation was Done. Then he agreed with Martin Harris to print. They therefore agreed with E Grandin to Print five thousand Coppies which was Printed and Bound at Palmiry in the Spring of 1830.[116]

117. Jesse Smith to Hyrum Smith (1829)

You state your Father cannot write by reason of a nervous affection this is a poor excuse, worse than none, he can dictate to others and they can write, ~~he can~~ If he knows not what to write, he can get your Brother's spectacles he would then be as able to ~~write~~ dictate a letter, as Joe is to decypher hieroglyphics, if more should be wanting he can employ the same scoundrel of a scribe, and then not only the matter but manner and style would be correct.[117]

118. *Wayne Sentinel* (1829)

Just about in this particular region, for some time past, much speculation has existed, concerning a pretended discovery, through superhuman means, of an ancient record, of a religious and divine nature and origin, written in ancient characters, impossible to be interpreted by any to whom the special gift has not been imparted by inspiration. It is generally known and spoken of as the "*Golden Bible*." . . . It is pretended that it will be published as soon as the translation is completed.[118]

119. *Rochester Advertiser and Telegraph* (1829)

It was said that the *leaves* of the Bible were *plates* of gold, about eight inches thick, on which were engraved characters or Hyeroglyphics. By placing the spectacles in a hat, and looking into it, Smith could (he said so, at least) interpret these characters.

. . . A few, however, believed the "*golden*" story, among them was *Martin Harris*, an honest and industrious farmer of this town, (Palmyra). So blindly credulous was Harris, that he took some of the characters interpreted by Smith and went in search of some one, besides the interpreter, who was learned enough to *English* them; but all to whom he applied (among the number was a Professor Mitchell of New York,) happened not to be possessed of sufficient knowledge to give satisfaction! Harris returned and set Smith to work at interpreting the Bible. He has at length performed the task, and the work is soon to be put to press in Palmyra.[119]

120. *Rochester Gem* (1829)

By placing the spectacles in a hat and looking into it, Smith interprets the characters into the English language.

Harris states that he went in search of some one to interpret the hieroglyphics, but found that no one was intended to perform that all important task but Smith himself.[120]

121. Lucius Fenn of Covert, Seneca County, New York, to Birdseye Bronson of Winchester, Connecticut (1830)

There is somthing that has taken place lately that is mysterious to us it is this there has been a bible found by 3 men but a short distance from us which is somthig remarkable we think. there was it is said an an [*sic*] angel appeared to these 3 men and told them there was a bible concealed in such a place and if one of them would go to that place he would find it he went and found as the angel said it was in a stone chest what is most to be wondered at is this that the man that found it could not read at all in the english language but he reald [read?] this bible and nobody else cannot it has been concealed there for fourteen hundred years it is written on a kind of gold leaf it is the same that our is only there is an addition to it they are a printing it in Palmyra it is expected that it will come out soon so that we can see it it speaks of the Millenniam day and tells when it is a goeing to take place and it talks that the man that is to find this bible his name as Joseph and his fathers name is Joseph. some people think that it is all a speculation and some think that somthing is going to take place different from what has been for my part I do not know how it will be but it is somthing singular to me, as it respects religion there has been considerable of an attention paid to it this winter between these lakes and there has been considerable many as we humbly hope have been [renewed?] by the grace of God there is a general solemnity upon the people generally in these parts and we hope that there will be a greater ourpouring of the spirit than ever.[121]

122. *Reflector* (Palmyra, N.Y.) (1830)

DIABOLICAL. Our readers must be aware of the great difficulty we labor under in translating our foreign correspondence. The inspired man who wrote the "Gold Bible" on "plates of brass," in the "*reformed* Egyptian" language, on account of its brevity, as we are informed, through the medium of one of these psuedo prophets, never had half the trouble that we experience in deciphering the unseemly scrolls of this dark representative of old Pluto's dominions.[122]

123. *Rochester Gem* (1830)

An ignoramous near Palmyra, Wayne county, pretended he had found some "Gold Plates," as he is pleased to call them, upon which is said to be engraved characters of marvelous and misunderstandable import, which he, nor no other mortal could divine. These characters he has translated into the English language, and lo! they appear to be no other than the mysticisms of an unrevealed Bible! A person more credulous or more cunning, than him who found the plates, ordered the translation thereof, mortgaged his farm, sold all he had, and appropriated it to the printing and binding of several thousand copies of this pearl, which is emphatically of GREAT PRICE! . . .The translator if we take his word for it, has been directed by an angel in this business, for the salvation and the edification of the world![123]

124. *Reflector* (1830)

2. Now Walters, the Magician, was a man unseemly to look upon, and to profound ignorance added the most consummate impudence,—he obeyed the summons of the idle and slothful, and produced an old book in an unknown tongue, (Cicero's Orations *in latin*,) from whence he read in the presence of the Idle and Slothful strange stories of hidden treasures and of the spirit who had the custody thereof.

3. And the Idle and Slothful paid tribute unto the Magician, and besought him saying, Oh! thou who art wise above all men, and can *interpret* the book that no man understandeth, and can discover hidden things by the power of thy enchantments, lead us, we pray thee to the place where the Nephites buried their treasure. . . .

10. Now the rest of the acts of the magician, how his *mantle* fell upon the *prophet* Jo. Smith Jun. and how Jo. made a league with the *Spirit*, who

afterwards turned out to be an angel, and how he obtained the "Gold Bible," Spectacles, and breast plate—will they not be faithfully recorded in the book of Pukei?[124]

125. Diedrich Willers (1830)

In the month of July [June 1829], Joseph Smith made his appearance in Seneca County. . . . There a certain David Whitmer claimed to have seen an angel of the Lord, so Smith proceeded to his house, in order to complete the translation of the above work [Book of Mormon] himself. According to the reports, only there could he work—where men who have had association with the other world also reside. . . .

. . . The Angel indicated that the Lord destined him to translate these things into English from the ancient language, that under these plates were hidden spectacles, without which he could not translate these plates, that by using these spectacles, he (Smith) would be in a position to read these ancient languages, which he had never studied, and that the Holy Ghost would reveal to him the translation in the English language. Therefore, he (Smith) proceeded to Manchester township, Ontario County, and found everything as described, the plates buried next to the spectacles in the earth, and soon he completed the translation of this work.[125]

126. *Reflector* (1830)

7. Knowest thou not, thou weak one of earth, that this same Mormon wrote a book on plates of gold, in the language I now speak . . . and knowest thou not, that thou art greater than all the "money-digging rabble," and art chosen to interpret the book, which Mormon has written, to wit, the gold Bible?

8. "And lo! I answered the spirit of the money diggers saying, how can these things be, as I can neither read nor write? And he said unto me: "I will give thee a breast plate, to keep thee from evil, and I will send thee an assistant, even Oliver, the pedagogue."[126]

127. *Reflector* (1830)

Although there may appear much of *jest*, in the self-conceits of our fellow mortals, it frequently has the faculty to impress upon our minds, a melencholy *tinge*; still the vices and follies of others, if rightly appreciated are full of instruction, & we only require *JO SMITH'S* Magic Spectacles, or some other powerful optical instrument to turn them to our own advantage.[127]

128. *Painesville Telegraph* (1830)

Some two or three years since, an account was given in the papers, of a book purporting to contain new revelations from Heaven, having been dug out of the ground, in Manchester in Ontario Co. N.Y. The book, it seems, has made its appearance in this vicinity.—It contains about 500 octavo pages, which is said to be translated from Egyptian Hieroglyphics, on metal plates, by one Smith, who was enabled to read the characters by instruction from Angels. About two weeks since some persons came along here with the book, one of whom pretends to have seen Angels, and assisted in translating the plates. . . . In the neighboring township of Kirtland, we understand that twenty or thirty have been immersed into the new order of things; many of whom had been previously baptised.—The name of the person here, who pretends to have a divine mission, and to have seen and conversed with Angels, is *Cowdray*.[128]

129. *Painesville Telegraph* (1830)

This new Gospel they say was found in Ontario co. N. Y. and was discovered by an Angel of light, appearing in a dream to a man by the name of Smith, who, as directed, went to a certain place and dug from the earth a stone box, containing plates of gold, on which this gospel was engraved in characters unknown. The said Smith though a man so illiterate that he cannot write, was, by divine inspiration, enabled to give the true interpretation, and the man who wrote from the mouth of Smith, is one of the four mentioned above.[129]

130. James Gordon Bennett (1831)

By the special interposition of God, the golden plates, on which was engraved the Book of Mormon, and other works, had been buried for ages in the hill by a wandering tribe of the children of Israel, who had found their way to western New York, before the birth of christianity itself. Joe Smith is discovered to be the second Messiah who was to reveal this word to the world and to reform it anew. . . .

At last a printer in Palmyra undertook to print the manuscript of Joe Smith, Harris becoming responsible for the expense. They were called translaters, but in fact and in truth they are believed to be the work of the Ex-Preacher from Ohio [Sidney Rigdon], who stood in the background and put forward Joe to father the new bible and the new faith. After the publication of the golden bible, they began to make converts rapidly.[130]

131. David Marks (1831)

Next day [March 29, 1830], we . . . tarried at the house of Mr. Whitmer. . . . They affirmed, that an angel had showed them certain plates of metal, having the appearance of gold, that were dug out of the ground by one Joseph Smith; that on these plates was written a history of the ten tribes of Israel which were lost, and revelations to different prophets that arose among them. They stated the writing could be read by no person, except by the said Smith; and, that the Lord had inspired him to translate and publish the book.[131]

132. W. W. Phelps to E. D. Howe (1831)

[H]e [Martin Harris] is honest, and sincerely declares upon his soul's salvation that the book is true, and was interpreted by Joseph Smith, through a pair of silver spectacles, found with the plates. The places where they dug for the plates, in Manchester, are to be seen. When the plates were said to have been found, a copy of one or two lines of the characters, were taken by Mr. Harris to Utica, Albany and New York; at New York, they were shown to Dr. Mitchell, and he referred to professor Anthon who translated and declared them to be the ancient short-hand Egyptian. So much is true. The family of Smiths is poor, and generally ignorant in common learning.[132]

133. *Painesville Telegraph* (1831)

He [Sidney Rigdon] then spoke of the supernatural gifts with which he said Smith was endowed: he said he could translate the scriptures from any language in which they were now extant, and could lay his finger on every interpolation in the sacred writings, adding, that he had proved him in all these things. But my friend knowing that Mr. Rigdon had no knowledge of any language but his own vernacular tongue, asked him how he knew these things, to which Mr. R. made no direct reply.[133]

134. *Reflector* (1831)

There remains but little doubt, in the minds of those at all acquainted with these transactions, that Walters, who was sometimes called the conjurer . . . first suggested to Smith the idea of finding a book. Walters . . . had procured an old copy of Cicero's Orations, in the latin language, out of which he read long and loud to his credulous hearers, uttering at the same time an unintelligible jargon, which he would afterwards pretend to interpret, and explain, as a record of the former inhabitants of America.[134]

135. *Evangelical Inquirer* (1831)

This golden bible consisted of metallic plates six or seven inches square, of the thickness of tin, and resembling gold, the surface of which was covered with hieroglyphic characters, unintelligible to Smith, the finder, who could not read English. However the angel (ghost!) that discovered the plates to him, likewise informed him that he would be inspired to translate the inscription without looking at the plates, while an amanuensis would record his infallible reading all of which was accordingly done. But now the book must be published, the translation of the inscriptions which Smith had been authorized to show to no man save a few accomplices, who subscribe a certificate of these pretended facts at the end of the volume.[135]

136. *Painesville Telegraph* (1831)

He [Martin Harris] told all about the gold plates, Angels, Spirits, and Jo Smith.—He had seen and handled them all, *by the power of God!*[136]

137. *Reflector* (1831)

Harris declares, that when he acted as *amanuenses*, and wrote the translation, as Smith dictated, such was his fear of the Divine displeasure, that a screen (sheet) was suspended between the prophet and himself. . . .

On opening that portion of the book which was not secured by the *seals*, he discovered inscribed on the aforesaid plates, divers and wonderful *characters*; some of them large and some small, but beyond the wisdom of man to understand without supernatural aid.[137]

138. *Painesville Telegraph* (1831)

The first idea of a "Book," was doubtless suggested to the Smiths by one Walters, a juggling fortune-teller, who made the ignorant believe that an old book in his possession, in the Latin language, contained an account of the anti-deluvians, & c. and the word was given out that the book Smith was about to find, was a history of hidden treasures. . . .

The [Book of Mormon] is chiefly garbled from the Old and New Testaments, the Apocraphy having contributed its share. . . . A quarto Bible now in this village, was borrowed and nearly worn out and defaced by their dirty handling. Some seven or eight of them spent many months in copying, Cowdery being principal scribe.[138]

139. *Evangelical Magazine and Gospel Advocate* (1831)

During the trial it was shown that the Book of Mormon was brought to light by the same magic power by which he pretended to tell fortunes, discover hidden treasures, &c. Oliver Cowdery, one of the three witnesses to the book, testified under oath, that said Smith found with the plates, from which he translated his book, two transparent stones, resembling glass, set in silver bows. That by looking through these, he was able to read in English, the reformed Egyptian characters, which were engraved on the plates.[139]

140. *Independent Messenger* (Worcester, Massachusetts) (1831)

He [Joseph Smith] has 10 years' translating to do; he looks in a small stone he has, and there reads the will of the Lord and writes it for the good of his fellow-men; he can read a person's heart by looking in his *face*.[140]

141. *Vermont Gazette* (Bennington, Vermont) (1831)

At last a printer in Palmyra undertook to print the translations of Joe Smith, Harris becoming responsible for the expense. They were called translations, but in fact and in truth they are believed to be the work of the ex-Preacher from Ohio, who stood in the back ground and put forward Joe to father the new bible and the new faith. After the publication of the golden bible, they began to make converts rapidly.[141]

142. Ezra Booth (1831)

[I]n translating.—The subject stands before his eyes in print, but it matters not whether his eyes are open or shut; he can see as well one way as the other.

You have probably read the testimony of the three witnesses appended to the Book of Mormon. These witnesses testify, that an angel appeared to them, and presented them the golden plates, and the voice of God declared it to be a Divine Record. To this they frequently testify, in the presence of large congregations. . . .

. . . These [buried] treasures were discovered several years since, by means of the dark glass, the same with which Smith says he translated most of the Book of Mormon.[142]

143. *New Hampshire Gazette* (1831)

At the place appointed he found in the earth a box which contained a set of thin plates resembling gold, with Arabic characters inscribed on them. The plates were minutely described as being connected with rings in the shape of the letter D, which facilitated the opening and shutting of the book. The preacher said he found in the same place two stones with which he was enabled by placing them over his eyes and putting his head in a dark corner to decypher the hieroglyphics on the plates![143]

144. Alexander Campbell (1832)

This prophet Smith, through his stone spectacles, wrote on the plates of Nephi, in his book of Mormon, every error and almost every truth discussed in N. York for the last ten years. . . .

. . . it is a translation made throu[g]h stone spectacles, in a dark room, and in the hat of the prophet Smith, from the *reformed Egyptian!!* . . . His three witnesses, I am credibly informed . . . represented Walter Scott and myself as employed in translating these plates, and as believers in the book of Mormon.[144]

145. Nathaniel W. Howell and Others to Ancil Beach (1832)

The neighbours of Smith and the others give the following account of them—Joseph Smith has lived in about Manchester for several years an idle worthless fellow; previous to the Mormon project he had been engaged for some time in company with several others of the same Character ~~Employed~~ in digging for money[.] They were poor as well as worthless and for a time were supported by a man Mr Fish an illiterate man of some property who was duped by them, and when he found that his money diggers were like to consume what he had gathered by his industry he turned them off—Joseph Smith then pretended to have found a box, in digging in the woods, containing some gold plates with Characters upon them which none but himself could decypher—Cowdry who certifies to the Book of Mormon was a school master in the town of Manchester and went away with Smith to the State of Pennsylvania and was employed by Smith to write down for him what he interpreted from the mystic characters upon the plates—They then induced Martin Harris a farmer of respectable property to become responsible for an edition of 5000 copies of the Book which was accordingly published in Palmyra.[145]

146. William E. McLellin (1832)

Some time in July 1831, Two men [Elders Samuel H. Smith and Reynolds Cahoon] came to Paris & held an evening meeting. . . . They said that in September 1827 an Angel appeared to Joseph Smith (in Ontario Co. New York) and showed to him the confusion on the earth respecting true religion. It also told him to go a few miles distant to a certain hill and there he should find some plates with engravings, which (if he was faithful) he should be enabled to translate. He went as directed and found plates (which had the appearance of fine Gold) about 8 inches long 5 or 6 wide and alltogether about 6 inches thick; each one about as thick as thin paste board fastened together and opened in the form of a book containing engravings of reformed Egyptian Hieroglyphical characters: which he was inspired to translate and the record was published in 1830 and is called the book of Mormon.[146]

147. Willard Chase (1833)

Samuel T. Lawrence . . . went with him [Joseph Smith] to a singular looking hill, in Manchester, and shewed him [Lawrence] where the treasure was. Lawrence asked him [Joseph Smith] if he had ever discovered any thing with the plates of gold; he said no: he then asked him to look in his stone, to see if there was any thing with them. He looked, and said there was nothing; he told him to look again, and see if there was not a large pair of specks with the plates; he looked and soon saw a pair of spectacles, the same with which Joseph says he translated the Book of Mormon. . . .

He [Joseph] met one day in the streets of Palmyra, a rich man, whose name was Martin Harris, and addressed him thus; "I have a commandment from God to ask the first man I meet in the street to give me fifty dollars, to assist me in doing the work of the Lord by translating the Golden Bible." Martin being naturally a credulous man, hands Joseph the money. . . .

In April, 1830, I again asked Hiram for the stone which he had borrowed of me; he told me I should not have it, for Joseph made use of it in translating his Bible.[147]

148. Henry Harris (1833)

I then asked him [Joseph Smith] what letters were engraved on them, he said italic letters written in an unknown language, and that he had copied some of the words and sent them to Dr. Mitchell and Professor Anthon of New York. By looking on the plates he said he could not understand the words, but it was made known to him that he was the person that must translate them, and on looking through the stone was enabled to translate.[148]

149. Aaron Wright (1833)

Spalding had many other manuscripts, which I expect to see when Smith translates his other plate. In conclusion, I will observe, that the names of, and most of the historical part of the Book of Mormon, were as familiar to me before I read it, as most modern history. If it is not Spalding's writing, it is the same as he wrote; and if Smith was inspired, I think it was by the same spirit that Spalding was, which he confessed to be the love of money.[149]

150. *The Evening and the Morning Star* (1833)

It [the Book of Mormon] was translated by the gift and power of God, by an unlearned man, through the aid of a pair of Interpreters, or spectacles—(known, perhaps, in ancient days as Teraphim, or Urim and Thummim).[150]

151. Barton Stafford (1833)

Even since he [Joseph Smith] professed to be inspired of the Lord to translate the Book of Mormon, he one day while at work in my father's field, got quite drunk on a composition of cider, molasses and water.[151]

152. Abigail Harris (1833)

In the early part of the winter in 1828, I made a visit to Martin Harris' and was joined in company by Jos[eph]. Smith, sen. and his wife. The Gold Bible business, so called, was the topic of conversation, to which I paid particular attention, that I might learn the truth of the whole matter.—They told me that the report that Joseph, jun. had found golden plates, was true, and that he was in Harmony, Pa. translating them—that such plates were in existence, and that Joseph, jun. was to obtain them, was revealed to him by the spirit of one of the Saints that was on this continent, previous to its being discovered by Columbus. . . . The old lady [Lucy Mack Smith] said also, that after the book was translated, the plates were to be publicly exhibited—admitance 25 cents.[152]

153. William Stafford (1833)

The two Josephs and Hiram, promised to show me the plates, after the book of Mormon was translated. But, afterwards, they pretended to have received an express commandment, forbidding them to show the plates. Respecting the manner of receiving and translating the book of Mormon, their statements were always discordant. The elder Joseph would say that he had seen the plates, and that he knew them to be gold; at other times he would say that they looked like gold; and other times he would say he had not seen the plates at all.[153]

154. Jesse Townsend to Phines Stiles (1833)

Joe visited a visionary fanatic by the name of Martin Harris, and told him he had received some golden plates of ancient records from the Lord, with a "revelation" to call on him for fifty dollars to enable him to go to Pennsylvania and translate the contents of the plates. . . .

. . . Some other men, having a great dislike to labor, joined Joe in his deceptions, among whom was a sort of schoolmaster named Cowdery, who assisted him in writing or transcribing the "Book of Mormon," as a pretended translation of the golden plates which he affirmed he had been directed by the Spirit of the Lord to dig from the earth. This was all done in the most secret manner. At the same time it was assumed to the uninitiated that it would be "immediate death" for any except the translators to see the plates.[154]

155. E. D. Howe (1834)

[Martin Harris] says he wrote a considerable part of the book, as Smith dictated, and at one time the presence of the Lord was so great, that a screen was hung up between him and the Prophet; at other times the Prophet would sit in a different room, or up stairs, while the Lord was communicating to him the contents of the plates. He does not pretend that he ever saw the wonderful plates but once, although he and Smith were engaged for months in deciphering their contents. . . .

Now, whether the two methods for translating, one by a pair of stone spectacles "set in the rims of a bow," and the other by one stone, were provided against accident, we cannot determine—perhaps they were limited in their appropriate uses—at all events the plan meets our approbation.

We are informed that Smith used a stone in a hat, for the purpose of translating the plates. The spectacles and plates were found together, but were taken from him and hid up again before he had translated one word, and he has never seen them since—this is Smith's own story. . . .

Before the publication of the book, Smith found many to believe its contents, from the ghost stories which he related concerning it. Soon after it was issued from the press, a person by the name of Parley P. Pratt *happened* to be passing on the canal through Palmyra, and hearing of the wonders of the gold plates and huge spectacles, called on the prophet, and was soon converted.[155]

156. Levi Lewis (1834)

Mr. Lewis says that he "knows Smith to be a liar;—that he saw him (Smith) intoxicated at three different times while he was composing the Book of Mormon."[156]

157. Joshua M'Kune (1834)

Joshua M'Kune states, that he "was acquainted with Joseph Smith Jr. and Martin Harris, during their residence in Harmony, Pa., and knew them to be artful seducers;"—That they informed him that "Smith had found a sword, breast-plate, and a pair of spectacles, at the time he found the gold plates"—that these were to be shewn to all the world as evidence of the truth of what was contained in those plates," and that "he (M'Kune) and others should see them at a specified time." He also states that "the time for the exhibition of the Plates, &c. has gone by, and he has not seen them." "Joseph Smith, Jr. told him that (Smith's) first-born child was to translate the characters, and hieroglyphics, upon the Plates into our language at the age of three years; but this child was not permitted to live to verify the prediction."[157]

158. Charles Anthon to E. D. Howe (1834)

Upon examining the paper in question, I soon came to the conclusion that it was all a trick, perhaps a *hoax*. When I asked the person, who brought it, how he obtained the writing, he gave me, as far as I can now recollect, the following account: A "gold book," consisting of a number of plates of gold, fastened together in the shape of a book by wires of the same metal, had been dug up in the northern part of the state of New York, and along with the book an enormous pair of "*gold spectacles*"! These spectacles were so large, that, if a person attempted to look through them, his two eyes would have to be turned towards *one* of the glasses merely, the spectacles in question being altogether too large for the breadth of the human face. Whoever examined the plates through the spectacles, was enabled not only to *read* them, but fully to *understand* their meaning. All this knowledge, however, was confined at that time to a young man, who had the trunk containing the book and spectacles in his sole possession. This young man was placed behind a curtain, in the garret of a farm house, and, being thus concealed from view, put on the spectacles occasionally, or rather, looked through one of the glasses, decyphered the characters in the book, and, having committed some of them to paper, handed copies from behind the curtain, to those who stood on the outside. Not a word, however, was said about the plates having been decyphered "by the gift of God." Every thing, in this way, was effected by the large pair of spectacles.[158]

159. Nathaniel C. Lewis (1834)

At one time, however, he came to my house, and asked my advice, whether he should proceed to translate the Book of Plates (referred to by Mr. Hale) or not. He said that God had commanded him to translate it, but he was afraid of the people: he remarked, that he was to exhibit the plates to the world, at a certain time, which was then about eighteen months distant. I told him I was not qualified to give advice in such cases. Smith frequently said to me that I should see the plates at the time appointed.[159]

160. Jesse Townsend to Elisha Camp (1834)

The Smiths used Martin [Harris]'s money freely—some other men, who had a great dislike to honest labor, about that time, joined Joe in his acts of deception. In that reinforcement was a ready writer by name [Oliver] Cowdry and a Whitney who declared he had once been in heaven, who assisted Joe in writing the Book of Mormon, as a pretended translation of the Golden Plates which Smith affirmed he had been directed by the Spirit of the Lord to dig from the earth. The whole was done in the most secret manner. At the same time, Smith affirmed that it would be immediate death for any one to see those plates besides himself & the writers of the Book of Mormon.[160]

161. W. R. Hine (1834?)

[Joseph] had a very clear stone about the size and shape of a duck's egg, and claimed that he could see lost or hidden things through it. He said he saw Captain Kidd sailing on the Susquehanna River during a freshet, and that he buried two pots of gold and silver. He claimed he saw writing cut on the rocks in an unknown language telling where Kidd buried it, and he translated it through his peep-stone. I have had it many times and could see in it whatever I imagined. Jo claimed it was found in digging a well in Palmyra, N.Y. He said he borrowed it. . . .

. . . About the spring of 1828, Jo . . . said he had found some metal plates which would be of great use to the world. He had them in a box in a handkerchief which he carried in one hand. I said, "Let me see them." Jo Smith said they must first be sent to Philadelphia to be translated. He said the only man in the world who could translate them lived there. After they were translated the world could see them. . . . Soon I learned that Jo claimed to be translating the plates in Badger's Tavern, in Colesville, three miles from my house. I went there and saw Jo Smith sit by a table and put a handkerchief to his forehead and peek into his hat and call out a word to Cowdery, who sat at the same table and wrote it down. Several persons sat near the same table and there was no curtain between them. Martin Harris introduced himself to me, and said they were going to bring the world from darkness into light. Martin's wife cooked for them, and one day while they were at dinner she put one hundred and sixteen pages, the first part they had translated, in her dress bosom and went out. . . .

. . . Newel Knight, who lived a few miles from me was brought before Justice N. K. Nobles as a witness for reporting Prophet Jo Smith had cast three devils out of him. . . . Jo was discharged. Noble told me later that it made his heart ache to hear the puppy swear. This occurred during the pretended translation of the plates.[161]

162. Orson Pratt, as recorded by the *Brookville Enquirer* (1835)

On last Saturday evening, for the first time, in this place, a gentleman, and minister belonging to this new sect, preached in the court house, to a very respectable audience; and discoursed briefly on the various subjects connected with his creed; explained his faith and gave a brief history of the book of Mormon—united it with the Holy Bible, &c. . . .

He believes the book of Mormon to be a series of revelations, and other matters appertaining to the Ephraimites, Lamanites, &c. whom he believes to have been the original settlers of this continent; and that an ancient Prophet caused the plates from which the book of Mormon was translated to be buried nearly two thousand years ago, in what is now called Ontario county; New York. He is also of the belief that Joseph Smith was cited to the plates by an angel from Heaven, and endowed with the gift to translate the engraving upon them into the known language of the country.[162]

163. *Christian Journal* (Exeter, N.H.) (1835)

Smith pretended that he had found some golden or brass plates, like the leaves of a book, hid in a box in the earth, to which he was directed by an *Angel*, in 1827,—that the writing on them was in the "Reformed Egyptian language,"—that he was *inspired* to interpret the writing, or engraving, by putting a plate in his hat, putting two smooth flat stones, which he found in the box, in the hat, and putting his face therein—that he could not write, but as he translated, one Oliver Cowdry wrote it down. . . .

. . . The probability is that Smith, who had been a book-pedlar, and was frequently about printing establishments, had procured some old copper plates for engravings, which he showed for his golden plates.

It is pretended that the "Book of Mormon," was translated by Joe Smith from these plates.[163]

164. John Corrill (1839)

Sometime in the fall of 1830, Oliver Cowdery, Parley P. Pratt, Peter Whitmer and Tiba [Ziba] Peterson, came through the county of Ashtabula, Ohio, where I then resided, on their way westward. They professed to be special messengers of the Living God, sent to preach the Gospel in its purity, as it was anciently preached by the Apostles. They had with them a new revelation, which they said had been translated from certain golden plates that had been deposited in a hill, (anciently called Camorah,) in the township of Manchester, Ontario county, New York. . . .

. . . Through much difficulty, on account of persecution and poverty, he [Joseph Smith] translated it by degrees, with the assistance of Oliver Cowdery and others, who wrote as he dictated. If I remember right, the language in which it was written on the plates, was the reformed Egyptian. And Martin Harris, who contributed much towards the publication of the Book, drew off several of the characters on paper, took them to the learned in New York, to see if they could be translated, but was requested to bring them the plates, which Smith was forbidden to do of the Lord, but was commanded to translate them himself, which he did, by the help of what he calls the Urim and Thummim, two stones set in a bow, and furnished by an Angel for that purpose.

After finishing the translation, the plates and stones of Urim and Thummim were again taken and concealed by the Angel for a wise purpose, and the translation published to the world in the winter of A. D. 1829 and '30.[164]

165. Charles Anthon to T. W. Coit (1841)

On my asking him by whom the copy was made, he gravely stated, that along with the golden book there had been dug up a very large *pair of spectacles!* so large in fact that if a man were to hold them in front of his face, his two eyes would merely look through one of the glasses, and the remaining part of the spectacles would project a considerable distance sideways! These spectacles possessed, it seems a very valuable property, of enabling any one who looked through them, (or rather through one of the lenses,) not only to decypher the characters on the plates, but also to comprehend their exact meaning, and be able to translate them!! My informant assured me that this curious property of the spectacles had been actually tested, and found to be true. A young man, it seems, had been placed in the garret of a farm-house, with a curtain before him, and having fastened the spectacles to his head, had read several pages in the golden book, and communicated their contents in writing to certain persons stationed on the outside of the curtain. He had also copied off one page of the book in the original character, which he had in like manner handed over to those who were separated from him by the curtain, and this copy was the paper which the countryman had brought with him.[165]

166. Brigham Young (1841)

I met with the Twelve at brother Joseph's. He conversed with us in a familiar manner on a variety of subjects, and explained to us the Urim and Thummim which he found with the plates, called in the Book of Mormon the Interpreters. He said that every man who lived on the earth was entitled to a seer stone, and should have one, but they are kept from them in consequence of their wickedness, and most of those who do find one make an evil use of it; he showed us his seer stone.[166]

167. Hiram Page (1848)

To say my mind was so treacherous that I had forgotten what I saw. To say that a man of Joseph's ability, who at that time did not know how to pronounce the word Nephi, could write a book of six hundred pages, as correct as the book of Mormon, without supernatural power. . . . [I]t would be treating the God of heaven with contempt, to deny these testimonies.[167]

168. Brigham Young (1855)

I will here relate a few of the circumstances which I personally knew concerning the coming forth of the plates, from a part of which the Book of Mormon was translated. This fact may be new to several, but I had a personal knowledge with regard to many of those circumstances.

I well knew a man who, to get the plates, rode over sixty miles three times the same season they were obtained by Joseph Smith. About the time of their being delivered to Joseph by the angel, the friends of this man sent for him, and informed him that they were going to lose that treasure, though they did not know what it was. . . .

When Joseph obtained the treasure, the priests, the deacons, and religionists of every grade, went hand in hand with the fortune-teller, and with every wicked person, to get it out of his hands, and, to accomplish this, a part of them came out and persecuted him.[168]

169. Solomon Chamberlain (1858)

When the boat came to Palmyra I felt as if some genii or good spirit told me to leave the boat. . . . [M]y guide directed me to put up for the night, which I did to a farm-house. In the morning the people of the house asked me if I had heard of the gold Bible [Book of Mormon]. When they said "gold Bible" there was a power like electricity went from the top of my head to the end of my toes. . . . I soon made my way across lots to father Smith's and found Hyrum walking the floor. . . .

They then called the people together which, consisted of five or six men who were out at the door. Father Smith was one of them and some of the Whitmer's. . . . They then made known to me that they had obtained a gold record, and just finished translating it here. No[w] the Lord revealed to me by the gift and power of the Holy Ghost that this was the work I had been looking for.[169]

170. Samuel Smith, as recorded by Phineas Young (1863)

I know the book to be a Revelation from God, translated by the gift adn [*sic*] power of the Holy Ghost, and that my brother Joseph Smith is a Prophet Sear and Revelator.[170]

171. Pomeroy Tucker (1867)

He [Joseph Smith] was "commanded" . . . [to] take out of the earth a metallic book of great antiquity in its origin . . . which was a record, in mystic letters or characters, of the long-lost tribes of Israel . . . and the power to translate which to the nations of the earth was also given to him only, as the chosen servant of God! . . .

. . . It was understood, however, that the custodian of the precious treasure afterward in some way procured a chest for his purpose, which, with its sacred deposit, was kept in a dark garret of his father's house, where the translations were subsequently made, as will be explained. . . .

With the book was also found, or so pretended, a huge pair of spectacles in a perfect state of preservation, or the *Urim* and *Thummim*, as afterward interpreted, whereby the mystic record was to be translated and the wonderful dealings of God revealed to man, by the superhuman power of Joe Smith. This spectacle pretension, however, is believed to have been purely an after-thought, for it was not heard of outside of the Smith family for a considerable period subsequent to the first story. . . .

. . . The Urim and Thummim, found with the records, were two transparent crystals set in the rims of a bow, in the form of spectacles of enormous size. This constituted the seer's instrument whereby the records were to be translated and the mysteries of hidden things revealed, and it was to supersede the further use of the magic stone. . . .

Translations and interpretations were now entered upon by the prophet, and manuscript specimens of these, with some of the literally transcribed characters, were shown to people, including ministers and other gentlemen of learning and influence. . . . The manuscripts were in the handwriting of one Oliver Cowdery, which had been written down by him, as he and Smith declared, from the translations, word for word, as made by the latter with the aid of the mammoth spectacles or Urim and Thummim, and verbally announced by him from behind a blanket-screen drawn across a dark corner of a room at his residence—for at this time the original revelation, limiting to the prophet the right of seeing the sacred plates, had not yet been changed, and the view with the instrument used was even too brilliant for his own spiritualized eyes in the light! This was the story of the first series of translations, which was always persisted in by the few persons connected with the business at this early period of its progress. The single significance of this theory will doubtless be manifest, when the facts are stated in explanation, that Smith could not write in a legible hand, and hence an amanuensis or scribe was necessary. Cowdery had been a schoolmaster, and was the only man in the band who could make a copy for the printer.

. . . Among others, Mr. George Crane, of the adjoining town of Macedon, a Quaker of intelligence, property, and high respectability (now deceased), was called upon by Smith with several foolscap quires of these so-called translations, for his perusal and opinion, and also for his pecuniary aid to get the work through the press. . . .

The work of translation this time [after the loss of the 116 pages] had been done in the recess of a dark artificial cave, which Smith had caused to be dug in the east side of the forest-hill near his residence. . . . [T]hough another version was, that the prophet continued to pursue his former mode of translating behind the curtain at his house, and only went into the cave to pay his spiritual devotions.[171]

172. Stephen S. Harding to Pomeroy Tucker (1867)

When I was in Palmyra in 1829, I went with Joe Smith, at his special request, to his father's house, in company with Martin Harris and Oliver Cowdery, for the purpose of hearing read his wonderful "translations" from the sacred plates.[172]

173. Orson Pratt (1871)

Thus the engravings were shown to three other witnesses. The angel at the same time placed his hands upon the head of David Whitmer and said, "Blessed be the Lord and they that keep his commandments.' At the time that the angel was showing the records, they heard a voice out of the heavens saying, that the records had been translated correctly by the gift and power of God, and they were commanded to bear witness of the same to all people to whom the work should be sent.[173]

174. Emily C. Blackman (1873)

It is a fact . . . that Susquehanna County harbored such a madman as Joe Smith at the period when he was engaged in the compilation, or, rather, the translation, of the Book of Mormon. . . .

. . . [I]t is certain he was here in 1825 and later; and, in 1829, his operations here were finished, and he had left the county. . . .

His [Isaac Hale's] sons were: Jesse, David, Alvah, Issac Ward, and Reuben. The last named "assisted Joe Smith to fix up some characters such as Smith pretended were engraven on his book of plates." . . .

From Dr. Peck's 'Early Methodism' we obtain the following:—

"Joe Smith married a niece of Nathaniel Lewis. . . . After the story of the Golden Bible, and the miracle-working spectacles had come out, Joe undertook to make a convert of Uncle Nat. The old gentleman . . . proceeded:

"'Joseph, can anybody else translate strange languages by the help of them spectacles?'

"'O, yes!' . . .

"'. . . I've got Clarke's Commentary, and it contains a great many strange languages; now if you will let me try the spectacles, and if, by looking through them, I can translate these strange languages into English, then I'll be one of your disciples.'

"This was a poser, and Joe had to run."[174]

175. Parley P. Pratt (1874)

We visited an old Baptist deacon by the name of Hamlin. After hearing of our appointment for evening, he began to tell of a *book*, a STRANGE BOOK, a VERY STRANGE BOOK! in his possession, which had been just published. This book, he said, purported to have been originally written on plates either of gold or brass, by a branch of the tribes of Israel; and to have been discovered and translated by a young man near Palmyra, in the State of New York, by the aid of visions, or the ministry of angels. I inquired of him how or where the book was to be obtained. He promised me the perusal of it, at his house the next day, if I would call. I felt a strange interest in the book. . . .

He [Hyrum Smith] also unfolded to me the particulars of the discovery of the Book; its translation; the rise of the Church of Latter-Day Saints, and the commission of his brother Joseph, and others, by revelation and the ministering of angels, by which the apostleship and authority had been again restored to the earth. . . .

This was the [Whitmer] family, several of whose names were attached to the Book of Mormon as witnesses—Mr. Joseph Smith having translated much of the book in Whitmer's chamber.[175]

176. Sidney Rigdon, as recorded by John Murdock (1876)

Joe, he said, was a very illiterate man, was unable either to read or write; but when he put on his nose the prophet's spectacles, and took the gold plates one by one, letter by letter and word by word presented themselves, and with the aid of an amanuensis the Bible that he held in his hand was a literal translation of the writing upon the gold plates.[176]

177. John H. Gilbert, as interviewed by the *Post and Tribune* (1877)

Upon the title page appears the name of Joseph Smith as "Author and Proprietor." In all subsequent editions he appears simply as "Translator." This change was rendered necessary to carry out the theory afterward adopted that Smith dug up these writings and translated them from "reformed Egyptian" by means of a pair of supernatural spectacles. . . .

As he claimed to be the author of the "Book of Mormon" his story was that by the aid of his wonderful stone he found gold plates on which were inscribed the writings in hieroglyphics. He translated them by means of a pair of magic spectacles which the Lord delivered to him at the same time that the golden tablets were turned up. But nobody but Joe himself ever saw the golden tablets or the far-seeing spectacles. He dictated the book, concealed behind a curtain, and it was written down by Cowdery. This course seemed to be rendered necessary by the fact that Joe did not know how to write.[177]

178. John H. Gilbert to James T. Cobb (1879)

I cannot say whether the entire work of "translation" was completed at the time the printing was commenced or not, but think it was. . . .

Late in 1827 or early in '28, was the first I heard Harris speak of Jo's finding the plates, and with the plates a pair of large spectacles, by looking through which Jo could translate the hieroglyphics on the plates into English.[178]

179. Michael Morse, as recorded by W. W. Blair (1879)

When Joseph was translating the Book of Mormon, he, (Morse), had occasion more than once to go into his immediate presence, and saw him engaged at his work of translation.

The mode of procedure consisted in Joseph's placing the Seer Stone in the crown of a hat, then putting his face into the hat, so as to entirely cover his face, resting his elbows upon his knees, and then dictating, word after word, while the scribes—Emma, John Whitmer, O. Cowdery, or some other, wrote it down.[179]

180. Hiel and Joseph Lewis (1879)

The statement that the prophet Joseph Smith, jr. made in our hearing, at the commencement of his translating his book, in Harmony, as to the manner of his finding the plates, was as follows: . . . He said that by a dream he was informed that at such a place . . . were some gold plates with curious engravings, which he must get and translate, and write a book. . . . That in the same box with the plates were spectacles; the bows were of gold, and the eyes were stone, and by looking through these spectacles all the characters on the plates were translated into English.[180]

181. Hiel Lewis (1879)

Smith translated his book of Mormon mostly with this same peep stone and hat—he, sitting in his house, and the plates hid far away. . . .

. . . Smith translated the book of Mormon by means of the same peep stone, and under the same inspiration that directed his enchantments and dog sacrifices; it was all by the same spirit.[181]

182. Joseph Lewis (1879)

[I]t is a fact that he translated nearly all of it [his "golden bible"] with this same stone and hat.[182]

183. Samuel Brush, as recorded by Frederic G. Mather (1880)

Among the callers was Samuel Brush, now a vigorous man of seventy-five, who carries on a large farm and a lumber-mill three miles south-west of Susquehanna. At the time of the translation he often called Reuben Hale away from his work, and the pair went for a walk. Reuben also explained the phenomenon of the peek-stone on the theory of "deflected light." Mr. Brush declares that Martin Harris was a believer in "second sight," and that "Smith was a good and kind neighbor,"—testimony which is also given by Mrs. McKune, Mrs. Squires and Mr. Skinner.[183]

184. Sidney Rigdon, as recorded by John M. Rigdon (ca. 1880)

Along come Parley Pratt, Oliver Cowdrey and one Zibe Paterson with the Book of Mormon. It was a bound volume and it was the first time Sidney Rigdon ever saw it or ever heard of the man called Joseph Smith. Parley Pratt presented the Book to my Father Sidney Rigdon in the presence of my mother and my oldest sister who was a young girl of 10 years of age. Parley Pratt . . . said, "Brother Rigdon, here is a book which is a revelation from God. One Joseph Smith, a young boy had an angel appear to him who told him where to go to find the Plates upon which the Book was engraved. They were gold. Joseph Smith went as directed by the angel and found the plates in a hill near Palmera New York and brought them to his home and there by the power of God translated them and it was the ever lasting Gospel given to the children of men."[184]

185. Nancy N. Tracy (1880)

At length [about 1833] it began to be rumoured around about a prophet Called Joseph Smith and that he had found ancient records in the hill Comorah shown to him by an Angel and he had translated the hieroglifics into the english language.[185]

186. Hiram Jackway, as interviewed by William H. Kelley (1881)

Where was Joe when he was translating his book?

"At home; it was translated in the farmhouse."

Mr. Gilbert, across here, said it was done in a cave; now you don't agree? What does Tucker say? (reading Tucker).

"They all differ. Now, Tucker has a statement from Willard Chase in his book, and Chase said Tucker never called on him at all to find out what he knew."[186]

187. Ezra Pierce, as interviewed by William H. Kelley (1881)

What about Joe's learning?

"I know that he was ignorant; and he knew no more about hieroglyphics than that stove," pointing to the stove in the room.[187]

188. Adeline M. Bernard to Thomas Gregg (1881)

Joe Smith said that as fast as he translated from the golden plates the B. of M., the angel took them from them and nothing was left him but the B. of M.[188]

189. William Lang to Thomas Gregg (1881)

The plates were never translated and could not be, were never intended to be. What is claimed to be a translation is the "Manuscript Found" worked over by C [Oliver Cowdery].[189]

190. Alice Grey Cowan to Ellen E. Dickinson (1881)

There was living three years ago, near the town of Gilroy, Santa Clara Co., California, a Mrs. Monroe, who claims that Joe Smith was living in her father's house when he discovered the golden plates on which the "Book of Mormon" was inscribed, and that the translation was made then.[190]

191. John H. Gilbert, as interviewed by William H. Kelley (1881)

". . . I am the party that set the type from the original manuscript for the Book of Mormon. They translated it in a cave. . . . [Hyrum Smith] said at the time it was translated from plates by the power of God, and they were very particular about it. We had a great deal of trouble with it. It was not punctuated at all. . . .

. . . If you ever saw a Book of Mormon you will see that they changed it afterwards."

. . . How is it changed now?

. . . "Here on the title page it says," (reading) "'Joseph Smith, Jr[.], author and proprietor.' Afterwards, in getting out other editions they left that out, and only claimed that Joseph Smith translated it."

Well, did they claim anything else than that he was the translator when they brought the manuscript to you?

"Oh, no; they claimed that he was translating it by means of some instruments he got at the same time he did the plates, and that the Lord helped him."[191]

192. Diedrich Willers (1882)

[T]o show how easily the Whitmers were duped, it is related, that by some contrivance of Smith and his associates a wooden image or representation was placed in a tree in a field where one of Whitmer's sons was engaged in ploughing, and that when interrogated as to whether he had not seen an angel, he answered in the affirmative. "Then," said Smith, "this is the place where the 'Book of Mormon' must be completed, since the angel has already appeared eleven times, and it has been revealed to me that at the place of the twelfth apearing of the angel, the book must be completed." Hence Whitmers', in West Fayette, became the resort of Smith and his fellow-impostors during the progress of this work.[192]

193. Josiah Quincy (1883)

I have quoted enough to show what really good material Smith managed to draw into his net. Were such fish to be caught with Spaulding's tedious romance and a puerile fable of undecipherable gold plates and gigantic spectacles?[193]

194. Thurlow Weed (1884)

About 1829 a stout, round, smooth-faced young man [Joseph Smith], between twenty-five and thirty, with the air and manners of a person without occupation, came into the "Rochester Telegraph" office and said he wanted a book printed, and added that he had been directed in a vision to a place in the woods . . . and that he found a "golden Bible," from which he was directed to copy the book which he wanted published. He then placed what he called a "tablet" in his hat, from which he read a chapter of the "Book of Mormon," a chapter which seemed so senseless that I thought the man either crazed or a very shallow impostor, and therefore declined to become a publisher.[194]

195. Lorenzo Saunders (1887)

I was frequently at the house of Joseph Smith from 1827 to 1830. That I saw Oliver Cowdery writing, I suppose the "Book of Mormon" with books and manuscripts laying on the table before him.[195]

196. Rhamanthus M. Stocker (1887)

It [the "golden Bible"] was written in an unknown language; hence its translation became necessary in the manner in which it was done. . . .

. . . Mrs. Squires says that Mrs. Harris destroyed about one hundred pages of her husband's manuscript, and that Smith dare not attempt another translation of it for fear that it would not conform with the first translation. . . .

. . . Joseph Fowler McCune . . . boarded in this neighborhood . . . while Smith was engaged in translating the Bible, and was quite often in Smith's house. Mr. McCune states that Reuben Hale acted as scribe a part of the time. He says Smith's hat was a very large one, and what is commonly called a "stove-pipe." The hat was on the table by the window and the stone in the bottom or rather in the top of the hat. Smith would bend over the hat with his face buried in it so that no light could enter it, and thus dictate to the scribe what he should write.[196]

197. John H. Gilbert (1892)

In the fall of 1827, [Martin Harris] told us what wonderful discoveries Jo Smith had made, and of his finding plates in a hill in the town of Manchester . . . also found with the plates a large pair of "spectacles," by putting which on his nose and looking at the plates, the spectacles turned the hyroglyphics into good English. The question might by [be] asked here whether Jo or the spectacles was the translator?[197]

198. John H. Gilbert, as interviewed by the *New York Herald* (1893)

I tried to learn something about the humbug, but they declared that everything they gave me was a direct translation from the golden plates. As I understood it, those golden plates were taken from the mountain to Smith's house and put in a bag. He was so frightened at first after he had recovered them from the guardianship of the angel that he hid them for a day and then took them to his house. Later the alleged plates were carried to a cave for translation.[198]

199. Albert Chandler to William A. Linn (1898)

My recollections of the early history of the Mormon Bible are vivid today. I knew personally Oliver Cowdery, who translated the Bible, Martin Harris, who mortgaged his farm to procure the printing, and Joseph Smith Jr., but slightly. What I knew of him was from hearsay, principally from Martin Harris, who believed fully in him. Mr. Tucker's "Origin, Rise, and Progress of Mormonism" is the fullest account I have ever seen. I doubt if I can add anything to that history.

The whole history is shrouded in the deepest mystery. Joseph Smith Jr., who read through the wonderful spectacles, pretended to give the scribe the exact reading of the plates, even to spelling, in which Smith was wofully deficient. Martin Harris was permitted to be in the room with the scribe, and would try the knowledge of Smith, as he told me, saying that Smith could not spell the word February, when his eyes were off the spectacles through which he pretended to work. This ignorance of Smith was proof positive to him that Smith was dependent on the spectacles for the contents of the Bible. Smith and the plates containing the original of the Mormon Bible were hid from view of the scribe and Martin Harris by a screen.[199]

200. Benjamin F. Johnson (not dated)

In the year 1829, in our village paper [in western New York], was published an account of some young man's professing to have seen an angel, who had shown and delivered to him golden plates, engraved in a strange language and hid up in the earth, from which he had translated a new Bible; and I could hardly refrain from wishing or hoping it might be so.[200]

201. Newel Knight (not dated)

During this time we were frequently visited by my young friend, Joseph Smith, who would entertain us with accounts of the wonderful things which had happened to him. It was evident to me that great things were about to be accomplished through him—that the Lord was about to use him as an instrument in His hands to bring to pass the great and mighty work of the last days. This chosen instrument told us of God's manifestations to him, of the discovery and receiving of the plates from which the Book of Mormon was translated, of his persecutions for the gospel's sake, and many other items of his eventful life. . . .

Joseph persevered, and the Lord raised up friends who aided him in the great work of translating and printing the record which the unsealed part of the sacred plates contained.[201]

202. Ebenezer Robinson (not dated)

They were both [two manuscripts of the Book of Mormon] mostly written in Oliver Cowdery's hand writing, as I have seen both. He was scribe for Joseph most of the time he was translating the Book of Mormon.[202]

Notes to the Documents of the Translation Chronology

1. Doctrine and Covenants 3:9, 12, 14. This revelation, given through Joseph Smith in July 1828, appeared initially as chapter 2 in the 1833 Book of Commandments.

2. Doctrine and Covenants 10:1–3, 8, 10–11, 30, 34, 40–41, 45. This revelation, given through Joseph Smith in part in summer 1828 and in May 1829, was first published as chapter 9 in the 1833 Book of Commandments.

3. Doctrine and Covenants 5:4, 30–31. This revelation, given through Joseph Smith in March 1829 at Harmony, Pennsylvania, following a request by Martin Harris, appeared initially as chapter 4 in the 1833 Book of Commandments. Discussed further in note 73 of the article above.

4. Doctrine and Covenants 6:17, 25. This revelation, given through Joseph Smith in April 1829 and directed to Oliver Cowdery and himself, was first published as chapter 5 in the 1833 Book of Commandments.

5. Doctrine and Covenants 8:11. This revelation, given through Joseph Smith to Oliver Cowdery in April 1829, was first published as chapter 7 in the 1833 Book of Commandments.

6. Doctrine and Covenants 9:1–5, 8–10. This revelation, given through Joseph Smith to Oliver Cowdery in April 1829, appeared initially as chapter 8 in the 1833 Book of Commandments.

7. Doctrine and Covenants 11:19. This revelation, given through Joseph Smith for his brother Hyrum, was received at Harmony, Pennsylvania, in May 1829, chapter 10 in the 1833 Book of Commandments.

8. Doctrine and Covenants 17:6. This revelation, given through Joseph Smith to Oliver Cowdery, David Whitmer, and Martin Harris in June 1829, first appeared in the *Messenger and Advocate* 1 (September 1835): 178.

9. Doctrine and Covenants 20:6–9. Also appeared as chapter 24 in the 1833 Book of Commandments. The section heading in the Book of Commandments refers to this revelation as the "Articles and Covenants of the church of Christ."

10. Preface to the 1830 edition of the Book of Mormon; cited in Dean C. Jessee, ed., *The Papers of Joseph Smith*, 2 vols. (Salt Lake City: Deseret Book, 1989–92), 1:287.

11. Minutes of conference at Orange, Ohio, October 25, 1831, in Donald Q. Cannon and Lyndon W. Cook, eds., *Far West Record* (Salt Lake City: Deseret Book, 1983), 23. For one explanation of Joseph's reticence to share his vision publicly, see Richard L. Bushman, "The Visionary World of Joseph Smith," *BYU Studies* 37, no. 1 (1997–98): 194–97.

12. Jessee, *Papers of Joseph Smith*, 1:10.

13. Jessee, *Papers of Joseph Smith*, 1:9. Until the phrase "I commenced," this portion of Joseph Smith's 1832 history was written in the Prophet's handwriting.

14. Nancy Towle, *Vicissitudes Illustrated in the Experience of Nancy Towle, in Europe and America* (Charleston: James L. Burges, 1832), 138–39. In October 1831, Towle visited Kirtland, where she attended Sabbath meetings, witnessed a baptism, and engaged in a contentious dialogue with W. W. Phelps, Martin

Harris, and Sidney Rigdon. She also met Joseph Smith and watched him give the gift of the Holy Ghost to several women and children.

15. Susa Young Gates ["Homespun"], *Lydia Knight's History* (Salt Lake City: Juvenile Instructor Office, 1883), 18.

16. Joseph Smith Jr., *History of The Church of Jesus Christ of Latter-day Saints*, ed. B. H. Roberts, 2d ed., rev., 7 vols. (Salt Lake City: Deseret Book, 1971), 1:315 (hereafter cited as *History of the Church*). N. E. Seaton (or Sexton) was the editor of a Rochester, New York, newspaper.

17. Peter Bauder, *The Kingdom and Gospel of Jesus Christ: Contrasted with That of Anti-Christ. A Brief Review of Some of the Most Interesting Circumstances, Which Have Transpired Since the Institution of the Gospel of Christ, from the Days of the Apostles* (Canajoharie, N.Y.: Printed by A. H. Calhoun, 1834), 36–37; cited in Dan Vogel, comp. and ed., *Early Mormon Documents*, 4 vols. (Salt Lake City: Signature Books, 1996–2002), 1:17.

18. Kirtland High Council Minutes, April 21, 1834, 43–44, Church Archives, The Church of Jesus Christ of Latter-day Saints, Salt Lake City; cited in Brian Q. Cannon and *BYU Studies* Staff, "Priesthood Restoration Documents," *BYU Studies* 35, no. 4 (1995–96): 177, and below on p. 257n10.

19. Oliver Cowdery to W. W. Phelps, "Letter IV," *Messenger and Advocate*, February 1835, 80.

20. Oliver Cowdery, Introduction to blessings, September 1835, in Patriarchal Blessing Book, 1:8–9, Church Archives; cited in Vogel, *Early Mormon Documents*, 2:452.

21. Oliver Cowdery to W. W. Phelps, "Letter VIII," *Messenger and Advocate*, October 1835, 198–200.

22. Joseph Smith, Diary, November 9, 1835, 25, recorded by scribe Warren Parrish; cited in Jessee, *Papers of Joseph Smith*, 1:128. On this occasion, Joseph Smith was relating the circumstances of the coming forth of the Book of Mormon to Robert Matthias [Robert Matthews], or Joshua "the Jewish minister," who had visited Joseph's home.

23. Truman Coe to Mr. Editor, *Hudson Ohio Observer*, August 11, 1836; cited in Vogel, *Early Mormon Documents*, 1:47.

24. "Answers to Questions," *Elders' Journal of the Church of Jesus Christ of Latter Day Saints* 1 (July 1838): 43.

25. Joseph Smith, "History of the Church," A-1, MS 5–30, Joseph Smith Collection, Church Archives; published in Jessee, *Papers of Joseph Smith*, 1:278–300; Joseph Smith—History 1:59, 62, 67, 75; and *History of the Church*, 1:12–71.

26. *History of the Church*, 4:79. Davis's letter to his wife (dated February 6, 1840) relates a speech given by Joseph Smith the previous evening in Washington, D.C. While History of the Church refers to Mathew L. Davis as a member of Congress, Robert N. Hullinger has identified Davis as a political correspondent.

Robert N. Hullinger, *Mormon Answer to Skepticism: Why Joseph Smith Wrote the Book of Mormon* (St. Louis, Mo.: Clayton Publishing House, 1980), 11.

27. Excerpts from the diary of Reverend George Moore, in Donald Q. Cannon, "Reverend George Moore Comments on Nauvoo, the Mormons, and Joseph Smith," *Western Illinois Regional Studies* 5 (Spring 1982): 11.

28. Joseph Smith, "Church History," *Times and Seasons* 3 (March 1, 1842): 707. This short history of the Restoration of the gospel had been taken from a letter Joseph Smith wrote to John Wentworth, editor of the *Chicago Democrat*.

29. "Joseph Smith to Editor of the Times and Seasons," *Times and Seasons* 4 (May 15, 1843): 194.

30. "Joseph Smith to James Arlington Bennett," *Times and Seasons* 4 (November 1, 1843): 373.

31. "History of Joseph Smith," *Millennial Star* 4 (December 1843): 116.

32. "Latter Day Saints," in I. Daniel Rupp, comp., *An Original History of the Religious Denominations at Present Existing in the United States* (Philadelphia: J. Y. Humphreys, 1844), 406.

33. Parley P. Pratt Jr., ed., *The Autobiography of Parley P. Pratt* (New York: Russell Brothers, 1874), 330. Parley P. Pratt was murdered in Arkansas in 1857; his autobiography was published by his son in 1874. The incident described occurred in 1839.

34. Joseph Curtis, "A Short History of Joseph Curtis," microfilm of journal, 6, Church Archives. Curtis states this happened in 1835, but Dan Vogel convincingly argues that the correct year is 1834. See Vogel, *Early Mormon Documents*, 1:36.

35. Emily M. Austin, *Mormonism; or Life among the Mormons* (Madison, Wis.: M. J. Cantwell, 1882), 34–35. Austin, the sister of Newel Knight's first wife, Sally Coburn, met Joseph Smith in the early 1830s and was baptized but eventually left the Church.

36. Addison Everett to Joseph F. Smith, January 16, 1882, holograph, microfilm, 2–3, Church Archives.

37. James Palmer, "James Palmer's Travels and Ministry in the Gospel," microfilm, 75, Church Archives. Palmer does not specify what year this occurred but says it happened at a meeting "near the Temple."

38. Edmund C. Briggs, "A Visit to Nauvoo in 1856," *Journal of History* 9 (October 1916): 454. Edmund C. Briggs and Samuel H. Gurley traveled to Nauvoo to visit Joseph Smith III and testify to him of the reorganization of the Church, which had recently occurred in Wisconsin. Briggs and Gurley arrived at the Mansion House in Nauvoo on December 5, 1856, and interviewed Emma Smith Bidamon three days later.

39. John T. Clark, "Translation of Nephite Records," *The Return* 4 (July 15, 1895): 2. Written from Nauvoo on March 27, 1870, the original letter is located

in the Emma Smith Papers, Library-Archives, Community of Christ, Independence, Mo. (hereafter cited as Community of Christ Library-Archives).

40. Nels Madsen, "Visit to Mrs. Emma Smith Bidamon," 1931, Church Archives. Madsen and Parley Pratt Jr. visited Bidamon in Nauvoo while they were missionaries.

41. Joseph Smith III, "Last Testimony of Sister Emma," *Saints' Herald* 26 (October 1, 1879): 289–90; and Joseph Smith III, "Last Testimony of Sister Emma," *Saints' Advocate* 2 (October 1879): 50–52. Joseph Smith III wrote that Emma reviewed the answers he had recorded for her. The answers "were affirmed by her" on the day before he left Nauvoo. Emma's husband Lewis C. Bidamon asserted that Emma's answers were "substantially what she had always stated" at times when they discussed the translation of the Book of Mormon.

42. Joseph Smith III to James T. Cobb, February 14, 1879, Community of Christ Library-Archives; cited in Vogel, *Early Mormon Documents*, 1:544.

43. Joseph Smith III to Mrs. E. Horton, March 7, 1900, Community of Christ Library-Archives; cited in Vogel, *Early Mormon Documents*, 1:546–47.

44. Fred C. Collier and William S. Harwell, eds., *Kirtland Council Minute Book* (Salt Lake City: Collier's, 1996), 23. The passage appears in the entry for February 12, 1834.

45. John A. Clark, *Gleanings By the Way* (Philadelphia: W. J. and J. K. Simon, 1842), 224, 228, 230–31; part of this chapter on the Mormons appeared as a letter in the *Episcopal Recorder* 18 (1846): 94. This interview was also reprinted in "Modern Superstition.—The Mormonites.—No. I," *Visitor, or Monthly Instructor* (1841): 62, 63–64.

46. David B. Dille, "Additional Testimony of Martin Harris (One of the Three Witnesses) to the Coming Forth of the Book of Mormon," *Millennial Star* 21 (August 20, 1859): 545. The interview occurred on September 15, 1853.

47. "Mormonism—No. II," *Tiffany's Monthly* 5 (May 1859): 163, 165–66.

48. Beatrice Cannon Evans and Janath Russell Cannon, eds., *Cannon Family Historical Treasury* (Salt Lake City: George Cannon Family Association, 1967), 250.

49. "A Witness to the Book of Mormon," *Des Moines Iowa State Register*, August 28, 1870; cited in Vogel, *Early Mormon Documents*, 2:330.

50. Rhett Stephens James, *The Man Who Knew: The Early Years. A Play About Martin Harris, 1824–1830* (Cache Valley, Utah: Martin Harris Pageant Committee, 1983), 97n3.

51. *Saints' Herald* 22 (October 15, 1875): 630. H. B. Emerson, of New Richmond, Ohio, wrote Martin Harris a series of letters seeking information about the early days of the Church. Two of Harris's replies were published in this issue of *Saints' Herald*.

52. Edward Stevenson to the editor, November 30, 1881, *Deseret Evening News*, December 13, 1881. The interview occurred in 1870.

53. Simon Smith to the editor, April 30, 1884, *Saints' Herald* 31 (May 24, 1884): 324. Smith visited Martin Harris in Clarkston, Utah, in July 1875.

54. Reuben P. Harmon Statement, *Naked Truths about Mormonism* 1 (April 1888): 1. Harmon's statement was witnessed by Arthur Deming and Granville Harmon.

55. "The Three Witnesses to the Book of Mormon," *Millennial Star* 48 (June 21, 1886): 389–90. Edward Stevenson gave a similar account in *Reminiscences of Joseph the Prophet and the Coming Forth of the Book of Mormon* (Salt Lake City: By the author, 1893), 30.

56. Andrew Jenson, ed., "The Three Witnesses," *Historical Record* 6 (May 1887): 216–17.

57. R. W. Alderman Statement, *Naked Truths about Mormonism* 1 (January 1888): 3. Alderman's statement was delivered on December 25, 1884, in Claridon, Geauga County, Ohio, and witnessed by Arthur B. Deming and Clara Alderman.

58. George Mantle to the editor, December 26, 1888, *Autumn Leaves* 2 (March 1889): 141.

59. Anthony Metcalf, *Ten Years before the Mast. Shipwrecks and Adventures at Sea. Religious Customs of the People of India and Burmah's Empire. How I Became a Mormon and Why I Became an Infidel* (Malad City, Idaho: n.p., 1888), 70–71. Metcalf visited Martin Harris in Smithfield, Utah, in winter 1875–76.

60. Ole A. Jensen, "Testimony of Martin Harris," holograph, microfilm, 3–4, Church Archives, n.d.

61. William Harrison Homer Statement, January 3, 1922, typescript, microfilm, Church Archives.

62. "Martin Harris and the Book of Mormon," *Improvement Era* 26 (September 1923): 980. The article contains a report of a statement made by William Waddoups at Benson Stake Conference in April 1923. Waddoups's interview occurred after Harris had moved to Utah.

63. William Harrison Homer, "The Last Testimony of Martin Harris," 1925, typescript, microfilm, 3, Church Archives. Homer interviewed Harris in winter 1869–70. For more information on Homer's visit with Martin Harris in Kirtland in December 1869, see Homer, "The Passing of Martin Harris," *Improvement Era* 29 (March 1926): 468–72; and William H. Homer, Jr., " . . . 'Publish It upon the Mountains': The Story of Martin Harris," *Improvement Era* 58 (July 1955): 505–7, 524–26.

64. John E. Godfrey, Affidavit, June [July] 2, 1933, typescript, microfilm, Church Archives.

65. Thomas Godfrey, Affidavit, July 2, 1933, typescript, microfilm, Church Archives.

66. William Pilkington, Affidavit, April 3, 1934, Church Archives; cited in Vogel, *Early Mormon Documents*, 2:353–56.

67. William Pilkington, Address delivered in the Lewisville Ward, Rigby Stake, April 23, 1939, typescript, 1–2, Church Archives. Pilkington gave several similar accounts, such as William Pilkington to Vern C. Poulter, February 28, 1930, holograph, microfilm, Church Archives.

68. Theodore Farley Sr., Address delivered at Priesthood Session of Sharon Stake Quarterly Conference, March 23, 1940, typescript, 2, Church Archives.

69. "A Mormon Interview," transcribed from Ashbel Kitchell, Pocket Journal (May [March] 7, 1831?), photocopy, L. Tom Perry Special Collections, Harold B. Lee Library, Brigham Young University, Provo, Utah. Kitchell was describing a visit of Oliver Cowdery that occurred in fall 1830.

70. Oliver Cowdery to W. W. Phelps, *Messenger and Advocate,* October 1834, 14. The letter was dated September 7, 1834. Phelps replied on December 25, 1834, declaring his spiritual anticipation of the Book of Mormon in 1823. *Messenger and Advocate*, February 1835, 65–67.

71. Josiah Jones, "History of the Mormonites," *Evangelist* 9 (June 1, 1841): 132–34. Jones wrote his history of the Mormons while living at Kirtland in 1831. According to the biographical blurb accompanying the article, Jones was "one of the faithful few belonging to the church of Kirtland, who refused to follow Rigdon when he made a surrender of himself and his flock to the Mormons."

72. Reuben Miller Journal, October 21, 1848, holograph, microfilm, Church Archives. Miller recorded Cowdery's testimony at a conference held at Council Bluffs. For more information on Reuben Miller, see Richard Lloyd Anderson, "Reuben Miller, Recorder of Oliver Cowdery's Reaffirmations," *BYU Studies* 8, no. 3 (1968): 277–93.

73. George Q. Cannon, in *Journal of Discourses*, 26 vols. (Liverpool: F. D. Richards, 1855–86), 22:254, September 18, 1881. Several others, including Brigham Young, Charles M. Nielsen, and Seymour B. Young, also gave accounts of this incident, but none of the accounts is firsthand. Historian Richard Lloyd Anderson, *Investigating the Book of Mormon Witnesses* (Salt Lake City: Deseret Book, 1981), 59–60, considers the Cannon account the most correct.

74. Edward Stevenson, "The Three Witnesses to the Book of Mormon," *Millennial Star* 48 (July 5, 1886): 420.

75. William M. Frampton to John E. Booth, September 15, 1901, typescript, microfilm, Church Archives.

76. Samuel W. Richards Statement, May 21, 1907, holograph, 2–3, Church Archives.

77. Jacob F. Gates Affidavit, January 30, 1912, 1, Church Archives. Jacob Gates's testimony of his meeting with Oliver Cowdery was recorded by his son, Jacob F. Gates.

78. Jenson, *Historical Record* 6, 210. Orson Pratt and Joseph F. Smith visited Whitmer on September 7, 1878, at Richmond, Missouri.

79. P. Wilhelm Poulson, *Deseret Evening News*, August 16, 1878.

80. Thomas Wood Smith, *Fall River Herald*, March 28, 1879; cited in Lyndon W. Cook, ed., *David Whitmer Interviews: A Restoration Witness* (Orem, Utah: Grandin Book, 1991), 10.

81. J. L. Traughber Jr., "Testimony of David Whitmer," *Saints' Herald* 26 (November 15, 1879): 341.

82. Thomas Wood Smith, Letter to the editor, *Saints' Herald* 27 (January 1, 1880): 13.

83. Eri B. Mullin, Letter to the editor, *Saints' Herald* 27 (March 1, 1880): 76.

84. *Kansas City Daily Journal*, June 5, 1881.

85. David Whitmer to the editor, *Kansas City Daily Journal*, June 19, 1881; cited in Cook, *David Whitmer Interviews*, 71–72.

86. *Chicago Times*, October 17, 1881; cited in Cook, *David Whitmer Interviews*, 74–76.

87. Interview conducted on January 15, 1882, in Richmond, Missouri; published in the *Saints' Herald* 29 (March 1, 1882): 68.

88. E. C. Briggs, Letter to the editor, *Saints' Herald* 31 (June 21, 1884): 396–97.

89. James H. Hart, "About the Book of Mormon," *Deseret Evening News*, March 25, 1884.

90. George Q. Cannon, interview, February 27, 1884, George Q. Cannon Journal, Church Archives; cited in Cook, *David Whitmer Interviews*, 108.

91. *St. Louis Republican*, July 16, 1884; cited in Cook, *David Whitmer Interviews*, 143.

92. Zenas H. Gurley, "Questions Asked of David Whitmer," holograph, 1, 3, 4, Gurley Collection, Church Archives; cited in Cook, *David Whitmer Interviews*, 152–58. The interview took place on January 14, 1885, and was recorded on January 21, 1885.

93. "The Book of Mormon," *Chicago Tribune*, December 17, 1885, 3. The *Tribune* correspondent visited and interviewed Whitmer on December 15, 1885, at Whitmer's home in Richmond, Missouri.

94. *Omaha Herald*, October 17, 1886; cited in Cook, *David Whitmer Interviews*, 199–200. See also *Chicago Inter-Ocean*, October 17, 1886; and *Saints' Herald* 33 (Nov. 13, 1886): 706. Although David Whitmer here states that the Urim and Thummim was not returned to Joseph Smith after the 116 pages were lost, Lucy Mack Smith quotes Joseph as saying the Urim and Thummim was returned on September 22, 1828. See Lucy Mack Smith, *Biographical Sketches of Joseph Smith, the Prophet, and His Progenitors for Many Generations* (London: Published for Orson Pratt by S. W. Richards, 1853), 125–26. In addition, David Whitmer was apparently unaware that rather than receiving the seer stone in 1828, Joseph Smith and others had discovered it while digging a well for Willard Chase in 1822. See Richard L. Bushman, *Joseph Smith and the Beginnings of Mormonism* (Urbana: University of Illinois Press, 1984), 69–70.

95. M. J. Hubble, interview, November 13, 1886; located at Missouri State Historical Society, Columbia, Missouri; cited in Cook, *David Whitmer Interviews*, 210–11.

96. David Whitmer, *An Address to All Believers in Christ: By a Witness to the Divine Authenticity of the Book of Mormon* (Richmond, Mo.: By the author, 1887): 6, 10–11, 12, 30, 32, 55–56.

97. *Richmond (Missouri) Democrat*, January 26, 1888; cited in Cook, *David Whitmer Interviews*, 228, 230. According to Cook, this account was probably borrowed from the *Omaha Herald* report mentioned above.

98. Nathan A. Tanner Jr. to Nathan A. Tanner, February 17, 1909, photocopy of typescript, 5, Church Archives. The interview occurred in May 1886.

99. John Whitmer, "Address," *Messenger and Advocate,* March 1836, 286–87.

100. *History of the Church*, 3:307–8.

101. S. F. Walker, "Synopsis of a Discourse Delivered at Lamoni, Iowa," *Saints' Herald* 26 (December 15, 1879): 370.

102. "An Angel Told Him: Joseph Smith's Aged Sister Tells about Moroni's Talk," *Kansas City Times*, April 11, 1895, 1; cited in Kyle R. Walker, "Katharine Smith Salisbury's Recollections of Joseph's Meetings with Moroni," *BYU Studies* 41, no. 3 (2002): 16. Katherine was born on July 28, 1813.

103. Fayette Lapham, "The Mormons," *Historical Magazine*, 2d ser., 7 (May 1870): 307–8. This interview with Joseph Smith's father reportedly occurred in 1830.

104. Lucy Mack Smith to Solomon Mack Jr., January 6, 1831, Church Archives. For other statements by Joseph Smith's mother, see documents 105 and 106. See further Janiece Johnson, "'Give Up All and Follow Your Lord': Testimony and Exhortation in Early Mormon Women's Letters, 1831–1839," *BYU Studies* 41, no. 1 (2002): 77–107, esp. 83–89.

105. Henry Caswall, *The City of the Mormons; or, Three Days at Nauvoo, in 1842* (London: J. G. F. and J. Rivington, 1842), 26–27. Caswell was an early anti-Mormon writer from England who visited Nauvoo on April 15–17, 1842. See Craig Foster, "Henry Caswell: Anti-Mormon Extraordinaire," *BYU Studies* 35 (1995–96): 144–59.

106. Lucy Mack Smith, "Preliminary Manuscript," 1845, Church Archives.

107. James Murdock, "The Mormons and Their Prophet," *Hartford and New Haven, Conn. Congregational Observer* 2 (July 3, 1841): 1; cited in Vogel, *Early Mormon Documents*, 1:479. Younger brother of Joseph Smith, William Smith was born in 1811.

108. William Smith, *William Smith on Mormonism* (Lamoni, Iowa: Herald Steam Book, 1883), 80. William was excommunicated in 1845 and joined the RLDS Church in 1878.

109. "The Old Soldier's Testimony," *Saints' Herald* 31 (October 4, 1884): 644. This is an excerpt from a sermon delivered by William B. Smith in the Saints' Chapel at Deloit, Iowa, on June 8, 1884, as reported by C. E. Butterworth.

110. "Statement of J. W. Peterson Concerning William Smith," May 1, 1921, Miscellaneous Letters and Papers, Community of Christ Library-Archives; cited in Vogel, *Early Mormon Documents*, 1:508.

111. Oliver B. Huntington, "History of the Life of Oliver B. Huntington," typescript, 49–50, Perry Special Collections. For Conrad's granddaughter's recollection, see Pearl Bunnell Newell, interview by Carma deJong Anderson, Orem, Utah, January 1970, copy of transcript in Perry Special Collections.

112. William E. McLellin to "My Dear Friends," February 1870, Community of Christ Library-Archives; cited in Cook, *David Whitmer Interviews*, 233–34. Elizabeth Whitmer, born in 1815, was the daughter of Peter Whitmer Sr. and Mary Whitmer (and the sister of David Whitmer). She was fourteen years old when the translation was completed at her parents' home in Fayette, New York. She married Oliver Cowdery in 1832.

113. Eber D. Howe, *Mormonism Unvailed: or, a Faithful Account of That Singular Imposition and Delusion, from Its Rise to the Present Time* (Painesville, Ohio: By the author, 1834), 268. Alva Hale was the brother of Emma Hale Smith; he was born in 1795.

114. Howe, *Mormonism Unvailed*, 264–65. Isaac Hale's statement also appears in "Modern Superstition.—The Mormonites.—No. II," *Visitor, or Monthly Instructor* (1841): 154–55. Isaac was the father of Emma Hale Smith.

115. "Joseph Knight's incidents of history from 1827 to 1844," microfilm, 1, Church Archives. Compiled from loose sheets in Joseph Knight's possession, this history was written by Thomas Bullock on August 16, 1862.

116. Dean C. Jessee, "Joseph Knight's Recollection of Early Mormon History," *BYU Studies* 17, no. 1 (1976): 33–36.

117. Jesse Smith to Hyrum Smith, June 17, 1829, in Joseph Smith Letterbook 2, MS, 60–61, Joseph Smith Collection, Church Archives. Jesse Smith was the oldest brother of Joseph Smith Sr. As this excerpt shows, he was hostile to the Restoration.

118. This is the first known published reference to the Book of Mormon and appeared before the translation was completed. *Wayne Sentinel*, June 26, 1829.

119. "Golden Bible," *Rochester Advertiser and Telegraph*, August 31, 1829; cited in Vogel, *Early Mormon Documents*, 2:221–22. This article is a reprint of one published that same month in the *Palmyra Freeman*. No original copies of the *Freeman* article have been found.

120. "Golden Bible," *Rochester Gem*, September 5, 1829, 70; cited in Vogel, *Early Mormon Documents*, 2:273.

121. Jeffrey R. Holland, "A Note on Mormon Americana at Yale," *BYU Studies* 10, no. 3 (1970): 387–88. The entire letter, with spelling and punctuation corrections, appears in William Mulder and Russell A. Mortensen, eds., *Among the Mormons* (New York: Alfred A. Knopf, 1958), 26–29.

122. "DIABOLICAL," *Palmyra (N.Y.) Reflector*, February 27, 1830, 66.

123. "Imposition and Blasphemy," *Rochester Gem*, May 15, 1830; cited in Francis W. Kirkham, *A New Witness for Christ in America*, rev. and enl., 2 vols. (Independence, Mo.: Zion's Printing and Publishing, 1947–51), 2:46–47.

124. "The Book of Pukei.—Chap. 1," *Reflector*, June 12, 1830, 36. The Book of Pukei was a parody of the Book of Mormon which offered a satirical alternative interpretation of the coming forth of the scriptural book.

125. Letter from Diedrich Willers to Reverend Brethren, June 18, 1830, original in Diedrich Willers Collection, the John M. Olin Library, Cornell University, Ithaca, N.Y.; cited in D. Michael Quinn, trans. and ed., "The First Months of Mormonism: A Contemporary View by Rev. Diedrich Willers," *New York History* 54 (July 1973): 326–27. Willers was the Reformed (German) minister at Fayette and wrote this letter to warn others about Mormonism.

126. "The Book of Pukei.—Chap. 2," *Reflector*, July 7, 1830, 60.

127. *Reflector*, August 28, 1830, 108.

128. "The Golden Bible," *Painesville (Ohio) Telegraph*, November 16, 1830.

129. "Beware of Impostors," *Painesville Telegraph*, December 14, 1830. This article had originally appeared in the *Milan (Huron County) Free Press*.

130. James Gordon Bennett, "Mormon Religion," *Morning Courier and Enquirer*, September 1, 1831; cited in Leonard J. Arrington, "James Gordon Bennett's 1831 Report on 'The Mormonites,'" *BYU Studies* 10, no. 3 (1970): 361–62.

131. David Marks, *The Life of David Marks, to the 26th Year of His Age* (Limerick, Me.: Morning Star, 1831), 340. David Marks was an itinerant preacher who stayed with the Whitmer family between the publication of the Book of Mormon and the organization of the Church. His reference to the Book of Mormon is the first known published account in a book.

132. W. W. Phelps to E. D. Howe, January 15, 1831, in Howe, *Mormonism Unvailed*, 273. Phelps wrote this letter before joining the Church.

133. "Mormonism," *Painesville Telegraph*, February 15, 1831.

134. "Gold Bible, No. 5," *Reflector*, February 28, 1831, 109.

135. *Evangelical Inquirer*, March 7, 1831; cited in Kirkham, *New Witness for Christ*, 2:112.

136. *Painesville Telegraph*, March 15, 1831.

137. "Gold Bible, No. 6," *Reflector*, March 19, 1831, 126.

138. *Painesville Telegraph*, March 22, 1831. This passage was taken from a letter dated March 12, 1831 and written by ten "individuals of the first respectability" residing in Palmyra.

139. From a letter to the editors signed "A. W. B."—probably A. W. Benton—and sent from South Bainbridge, New York; cited in John Phillip Walker, ed., *Dale Morgan on Early Mormonism: Correspondence and a New History* (Salt Lake City: Signature Books, 1986), 338. The letter describes a trial reportedly held in 1826. For more on Joseph Smith's 1826 trial, see Marvin S. Hill, "Joseph Smith and the 1826 Trial: New Evidence and New Difficulties," *BYU Studies* 12, no. 2 (1972): 223–33.

140. Letter from "A Presbyterian," *Worcester (Mass.) Independent Messenger*, May 27, 1831, 96. The letter was dated February 22, 1831.

141. "Mormon Religion," *Bennington Vermont Gazette*, September 13, 1831. This article was reprinted from New York Courier and Enquirer.

142. Ezra Booth, "Mormonism—No. III," *Ravenna Ohio Star*, October 24, 1831.

143. *New Hampshire Gazette*, October 25, 1831; cited in Kirkham, *New Witness for Christ*, 2:405–6.

144. Alexander Campbell, *Delusions: An Analysis of the Book of Mormon* (Boston: Benjamin H. Greene, 1832), 13, 15.

145. Nathaniel W. Howell and Others to Ancil Beach, January 1832; cited in Vogel, *Early Mormon Documents*, 3:14–16. Howell (1770–1850), first judge of Ontario County, New York, from 1819 to 1833, was a resident of Canandaigua. Five other Canandaigua citizens signed this letter: W. Hubbell, master in chancellery; A. D. Eddy, pastor; Henry Chapin, commissioner of judiciary; Jared Wilson, surrogate; and Lewis Jenkins, postmaster. Ancil Beach was a Methodist minister living in Indiana who had sent a letter to Canandaigua seeking information on the "character of individuals who have published the Book of Mormon."

146. William E. McLellin to Beloved Relatives, August 4, 1832, microfilm, photocopy of holograph, Church Archives. The original letter is found in the Community of Christ Library-Archives; published in Jan Shipps and John W. Welch, eds., *The Journals of William E. McLellin: 1831–1836* (Provo, Utah: BYU Studies; Urbana: University of Illinois, 1994), 79.

147. Howe, *Mormonism Unvailed*, 243–47. Such statements were collected by the excommunicated apostate Doctor Philastus Hurlbut. While attempting to damage Joseph Smith's reputation, these statements also confirm that the miraculous nature of the translation was openly being claimed, although not accepted by all. For a forensic and historical discrediting of these affidavits, see Richard Lloyd Anderson, "Joseph Smith's New York Reputation Reappraised," *BYU Studies* 10, no. 3 (1970): 283–314. For an 1843 testimonial of the youthful prophet's good character, see Mark Ashurst-McGee, "The Josiah Stowell Jr.–John S. Fullmer Correspondence," *BYU Studies* 38, no. 3 (1999): 109–17, with Josiah Stowell Jr. stating, "I never new him to git drunk," 113.

148. Howe, *Mormonism Unvailed*, 252. See note 147.

149. Howe, *Mormonism Unvailed*, 284. See note 147. The Spaulding theory of Book of Mormon origins is no longer tenable. See generally Lance D. Chase, "Spaulding Manuscript," in *Encyclopedia of Mormonism*, ed. Daniel H. Ludlow, 4 vols. (New York: Macmillan, 1992), 3:1402–3.

150. "The Book of Mormon," *Evening and the Morning Star*, January 1833.

151. Howe, *Mormonism Unvailed*, 250–51. See note 147 above.

152. Howe, *Mormonism Unvailed*, 253. See note 147 above.

153. Howe, *Mormonism Unvailed*, 240. See note 147 above.

154. Jesse Townsend to Phines Stiles, December 24, 1833, printed by the Christian Tract Society as "A Minister's Opinion of Joseph Smith, Jr.," Perry Special Collections. Townsend (1766–1838) served as pastor of the Western Presbyterian Church of Palmyra from 1817 to 1820. He was one of fifty-seven Palmyra residents who signed a statement criticizing the Smith family and Martin Harris. See Vogel, *Early Mormon Documents*, 2:48–55.

155. Howe, *Mormonism Unvailed*, 14, 77, 100. Based on reports by Doctor Philastus Hurlbut.

156. Howe, *Mormonism Unvailed*, 268. See note 147 above.

157. Howe, *Mormonism Unvailed*, 267–68. See note 147 above.

158. Howe, *Mormonism Unvailed*, 270–71. Here, Howe reprints a letter, dated February 17, 1834, written by Charles Anthon. See also documents 165 and note 26 in the chronology above.

159. Howe, *Mormonism Unvailed*, 266. See note 147 above.

160. Jesse Townsend to Elisha Camp, August 16, 1834, in Vogel, *Early Mormon Documents*, 3:26. Camp, a lawyer in Jefferson County, New York, where the Mormons had missionary success, wrote Townsend, a Presbyterian minister in Palmyra, on August 5, 1834, "requesting information concerning the people called Mormonites." The letter quoted here is Townsend's reply. See also note 155.

161. W. R. Hine's Statement, *Naked Truths about Mormonism* 1 (January 1888): 2.

162. *Messenger and Advocate*, February 1835, 77. Elders Pratt and Barnes spoke twice in the courthouse at Brookville, Indiana. See also document 173.

163. "Mormonism," *Exeter (N.H.) Christian Journal*, May 28, 1835.

164. John Corrill, *A Brief History of the Church of Christ of Latter Day Saints (Commonly Called Mormons; Including an Account of Their Doctrine and Discipline; with the Reasons of the Author for Leaving the Church* (St. Louis: By the author, 1839), 7, 12. John Corrill wrote this work after leaving the Church in 1838 and being elected to the Illinois legislature. Prior to that time he served faithfully and was a counselor to Edward Partridge, first bishop in the Church.

165. Charles Anthon to Reverend T. W. Coit, April 3, 1841, in Clark, *Gleanings By the Way*, 234–35.

166. Elden J. Watson, ed., *Manuscript History of Brigham Young 1801–1844* (Salt Lake City: Smith Secretarial Service, 1968), 112a. See also document 168.

167. Hiram Page to William McLellin, *The Ensign of Liberty of the Church of Christ* (Kirtland, Ohio) 1 (January 1848): 63. The letter was written from Ray County, Missouri, on May 30, 1847.

168. Brigham Young, in *Journal of Discourses*, 2:180–81, February 18, 1855.

169. "Life Sketch of Solomon Chamberlain," typescript, 2, Perry Special Collections. See further Larry C. Porter, "Solomon Chamberlin's Missing Pamphlet: Dreams, Visions, and Angelic Ministrants," *BYU Studies* 37, no. 2 (1997–98): 113–40.

170. "Life of Phineas Howe Young," typescript, Perry Special Collections, 3. Samuel Smith (1808–44) was a brother of Joseph Smith.

171. Pomeroy Tucker, *Origin, Rise, and Progress of Mormonism* (New York: D. Appleton, 1867), 29–49.

172. Tucker, *Progress of Mormonism*, 284. The passage appears in a letter from Stephen S. Harding to Tucker. Harding had previously served as governor of the Utah Territory.

173. Orson Pratt, in *Journal of Discourses*, 14:144, March 19, 1871.

174. Emily C. Blackman, *History of Susquehanna County Pennsylvania* (Philadelphia: Claxton, Remsen, and Haffelfinger, 1873), 577, 104–5.

175. Pratt, *Autobiography of Parley P. Pratt*, 37, 39, 43. The incident described occurred in 1830.

176. [John Murdock], "Sidney Rigdon. A Report of a Lecture He Delivered Forty Years Ago in Meadville [Pennsylvania]—Rigdon's Account of Joe Smith's Revelation," *Pittsburgh Telegraph*, August 24, 1876; cited in Vogel, *Early Mormon Documents*, 1:50. Compare document 184.

177. "Joe Smith. Something about the Early Life of the Mormon Prophet," *Detroit Post and Tribune*, December 3, 1877, 3; cited in Vogel, *Early Mormon Documents*, 2:517, 520. John Gilbert (1802–95) was principal typesetter and proofreader when the Book of Mormon was printed in 1829–30. Compare documents 178, 191, 197, 198.

178. John H. Gilbert to James T. Cobb, February 10, 1879, Theodore A. Schroeder Papers, Rare Books and Manuscript Division, New York Public Library, New York; cited in Vogel, *Early Mormon Documents*, 2:523–24.

179. W. W. Blair, Letter to the editor, *Saints' Herald* 26 (June 15, 1879): 191. Michael Morse was married to Tryal Hale, Emma Hale Smith's sister, and is quoted here by W. W. Blair, a member of the First Presidency of the RLDS Church, in 1879.

180. Joseph Lewis and Hiel Lewis, "Mormon History," *Amboy (Ill.) Journal*, April 30, 1879. Hiel and Joseph Lewis, brothers, were cousins of Emma Hale Smith.

181. Hiel Lewis, "Review of Mormonism," *Amboy Journal*, June 4, 1879.

182. Joseph Lewis, "Review of Mormonism," *Amboy Journal*, June 11, 1879.

183. Frederic G. Mather, "Early Days of Mormonism," *Lippincott's Magazine* (August 1880): 201.

184. "Lecture Written by John M. Rigdon on the Early History of the Mormon Church," typescript, Perry Special Collections. John Rigdon was Sidney Rigdon's son, born in 1833.

185. Nancy N. Tracy (1814?–1902), Narrative, November 4, 1880, holograph, microfilm, 4, Church Archives; the original document is located at the Bancroft Library. She was present at the August 8, 1844, meeting in Nauvoo when Brigham Young appeared as Joseph Smith.

186. William H. Kelley, "The Hill Cumorah, and the Book of Mormon," *Saints' Herald* 28 (June 1, 1881): 166.

187. Kelley, "Hill Cumorah," 163.

188. Charles A. Shook, *The True Origin of the Book of Mormon* (Cincinnati, Ohio: Standard Publishing, 1914), 57. According to Shook, Adeline Bernard was Oliver Cowdery's adopted daughter.

189. Shook, *Origin of the Book of Mormon*, 55. Lang was Oliver Cowdery's friend and legal associate in Tiffin, Ohio, in the early 1840s. Although he claims that the Book of Mormon was produced from an alleged Solomon Spaulding manuscript, he admits in the same letter that Oliver Cowdery "would never allow any man to drag him into a conversation on the subject [Mormonism]" (56). Henry Gibson, another prominent Tiffin resident agreed that Oliver Cowdery "never conversed on the subject [Mormonism] with his most intimate friends" (57).

190. Ellen E. Dickinson, *New Light on Mormonism* (New York: Funk and Wagnalls, 1885), 263.

191. Kelley, "Hill Cumorah," 165. In a letter to Thomas Gregg, dated June 19, 1881, Gilbert claimed that Kelley's "report of the conversation had with me is full of misrepresentations. In the first paragraph, Hyrum said, 'It was translated from plates by the power of God,' etc., is utterly false. I never had any conversation with Hyrum in regard to the translation. . . . In regard to Smith claiming to be author, etc., I told him I understood in later editions he only claimed to be translator, etc.; the balance of the story in regard to this authorship, is all his own coining and answering." Charles A. Shook, *The True Origin of Mormon Polygamy* (Cincinnati, Ohio: Standard Publishing, 1914), 37–38.

192. Dickinson, *New Light on Mormonism*, 251.

193. Josiah Quincy, *Figures of the Past from the Leaves of Old Journals* (Boston: Roberts Brothers, 1883), 395. See further Jed Woodworth, "Josiah Quincy's 1844 Visit with Joseph Smith," *BYU Studies* 39, no. 4 (2000): 71–87.

194. Harriet A. Weed, ed., *The Autobiography of Thurlow Weed* (Boston: Houghton Mifflin, 1884), 358–59. Thurlow Weed made a similar statement in 1880. His memory of Joseph Smith—calling him "stout," and "compactly built, about five feet eight inches in height"—is not accurate. See Dickinson, *New Light on Mormonism*, 261.

195. Lorenzo Saunders Statement, *Naked Truths about Mormonism*, 2. A variety of sources agree that Oliver Cowdery taught school in the Palmyra area. Lucy Mack Smith reports that he boarded with the Smiths. Therefore, it hardly seems unusual that a schoolteacher would be working at a table with books and manuscripts. In addition, Joseph Smith was in Pennsylvania during this time (1828–29 school year), and he and Oliver Cowdery had not yet met.

196. Rhamanthus M. Stocker, *Centennial History of Susquehanna County, Pennsylvania* (Philadelphia: R. T. Peck, 1887), 555–56.

197. John H. Gilbert, "Memorandum made by John H. Gilbert, Esq., Sep[tember] 8, 1892[,] Palmyra, N.Y.," Palmyra King's Daughters' Free Library, Palmyra, N.Y.; cited in Vogel, *Early Mormon Documents*, 2:546.

198. "Mormon Leaders at Their Mecca," *New York Herald*, June 25, 1893, 12; cited in Vogel, *Early Mormon Documents*, 2:551.

199. William A. Linn, *The Story of the Mormons* (New York: Macmillan, 1902), 48. Chandler was eighty-five years old when he wrote this letter; he reports that he was an apprentice in the Sentinel bookbindery in 1829.

200. Benjamin F. Johnson, *My Life's Review* (Provo, Utah: Grandin Book, 1997), 3.

201. "Scraps of Biography—Newel Knight's Journal," in *Classic Experiences and Adventures* (Salt Lake City: Bookcraft, 1969), 48–49.

202. Ebenezer Robinson (1816–91), Autobiography (1832–1843), appears in *The Return* 2 (August 1890): 314, 316. Robinson was a printer and editor for Church publications in Kirtland and Nauvoo.

Main room in the restored Peter Whitmer home, Fayette, New York, where the Church was organized on April 6, 1830, and priesthood ordinances were performed.

Seventy Contemporaneous Priesthood Restoration Documents

Brian Q. Cannon and BYU Studies *Staff*

Few events in the history of the Restoration are as consequential as the bestowal of the priesthood upon Joseph Smith and Oliver Cowdery. The following excerpts from early Church documents recount all the known direct statements from the first twenty years of Church history specifically concerning the restoration of the Aaronic and Melchizedek Priesthoods. In addition to compiling the descriptions that were written or dictated by Joseph Smith and Oliver Cowdery, this collection also includes the accounts by contemporaries of Joseph and Oliver up to the time of Cowdery's death in 1850. Reflecting information that was probably gleaned from conversations or unrecorded discourses of Joseph and Oliver, a few of these statements offer details unavailable elsewhere. Additionally, these statements help to reveal early Church members' understanding of the restoration of the priesthood and show how they described the priesthood restoration to others.

Long before he received the priesthood, Joseph Smith learned of it from Moroni. According to an Oliver Cowdery account published in 1835, Moroni appeared to Joseph in September 1823 and informed him, "When they [the golden plates] are interpreted the Lord will give the holy priesthood to some, and they shall begin to proclaim this gospel and baptize by water, and after that they shall have power to give the Holy Ghost by the laying on of their hands."[1] While it is unclear to what extent this retrospective account may contain details that were actually learned after 1823, Joseph definitely learned more about the priesthood as he translated the Book of Mormon in 1829. From the golden plates, Joseph learned that power was necessary to perform ordinances including baptism (3 Ne. 11:22), the sacrament (3 Ne. 18:5), and conferring the Holy Ghost (3 Ne. 18:37; Moro. 2:1–3); that this power was conferred by the laying on of hands (3 Ne. 18:38; Moro. 2:1; 3:2); that one could be ordained to the calling of disciple or elder, who in turn could ordain priests and teachers (Moro. 3:1); and that elders or disciples, unlike priests and teachers, could confer the gift of the Holy Ghost by the laying on of hands (Moro. 2:1–2). Additionally, a passage in Alma 13 discussed the calling and ordination of high priests including Melchizedek to the "high priesthood of the holy order of God" (Alma 13:6, 14, 18).

Having learned through the writings of ancient prophets that baptism by proper authority was necessary, Joseph Smith and Oliver Cowdery sought that ordinance. In response to their supplication, John the Baptist appeared and conferred the priesthood of Aaron upon them. At a later date, Peter, James, and John appeared and bestowed what is known today as the Melchizedek Priesthood.[2]

The Restoration of the Aaronic Priesthood

The historical record clearly identifies the circumstances surrounding the restoration of the Aaronic Priesthood, including the date that it occurred, and unambiguous evidence links Joseph and Oliver's quest for that priesthood to knowledge they gained while translating the Book of Mormon. An 1829 document in Oliver Cowdery's handwriting entitled "Articles of the Church of Christ" testified that Cowdery had been given power to baptize "of Jesus Christ" (document 1 below), and Cowdery made similar statements in 1830 (documents 20, 21).

Details regarding the restoration of the Aaronic Priesthood, including John the Baptist's role in that event, however, were seldom if ever shared prior to 1832 "owing to a spirit of persecution," as Joseph Smith indicated in 1838.[3] Two of Joseph and Oliver's close associates, David Whitmer and William McLellin, recalled in 1885 and 1878, respectively, that they first learned of John the Baptist's 1829 appearance two to four years after the Church's organization.[4] In writing, Joseph Smith first referred to this event in 1832 (document 6), describing "the reception of the holy Priesthood by the ministring of Aangels [*sic*] to adminster the letter of the Gospel." Oliver Cowdery offered the first detailed, recorded account of the restoration of the lower priesthood in 1834 (document 23). The following year, Cowdery specified the date and location of the restoration of the Aaronic Priesthood (document 25). Joseph Smith's fullest account of the event (document 12) corroborated Oliver's record and added new details: for instance, Joseph recorded words used by John regarding the nature of the keys that he bestowed; explained that John had acted under the direction of Peter, James, and John; and indicated that John promised them that later they would receive power to bestow the gift of the Holy Ghost. In 1844 (documents 17–19), Joseph Smith referred to the preparatory priesthood as "the power of Elias" and indicated that John the Baptist, the forerunner of the Savior, was "the Spirit of Elias."[5]

Early members read Joseph's and Oliver's testimonies regarding the restoration of the Aaronic Priesthood and used the information in their missionary work. For instance, Orson Hyde (documents 49, 50) quoted directly from Oliver Cowdery's 1834 account (document 23), while Reuben Miller in an 1847 publication (document 66) relied on Joseph Smith's accounts of John's visitation (documents 12, 14). Many accounts mention John the Baptist by name (documents 4, 12, 28, 31, 65, 68, 69); others call him "the angel John" (document 25), "the angel of the Lord" (document 41), simply "the angel" (documents 13, 14, 22), or some other similar appellation (documents 8, 12, 29, 67).

Despite detailed accounts by Joseph and Oliver, some errors crept into the record: William Appleby, for instance, erroneously indicated in a tract published in 1844 that the power to baptize had been restored in 1830 (document 61). Additionally, ambiguity and imprecision arose through leaders' and members' frequent use of the phrase "the holy priesthood" to refer to the Aaronic Priesthood on some occasions (document 23), to the Melchizedek Priesthood on others (documents 8, 25, 57, 70), and to the priesthood in general on yet other occasions (documents 26, 30, 37, 47, 48, 58, 61, 62). Still, the documentary record demonstrates that detailed accounts of the restoration of the Aaronic Priesthood were available to members of the Church as early as 1834 and that early members used those accounts in teaching others about the Aaronic Priesthood's restoration.

The Events of the Restoration of the Melchizedek Priesthood

The written record regarding the restoration of the Melchizedek Priesthood is less complete. Although repeatedly testifying that Peter, James, and John had appeared to them and restored this high priesthood authority (documents 4, 15, 16, 31) or referring alternatively to "apostles" (document 7), "Peter" (document 28), "angels" (documents 6, 29), or "those who had been held in reserve" (document 8), neither Joseph Smith nor Oliver Cowdery specified the date of that restoration or reported the words used by Peter in ordaining them to this priesthood beyond "declaring themselves as possessing the keys" (document 16; see also 40). Oliver Cowdery's accounts concerning the restoration of the Melchizedek Priesthood corroborate the accounts of Joseph; whereas Oliver Cowdery provided the earliest detailed report of the visit of John the Baptist, his accounts of the visit of Peter, James, and John seldom add new information.

Significant evidence suggests that the Melchizedek Priesthood may have been restored in connection with the translation of the Book of Mormon. A revelation dated June 1829 (documents 1, 3) referred to the apostolic calling of David Whitmer and Oliver Cowdery, likening their calling to Paul's, although the revelation did not detail the restoration of priesthood authority or any ordination in connection with that calling. Additionally, David Whitmer recalled in 1887 that he was "baptized, confirmed, and ordained an Elder" in June 1829 and that "previous to this, Joseph Smith and Oliver Cowdery had baptized, confirmed and ordained each other to the office of an Elder."[6] The Book of Mormon, which was being translated at that time, described the ancient ordination of disciples, known as elders, who had power to confer the gift of the Holy Ghost (3 Ne. 18; Moro. 2–3). Inasmuch as the translation of 3 Nephi 11 had made Joseph and Oliver sensitive to their lack of power to baptize and impelled them to seek that power, it is possible that the translation of 3 Nephi 18 and Moroni 2–3 had a similar effect upon them, motivating them to pray to receive by the laying on of hands the additional power to bestow the gift of the Holy Ghost.

The first printed reference to Joseph's and Oliver's ordination as apostles appeared in 1831. It indicated that Joseph and Oliver were each "called of God and ordained an apostle of Jesus Christ" (document 2). In 1833, Joseph Smith discussed the restoration of apostolic authority in greater detail. Thereafter, most of his and Oliver's written accounts expressly mentioned that angels played a role in the restoration of apostolic authority and of the power to bestow the gift of the Holy Ghost. In 1833 (document 7), Joseph Smith testified that he had seen "the Apostles" and could perform miracles. The following year, Joseph met with the Kirtland Stake High Council. On February 12, 1834, he discussed "the dignity of the office which has been conferred upon me by the ministring of the Angel of God" (document 9). While this might have been a reference to John the Baptist, it is also possible that Joseph was referring to Peter's role in conferring the Melchizedek Priesthood upon him. Five days later he instructed the same group that anciently "the apostle Peter was the president of the Council and held the keys of the Kingdom of God."[7] In a blessing which Oliver Cowdery dated 1833 and copied in 1835, Joseph Smith referred to the reception of "the holy priesthood under the hands of those who . . . received it under the hand of the Messiah" (document 8).

In 1835 the original edition of the Doctrine and Covenants gave the first precise published account of the appearance of Peter, James, and John to Joseph and Oliver.[8] This edition indicated that the three ancient apostles had "ordained" and "confirmed" Joseph and Oliver as "apostles" and granted them "the keys of your ministry" (document 4). In subsequent statements, Joseph reiterated the role of Peter, James, and John in the restoration of the "priesthood" and "the keys" of the kingdom (documents 15, 16) and indicated that

Courtesy Museum of Church History and Art

The Restoration of the Melchizedek Priesthood, by Minerva Teichert, oil on canvas, 1934.

the angelic ministrants' voices had come to them "in the wilderness" between Harmony, Pennsylvania, and Colesville, New York (document 16).[9] Following the Prophet's death, Oliver Cowdery testified repeatedly and fervently that he had received the higher priesthood under the hands of angelic ministrants (documents 28–31).[10] In 1846 he mentioned only Peter's role in the restoration of the Melchizedek Priesthood (document 28), but in 1849 he confirmed that James and John had also been present (document 31).

Supplementing Joseph's and Oliver's own accounts in several respects are Addison Everett's recollections, written in 1881, 1882, and 1883, of statements he had heard Joseph Smith make in a conversation in 1844. According to Everett's longest account, Joseph Smith indicated that while translating the Book of Mormon in Harmony, Pennsylvania, he and Oliver had been arrested; after escaping from a courtroom, they spent the night in the woods eluding their enemies. At daybreak, Peter, James, and John appeared to them and "ordained us to the Holy Apostelship and gave unto us the Keys of the Dispensation of the fullness of times."[11]

The foregoing accounts all seem to describe a single event: a restoration between Harmony and Colesville of (what came to be known as) the Melchizedek Priesthood under the Savior's direction by Peter with the assistance of James and John. However, the draft and final version of an 1839 account by Joseph Smith may describe a separate set of events connected with the restoration of "the Melchesidec Priesthood, which holds the authority of the laying on of hands for the gift of the Holy Ghost" (documents 13, 14). Those documents indicate that after Joseph and Oliver had prayed for this authority, "the word of the Lord" came to them in a second location, the Whitmer home in Fayette, commanding them to ordain one another to the office of Elder once they had "called together our brethren and had their sanction" and then to "attend to the laying on of hands for the Gift of the Holy Ghost."[12]

No single document written by the principals discusses both the appearance of Peter, James, and John and the revelation received in the Whitmer home, specifying the chronological order of these revelations, but the revelation described in documents 13 and 14 was definitely received prior to the organization of the Church, since Joseph Smith carried out its instructions on April 6, 1830. Joseph Smith's history indicates that he and Oliver ordained each other on April 6 "according to previous commandment."[13]

In their written accounts, most of which were produced for didactic purposes, many early members compressed all the events of priesthood restoration into a general reference to a visitation by a holy messenger or angel (documents 33, 34, 35, 39, 43, 49, 51, 52, 54, 55, 59, 60, 61, 62). Although a published revelation (document 4) referring to separate ministrations by John the Baptist and by Peter, James, and John was widely disseminated and readily available beginning in 1835, more details were circulated about the restoration of the Aaronic Priesthood, probably because that authority was more immediately relevant to the issue of conversion and baptism. Under these circumstances, it is possible that some members regarded the restoration of the authority to baptize as the primary facet of priesthood restoration and therefore focused on that restoration in their teachings.

It is also likely that some writers focused on a single messenger's role in the restoration of the priesthood in order to simplify the Restoration for hymns or missionary work, particularly when they desired to draw a parallel between the other angel mentioned in Revelation 14:6 and the Restoration of the gospel. Charles Thompson, for instance, borrowed heavily from John's prophecy in Revelation when he wrote, "God sent an holy angel from the midst of heaven, with the Priesthood and authority of Jesus Christ, to preach the everlasting Gospel unto them who dwell on the earth, and to every nation, kindred, tongue and people" (document 52).

Statements by William McLellin (document 67) and David Patten (document 41) demonstrate that some members who had studied Doctrine and Covenants 27 understood clearly that the Aaronic and Melchizedek Priesthoods were restored on separate occasions. Similarly, other leaders and missionaries, including Brigham Young (document 69) and Reuben Miller (documents 65, 66), referred to two separate appearances in their sermons and writings.

The accounts by Joseph's and Oliver's contemporaries show that early members arrived at different conclusions regarding the timing of the restoration of the Melchizedek Priesthood. In the 1880s, Everett calculated that it probably occurred in August 1829. Although William McLellin recognized the importance of Peter, James, and John's visitation (document 67), he seems to trace the reception of the Melchizedek Priesthood to the ordination of Joseph and Oliver as elders on April 6, 1830 (document 68). Hiram Page, one of the Eight Witnesses to the Book of Mormon, was convinced that Joseph and Oliver received the Melchizedek Priesthood from Peter, James, and John "before the 6th of april 1830" (document 70). Agreeing with Hiram Page, in 1853 and again in 1874, Brigham Young emphasized that Joseph Smith received apostolic power from Peter, James, and John prior to the organization of the Church. Independent historian D. Michael Quinn's reading of Brigham Young's comment that "Peter, James, and John came to him [Joseph Smith] in Kirtland" led Quinn to conclude that key words and contextual information found in that discussion by President Young concerning several revelations regarding the priesthood were omitted.[14]

Modern readers have also arrived at divergent conclusions regarding the timing of the Melchizedek Priesthood restoration and Joseph Smith's early understanding of the distinction between the Aaronic and Melchizedek Priesthoods. Two recent interpretations are illustrative. Larry C. Porter, a Senior Research Fellow of the Joseph Fielding Smith Institute for Latter-day Saint History at Brigham Young University, maintains that "the evidence suggests a date near the end of May 1829" and "certainly before the organization of the Church on 6 April 1830."[15] In support of this conclusion, Porter highlights the revelation received prior to June 14, 1829, and first printed in the "Articles of the Church of Christ" (documents 1, 3) that identifies Oliver Cowdery and David Whitmer as apostles who are "called even with that same calling" as "Paul mine apostle." As evidence that this call to the apostleship included priesthood authority, Porter highlights the Prophet's preface to a later publication of this revelation: "The following commandment will further illustrate the nature of our calling to this Priesthood as well as that of others who were yet to be sought after" (document 14). Porter also notes that Joseph and Oliver conferred the gift of the Holy Ghost upon members of the Church on April 6, 1830, and assumes that they used the priesthood that they had received from Peter, James, and John to do so. Based on Joseph Smith's later recollections of instructions he had received in 1829 from John the Baptist, Porter infers that by April 1830 "Joseph Smith recognized the limitations of John's power"[16] and thus would not have conferred the Holy Ghost on members unless he had already received the power to do so from Peter, James, and John. To support this view, Porter cites Joseph Smith's 1844 statement:

> John's mission was limited to preaching and baptizing; but what he did was legal; and when Jesus Christ came to any of John's disciples, He baptized them with fire and the Holy Ghost.
>
> We find the Apostles endowed with greater power than John. . . . John did not transcend his bounds, but faithfully performed that part belonging to his office.[17]

Whereas Porter identifies spring 1829 as the time for the restoration of the Melchizedek Priesthood, D. Michael Quinn concludes that Joseph Smith did not receive the higher priesthood from Peter, James, and John until July 1830.[18] He acknowledges the 1829 reference to the calling of apostles (documents 1, 3), but he argues that the revelation merely likens Oliver Cowdery and David Whitmer to Paul. Then, overlooking Paul's assertion in 1 Timothy 2:7, "I am ordained a preacher, and an apostle, (I speak the truth in Christ, and lie not)," Quinn follows Dan Vogel's interpretation and suggests that Paul may have been an unordained "charismatic apostle and special witness"[19] rather than an ordained apostle, citing the LDS Bible Dictionary for general support. Quinn argues that Cowdery and Whitmer as witnesses of the Book of Mormon were called apostles in that sense prior to 1830.[20] Quinn admits that elders were ordained as early as mid-1829, but he suggests that those ordinations and all confirmations prior to that time might have been performed solely on the basis of the revelation received in June 1829 instructing Joseph and Oliver to ordain each other (documents 13, 14). He suggests further that the ordinations carried out on April 6, 1830, were reordinations.[21]

Quinn looks mainly to documents 10 and 16, and to the 1881 and 1882 Addison Everett accounts to support his conclusion that the

Melchizedek Priesthood was formally restored by Peter, James, and John in July 1830. In document 10, Joseph Smith mentions the restoration of the Melchizedek Priesthood and the pouring out of "the gift of the Holy Spirit" upon the Church after referring to the Church's organization. Quinn infers that this document as well as document 16 (also found in D&C 128:20) are a chronological listing of events. But document 16 helps Quinn's case only if one assumes that one can date to June 1830 the event referred to in document 16 as "the voice of Michael on the banks of the Susquehanna, detecting the devil when he appeared as an angel of light."[22] While he acknowledges that the date specified by Everett for the restoration of the higher priesthood is 1829, Quinn notes that this date does not match the events that Everett described surrounding Joseph's arrest and court trial, which occurred in June and July 1830. Thus, for Quinn, Everett's account "seems to confirm the July 1830 date."[23]

While Porter acknowledges the statements by Everett and believes that "Addison Everett was a man of veracity," he is more skeptical of Everett's statements because thirty-seven years had passed between the time that Everett heard the Prophet's statements and the time that he recorded them, and because Everett admitted his limitations and "lack of technical skills" as a historian. Porter concludes that "portions of his [Everett's] remembrance are inconsistent enough to warrant some obvious cautions when attempting to reconstruct the sequence of events surrounding the restoration process from his citations."[24]

Conclusion

The fact that the historical record can be used to support different interpretations demonstrates how puzzling any fragmentary record of the past can be. Because Joseph and Oliver never identified a date for the restoration of the Melchizedek Priesthood, they left room for speculation about the date of that priesthood's restoration. Further complicating the task is our inability using extant documents to determine with certainty Joseph Smith's full understanding of the nature of the priesthood at the time of the Church's organization.

While the documentary record is fragmentary regarding the date for the restoration of the Melchizedek Priesthood, and further work remains to be done in analyzing and interpreting these documents, the record is extensive and rich in many respects. It strongly shows that Joseph Smith and Oliver Cowdery repeatedly testified that they received power from on high to perform ordinances, first from John the Baptist and then from Peter, James, and John. Their testimonies began early in Church documents and intensified as these first and second elders drew closer to their own impending deaths. The powerful thrust of these accounts, corroborated by numerous statements from other early members of the Church, is intellectually challenging and spiritually invigorating.

Brian Q. Cannon is Associate Professor of History at Brigham Young University and member of the BYU Studies *Church History editorial board. John W. Welch, Professor of Law, Editor-in-Chief of* BYU Studies, *and Director of Publications for the Joseph Fielding Smith Institute for Latter-day Saint History; and several editorial interns at* BYU Studies, *particularly Trevor Packer, assisted in preparing these materials for publication.* BYU Studies *expresses appreciation to members of the staff at Church Archives for their valuable assistance in locating and verifying these priesthood restoration documents.*

This article was originally published in BYU Studies *35, no. 4 (1995–96): 162–207.*

Notes

1. *Messenger and Advocate*, October 1835, 199. Further words given by Moroni at that time, now found in Doctrine and Covenants 2, were provided by Joseph Smith in 1838: "Behold, I will reveal unto you the Priesthood, by the hand of Elijah" (D&C 2:1).

2. As Gregory Prince has observed, the earliest occurrences of the word *priesthood* in written Mormon sources outside the Book of Mormon begin in 1831 (27). Moreover, although priesthood authority had been restored prior to

that time, the terms *Aaronic Priesthood* and *Melchizedek Priesthood* "were not adopted until 1835" (14). Gregory A. Prince, *Having Authority: The Origins and Development of Priesthood during the Ministry of Joseph Smith* (Independence, Mo.: Independence Press, 1993). William E. McLellin's journal entry for October 25, 1831, speaks of "the High-Priesthood" and "the lesser Priest-Hood." Jan Shipps and John W. Welch, eds., *The Journals of William E. McLellin, 1831–1836* (Provo, Utah: BYU Studies; Urbana: University of Illinois Press, 1994), 45, 283.

3. Joseph Smith Jr., *History of The Church of Jesus Christ of Latter-day Saints*, ed. B. H. Roberts, 2d ed., rev., 7 vols. (Salt Lake City: Deseret Book, 1971), 1:43 (hereafter cited as *History of the Church*).

4. While remaining true to his testimony as a witness to the Book of Mormon, David Whitmer rejected any aspect of the Restoration that recognized or promoted central Church authority. In 1885, Whitmer stated:

> I moved Joseph Smith and Oliver Cowdery to my fathers house in Fayette Seneca County New York, from Harmony, Penn. in the year 1829, on our way I conversed freely with them upon this great work they were bringing about, and Oliver stated to me in Josephs presence that they had baptized each other seeking by that to fulfill the command—And after our arrival at fathers sometime in June 1829, Joseph ordained Oliver Cowdery to be an Elder, and Oliver ordained Joseph to be an Elder in the church of Christ and during that year Joseph both baptized and ordained me an elder in the church of Christ. . . . I never heard that an Angel had ordained Joseph and Oliver to the Aaronic priesthood until the year 1834 5. or 6—in Ohio.

Notwithstanding numerous attestations to the contrary by Joseph Smith and Oliver Cowdery, David Whitmer in 1885 maintained, "I do not believe that John the Baptist ever ordained Joseph and Oliver as stated and believed by some." Zenas H. Gurley, Interview, January 14, 1885, Gurley Collection, Church Archives, The Church of Jesus Christ of Latter-day Saints, Salt Lake City, quoted in Lyndon W. Cook, ed., *David Whitmer Interviews: A Restoration Witness* (Orem, Utah: Grandin Book, 1991), 154–55. Earlier, Whitmer had been very impressed, however, by Oliver Cowdery's testimony regarding the visitation of Peter, James, and John; see note 10 below.

In 1878, William E. McLellin wrote:

> In 1831 I heard Joseph tell his experience about angel visits many times, and about finding the plates, and their contents coming to light. . . . But I never heard one word of John the baptist, or of Peter, James, and John's visit and ordination till I was told some year or ~~two~~ afterward [that is, in 1832] in Ohio. (William E. McLellin statement, 10, numbered item 28, quoted in D. Michael Quinn, *The Mormon Hierarchy: Origins of Power* [Salt Lake City: Signature Books, 1994], 19)

5. Part of a revelation dated August and September 1830 (D&C 27) and published for the first time in 1835 stated that Elias had informed Zacharias, the father of John the Baptist, that John would "be filled with the spirit of Elias" (D&C 27:7).

6. David Whitmer, *An Address to All Believers in Christ: By a Witness to the Divine Authenticity of the Book of Mormon* (Richmond, Mo.: By the author, 1887), 32.

7. Kirtland High Council Minutes, February 17, 1834, Church Archives.

8. These verses did not appear in the earlier text of the revelation printed in the Book of Commandments, 1833. Joseph Smith recalled in 1839 that all of section 27 was received as a revelation in August 1830 but that most of the revelation, including these words, was not recorded until September 1830. Dean C. Jessee, ed., *The Papers of Joseph Smith*, 2 vols. (Salt Lake City: Deseret Book, 1989–1992), 1:320–21.

9. This passage mentions "the voice of Peter, James, and John" but does not discuss a physical ordination. The reason is that this is part of a response to the preceding question, "What do we *hear*?" (italics added).

10. During an 1861 visit with David Whitmer, David H. Cannon reported that Whitmer recalled yet another testimony given by Cowdery regarding the appearance of Peter, James, and John:

> The thing which impressed me most of all was, as we stood beside the grave of Oliver Cowdery the other Witness, who had come back into the Church before his death, and in describing Olivers action, when bearing his testimony, said to the people in his room, placing his hands like this upon his head, saying "I know the Gospel to be true and upon this head has Peter James and John laid their hands and confered the Holy Melchesdic Priestood," the manner in which this tall grey headed man went through the exhibition of what Oliver had done was prophetic. I shall never forget the impression that the testimony of . . . David Whitmer made upon me.

David H. Cannon, Autobiography, March 13, 1917, 5, photocopy of holograph in possession of Richard L. Anderson, quoted in Larry C. Porter, "The Restoration of the Priesthood," *Religious Studies Center Newsletter* 9, no. 3 (May 3, 1995): 10.

11. Addison Everett wrote:

> A few days Before Br Joseph & Hiram ware calld to Carthage By Gov. Ford I wus Passing the Mansheon House I observed Bro Joseph & Hiram & some five or six Brethren in earnest conversation Before the Door of the House. I opened the gate and steped in. . . . Br Joseph Ex[p]resed Greate simpathy for Br Oliver saying Poor Boy[,] Poor

Boy[,] casting his eyes to the ground. And then Said as they Ware Tran[s]lating the Book of Mormon at His Father In Laws in Susquhanah County Penny. T[h]ey ware thretned By a Mob and in the same time Father Kn<i>ghts came Down from Cole[s]vill[e] Broom[e] County New York and Desired them to go home with him and preach to them in his Neighbourhood And on Account of the Mob Spirit prevailing they concluded to goe. And they ware teachi[n]g And preaching the Gospele they ware taken with <a> writ and Before a Judge as fals[e] Prophets. And the Prossecuting Atorny had conceived in his own Mind That A few simple qu[e]stions would Convince the Court By the Answers Bro Joseph would giv[e] <to> that <the> charge was Correct. So he calls out Jo which was the first Merical Jesus raught [wrought.] Why <said Br Joseph> we read He Created the worlds And what He done previous to that I have not as yet Learned. This answer completly confounded the Prossicuting Atorny that he requested the Judge to Dismis the case. and went out To Organ<ize> the Mob that was on the Out Side. At about this time a Lawyer By the Name of Reede I think was his name came in to the court and Stated He was Mr Smiths Atorney and wished to see him <in> a Private room And was <put> in to <a> Back room and when in he hoisted a window and told Br Joseph & Oliver to flee in to the forest which was close at hand. And they wandered in a dense Forest all Night and often times in Mud and water up to thare Knees. And Brother Oliver got quite exausted in the After Part of the Night and Brother Joseph had to put his arm arround him and allmost carry him. And Just as the day Broke in the East Brother Oliver gave out Entirely and he[,] Br Joseph[,] leaned him against an Oake tree Just out side a field fenc[e] Br Oliver Crying out how long O Lord O how Long Br Joseph hav[e] we got to suffer these things[?] Just this moment Peter James & John came to us and Ordained ~~to~~<us to> the Holy Apostelship and gave <unto> us the Keys of the Disp<e>nsation of the fullness of times. And we had some 16 or 17 miles to goe to reach our place of residence and Brother Oliver could travel as well as I could <after the Endowment>. Now as to time and Place. I heard the Name of the Banks of the Susquehanah river spoken <of> But whare it was pla[c]ed I cannot till. No doubt the Oake tree and the field fence was ajacent to the river. As to time I cannot Be Very Explsit. But as the Mob spirit had not abated when they returned they had to remove to Father Whitmores <at Fayet[te] Seneca Co> to finish the Translation. I should <jud[g]e> it to <Be> the Latter part of August.

> Now Beloved Brother I am Not Writing as wone of the Lords Historians But as your friend reproduc<i>ng the last words I heard our Beloved and Gods Holy Prophet Speake before his depart[ure] Into the Eternal Heavens to Dwell with the Holy & Eternal gods forever & Ever!

Addison Everett to Joseph F. Smith, January 16, 1882, Joseph F. Smith Collection, Personal Papers, Church Archives (underlining in the original), quoted in Porter, "Restoration of the Priesthood," 8. Angle brackets < > designate material inserted by Everett above the line. See also Addison Everett to Oliver B. Huntington, February 17, 1881, recorded in "Oliver Boardman Huntington Journal no. 14," under backdate of January 31, 1881; and "Oliver Boardman Huntington Journal no. 15," entry for February 18, 1883, L. Tom Perry Special Collections, Harold B. Lee Library, Brigham Young University, Provo, Utah, quoted in Porter, "Restoration of the Priesthood," 7. The 1881 entry reads as follows:

> Joseph went on to state that "at Coalville he & Oliver were under arrest on charge of Deceiving the people & in court he stated that the first miracle done was to create this earth. About that time his attorney told the court that he wanted to see Mr. Smith alone a few moments. When alone Mr. Reid said that there was a mob in front of the house, & ho[i]sting the window, Joseph & Oliver went to the woods in a few rods, it being night, and they traveled until Oliver was exhausted & Joseph almost carried him through mud and water. They traveled all night and just at the break of day Olive[r] gave out entirely and exclaimed "O! Lord! How long Brother Joseph have we got to endure this thing,"
>
> Brother Joseph said that at that very time Peter, James, & John came to them and ordained them to the Apostleship.
>
> They had 16 or 17 miles to travel to get back to Mr. Hales his father in law and Oliver did not complain anymore of fatigue."

Compare these comments with the early history of Joseph Smith by Joseph Knight, "Joseph Knight's Recollection of Early Mormon History," ed. Dean Jessee, *BYU Studies* 17, no. 1 (1976): 37–38.

12. The first ordinations to the office of elder occurred in 1829. On April 6, 1830, Joseph and Oliver reordained one another as First and Second Elder and then "laid our hands on each individual member of the Church present, that they might receive the gift of the Holy Ghost, and be confirmed members of the Church of Christ." *History of the Church*, 1:78. Both Joseph and Oliver were elders prior to this time. See Porter, "Restoration of the Priesthood," 3.

13. *History of the Church*, 1:77–78.

14. On April 6, 1853, President Young said, "I know that Joseph received his Apostleship from Peter, James, and John, before a revelation on the subject was printed, and he never had a right to organize a Church before he was an Apostle." Brigham Young and others, in *Journal of Discourses*, 26 vols. (Liverpool: F. D. Richards, 1855–86), 1:137. On June 23, 1874, Brigham Young indicated:

> [Joseph Smith] received the Aaronic Priesthood, and then he received the keys of the Melchisedek Priesthood, and organized the Church. He first received the power to baptise, and still did not know that he was to receive any more until the Lord told him there was more for him. Then he received the keys of the Melchisedek Priesthood, and had power to confirm after he had baptized, which he had not before. He would have stood precisely as John the Baptist stood, had not the Lord sent his other messengers, Peter, James and John, to ordain Joseph to the Melchisedek Priesthood. (*Journal of Discourses*, 18:240)

In 1861, in a discourse on the priesthood, President Young said:

> How came these Apostles, these Seventies, these High Priests, and all this organization we now enjoy? It came by revelation. Father Cahoon, who lately died in your neighbourhood, was one of the first men ordained to the office of High Priest in this kingdom. In the year 1831 the Prophet Joseph went to Ohio. He left the State of New York on the last of April, if my memory serves me, and arrived in Kirtland sometime in May. They held a General Conference, which was the first General Conference ever called or held in Ohio. Joseph then received a revelation, and ordained High Priests. You read in the Book of Doctrine and Covenants how he received the Priesthood in the first place. It is there stated how Joseph received the Aaronic Priesthood. John the Baptist came to Joseph Smith and Oliver Cowdery. When a person passes behind the vail, he can only officiate in the spirit-world; but when he is resurrected he officiates as a resurrected being, and not as a mortal being. You read in the revelation that Joseph was ordained, as it is written. When he received the Melchisedek Priesthood, he had another revelation. Peter, James, and John came to him. You can read the revelation at your leisure. When he received this revelation in Kirtland, the Lord revealed to him that he should begin and ordain High Priests; and he then ordained quite a number, all whose names I do not now recollect; but Lyman Wight was one; Fathers Cahoon and Morley, John Murdock, Sidney Rigdon, and others were also then ordained. These were the first that were ordained to this office in the Church. I relate this to show you how Joseph proceeded step by step

> in organizing the Church. At that time there were no Seventies nor Twelve Apostles. (*Journal of Discourses*, 9:88–89)

Readers may judge for themselves if the Kirtland revelation referred to here was the visit of Peter, James, and John or the revelation instructing Joseph Smith to begin ordaining high priests. Likewise, when Brigham Young said that Joseph Smith "was taken in the spirit to the 3d heavens & all this with the aronic priesthood" (Quinn, *Mormon Hierarchy*, 26) before he was ordained an apostle, Brigham need not have been referring to the vision of the three degrees of glory received by Joseph Smith and Sidney Rigdon in February 1832, as Quinn argues. It was common for people to use the phrase "third heaven" from 2 Corinthians 12:2 in connection with Paul's gift of vision in general, as in *History of the Church*, 5:30, but this phrase is ambiguous.

15. Porter, "Restoration of the Priesthood," 3, 6–7.

16. Porter, "Restoration of the Priesthood," 3.

17. Joseph Fielding Smith, comp., *Teachings of the Prophet Joseph Smith* (Salt Lake City: Deseret Book, 1976), 336, quoted in Porter, "Restoration of the Priesthood," 3.

18. Quinn, *Mormon Hierarchy*, 22.

19. Dan Vogel, *Religious Seekers and the Advent of Mormonism* (Salt Lake City: Signature Books, 1988), 144–45; Quinn, *Mormon Hierarchy*, 10.

20. Quinn, *Mormon Hierarchy*, 10; "Bible Dictionary," in Holy Bible (Salt Lake City: The Church of Jesus Christ of Latter-day Saints, 1983), 612, s.v. *Apostle*.

21. Quinn, *Mormon Hierarchy*, 10, 27–30. Quinn argues that Joseph and Oliver could have felt justified in ordaining elders using the authority that they received from John the Baptist because they did not at that time associate the office of elder exclusively with the Melchizedek Priesthood. In support of this position, Quinn indicates that Joseph Smith conferred the Melchizedek Priesthood upon several who had previously been ordained elders in June 1831. At the October 1831 conference in Kirtland, "the authority of the Melchizedek Priesthood was manifested and conferred for the first time upon several of the Elders." *History of the Church*, 1:175–76. A September 1832 revelation specified that "elder and bishop are necessary appendages belonging unto the high priesthood" (D&C 84:29).

22. Quinn dates this event only by indirect association with two other events. Quinn, *Mormon Hierarchy*, 23.

23. Quinn, *Mormon Hierarchy*, 25. Quinn also cites a discourse by Erastus Snow in 1882:

> In due course of time, as we read in the history which he has left, Peter, James and John appeared to him—it was at a period when they were being pursued by their enemies and they had to travel all night, and

in the dawn of the coming day when they were weary and worn who should appear to them but Peter, James and John, for the purpose of conferring upon them the Apostleship, the keys of which they themselves had held while upon the earth, which had been bestowed upon them by the Savior. This Priesthood conferred upon them by those three messengers embraces within it all offices of the Priesthood from the highest to the lowest. (*Journal of Discourses*, 23:183)

24. Porter, "Restoration of the Priesthood," 8–9.

Documents of the Priesthood Restoration

The following collection of historical sources seeks to display all known statements directly concerning the restoration of the Aaronic or Melchizedek Priesthoods that were made during the lifetimes of Joseph Smith (who died in 1844) and Oliver Cowdery (who died in 1850). About half of these documents are firsthand declarations by Joseph or Oliver or secondhand reports of their words. In most other cases, Joseph or Oliver could have known of the statement. The documents are arranged by author (or speaker) in chronological order. The authors appear in the order of their earliest priesthood restoration statement. The statements by that author are then grouped in chronological order. A few later or additional statements appear in the footnotes. In a few documents, punctuation has been added for clarity. Underlining is reproduced from the original document. Editorial marks include angle brackets < > to indicate insertions made by the author of the document. Strikeouts are shown by ~~strikeouts~~. Brackets [ ] indicate editorial comments. In most cases, the entries are an excerpt of the document.

1. Articles of the Church of Christ (1829)

A commandment from God unto Oliver how he should build up his church & the manner thereof. . . . I command all men every where to repent & I speak unto you even as unto Paul mine apostle for ye are called even with that same calling with which he was called Now therefore whosoever repenteth & humbleth himself before me & desireth to be baptized in my name shall ye baptize them And after this manner did he command me that I should baptize them Behold ye shall go down & stand in the water & in my name shall ye baptize them And now behold these are the words which ye shall say calling them by name saying Having authority given me of Jesus Christ I baptize you.[1]

2. Doctrine and Covenants 20 ([1830]/April 1831)

The rise of the Church of Christ in these last days, being 1830 years since the coming of our Lord and Saviour Jesus Christ in the flesh, it being regularly organized and established agreeable to the laws of our country, by the will and commandments of God, in the 4th month, and on the 6th day of the same, which commandments were given to Joseph Smith, jun. who was called of God and ordained an apostle of Jesus Christ, an elder of the church, and also to Oliver Cowdery, who was also called of God an apostle of Jesus Christ, an elder of the church, and ordained under his hand, and this according to the grace of God the Father, and our Lord Jesus Christ, to whom be all glory both now and ever—amen.[2]

3. Doctrine and Covenants 18 ([June 1829]/1833)

And now Oliver, I speak unto you, and also unto David, by way of commandment: For behold I command all men every where to repent, and I speak unto you, even as unto Paul mine apostle, for you are called even with that same calling with which he was called.[3]

4. Doctrine and Covenants 27 ([September 1830]/1835)

John I have sent unto you, my servants, Joseph Smith, jr. and Oliver Cowdery, to ordain you unto this first priesthood which you have received, that you might be called and ordained even as Aaron. . . . And also with Peter, and James, and John, whom I have sent unto you, by whom I have ordained you and confirmed you to be apostles and especial witnesses of my name, and bear the keys of your ministry: and of the same things which I revealed unto them: unto whom I have committed the keys of my kingdom, and a dispensation of the gospel for the last times; and for the fulness of times.[4]

5. Doctrine and Covenants 112 (July 23, 1837)

For unto you, (the Twelve,) and those (the First Presidency) who are appointed with you to be your councilors and your leaders, is the power of this Priesthood given, for the last days and for the last time, in the which is the dispensation of the fulness of times. . . . For verily I say unto you, the keys of the dispensation, which ye have received, have come down from the Fathers, and last of all, being sent down from Heaven unto you.[5]

6. Joseph Smith (1832)

A History of the life of Joseph Smith Jr. an account of his marvilous experience and of all the mighty acts which he doeth in the name of Jesus Chist the son of the living God of whom he beareth record and also an account of the rise of the church of Christ in the eve of time according as the Lord brought forth and established by his hand firstly he receiving the testamony from on high seccondly the ministering of Angels thirdly the reception of the holy Priesthood by the ministring of Aangels [*sic*] to adminster the letter of the Gospel—the Law and commandments as they were given unto him—and the ordinencs, forthly a confirmation and reception of the high Priesthood after the holy order of the son of the living God power and ordinence from on high to preach the Gospel in the administration and demonstration of the spirit the Kees of the Kingdom of God confered upon him and the continuation of the blessings of God to him &c.[6]

7. Joseph Smith (March 2, 1833)

The following Curious occurrence occurred last week in Newburg about 6 miles from this Place [Cleveland, Ohio]. Joe Smith the great Mormonosity was there and held forth, and among other things he told them he had seen Jesus Christ and the Apostles and conversed with them, and that he could perform Miracles.[7]

8. Joseph Smith ([December 18, 1833]/1835)

These blessings shall come upon him according to the blessings of the prophecy of Joseph, in ancient days, which he said should come upon the Seer of the last days and the Scribe that should sit with him, and that should be ordained with him, by the hand of the angel in the bush, unto the lesser priesthood, and after receive the holy priesthood under the hands of those who had been held in reserve for a long season, even those who received it under the hand of the Messiah while he should dwell in the flesh, upon the earth, and should receive the blessings with him, even the Seer of the God of Abraham, Isaac and Jacob, saith he, even Joseph of old, by his hand, even God. And he shall inherit a crown of eternal life, at the end; and while in the flesh shall stand up in Zion and assist to crown the tribes of Jacob; even so. Amen.[8]

9. Joseph Smith (February 12, 1834)

Thursday evening, February 12, 1834. This evening the high Priests and Elders of the Church in Kirtland at the house of bro. Joseph Smith Jun. in Council for Church business. The council was organized, and opened by bro. Joseph Smith Jun in prayer. Bro. Joseph then rose and said: I shall now endeavor to set forth before this council, the dignity of the office which has been conferred upon me by the ministring of the Angel of God, by his own will and by the voice of this Church.[9]

10. Joseph Smith (April 21, 1834)

Norton Medina Co. Ohio April 21, 1834. . . . Bro. Joseph Smith Jun. . . . then gave a relation of obtaining and translating the Book of Mormon, the revelation of the priesthood of Aaron, the organization of the Church in the year 1830, the revelation of the high priesthood, and the gift of the Holy Spirit poured out upon the Church, &c. Take away the book of Mormon, and the revelations, and where is our religion? We have none.[10]

11. Joseph Smith (March 27, 1836)

Joseph Smith Jun. testified of the Angel of the Lord's appearing unto him to call him to the work of the Lord, & also of being ordained under the hands of the Angel of of [*sic*] the covenant.[11]

12. Joseph Smith (1839)

While we were thus employed, praying, and calling upon the Lord, a Messenger from heaven, descended in a cloud of light, and having laid his hands upon us, he ordained us, saying unto us; "Upon you my fellow servants, in the name of Messiah I confer the priesthood of Aaron, which holds the keys of the ministring of angels, and of the gospel of repentance, and of baptism by immersion for the remission of sins; and this shall never be taken again from the earth, untill the sons of Levi do offer again an offering unto the Lord in righteousness." He said this Aaronic priesthood had not the power of laying on of hands, for the gift of the Holy Ghost, but that this should be conferred on us hereafter and he commanded us to go and be baptized, and gave us directions that I should baptize Oliver Cowdery, and afterward that he should baptize me.

Accordingly we went and were baptized, I baptized him first, and afterwards he baptized me, after which I laid my hands upon his head and ordained him to the Aaronick priesthood, and afterward he laid his hands on me and ordained me to the same priesthood, for so we were commanded. The messenger who visited us on this occasion and conferred this priesthood upon us said that his name was John, the same that is called John the Baptist, in the new Testament, and that he acted under the direction of Peter, James, and John, who held the keys of the priesthood of Melchisedeck, whi[c]h priesthood he said should in due time be conferred on us. . . . we were forced to keep secret the circumstances of our having been baptized, and having received the priesthood; owing to a spirit of persecution which had already manifested itself in the neighborhood.[12]

13. Joseph Smith (1839—Draft)

We now became anxious to have that promise realized to us, which the angel that conferred upon us the Aaronick Priesthood had given us, viz, that provided we continued faithful, we should also have the Melchesidec Priesthood, which holds the authority of the laying on of hands for the gift of the Holy Ghost. We had for some time made this matter a subject of humble prayer, and at length we got together in the Chamber of Mr Whitmer's house in order more particularly to seek of the Lord information, and if possible obtain what we now so earnestly desired. After some time spent in solemn and fervent prayer, the word of the Lord came unto us, in the Chamber, commanding us, that I should ordain Oliver Cowdery to be an Elder in the Church of Jesus Christ, and that he also should ordain me to the same office, and that after having been thus ordained, we should proceed to ordain others to the same office, according as it should be made known unto us, from time to time, also commanding us, that as soon as practicable we should call together all those who had already been baptized by us, to bless bread, and break it with them, also to take wine, bless it, and drink it with them doing all these things in the name of the Lord, but to defer our own ordination untill we had called together our brethren and had their sanction, and been accepted by them as their teachers, after which we were commanded to proceed to ordain each other and call out such men as the spirit should dictate unto us, and ordain them, and then attend to the laying on of hands for the Gift of the Holy Ghost.

The following commandment [Doctrine and Covenants 18] will further illustrate the nature of our calling to this Priesthood as well as others who were yet to be sought after.[13]

14. Joseph Smith (1839)

We now became anxious to have that promise realized to us, which the Angel that conferred upon us the Aaronick Priesthood had given us, viz: that provided we continued faithful; we should also have the Melchesidec Priesthood, which holds the authority of the laying on of hands for the gift of the Holy Ghost. We had for some time made this matter a subject of humble prayer, and at length we got together in the Chamber of Mr Whitmer's house in order more particularly to seek of the Lord what we now so earnestly desired: and here to our unspeakable satisfaction did we realize the truth of the Saviour's promise; "Ask, and you shall recieve, seek, and you shall find, knock and it shall be opened unto you;" for we had not long been engaged in solemn and fervent prayer, when the word of the Lord, came unto us in the Chamber, commanding us; that I should ordain Oliver Cowdery to be an Elder in the Church of Jesus Christ, And that he also should ordain me to the same office, ~~accordin~~ and then <to> ordain others as it should be made known unto us, from time to time: we were however commanded to defer this our ordination untill, such times, as it should be practicable to have our brethren, who had been and who should be baptized, assembled together, when we must have their sanction to our thus proceeding to ordain each other, and have them decide by vote whether they were willing to accept us as spiritual teachers, or not, when also we were commanded to bless bread and break it with them, and to take wine, bless it, and drink it with them, afterward proceed to ordain each other according to commandment, then call out such men as the Spirit should dictate, and ordain them, and then attend to the laying on of hands for the gift of the Holy Ghost, upon all those whom we had previously baptized; doing all things in the name of the Lord.

The following commandment [Doctrine and Covenants 18] will further illustrate the nature of our calling to this Priesthood as well as that of others who were yet to be sought after.[14]

15. Joseph Smith (1839)

The Priesthood is everlasting. The Savior, Moses, & Elias—gave the Keys to Peter, James & John on the Mount when they were transfigured before him. The Priesthood is everlasting, without beginning of days or end of years, without Father, Mother &c,—

If there is no change of ordinances there is no change of Priesthood. Wherever the ordinances of the Gospel are administered there is the priesthood. How have we come at the priesthood in the last days? They it came down, down in regular succession. Peter James & John had it given to them & they gave it up.[15]

16. Joseph Smith (September 6, 1842)

And again, what do we hear? Glad tidings from Cumorah! Moroni, an Angel from heaven, declaring the fulfilment of the prophets—the book to be revealed. A voice of the Lord in the wilderness of Fayette, Seneca county, declaring the three witnesses to bear record of the book. The voice of Michael on the banks of the Susquehanna, detecting the devil when he appeared as an angel of light. The voice of Peter, James, and John, in the wilderness between Harmony, Susquehanna county, and Colesville, Broom county, on the Susquehanna River, declaring themselves as possessing the keys of the kingdom, and of the dispensation of the fulness of times. And again, the voice of God in the chamber of old Father Whitmer, in Fayette, Seneca county, and at sundry times, and in divers places through all the travels and tribulation of this Church of Jesus Christ of Latter-day Saints! And the voice of Michael, the archangel; the voice of Gabriel, and of Raphael, and of divers angels, from Michael or Adam down to the present time, all declaring their dispensation, their rights, their keys, their honors, their majesty and glory, and the power of their priesthood.[16]

17. Joseph Smith (March 10, 1844)

Showing the difference between the Spirit of Elias, Elijah and the messiah. J Smith P[rophet]. of the spirit of Elias I must go back to the time at Susquehannah river when I retired in the woods pouring out my soul in prayer to Almighty God. An Angel came down from heaven and laid his hands upon me and ordained me to the power of Elias and that authorised me to babtise with water unto repentance. It is a power or a preparatory work for something greater. you have not power to lay on hands for the gift of the holy ghost but you shall have power given you hereafter, that is the power of the Aronick preisthood.[17]

18. Joseph Smith (March 10, 1844)

On Sunday March 10 Joseph the Priest delivered the following concernin [*sic*] the Spirits & Powers of Elias Elijah ~~& of Messiah~~ The power of Elias is not the power of Elijah related the vision of his ordination to the priesthood of Aaron on the Susquehannah river to preach the preparatory gospel. This said the Angel is the *Spirit of Elias*.[18]

19. Joseph Smith (March 10, 1844)

I went into the woods to inquire of the Lord by prayer his will concerning me— & I saw an angel & he laid his hands upon my head & ordained me to be a priest after the order of Aaron & to hold the keys of this priesthood which office was to preach repentance & Baptism for the remission of sins & also to baptise but was informed that this office did not extend to the laying on of hands for the giving of the Holy Ghost that that office was a greater work & was to be given afterwards but that my ordination was a preparetory work or a going before which was the spirit of Elias for the spirit of Elias was a going before to prepare the way for the greater, which was the Case with John the Baptist.[19]

20. Oliver Cowdery (November 16, 1830)

About two weeks since some persons came along here with the book, one of whom pretends to have seen Angels, and assisted in translating the plates. He proclaims destruction upon the world within a few years,—holds forth that the ordinances of the gospel, have not been regularly administered since the days of the Apostles, till the said Smith and himself commenced the work. . . . The name of the person here, who pretends to have a divine mission, and to have seen and conversed with Angels, is *Cowdray*.[20]

21. Oliver Cowdery (December 7, 1830)

Those who are the friends and advocates of this wonderful book [Book of Mormon], state that Mr. Oliver Cowdry has his commission directly from the God of Heaven, and that he has credentials, written and signed by the hand of Jesus Christ, with whom he has personally conversed, and as such, said Cowdry claims that he and his associates are the only persons on earth who are qualified to administer in his name. By this authority, they proclaim to the world, that all who do not believe *their* testimony, and be baptised by them for the remission of sins, and come under the imposition of *their* hands for the gift of the Holy Ghost . . . must be forever miserable.[21]

22. Oliver Cowdery (December 5, 1834)

The reader may further understand, that the reason why High Counsellor Cowdery was not previously ordained to the Presidency, was, in consequence of his necessary attendance in Zion, to assist Wm. W. Phelps in conducting the printing business; but that this promise was made by the angel while in company with President Smith, at the time they received the office of the lesser priesthood.[22]

23. Oliver Cowdery (1834)

From *his* [Joseph Smith's] hand I received baptism, by the direction of the angel of God—the first received into this church, in this day. . . . On a sudden, as from the midst of eternity, the voice of the Redeemer spake peace to us, while the vail was parted and the angel of God came down clothed with glory, and delivered the anxiously looked for message, and the keys of the gospel of repentance! . . . [O]ur eyes beheld—our ears heard. . . . We listened—we gazed—we admired! 'Twas the voice of the angel from glory. . . . [W]e were rapt in the vision of the Almighty! . . . [W]e received under [the angel's] hand the holy priesthood, as he said, "upon you my fellow servants, in the name of Messiah I confer this priesthood and this authority, which shall remain upon earth, that the sons of Levi may yet offer an offering unto the Lord in righteousness!" . . . The assurance that we were in the presence of an angel; the certainty that we heard the voice of Jesus, and the truth unsullied as it flowed from a pure personage, dictated by the will of God, is to me, past description.[23]

24. Oliver Cowdery (February 1835)

Brethren, you have your duty presented in this revelation. You have been ordained to the Holy Priesthood. You have received it from those who had their power and authority from an angel. You are to preach the gospel to every nation.[24]

25. Oliver Cowdery (October 2, 1835)

The following blessings by the spirit of prophecy, were pronounced by Joseph Smith, jr. the first elder, and first patriarch of the church: for although his father laid hands upon, and blessed the fatherless, thereby securing the blessings of the Lord unto them and their posterity, he was not the first elder, because God called upon his son Joseph and ordained him to this power and delivered to him the keys of the kingdom, that is, of authority and spiritual blessings upon the Church, and through him the Lord revealed his will to the Church: he [Joseph Smith] was ministered unto by the angel, and by his direction he obtained the Records of the Nephites, and translated by the gift and power of God: he was ordained by the angel John, unto the lesser or Aaronic priesthood, in company with myself, in the town of Harmony, Susquehannah County, Pennsylvania, on Fryday, the 15th day of May, 1829, after which we repaired to the water, even to the Susquehannah River, and were baptized, he first ministering unto me and after I to him. But before baptism, our souls were drawn out in mighty prayer to know how we might obtain the blessings of baptism and of the Holy Spirit, according to the order of God, and we diligently sought for the right of the fathers and the authority of the holy priesthood, and the power to admin[ister] in the same: for we desired to be followers of righteousness and the possessors of greater knowledge, even the knowledge of the mysteries of the kingdom of God. Therefore, we repaired to the woods, even as our father Joseph said we should, that is to the bush, and called upon the name of the Lord, and he answered us out of the heavens, and while we were in the heavenly vision the angel came down and bestowed upon us this priesthood: and then, as I have said, we repaired to the water and were baptized. After this we received the high and holy priesthood: but an account of this will be given elsewhere, or in another place. Let it suffice, that others had authority to bless, but after these blessings were given, of which I am about to write, Joseph Smith, Sen. was ordained a president and patriarch, under the hands of his son Joseph, myself, Sidney Rigdon, and Frederick G. Williams, presidents of the Church. These blessings were given by vision and the spirit of prophecy, on the 18th of December, 1833, and written by my own hand at the time; and I know them to be correct and according to the mind of the Lord.[25]

26. Oliver Cowdery (October 1835, relating Moroni's instructions to Joseph Smith on September 22, 1823)

When they [the golden plates] are interpreted the Lord will give the holy priesthood to some, and they shall begin to proclaim this gospel and baptize by water, and after that they shall have power to give the Holy Ghost by the laying on of their hands.[26]

27. Oliver Cowdery (April 1836)

The least among us values more highly his profession, and holds too sacredly that heavenly communication bestowed by the laying on of the hands of those who were clothed with authority, than all that frail, worse than thread-bare hypocritical pretention, which came down through the mother of abominations, of which himself [a reverend] and all others of his profession can boast.[27]

28. Oliver Cowdery (March 23, 1846)

I have cherished a hope, and that one of my fondest, that I might leave such a character as those who might believe in my testimony, after I shall be called hence, might do so, not only for the sake of the truth, but might not <u>blush</u> for the private character of the man who bore that testimony. I have been sensitive on this subject, I admit; but I ought to be so—you would be, under the circumstances, had you stood in the presence of John, with our departed brother Joseph, to receive the Lesser Priesthood—and in the presence of Peter, to receive the Greater, and look down through time, and witness the effects these two must produce.[28]

29. Oliver Cowdery (October 21, 1848)

The priesthood is here. I was present with Joseph when an holy angle from god came down from heaven and confered or restored the Aronic priesthood. And said at the same time that it should remain upon the earth while the earth stands. I was also present with Joseph when the Melchesideck priesthood was confered by the holy angles of god—this was the more necessary in order that by which we then confirmed on each other by the will and commandment of god. This priesthood is also to remain upon the earth until, the Last remnant of time.[29]

30. Oliver Cowdery, as Reported by George A. Smith (October 31, 1848)

Oliver Cowdery, who had just arrived from Wisconsin with his family, on being invited, addressed the meeting. He bore testimony in the most positive terms of the truth of the Book of Mormon—the restoration of the priesthood to the earth, and the mission of Joseph Smith as the prophet of the last days; and told the people if they wanted to follow the right path, to keep the main channel of the stream—where the body of the Church goes, there is the authority; and all these lo here's and lo there's, have no authority; but this people have the true and holy priesthood; "for the angel said unto Joseph Smith Jr., in my hearing, that this priesthood shall remain on earth unto the end." His [Oliver Cowdery's] testimony produced quite a sensation among the gentlemen present who did not belong to the Church, and it was gratefully received by all the saints.[30]

31. Oliver Cowdery (January 13, 1849)

While darkness covered the earth and gross darkness the people; long after the authority to administer in holy things had been taken away, the Lord opened the heavens and sent forth his word for the salvation of Israel. In fulfilment of the sacred Scripture the everlasting Gospel was proclaimed by the mighty angel, (Moroni) who, clothed with the authority of his mission, gave glory to God in the highest. This Gospel is the "stone taken from the mountain without hands." John the Baptist, holding the keys of the Aaronic Priesthood; Peter, James and John, holding the keys of the Melchisedek Priesthood, have also ministered for those who shall be heirs of salvation, and with these ministrations ordained men to the same Priesthoods. These Priesthoods, with their authority, are now, and must continue to be, in the body of the Church of Jesus Christ of Latter-day Saints. Blessed is the Elder who has received the same, and thrice blessed and holy is he who shall endure to the end. Accept assurances, dear Brother, of the unfeigned prayer of him, who, in connection with Joseph the Seer, was blessed with the above ministrations, and who earnestly and devoutly hopes to meet you in the celestial glory.[31]

32. *Reflector* (Palmyra, N.Y.) (1831)

They [missionaries] then proclaimed that there had been no religion in the world for 1500 years,—that no one had been authorized to preach &c. for that period—that Jo Smith had now received a commission from God for that purpose. . . . Smith (they affirmed) had seen God frequently and personally—Cowdery and his friends had frequent interviews with angels.[32]

33. William W. Phelps (December 25, 1834)

The next item I shall notice, is, (a glorious one,) when the angel conferred the "priesthood upon you, his fellow servants." That was an august meeting of men and angels, and brought again, upon earth, the keys of the mysteries of the kingdom of God.[33]

34. LDS Hymnal (1835)

Hymn 26. P.M.

And an angel surely, then,
For a blessing unto men,
Brought the priesthood back again,
In its ancient purity.[34]

35. Parley P. Pratt (1835)

Song III. Long Metre.

The Opening of the Dispensation
of the Fulness of Times.
A voice commissioned from on high,
Hark, hark, it is the angel's cry,
Descending from the throne of light,
His garments shining clear and white.
He comes the gospel to reveal
In fulness, to the sons of men;
Lo! from Cumorah's lonely hill,
There comes a record of God's will!
Translated by the power of God,
His voice bears record to his word;
Again an angel did appear,
As witnesses do record bear.

Restored the priesthood, long since lost,
In truth and power, as at the first;
Thus men commissioned from on high,
Came forth and did repentance cry.[35]

36. Parley P. Pratt (1840)

the church of jesus christ of latter day saints was first organized in the State of New York, in the year of our Lord one thousand eight hundred and thirty, on the sixth day of April. At its first organization, it consisted of six members. The first instruments of its organization were Joseph Smith, jun., and Oliver Cowdery, who profess to have received their authority and priesthood, or apostleship, by direct revelation from God—by the voice of God—by the ministering of angels—and by the Holy Ghost.[36]

37. Parley P. Pratt (January 1842)

Some of those who held the holy priesthood in ancient times, the priesthood which is after the power of an endless life, without beginning of days or end of years—some of those, I say, being raised from the dead, and others translated, still hold the apostleship and priesthood; and it has pleased God to send them as holy angels to earth to reintroduce the pure gospel, and to commission and ordain the first instruments of the Latter-day Saints.[37]

38. Orson Pratt (June 26, 1836)

June 26th [1836]. Being the Sabbath preached in Antwerp village in the forenoon and also in the afternoon upon the faith once delivered to the saints, the falling away of the church, the losing of the authority of the priesthood, the restoration of the church by Ministering of an Angel, Rev. [1]4th chap. In the afternoon at 5 o'clock the members of the church with several others that were favorable met together. The sacrament was administered and also confirmation was administered to three.[38]

39. Orson Pratt (1840)

Also, in the year 1829, Mr Smith and Mr Cowdery, having learned the correct mode of baptism, from the teachings of the Saviour to the ancient Nephites, as recorded in the "Book of Mormon," had a desire to be baptized; but knowing that no one had authority to administer that sacred ordinance in any denomination, they were at a loss to know how the authority was to be restored, and while calling upon the Lord with a desire to be informed on the subject, a holy angel appeared and stood before them, and laid his hands upon their heads, and ordained them, and commanded them to baptize each other, which they accordingly did. . . . In the foregoing, we have related the most important facts concerning the visions and the ministry of the angel to Mr Smith; the discovery of the records; their translation into the English language, and the witnesses raised up to bear testimony of the same. . . . We have also given an account of the restoration of the authority in these days, to administer in the ordinances of the gospel; and of the time of the organization of the church; and of the blessings poured out upon [t]he same [while yet] in its infancy.[39]

40. Orson Pratt (September 30, 1848)

A revelation and restoration to the earth of the *"everlasting gospel"* through the angel Moroni would be of no benefit to the nations, unless some one should be ordained with authority to preach it and administer its ordinances. . . . But why not confer authority by ordination, as well as reveal the everlasting gospel [referring to Moroni]? Because in all probability he had not the right so to do. . . . How then did Mr. Smith obtain the office of an apostle, if Moroni had no authority to ordain him to such office? Mr. Smith testifies that Peter, James, and John came to him in the capacity of ministering angels, and by the laying on of hands ordained him an apostle, and commanded him to preach, baptize, lay on hands for the gift of the Holy Ghost, and administer all other ordinances of the gospel as they themselves did in ancient days. . . . If Mr. Smith had pretended that he received the apostleship by the revelation of the Holy Ghost, without an ordination under the hands of an apostle, we should at once know that his pretensions were vain, and that he was a deceiver. . . . Did John predict the restoration of the gospel by an angel? It is included in Mr. Smith's system. . . . Can any man show that the gospel will not be restored by an angel?[40]

41. David W. Patten (July 1838)

[Referring to Revelation 14:6–7, previously mentioned in the text.] The authority connected with the ordinances, renders the time very desirable to the man of God, and renders him happy, amidst all his trials, and afflictions. To such an one, through the grace of God, we are indebted for this dispensation, as given by the angel of the Lord. . . . And they who sin against this authority given to him—(the before mentioned man of God,)—sins not against him only, but against Moroni, who holds the keys of the stick of Ephraim. And also with Elias, who holds the keys of bringing to pass the restitution of all things, or the restoration of all things. And also John, the son of Zacharias which Zacharias Elias visited, and give promise that he should have a son, and his name should be John, and he should be filled with the spirit of Elias, which John I have sent unto you, my servants Joseph Smith Jr. and Oliver Cowdery, to ordain you to this first priesthood, even as Aaron. . . . And also, Peter, and James and John, whom I have sent unto you, by whom I have ordained you, and confirmed you to be apostles, and especial witnesses of my name, and bear the keys of your ministry, and of the same things I revealed unto them; unto whom I have committed the keys of my kingdom, and a dispensation of the gospel for the last time, and for the fulness of times.[41]

42. Oliver Granger (September 10, 1839)

Br. [Oliver] Granger occupied the fore part of the day, and gave a very interesting account of his life; of the administration of angels, who testified of the work of God in the world; a vision of the Book of Mormon, the means by which he was brought into the church, and then bore testimony to the restoration of the Priesthood.[42]

43. John Taylor (February 11, 1840)

11 [February 1840] Tuesday. . . . Mr Bradshaw said he could tell if [a] man had the Holy Ghost—yet could not tell how. We shewd him a Man might have the Gift of Wisdom, etc. and he not see it—told him he did not know what the H[oly]. G[host]. was. Mr. M[atthews] asked Bro. [John] Taylor where he got his Authority. Ans: By Prophecy and laying on of hands of those who had Authority, etc. This came by the Ministration of an holy Angel. Bro. T[aylor]. then asked where he got his. Ans: from the Bishop of Lincoln, and that was as good as his Angel, "and you have no more Power than I have and if you have, let us see it. I say if you have any Power shew it, either from Heaven or Hell. I don't fear you. I say if you have any Power from Heaven or Hell shew it." We said we were sent not [to] shew Signs but to call on all to repent, Priests and People.[43]

44. Erastus Snow (December 1840)

(Erastus Snow to Benjamin Winchester, Letter, December 1840, Philadelphia.) Little more than ten years has passed since the organization of the church of Christ in these last days; since the angel of the Lord said to our much esteemed brother J. Smith, and his faithful companion, O. Cowdery, "To you my fellow servants am I sent to confer this pristhood, that through you it may be conferred upon others." The morning that heavenly messenger executed this important mission, is one long to be remembered by all the saints.[44]

45. Erastus Snow and Benjamin Winchester (1841)

We also believe and testify, that the Lord has renewed the gospel dispensation and in fulfilment of numerous predictions of the prophets and apostles, sent his holy angel to commission men to preach the fulness of the everlasting gospel to all nations.[45]

46. Benjamin Winchester (February 15, 1841)

God does not send his angels to act as priests on earth, but to bear his messages to men; also to make known his covenants to them. It is not said that this angel in person should preach the gospel to all nations [referring to the angel prophesied of in Revelation 14:6–7]; but that he should come with it, or have it to preach to all nations. It is the work of the servants of God, to preach the gospel to all nations. Indeed, in consequence of apostacy, the Lord has taken the priesthood, or authority from the church; therefore, this angel was to be sent to restore this authority, or commission men to preach the gospel to all nations.[46]

47. Benjamin Winchester (April 1, 1841)

As soon as the Book of Mormon was translated, the Lord sent his holy angel with the holy priesthood, which was conferred upon men; thus fulfilling the saying of John: "I saw another angel fly in the midst of heaven having the everlasting gospel to preach unto them that dwell on the earth, &c." . . . the Book of Mormon has come forth on this land, and the Lord has sent his angel to confer the holy priesthood upon his servants once more, or renewed the gospel dispensation, and organized his kingdom, &c. . . . the

Lord has sent forth the Book of Mormon, also his angel to confer the holy priesthood and organized his church.[47]

48. Benjamin Winchester (1843)

Soon after this Book was discovered, the Lord sent His angel with the Holy priesthood, which was conferred upon Mr. Smith, and O. Cowdery who as a scribe assisted in the work of translation: they immediately baptized each other, and also others that believed the work.[48]

49. Orson Hyde (June 15, 1841)

I began with the Priesthood, and showed that the saints were not under the necessity of tracing back the dark and bloody stream of papal superstition to find their authority, neither were they compelled to seek for it among the floating and trancient notions of Protestant reformers; but God has sent his holy angel directly from heaven with this seal and authority, and conferred it upon men with his own hands: quoting the letter and testimony of O. Cowdery.[49]

50. Orson Hyde (1842)

While calling upon the Lord with a desire to be informed on the subject, a holy angel appeared, stood before them, and laid his hands upon their heads and ordained them. Then he commanded these two men to baptize each other, which they did accordingly. [Hyde then gives Oliver Cowdery's 1834 *Messenger and Advocate* account, document 23.][50]

51. Heber C. Kimball and Wilford Woodruff (September 15, 1841)

[The Lord] sent a holy angel, who hath committed the everlasting Gospel, and restored the priesthood.[51]

52. Charles Thompson (1841)

Immediately after it was translated God sent an holy angel from the midst of heaven, with the Priesthood and authority of Jesus Christ, to preach the everlasting Gospel unto them who dwell on the earth, and to every nation, kindred, tongue and people, saying, with a loud voice, fear God and give glory to him, for the hour of his judgment is come; and worship him that made heaven and earth, and the sea, and the fountains of water. And this Priesthood and authority has been conferred upon many men, (and will be conferred upon many more,) who have escaped the corruptions that are in the world through lust.[52]

53. George J. Adams (1841)

The Church of Jesus Christ of Latter Day Saints was first organized in the State of New York, in the year of our Lord one thousand eight hundred and thirty, on the sixth day of April. At its first organization, it consisted of six members. The first instruments of its organization were Joseph Smith, Jun. and Oliver Cowdery, who received their authority and priesthood, or apostleship, by direct revelation from God—by the voice of God—by the ministering of angels—and by the Holy Ghost.[53]

54. George J. Adams (1849)

[Joseph Smith and Oliver Cowdery] were at a loss to know how the authority was to be restored, and while calling upon the Lord with a desire to be informed upon the subject, a holy angel appeared—stood before them—laid his hands upon their heads—ordained them—and commanded them to baptize each other, which they accordingly did.[54]

55. Ebenezer Robinson (January 1, 1842)

These preachers profess no authority from antiquity to administer gospel ordinances, but say that an angel has come down from the midst of heaven, and conferred on them the priesthood and authority to preach and administer the everlasting gospel unto them that dwell on the earth.[55]

56. Alfred Cordon (April 18, 1842)

Monday 18th [April 1842] . . . as soon has I got home I discovered that Mr Brabazon Ellis, Incumbent of St Pauls Church Burslem, had sent desiring to hold a little conversation with one or more of the Latter Day Saints, immediately I went Elder Wm Lloyd accompanied me we found another Minister with him, and after the usual compliments he said let us pray we kneeled down and he prayed that the Lord would enlighten both our hearts that we might be blessd with wisdom and Intelligence, and I felt in my heart to say—Amen—After Prayer He asked me who Ordained me in the Church of Latter Day Saints I told him Wm Clayton, I then said and Sir, Who ordained you He answered The Bishop, He then asked me who Ordained Wm Clayton I answered Heber C. Kimball, I then asked him who Ordained the Bishop; He answered; Another Bishop; He then asked me who Ordained Heber C. Kimball; I answered, Joseph Smith and said I; Joseph Smith was Ordained by Holy Angels that were sent by commandment from the Most High God.[56]

57. Warren Foote (August 29, 1842)

29th [August 1842] We returned home, satisfied with sectarian nonsense, and feeling thankful to the Lord for the revelation of His gospel through His servant Joseph Smith, on whom he bestowed his Holy Priesthood through the laying on of hands of the ancient Apostles' Peter James and John thereby opening up the way whereby mankind can be saved and exalted in His Celestial Kingdom, through repentance and baptism and the laying on of hands for the reception of the Holy Ghost, by those ordained into this Holy Priesthood.[57]

58. Moses Martin (1842)

I, now, as a living witness of God, feel it my indispensable duty, to declare to all men, who may chance to peruse this little work, that the Angel of God has committed the everlasting gospel, with the Holy Priesthood, unto man, in fulfilment of John's prediction: that God has now a church on earth, organized after the apostolic order, with all the gifts and graces which belong to it.[58]

59. James Henry Flanigan (April 14, 1844)

Sunday 14 [April 1844] Mr Fishers ____ 21, & 22 verses of 28 cptr of Isa _________ Book of Mormon, Gathering of Israel, 2nd coming of Christ, restoration of ______, Reserection of ________, Milenium, & the manner & means ____ will make use of bringing ________ about, for ______ by giving ________, sending his Angel with______ Priesthood, ___ up a Prophet, sending Fishers & hunters to gather sons of Irael & build up Zion &c &c.[59]

60. Lorenzo Snow (1844)

I now bear testimony, having the highest assurance, by revelation from God, that this prophecy [Revelation 14:6] has already been fulfilled, that an *Angel from God* has visited man in these last days, and restored that which has long been lost, even the priesthood,—the keys of the kingdom,—the fulness of the everlasting Gospel.[60]

61. William I. Appleby (1844)

In the year 1830, after the Book was translated and published, the Angel of God according to promise conferred the Holy priesthood upon Mr. Smith, and gave unto him commandments to Baptize with water in the name of Jesus, and build up the Church of Christ; which accordingly was organized April 6th, A.D. 1830, with six members.[61]

62. William I. Appleby (December 30, 1848)

He [Oliver Cowdery] was one of the first Apostles in this Church, and baptised Br. Joseph the Prophet at first, and then Br. Joseph administered to him the same ordinance, after they had both received the Holy Priesthood from under the hands of the angel of God![62]

63. Jedediah M. Grant (1844)

After he had obtained and translated the ancient American Records, (commonly called the Book of Mormon,) and had received authority from the Legates of Heaven, delegated and sent unto him by the Lord to ordain him to the Holy Priesthood, giving him the right to ordain others, that the Gospel might be preached in all the world for a witness unto all nations.[63]

64. Quorum of the Twelve (April 6, 1845)

The great Elohim, Jehovah, had been pleased once more to speak from the heavens, and also to commune with man upon the earth, by means of open visions, and by the ministration of HOLY MESSENGERS.

By this means the great and eternal High Priesthood, after the order of his Son (even the Apostleship) has been restored or returned to the earth.

This High Priesthood or Apostleship, holds the keys of the kingdom of God, with power to bind on earth that which shall be bound in heaven, and to loose on earth that which shall be loosed in heaven; and, in fine, to do and to administer in all things pertaining to the ordinances, organization, government, and direction of the kingdom of God.[64]

65. Reuben Miller (September 1846)

Who was Joseph Smith? A man appointed of God to lay the foundation of this, "The Dispensation of the fullness of Times." He was ordained to the Aaronic Priesthood by John the Baptist, and received the keys of the kingdom and the keys of "the Dispensation of the fulness of Times" from Peter, James and John: and the restoring power of the Melchisedek Priesthood from Elias, and the sealing and binding powers of the same from Elijah.[65]

66. Reuben Miller (1847)

[Miller briefly retells Joseph Smith's account of the Aaronic Priesthood restoration as given in the *Times and Seasons*, then] . . . Now when I speak of the Melchisedek priesthood, I wish so to be understood. And when I speak of the Aaronic, I do not wish the reader to understand that I hold its jurisdiction or authority as being over that of the greater, or Melchisedek. They are two priesthoods and when restored to earth through Joseph, by different angels, and at different times. . . . He [Joseph Smith] received from John the baptist, according to promise, the priesthood after the order of Aaron, on the 15th day of May, 1829, in the manner and form as I have already shown. And a short time after, the Melchisedek priesthood from Peter, James, and John, the ancient Apostles.[66]

67. William E. McLellin (March and April 1847)

[The Church] very soon increased in numbers, and branches of it were organized and established in various places, by the labors, and through the instrumentality of its first Ministers, who had received their authority direct from Heaven—from the great Head of the Church—even Christ the Lord; as did men in days of old—by the ministrations of holy Angels, and by the direct commandments of God from heaven. . . . Joseph was first called by an holy angel, Strang was first called by Joseph—not a like here Again, when the holy angel visited and ordained Joseph, Oliver was with him, that it might be as the Lord had said: "In the mouth of TWO or three witnesses shall every word be established." 2 Cor. 13:1. Who was with Strang, when he was ordained? No person. Not alike here. "And also with Peter and James and John, whom I have sent unto you [Joseph and Oliver,] by whom I have ordained you, and confirmed you to be Apostles, and especial witnesses of my name."[67]

68. William E. McLellin (March 1848)

We hold that JOSEPH SMITH and OLIVER COWDERY, in May 1829, received the authority of the lesser priesthood, and the keys of it, by the visitation and the administration of the angel John, the Baptist: and that on the 6th day of April, 1830, the day on which the *church* was organized, they by a revelation from *Jesus Christ* by the unanimous consent and vote of those whom they had baptised, and by the laying on of hands Oliver Cowdery and Joseph Smith were ordained to the office of Elder, in the *high* priesthood: And that on the same day JOSEPH SMITH was ordained under the hands of O. Cowdery, to the offices in the Melchisedek priesthood.[68]

69. Brigham Young (August 15, 1847)

When Brother Joseph received the Preisthood He did not recieve all at once, but He was A prophet Seer & Revelator before He recieved the fulness of the Priesthood & keys of the kingdom.

He first recieved the Aronick Priesthood and Keys from under the hands of John the Baptist. He then had not power to lay on hands to confirm the Church but afterwards He recieved the Patriarchal or Melchisedick Priesthood from under the Hands of Peter James & John who were of the Twelve Apostles & were the Presidency when the other Apostles were Absent. From those Apostles Joseph Smith recieved every key power, Blessing, & Privilege of the Highest Authority of the Melchezedick Priesthood ever committed to man on the earth which they held.[69]

70. Hiram Page (March 4, 1848)

In the beginning we find the first ordinations were by Peter James and John they ordained Joseph and Oliver; to what priesthood were they ordained; the answer must be to the Holy priesthood on the office of an elder or an apostle which is an additional grace added to the office of an elder these offices Oliver received from those holy messengers before the 6th of april 1830.[70]

Notes to the Documents of the Priesthood Restoration

1. Oliver Cowdery's 1829 manuscript, "A Commandment from God" (or "Articles of the Church of Christ"), Church Archives, The Church of Jesus Christ of Latter-day Saints, Salt Lake City, quoted in Robert J. Woodford, "The Historical Development of the Doctrine and Covenants," 3 vols. (Ph.D. diss., Brigham Young University, 1974), 1:288. This document ends with the declaration: "Behold I am Oliver I am an Apostle of Jesus Christ by the will of God the Father & the Lord Jesus Christ." See p. 113n90 above.

2. "The Mormon Creed," *Painesville (Ohio) Telegraph*, April 19, 1831, 4. The same text with minor changes was also published in *Evening and the Morning Star*, June 1832, 1; and Book of Commandments (1833), ch. 24, pp. 47–48. For a listing of early printings of this text, see Woodford, "Historical Development of the Doctrine and Covenants," 1:296–97. In addition to changes in punctuation, the Book of Commandments and the *Evening and the Morning Star* versions contain the following differences from the *Telegraph* printing: both later renditions spell out the dates instead of using numbers and write "sixth day of the month" instead of "sixth day of the same." In these versions, the last names "Smith" and "Cowdery" are omitted, and the repeated phrase is "elder of this church" instead of "elder of the church." They do not contain the words "God the Father," but read "Lord and Savior" instead of just "Lord." They close with the word "forever" as opposed to the "ever" of the earlier version. Furthermore, the Book of Commandments rendition opens with a lowercase "church of Christ," and the *Evening and the Morning Star* capitalizes "Elder," "Apostle," and "Amen."

3. Book of Commandments (1833), ch. 15, p. 35.

4. *Doctrine and Covenants of the Church of the Latter Day Saints*, comp. Joseph Smith and others (Kirtland, Ohio: F. G. Williams, 1835), 180; see also *Evening and the Morning Star*, March 1833, 78; May 1836, 155; *Times and Seasons* 4 (March 1, 1843): 122; and *Millennial Star* 4 (February 1844): 151. These verses did not appear in the earlier text of the revelation printed in the Book of Commandments, 1833. Joseph Smith recalled in 1839 that all of Section 27 was received as a revelation in August 1830 but that most of the revelation, including these verses, was not recorded until September 1830.

> Early in the month of August Newel Knight and his wife paid us a visit at my place in Harmony; Neither his wife nor mine had been as yet confirmed, it was proposed that we should confirm them, and partake together of the sacrament, before he and his wife should leave us—In order to prepare for this I set out to procure some wine for the occasion, but had gone only a short distance when I was met by a heavenly messenger, and received the following revelation, the first paragraph

> of which was written at this time, and the remainder in the September following. (Dean C. Jessee, ed., *The Papers of Joseph Smith*, 2 vols. [Salt Lake City: Deseret Book, 1989–92], 1:320–21)

No manuscript copy of these verses dating from before the publication of the Doctrine and Covenants in 1835 has been identified. See Woodford, "Historical Development of the Doctrine and Covenants," 1:395–97.

5. 1844 Doctrine and Covenants version of current D&C 112:30–32. The 1844 text is the same as Vilate Kimball's copy sent to Heber C. Kimball in her September 6, 1837, letter from Kirtland, in which she says, "I copyed it from Elder Marshs book as he wrote it from Joseph's mouth." The entire letter is found in Woodford, "Historical Development of the Doctrine and Covenants," 3:1477, 1480, 1490–94.

6. Joseph Smith, History (dated between July 20 and November 27, 1832, by Dean C. Jessee), in Jessee, *Papers of Joseph Smith*, 1:3.

7. Reported by Reverend Richmond Taggart to Reverend Jonathon Goings, Cleveland, Ohio, March 2, 1833, in Jonathon Goings Collection, American Baptist Historical Society, Rochester, New York.

8. Patriarchal Blessings, Book 1 (1835), 12, Church Archives, The Church of Jesus Christ of Latter-day Saints, Salt Lake City. The end of this blessing contains this information about its origin: "Oliver Cowdery, Clerk and Recorder. Given December 18th, 1833, and recorded in this book October 2, 1835." This particular blessing was evidently given for Oliver Cowdery, but the name specifying the recipient has been omitted. This passage comes from the last sixth of the blessing.

9. Found in the Kirtland High Council Minutes, February 12, 1834, 27, Church Archives. Compare the further report by Orson Hyde of the following testimony by Joseph Smith:

> Brother Joseph observed to Bishop that he knew he had lied before he confessed it; that his declarations were not only false in themselves, but they involved a false principle. An angel, said Joseph, may administer the word of the Lord unto men, and bring intelligence to them from heaven upon various subjects; but no true angel from God will ever come to ordain any man, because they have once been sent to establish the priesthood by ordaining me thereunto; and the priesthood being once established on earth, with power to ordain others, no heavenly messenger will ever come to interfere with that power by ordaining any more. He referred to the angel that came to Cornelius and told Cornelius to send for Peter; but if there had been no Peter with keys and power to administer, the angel might have done it himself; but as there was, the angel would not interfere. Saul was directed to go to Ananias for instruction and to be administered to by him;

but if there had been no Ananias with power and authority on the earth to administer in the name of Christ, the Lord might have done it himself. You may therefore know, from this time forward, that if any man comes to you professing to be ordained by an angel, he is either a liar or has been imposed upon in consequence of transgression by an angel of the devil, for this priesthood shall never be taken away from this church.

This testimony was delivered in an upper room, in the south-west corner of the White Store and dwelling-house, formerly occupied by Whitney and Gilbert, situated on Kirtland Flats. (*Millennial Star* 8 [November 20, 1846]: 139)

10. Kirtland High Council Minutes, April 21, 1834, 43–44.

11. Stephen Post, Journal, Stephen Post Papers, March 27, 1836, microfilm, Church Archives.

12. Joseph Smith, History, 1839, in Jessee, *Papers of Joseph Smith*, 1:290–91; also published with minor changes in spelling, punctuation, and capitalization in *Times and Seasons* 3 (August 1, 1842): 865–66.

13. Joseph Smith, History [1839 Draft], in Jessee, *Papers of Joseph Smith*, 1:238–39.

14. Joseph Smith, History, 1839, in Jessee, *Papers of Joseph Smith*, 1:299–300; also published with only slight changes in spelling, capitalization, and punctuation in *Times and Seasons* 3 (September 15, 1842): 915. Angle brackets indicate an insertion above the line.

15. Joseph Smith, Sermon (ca. 1839), Willard Richards Pocket Companion, in *The Words of Joseph Smith: The Contemporary Accounts of the Nauvoo Discourses of the Prophet Joseph*, ed. Andrew F. Ehat and Lyndon W. Cook, Religious Studies Monograph Series, no. 6 (Provo, Utah: Religious Studies Center, Brigham Young University, 1980), 9. James Burgess apparently had access to and copied this passage into his own journal around 1841. James Burgess, Journals, 1841–48, Church Archives. See also *History of the Church*, 3:387. On March 22, 1839, Joseph Smith had affirmed in a letter from Liberty Jail to Isaac Galland the following related general principle: "We believe that no man can administer salvation through the gospel, to the souls of men, in the name of Jesus Christ, except he is authorized from God, by revelation, or by being ordained by some one whom God hath sent by revelation." Dean C. Jessee, ed. and comp., *The Personal Writings of Joseph Smith*, rev. ed. (Salt Lake City: Deseret Book; Provo, Utah: Brigham Young University Press, 2002), 459.

16. Joseph Smith to The Church of Jesus Christ of Latter Day Saints, September 6, 1842, Nauvoo, Illinois, in *Times and Seasons* 3 (October 1, 1842): 935–36; Doctrine and Covenants 128:20–21.

17. Joseph Smith, Sermon, March 10, 1844, recorded by James Burgess in his notebook, in Ehat and Cook, *Words of Joseph Smith*, 332–33. For an 1870 recollection of these words of Joseph Smith, see "Biography of David Osborne, Senior," typescript, 63–64, L. Tom Perry Special Collections, Harold B. Lee Library, Brigham Young University, Provo, Utah:

> He spoke of Adam, Enoch, Noah, Moses, The patriarchs and some of the Prophets, telling what keys each one held, and the work he accomplished in his day, down to Jesus and the apostles. Now, says he, having told you so much about these ancient men of God, I will proceed to tell you something of myself. . . . He told us that Peter, James, and John, having held the Keys of the Kingdom in their day had come and confered the same upon him and his brethren.

18. Joseph Smith, Sermon, March 10, 1844, in Franklin D. Richards, "Scriptural Items," in Ehat and Cook, *Words of Joseph Smith*, 334.

19. Joseph Smith, Sermon, March 10, 1844, recorded by Wilford Woodruff in his journal, in Ehat and Cook, *Words of Joseph Smith*, 327.

20. "The Golden Bible," *Painesville (Ohio) Telegraph*, November 16, 1830, 3.

21. *Painesville Telegraph*, December 7, 1830.

22. Joseph Smith, History, 1834–36, in Jessee, *Papers of Joseph Smith*, 1:21.

23. Oliver Cowdery to W. W. Phelps, September 7, 1834, Norton, Ohio, in *Messenger and Advocate*, October 1834, 14–16.

24. Kirtland High Council Minutes, under heading of February 21, 1835, 159. The occasion was the blessing of several new members of the Twelve Apostles. Following their blessings, Oliver Cowdery gave them this charge.

25. Patriarchal Blessings, Book 1 (1835): 8–9. The end of this blessing contains this information about its origin: "Oliver Cowdery, Clerk and Recorder. Given in Kirtland, December 18, 1833, and recorded September 1835."

26. *Messenger and Advocate*, October 1835, 199.

27. Oliver Cowdery, "The Atlas Article," *Messenger and Advocate*, April 1836, 303.

28. Oliver Cowdery to Phineas Young, March 23, 1846, Tiffin, Seneca County, Ohio. Quoted in Stanley R. Gunn, *Oliver Cowdery: Second Elder and Scribe* (Salt Lake City: Bookcraft, 1962), 161.

29. Reuben Miller, Journal, October 21, 1848, microfilm of holograph, 14, Church Archives. Report of "Conference held on Misqueto Creek Council Bluffs October 21st ["21st" may have been added later, as it was written in a different color ink] 1848."

30. George A. Smith to Orson Pratt, October 20 and 31, 1848, Carbonca, Council Bluffs, Iowa, photocopy of typescript; reprinted, with a few minor differences, in Manuscript History of Brigham Young, October 31, 1848, 78, Church Archives.

31. Oliver Cowdery to Elder Samuel W. Richards, January 13, 1849, in *Deseret Evening News*, March 22, 1884, 2. The location of the original letter is unknown, but scholars find little reason to doubt the authenticity of this piece and its 1849 date.

32. *Palmyra (N.Y.) Reflector*, February 14, 1831, 102.

33. William W. Phelps, "Letter No. 4," *Messenger and Advocate*, February 1835, 66.

34. Emma Smith, *A Collection of Sacred Hymns for The Church of the Latter Day Saints* (Kirtland, Ohio: F. G. Williams, 1835), 33; also published in *A Collection of Sacred Hymns for the Church of the Latter Day Saints*, selected and published by David W. Rogers (New York: C. Vinten, 1838), 12; and in Benjamin C. Elsworth, *A Collection of Sacred Hymns for the Church of Christ of the Latter Day Saints* (n.p.: Benjamin C. Elsworth, 1839), 13. See also LDS Hymnal (1835), Hymn no. 72: "The keys which Peter did receive, / To rear a kingdom God to please. / Have once more been confer'd to man, / To bring about Jehovah's plan"; and LDS Hymnal (1835), Hymn 76: "Such blessings to the human race, / Once more are tender'd by God's grace; / The Priesthood is again restor'd, / For this let God be long ador'd." See further *A Collection of Sacred Hymns, for the Use of All Saints, Selected by a Committee in a Branch of The Church of Jesus Christ of Latter Day Saints* (Austin: New Era Office, 1847), 77, Hymn no. 55: "The chosen of God and the friend of men, / He [Joseph Smith] brought the priesthood back again."

35. Parley P. Pratt, *The Millennium, a Poem* (Boston: Parley P. Pratt, 1835), 38. Also published without the title and with several minor punctuation changes in Rogers, *Collection of Sacred Hymns*, 104; and in Elsworth, *Collection of Sacred Hymns*, 105–6.

36. Parley P. Pratt, *Late Persecution of The Church of Jesus Christ of Latter Day Saints* (New York: J. W. Harrison, 1840), iii.

37. Parley P. Pratt, "Dialogue between a Latter-day Saint and an Enquirer after Truth," *Millennial Star* 2 (January 1842): 131; also published as a pamphlet by the author in Manchester, England (1842).

38. Elden Jay Watson, comp., *The Orson Pratt Journals* (Salt Lake City: Watson, 1975), 84–85.

39. Orson Pratt, *Interesting Account of Several Remarkable Visions, and the Late Discovery of Ancient American Records* (Edinburgh: Ballantyne and Hughes, 1840), 23–24.

40. Orson Pratt, *Divine Authority; or, The Question Was Joseph Sent of God?* (Liverpool: R. James, 1848, 1851), 4–5, 7; an almost exact duplicate of this is in *The Frontier Guardian* 1 (February 7, 1849): 1.

41. David W. Patten, "To the Saints Scattered Abroad," *Elders' Journal of the Church of Christ of Latter Day Saints* 1 (July 1838): 41–42. This passage

includes a quotation from what was at that time section L in the Doctrine and Covenants.

42. John P. Green[e] to D. C. Smith and E. Robinson, September 10, 1839, Monmouth County, N.J., in *Times and Seasons* 1 (December 1839): 28.

43. Joseph Fielding Diary, typescript, 55, Perry Special Collections.

44. *The Gospel Reflector* 1 (January 1, 1841): 22.

45. Erastus Snow and Benjamin Winchester, *An Address to the Citizens of Salem and Vicinity*, photocopy of original (n.p., [1841]), 5, Perry Special Collections.

46. *Gospel Reflector* 1 (February 15, 1841): 89.

47. *Gospel Reflector* 1 (April 1, 1841): 177, 183, 187.

48. Benjamin Winchester, *A History of the Priesthood from the Beginning of the World to the Present Time* (Philadelphia: Brown, Bicking, and Guilbert, 1843), 147.

49. Orson Hyde to President [Joseph] Smith, *Times and Seasons* 2 (October 1, 1841): 551.

50. Orson Hyde, *Ein Ruf aus der Wüste, eine Stimme aus dem Schoose der Erde* (A Cry from the Wilderness, a Voice from the Dust of the Earth) (Frankfurt: n.p., 1842), typescript (translated from the German by Justus Ernst), 27, Church Archives; reprinted with translation in Jessee, *Papers of Joseph Smith*, 1:402–25.

51. Heber C. Kimball and Wilford Woodruff, "The Word of the Lord to the Citizens of London of Every Sect and Denomination: And to Every Individual into Whose Hands It May Fall," *Times and Seasons* 2 (September 15, 1841): 538.

52. Charles Thompson, *Evidence in Proof of the Book of Mormon Being a Divinely Inspired Record* (Batavia, N.Y.: D. D. Waite, 1841), 144–45. Similarly, Benjamin Winchester held that Revelation 14:7 "relates to the renewal of the gospel covenant, the restoration of the priesthood." *Gospel Reflector* 1 (February 15, 1841): 86.

53. George J. Adams, *A Few Plain Facts, Shewing the Folly, Wickedness, and Imposition of the Rev. Timothy R. Matthews; also a Short Sketch of the Rise, Faith, and Doctrine of the Church of Jesus Christ of Latter Day Saints* (Bedford, England: C. B. Merry, 1841), 12; reprinted in *Times and Seasons* 4 (March 15, 1843): 141.

54. George J. Adams, *A True History of the Rise of The Church of Jesus Christ of Latter Day Saints—of the Restoration of the Holy Priesthood, and of the Late Discovery of Ancient American Records* (Baltimore: Hoffman, [1849]), 27.

55. Ebenezer Robinson, ed., "Evidences in the Proof of the Book of Mormon," *Times and Seasons* 3 (January 1, 1842): 644.

56. Alfred Cordon, Reminiscences and Journals, April 18, 1842, microfilm, 77–79, Church Archives.

57. Warren Foote, Autobiography and Journals, August 29, 1842, typescript, 53, Perry Special Collections. Because this diary appears to be a combination of reminiscences and other texts copied from a journal that was kept earlier, it is difficult to ascertain whether this is a reflection or a contemporary observation.

58. Moses Martin, *A Treatise on the Fulness of the Everlasting Gospel* (New York: J. W. Harrison, 1842), 54–55.

59. James Henry Flanigan Diaries, April 14, 1844, 105. Much of this section is in a form of shorthand and undecipherable to this writer. Blank lines have been inserted in those areas that cannot be read.

60. Lorenzo Snow, *The Only Way to Be Saved* (London: F. Shephard, 1844), 11–12.

61. William I. Appleby, *A Dissertation on Nebuchadnezzar's Dream . . . Together with a Synopsis of the Origin and Faith of the Church of "Latter-day Saints"* (Philadelphia: Brown, Bicking, and Guilbert, 1844), 23.

62. William I. Appleby, Biography and Journal, December 30, 1848, microfilm, 247, Church Archives.

63. Jedediah M. Grant, *Collection of Facts Relative to the Course Taken by Elder Sidney Rigdon* (Philadelphia: Brown, Bicking, and Guilbert, 1844), 1.

64. Parley P. Pratt, *Proclamation of the Twelve Apostles of the Church of Jesus Christ of Latter-day Saints. To all the Kings of the World, to the President of the United States of America; to the Governors of the Several States, and to the Rulers and People of all Nations* (Liverpool: Wilford Woodruff, 1845), 1–2 (written from New York).

65. Reuben Miller, *James J. Strang, Weighed in the Balance of Truth, and Found Wanting. His Claims as First President of the Melchisedek Priesthood Refuted* (Burlington, Wis.: n.p., September 1846), 12–13.

66. Reuben Miller, *Truth Shall Prevail: A Short Reply to an Article Published in the Voree Herald (Reveille), by J. C. Bennett and the Willful Falsehoods of J. J. Strang* (Burlington, Wis.: n.p., 1847), 7, 9.

67. *The Ensign of Liberty of the Church of Christ* 1 (March and April 1847): 2, 31.

68. *The Ensign of Liberty of the Church of Christ* 1 (March 1848): 67.

69. Wilford Woodruff, *Wilford Woodruff's Journal, 1833–1898, Typescript*, ed. Scott G. Kenney, 9 vols. (Midvale, Utah: Signature Books, 1983–84), 3:257.

70. Hiram Page to William, March 4, 1848, Fishing River, photocopy of original, Library-Archives, Community of Christ, Independence, Missouri.

Desk in the room of the restored John Johnson home, Hiram, Ohio, in which "The Vision," now known as Doctrine and Covenants 76, was received concurrently by Joseph Smith and Sidney Rigdon.

Parting the Veil: Joseph Smith's Seventy-six Documented Visionary Experiences

Alexander L. Baugh

Joseph Smith the seer ushered in the dispensation of the fullness of times. His role was known and prophesied of anciently. The Lord promised Joseph of Egypt that in the last days a "choice seer" would come through his lineage and would bring his seed to a knowledge of the covenants made to Abraham, Isaac, and Jacob (2 Ne. 3:7; JST Gen. 50:27–28). "That seer will the Lord bless," Joseph prophesied, specifically indicating that "his name shall be called after me" (2 Ne. 3:14–15; see also JST Gen. 50:33). Significantly, in the revelation received during the organizational meeting of the Church on April 6, 1830, the first title given to the first elder was that of seer: "Behold, there shall be a record kept . . . and in it thou [Joseph Smith] shalt be called a seer, a translator, a prophet, an apostle of Jesus Christ" (D&C 21:1).

In the Book of Mormon, Ammon defined a seer as one who possessed "a gift from God" to translate ancient records (Mosiah 8:13; see also 28:11–16). However, the seeric gift is not limited to translation, hence Ammon's additional statement that "a seer is a revelator and a prophet also; and a gift which is greater can no man have" (Mosiah 8:16). In actuality, a seer is a see-er.[1] Among other gifts and powers, he sees visions that are seen with spiritual eyes.[2] This study attempts to compile and analyze all of the known visions, visitations, or visual revelations experienced by the Prophet Joseph Smith.

Visions can take various forms. Personal visitations or appearances of deity, angels, or even Satan and his emissaries certainly come under the heading of visions. Visions can also include seeing vivid images where the veil is lifted from an individual's mind in order to see and comprehend the things of God. Certain dreams could be considered visions, particularly when heavenly or spiritual messages are conveyed. Finally, certain revelations received through the Urim and Thummim mediums such as the Nephite interpreters and the seer stone may also be classified, in the ancient sense, as visions.

While the visions received by Joseph Smith were also revelatory experiences, revelations were not always visionary. Hence, in researching Joseph Smith's visions, I attempted to distinguish between visions and other kinds of inspiration or revelation. More often than not, when a vision was involved, the wording of the source material indicated that a vision—not a more general "revelation"—had been received. However, in some instances, the visual nature of the experience was not quite clear, so I made some judgment calls as to whether a particular revelation involved a vision based on the graphic detail in the account and the perceptual circumstances of the manifestation.

This difficulty in determining what actually constitutes a vision is illustrated by the following example. In January 1841, Joseph Smith gave a detailed description of the Apostle Paul's physical appearance and mannerisms:

> He is about five foot high; very dark hair; dark complexion; dark skin; large Roman nose; sharp face; small black eyes, penetrating as eternity; round shoulders; a whining voice, except when elevated and then it almost resembles the roaring of a Lion. He was a good orator active and deligent, always employing himself in doing good to his fellow men.[3]

A cursory reading of the Prophet's statement might lead to the conclusion that his knowledge of Paul's physical characteristics could have been learned only by means of a vision. However, the Prophet's description resembles depictions of Paul found in familiar apocryphal writings.[4] Thus, while Joseph may have received an actual vision of Paul, he possibly gained his understanding of the ancient Apostle's appearance from the traditional Christian literature of the day and accepted it as accurate. Due to this ambiguity and in the interest of cautious scholarship, I have not included the Prophet's statement on Paul among the visions listed in the documents below.

Three major points became apparent as I researched Joseph Smith's visions. First, and perhaps most remarkable, is the sheer number of visions the Prophet received. The majority of these visions are not found in the standard works but pervade the Prophet's own history and the records kept by contemporaries who were present when a vision was received or when Joseph Smith spoke about his sacred communications. The major purpose of this study is simply to catalogue those visions, many of which are not generally known. As I began collecting the accounts of the visions, I realized that any attempt to number the visions would risk miscounting, since evidence of visions relies upon documentation, and some visions may have been purposely unrecorded. Of one vision Joseph remarked, "I could explain a hundred fold more than I ever have of the glories of the kingdoms manifested to me in the vision were I permitted, and were the people prepared to receive them."[5]

Second, the Prophet was privileged to receive so many visions that they might seem almost commonplace experiences for him, but they were not. Each was supernal. In 1843 he said, "It is my meditation all the day, and more than my meat and drink, to know how I shall make the Saints of God comprehend the visions that roll like an overflowing surge before my mind."[6] Because his visionary experiences were so frequent, it is understandable if he left out several details or failed to record certain events altogether.

Finally, in a number of instances, others witnessed Joseph Smith's visionary experiences. Oliver Cowdery, David Whitmer, Martin Harris, Sidney Rigdon, Heber C. Kimball, Frederick G. Williams, John Murdock, Zebedee Coltrin, and others were present when the Prophet had visions, often seeing the manifestation with him. The recorded statements of these witnesses and co-participants give additional testimony and credibility to the reality of the Prophet's seeric experiences.[7]

For clarity and organization, the Prophet's visions will be discussed in a historical context using two periods: 1820 to 1830 and 1831 to 1844.

Joseph Smith's Visions, 1820–1830

Joseph Smith's visions between 1820 and 1830 fall into three of the broad categories mentioned earlier: personal visitations of deity, angels, and Satan; visions received via the seer stone and the Urim and Thummim; and visions opened to the mind. One vision in particular seems to be in a category of its own.

Visitations

In the Book of Mormon, Ammon said that through a seer "secret things [shall] be made manifest, and hidden things shall come to light" (Mosiah 8:16). Joseph Smith brought to light many truths he learned from heavenly beings, and he learned to distinguish those truths from their opposites through his encounters with Satan.

The First Vision. The most magnificent and certainly the most historically and doctrinally significant theophany occurred in the Sacred Grove in spring 1820, when the Father and the Son—and "many angels," according to Joseph's 1835 account—ushered in the opening of the Restoration. This initial spiritual manifestation has appropriately come to be known among Latter-day Saints as the "First Vision," a title that recognizes that more visions soon followed. Although Joseph Smith was privileged to have additional visions of the Father and the Son later, the First Vision is the only known instance during this ten-year period that the young prophet was privileged to have a vision of either of these two members of the Godhead. Historical evidence demonstrates that the Restoration was brought to pass primarily through the ministration of angels and other forms of revelation rather than by direct appearances of either of these two supreme deities.

Visions of Heavenly Messengers. Of the heavenly messengers who personally appeared to the youthful prophet in the years 1820 to 1830, Moroni was the most regular visitor. Best known are the three visits that occurred during the night of September 21–22, 1823; the appearance while Joseph returned from work in his father's field the next day; the meeting with Moroni at the Hill Cumorah; and the four annual visits that subsequently took place each September until 1827. In total over twenty appearances by the last Nephite have been documented notably by H. Donl Peterson.[8]

Library of Congress

The Angel Moroni Delivering the Plates of the Book of Mormon to Joseph Smith Jun. Print, ca. 1886, C. C. A. Christensen.

One of Moroni's visits, in particular, is worth recounting. During Joseph and Emma's move from Palmyra, New York, to Harmony, Pennsylvania, in December 1827, Joseph protected the plates and the other Nephite artifacts by placing them in a barrel of beans. Shortly after departing, he and his wife were accosted by a group of men intent on taking the plates. After a thorough search, the men left empty-handed, and the couple and the plates eventually arrived safely in Harmony. A year and a half later, because of increased persecution, Joseph and Oliver were forced to leave Harmony, departing for Fayette, New York, around June 1. David Whitmer came from Fayette to transport them to his father's home. However, on this move, the plates were not in their possession. Prior to the trio's departure, Joseph had returned the plates and sacred relics to Moroni, who had informed him they would be returned upon arrival at the Whitmer homestead. Soon after the party's departure by wagon, Moroni paid them an interesting visit. David Whitmer told the following incident on numerous occasions over the years. One account reads:

> When I was returning to Fayette with Joseph and Oliver, all of us riding in the wagon, Oliver and I on an old fashioned wooden spring seat and Joseph behind us, we were suddenly approached by a very pleasant, nice looking old man in a clear open place,

> who saluted us with "Good morning, it is very warm," at the same instant wiping his face or forehead with his hand. We returned the salutation and by a sign from Joseph I invited him to ride if he was going our way, but he said very pleasantly, "No, I am going to Cumorah." This was something new to me, I did not know what Cumorah meant, and as I looked enquiringly at Joseph, the old man instantly disappeared so that I did not see him again.
>
> . . . He was, I should think, about 5 feet 9 or 10 inches and heavy set. . . . He was dressed in a suit of brown, woolen clothes; his hair and beard were white. . . . I also remember that he had a sort of knapsack on his back, and something was in it which was shaped like a book. It was the messenger who had the plates.[9]

In this fascinating account, Whitmer gives some idea of Moroni's physical stature and demonstrates that angels are occasionally given to informal pleasantries when executing their missions among mortals. This incident further illustrates that celestial, glorified messengers can appear in an earthly form and condition.

Moroni was not Joseph's only seeric tutor. Statements and testimonies by some of the Prophet's contemporaries reveal that the young seer was visited and taught by numerous ancient prophets and apostles. In the Wentworth Letter, published in March 1842, Joseph Smith stated, "After having received many visits from the angels of God unfolding the majesty and glory of the events that should transpire in the last days, on the morning of the 22nd of September, A.D. 1827, the angel of the Lord delivered the records into my hands."[10]

Three major points stand out in this statement. First, Joseph Smith received "many visits from the angels of God." Second, these angels visited him to unfold events that would soon transpire. And third, these visits occurred before he obtained the plates in September 1827 and thus took place concurrently with his years of instruction by Moroni at Cumorah. Orson Pratt stated that during the years 1823 to 1827, Joseph "was often ministered to by the angels of God, and received instruction concerning the work that was to be performed in the latter days."[11] George Q. Cannon taught that during these preparatory years Joseph "was visited constantly by angels. . . . He had vision after vision in order that his mind might be fully saturated with a knowledge of the things of God, and that he might comprehend the great and holy calling that God has bestowed upon him."[12]

Joseph never mentioned publicly, as far as we know, who these angelic ministrants were, but his close associates spoke of these appearances. John Taylor gave some indication of their identity in these two typical statements:

> And when Joseph Smith was raised up as a Prophet of God, Mormon, Moroni, Nephi and others of the ancient Prophets who formerly lived on this Continent, and Peter and John and others who lived on the Asiatic Continent, came to him and communicated to him certain principles pertaining to the Gospel of the Son of God.[13]

> The principles which he had, placed him in communication with the Lord, and not only with the Lord, but with the ancient apostles and prophets; such men, for instance, as Abraham, Isaac, Jacob, Noah, Adam, Seth, Enoch, and . . . the apostles that lived on this continent as well as those who lived on the Asiatic continent. He seemed to be as familiar with these people as we are with one another. Why? Because he had to introduce a dispensation which was called the dispensation of the fulness of times.[14]

Lucy Mack Smith had fond memories of Joseph's maturing years and recalled some of the things her son learned from these interviews, particularly from the ancient American prophets. "During our evening conversations, Joseph would occasionally give us some of the most amusing recitals that could be imagined," Lucy said, continuing:

> He would describe the ancient inhabitants of this continent, their dress, mode of travelling, and the animals upon which they rode; their cities, their buildings, with every particular; their mode of warfare; and also their religious worship. This he would do with as much ease, seemingly, as if he had spent his whole life with them.[15]

The Prophet left specific record that on May 15, 1829, John the Baptist appeared and conferred Aaronic Priesthood keys and authority upon Joseph Smith and Oliver Cowdery. Besides Joseph's brief account describing this visitation, Oliver Cowdery also left his written testimony of that event. Significantly, by the time John the Baptist appeared, Joseph had received numerous heavenly visitors, but this was one of Cowdery's first visions. When Cowdery wrote about the incident five years later, his words still expressed exhilaration and spiritual elation. "The vail was parted and the angel of God came down clothed with glory, and delivered the anxiously looked for message," he wrote.

> What joy! what wonder! what amazement! . . . our eyes beheld—our ears heard. . . . Then his voice, though mild, pierced to the center, and his words, "I am thy fellow servant," dispelled every fear. We listened—we gazed—we admired! 'Twas the voice of the angel from glory—'twas a message from the Most High! and as we heard we rejoiced, while his love enkindled upon our souls, and we were rapt in the vision of the Almighty! . . .
>
> . . . The assurance that we were in the presence of an angel . . . is to me, past description, and I shall ever look upon this expression of the Savior's goodness with wonder and thanksgiving.[16]

The appearance of Peter, James, and John and their bestowal of the Melchizedek Priesthood upon Joseph and Oliver followed. While Joseph and Oliver left no record of the exact date of this event, the traditional view is that the higher priesthood was conferred during the visitation of these ancient Apostles in late May or early June 1829, approximately two weeks following the bestowal of the Aaronic Priesthood.[17]

Another heavenly visitor whom Joseph Smith saw during the 1820–30 period was an angel who is not identified in surviving records. This messenger appeared during the first week of August 1830 to instruct Joseph concerning the emblems of the sacrament. Newel Knight and his wife, Sally, had traveled from Colesville, New York, to Harmony, Pennsylvania, to visit Joseph and Emma. Both women had been baptized, but neither had been confirmed nor had yet partaken of the sacrament. Joseph authorized both ordinances and "set out to procure some wine for the occasion," wrote Newel Knight. "He had gone only a short distance, when he was met by a heavenly messenger and received the first four verses of the revelation" (that is, D&C 27:1–4). The Prophet returned to the small group, which also included John Whitmer, prepared some wine in accordance with the instructions from the angel, partook of the sacrament, confirmed the two sisters, and "spent the evening in a glorious manner."[18]

Visions of Satan. Joseph had at least two personal encounters with Lucifer during the 1820s. The best-known confrontation occurred prior to his theophany in the Sacred Grove, when Satan sought to physically destroy him as discussed in the two articles about the First Vision in this volume. The other confrontation with Satan is mentioned only briefly, in Doctrine and Covenants 128. In verse 20, the Prophet wrote of hearing "the voice of Michael on the banks of the Susquehanna, detecting the devil when he appeared as an angel of light." Clearly, he heard Adam's (Michael's) voice and also saw the devil. Satan's appearance also seems to be associated with the restoration of the Melchizedek Priesthood since Joseph refers to Peter, James, and John's appearance on the Susquehanna in the very next sentence. Simply interpreted, Satan appeared as an angel of light, hoping to deceive Joseph and Oliver in some manner and thereby thwart the restoration of authority. Satan's presence, however, was detected by Michael, who informed Joseph and Oliver of the deception, concluding the incident.

Visions through the Urim and Thummim or Seer Stone

During this early period, the youthful prophet received many visions through the medium of "Urim and Thummim"—sometimes a seer stone and, more particularly, the Nephite interpreters. Both of these instruments apparently operated in much the same spiritual manner, and through them Joseph received an undetermined number of visions in addition to the translation of the Book of Mormon. The young prophet obtained a seer stone, described as dark brown in color, while digging a well for Willard Chase around 1822.[19] This discovery occurred only two years after the First Vision and one year before Moroni's first visits. Joseph made use of the seer stone for five years before obtaining the Nephite interpreters from Moroni in 1827. Latter-day Saints should not be surprised to learn that prior to being engaged specifically in the work of the Lord—that is, prior to beginning the work of the translation of the plates—the youthful Joseph apparently recognized that God had given him visionary powers enabling him to see supernatural visions in a wide variety of areas. Between 1822 and 1827, he successfully obtained an unspecified number of visions by means of the seer stone. He even gained a reputation for such activities, which may explain why men such as Josiah Stowell, who lived more than one hundred miles away, near South Bainbridge, New York, sought out Joseph Smith and employed him to locate buried treasure in fall 1825.[20]

Several examples of Joseph's ability to receive visions by means of a seer stone illustrate the power associated with the Prophet and this instrument. Martin Harris steadfastly believed Joseph possessed an uncanny ability of seership. This was perhaps due in part to the following incident:

> I was at the house of his father in Manchester, two miles south of Palmyra village, and was picking my teeth with a pin while sitting on the bars. The pin caught in my teeth, and dropped from my fingers into shavings and straw. I jumped from the bars and looked for it. . . . I then took Joseph on surprise, and said to him—I said, "Take your stone." I had never seen it, and did not know that he had it with him. He had it in his pocket. He took it and placed it in his hat—the old white hat—and placed his face in his hat. I watched him closely to see that he did not look [to] one side; he reached out his hand beyond me on the right, and moved a little stick, and there I saw the pin, which he picked up and gave to me.[21]

Joseph's use of the stone may have also encouraged him to propose marriage to Emma Hale. At Joseph's annual visit to the Hill Cumorah in September 1826, Moroni told him that he could have the plates the following year if, in Joseph Knight's words, "he Brot the right person." Knight recounted this conversation further:

> "Who is the right Person?" The answer was you will know. Then he looked in his glass and found it was Emma Hale, Daughter of old Mr Hail of Pensylvany, a girl that he had seen Before, for he had Bin Down there Before with me. . . . He came to me perhaps in November and worked for me until about the time that he was Married . . . and I furnished him with a horse and Cutter to go and see his girl Down to Mr. Hails. And soon after this he was Married

> and Mr Stowel moved him and his wife to his fathers in Palmyra Ontario County.[22]

David Whitmer learned during his very first meeting with Joseph that, by means of the seer stone, Joseph was able to see in detail actions many miles away. In late May 1828, at the request of Oliver Cowdery and Joseph, David traveled from Fayette, New York, over one hundred miles to Harmony, Pennsylvania, to take the two men back to his father's farmhouse so they could complete the translation. As he neared Harmony, he was surprised to meet Joseph and Oliver, who "were coming toward me, and met me some little distance from the house." David reported further:

> Oliver told me that Joseph had told him when I started from home, where I had stopped the first night, how I read the sign at the tavern, where I stopped the next night and that I would be there that day before dinner, and this was why they had come out to meet me, all of which was exactly as Joseph had told Oliver, at which I was greatly astonished.[23]

Moroni gave Joseph possession of the plates, breastplate, and interpreters on September 22, 1827. When Joseph Smith first put on the spectacles, "his entire past history [was] revealed to him," David Whitmer recounted. This experience, David believed, helped Joseph recognize the greater supernatural power God had now given him.[24] Joseph Knight Sr., who was at the Smith home in Palmyra when Joseph returned from the Hill Cumorah, remembered conversing with Joseph about the sacred relics the morning after he gained possession of them. "It is ten times Better than I expected," he remembered Joseph saying. He recalled further the Prophet's particular fascination with the spectacles. "He seamed to think more of the glasses or the urim and thummem then [than] he Did of the Plates," wrote Knight, "for, says he, 'I can see any thing; they are Marvelus.'"[25] Indeed they were, for as the Prophet's mother, Lucy Mack Smith, recalled, by means of the instrument "the angel showed him many things which he saw in vision."[26] These tools were not used for trivial or spectacular sensations. One major purpose of the spectacles (and perhaps also the seer stone) was to help protect the plates and Joseph's life. Lucy said her son "always kept the Urim and Thummim about his person" so "he could also ascertain, at any time, the approach of danger, either to himself or the Record."[27] Lucy Mack Smith and Martin Harris mention three incidents where the plates were kept safe because of information received by means of the Urim and Thummim.[28]

Soon after acquiring the ancient relics, Joseph wondered how he could proceed without some personal assistance, particularly financial aid, so that he could devote himself entirely to the work of translation. The answer came in a vision through the holy interpreters. During one of his interviews with the angel Moroni, probably in September 1827, Joseph asked who could assist him. He was told "to go and look in the spectacles, and he would show him the man that would assist him." The man he saw was Martin Harris. A short while later, the Prophet told Harris what had been made known to him. The Palmyra farmer later recalled how the message "struck me with surprise. I told him I wished him to be careful about these things. 'Well,' said [Joseph], 'I saw you standing before me as plainly as I do now.'"[29] Martin subsequently received a testimony of Joseph Smith's divine calling to translate the Book of Mormon and later gave liberally of his wealth to the work.

Joseph Smith never detailed the method or procedure of translation.[30] However, Martin Harris, who assisted with the translation of the first 116 pages in 1828, and David Whitmer, a firsthand observer who lent assistance beginning in June 1829, gave some particulars. Harris gave the following testimony to Edward Stevenson:

> Sentences would appear and were read by the Prophet and written by Martin, and when finished he would say, "Written," and if correctly written, that sentence would disappear and another appear in its place, but if not written correctly it remained until corrected, so that the translation was just as it was engraven on the plates, precisely in the language then used.[31]

David Whitmer stated a similar procedure for the translation:

> Joseph Smith would put the seer stone into a hat, and put his face in the hat, drawing it closely around his face to exclude the light; and in the darkness the spiritual light would shine. A piece of something resembling parchment would appear, and on that appeared

> the writing. One character at a time would appear, and under it was the interpretation in English. Brother Joseph would read off the English to Oliver Cowdery, who was his principal scribe, and when it was written down and repeated to Brother Joseph to see if it was correct, then it would disappear, and another character with the interpretation would appear. Thus the Book of Mormon was translated by the gift and power of God, and not by any power of man.[32]

Clearly, the main purpose of the interpreters was to assist the seer in the translation of the Book of Mormon. The testimonies of Emma Smith and David Whitmer agree that the Prophet used the Nephite interpreters to translate the first 116 pages, after which this instrument was returned to the angel in consequence of the incidents surrounding the lost manuscript. Thereafter, the seer stone was used, both instruments being essentially a "urim and thummim."[33] In such cases, when Joseph translated he was seeing some kind of vision. Furthermore, in the Doctrine and Covenants at least nine revelations were received by means of the Urim and Thummim and the seer stone—sections 3, 6, 7, 10, 11, 14, 15, 16, and 17.[34] Since it is likely the information was conveyed to the Prophet in much the same manner as the translation of the Book of Mormon (that is, the words would appear in some fashion within the instruments), perhaps these revelations could be better described as "visions" received through the Nephite interpreters or the seer stone. Soon after the translation of the Book of Mormon was complete, visions using the seer stone as a medium seemed to cease. David Whitmer remembered Joseph saying that "we would all have to depend on the Holy Ghost hereafter to be guided into truth and obtain the will of the Lord."[35]

Visions Opened to the Mind

Documentation exists for three visions received in the mind of the youthful prophet during the ten-year period of 1820 to 1830, each associated with his initial interviews with Moroni. The first two occurred in conjunction with Moroni's inaugural appearance on the evening of September 21–22, 1823, in the Joseph Smith Sr. log house. In the Prophet's 1839 history, he related that as the heavenly messenger was telling him about the gold plates, "the vision was opened to my mind that I could see the place where the plates were deposited, and that so clearly and distinctly that I knew the place again when I visited it" (Joseph Smith—History 1:42). In the 1842 Wentworth Letter, he added that during this initial interview he was informed about the ancient American inhabitants and "shown who they were, and from whence they came; a brief sketch of their origin, progress, civilization, laws, governments, of their righteousness and iniquity, and the blessings of God being finally withdrawn from them as a people."[36] A similar experience occurred the following day at the hill. After determining where the stone box was located, and after removing the large stone that covered it, Joseph made several attempts to obtain the record. As Joseph began to pray, Moroni appeared. He then told the young seer to

> "Look!" and as he thus spake he beheld the prince of darkness, surrounded by his innumerable train of associates. All this passed before him, and the heavenly messenger said, "All this is shown, the good and the evil, the holy and impure, the glory of God and the power of darkness, that you may know hereafter the two powers and never be influenced or overcome by that wicked one."[37]

In a very real sense, what Joseph experienced on these three occasions was a "vision within a vision" since he received visual instruction at the same time he was in the presence of a celestial personage.

A Unique Visionary Experience

A well-known vision of this period warrants a brief examination, but it is difficult to classify and explain. After the completion of the translation, Joseph returned the plates to Moroni, who appeared a very short time later at a location near the Whitmer farm to show the plates to the Three Witnesses of the Book of Mormon. The plates were then loaned back to the Prophet, who showed them to the Eight Witnesses, who were in the vicinity of Manchester. The Prophet and Oliver Cowdery then went to Cumorah to return the record for the last time. While at the hill, an unusual phenomenon took place. Brigham Young explained:

> I believe I will take the liberty to tell you of another circumstance that will be as marvelous as anything can be. This is an incident in the life of Oliver Cowdery, but he did not take the liberty of telling such things in meeting as I take. . . . Oliver Cowdery went with the Prophet Joseph when he deposited [returned] these plates. . . . When Joseph got the plates, the angel instructed him to carry them back to the hill Cumorah, which he did. Oliver says that when Joseph and Oliver went there, the hill opened, and they walked into a cave, in which there was a large and spacious room. He says he did not think, at the time, whether they had the light of the sun or artificial light; but that it was just as light as day. They laid the plates on a table; it was a large table that stood in the room. Under this table there was a pile of plates as much as two feet high, and there were altogether in this room more plates than probably many wagon loads; they were piled up in the corners and along the walls. The first time they went there the sword of Laban hung upon the wall; but when they went again it had been taken down and laid upon the table across the gold plates; it was unsheathed, and on it was written these words: "This sword will never be sheathed again until the kingdoms of this world become the kingdom of our God and his Christ." I tell you this as coming not only from Oliver Cowdery, but others who were familiar with it.[38]

The incident is substantiated by two other statements made by Brigham Young and recorded by William H. Dame and Wilford Woodruff.[39] Others of the Prophet's contemporaries giving similar reports included Heber C. Kimball, Orson Pratt, and David Whitmer.[40]

Summary of the 1820–1830 Period

This decade was distinguished by the following: First, the most significant experience of Joseph Smith during this period was the personal visitation of the Father and the Son, who opened the latter-day dispensation with a personal appearance. This vision is also the only recorded appearance of the two supreme beings during the decade of the 1820s. Second, the period is characterized by a series of visitations from heavenly messengers, including ancient prophets from both hemispheres who appeared to indoctrinate and teach the young seer. Third, Joseph had at least two spiritual encounters with Satan, the first being a vision involving a destructive force immediately before the appearance of the Father and the Son, and the second, a more subtle appearance where Satan was disguised as an angel of light. Fourth, around 1822, Joseph Smith began to receive visions by means of a seer stone. Later, in 1827, he received the Nephite spectacles. Both of these instruments acted as a Urim and Thummim, and by them Joseph Smith received divine light and knowledge. Evidence further suggests that the entire translation process of the Book of Mormon and the receipt of several early revelations through the Urim and Thummim were in essence visionary experiences. Fifth, the Prophet had visions opened to his mind, albeit rarely, during this time period. Sixth, the Prophet and Oliver Cowdery experienced a singular visionary phenomenon when they returned the plates to the Hill Cumorah.

Joseph Smith's Visions, 1831–1844

From 1831 to 1844, Joseph received personal visitations from the Father and the Son together, the Son alone, other heavenly beings, and Satan. The Prophet also received visions where the method of receiving the vision is not clearly recorded. Examples of those visions will be discussed according to subject or event.

Visions of Beings

Joseph the seer continued to have visions of heavenly and satanic personages. These experiences gave him increasing knowledge of the unseen world.

Visions of the Father and the Son. During the first five years of the 1831–44 period, Joseph Smith was privileged to see both the Father and the Son in vision on at least four occasions. On June 4, 1831, during a four-day conference held in Kirtland, Joseph had a vision of these two beings. Levi Hancock was present and stated that the vision occurred in a schoolhouse on the hill above the Isaac Morley farmhouse, about one mile northeast of the Newel K. Whitney store. Hancock reported that the elders were meeting together when Joseph "stepped out on the floor and said, 'I now see God, and Jesus Christ at his right hand, let them kill me, I should not feel death as I am now.'"[41] Hancock's wording suggests a vision similar to that experienced by Stephen, who saw the Father and the Son prior to being stoned before Jewish accusers (Acts 7).

Joseph Smith and his spokesman, Sidney Rigdon, saw the Father and the Son in 1832 in the vision now canonized as Doctrine and Covenants 76. Classroom discussions of this vision often focus on the degrees of glory, perdition, and the attendant requirements for each. However, the highlight of the section is a vision of the Father and the Son, the premortal life, and Lucifer's fall. The vision of the two supreme members of the Godhead was rich and glorious. The manifestation led them to write, "The glory of the Lord shone round about. And we beheld the glory of the Son, on the right hand of the Father, and received of his fulness; And saw the holy angels, and them who are sanctified before his throne, worshiping God, and the Lamb, who worship him forever and ever" (D&C 76:19–21). So powerful was the vision of what they both saw and heard, they chose to bear testimony of the Savior, a testimony declaring "that he lives! For we saw him, even on the right hand of God; and we heard the voice bearing record that he is the Only Begotten of the Father" (D&C 76:22–23).

On March 18, 1833, God the Father and the Son also made a brief personal appearance to members of the School of the Prophets. Two eyewitnesses left a dramatic record of their experience. The first comes years later from Zebedee Coltrin:

> At one of these meetings after the organization of the school, . . . when we were all together, Joseph having given instructions, and while engaged in silent prayer, kneeling, with our hands uplifted each one praying in silence, no one whispered above his breath, a personage walked through the room from East to west, and Joseph asked if we saw him. I saw him and suppose the others did, and Joseph answered that is Jesus, the Son of God, our elder brother. Afterward Joseph told us to resume our former position in prayer, which we did. Another person came through; He was surrounded as with a flame of fire.[42]

In the presence of this personage, Coltrin "experienced a sensation that it might destroy the tabernacle as it was of consuming fire of great brightness." Joseph Smith identified this personage as "the Father of our Lord Jesus Christ," and Coltrin gave the following description:

> I saw His hands, His legs, his feet, his eyes, nose, mouth, head and body in the shape and form of a perfect man. . . . This appearance was so grand and overwhelming that it seemed I should melt down in His presence, and the sensation was so powerful that it thrilled through my whole system and I felt it in the marrow of my bones.[43]

On another occasion, Coltrin stated that as the Father passed through the room, the "glory and brightness was so great . . . that had it continued much longer, I believe it would have consumed us."[44] The second testimony of this vision comes from John Murdock:

> During the winter that I boarded with Brother Joseph . . . we had a number of prayer meetings, in the Prophet's chamber. . . . In one of those meetings the Prophet told us, "If we could humble ourselves before God, and exercise strong faith, we should see the face of the Lord." And about midday the visions of my mind were opened, and the eyes of my understanding were enlightened, and I saw the form of a man, most lovely, the visage of his face was sound and fair as the sun. His hair a bright silver grey, curled in most majestic form; His eyes a keen penetrating blue, and the skin of his neck a most beautiful white and he was covered from the neck to the feet with a loose garment, pure white: Whiter than any garment I have ever before seen. His countenance was most penetrating, and yet most lovely. And while I was endeavoring to comprehend the whole personage from head to feet it slipped from me, and the vision was closed up. But it left on my mind the impression of love, for months, that I had never felt before to that degree.[45]

On January 21, 1836, Joseph Smith was more in heaven than on earth. That day he received at least two, and possibly three, visions of different events. In one of these visions, he saw "the blazing throne of God, whereon was seated the Father and the Son" and those who became heirs of the celestial kingdom. It is this portion of the vision that has been canonized as Doctrine and Covenants 137. However, in addition, Joseph observed William E. McLellin proselyting in the South, Brigham Young working in the Southwest, and others bringing about the redemption of Zion. He also saw the Twelve standing together in a foreign land (probably Great Britain). The Prophet indicated they were "much fatigued, with their clothes tattered and feet swollen, with their eyes cast downward, and Jesus standing in their midst, and they did not behold Him. The Savior looked upon them and wept."[46] Subsequently, he observed that the Twelve had successfully accomplished their work on earth and had entered the celestial city, where the Savior embraced and kissed each one and then crowned them in the presence of God the Father. This vision left such a powerful impression on the Prophet, wrote Heber C. Kimball, "that he never could refrain from weeping while rehearsing it."[47]

Visions of the Son. In addition to the four appearances of the Father and Son during this five-year span (1831–36), historical sources reveal that Joseph Smith saw Jesus Christ separately on four occasions. Thirteen-year-old Mary Elizabeth Rollins was present when one of these visitations transpired. She remembered the event occurring in 1831, at a meeting of Saints held at the Isaac Morley farm, where the Prophet was the main speaker. She recalled Joseph speaking very solemnly during the meeting. "All at once his countenance changed and he stood mute," Rollins recounted. "Those who looked at him . . . said there was a search light within him, over every part of his body. I never saw anything like it on the earth. I could not take my eyes off of him. He got so white that anyone who saw him would have thought he was transparent. I . . . thought I could almost see the bones through the flesh." The Prophet stood silent for several minutes before he asked those present if they knew who had been in their midst. Martin Harris told them it was the Savior, to which the Prophet responded that God had revealed that truth to Martin. He then said, "Brothers and Sisters, . . . the Savior has been here this night and I want to tell you to remember it. There is a vail over your eyes for you could not endure to look upon Him."[48]

During an intimate meeting in Kirtland on December 18, 1833, the Prophet experienced a singular vision of the premortal Jehovah ministering to Father Adam in mortality. Scribe Oliver Cowdery noted that while Joseph Smith was setting apart his father, Joseph Smith Sr., as Patriarch to the Church, "the visions of the Almighty were open to his view," and he beheld a great ancient council meeting at Adam-ondi-Ahman held three years previous to Adam's death. "The Lord appeared unto them," Cowdery recorded, and "administered comfort unto Adam."[49] In July 1839 during a meeting with the Twelve and the Seventy, Joseph Smith briefly recounted the vision. "I saw Adam in the valley of Adam-ondi-Ahman," he said. "The Lord appeared in their midst, and he (Adam) blessed them all."[50]

Joseph Smith had two additional visions of the Savior during the week of the dedication of the Kirtland Temple. The Prophet's history for March 30, 1836, three days after the formal dedication, states that "the Savior made His appearance," while "angels minestered unto others."[51] Although Joseph did not give any additional information concerning this manifestation, Harrison Burgess, a member of the Seventy, was present and provided the following recollection:

> I was in a meeting for instruction in the upper part of the [Kirtland] Temple, with about a hundred of the High Priests, Seventies and Elders . . . and I beheld the room lighted up with a peculiar light such as I had never seen before. It was soft and clear and the room looked to me as though it had neither roof nor floor to the building and I beheld the Prophet Joseph and Hyrum Smith and Roger Orton enveloped in the light: Joseph exclaimed aloud, "I behold the Savior, the Son of God." Hyrum said, "I behold the angels of heaven." Brother Orton exclaimed, "I behold the chariots of Israel." All who were in the room felt the power of God to that degree that many prophesied, and the power of God was made manifest, the remembrance of which will remain with me while I live upon the earth.[52]

On Sunday, April 3, 1836, Joseph and Oliver, perhaps feeling that a manifestation was about to take place, retired to the veiled Melchizedek Priesthood pulpits in the Kirtland Temple, where a glorious vision of the Lord was opened to them. As stated in Doctrine and Covenants 110, the first and second elder saw Jesus Christ "standing upon the breastwork of the pulpit. . . . His eyes were as a flame of fire; the hair of his head was white like the pure snow; his countenance shone above the brightness of the sun" (110:2–3). This occasion is the last documented vision of Joseph Smith seeing the Lord Jesus Christ. Including the First Vision, there is documentation for five visions of the Father and the Son together, and four visions of the Savior individually, totaling nine.

Visions of Other Heavenly Beings. During his years as Church President, Joseph Smith also had visions of, manifestations about, and visitations from ancient prophets and apostles and other heavenly messengers. Father Adam was among the prophets most frequently seen. As stated above, Joseph heard Adam detect Satan as an angel of light during the 1820–30 period. In addition, on at least three instances Joseph Smith saw Adam in vision during the 1830s. The two most familiar accounts are included in scripture. Joseph saw in vision the great council at Adam-ondi-Ahman, where Adam and other patriarchs—including Seth, Enos, Cainan, Mahalaleel, Jared, Enoch, and Methuselah—as well as all of Adam's righteous posterity, assembled three years prior to Adam's death (D&C 107:53–57).[53]

Joseph later saw Adam in his vision of the celestial kingdom, as recorded in Doctrine and Covenants 137. Concerning this vision, Heber C. Kimball stated that Joseph also "saw Adam open the gate of the Celestial City and admit the people one by one."[54] The most personal account of Adam in vision is not recorded in scripture. In April 1834, the Prophet held a conference of the Church at New Portage, Ohio. There Joseph asked Oliver Cowdery and Zebedee Coltrin to walk with him "to a place where there was some beautiful grass, and grapevines," Coltrin later recounted. The Prophet then requested they each pray in turn. After praying, Joseph said, "Now breth[r]en . . . we will see some visions." Joseph lay on the ground, and Oliver and Zebedee rested their heads on his outstretched arms. "The heavens gradually opened," Coltrin recalled, and the brethren "saw a golden throne, on a circular foundation, something like a light house, and on the throne were two aged personages, having white hair, and clothed in white garments." These personages were "the two most beautiful and perfect specimens of mankind" Coltrin had ever seen. Joseph called them "our first parents, Adam and Eve." Coltrin remembered Adam as a "large broadshouldered man, and Eve as a woman . . . large in proportion."[55] That the Prophet knew Adam's visage is also evident from a brief statement he made in January 1843, while reminiscing about his deceased brother, Alvin, where Joseph called his oldest brother "a very handsome man, surpassed by none but Adam and Seth."[56]

The Prophet also saw other angelic ministrants and prophets during this period. As the Kirtland Temple neared completion in early 1836, an outpouring of spiritual appearances by heavenly beings began. On January 21, at a meeting held in the not-yet-dedicated temple, angels ministered unto those present, the Prophet reported, "as well as my self. . . . For we all communed with the h[e]avenly host's."[57] Bishop Edward Partridge stated that "a number saw visions & others were blessed with the outpouring of the Holy Ghost."[58] Oliver Cowdery called the scene "too great to be described, . . . therefore, I only say, that the heavens were opened to many, and great and marvelous things were shown."[59] Recorded in the Prophet's journal for the next day, January 22, is a comparable occurrence: "The heavens were opened, and angels ministered unto us. . . . [They] mingled their voices with ours, while their presence was in our midst."[60] On January 28, Joseph saw another glorious vision, which he did not describe.[61]

Divine messengers attended the dedicatory services of the Kirtland Temple on March 27, 1836. As the Prophet read the dedicatory prayer, "we, having our heads bowed," Truman O. Angell later testified, "felt a sensation very elevating to the soul." At the completion of the prayer, President Frederick G. Williams arose "and testified that midway during the prayer an Holy Angel came and seated Himself in the stand."[62] Heber C. Kimball could see the personage from where he sat, describing him as "very tall . . . [with] black eyes, white hair, and stoop shouldered; his garment was whole, extending to near his ankles; on his feet he had sandals. He was sent as a messenger to accept of the dedication."[63] After a midday adjournment, the first thing Joseph Smith did was announce to those assembled that "the Personage who had appeared in the morning was the Angel Peter [who] had come to accept the dedication."[64] David Whitmer testified that at the dedication he also saw angels in the house.[65]

On the evening of the dedication day, the priesthood quorums again met in the temple. It was during this meeting that a pentecostal outpouring transpired. The Prophet's history states:

> A noise was heard like the sound of a rushing mighty wind, which filled the Temple, and all the congregation simultaneously arose, being moved upon by an invisible power; many began to speak in tongues and prophesy; others saw glorious visions; and I beheld the Temple was filled with angels, which fact I declared to the congregation. The people of the neighborhood came running together (hearing an unusual sound within, and seeing a bright light like a pillar of fire resting upon the Temple), and were astonished at what was taking place.[66]

Two or three days later, the leading brethren and quorums met to perform anointings. On this occasion, noted Heber C. Kimball, another heavenly personage appeared—"the beloved disciple John was seen in our midst by the Prophet Joseph, Oliver Cowdery, and others."[67]

The most significant manifestation during this spiritual season in Kirtland occurred a week after the dedication, when the Lord appeared and accepted the temple and the sacrifice of the Saints. Then, following that theophany, the great lawgiver, Moses, appeared and bestowed the keys of gathering. His appearance was followed by a personage, whom the Prophet simply called Elias, who restored the keys associated with the dispensation of the gospel of Abraham. Finally, Elijah, an ancient Israelite prophet, bestowed the keys of the sealing power upon the first and second elders, Joseph Smith and Oliver Cowdery (D&C 110:11–16). So ended the week in which, according to Orson Pratt, heaven and earth were brought so close together that "people were blessed as they never had been blessed for generations and generations that were passed and gone."[68]

Several of Joseph Smith's close associates left record of an angel, whose identity was not recorded, visiting him on several occasions. The purpose of these appearances was to encourage the Prophet to move ahead with the principle of celestial marriage. According to one of the Prophet's celestial wives, this angel appeared three times between 1834 and 1842.[69] Another plural wife, Eliza R. Snow, described an angel that "stood by him with a drawn sword, [who] told him that, unless he moved forward and established plural marriage, his Priesthood would be taken from him."[70] Documents currently available do not record Joseph Smith receiving visitations from heavenly beings after 1842.

Visions of Satan. The Prophet encountered the adversary face-to-face during the 1830s and 40s. In 1831, while returning to Ohio from his first excursion to Missouri, the Prophet received a revelation at McIlwaine's Bend on the Missouri River. This revelation came, according to the Prophet's history, after W. W. Phelps saw Satan, in broad daylight, moving in power upon the surface of the water. Although the record does not indicate how much of this manifestation the Prophet also saw, he knew distinctly who was involved and what had taken place in the vision.

A more direct encounter took place shortly after the Prophet moved into his home in Far West in 1838. Heber C. Kimball related the incident:

> One of his children was taken very sick; he laid his hands upon the child, [but] when it got better; as soon as he went out of doors, the child was taken sick again; he again laid his hands upon it, so that it again recovered. This occurred several times, when Joseph inquired of the Lord what it all meant; . . . he had an open vision, and saw the devil in person, who contended with Joseph, face to face, for some time. He said it was his house, it belonged to him, and Joseph had no right there. Then Joseph rebuked Satan in the name of the Lord, and he departed and touched the child no more.[71]

As early as June 1839, Joseph Smith instructed the Twelve, prior to their departure to England, how to differentiate messengers of God from messengers of Satan. At the time the Prophet gave these instructions, Parley P. Pratt was imprisoned in the Columbia, Missouri, jail and did not receive these instructions until returning from Great Britain in 1843, when the Prophet taught these principles to him personally. On that occasion, William Clayton recorded Joseph's words, which now comprise section 129, outlining the three grand keys for discerning spirits. This revelation shows that the Prophet evidently had firsthand experience in such matters. When Heber C. Kimball returned from his first mission to Great Britain, he and Joseph took a walk down by the Mississippi River. Heber told the Prophet how he, Orson Hyde, and Willard Richards had been buffeted by Satan when they first arrived in Preston, England. The Prophet then told Brother Kimball about his own contests with the prince of darkness, in which Joseph saw Satan "face to face" and was "handled and afflicted" by him.[72]

Visions of Zion

Although Kirtland was the hub of Mormonism between 1831 and 1838, Joseph focused on the establishment of Zion in Missouri during these years. Through revelations and visionary experiences, the Lord revealed many truths to this modern-day seer about the land where the New Jerusalem would be established. In June 1831, just four months after moving to Ohio from New York, Joseph received a revelation in which the Lord instructed Joseph, Sidney Rigdon, and thirteen pairs of elders to travel to Missouri, where "the land of their inheritance" would "be made known unto them" (D&C 52:5). Joseph later stated that the commandment to travel "to the western boundaries of the State of Missouri" was received "by a heavenly vision" and that the main purpose of the expedition was to "designate the very spot which was to be the central place for the commencement of the gathering together of those who embrace the fullness of the everlasting Gospel."[73] Soon after the elders' arrival in Missouri in mid-July, the Prophet alluded to another vision, giving the precise location of Zion: "He manifested Himself unto us, and designated, to me and others, the very spot upon which He designed to commence the work of the gathering, and the upbuilding of an 'holy city,' which should be called Zion."[74]

Visions Received during Zion's Camp

The Prophet received two unusual visions in 1834. Following the expulsion of some 1,200 Latter-day Saints from Jackson County in 1833, the Prophet called for a contingent of Saints to travel to Missouri and there assist the exiled Saints in reclaiming their lands. The expedition, known as Zion's Camp, was led by Joseph Smith. After traveling for over a month, on June 3, 1834, near the Illinois River, the expedition came across some peculiar mounds. While surveying one of these formations, the Prophet received a remarkable vision. Seven members of the camp wrote about this event, now known simply as the Zelph story.[75] Regardless of the many differences in these accounts, Joseph received some divine understanding concerning Zelph, apparently through visionary means, as noted in the following published report:

> We encamped on the bank of the river until Tuesday the 3rd during our travels we visited several of the mounds which had been thrown up by the ancient inhabitants of this county, Nephites, Lamanites, &c., and this morning I went up on a high mound, near the river, accompanied by the brethren. . . .
>
> On the top of the mound were stones which presented the appearance of three alters, . . . and human bones were strewn over the surface of the ground. The brethren procured a shovel and hoe, and removing the earth to the depth of about one foot discovered [the] skeleton of a man, almost entire, and between his ribs was a Lamanitish arrow, which evidently produced his death. Elder Brigham Young retained the arrow and the brethren carried some pieces of the skeleton to Clay county. The contemplation of the scenery before us produced peculiar sensations in our bosoms; and the visions of the past being opened to my understanding by the spirit of the Almighty I discovered that the person whose skeleton was before us, was a white Lamanite, a large thick set man, and a man of God. He was a warrior and chieftain under the great prophet Omandagus, who was known from the hill Cumorah, or Eastern sea, to the Rocky Mountains. His name was Zelph. The curse was taken from him, or at least, in part; one of his thigh bones was broken, by a stone flung from a sling, while in battle years before his death. He was killed in battle, by the arrow found among his ribs, during the last great struggle of the Lamanites and Nephites.[76]

Joseph received at least one other vision while leading Zion's Camp. It illustrates how the Prophet could receive a vision at almost any time and on almost any matter. Nathan Tanner stated that while traveling with the camp

> I had the pleasure of seeing him [Joseph] in a vision when he saw the country over which we had traveled in a high state of cultivation. This was while he was riding, and when he camped, he had a wagon run out in the middle of the corral of wagons, and got up into it, and told the camp what he had seen while in the Spirit. It was glorious and grand to hear.[77]

Visions of Church Organization

The Prophet received visionary instruction concerning Church structure and organization. During the first part of February 1835, Joseph Smith called for a meeting of the men who had participated in Zion's Camp. Brigham and Joseph Young met with the Prophet a week prior to the meeting. At that time, President Smith told the two brothers, "I have seen those men who died of the cholera in our camp; and the Lord knows, if I get a mansion as bright as theirs, I ask no more." As Joseph Young remembered this meeting, the Prophet "wept, and for some time could not speak." This vision apparently included information about the organization of the Council of the Twelve and the Quorums of Seventy. After Joseph Smith told the Young brothers about his vision, he informed Brigham that he would be called to the Quorum of the Twelve Apostles, not yet organized, and "proceeded to enlarge upon the duties of [the Twelve's] calling." Turning next to Joseph Young, the Prophet said, "Brother Joseph, the Lord has made you President of the Seventies."[78] These councils were organized later in the month—the Quorum of the Twelve on February 14, 1835, and the Seventy on February 28. The following month, the Prophet dictated section 107, which connects these councils to a visionary experience. "And it is according to the vision showing the order of the Seventy, that they should have seven presidents to preside over them, chosen out of the number of the seventy" (D&C 107:93). Perhaps it was in part this vision of Church councils to which Joseph Smith referred when, according to Parley P. Pratt, he explained to the Twelve shortly before his death, "I have now finished the work which was laid upon me, by committing to you all things for the building up of the kingdom according to the heavenly vision, and the pattern shown me from heaven."[79]

Visions of the Future

Joseph Smith saw events in the near and distant future. The year 1831 opened with Joseph Smith and several other leading elders receiving a unique vision of the Church in the future. Among these elders was Sidney Rigdon, who was converted to Mormonism in Kirtland in November 1830 by four missionaries en route to Indian Territory on the western borders of Missouri (see D&C 32). Soon after his conversion, Rigdon journeyed to New York to meet the Prophet. He took with him Edward Partridge, who was not yet baptized. The two men arrived at Joseph Sr. and Lucy's home on the Seneca River on December 10, 1830. They stayed for several weeks and were present at the conference held in Fayette during the first week of January. Fourteen years later, while addressing the Saints in Nauvoo, Rigdon reflected on this conference and recalled how small the Church had been in 1831. He remarked, "All the members met in conference in a room twenty feet square"—referring to the Whitmer farmhouse. Then continuing, he added, "We knew fourteen years ago that the Church would become as large as it is today," for, "we saw by vision the Church of God, a thousand times larger."[80]

The Prophet received another interesting vision either prior to his departure to Ohio in January 1831 or while en route. Like Rigdon, Newel K. Whitney encountered Mormonism through the preaching of the missionaries on their way to teach the Lamanites. After joining the Church, Whitney was unable to travel with Rigdon and Partridge to New York to meet Joseph Smith and instead remained behind, apparently petitioning the Lord to bring Joseph to Ohio. According to Whitney family tradition, Joseph had a vision of Whitney praying for the Prophet to come to Kirtland. When the Prophet and his company pulled up in front of Whitney's store on February 1, Joseph

> alighted, and springing up the steps, walked into the store. Upon seeing Whitney the Prophet said, "Newel K. Whitney! Thou art the man!" meaning that he was the person whom he had seen in his vision. The storekeeper "could not call [Joseph] by name" so he enquired as to who he was. With obvious reference to his vision the Mormon leader responded, "I am Joseph, the Prophet. . . . You've prayed me here; now what do you want of me?"[81]

The experience no doubt helped confirm in Whitney's mind the power that attended the youthful prophet.

Joseph's visions of the future included views of kingdoms and eternal worlds. Doctrine and Covenants 76 and 137 are the best examples. He also saw the tragic events of the last days as well as the glories of the Resurrection.

On July 2, 1839, the Prophet addressed several members of the Twelve prior to their departure to Great Britain. During his remarks, he referred to some of the things the Lord had revealed to him concerning the wickedness of men, future wars, and the destruction that awaits the disobedient. "I saw men hunting the lives of their own sons," Joseph explained, "brother murdering brother, women killing their own daughters, and daughters seeking the lives of their mothers. I saw armies arrayed against armies. I saw blood, desolation, fires. . . . These things are at our doors."[82]

Tragic visions such as these were offset by more hopeful visionary experiences. While speaking at the funeral of Lorenzo D. Barnes in 1843, Joseph Smith reflected on the death of some of his own family members, particularly his father. He discussed the sanctity of the body and the need for a proper and honorable burial, and then he stated his desire to be buried beside his father and mother and other family members and friends. "Would you think it strange if I relate what I have seen in vision in relation to this interesting theme?" he asked.

> I actually saw men, before they had ascended from the tomb, as though they were getting up slowly. They took each other by the hand and said to each other, "My father, my son, my mother, my daughter, my brother, my sister." And when the voice calls for the dead to arise, suppose I am laid by the side of my father, what would be the first joy of my heart? To meet my father, my mother, my brother, my sister; and when they are by my side, I embrace them and they me.[83]

Visions of Temple Patterns

Like Moses, David, and Solomon, who obtained divine knowledge pertaining to the construction of Israel's tabernacle in the wilderness and temple in Jerusalem, Joseph Smith received visionary understanding on the basic architectural design, construction, and function of four temples—Kirtland, Independence, Far West, and Nauvoo. Joseph received a divine commission to erect a temple in Kirtland in late 1832, several months before the pattern was revealed to him (see D&C 88:119–20). The Lord instructed the Saints to build "after the manner which I shall show unto three of you" (D&C 95:14). Those three, according to Truman O. Angell, the temple's primary craftsman, comprised the First Presidency of the Church. Frederick G. Williams, the Prophet's Second Counselor, told Angell, "Joseph received the word of the Lord for him to take his two counselors . . . and come before the Lord and He would show them the plan or model of the House to be built." Williams continued:

> We went upon our knees, called on the Lord, and the Building appeared within viewing distance. I being the first to discover it. Then all of us viewed it together. After we had taken a good look at the exterior, the Building seemed to come right over us, and the Makeup of this Hall [the lower auditorium] seemed to coincide with what I there saw to a minutia.[84]

Scriptural evidence indicates that patterns for the Independence, Far West, and Nauvoo Temples were also given in vision. Concerning the temple in Jackson County, the Lord stated on August 2, 1833, "Verily I say unto you, that it is my will that a house should be built unto me in the land of Zion, like unto the pattern which I have given you" (D&C 97:10). On June 25, 1833, over a month before receiving section 97, Joseph Smith had sent Church leaders in Jackson County detailed instructions concerning the size, features, and function of the temple complex in Independence plus an explanation of the layout and arrangement of the city of Zion. From this information, one might infer that Joseph Smith received the pattern of the city of Zion together with the vision shown to him for the temples of that early era.[85]

Concerning the temple at Far West, Joseph Smith received the following set of instructions:

> But let a house be built unto my name according to the pattern which I will show unto them. And if my people build it not

> according to the pattern which I shall show unto their presidency, I will not accept it at their hands. But if my people do build it according to the pattern which I shall show unto their presidency, even my servant Joseph and his counselors, then I will accept it at the hands of my people. (D&C 115:14–16; see also vv. 10–13)

This particular revelation specifically states the pattern would be given to the First Presidency. Any such revelation was not documented but must have been received before summer 1838, when the cornerstones were laid and construction began.[86]

The Nauvoo Temple stood as a crowning monument to the life and mission of the Prophet. God was the architect, but Joseph was the engineer. "And I will show unto my servant Joseph all things pertaining to this house, and the priesthood thereof, and the place whereon it shall be built. And ye shall build it on the place where you have contemplated building it, for that is the spot which I have chosen for you to build it" (D&C 124:42–43). Three other temple-building passages specifically state that the pattern would be revealed by the Lord, and the Prophet's history makes it clear that a pattern was indeed given. In February 1844, the Prophet called on William Weeks, temple architect. In Weeks's drawings, Joseph Smith noticed semicircular windows in the half stories separating the upper and lower halls. The Prophet politely instructed Weeks that the windows should be completely circular. Weeks protested, stating that circular windows "were a violation of all the known rules of architecture." Determined to have circular windows, Joseph responded, "I wish you to carry out *my* designs. I have seen in vision the splendid appearance of that building . . . and will have it built according to the pattern shown me."[87]

Visionary Dreams

Holy writ teaches that certain dreams can be visions or views sent from God. Ancient scripture contains numerous examples of God communicating to his servants visually through dreams. However, an examination of the historical sources leads to the conclusion that Joseph Smith did not receive most of his divine understanding through dreams in the night. Apparently, God chose more direct methods of communicating to him. Although the Prophet told of some of his dreams, he did not usually detail or interpret what he envisioned in those dreams.[88]

Conclusion

On October 9, 1843, Joseph Smith spoke at the funeral services of James Adams. "Could you gaze into heaven five minutes," he remarked, "you would know more than you would by reading all that ever was written on the subject."[89] He was privileged to view the heavens not just for five minutes but for extended periods on many occasions. As far as historical records indicate, Joseph Smith received more documentable visions than any other prophet, past or present. His receiving numerous visions occurred in part because he was called and appointed to bring about the "restitution of all things, which God hath spoken by the mouth of all his holy prophets since the world began" (Acts 3:21).

But Joseph's calling as a seer also came because of his spiritual capacity and sensitivity. As Brigham Young taught, "There are thousands in the world who are natural born Seers, but when the Lord selected Joseph Smith to be his vice-regent and mouthpiece upon the earth in this dispensation, he saw that he would be faithful and honor his calling."[90]

Extolling the visionary gifts of Joseph Smith, President John Taylor penned a poem entitled "The Seer," which was later set to music by Ebenezer Beesley. A portion of its first stanza follows:

> The seer;—the seer:—Joseph the seer—
> I'll sing of the Prophet ever dear:
> His equal now cannot be found,—
> By searching the wide world around.
> With Gods he soared, in the realms of day;
> And men he taught the heavenly way.
> The earthly seer! the heavenly seer,
>
> . . . .
>
> He gazed on the past, on the present too;—
> And ope'd the heav'nly world to view.[91]

Alexander L. Baugh is Associate Professor of Church History and Doctrine at Brigham Young University.

An earlier version of this article originally appeared in BYU Studies *38, no. 1 (1999): 22–69.*

Notes

1. The Hebrew *chāzāh* comes from "the usual word for 'see' in the various dialects of Aramaic, . . . referring both to the natural vision of the eyes and to supernatural visions of various kinds." G. Johannes Botterweck and Helmer Ringgren, eds., *Theological Dictionary of the Old Testament* (Grand Rapids, Mich.: Eerdmans, 1980), 4:281–82. The manner in which revelation was received by the Old Testament seers is not entirely clear, but it predominantly involved hearing the word of the Lord at night, although the eyes were also "somehow involved" (4:285). The obscure Hebrew term *chāzāh* is translated in the Greek LXX as *blepōn*, literally "looker," and then translated into English as "seer."

2. John A. Widtsoe, *Evidences and Reconciliations* (Salt Lake City: Bookcraft, 1987), 258. Orson F. Whitney stated: "A seer is one who sees. But it is not the ordinary sight that is meant. The seeric gift is a supernatural endowment." Orson F. Whitney, *Saturday Night Thoughts: A Series of Dissertations on Spiritual, Historical and Philosophic Themes* (Salt Lake City: Deseret News, 1921), 39. See also Steven C. Walker, "Seer," in *Encyclopedia of Mormonism*, ed. Daniel H. Ludlow, 4 vols. (New York: Macmillan, 1992), 3:1292–93.

3. Andrew F. Ehat and Lyndon W. Cook, eds., *The Words of Joseph Smith: The Contemporary Accounts of the Nauvoo Discourses of the Prophet Joseph* (Orem, Utah: Grandin, 1991), 59. See also Joseph Fielding Smith, comp., *Teachings of the Prophet Joseph Smith* (Salt Lake City: Deseret Book, 1972), 180. The Prophet compared his description of Paul to John C. Bennett's appearance. For more on how Bennett may have resembled the ancient apostle, see Ehat and Cook, *Words of Joseph Smith*, 82n2.

4. See J. K. Elliott, *The Apocryphal New Testament: A Collection of Apocryphal Christian Literature in an English Translation* (Oxford: Clarendon, 1993), 364.

5. Joseph Smith Jr., *History of The Church of Jesus Christ of Latter-day Saints*, ed. B. H. Roberts, 2d ed., rev., 7 vols. (Salt Lake City: Deseret Book, 1958), 5:402 (hereafter cited as *History of the Church*).

6. *History of the Church*, 5:362.

7. For a general discussion and overview of Joseph Smith's visionary experiences, see Larry C. Porter, "Visions of Joseph Smith," in *Encyclopedia of Mormonism*, 4:1512–16. For an examination of Joseph Smith's visionary contemporaries, see Richard L. Bushman, "The Visionary World of Joseph Smith," *BYU Studies* 37, no. 1 (1997–98): 183–204.

8. See H. Donl Peterson, "Moroni: Joseph Smith's Tutor," *Ensign* 22 (January 1992): 22–29; Peterson, "Moroni: Joseph Smith's Tutor," in Larry C. Porter, Milton V. Backman Jr., and Susan Easton Black, eds., *Regional Studies in Latter-day Saint Church History: New York* (Provo, Utah: Department of Church History and Doctrine, Brigham Young University, 1992), 49–70; and Robert J. Woodford, "Book of Mormon Personalities Known by Joseph Smith," *Ensign* 8 (August 1978): 12–15. See also H. Donl Peterson, *Moroni: Ancient Prophet, Modern Messenger* (Bountiful, Utah: Horizon, 1983).

9. Lyndon W. Cook, ed., *David Whitmer Interviews: A Restoration Witness* (Orem, Utah: Grandin Book, 1991), 27. Whitmer told the story on a number of occasions, leaving at least five additional versions of the incident. See Cook, *David Whitmer Interviews*, 13, 41–42, 49–50, 181–82, 213–16.

10. Dean C. Jessee, ed., *The Papers of Joseph Smith*, 2 vols. (Salt Lake City: Deseret Book, 1989–92), 1:431.

11. Orson Pratt, in *Journal of Discourses*, 26 vols. (Liverpool: F. D. Richards, 1855–86), 15:185, September 22, 1872. On another occasion, Orson Pratt stated, "After having received from time to time, visits from . . . glorious personages, and talking with them, . . . he was permitted to go and take [the] plates from the place of their deposit." Orson Pratt, in *Journal of Discourses*, 13:66, December 19, 1869.

12. George Q. Cannon, in *Journal of Discourses*, 23:362, October 29, 1882.

13. John Taylor, in *Journal of Discourses*, 17:374, April 8, 1875.

14. John Taylor, in *Journal of Discourses*, 21:94, April 13, 1879. For additional statements concerning the heavenly beings who appeared to Joseph Smith, see *Journal of Discourses*, 13:47; 18:326; 20:174–75; 21:65; 21:161, 163; and 23:48–49.

15. Lucy Mack Smith, *Biographical Sketches of Joseph Smith, the Prophet, and His Progenitors for Many Generations* (London: Published for Orson Pratt by S. W. Richards, 1853), 85. See also Woodford, "Book of Mormon Personalities," 12.

16. Oliver Cowdery, *Messenger and Advocate*, October 1834, 15–16; and Jessee, *Papers of Joseph Smith*, 1:30–32. It is significant to note that in his narrative Cowdery twice mentions that the voice of the Lord was heard. The Prophet's history does not mention this fact.

17. Larry C. Porter, "Dating the Restoration of the Melchizedek Priesthood," *Ensign* 9 (June 1979): 4–10; Larry C. Porter, "The Restoration of the Priesthood," *Religious Studies Center Newsletter* 9 (May 3, 1995): 3–7; Larry C. Porter, "The Restoration of the Aaronic and Melchizedek Priesthoods," *Ensign*

26 (December 1996): 30–47. For additional information on the restoration of the priesthood, see Brian Q. Cannon and *BYU Studies* staff, "Priesthood Restoration Documents," *BYU Studies* 35, no. 4 (1995–96): 162–207, reprinted herein as "Seventy Contemporaneous Priesthood Restoration Documents."

18. Newel Knight, "Newel Knight's Journal," in *Scraps of Biography*, Faith-Promoting Series, no. 10, published in *Classic Experiences and Adventures* (Salt Lake City: Bookcraft, 1969), 62–63.

19. Willard Chase, in Eber D. Howe, *Mormonism Unvailed* (Painesville, Ohio: By the author, 1834), 241–42. For eyewitness descriptions of the seer stone, see Richard Van Wagoner and Steve Walker, "Joseph Smith: 'The Gift of Seeing,'" *Dialogue: A Journal of Mormon Thought* 15 (Summer 1982): 59.

20. See Richard L. Bushman, *Joseph Smith and the Beginnings of Mormonism* (Urbana: University of Illinois Press, 1984), 69–70, 97, 103.

21. Martin Harris, in [Tiffany,] "Mormonism—No. II," *Tiffany's Monthly* 5 (May 1859): 164.

22. Dean Jessee, "Joseph Knight's Recollection of Early Mormon History," *BYU Studies* 17, no. 1 (1976): 31–32.

23. Cook, *David Whitmer Interviews*, 27. For slightly different accounts, see Cook, *David Whitmer Interviews*, 41, 48–49, 114–15, 123, 191, 213, 215.

24. Cook, *David Whitmer Interviews*, 150.

25. Jessee, "Joseph Knight's Recollection," 33.

26. Smith, *Biographical Sketches*, 106.

27. Smith, *Biographical Sketches*, 106.

28. Smith, *Biographical Sketches*, 102–8. The three incidents were: (1) taking the plates from the old birch log where he had initially deposited them, (2) concealing the plates beneath the hearth, and (3) hiding the plates in some flax in the loft of the cooper's shop. Harris's recollections parallel that of Mother Smith. See [Tiffany,] "Mormonism," 166–67.

29. [Tiffany,] "Mormonism," 169.

30. For recent discussions of translation, see Neal A. Maxwell, "By the Gift and Power of God," *Ensign* 27 (January 1997): 36–41; Royal Skousen, "Translating the Book of Mormon: Evidence from the Original Manuscript," in Noel B. Reynolds, ed., *Book of Mormon Authorship Revisited: The Evidence for Ancient Origins* (Provo, Utah: FARMS, 1997), 61–93; John W. Welch, *The Sermon at the Temple and the Sermon on the Mount: A Latter-day Saint Approach* (Salt Lake City: Deseret Book and FARMS, 1990), 130–44; Stephen D. Ricks, "Joseph Smith's Means and Methods of Translating the Book of Mormon" (Provo, Utah: FARMS paper, 1986); and John W. Welch, "The Miraculous Translation of the Book of Mormon," herein.

31. Edward Stevenson, "One of the Three Witnesses: Incidents in the Life of Martin Harris," *Millennial Star* 44 (February 6, 1882): 86–87.

32. David Whitmer, *An Address to All Believers in Christ* (Richmond, Mo.: n.p., 1887), 12.

33. "Now the first that my <husband> translated, [the book of Lehi] was translated by the use of the Urim, and Thummim, and that was the part that Martin Harris lost, after that he [Joseph] used a small stone [to translate the plates]." Emma Smith Bidamon to Emma Pilgrim, March 27, 1870, in John T. Clark, "Translation of Nephite Records," *The Return* 4 (July 15, 1895): 2. Written from Nauvoo, the original letter is located in the Emma Smith Papers, Library-Archives, Community of Christ, Independence, Mo. David Whitmer stated:

> This unpardonable carelessness [of giving Martin Harris the manuscript] evoked the stormiest kind of chastisement from the Lord, who took from the prophet the urim and thummum and otherwise expressed his condemnation. By fervent prayer and by otherwise humbling himself, the prophet, however, again found favor, and was presented with a . . . stone . . . which, it was promised, should serve the same purpose as the missing urim and thummim. . . . With this stone all of the present Book of Mormon was translated. (Cook, *David Whitmer Interviews*, 200; see also 72, 156–57, 175, 230)

34. Although not indicated in the historical record, it is likely that section 10 was received through the Urim and Thummim. Sections 3 and 10 were probably received through the Nephite interpreters since these revelations were given in conjunction with the loss of the 116 pages.

35. Whitmer, *Address to All Believers*, 32. The seer stone passed through a series of owners. Soon after the translation of the Book of Mormon was complete, Joseph Smith gave the stone to Oliver Cowdery, who possessed the stone until his death in 1848. That same year Phineas Young visited Oliver's widow, Lucy Cowdery, and persuaded her to give it to him. He returned to Salt Lake City and presented it to his brother, Brigham Young. The stone has remained in the possession of the Church since that time. See Whitmer, *Address to All Believers*, 32; Cook, *David Whitmer Interviews*, 200; and Zina Young Card to F. D. Richards, July 31, 1896, F. D. Richards Letter Collection, Church Archives, The Church of Jesus Christ of Latter-day Saints, Salt Lake City, as cited in Van Wagoner and Walker, "Gift of Seeing," 66n53. Edward Stevenson remembered Joseph Smith using a seer stone at least four years after the Book of Mormon was translated. See Edward Stevenson, *Reminiscences of Joseph the Prophet and the Coming Forth of the Book of Mormon* (Salt Lake City: By the author, 1893), 6.

36. *History of the Church*, 4:537; also Jessee, *Papers of Joseph Smith*, 1:431.

37. Oliver Cowdery to [W. W. Phelps], *Messenger and Advocate*, October 1835, 198; Jessee, *Papers of Joseph Smith*, 1:87. Although this was a vision of Satan

and his associates, it was given to Joseph Smith by Moroni and the powers of heaven.

38. Brigham Young, in *Journal of Discourses*, 19:38, June 17, 1877.

39. The two additional statements by Brigham Young concerning the cave and the plates are given here. William H. Dame was present when Brigham Young

> related a story told to him by Hyrum Smith which was as follows: Joseph, Hyrum, Cowdery, and Whitmere went to the hill Cormorah. As they were walking up the hill, a door opened and they walked into a room about 16 ft square. In that room was an angel and a trunk. On the trunk lay a book of Mormon & gold plates, Laban's sword, Aaron's brestplate. (William H. Dame, Diary, manuscript, January 14, 1855, L. Tom Perry Special Collections, Harold B. Lee Library, Brigham Young University, Provo, Utah)

On December 11, 1869, Wilford Woodruff heard Brigham Young relate to the Salt Lake School of the Prophets,

> President Young said in relation to Joseph Smith returning the Plates of the Book of Mormon that He did not return them to the Box from wh[ence?] He had Received But He went [in?] a Cave in the Hill Comoro with Oliver Cowdry & deposited those plates upon a table or shelf. In that room were deposited a large amount of gold plates Containing sacred records & when they first visited that Room the sword of Laban was Hanging upon the wall & when they last visited it the sword was drawn from the scabbard & [laid?] upon a table & a Messenger who was the keeper of the room informed them that that sword would never be returned to its scabbard untill the Kingdom of God was Esstablished upon the Earth & untill it reigned triumphant over Evry Enemy. Joseph Smith said that Cave Contained tons of Choice Treasures & records. (Wilford Woodruff, *Wilford Woodruff's Journal, 1833–1898,* ed. Scott G. Kenney, 9 vols. [Midvale, Utah: Signature Books, 1983–85], 6:508–9)

40. In 1856, Heber C. Kimball made brief mention of the Nephite depository in the Hill Cumorah. "How does it [the crossing of the plains] compare with the vision that Joseph and others had, when they went into a cave in the hill Cumorah, and saw more records than ten men could carry? There were books piled up on tables, book upon book." *Journal of Discourses*, 4:105, September 28, 1856. Several years later, Kimball spoke to a missionary meeting at the Church Historians' Office and "related about Father Smith, Oliver Cowdery and others walking into the Hill Cumorah and seeing records upon

records piled upon tables, they walked from cell to cell and saw the records that were piled up." Brigham Young Manuscript History, May 5, 1867, microfilm of holograph, Church Archives. Orson Pratt made at least four statements attesting to his belief in the Cumorah library. See *Journal of Discourses*, 14:331; 15:183; 17:30; and 17:281–82. David Whitmer believed the cave existed but felt it was in a location other than the Hill Cumorah. See Cook, *David Whitmer Interviews*, 22; A. Karl Larson and Katharine Miles Larson, eds., *Diary of Charles Lowell Walker*, 2 vols. (Logan: Utah State University Press, 1980), 2:525–26; and Stevenson, *Reminiscences of Joseph*, 14–15.

41. Levi W. Hancock, "The Life of Levi Ward Hancock," typescript, 33, Perry Special Collections, quoted in Karl Ricks Anderson, *Joseph Smith's Kirtland: Eyewitness Accounts* (Salt Lake City: Deseret Book, 1989), 107–8.

42. "Salt Lake School of the Prophets Minute Book, 1883," October 3, 1883, typescript, 56–57, Perry Special Collections.

43. "Salt Lake City School of Prophets Minute Book, 1883," October 3, 1883, 57.

44. Zebedee Coltrin, in Utah Stake Minutes, Spanish Fork High Priests, February 5, 1870, Church Archives.

45. John Murdock, Journal, typescript, 13, Perry Special Collections; also quoted in Milton V. Backman Jr., *The Heavens Resound: A History of the Latter-day Saints in Ohio, 1830–1838* (Salt Lake City: Deseret Book, 1983), 267. Joseph Smith made brief reference to the appearance of the Father and the Son on this occasion. See *History of the Church*, 1:334–35.

46. Jessee, *Papers of Joseph Smith*, 2:157.

47. Orson F. Whitney, *Life of Heber C. Kimball: An Apostle, the Father and Founder of the British Mission* (Salt Lake City: Bookcraft, 1974), 93–94.

48. Mary Elizabeth Rollins Lightner, in Anderson, *Joseph Smith's Kirtland*, 112–13.

49. See Smith, *Teachings*, 38–39; and Joseph Fielding Smith, *Life of Joseph F. Smith, Sixth President of The Church of Jesus Christ of Latter-day Saints* (Salt Lake City: Deseret News Press, 1938), 34–35. A careful reading of Doctrine and Covenants 107:53–57 indicates that these verses are given almost verbatim with those of the Joseph Smith Sr. December 1833 blessing, thus revealing the initial source.

50. *History of the Church*, 3:388.

51. The Prophet's history indicates the Savior made his appearance "to some." Although the record does not state Martin actually saw Christ, the fact that Martin knew the being was Christ indicates he more than likely did see the Savior. See Jessee, *Papers of Joseph Smith*, 2:207; reprinted in *History of the Church*, 2:432–33.

52. Harrison Burgess, "Sketch of a Well-Spent Life," in *Labors in the Vineyard: Twelfth Book of the Faith-Promoting Series* (Salt Lake City: Juvenile

Instructor Office, 1884), 67. For a discussion of the dating of this vision, see the document section of this article, n53.

53. See notes 49 and 50 above.

54. Heber C. Kimball, in *Journal of Discourses*, 9:41, March 17, 1861. See also Whitney, *Life of Heber C. Kimball*, 93–94.

55. "Salt Lake City School of the Prophets Minute Book, 1883," October 11, 1883, 67. The Prophet's history is the source for the date of the conference that took place April 21, 1834. See *History of the Church*, 2:52–54.

56. *History of the Church*, 5:247.

57. Jessee, *Papers of Joseph Smith*, 2:158.

58. Edward Partridge, Journal, January 21, 1836, typescript, Church Archives.

59. Leonard J. Arrington, "Oliver Cowdery's Kirtland, Ohio, 'Sketch Book,'" *BYU Studies* 12, no. 4 (1972): 419.

60. Jessee, *Papers of Joseph Smith*, 2:160.

61. Jessee, *Papers of Joseph Smith*, 2:164.

62. Truman O. Angell Sr., "His Journal," in *Our Pioneer Heritage*, comp. Kate B. Carter, 20 vols. (Salt Lake City: Daughters of Utah Pioneers, 1958–77), 10:198.

63. Whitney, *Life of Heber C. Kimball*, 91.

64. Angell, "His Journal," 198. In her reminiscence of the Kirtland Temple dedication, Lydia Knight indicated that the personage who appeared during the services was none other than Jesus. See Lydia Knight, *Lydia Knight's History: The First Book of the Noble Women's Lives Series* (Salt Lake City: Juvenile Instructor Office, 1883), 33. In an 1864 address, George A. Smith also identified the messenger as being the Savior. *Journal of Discourses*, 11:10, November 15, 1864. Angell's account is accepted as being the most accurate since he claims to have received the information from Joseph Smith.

65. *History of the Church*, 2:427. Reminiscing about the dedication of the Kirtland Temple, Orson Pratt later declared:

> God was there, his angels were there, the Holy Ghost was in the midst of the people, the visions of the Almighty were opened to the minds of the servants of the living God; the vail was taken off from the minds of many; they saw the heavens opened; they beheld the angels of God; they heard the voice of the Lord; and they were filled from the crown of their heads to the soles of their feet with the power and inspiration of the Holy Ghost. . . .
>
> . . . In that Temple, set apart by the servants of God, and dedicated by a prayer that was written by inspiration, the people were blessed as they never had been blessed for generations and generations. (*Journal of Discourses*, 18:132, October 9, 1875)

66. *History of the Church*, 2:428.

67. Whitney, *Life of Heber C. Kimball*, 92. Kimball did not state on what day the anointings took place. However, the events of March 29–30 seem to indicate the appearance must have occurred on one of those two dates. See *History of the Church*, 2:428–34.

68. See Orson Pratt, in *Journal of Discourses*, 18:131–32, October 9, 1875.

69. Mary Elizabeth Rollins Lightner [1905], as cited in Danel W. Bachman, "A Study of the Mormon Practice of Plural Marriage before the Death of Joseph Smith" (master's thesis, Purdue University, 1975), 74.

70. Eliza R. Snow Smith, *Biography and Family Record of Lorenzo Snow, One of the Twelve Apostles of The Church of Jesus Christ of Latter-day Saints* (Salt Lake City: Deseret News, 1884), 69–70. Additional statements about the angel are Joseph B. Noble Affidavit, [1869], as quoted in Bachman, "A Study of the Mormon Practice of Plural Marriage," 74; and Benjamin F. Johnson to George S. Gibbs, April–October 1903, in E. Dale LeBaron, *Benjamin F. Johnson: Friend to the Prophets* (Provo, Utah: Grandin, 1997), 227.

71. Whitney, *Life of Heber C. Kimball*, 258–59.

72. Heber C. Kimball, in *Journal of Discourses*, 3:229–30, March 2, 1856.

73. *History of the Church*, 2:254.

74. *History of the Church*, 2:254.

75. Kenneth W. Godfrey has made a thorough examination of each of the accounts, noting their similarities and differences. See Kenneth W. Godfrey, "The Zelph Story," *BYU Studies* 29, no. 2 (1989): 31–56.

76. "History of Joseph Smith," *Times and Seasons* 6 (January 1, 1846): 1076; History of the Church, 2:79–80. These accounts are written as if Joseph Smith were telling the story.

77. Nathan Tanner, "Reminiscences," in George S. Tanner, *John Tanner and His Family* (Salt Lake City: Publishers Press, 1974), 382–83.

78. *History of the Church*, 2:181n.

79. Parley P. Pratt, "Proclamation," in *Millennial Star* 5 (March 1845): 151. See also Robert J. Matthews, *"A Plainer Translation": Joseph Smith's Translation of the Bible* (Provo, Utah: Brigham Young University Press, 1975), 258–60. It is likely Joseph Smith received a vision of the purpose and function of other types of Church councils, particularly the high council, at least a year prior to receiving his understanding concerning the Twelve and the Seventy. At a meeting of high priests in February 1834, he explained in explicit detail the decorum that existed in ancient councils. See *History of the Church*, 2:25–26. One week later he proceeded to organize the Kirtland High Council (see D&C 102). Then in July of that same year, while in Clay County with Zion's Camp, he organized the high council in Missouri. See *History of the Church*, 2:122–24.

At one time the Mormon leader declared that all Church councils were to be conducted according to an ancient pattern that had been shown him by "vision." Joseph Smith, February 17, 1834, in Fred C. Collier and William S. Harwell, eds., *Kirtland Council Minute Book* (Salt Lake City: Collier's, 1996), 24.

80. *History of the Church*, 6:289.

81. Orson F. Whitney, "Newel K. Whitney," *Contributor* 6 (January 1885): 125; also in *History of the Church*, 1:146n.

82. *History of the Church*, 3:391.

83. *History of the Church*, 5:361–62. Wilford Woodruff recorded portions of this sermon in his journal. He quoted the Prophet as saying: "In speaking of the resurrection I would say that God hath shown unto me a vision of the resurrection of the dead & I saw the graves open & the saints as they arose took each other by the hand even before they got up or while getting up & great Joy & glory rested upon them." Woodruff, *Journal*, 2:227 [April 16, 1843].

84. Angell, "His Journal," 10:198. Lyndon W. Cook has given substantial historical evidence that indicates section 95 was actually received in early June 1833, while section 94 was received in August, some two months after section 95. As further evidence of this, Cook states that "verses 1–2 of section 94 indicate that the pattern for constructing the Kirtland Temple had already been given." Lyndon W. Cook, *The Revelations of the Prophet Joseph Smith* (Salt Lake City: Deseret Book, 1985), 195. In D&C 94:3–12, Joseph Smith was instructed to build a house for the Presidency and a house for printing, the patterns of which were also to be revealed. Whether the patterns for these two buildings were ever given is not known. For more on the pattern of the Kirtland Temple, see Elwin C. Robison, *The First Mormon Temple: Design, Construction, and Historic Context of the Kirtland Temple* (Provo, Utah: Brigham Young University Press, 1997), 7–26.

85. See *History of the Church*, 1:357–62.

86. The Far West Temple revelation was received on April 26, 1838. Four days later, Thomas B. Marsh wrote a letter wherein he indicated the "plan is yet to be shown to the First presidency." See Thomas B. Marsh to Wilford Woodruff, April 30, 1838, Wilford Woodruff Papers, Church Archives. This letter was published in Thomas B. Marsh to Wilford Woodruff [April 30, 1838], in *Elders' Journal* 1 (July 1838): 38. The cornerstones of the temple were subsequently laid on July 4, 1838. "Celebration of the 4th of July," *Elders' Journal* 1 (August 1838): 60. During summer and fall 1838, work on the temple proceeded slowly due to the Missouri persecutions. According to Missourian William A. Wood, the walls were built to a height of two or two and a half feet. See William A. Wood, "An Old Mormon City in Missouri," *Magazine of American History* 16 (1886): 99; and Cook, *Revelations of the Prophet Joseph Smith*, 237.

87. *History of the Church*, 6:196–97; italics in original.

88. The recorded dreams of Joseph Smith are in *History of the Church*, 2:387; 5:254–55, 394; 6:194–95, 461–62, 609–10.

89. *History of the Church*, 6:50.

90. "Report of Remarks Made at the Tabernacle, 23 December 1860," *Deseret News Weekly*, December 26, 1860, 341, quoted in Ronald W. Walker, "Joseph Smith: The Palmyra Seer," *BYU Studies* 24 (fall 1984): 468.

91. John Taylor, "The Seer," broadside (n.p.: John Taylor, ca. 1844–45), Perry Special Collections; reprinted as "The Seer, Joseph the Seer," in *Hymns of The Church of Jesus Christ of Latter-day Saints* (Salt Lake City: Deseret Book, 1927), no. 96.

Documented Visions of Joseph Smith

The following collection of historical documents attempts to bring together all the known visions of Joseph Smith with the exception of various forms of visionary inspiration received as part of the translation of the words of the Bible, Book of Mormon, or Pearl of Great Price, which are too numerous to mention here. Synopses of visions are arranged chronologically. Listed first is the date, either exact or approximate, that Joseph Smith received the vision, followed by a close paraphrase of each vision taken from a document judged to be the most comprehensive account available. The source for this account follows each paraphrase. Some details in a paraphrase may derive from a second source, listed in the footnotes. Following each main source is the date when the document was written. Date spans indicate the period of time within which the vision was received, not the length of the vision. A "ca." (circa) before a date means the date is unknown but assumed based on historical evidence. Footnotes do not include every known account of each vision, but instead give some sources where readers can go to learn more. Because this collection depends on record keeping and the preservation of historical documents and because some manifestations are grouped here for the reader's convenience, this list should not be taken as an exhaustive compilation of Joseph Smith's visions.

1. Spring 1820

God the Father, Jesus Christ, and many angels appeared to Joseph Smith. Main source: Joseph Smith (1839).[1]

2A–2E. September 21–22, 1823

The angel Moroni appeared to Joseph Smith on five separate occasions. Main source: Joseph Smith (1839).[2]

3. September 21–22, 1823

Joseph Smith saw the location of the plates from which the Book of Mormon was translated. Main source: Joseph Smith (1839).[3]

4. September 21–22, 1823

Joseph Smith was shown the ancient inhabitants of "this country." Main source: Joseph Smith (1842).[4]

5. September 22, 1823

Joseph Smith saw the prince of darkness and his innumerable associates. Main source: Oliver Cowdery (1835).[5]

6. September 22, 1823–September 22, 1827

Joseph Smith received many visits from God's angels. Main source: Joseph Smith (1842).[6]

7A–7C. September 22, 1824–September 22, 1826

Joseph Smith met with Moroni at three annual intervals. Main source: Joseph Smith (1839).[7]

8. September 22, 1826

Joseph Smith saw that he should take Emma Hale with him to the Hill Cumorah the following year. Main source: Joseph Knight (ca. 1833–47).[8]

9. Early 1827

Moroni instructed Joseph Smith near the Hill Cumorah. Main source: Lucy Mack Smith (1845).[9]

10. September 22, 1827

Moroni delivered the plates and sacred relics to Joseph Smith. Main source: Joseph Smith (1839).[10]

11. Late 1827

Joseph Smith saw his "entire past history" through the Urim and Thummim. Main source: David Whitmer (1884).[11]

12A–12C. Late 1827–Early 1828

At various times after receiving the plates, Joseph Smith saw when he or the plates were in danger. Main source: Lucy Mack Smith (1845).[12]

13. Late 1827–Early 1828

Joseph Smith was shown the man who would assist him in translation, Martin Harris. Main source: Martin Harris (1859).[13]

14. 1827–1828

Joseph Smith was shown the location of a pin lost by Martin Harris. Main source: Martin Harris (1859).[14]

15. June–July 1828

Moroni took the Urim and Thummim from Joseph Smith. Main source: Joseph Smith (1839).[15]

16. June–July 1828

Moroni returned the Urim and Thummim to Joseph Smith. Main source: Joseph Smith (1839).[16]

17. Summer 1828

Moroni took the plates and, again, the Urim and Thummim from Joseph Smith. Main source: Joseph Smith (1839).[17]

18A–18I. September 22, 1828

Moroni returned the plates and the Urim and Thummim through which at least nine revelations were seen. Main source: Lucy Mack Smith (1845).[18]

19. May 15, 1829

John the Baptist appeared to Joseph Smith and Oliver Cowdery. Main source: Joseph Smith (1839).[19]

20. ca. May–June 1829

Satan appeared to Joseph Smith as an angel of light. Main source: Joseph Smith (1842).[20]

21. ca. May–June 1829

Peter, James, and John appeared to Joseph Smith and Oliver Cowdery. Main source: Joseph Smith (1830).[21]

22. May–June 1829

Joseph Smith saw David Whitmer en route from Fayette, New York, to Harmony, Pennsylvania. Main source: David Whitmer (1884).[22]

23. May–June 1829

Joseph Smith gave the plates to Moroni before proceeding to Fayette, New York. Main source: Lucy Mack Smith (1845).[23]

24. May–June 1829

Joseph Smith, Oliver Cowdery, and David Whitmer saw Moroni along the road to Fayette, New York. Main source: David Whitmer (1886).[24]

25. May–June 1829

Joseph Smith received the plates from Moroni after arriving in Fayette, New York. Main source: Lucy Mack Smith (1845).[25]

26. June 1829

Joseph Smith, Oliver Cowdery, and David Whitmer saw an angel who showed them the plates and other sacred relics. Main source: Joseph Smith (1839).[26]

27. June 1829

Joseph Smith and Martin Harris saw an angel who showed them the plates and other sacred relics. Main source: Joseph Smith (1839).[27]

28. June 1829

Moroni delivered the plates so that Joseph could show them to the Eight Witnesses. Main source: Lucy Mack Smith (1845).[28]

29. ca. June 1829

Joseph Smith returned the plates to the angel. Main source: Joseph Smith (1839).[29]

30. August 1830

Joseph Smith received a revelation on the sacrament from a heavenly messenger. Main source: Joseph Smith (1839).[30]

31. January 1831

Joseph Smith and others saw by vision the growth of the Church. Main source: Sidney Rigdon (1844).[31]

32. January 1831

Joseph Smith saw Newel K. Whitney in vision. Main source: Orson F. Whitney (1885).[32]

33. June 3–6, 1831

Joseph Smith saw God and Jesus Christ. Main source: Levi W. Hancock (before 1883).[33]

34. June 1831

By heavenly vision, Joseph Smith was commanded to travel to western Missouri and there designate the location for a temple and central gathering place of Zion. Main source: Joseph Smith (1835).[34]

35. July 1831

Joseph Smith and others were shown where the temple at Independence and the city of Zion would be located. Main source: Joseph Smith (1835).[35]

36. 1831

Joseph Smith identified the presence of Jesus Christ in a meeting of the Saints. Main source: Mary Elizabeth Rollins Lightner (1905).[36]

37. February 16, 1832

Joseph Smith and Sidney Rigdon saw the Son of Man on the right hand of God, events in the premortal life, and postmortal glories. Main source: Joseph Smith (1832).[37]

38. May–June 1832

Joseph Smith was shown the mode of travel he and Newel K. Whitney would take after leaving Greenville, Indiana. Main source: Joseph Smith (1839).[38]

39. March 18, 1833

Joseph Smith identified the physical presence of God the Father and Jesus Christ in the School of the Prophets. Main source: Zebedee Coltrin (1883).[39]

40. June 1833

Joseph Smith, Frederick G. Williams, and Sidney Rigdon viewed the plan for the Kirtland Temple. Main source: Truman O. Angell (1885).[40]

41. December 18, 1833

Joseph Smith saw Jehovah appear to Adam at Adam-ondi-Ahman. Main source: Patriarchial Blessing Book (1833).[41]

42. ca. February 1834

Joseph Smith saw the pattern and organization of Church councils. Main source: Joseph Smith (1834).[42]

43. April 18, 1834

Joseph Smith, Oliver Cowdery, and Zebedee Coltrin saw Adam and Eve. Main source: Zebedee Coltrin (1870).[43]

44. May–June 1834

Joseph Smith saw land passed over by Zion's Camp in a high state of cultivation. Main source: Nathan Tanner (1884).[44]

45. June 1834

By vision, Joseph Smith was taught about Zelph, a Lamanite warrior. Main source: Wilford Woodruff (1834).[45]

46. ca. February 1835

Joseph Smith saw the postmortal condition of those who died in Zion's Camp and the order of the priesthood. Main source: Joseph Smith (1835).[46]

47. ca. 1835

Joseph Smith saw Christian martyrs' condition. Main source: Edward Stevenson (1893).[47]

48. January 21, 1836

Joseph Smith saw the celestial kingdom, some of its inhabitants, the Twelve in foreign lands, the Savior standing in their midst, the redemption of Zion, and many other things that the tongue of man cannot fully describe. Main source: Joseph Smith (1836).[48]

49. January 22–23, 1836

Visions of God attended Joseph Smith through the night. Main source: Joseph Smith (1836).[49]

50. January 28, 1836

Joseph Smith saw a glorious vision in the Kirtland Temple. Main source: Joseph Smith (1836).[50]

51. January 28–29, 1836

Visions of the Lord attended Joseph Smith through the night. Main source: Joseph Smith (1836).[51]

52. March 27, 1836

Joseph Smith beheld the Kirtland Temple filled with angels, including Peter. Main source: Joseph Smith (1836).[52]

53. ca. March 30, 1836

Joseph Smith saw Jesus Christ and angels, including John the Beloved, in the Kirtland Temple. Main source: Harrison Burgess (before 1885).[53]

54. April 3, 1836

Joseph Smith and Oliver Cowdery saw Jesus Christ, Moses, Elijah, and Elias in the Kirtland Temple. Main source: Joseph Smith (1836).[54]

55. April–May 1836

Joseph Smith saw Frederick G. Williams's daughter and her family en route to Missouri. Main source: Caroline Barnes Crosby (before 1885).[55]

56. April 6, 1837

Joseph Smith saw the future of Kirtland. Main source: Wilford Woodruff (1837).[56]

57. Summer 1837

Joseph Smith was blessed with glorious visions during an illness. Main source: Mary Fielding (1837).[57]

58. September 1837

Joseph Smith was shown in vision the enlargement of Zion's borders. Main source: Mary Fielding (1837).[58]

59. March 1838

Joseph Smith saw William Marks carried away by an angel. Main source: Joseph Smith (1838).[59]

60. March–October 1838

Joseph Smith saw Satan face to face. Main source: Heber C. Kimball (before 1869).[60]

61. Before 1839

Joseph Smith was shown the pattern for the temple in Far West, Missouri. Main source: Thomas B. Marsh (1838).[61]

62. April 11–12, 1839

Joseph Smith saw the means of escape from Liberty Jail and danger awaiting Stephen Markham. Main source: *History of the Church* (1845).[62]

63. Before July 2, 1839

Joseph Smith saw persecutions and judgments that would occur prior to the Second Coming. Main source: *History of the Church* (1845).[63]

64. Before March 4, 1840

By the visions of the Almighty, Joseph Smith saw the end of the United States if she disregards the cries of virtuous citizens. Main source: *History of the Church* (1845).[64]

65. August 6, 1842

Joseph gazed upon the valleys of the Rocky Mountains. Main source: Anson Call (ca. 1854).[65]

66. August 15–16, 1842

Through dream and vision, Joseph was persuaded against traveling to the "Pine country." Main source: Joseph Smith (1842).[66]

67A–67C. Before 1843

At least three times since 1834, an angel appeared to Joseph Smith and commanded him to enter into the practice of plural marriage. Main source: Joseph B. Noble (1869).[67]

68. Before January 20, 1843

Joseph Smith dreamed that he was in the Illinois statehouse among enemies. Main source: *History of the Church* (1845–46).[68]

69. Before April 16, 1843

Joseph Smith saw in vision the resurrection of the dead. Main source: Wilford Woodruff (1843).[69]

70. Before May 19, 1843

Joseph Smith dreamed that writing and compiling the history of the Church must move forward. Main source: *History of the Church* (1854–56).[70]

71. Before February 3, 1844

Joseph Smith saw himself in a dream swimming safely in troubled waters. Main source: Wilford Woodruff (1844).[71]

72. Before February 5, 1844

Joseph Smith saw in vision the pattern for the Nauvoo Temple. Main source: *History of the Church* (1854–56).[72]

73. June 1844

Joseph Smith saw in vision what would happen to the Saints if the *Nauvoo Expositor* press was not destroyed. Main source: George Laub (1845).[73]

74. Before June 13, 1844

Joseph Smith dreamed that he escaped a pit where his enemies had thrown him. Main source: *History of the Church* (1854–56).[74]

75. June 26–27, 1844

Joseph Smith dreamed that his life was threatened. Main source: *History of the Church* (1854–56).[75]

76. Date Unknown

Joseph Smith saw the common progenitors of several early Church leaders. Main source: Heber C. Kimball (1856).[76]

Notes to the Documented Visions

1. Joseph Smith, History, 1839, in Dean C. Jessee, ed., *The Papers of Joseph Smith*, 2 vols. (Salt Lake City: Deseret Book, 1989–92), 1:267–75; Joseph Smith, History, 1834–1836, in Jessee, *Papers of Joseph Smith*, 1:125–27. The account of the vision in the 1839 history was canonized in Joseph Smith—History 1:1–20. See also Doctrine and Covenants 20:5. For other accounts of this vision prepared under Joseph Smith's direction, see Jessee, *Papers of Joseph Smith*, 1:3–7, 429–30, 448–49. For accounts written by those who claimed to hear Joseph rehearse this vision, see Jessee, *Papers of Joseph Smith*, 1:443–44, 461; and Andrew F. Ehat and Lyndon W. Cook, eds., *The Words of Joseph Smith: The Contemporary Accounts of the Nauvoo Discourses of the Prophet Joseph*, Religious Studies Monograph Series, no. 6 (Provo, Utah: Religious Studies Center, Brigham Young University, 1980), 215. For contemporaneous accounts prepared by Joseph Smith's close associates, see Jessee, *Papers of Joseph Smith*, 1:389–91, 405–9. See also Dean C. Jessee, "The Early Accounts of Joseph Smith's First Vision," *BYU Studies* 9, no. 3 (1969): 275–94, reprinted herein as "Ten Documented Accounts of Joseph Smith's First Vision"; and James B. Allen, "Eight Contemporary Accounts of Joseph Smith's First Vision: What Do We Learn from Them?" *Improvement Era* 73 (April 1970): 4–13, reprinted herein as James B. Allen and John W. Welch, "The Appearance of the Father and the Son to Joseph Smith in 1820."

Many of the accounts listed in this appendix have been published previously, some of them with minor changes in spelling and punctuation, in Joseph Smith Jr., *History of The Church of Jesus Christ of Latter-day Saints*, ed. B. H. Roberts, 2d ed., rev., 7 vols. (Salt Lake City: Deseret Book, 1971) (hereafter cited as *History of the Church*). Primary source documents, when available, are cited first, followed by reprints in History of the Church and Joseph Smith—History in the Pearl of Great Price. References to *History of the Church* have been omitted when the same material appears in the Doctrine and Covenants or Pearl of Great Price.

2. Joseph Smith, History, 1839, in Jessee, *Papers of Joseph Smith*, 1:275–82; Joseph Smith—History 1:27–53. See also Doctrine and Covenants 2; 20:5–9; 27:5. For other accounts of this vision prepared under Joseph Smith's direction, see Jessee, *Papers of Joseph Smith*, 1:8–9, 127–28, 430–31, 449–50. For contemporary accounts prepared by Joseph Smith's close associates, see Jessee, *Papers of Joseph Smith*, 1:50–54, 73–76, 85–90, 392–94, 409–21. Context is provided by Lucy Mack Smith, *Biographical Sketches of Joseph Smith, the Prophet, and His Progenitors for Many Generations* (London: Published for Orson Pratt by S. W. Richards, 1853), 78–85.

3. Joseph Smith, History, 1839, in Jessee, *Papers of Joseph Smith*, 1:279; Joseph Smith—History 1:42. Joseph Knight said Joseph Smith had a "vision" of the location. Dean C. Jessee, "Joseph Knight's Recollection of Early Mormon History," *BYU Studies* 17, no. 1 (1976): 30–31.

4. Joseph Smith, "Church History," 1842, in Jessee, *Papers of Joseph Smith*, 1:431; reprinted in *History of the Church*, 4:537.

5. Joseph Smith, History, 1834–1836, in Jessee, *Papers of Joseph Smith*, 1:87. See also Smith, *Biographical Sketches*, 83–85. Cowdery's account was first published in the October 1834 issue of the *Messenger and Advocate* as the eighth of a series of letters projected to give "a full history of the rise of the church of the Latter Day Saints." *Messenger and Advocate*, October 1834, 13. Joseph offered his assistance at the beginning of the writing stage and later directed copying the letters into his journal. See Jessee, *Papers of Joseph Smith*, 1:16–17.

6. Joseph Smith, "Church History," 1842, in Jessee, *Papers of Joseph Smith*, 1:431; reprinted in *History of the Church*, 4:537. The Doctrine and Covenants alludes to Joseph Smith's experience with some of these angels. In 1842, Joseph described hearing the "voice" of "divers angels" from Adam "down to the present time, all declaring their dispensation, their rights, their keys, their honors, their majesty and glory, and the power of their priesthood" (D&C 128:20–21). The voices of Gabriel, Raphael, and Michael were among those Joseph heard (D&C 128:20). Several of the Prophet's associates later made reference to some of these visits. See John Taylor, in *Journal of Discourses*, 26 vols. (Liverpool: F. D. Richards, 1855–86), 17:374, April 8, 1875; John Taylor, in *Journal of Discourses*, 18:326, December 31, 1876; John Taylor, in *Journal of Discourses*, 20:174–75, April 8, 1879; John Taylor, in *Journal of Discourses*, 21:65, January 4, 1880; John Taylor, in *Journal of Discourses*, 21:94, April 13, 1879; John Taylor, in *Journal of Discourses*, 21:161–63, December 7, 1879; John Taylor, in *Journal of Discourses*, 23:48–49, April 9, 1882; Orson Pratt, in *Journal of Discourses*, 13:67, December 19, 1869; Orson Pratt, in *Journal of Discourses*, 15:185, September 22, 1872; George Q. Cannon, in *Journal of Discourses*, 13:47, December 5, 1869; George Q. Cannon, in *Journal of Discourses*, 23:362, October 29, 1882.

7. Smith, History, 1839, in Jessee, *Papers of Joseph Smith*, 1:282; Joseph Smith—History 1:54. See also Smith, *Biographical Sketches*, 85–86.

8. Jessee, "Joseph Knight's Recollection," 31.

9. Smith, Biographical Sketches, 98–99. Lucy's account was published in 1853 but dictated in 1845. See Richard Lloyd Anderson, "Circumstantial Confirmation of the First Vision through Reminiscences," *BYU Studies* 9, no. 3 (1969): 386–88. According to Lucy, the angel told Joseph that he had "not been engaged enough in the work of the Lord," and that he "must be up and doing." Smith, *Biographical Sketches*, 99.

10. Joseph Smith, History, 1839, in Jessee, *Papers of Joseph Smith*, 1:283; Joseph Smith—History 1:59. See also Smith, *Biographical Sketches*, 99–106; and Jessee, "Joseph Knight's Recollection," 32–33.

11. David Whitmer interview with the *St. Louis Republican*, July 16, 1884, as cited in Lyndon W. Cook, ed., *David Whitmer Interviews: A Restoration Witness* (Orem, Utah: Grandin Book, 1991), 150.

12. Smith, *Biographical Sketches*, 103–9. Among the places Joseph Smith hid the plates from those intent on seizing them was beneath the floor of the local cooper's shop. Martin Harris remembered Joseph Smith saying an angel warned him when the plates were no longer safe underneath the floor. See [Joel Tiffany,] "Mormonism—No. II," *Tiffany's Monthly* 5 (May 1859), 167.

13. [Tiffany,] "Mormonism," 169.

14. [Tiffany,] "Mormonism," 164.

15. Smith, History, 1839, in Jessee, *Papers of Joseph Smith*, 1:287; reprinted in *History of the Church*, 1:21–22. This vision is implied; Joseph said he was required to give the plates up "in consequence of my having wearied the Lord in asking for the privilege of letting Martin Harris take the writings." Jessee, *Papers of Joseph Smith*, 1:287; reprinted in *History of the Church*, 1:21.

16. Smith, History, 1839, in Jessee, *Papers of Joseph Smith*, 1:287, reprinted in *History of the Church*, 1:21–22.

17. Smith, History, 1839, in Jessee, *Papers of Joseph Smith*, 1:287; reprinted in *History of the Church*, 1:23; Smith, Biographical Sketches, 124–25.

18. Smith, *Biographical Sketches*, 124–25; Smith, History, 1839, in Jessee, *Papers of Joseph Smith*, 1:287; reprinted in *History of the Church*, 1:23. From July 1828 to June 1829, Joseph Smith received at least nine revelations from the Urim and Thummim (D&C 3, 6, 7, 10, 11, 14, 15, 16, 17).

19. Joseph Smith, History, 1839, in Jessee, *Papers of Joseph Smith*, 1:290; Joseph Smith—History 1:68–73. See also Doctrine and Covenants 13; 27:7–8. All presently known primary source accounts of this event are published in Brian Q. Cannon and *BYU Studies* Staff, "Priesthood Restoration Documents," *BYU Studies* 35, no. 4 (1995–96): 175–96, reprinted herein as "Seventy Contemporaneous Priesthood Restoration Documents."

20. Doctrine and Covenants 128:20. The date of the vision assumes the contiguity of Satan's appearance with the appearance of Peter, James, and John,

listed in this verse of scripture, and the placement of both events in Pennsylvania. See also note 6. The import of the Melchizedek Priesthood would seem to warrant some resistance from Satan, as was the case with the First Vision.

21. Doctrine and Covenants 27:12–13. See also Joseph Smith—History 1:72 and Doctrine and Covenants 128:20. All presently known primary source accounts of this event are published in this volume in Brian Q. Cannon and *BYU Studies* Staff, "Priesthood Restoration Documents." For a discussion of the May–June 1829 date, see Larry C. Porter, "The Restoration of the Aaronic and Melchizedek Priesthoods," *Ensign* 26 (December 1996): 30–47; Larry C. Porter, "The Restoration of the Priesthood," *Religious Studies Center Newsletter* 9, no. 3 (May 3, 1995): 1–12; and Larry C. Porter, "Dating the Melchizedek Priesthood," *Ensign* 9 (June 1979): 4–10.

22. David Whitmer interview with James H. Hart, March 10, 1884, in Cook, *David Whitmer Interviews*, 123. See also Cook, *David Whitmer Interviews*, 27, 41, 48–49, 114–15, 191, 213, 215.

23. Smith, *Biographical Sketches*, 137. Although Lucy did not name the angel, David Whitmer identified him as Moroni. See Cook, *David Whitmer Interviews*, 50, 181–82. David said the translation in Fayette occupied "about one month," beginning on June 1, 1829, placing Moroni's appearance around this date. Cook, *David Whitmer Interviews*, 62.

24. David Whitmer interview with Edward Stevenson, February 9, 1886, in Cook, *David Whitmer Interviews*, 180–82. For other Whitmer accounts of this event, see Cook, *David Whitmer Interviews*, 13, 27, 41–42, 49–50, 213–16.

25. Smith, *Biographical Sketches*, 137.

26. Smith, History, 1839, in Jessee, *Papers of Joseph Smith*, 1:296; reprinted in *History of the Church*, 1:54–55. See also Doctrine and Covenants 20:10; 128:20. Oliver Cowdery and David Whitmer testified of the vision in "The Testimony of Three Witnesses," which appeared in the first edition of the Book of Mormon (1830) and in every edition thereafter. For David Whitmer's testimony of the vision, see Cook, *David Whitmer Interviews*, 11, 15, 18–20, 25–26, 40–41, 63, 75–76, 86–87, 127, 166, 175–76, 181, 192–93, 197–98, 213, 229, 250–51. This vision was used by participants as a missionary tool to help convince listeners of the divinity of the Book of Mormon. William McLellin first heard the gospel preached in 1831 near Paris, Illinois, when David Whitmer "bore testimony to having seen an Holy Angel who had made known the truth of this record to him." Jan Shipps and John W. Welch, eds., *The Journals of William E. McLellin, 1831–1836* (Provo, Utah: BYU Studies; Urbana: University of Illinois Press, 1994), 29.

27. Joseph Smith, History, 1839, in Jessee, *Papers of Joseph Smith*, 1:296–97; reprinted in *History of the Church*, 1:55. See also Doctrine and Covenants 20:8–10; 128:20; and Cook, *David Whitmer Interviews*, 21, 64, 76. As one of the Three Witnesses, Martin Harris testified of this vision in "The Testimony of

Three Witnesses," printed in all editions of the Book of Mormon. Joseph Smith's exultation immediately after his vision with the Three Witnesses is recorded in Smith, *Biographical Sketches*, 139.

28. Smith, *Biographical Sketches*, 140. Lucy said the site where the Eight Witnesses saw the plates was "a place where the family were in the habit of offering up their secret devotions to God." Joseph went there because "it had been revealed" to him that the "plates would be carried thither" by "one of the ancient Nephites." Smith, *Biographical Sketches*, 140.

29. Smith, *Biographical Sketches*, 141. Lucy placed the timing of this meeting after the Eight Witnesses had handled the plates and had "returned to the house." Smith, *Biographical Sketches*, 141. More descriptions of this vision can be found in Brigham Young, in *Journal of Discourses*, 19:38, June 17, 1877; Wilford Woodruff, *Wilford Woodruff's Journal, 1833–1898, Typescript*, ed. Scott G. Kenney, 9 vols. (Midvale, Utah: Signature Book, 1983–84), 6:508–9 [December 11, 1869] (hereafter cited as Woodruff, *Journal*). Heber C. Kimball called Joseph and Oliver's experience a "vision" in which they "went into a cave in the hill Cumorah." Heber C. Kimball, in *Journal of Discourses*, 4:105, September 28, 1856. Oliver Cowdery's brother-in-law David Whitmer heard Oliver recount his experience in the cave. P. Wilhelm Poulson asked David in 1878 where the plates were then, and David told him they were "in a cave, where the angel has hidden them up till the time arrives when the plates, which are sealed, shall be translated." Cook, *David Whitmer Interviews*, 22. See also Edward Stevenson, *Reminiscences of Joseph the Prophet and the Coming Forth of the Book of Mormon* (Salt Lake City: By the author, 1893), 14–15; and William H. Dame, Journal, January 14, 1855, typescript, L. Tom Perry Special Collections, Harold B. Lee Library, Brigham Young University, Provo, Utah.

30. Joseph Smith, History, 1839, in Jessee, *Papers of Joseph Smith*, 1:321; reprinted in *History of the Church*, 1:106. See also Doctrine and Covenants 27:1–4. Joseph said the "first four paragraphs" of the revelation now canonized as Doctrine and Covenants 27 were received "at this time," that is, at the time the angel appeared in August 1830, near Harmony, Pennsylvania. The remainder of the revelation was received a month later. See Robert J. Woodford, "The Historical Development of the Doctrine and Covenants," 3 vols. (Ph.D. diss., Brigham Young University, 1974), 1:393–94.

31. Sidney Rigdon, in General Church Minutes, April 6, 1844, Church Archives, The Church of Jesus Christ of Latter-day Saints, Salt Lake City; reprinted in *History of the Church*, 6:289.

32. Orson F. Whitney, "Newel K. Whitney," *Contributor* 6 (January 1885): 125; reprinted in History of the Church, 1:146n.

33. Levi Hancock, "Diary of Levi W. Hancock," typescript, 48, Perry Special Collections.

34. Joseph Smith to the Elders of the Church of Latter Day Saints [1835], in *Messenger and Advocate*, September 1835, 179; reprinted in *History of the Church*, 2:254. Joseph departed Kirtland for Missouri on June 19, 1831, after receiving a revelation on June 7 commanding him and Sidney Rigdon to "journey to the land of Missouri" where "the land of your inheritance" should be revealed to them. *History of the Church*, 1:177, 188; Doctrine and Covenants 52:3, 5. Joseph did not indicate whether this June 7 revelation is the same June vision mentioned in his 1835 letter to the elders.

35. Smith to the Elders, September 1835, 179; reprinted in *History of the Church*, 2:254. See also Doctrine and Covenants 52:3–5; 57:1–3.

36. Mary Elizabeth Rollins Lightner, in Karl Ricks Anderson, *Joseph Smith's Kirtland: Eyewitness Accounts* (Salt Lake City: Deseret Book, 1989), 112–13.

37. Doctrine and Covenants 76. See also Jessee, *Papers of Joseph Smith*, 1:372. Of this vision Joseph later said: "I could explain a hundred fold more than I ever have of the glories of the kingdoms manifested to me in the vision, were I permitted, and were the people prepared to receive them." *History of the Church*, 5:402. Philo Dibble was present when Joseph and Sidney had the vision and later recounted the event in "Recollections of the Prophet Joseph Smith," *Juvenile Instructor* 27 (May 15, 1892): 303–4.

38. Smith, History, 1839, in Jessee, *Papers of Joseph Smith*, 1:383–84; reprinted in *History of the Church*, 1:272.

39. Zebedee Coltrin, in "Salt Lake School of the Prophets Minute Book, 1883," October 3, 1883, typescript, 56–57, Perry Special Collections. See also Zebedee Coltrin, in Utah Stake Minutes, Spanish Fork High Priest's Quorum, February 5, 1870, Church Archives; and *History of the Church*, 1:334–35.

40. Truman O. Angell to John Taylor and Council, March 11, 1885, John Taylor Presidential Papers, Church Archives. Angell, who did much of the interior work on the Kirtland Temple, was informed by Frederick G. Williams, a member of the First Presidency and a participant in the vision. The First Presidency was given the vision in accordance with a promise given on June 1, 1833: "Let [the house] be built after the manner which I shall show unto three of you." (D&C 95:14; see also D&C 94:1–2). Orson Pratt confirmed that the plan came through a vision. *Journal of Discourses*, 13:357, May 5, 1870; *Journal of Discourses*, 14:273, April 9, 1871. For more on the design of the Kirtland Temple, see Elwin C. Robison, *The First Mormon Temple: Design, Construction, and Historic Context of the Kirtland Temple* (Provo, Utah: Brigham Young University Press, 1997), 7–25.

41. Patriarchial Blessing Book, Church Archives, 9.

42. Joseph Smith, February 17, 1834, in Fred C. Collier and William S. Harwell, eds., *Kirtland Council Minute Book* (Salt Lake City: Collier's, 1996), 24. See also *History of the Church*, 2:25–26, 122–24.

43. Zebedee Coltrin, in Utah Stake Minutes, Spanish Fork High Priest's Quorum, February 5, 1870, Church Archives. See also *History of the Church*, 2:50.

44. Nathan Tanner, "Reminiscences," in George S. Tanner, *John Tanner and His Family* (Salt Lake City: Publishers Press, 1974), 382.

45. Woodruff, *Journal*, 1:10 [June 1834]. See also *History of the Church*, 2:79–80. This vision came after the Prophet and the other members of Zion's Camp, including Woodruff, marching to Missouri, unearthed human remains from a burial mound located in Pike County, Ohio. For additional accounts of the vision, see Kenneth W. Godfrey, "The Zelph Story," *BYU Studies* 29, no. 2 (1989): 31–56.

46. *History of the Church*, 2:181–82. See also Doctrine and Covenants 107:93–97. Joseph Young recalled hearing Joseph Smith discuss this vision on February 8, 1835. "I have seen those men who died of the cholera in our camp," Joseph Smith told Young and his brother, Brigham. "At this relation he [Joseph Smith] wept, and for some time could not speak," said Joseph Young. When the Prophet regained his composure, Joseph Young believed the Prophet picked up where he left off, again relaying information he had received in vision. Addressing himself to Brigham, Joseph Smith continued: "I wish you to notify all the brethren living in the branches, within a reasonable distance from this place, to meet at a general conference on Saturday next." The Prophet then told Brigham Young that he would be one of twelve special witnesses—the Quorum of the Twelve Apostles—who would be called at the conference to "open the door of the Gospel to foreign nations." To Joseph Young the Prophet said, "The Lord has made you President of the Seventies." *History of the Church*, 2:181n. See also Parley P. Pratt Jr., ed., *The Autobiography of Parley P. Pratt*, 4th ed. (Salt Lake City: Deseret Book, 1985), 97.

47. Stevenson, *Reminiscences of Joseph*, 6.

48. Doctrine and Covenants 137; Joseph Smith, Journal, January 21, 1836, in Jessee, *Papers of Joseph Smith*, 2:156–58; reprinted in *History of the Church*, 2:380–82. Heber C. Kimball said Joseph saw "Father Adam" admit people one by one through the "gate of the Celestial City" and thereafter "conduct them to the throne" where "they were crowned Kings and Priests of God." Heber C. Kimball, in *Journal of Discourses*, 9:41, March 17, 1861. See also Orson F. Whitney, *Life of Heber C. Kimball, an Apostle* (Salt Lake City: Kimball Family, 1888), 105–6. According to Joseph's journal for this period, others were present when Joseph had his vision, and some of them also had visions of the Savior and other heavenly beings. See Joseph Smith, Journal, January 21, 1836, in Jessee, *Papers of Joseph Smith*, 2:158. See also Leonard J. Arrington, "Oliver Cowdery's Kirtland, Ohio, 'Sketch Book,'" *BYU Studies* 12, no. 4 (1972): 419.

49. Joseph Smith, Journal, January 22, 1836, in Jessee, *Papers of Joseph Smith*, 2:160; reprinted in *History of the Church*, 2:383.

50. Joseph Smith, Journal, January 28, 1836, in Jessee, *Papers of Joseph Smith*, 2:164; reprinted in *History of the Church*, 2:387. Immediately before Joseph's vision, Zebedee Coltrin, one of the Seven Presidents of Seventy, saw the Savior "extended before him as upon the cross." Joseph Smith, Journal, January 28, 1836, in Jessee, *Papers of Joseph Smith*, 2:164; reprinted in *History of the Church*, 2:387.

51. Joseph Smith, Journal, January 28, 1836, in Jessee, *Papers of Joseph Smith*, 2:164; reprinted in *History of the Church*, 2:387.

52. Joseph Smith, Journal, March 27, 1836, in Jessee, *Papers of Joseph Smith*, 2:203; reprinted in *History of the Church*, 2:428. See also Whitney, *Life of Heber C. Kimball*, 103.

53. Harrison Burgess, "Sketch of a Well-Spent Life," in *Labors in the Vineyard: Twelfth Book of the Faith-Promoting Series* (Salt Lake City: Juvenile Instructor Office, 1884), 67. Burgess, writing years later, dated this vision to 1835. The anointings he described in connection with the vision, however, did not begin until the Kirtland Temple neared completion in early 1836. Milton V. Backman, personal conversation with author, Provo, Utah, September 15, 1998. An entry from Joseph's journal on this date confirms the setting and content of the Burgess account. "The Savior made his appearance to some," said the Prophet, "while angels minestered unto others." Joseph Smith, Journal, March 30, 1836, in Jessee, *Papers of Joseph Smith*, 2:207; reprinted in *History of the Church*, 2:432; see also Whitney, *Life of Heber C. Kimball*, 92.

54. Doctrine and Covenants 110; Joseph Smith, Journal, April 3, 1836, in Jessee, *Papers of Joseph Smith*, 2:209–10; reprinted in *History of the Church*, 2:435.

55. Caroline Barnes Crosby, Memoirs, as cited in Kenneth W. Godfrey, Audrey M. Godfrey, and Jill Mulvay Derr, eds., *Women's Voices: An Untold History of the Latter-day Saints, 1830–1900* (Salt Lake City: Deseret Book, 1982), 51.

56. Woodruff, *Journal*, 1:134 [April 6, 1837].

57. Mary Fielding to Mercy Thompson, July 1837, as cited in Dean C. Jessee, "The Spirituality of Joseph Smith," *Ensign* 8 (September 1978): 20.

58. Mary Fielding to Mercy Thompson and Robert Thompson, October 7, 1837, as cited in Godfrey, Godfrey, and Derr, *Women's Voices*, 67–68. In the letter, Fielding dated Joseph's vision to "soon before" his departure from Kirtland. He departed on September 27, 1836. *History of the Church*, 2:518.

59. Joseph Smith to the Presidency of The Church of Jesus Christ of Latter-day Saints in Kirtland, March 29, 1838, in Jessee, *Papers of Joseph Smith*, 2:223–24; reprinted in *History of the Church*, 3:10–12. Joseph described the vision in a letter dated March 29, 1838, written from Far West, to Marks and his counselors in the stake presidency at Kirtland. In the letter, Joseph reported events from January 12, 1836, when he departed from Kirtland, through his arrival in Far West on March 14, to the end of that month. Joseph's statement that the vision

took place "while on the road" apparently means during the eight weeks he was traveling from Ohio to Missouri. For dates of Joseph's journey, see *History of the Church*, 3:1, 8.

60. Whitney, *Life of Heber C. Kimball*, 269–70. Heber C. Kimball died June 22, 1868.

61. Thomas B. Marsh to Wilford Woodruff, April 30, 1838, Wilford Woodruff Papers, Church Archives. See also Doctrine and Covenants 115:13–16.

62. *History of the Church*, 3:316. By the time Joseph Smith was martyred, Willard Richards had written the *History of the Church*, under the Prophet's direction, through August 5, 1838. From that point, Thomas Bullock resumed the writing of the history in February 1845, and within two months he had completed through the year 1839. See Dean C. Jessee, "The Writing of Joseph Smith's History," *BYU Studies* 11, no. 4 (1971): 466–67. Bullock, who was not present with Joseph Smith at Liberty Jail or at the trial that immediately followed, relied on the testimonies of those who were—including Stephen Markham, the Prophet's bodyguard. Markham, present with the Prophet the first few days of the trial, April 9–12, 1839, informs Bullock's writing of *History of the Church* for this time period. For evidence of this, see *History of the Church*, 3:309–19.

63. *History of the Church*, 3:391. Joseph mentioned the vision in a discourse dated July 2, 1839. The account in *History of the Church* was written into the history by Thomas Bullock in 1845. See Jessee, "Joseph Smith's History," 467. Wilford Woodruff's account of this discourse was not, apparently, the only source Bullock used in his compilation. Compare the account in *History of the Church* with Ehat and Cook, *Words of Joseph Smith*, 6–8.

64. *History of the Church*, 4:89. On March 4, 1840, Joseph returned to Nauvoo from Washington, D.C., after seeking unsuccessfully to obtain redress from President Martin Van Buren for losses the Saints suffered in Missouri. Thomas Bullock wrote this portion of the history in 1845. See Jessee, "Joseph Smith's History," 467.

65. Anson Call, Statement [ca. 1854], Church Archives; Anson Call, Autobiography and Journal, 22, LDS Church Archives. See also *History of the Church*, 5:85–86; Brigham Young, in *Journal of Discourses*, 3:257–58, March 16, 1856.

66. Joseph Smith to Emma Smith, August 16, 1842, in Jessee, *Papers of Joseph Smith*, 2:430; reprinted in *History of the Church*, 5:104. In a letter he wrote to Emma Smith while in exile from his enemies, Joseph mentioned the dream and vision. The "Pine country" was probably Joseph's term for the region along the Black River of Wisconsin where the Saints obtained lumber for the Nauvoo Temple. See Dennis Rowley, "The Mormon Experience in the Wisconsin Pineries, 1841–1845," *BYU Studies* 32, nos. 1, 2 (1992): 119–48.

67. Joseph B. Noble [1869] and Mary Elizabeth Rollins Lightner [1905], as cited in Danel W. Bachman, "A Study of the Mormon Practice of Plural Marriage

before the Death of Joseph Smith" (master's thesis, Purdue University, 1975), 74. See also Eliza R. Snow Smith, *Biography and Family Record of Lorenzo Snow, One of the Twelve Apostles of the Church of Jesus Christ of Latter-day Saints* (Salt Lake City: Deseret News, 1884), 69–70; Benjamin F. Johnson to George F. Gibbs, April–October 1903, in E. Dale LeBaron, *Benjamin F. Johnson: Friend to the Prophets* (Provo, Utah: Grandin Book, 1997), 227.

68. *History of the Church*, 5:254–55. Willard Richards and Thomas Bullock compiled this portion of the history during the winter months of 1845–46. Jessee, "Joseph Smith's History," 468.

69. Woodruff, *Journal*, 2:226–27 [April 16, 1843]; reprinted in *History of the Church*, 5:361–62.

70. *History of the Church*, 5:394. That portion of *History of the Church* where Joseph's dream is recorded was completed under the direction of George A. Smith, who began his work on April 10, 1854, and finished in August 1856. Jessee, "Joseph Smith's History," 469–72.

71. Woodruff, *Journal*, 2:346–47 [February 3, 1844]; reprinted in *History of the Church*, 6:194–95.

72. *History of the Church*, 6:196–97. Joseph Smith mentions this vision under the date of February 5, 1844, in a conversation with William Weeks, an architect of the Nauvoo Temple. Weeks, who lived in Utah Territory during the time George A. Smith compiled this portion of the history, could have easily supplied Smith with the 1844 conversation. See J. Earl Arrington, "William Weeks, Architect of the Nauvoo Temple," *BYU Studies* 19, no. 3 (1979): 337–59. George A. Smith and Wilford Woodruff said that the clerks and historians who did this work were "eye and ear witnesses of nearly all the transactions recorded," and in cases where they were not, "had access to those who were." Jessee, "Joseph Smith's History," 473. The pretext to Weeks's recollection is a revelation, dated January 19, 1841, in which the Lord promised, "I will show unto my servant Joseph all things pertaining to this house" (D&C 124:42).

73. George Laub, Journal, in Eugene England, ed., "George Laub's Nauvoo Journal," *BYU Studies* 18, no. 2 (1978): 160.

74. *History of the Church*, 6:461–62.

75. *History of the Church*, 6:609–10.

76. Heber C. Kimball, in *Journal of Discourses*, 5:215–16, September 6, 1856.

"A Pentecost and Endowment Indeed": Six Eyewitness Accounts of the Kirtland Temple Experience

Steven C. Harper

Mankind's knowledge and power from God expanded exponentially in the temple at Kirtland, Ohio, from January through April 1836. This promised outpouring served as a reward for early obedience and a catalyst for further blessings described finally as "an infinity of fulness" (D&C 38:32–33; 105:9–12; 109:77). An abundant historical record affirms and embodies this remarkable endowment of divine power.[1] The richest documents—the contemporary writings of eyewitnesses—are reproduced in this chapter. They are published here together as a collective testimony of the fulfillment of divine promises to reward righteousness and sacrifice by the bestowal of spiritual gifts, ministering angels, and restoration of priesthood keys to endow the faithful with power, "so" in the words of Joseph Smith, "that satan cannot over throw us, nor have any power over us."[2]

The Religious and Historical Context of the Kirtland Manifestations

The Saints regarded their experiences as continuation of the pentecostal experience recorded in the Acts of the Apostles. What occurred in the Kirtland Temple was, as Benjamin Brown writes in his account, "even greater than at the day of Pente[cost]." We can

Historic American Survey Collection, Library of Congress

Kirtland Temple exterior, ca. 1930s.

say, at least, that the historical record of the Kirtland manifestations is greater than the biblical record of the day of Pentecost (Acts 2). A non–Latter-day Saint living in Kirtland reported specifically on the manifestations in a letter to his sister. Writing on April 10, 1836, a week after the Savior appeared to Joseph Smith and Oliver Cowdery, Lucius Pomeroy Parsons noted,

> They have lately had what they term a solemn assembly. This was at the completion of the lower story of the Temple which is finished in a very singular order having four Pulpits on each end of the House and curtains between each. Also, curtains dividing the house in the center. They have had wonderful manifestations there of late behind the curtains. This was in the night. Their meeting held for several nights in succession. None but the Prophets and Elders were admitted. The number of Prophets now amounts to twelve. Some can see angels and others cannot. They report that the Savior appeared personally with angels and endowed the Elders with powers to work Miracles.[3]

Even hostile observers seemed to testify of the relationship between the pentecostal manifestations of first-century Jerusalem and nineteenth-century Kirtland. John Corrill wrote of a meeting in the Kirtland Temple, "The sacrament was then administered, in which they partook of the bread and wine freely, and a report went abroad that some of them got drunk: as to that every man must answer for himself. A similar report, the reader will recollect, went out concerning the disciples, at Jerusalem, on the day of pentecost."[4]

Historians tend to situate these accounts of the "many Miracilous Experiences" and "Many Visions told" as examples of a visionary subculture in the early American republic.[5] The experiences of these eyewitnesses can partly be understood as a believing response to skepticism, confirmed by intense personal experience with God. The renewal of biblical revelation solidified faith in the Bible. As many increasingly doubted the possibility of biblical miracles in modernity and, finally, even in antiquity, the Saints believed in the gifts of the Spirit and pentecostal outpourings because they experienced them. The Kirtland Temple made these witnesses heirs of the Israelite Patriarchs and the Apostolic Church.

Those who recorded events surrounding the Kirtland Temple dedication did not overtly try to explain them. They assumed, instead, an affinity of understanding with the few who shared their experiences. Benjamin Brown wrote in 1853, for example, "Such a chain of testimonies, and an interweaving of evidences, accompanied with that perception and comprehension which the Holy Ghost alone can give, none can realize, but those who have received that Spirit and revelations unto themselves. Such persons know just how it is."[6] In the first months of 1836, Benjamin Brown, Oliver Cowdery, Edward Partridge, William Phelps, Stephen Post, and Joseph Smith were among those who gathered in solemn meetings with other Saints in the Kirtland Temple.[7] Thanks to their lengthy, detailed, contemporaneous documents, modern readers have the benefit of several independent eyewitness accounts of these events, the power and significance of which prompted each immediately to commit their experiences to writing.

Revelations had promised the Saints that if they sacrificed to build the temple as commanded, they would be endowed with divine power to transcend the temporal and mortal.[8] They anticipated an endowment of power through communion with heaven.[9] The documents that follow largely capture the effulgence of that endowment. Though some documents have suffered frustrating damage and are subject to other limitations, each confirms the general and specific testimonies of other participants of the Kirtland Pentecost. Some eyewitnesses captured more of the experience than Joseph Smith recorded in his characteristically understated journal entries. Where Joseph's entry for the evening of March 29, 1836, says, for instance, "The Holy Spirit rested down upon us and we continued in the Lord's house all night prophesying and giving glory to God," Benjamin Brown both confirms and enhances Joseph's record by noting the ministering of angels, prophesying in tongues, and visions of the Savior and eternity as part of the "many Miraculous Experiences told [and] Many Visions told."

Priesthood leaders began meeting in the Kirtland Temple January 21, 1836. In a series of meetings leading up to the March 27 dedication, members of the priesthood quorums washed and were anointed with oil consecrated for the sacred purpose of designating them clean from the sinfulness of their world. William Phelps wrote to his wife, Sally, in January 1836, "Our meeting[s] will grow more and more solemn, and will continue till the great solemn assembly when the house is finished! We are preparing to make ourselves clean, by first cleansing our hearts, forsaking our sins, forgiving every body; putting on clean decent clothes, by anointing our heads and by keeping all the commandments. As we come nearer to God we see our imperfections and nothingness plainer and plainer."[10] In the temple meetings in January brethren sang, prayed, testified, prophesied, beheld visions, received ministering angels, spoke in and interpreted tongues, and shouted hosannas.

Then, on March 27, Joseph dedicated the temple. That night he and those who had been anointed tarried all night in the temple, where spiritual gifts were richly bestowed. On March 29 the first presidency met in the temple with the stake presidencies and bishoprics of Kirtland and Missouri and washed their feet, following the pattern of Jesus as recorded in John 13. The next night, March 30, the other elders who had been anointed earlier received the same culminating ordinance, which Joseph had previously described as "calculated to unite our hearts, that we may be one in feeling and sentiment and that our faith may be strong, so that satan cannot over throw us, nor have any power over us."[11] On March 31 the dedicatory services were repeated for those unable to attend on March 27. On Sunday April 3, 1836, the Lord Jesus Christ appeared to Joseph Smith and Oliver Cowdery and accepted the Temple, as recorded in Joseph Smith's journal entry for that day. Ministering angels followed. Elias, Moses, and Elijah each committed priesthood keys needed to gather Israel, endow the Saints with power, and seal the human family together in anticipation of the "great and dreadful day of the Lord" (D&C 110:16). Thus was accomplished the endowment of priesthood power Moroni foretold when he appeared to Joseph Smith on September 21, 1823 (D&C 2). As Joseph Smith's March 30, 1836, journal entry reports, "it was a penticost and enduement [endowment] indeed, long to be remembered for the sound shall go forth from this place into all the world, and the occurrences of this day shall be hande[d] down upon the pages of sacred history to all generations, as the day of Pentecost."[12]

Six Contemporary Eyewitness Accounts of the Kirtland Temple Pentecost, 1836

	Brown	Cowdery	Partridge	Phelps	Post	Smith
January 21 preparation, blessing meeting, visions		✓				✓
Washing and anointing ordinances	✓	✓	✓	✓		✓
First Presidency			✓			
High Councils		✓	✓			
Twelve Apostles		✓	✓			✓
Bishoprics		✓	✓			
High Priests		✓	✓			✓
Elders		✓				
Seventies		✓	✓			✓
Aaronic Priesthood holders		✓	✓			
Hosannah shout	✓	✓	✓	✓	✓	✓
March 27 solemn assembly	✓	✓	✓	✓	✓	✓
Frederick Williams vision of angel/Savior	✓	✓	✓		✓	✓
Visions	✓	✓	✓		✓	✓
Gifts of prophesy, tongues	✓	✓	✓	✓	✓	✓
March 27–28 priesthood meeting	✓		✓	✓	✓	
March 29 washing of feet of First Presidency, stake presidencies, bishoprics			✓	✓		✓
March 30 washing of feet of priesthood holders generally			✓	✓	✓	✓
March 31 solemn assembly			✓	✓	✓	✓
April 3 vision of Savior and reception of priesthood keys from ministering angels				✓		✓

Description of Documents

Each of the documents reproduced below has different characteristics and provenance. Oliver Cowdery published his lengthy account in the *Messenger and Advocate* shortly after the March 1836 dedication of the Kirtland Temple.[13] Benjamin Brown's unpolished account was recently discovered in a private collection.[14] The accounts of Edward Partridge and Stephen Post have been quoted and cited repeatedly, but both are published in extended form here for the first time; also, an especially rich April 1836 letter from William Phelps to his wife Sally is published here for the first time. Joseph Smith's diary entries have been published in various places but are set forth best in *The Papers of Joseph Smith*.[15] While the Phelps and Brown letters are reproduced in full, only the relevant diary entries of Edward Partridge, Oliver Cowdery, Stephen Post, and Joseph Smith are reproduced below. Likewise, Cowdery's *Messenger and Advocate* report of the dedication is reproduced only in part. Each document is preceded by a brief description of its author, composition, and provenance. Underlining is reproduced from the original document. Editorial marks include angle brackets < > to indicate insertions made by the author of the document. Strikeouts are shown by ~~strikeouts~~. Brackets [ ] indicate editorial comments.

1. Benjamin Brown, Letter (March 27, 1835)

Even before his introduction to the gospel in 1835, Benjamin Brown (1794–1878) seemed to be blessed with spiritual gifts and impressions that led him to the pentecostal season centered in the Kirtland Temple. "There," Benjamin wrote, "the Spirit of the Lord, as on the day of Pentecost, was profusely poured out. . . . We had a most glorious and never-to-be forgotten time."[16]

On a sheet of weathered, now-torn paper measuring nearly 12 x 8 inches, Benjamin began to compose a letter to his wife, Sarah.[17] Though undated, an internal reference to "the sol[e]mn assembly which will be called next Sunday," meaning March 27, 1836, narrows its composition to the week beginning March 20. As it continues, the writing on this sheet begins to sound less like a letter and more like a chronicle of events of that marvelous week of dedication. A second sheet of paper in much better condition and almost an inch and a half shorter seems to continue this account. Generally it reads more like a journal than a letter, and no formal epistolary closing is evident, but some internal evidence suggests that Benjamin is still addressing Sarah and intending to send the letter by way of a neighbor.

Although the handwriting appears consistent throughout, a third-person reference to B. Brown toward the end of the document suggests the possibility that Benjamin did not write it all himself. Whether Benjamin Brown intended that the two sheets form a coherent single document cannot be determined. That they both stem from an effort to record his witness of a pentecostal experience is certain. The line endings where the document is torn are preserved below.

> Dear wife I last night heard from you [*page torn*]
> which I thank the Lord, Brother Bovee[18] said [*page torn*]
> Gospel <to father> for which my heart rejoiced for [*page torn*]
> and great is thy reward. Rejoice in the Lord [*page torn*]
> Rejoice, let your moderation be known [*page torn*]
> Now be careful for nothing but in eve [*page torn*]
> [*illegible*] and with thanksgiving let your requests be made known to [*page torn*]
> [*illegible*] God, And the peace of God which passeth all understanding [shall] [*page torn*]
> fill your heart through Christ Jesus.[19]
>
> Now to let you know a few of the thousand great things of God that is passing in this place, there has been no mobs as you have heard. But the work of the Lord is increascing daily. There has been from one to ten Baptized every day this week, some of the Elders have been out for a few days some have baptized 16 some five &c [*page torn*]
>
> Elders still continue to come in and wash and anoint for the solmn assembly which will be called next sunday for tithin[g] [*page torn*]
> & sacrifice with fasting & Prayr in the house of the Lord fr[*page torn*]
> 8 oclock in the morning until 4 in the afternoon [*page torn*]
> known how long the meeting will hold probaly [*page torn*]

we have meetings almost every evening and [*page torn*]
and hold till 9. Many marvelous things [*page torn*]
transpired even greater than at the day of Penti[cost] [*page torn*]
are increasing in faith and expecting greater [*page torn*]
endowment it is expected that there is three hundred of [*page torn*]
in Prayer with one accord as at Jerusalem[20]

Many visions are given and also Revelations by night & by day some have already come to pass, and many have no[t] yet but will soon.[21] I was present when father Smith Blest a man who lived in Niagara County who was in a streight whether to go home, on Business or stay at the solem assembly the old patriarch[22] said you want to go home, But the Lord will give you a Sign between this and tomorning and the man asked the Lord for a sign about 2 hours after as he came out of the house to go to meeting there appeared a light over the Hou[se] [*page torn*]
of the Lord and extended from west to East But that part [*page torn*]
the heavens over his house or home was dark & he said it eno[ugh][*page torn*][23]

some have seen the heavens opend & seen the savior others have seen angels on the four corners of the house of the Lord with drawn swords & also stood thick on the ridge Elisha with his chariot of Fire, Peter John & James, & the highway cast up the ten tribes returning in chariots as far as the eye could extend some saw the Redemtion of Zion and other thing to num [p. 1]

[*page torn*] not the wine & oil. Deeds to the church
[*page torn*] [w]hether the wicked will be raised
[*page torn*] 318 page and now my brethren
[*page torn*]nd prophet of old has testified
[*page torn*] of God and the people stoned him to death.

[*Illegible*]

Whether the Saints that are raised will remain on earth during the thousand, years, for they lived & reigned with Christ a thousand years Rev 20th 4th

Book of Mormon 424th page Cain & his followers[24]

Old father Adam was seen Butiful man his hair stood back & curled most butiful even down on his shoulders. . . .

Sunday Evening after Joseph spoke opened & told them the day of Penticost was continued[25] the the [*sic*] Brethren began to to [*sic*] prophesy many prophesied in the name of the Lord then began speaking in tongues and it filled as it were the whole house, perhaps there were forty speaking at once Cloven tongues of fire was seen to sit on many of them an hand was seen laid upon one when he spake in tongues to the lamanites many Visions seen, one saw a pillow or cloud rest down upon the house bright as when the sun shines on a cloud like as gold, two others saw three personages hovering in the room with bright keys in their hands, and also a bright chain in their hands ~~the~~ I did not intend this for a letter But this morning while writing Brother Bovee concluded to start for home

Sunday March 27th 1836 the order of the House of the Lord was there was no small children admitted, one woman however not knowing the order brought her child about 2 months old she stood out of the door for a long time, manifested an anxious desire to enter at length one of the Elders said Brethren we do not Exercise faith my faith is this child will not cry a word in the House to day on this the woman & child entered and the child did not cry a word from 8 till 4 in the after noon. But when the saints all shouted Hosana the child was nursing But let go & shouted also when the saints paused it paused when they shouted it shouted for three times when they shouted amen it shouted also for three times then it resumed its nursing without any alarm[26]

Monday a young man fell and sprained his ancle so as he could not stand the Elders laid hand on him he was healed imediately

On the Penticost evening the west end of the House was illuminated by a light from heaven seen on the outside by many [p. 2]

Brother Benjamin Lewis laid hands on a boy that had his arm Broken so as it laid back on his elbow. he placed the bones raped a rag around it his wife poured on some vinegar he then asked the boy to move his fingers the boy did so this was at noon. the next morning the boy went to pulling weed in the garden with that hand no more trouble about it——

B. Brown heard Brother Colonel Parks of Uclid[27] testify that heard in the evening between 8&9 the Report of a rifle apparently about forty rods off then they began as in an action passing a long the road then took a turn & came accross the lot up to the house

But the report grew more faint untill it was nothing but a snap and the noise of a flash in the pan was heard by all of the family and ~~all~~ many of the brethren in that place the interpilation Given to two present which was judgements of God on that place——

Father Stephens[28] saw on sunday evening two rows of Angels through the House, at another time the glory of God came down on the Elders from the head down half way——

~~Br~~ April 29th an angel~~s~~ was seen over the Elders Many Propesys given & speaking in tongues, this 29th of March two corums continued all night in the House the twelve guarded it the Heavens was opened two saw the savior some saw chariots and other thing one lay about half an hour & saw from Eternity to Eternity many Miracilous Experiences told Many Visions told[29]

2A. Oliver Cowdery, Sketch Book (1836)

Along with Joseph Smith, Oliver Cowdery (1806–50) received power and authority in each of the landmark events in the restoration of holy priesthood powers and keys. On May 15, 1829, John the Baptist conferred the Aaronic Priesthood on their heads (D&C 13). Soon thereafter Peter, James, and John ordained Joseph and Oliver to the Melchizedek Priesthood and conferred the keys of the holy apostleship (D&C 7:7; 27:12–13). Then on April 3, 1836, these two witnesses envisioned the Savior and received an endowment of priesthood keys from Elias, Moses, and Elijah. (See Joseph Smith's account below.) Oliver Cowdery kept a private "Sketch Book"[30] in which he included more details of his involvement in the solemn meetings leading up to the March 27 dedication. He also penned the Church's official news account of the Kirtland Temple dedication, published in the *Messenger & Advocate* immediately after the occasion.

January 1836. Thursday, the 21st.

. . . At about three o'clock P.M. I assembled in our office garret, having all things prepared for the occasion, with presidents Joseph Smith, jr. F. G. Williams, Sidney Rigdon Hyrum Smith, David Whitmer, John Whitmer and elder John Corrill, and washed our bodies with pure water before the Lord, preparatory to the annointing with the holy oil. After we were washed, our bodies were perfumed with a sweet smelling oderous wash. At evening the presidents of the Church, with the two bishop[s] and their counsellors, and elder Warren Parrish, met in the presidents' room, the high cou[n]cils of Kirtland and Zion in their rooms. Those named in the first room were annointed with the same kind of oil and in the man[ner] that were Moses and Aaron, and those who stood before the Lord in ancient days, and those in the other rooms with annointing oil prepared for them. The glorious scene is too great to be described in this book, therefore, I only say, that the heavens were opened to many, and great and marvelous things were shown.

January 1836 Friday, the 22nd.

Copied blessings. At evening met in the president's room where were the presidents, the twelve, the presidents of the 70, the high councils of Kirtland and Zion, and the bishops and their counsellors. The presidents proceeded and annointed Thomas B. Marsh, the president of the twelve, and he annointed the other eleven. The twelve then proceeded, president Marsh taking the lead, and annointed the presidents of the Seventy. Elder Don Carlos Smith was ordained and annointed president of the high priesthood of the Melchisedek priesthood,[31] by the presidents of the Church. Near the close of the meeting, 2 o'clock in the morning, almost all present broke out in tongues and songs of Zion. . . .

P[ost]. S[cript]. To Monday [January 25, 1836]: In the evening the high priests and elders, all who did not belong to the quorums, met in the Lord's house, and also the Lesser priesthood, with the bishop at their head, to receive instructions relative to washing and annointing a large number of elders convened; more than I had supposed resided in Kirtland. . . .

Saturday, 6 [February 1836]. . . . In the evening met with the presidency and quorums in the Lord's house, when their anointing blessings were sealed by uplifted hands and praises to God. Many saw visions, many prophesied, and many spoke in tongues. Closed a little before 12 o'clock. . . .

From Saturday 19th [March 1836] attended Heb[rew]. School, up to Saturday the 26. Nothing of note's transpiring. This day our school did not keep, we prepared for the dedication of the Lord's house. I met in the president's room, pres. J. Smith, jr. S. Rigdon, my brother W. A. Cowdery & Elder W. Parrish, and assisted in writing a prayer for the dedication of the house. [See D&C 109].

Sunday the 27[the] [March 1836] attended on the dedication of the Lord's house. For the particulars of this great event see my account written by myself, and printed in the March No. of The Messenger and Advocate, signed C. In the evening I met with the officers of the church in the Lord's house. The Spirit was poured out—I saw the glory of God, like a great cloud, come down and rest upon the house, and fill the same like a mighty rushing wind. I also saw cloven tongues, like as of fire rest upon many, (for there were 316 present,) while they spake with other tongues and prophesied.[32]

2B. Oliver Cowdery, *Messenger & Advocate* Account (March 27, 1836)

[March 27] Previous notice having been given, the Church of the Latter Day Saints met this day in the House of the Lord to dedicate it to him. The congregation began to assemble before 8 o'clock A.M. and thronged the doors until 9, when the Presidents of the church who assisted in seating the congregation, were reluctantly compelled to order the door keepers to close the doors; every seat and aisle were crowded. — One thousand persons were now silently and solemnly waiting to hear the word of the Lord from the mouth of his servants in the sacred desk. President S. Rigdon began the services of the day, by reading the 96th and 24th Psalms. An excellent choir of singers, led by M.C. Davis sung the following Hymn: ["Ere Long the Vail Will Rend in Twain."]

President Rigdon then in an able, devout and appropriate manner, addressed the throne of Grace. The following Hymn was then sung: ["O Happy Souls Who Pray."]

The speaker (S. Rigdon,) selected the 8th chapter of Matthew, the 18, 19 and 20th verses from which, he proposed to address the congregation, continuing himself more closely to the 20th verse — He spoke two hours and a half in his usual, forcible and logical manner. At one time in the course of his remarks he was rather pathetic, than otherwise, which drew tears from many eyes. He was then taking a retrospective view of the toils, privations and anxieties of those who had labored upon the walls of the house to erect them. And added, there were those who had wet them with their tears, in the silent shades of night, while they were praying to the God of heaven, to protect them, and stay the unhallowed hands of ruthless spoilers, who had uttered a prophecy when the foundation was laid, that the walls would never be reared. This was only a short digression from the main thread of his discourse, which he soon resumed.

Here it may be not improper to give a synopsis of the discourse for the satisfaction of our readers who were not privileged as we were with hearing it. The speaker assumed as a postulate, what we presume no one was disposed to deny, (viz:) that in the days of the Savior there were Synagogues, where the Jews worshipped God, and in addition to them, the splendid Temple at jerusalem. Yet, when on a certain occasion, one proposed to follow him whithersoever he went, he though heir of all things cried out like on in the bitterness of his soul in abject poverty, The Foxes have holes, &c. This, said the speaker, was evidence to his mind, that the Most High did not put his name there, and that he did not accept the worship of those who payed their vows and adorations there. This was evident from the fact that they would not receive him, but thrust him from them, saying, away with him, crucify him! crucify him! It was therefore abundantly evident that his spirit did not dwell in them. They were the degenerate sons of noble sires: but they had long since slain the Prophets and Seers through whom the Lord revealed himself to the children of men. They were not led by revelation, This, said the speaker, was the grand difficulty among them. Their unbelieve in present revelation. He further remarked, that, their unbelief in present revelation was the means of dividing that generation into the various sects and parties that existed. They were sincere worshipers, but their worship was not required of them, nor was it acceptable to God. — The Redeemer himself who knew the hearts of all men, called them generation of vipers. It was proof positive to his mind, that there being Pharisees, Sadducees, Herodians and Essens, and all differing from each other, that they were led by the precepts and commandments of men. Each had something peculiar to himself. But all agreed in one point, (viz:) to oppose the Redeemer. So that we discover he would with the utmost propriety, exclaim, notwithstanding their synagogue and Temple worship, The foxes have holes, the birds of the air have nests, but the Son of man hath not where to lay his head. He took occasion here to remark that such diversity of sentiment ever had, and ever would obtain when people were not led by present revelation. This brought him to the inevitable conclusion that the various sects of the present day, from their manifesting the same spirit, rested under the same condemnation with those who were coeval with the Savior. He admitted there were many houses; many sufficiently great, built for the worship of God, but not one except his, on the face of the whole earth, that was built by divine revelation, and were it not for this, the dear Redeemer might in this day of science, this day of intelligence, this day of religion, say to those who would follow him, The foxes have holes, the birds of the air have nests, but the Son of man hath not where to lay his head.

Here his whole soul appeared to be fired with his subject. Arguments, strong and conclusive seemed almost to vie with each other for utterance. Indeed, there was no sophistry in his reasoning, no plausible hypothesis on which the whole rested, but on the contrary plain scripture facts. Therefore his deductions and inferences were logical and conclusive.

The comparison drawn between the different religious sects of ancient and modern times, was perfectly natural, and simple yet it was done in that confident, masterly manner, accompanied with those incontrovertable proofs of his position, that was directly calculated to cheer and gladden the hearts of the Saints, but to draw down the indignation of the sectarian world upon him and we have no doubt had our speaker uttered the same sentiments, with the same proof of their correctness, had there been those present that we might name, his voice would doubtless have been drowned as was that of the ancient apostle in the Athenian Temple, when his auditors cried incessantly for about two hours "Great is Diana of the Ephesians."

But to conclude, we can truly say no one unacquainted with the manner of delivery and style of our speaker can, from reading form any adequate idea of the powerful effect he is capable of producing in the minds of his hearers.: And to say on this occasion he showed himself mater of his subject and did well, would be doing him injustice; to say he acquitted himself with honor or did very well, would be detracting from him real merit; and to say that he did exceeding well; would be only halting praise.

After closing his discourse he presented Joseph Smith jr. to the church as a Prophet and Seer. The Presidents of the church then all in their seats, acknowledged him as such by rising. The vote was unanimous in the affirmative.

The question was then put, and carried without a manifest dissenting sentiment to each of the different grades or quorums of church officers respectively and then to the congregation. The following hymn was then sung: ["Now Let Us Rejoice."]

Services closed for the forenoon.

Intermission was about 15 minutes during which none left their seats except a few females, who from having left their infants with their friends, were compelled to do so to take care of them. The P.M. services commenced by singing the following hymn: ["Adam-ondi-Ahman."]

President J. Smith jr. then rose, and after a few preliminary remarks, presented the several Presidents of the church, then present, to the several quorums respectively, and then to the church as being equal with himself, acknowledging them to be Prophets and Seers. The vote was unanimous in the affirmative in every instance. — Each of the different quorums was presented in its turn to all the rest, and then to the church, and received and acknowledged by all the rest, in their several stations without a manifest dissenting sentiment.

President J. Smith jr. then addressed the congregation in a manner calculated to instruct the understanding, rather than please the ear, and at or about the close of his remarks, he prophesied to all that inasmuch as they would uphold these men in their several stations, alluding to the different quorums in the church, the Lord would bless them; yea, in the name of Christ, the blessings of Heaven shall be yours. And when the Lord's anointed go forth to proclaim the word, bearing testimony to this generation, if they receive it, they shall be blessed, but if not, the judgments of God will follow close upon them, until that city of that house, that rejects them, shall be left desolate. The following hymn was then sung: ["How Pleased and Blest I Was."]

He then offered the dedication prayer, which was as follows: [See D&C 109.]

The choir then sung a hymn. ["The Spirit of God."]

President Smith then asked the several quorums separately and then the congregation, if they accepted the prayer. The vote was, in every instance, unanimous in the affirmative.

The Eucharist was administered. D[on]. C[arlos]. Smith blessed the bread and wine and they were distributed by several Elders present, to the church.

President J. Smith jr. then arose and bore record of his mission. D. C. Smith bore record of the truth of the work of the Lord in which we are engaged.

President O. Cowdery spoke and testified of the truth of the book of Mormon, and of the work of the Lord in these last days.

President F. G. Williams bore record that a Holy Angel of God, came and set between him and J. Smith sen. while the house was being dedicated.

President Hyrum Smith, (one of the building committee) made some appropriate remarks concerning the house, congratulating those who had endured so many toils and privations to erect it, that it was the Lord's house built by his commandment and he would bless them.

President S. Rigdon then made a few appropriate closing remarks; and a short prayer which was ended with loud acclamations of Hosanna! Hosanna! Hosanna to God and the Lamb, Amen, Amen and Amen! Three times. Elder B. Young, one of the Twelve, gave a short address in tongues; Elder D. W. Patten interpreted and gave a short exhortation in tongues himself; after which, President J. Smith jr. blessed the congregation in the name of the Lord, and at a little past four P.M. the whole exercise closed and the congregation dispersed.

We further add that we should do violence to our own feelings and injustice to the real merit of our brethren and friends who attended the meeting, were we here to withhold a meed of praise, which we think is their just due; not only for their qui[e]t demeanor during the whole exercise, which lasted more than eight hours, but for their great liberality in contributing of their earthly substance for the relief of the building committee, who were yet somewhat involved. As this was to be a day of sacrifice, as well as of fasting, There was a man placed at each door in the morning to receive the voluntary donations of those who entered. On counting the collection it amounted to nine hundred and sixty three dollars.

Kirtland, Ohio, March, 1836.[33]

3. Edward Partridge, Diary (1836)

A Painesville, Ohio, industrialist and merchant, Edward Partridge (1793–1840) joined the Church of Jesus Christ on December 11, 1830, after visiting Joseph Smith in upstate New York.[34] On February 4, 1831, the Lord called him to serve as the first bishop in the Restored Church. In that capacity Partridge was among the priesthood leaders intimately involved in the Kirtland Temple meetings. Partridge's thorough diary, housed at Church Archives, describes the ordinances in detail, documents his involvement, and testifies of rich spiritual outpourings.[35]

> 21st [January 1836] Having previously washed once or twice, The presidency with Bishop Whitney and his counsel, myself & my counselors[36] met for the purpose of being anointed with Holy oil. Meeting was opened by Prest. Joseph Smith Jnr. in behalf of the Presidency Bishop Whitney in behalf of himself and counsellors, and myself in behalf of myself & counsellors. Then the Presidency proceeded to sanctify the oil, br. Smith Jun: first annointed his father pronouncing blessings upon him, then all the president beginning at the oldest rubbed their hand over his head & face which had been anointed, then br. J. prayed to the Lord to accept of the annointing and all of the presidency with right hand uplifted to heaven said amen. Father Smith then proceeded to take the lead and pour on the oil, then br J. followed and then in rotation as before described, prophesying &. c. on one anothers heads. After the presidents bishop Whitney & his counsel were annointed after the same manner then myself & my counsel, then br. Parrish as scribe for the presidency. After this Hyrum Smith annointed father John Smith who annointed the rest of the high council of Kirtland, br. David Whitmer annointed br. Simeon Carter who annointed the high council from Zion. Hymns were sung & a number saw visions & others were blessed with the outpouring of the Holy Ghost and we shouted hosanna to the most high, the meeting was dismissed by br. J. S. Jun confering the benedictions of heaven upon us. The 22d the forenoon was taken up in telling the visions of the preceeding evening. We met in the evening for the purpose, of anointing the traveling high council, and the 7 Presidents of the 70. The Presidents of the church, first consecrated the oil, they then proceeded to anoint br. Thomas B. Marsh

as the oldest of the 12. br. Marsh then proceeded to anoint the 12, after which he anointed the presidents of the 70. The Presidents of the church anointed br. Carlos Smith as president of the high priests in Kirtland. Prest. J. S. Jur. requested Prest. Sidney Rigdon, to ask the Lord to accept the performances of the evening, and instructed us, when he was done, to shout hosannah blessed be the name of the most high God.

These things were performed; the shout & speaking in unknown tongues lasted 10 or 15 minutes. During the evening, more especially at the time of shouting, a number saw visions as they declared unto us.

The priests, teachers, and deacons met 2 or 3 evenings, about the last of Jan., for the purpose of being anointed. Bishop Whitney and counsel and myself and my counsel met and anointed them, after the anointing was over, each man asked the Lord to belss [*sic*] them and seal upon them the blessings that had been pronounced upon their heads by the bishops and their counsellors. bishop Whitney then asked the Lord to seal the blessings that had been pronounced upon the heads of his brethren after he was through we shouted hosanna 3 times, to God and the Lamb, amen, amen, and amen. The 6 [February] evening all the quorums met and had all the blessings sealed by the presidency of the church; at the close of the ceremony we all shouted, agreeably to the above described order.

Sunday the 27 [March 1836] met and dedicated the House of the Lord. Prest. Rigdon preached in the forenoon. Prest. J Smith Jun. made many remarks and delivered the dedication prayer. meet at 8 morn & dismissed ? past 4 afternoon Met again in the evening that is the authorities of the church. many spoke in tongues some saw visions &c. Doct. F. G. Williams saw an angel or rather the Savior during the forenoon service.

Tuesday the 29, the 9 prest. the two bishops and their counsel met in the afternoon in the house of the Lord. We cleansed our hands and faces and feet after which we had our feet washed in the name of the Lord, this took till about dusk we then partook of bread and wine a feast, we prophesied and spoke in tongues & shouted hosannas. the meeting lasted till day light.

Wednesday [March 30, 1836] all the officers of the church met at 9 oclock in the Lords house, the priests teachers & deacons in

> one corner the vails having been let down, and the other officers occupied the rest of the lower room, the washing of feet was performed by noon, then they began to prophesy and speak in tongues adding shouts of hosannas to God and the Lamb with amen and amen this continued till dark when they partook of a feast of bread and wine, the meeting was kept up till morning the shouts were omitted during the night.[37]
>
> Thursday [March] 31st we met from 8 to 9 to accommodate those who could not get in the Sunday dedication the house was about filled and similar ceremonies performed that were performed on Sunday this meeting rather surpassed the Sunday meeting both in length & goodness.

4. William W. Phelps, Letter to Sally Phelps (April 1–3, 1836)

William Wines (W. W.) Phelps (1792–1872), a New Jersey native, married Sally Waterman in 1815 and was editor of the Ontario Phoenix newspaper in Canindaigua, New York, when they joined the Church of Jesus Christ in 1831. A valuable asset to the Church for his literary gifts, Phelps composed some of the hymns sung during the solemn assembly in the Kirtland Temple. "You can perceive that my letters are my private Journal," he wrote in January 1836 from Kirtland to Sally in Clay County, Missouri.[38] Along with the other leaders of the Church from Missouri, Phelps had come to Kirtland to receive an endowment of priesthood power. His remarkable letter to Sally, written between April 1 and 6, is perhaps the most detailed yet succinct summary of all that transpired in the temple during the week of the solemn assembly.[39] Sally dutifully copied or had copied the letter into a book Phelps called his journal. In 2002 a descendant of Phelps donated this journal to the L. Tom Perry Special Collections at the Harold B. Lee Library at Brigham Young University.

> Sally: The house of the Lord at Kirtland, Ohio, was
> Dedicated on Sunday, the 27 of March, 1836. The con=
> gregation to the number of about 1000, convened in
> the house at 8 oclock A.M. There was probably
> as many more without the house. Opened the mee=
> ting by singing. "Er long the vail will rend in twain". Starting

Prayer by President Rigdon. A Angel came in on the first
seat during the prayer. Sung "O happy souls who
pray"_ [- -]mouth . . . President Rigdon preached from the
18,19, & 20 verses of <8 chap> Matthew, about 2½ hours. After
this President J. Smith Jr. was acknowledged prophet
and Seer, by the different Quorums, and by all the
congregation of the Saints by rising alternately.
The remaining presidents [was] ~~then acknowledge~~
the same ~~by the same~~ sung "Now let us rejoice
in day of Salvation" Hosanna. Intermission 15 ms
Recommenced by Singing "This earth was once a garden place".
Adam=ondi-Ahman." Here the presidents, and all the
quorums were acknowledged in their several offices
as the seer and prophet had been. and it was
one of the solemnest as well as sublimest
scenes I ever witnessed. Sung "How pleased and
blesst was I" President Smith then delivered the
following prayer [Here the Phelps letterbook includes the parenthetical comment "see page 130 & 131 of this letter." The dedicatory prayer to which this refers is in D&C 109.] sung
"Hosanna to God and the Lamb
Several then bore record after the sacrament
was administered. The scene now became anima=
ting: the whole congregation Shouted "Hosanna, hosan=
na, hosanna, to God and the Lamb. Henceforth and
forever; Amen, Amen, And Amen" three times. One
song of Zion sung in tongues, and the services
concluded. A meeting of the Elders was held in
the evening when much speaking in tongues was witnessed

On Tuesday, the 29th, The washing of feet among the
presidents & Bishops and their councillors to place: it
was a solemn scene; at night they partook of the
sacrament, as the passover, having fasted all day
they feasted on bread and wine; were filled with
the spirit of their endowment, and prophesied many
terrible things: The meeting continued till day light
in the morning: At 8 oclock the Several Quorums
of the church, embracing all the ordained members
came in and, let be remembered that on that 30th

day of March, 1836, their feet were washed, and
they commenced prophecying and shouting Hosanna
to God and the Lamb. At Evening the sacrament
was administered, as the feast of the Passover for
the first time in more than 1800 years: then
spake they with tongues and prophesied.
On Thursday the 31st March, a second Ded=
ication was held for the Lord's House. It was
a sublime scene, surpassing the first in
sublimity and solemnity as well as in order.
The singing was grand. The Addresses were
the best that could be and majesty exceeded
anything I have witnessed in the last days.
On Friday, April 1, the elders began to go
forth to bind up the [Saints?] and seal up their
testimony: and though the going was very hard,
not a word was heard, every [many] was anxious
to be in the field. May God bless them in their
labors. The whole has been a grand sol=
emn scene. The last endowment. Now

Courtesy Museum of Church History and Art

Jesus Christ Appears to the Prophet Joseph Smith and Oliver Cowdery, by Walter Rane, oil on canvas, 2003.

may the Lord speed his work, and cut it short
in righteousness. Amen. April 1, 1836

On Sunday, April 3, the twelve held meeting and
administered the sacrament. It was a glorious time.
The curtains were dropt in the afternoon. And
There was a manifestation of the Lord to Br Joseph
and Oliver, [by?] which they [learned?] thus the great &
terrible day of the Lord as mentioned by Malichi,
was near, even at the doors. Could not
get ready to start for Missouri, on Monday-
had to wait to raise Money to purchase
land: Monday & Tuesday went heavily though
I attended a feast at Father Johnson's on Tuesday
afternoon. Wednesday was set apart as day
of prayer, to end The feast of the passover.
and in honor of the Jubilee of the church:
it being Six years to this day:
The Elders had been leaving for Mo. every
day since last Thursday, and myself and Br
P. & C. & M. hated to stay so long, but we could not
help it.[40]
This last letter is from your husband, Sally, who, to save
you the postage, as well as, to have a little More of
your sweet "Satisfaction", brings it to you in person
hoping you will receive both in welcome &

Forever

WW Phelps

5. Stephen Post, Papers (March 27–31, 1836)

Stephen Post (1810–1879) joined the Church in 1835 at age twenty-five. He moved from his New York home to Kirtland, Ohio, where he participated in the ordinances and dedication ceremonies as a member of the second quorum of Seventy. One of the best chroniclers of the Restoration, Post kept a journal from his baptism until his death in 1879, amounting to twelve volumes, now housed in Church Archives, and including the entries featured here.[41] After the

Kirtland Temple dedication, Post began a series of missions. He was, in fact, serving in Pennsylvania when Joseph Smith was murdered in 1844. Post followed James Strang and then allied closely with Sidney Rigdon. He was leading Rigdon's followers in Manitoba, Canada, when he died in 1879. Since the Church acquired Post's journals from a descendant in 1971, historians have recognized their value.[42] The following passages are especially valuable for their straightforward reporting of the key events, including the ordinances and manifestations of the Kirtland Temple experience.

> March 27 1836 This day was appointed to be a day when the house of the Lord built by the Church of the Latter day Saints was to be dedicated unto the Lord of the whole earth: there was also a contribution: each individual as they came into the house of the Lord donated as they could in order to defray the expense of the building as the committee had incurred much expense above what had before been contributed. The doors were opened at 8 to be closed at 9 A.M. however they were closed before 9 on account of the house being full many retired to & filled the school room, under the printing office which holds 400 to 450 & many went home. The congregation came to order & President Sidney Rigdon commenced the services of the day by reading the 96 Psalm & then the 24 Ps[alm]. Then a song of praise then a prayer by President S. Rigdon Then another song of praise & next a discourse from S. Rigdon from Matthew VIII 18-19-20 particularly the 20 verse: after the sermon the several quorums voted & arose as they were called upon to declare that they acknowledged Joseph Smith Jun. as a prophet, seer, & revelator to Israel. There was a song of praise & a short intermission the order of the house was for the people to keep their seats: as this day was appointed as a fast day unto the Lord from morning until evening. PM. a song of praise. Joseph Smith Jun. first president of the church of Latter day Saints; took the lead & called upon the several quorums separately to acknowledge each other in their separate capacities. There was present the following & they voted in the following order, to acknowledge the Prophet first the presidency 2nd the 12 apostles 3rd the High Council. 4th the Bishopric including the Bishop of Zion & his counsellors. 5th the Zion council on the right of the Bishopric 6: the 7 presidents of the 70's on the left of the Bishopric. 7th the Presidency &

council of High Priests, 8th the President and Council of Elders 9th the whole congregation when the Bishoprick voted the whole Bishoprick was included viz Bishop of Kirtland of Zion, Presidents of the Priests Teachers & Deacons with their councils. President Joseph Smith Jun. offered up a dedication prayer unto the Lord President Sidney Rigdon offered a short prayer & then led the way followed by the whole congregation acknowledging the Lord to be King. This is the sample of the shout with uplifted hands unto the most high, by the Lord's anointed Hosanna! Hosanna! Hosanna to God & the Lamb Amen! Amen & Amen. This was done three times making 9 hosannas & 9 amens. They next partook of the sacrament & then were dismissed after after [*sic*] some testimony during the partaking by the congregation of the bread & wine in remembrance of our Lord & Savior Jesus Christ. Joseph Smith Jun. testified of the Angel of the Lord appearing unto him to call him to the work of the Lord, & also of being ordained under the hands of the Angel of the covenant. President Hyrum Smith & President O. Cowdery testified of the truth of the work which was made known to them by the power of God. Carlos Smith President of the High Priests testified of the truth of the book. President F. G. Williams arose & testified that in the A. M. an angel of God came into the window (at the back of the pulpit) while Pt. Rigdon was at prayer & took his seat between him & Father Joseph Smith Sr. & remained there during the prayer. The ordained members of the church are requested to meet in the Lords house this evening to receive instruction previous to their going forth to proclaim the gospel. The congregation were now dismissed. The eve assembled in the house of the Lord Joseph Smith Jun. read the 6 chap. II Chron. & showed us the order of dedicating a house to God anciently. This evening was designed as a continuation of our Pentecost, Angels of God came into the room, cloven tongues rested upon some of the servants of the Lord like unto fire & they spake with tongues & prophesied. . . .

March 28 . . . It was ascertained and told to us last eve that there was 1000 persons in the house of the Lord yesterday & they contributed as they went in $960. I will mention here that two of the Apostles Brigham Young & David Patten sang each a song of Zion in tongues & each spake in tongues & Elder Patten interpreted Brother Young's tongue which he spake. . . . There was about

316 ordained members met in the house of the Lord Sunday eve & we received instruction from Joseph Smith Jr. relative to our preaching & to our endowment this eve the Spirit of the Lord rested on the congregation many spake in tongues many prophesied, angels were in our midst, & ministered unto some. Cloven tongues like unto fire rested upon those who spake in tongues & prophesied when they ceased to speak the tongues ascended.

Wed. [March] 30 this day between the hours of 8 & 9 the ordained members met in the house of the Lord to attend to the last ordinance of the endowment viz: the ordinance of the washing of feet. This ordinance is administered to none but those who are clean from blood of the generation in which they live. I did not expect much to receive the ordinance as I had not laboured much in the vineyard, but I had endeavored to do as well as I could. However when we came together the Word of the Lord was that we all should receive the ordinance. O the goodness & condescension of God. The washing was commenced by the Presidents who first washed the 12 & the 7 Presidents of the Seventies the 12 & 7 then commenced washing until the whole were washed. The order of the house was that we tarry until tomorrow morning in the house of the Lord & not go out only in case of necessity. After the washing the Brethren commenced prophesying for the Spirit of prophecy was poured out upon the congregation: the house was divided into parts by curtains & they prophesied spake and sang in tongues in each room. We fasted until even when we partook of bread & wine in commemoration of the marriage supper of the Lamb. Now having attended through the endowment I could form an idea of the endowment anciently for Gods ordinances change not.

Thursday [March] 31 This morning I came home, partook of some breakfast & then went to another dedication meeting for those who could not be accommodated Sunday the house was filled, the services were the same & some more was contributed to the house of the Lord.

6. Joseph Smith, Journal (1836)

The entries in the journal[43] of Joseph Smith (1805–1844) that lead up to and describe the Kirtland Temple experience are characterized by an informed determination to see the Temple completed and hold the solemn assembly as commanded. In January 1833 he wrote to William Phelps in Missouri,

> the Lord commanded us in Kirtland, to build an house of God, & establish a school for the Prophets, this is the word of the Lord to us, & we must—yea the Lord helping us we will obey, as on conditions of our obedience, he has promised <us> great things, yea <even> a visit from the heavens to honor us with his own presence. (D&C 88)[44]

Joseph understood the significance of the Temple and what would occur within it better than anyone else. During a meeting with the apostles on November 12, 1835, he urged,

> we must have all things prepared and call our solem assembly as the Lord has commanded us, that we may be able to accomplish his great work: and it mu[s]t be done in Gods own way, the house of the Lord must be prepared, and the solem assembly called and organized in it according to the order of the house of God and in it we must attend to the ordinance of washing of feet.

Joseph continued, "the endowment you are so anxious about you cannot comprehend now," nevertheless he urged them to prepare personally. "You need an endowment brethren," he said, "in order that you may be prepared and able to over come all things."[45] Joseph's descriptions of the pentecostal experiences at Kirtland are characteristically straightforward, lacking hyperbole, affirming matter-of-factly that the promised blessings were obtained. Because the following entries were recorded by various clerks, they are sometimes rendered in the third-person voice.

> [January 21, 1836, Thursday; p. 135] At about 3. oclock P. M I dismissed the school and the presidency; retired to the loft of the printing office, where we attended to the ordinance of washing our bodies in pure water, we also perfumed our bodies and our heads, in the name of the Lord at early candlelight, I met with the presidency, at the west school room in the Chapel to attend to the ordinance of annointing our heads with holy oil—also the councils of ~~Zion~~ Kirtland and Zion, met in the two adjoining rooms, who waited in prayer while we attended to the ordinance;— I took

the oil in my <left> ~~right~~ hand, father Smith being seated before me and the rest of the presidency encircled him round about.—we then streched our right hands to heaven and blessed the oil and concecrated it in the name of Jesus Christ—we then laid our hands on our aged fath[er] Smith, and invoked, the blessings of heaven,—I then annointed his head with the concecrated oil, and sealed many blessings upon him, ~~head,~~ the presidency then in turn, laid their hands upon his head, beginning at the eldest, untill they had all laid their hands on him, and pronounced such blessings, upon his head as the Lord put into their hearts—all blessing him to be our patraarch, ~~and~~ <to> annoint our [p. 136] heads, and attend to all duties that purtain to that office.—I then took the seat, and father annoint[ed] my head, and sealed upon me the blessings, of Moses, to lead Israel in the latter days, even as moses led him in days of old.—also the blessings of Abraham Isaac and Jacob.—all of the presidency laid their hands upon me and pronounced upon my head many prophesies, and blessings, many of which I shall not notice at this time, but as Paul said, so say I, let us come to vissions and revelations,— The heavens were opened upon us and I beheld the celestial kingdom of God, and the glory thereof, whether in the body or out I cannot tell,—I saw the transcendant beauty of the gate ~~that enters~~, through which the heirs of that Kingdom will enter, which was like unto circling flames of fire, also the blasing throne of God, where on was seated the Father and the Son,—I saw the beautiful streets of that Kingdom, which had the appearance of being paved with gold— I saw father Adam, and Abraham and Michael and my father and mother, my brother Alvin that has long since slept, and marvled how it was that he had obtained ~~this~~ an inheritance <in> that Kingdom, seeing that he had departed this life, before the Lord <had> set his hand to gather Israel <the second time> and had not been baptised for the remission of sins— Thus ~~said~~ came the voice <of the Lord unto> me saying all who have [p. 137] died with[out] a knowledge of this gospel, who would have received it, if they had been permited to tarry, shall be heirs of the celestial kingdom of God— also all that shall die henseforth, with<out> a knowledge of it, who would have received it, with all their hearts, shall be heirs of that kingdom, for I the Lord <will> judge all men according to their works according to the desires of their hearts— and ~~again I also beheld the Terrestial Kingdom~~ I also beheld that all children who die before they arive to the years of accountability, are saved in the celestial kingdom of heaven— I saw the 12, apostles of the Lamb, who are now upon the earth who hold the keys of this last ministry, in foreign lands, standing together in a circle much fatiegued, with their clothes tattered and feet swolen, with their eyes cast downward, and Jesus <standing> in their midst, and they did not behold him, the Saviour looked upon them and wept— I also beheld Elder McLellen in the south, standing upon a hill surrounded with a vast multitude, preaching to them, and a lame man standing before him, supported by his crutches, he threw them down at his word, and leaped as an heart, by the mighty power of God

Also Eld[e]r Brigham Young standing in a strange land, in the far southwest, in a desert place, upon a rock in the midst of about a dozen men of colour, who, appeared hostile [p. 138] He was preaching to them in their own toung, and the angel of God standing above his head with a drawn sword in his hand protec[t]ing him, but he did not see it,—and I finally saw the 12 in the celestial kingdom of God,— I also beheld the redemption of Zion, and many things which the toung of man, cannot discribe in full.— Many of my brethren who received this ordinance with me, saw glorious visions also,—angels ministered unto them, as well as my self, and the power of the highest rested upon, us the house was filled with the glory of God, and we shouted Hosanah to ~~the~~ God and the Lamb

I am mistaken, concerning my receiving the holy anointing first after father Smith, we received <it> in turn according to our age, (that is the presidency,)

My Scribe also recieved his anointing <with us> and saw in a vision the armies of heaven protecting the Saints in their return to Zion—& many things that I saw[46]

The Bishop of Kirtland with his counsellors and the Bishop of Zion with his counsellors, were present with us, and received their, annointing under the hands of father Smith and confirmed by the presidency and the glories of heaven was unfolded to them also—

We then invited the counsellors of Kirtland and Zion ~~and Kirtland~~ into our room, and President Hyrum [p. 139] Smith annointed the head of the president of the counsellors in Kirtland

and President D. Whitmer the head of the president, of the counsellors of Zion.

The president of each quorum then annointed the heads of his colleagues, each in his turn beginning, at the eldest

The vision of heaven was opened to them also, some of them saw the face of the Saviour, and others were ministered unto by holy angels, and the spirit of prop[h]esy and revelation was poured out in mighty power, and loud hosanahs and glory to God in the highest, saluted the heavens for we all communed with the h[e]avenly host's,—and I saw in my vision all of the presidency in the Celestial Kingdom of God, and, many others who were present.

Our meeting was opened by singing and prayer offered up by the head of each quorum, and closed by singing and invoking the benediction of heaven with uplifted hands, and retired between one and 2. oclock in the morning [p. 140]

Friday morning the 22nd attended at the school room at the us[u]al hour,—But insted of persuing our studies we ~~commenced~~ spent the time in rehearsing to each other the glorious scenes that transpired on the preceding evening, while attending to the ordinance of holy anointing.—At evening we met at the same place, with the council of the 12 and the presidency of the 70 who were to receive this ordinance; the high councils of Kirtland and Zion were present also: we called to order and organized; the Presidency then proceeded to consecrate the oil; we then laid our hands upon Elder Thomas B. Marsh who is the president of the 12 and ordained him to the authority of anointing his brethren, I then poured the concecrated oil upon his head in the name of Jesus Christ and sealed such blessings upon him as the Lord put into my heart; the rest of the presidency then laid their hands upon him and blessed him each in their turn beginning at the eldest; he then anointed <and blessed> his brethren from the oldest to the youngest, I also laid my hands upon them and prounounced many great and glorious [blessings] upon their heads; the heavens were opened and angels ministered unto us.

The 12 then proceeded to anoint and bless the presidency of the 70 and seal upon their heads power and authority to anoint their brethren; the heavens were opened upon Elder Sylvester Smith and he leaping up exclaimed, The horsemen of Israel and the chariots thereof. ~~President Rigdon arose~~ Br. [Don] Carloss Smith was also, annointed and ~~ordained~~ blessed to preside over the high priesthood. — President Rigdon, arose to conclude the servises of the evening [p. 141] by invoking the benediction of heaven ~~of heaven~~ upon the Lords anointed <which he did> in an eloquent manner the congregation shouted a loud hosannah the gift of toungs, fell upon us in mighty power, angels mingled ~~themselves~~ their voices with ours, while their presence was in our midst, and unseasing prasis swelled our bosoms for the space of half an hour, — I then observed to the brethren that it was time to retire, we accordingly <closed> our interview and returned home at about 2. oclock in the morning/ & the spirit & visions of God attended me through the night. . . .

[p. 143] Thursday <28> [January 1836] attended school at the usual hours In the evening met the quorems of High Priests in the west room of the upper loft of the Lord,s house & in company with my council of the presidency— consecrated & anointed the cou[n]sellors of the President of the High priesthood & having instructed them & set the quorem in order I left them to perform the holy anointing—& went to the quorem of Elders in the other end of the room. I assisted in anointing the counsellors of the President of the Elders & gave them the instruction necessary for the occasion & left the President & his council to anoint the Elders while I should go to the adjoining room & attend to organizing & instructing of the quorem of the Seventy—

I found the Twelve Apostles assembled with this quorem & I proceeded with the quorem of the presedincy to instruct them & also the seven presidents of the seventy Elders to call upon God with uplifted hands to seal the blessings which had been promised to them by the holy anointing As I organized this quorem with the presedincy in this room, Pres. Sylvester Smith saw a piller of fire rest down & abide upon the heads of the quorem as we stood in the midst of the Twelve.[47]

When the Twelve & the seven were through with their sealing prayers I called upon Pres. S. Rigdon to seal them with uplifted hands & when he had done this & cried hossannah that all [the] congregation should join him & shout hosannah to God & the Lamb & glory to God in the highest—It was done so & Etc. Roger [p. 144] Orton saw a ~~flaming~~ <mighty> Angel riding upon a horse of fire with a flaming sword in his hand followed by five others—

Encircle the house & protect the saints even the Lords anointed from the power of Satan & a host of evil spirits which were striving to disturb the saints—

Pres. Wm Smith one of the Twelve saw the h[e]avens op[e]ned & the Lords host protecting the Lords anointed. Pres. Z[ebedee] Coltrin one of the seven saw the saviour extended before him as upon the cross & [a] little after crowned with a glory upon his head above the brightness of the sun after these things were over & a glorious vision which I saw had passed I instructed the seven presidents to proceede & anoint the seventy & returned to the room of the High Priests & Elders & attended to the sealing of what they had done with uplifted hands, the Lord had assisted my bro. Carloss the Pres. of the High Priests to go forward with the anointing of the High priests so that he had performed it to the acceptance of the Lord, notwithstanding he was verry young & inexperienced in such duties & I f[e]lt to praise God with a loud hossannah for his goodness to me & my fathers family & to all the children of men—praise the Lord all ye his saints—praise his holy name after these quorems were dismissed I retired to my home filled with the spirit & my soul cried hossannah to God & the Lamb through <the> silent watches of the night & while my eyes were closed in sleep the visions of the Lord were sweet unto me & his glory was round about me praise the Lord [p. 145] . . .

Saturday 30 [January 1836] Attended school as usual, & waited upon several visiters & showed them the record of Abraham— Mr Seixas our hebrew teacher examined them with deep interest & pronounced them to be original beyound all doubt, he is a man of excellent understanding—& has a knowledge of many languages which were spoken by the Ancients— he is an honored man so far as I can judge as yet— in the evening went to the upper rooms of the Lord's house & set the different quorems in order— instructed the Presidents of the seventy concerning the order of their anointing & requested them to proceed & anoint the seventy having set all the quorems in order I returned [p. 149] to my house being weary with continual anxiety & labour in puting all the Authorities in & in striving to purify them for the solemn assembly according to the commandment of the Lord . . .

[p. 151] Saturday 6 [February 1836] called the anointed together to receive the seal of all their blessings, The High Priests & Elders in the council room as usual— The Seventy with the Twelve in the second room & the Bishop in the 3— I laboured with each of these quorems for some time to bring to the order which God had shown to me which is as follows— first part to be spent in solemn prayer before god without any talking or confusion & the conclusion with a sealing prayer by Pres. Sidney Rigdon when all the quorems are to shout with one accord a solemn hosannah to God & the Lamb with an Amen——amen & amen— & then all take seats & lift up their hearts in silent prayer to God & if any obtain a prophecy or vision to rise & speak that all may be edified & rejoice together I had considerable trouble to get all the quorems united in this order— I went from room to room repeatedly & charged each separately—assuring them that it was according to the mind of God yet notwithstanding all my labour—while I was in the east room with the Bishops quorems I f[e]lt by the spirit that something was wrong in the quorem of Elders in the west room— & I immediately requested Pres. O. Cowdery & H. Smith to go in & see what was the matter—The quorem of Elders had not observed the order which I had given them & were reminded of it by Pres. [Don] Carloss Smith & mildly requested to observe order & continue in prayer & requested—some of them replied that they had a teacher of their own & did not wish to be troubled by others this caused the spirit of the Lord to withdraw [p. 151[48]] This interrupted the meeting & this quorem lost th[e]ir blessing in a great measure— the other quorems were more careful & the quorem of the seventy enjoyed a great flow of the holy spirit many arose & spok[e] testifying that they were filled with the holy spirit which was like fire in their bones so that they could not hold their peace but were constrained to cry hosannah to God & the Lamb & glory in the highest. Pres. Wm Smith one of the twelve saw a vision of the Twelve & seven in council together in old England & prophecied that a great work would be done by them in the old co[u]ntries & God was already beginning to work in the hearts of the p[e]ople— Pres. Z. Coltrin one of the seven saw a vision of the Lords Host—& others were filled with the spirit & spake in tongues & prophecied— This was a time of rejoicing long to be remembered! praise the Lord— . . .

[p. 172] Saturday the 26th [March 1836] At home attending to my domestick concerns in the morning.— after brekfast met with the presidency to make arangements for the solemn assembly which occupied the remainder of the day

Sunday morning the 27th [March 1836] The congregation began to assemble <at the chapel> at about 7 oclock one hour earlier than the doors were to be opened many brethren had come in from the region's [p. 173] round about to witness the dedication of the Lords House and share in his blessings and such was the anxiety on this occasion that some hundreds, (probably five or six,) assembled ~~collected~~ before the doors were opened—

The presidency entered with the door ke[e]pers and aranged them at the inner and outer doors also placed our stewards to rec[e]iv[e] donations from those who should feel disposed to contribute something to defray the expenses of building the House of the Lord— <we also dedicated the pulpits & consecrated them to the Lord> The doors were then opened President Rigdon President Cowdery and myself seated the congregation as they came in, ~~we received about~~ and according to the best calculation we could make we received between 9 <hundred> and 10,00 [*sic*] which is as many as can be comfortably situated we then informed the door keepers that we could rec[e]iv[e] no more, and a multitude were deprived of the benefits of the meeting on account of the house not being sufficiently capacious to rec[e]ive them, and I felt to regret that any of my brethren and sisters should be deprived of the meeting, and I recommended them to repair to the School-house and hold a meeting which they did and filled that house <also> and yet many were left out—

The assembly were then organized in the following manner. viz— [p. 174]

West end of the. house—

Presdt. F G. Williams Presdt. Joseph Smith, Sen and Presdt. W W. Phelps occupied the lst pulpit for the Melchisedic priesthood— Presdt. S. Rigdon myself and Presdt Hyrum Smith in the 2nd— Presdt. D. Whitmer Presdt. O. Cowdery and Presdt. J. Whitmer in the 3d—The 4th was occupied by the president of the high-priests and his counsellors, and 2 choiresters—The 12. Apostles on the right in the 3 highest seats— The presdt of the Eld[e]rs his clerk & counsellors in the seat immediatly below the 12—The high council of Kirtland consisting of 12, on the left in the 3, first seats— the 4th seat below them was occupied by

Historic American Buildings Survey Collection, Library of Congress

Kirtland Temple interior, west window and pulpits, lower court. Photographed April 1934 by Carl F. Waite. Flanking the pulpits are an organ and sacrament (communion) table, which have since been removed.

~~the presidencys~~ Eldr's W A. Cowdery & W. Parrish who served as scribes.—The pulpits in the east end of the house for the Aaronic priesthood were occupied as follows.—The Bishop of Kirtland and his counsellors in the 1st pulpit.—The Bishop of Zion and his counsellors in the 2nd—The presdt. of the priests and his counsellors in the 3d—The presdt. of the Teachers and his counsellors <& one choirister> in the 4th—The high council of Zion consisting of [p. 175] 12 counsellors on the right—The presdt of the Deacons and his counsillors in the seat below them— The 7 presdts of the Seventies on the left—The choir of singers were seated in the 4 corners of the room in seats prepared for that purpose—rec[eive]d by contribution $960.00

9 oclock A. M the servises of the day were opened by Presdt S. Rigdon by reading 1st the 96 Psalm secondly the 24th Psalm—the choir then sung hymn on the 29th page of Latter day Saints collection of hymn's—prayer by Presdt Rigdon choir then sung hymn on 14th page[49] Presdt Rigdon then <read> the 18, 19, & 20, verses

of the 8th Chapter of Mathew and preached more particularly from the 20th verse.—his prayer and address were very forcible and sublime, and well adapted to the occasion.—after he closed his sermon, he called upon the several quorums commenceing with the presidency, to manifest by rising up, their willingness to acknowledge me as a prophet and seer and uphold me as such by their p[r]ayers of faith, all the quorums in their turn, cheerfully complyed with this request he then called upon all the congregation of Saints, also to give their assent by rising on their feet which they did unanimously

After an intermission of 20, minutes the servises of the day were resumed, by singing Adam ondi ahman.[50] I then made a short address and called upon the several quorums, and all the congregation of saints to acknowledge the Presidency as Prophets and Seers, and uphold them by their prayers, they all covenanted to do so by rising; I then called upon the quorums and congregation of saints to acknowledge the 12 [p. 176] Apostles who were present as Prophets and Seers and special witnesses to all the nations of the earth, holding the keys of the kingdom, to unlock it or cause it to be done among ~~all nations~~ them; and uphold them by their prayers, which they assented to by rising, # I then called upon the quorums and congregation of saints to acknowledge the high council of Kirtland in all the authorities of the Melchisedec priesthood and uphold them by their prayers which they assented to by rising. I then called upon the quoru<ms> and congregation of saints to acknowledge and upho<ld> by their prayer's the Bishops of Kirtland and Zion and their counsellors, ~~the Presidents of the Priests~~ in all the authority of the Aaronic priesthood, which they did by rising. I then called upon the quorums and congregation of saints to acknowledge the high-council of Zion, and uphold them by their prayers in all the authority of the high priesthood which they did by rising. I next called upon the quorums and congregation of saints to acknowledge the Presidents of the seventys who act as their represent[at]ives as <Apostles and> special witnesses to the nations to assist the 12 in opening the gospel kingdom, among all people and to uphold them by their prayer's which they did by rising—I then called upon the quorums and all the saints to acknowledge [the] president of the Elders and his counsellors and uphold them by their prayers which they did by rising—The quorums and congregation of saints were then called upon to acknowledge and uphold by their prayers the Presidents of the Priests, Teachers, and Deacons and their counsellors, which they did by rising.

N. B. The Presidents ~~were~~ of the seventy's were acknowledged first after the 12 Apostles [p. 177]

The hymn on the hundred and 14 page was then sung,[51] after which I offered to God the following dedication prayer. [See D&C 109.] . . .

Sung Hosanah to God and the Lamb[52] after which the Lords supper was administered

I then bore testimony of the administering of angels.—Presdt Williams also arose and testified that while Presdt Rigdon was making [p. 185] his first prayer an angel entered the window and <took his> seated ~~himself~~ between father Smith, and himself, and remained their during his prayer Presdt David Whitmer also saw angels in the house

We then sealed the proceedings of the day by ~~a~~ shouting hosanah to God and the Lamb 3 times sealing it each time with Amen, Amen, and Amen and after requesting all the official members to meet again in the evening we retired—met in the evening and instructed the quorums respecting the ordinance of washing of feet which we were to attend to on wednesday following . . .

[pp. 185–86] Tuesday the 29th [March 1836][53] . . . Soon after this, the word of the Lord came to us through Presdt J. Smith Jun that those who had entered the holy place must not leave the house untill morning but send for such things as were necessary, and also, that during our stay we must cleans[e] our feet and partake of the sacrament that we might be made holy before Him, and thereby be qualified to officiate in our calling upon the morrow in washing the feet of the Elders.[54]

Accordingly we proceeded and cleansed our faces and our feet, and then proceeded to wash each others feet.—president S. Rigdon first washed presdt J. Smith jun and then in [p. 187] turn was washed by him—after which president Rigdon washed presdt J. Smith Sen. and Hyrum Smith <prsdt> J. Smith Jun washed presdt F. G Williams, and then pres. Hyrum Smith washed president David Whitmer's feet and president Oliver Cowdery's, then pres D. Whitmer washed pres. W. W. Phelps feet and in turn pres Phelps washed pres John Whitmers feet.

The Bishops and their councils were then washed: After which we partook of the bread and wine. The Holy S[p]irit rested down upon us and we continued in the Lords house all night prophesying and giving glory to God

Wednesday morning 8 O clock March 30th 1836

According to appointment the presidency, the 12, the seventies, the high ~~co<u>ncils~~ councils, the Bishops and their entire quorums, the Elders, and all the official members in this stake of Zion amounting to about 300 met in the temple of the Lord to attend to the ordinance of washing of feet, I ascended the pulpit and remarked to the congregation that we had passed through many trials and afflictions since the organization of this church and that this is a year of Jubilee to us and a time of rejoicing, and that it was expedient for us to prepare bread and wine sufficient to make our hearts glad, as we should not probably leave this house until morning; to this end we should call on the brethren to make a contribution, the stewards passed round and took up a liberal contribution and messengers were dispatched for bread and wine, tubs [of] water and towels were prepared and I called the house to order, and the presidency proceeded to wash the feet of the 12 pronouncing many prophecys and blessings upon them in the name of the Lord Jesus, the brethren began to prophesy [p. 187] upon each others heads, and cursings upon the enimies of Christ who inhabit Jackson county Missouri continued prophesying and blessing and sealing them with Hosanna and Amen until nearly 7 oclock P.M. the bread <& wine> was then brought in, and I observed that we had fasted all the day, and lest we faint; as the Saviour did so shall we do on this occasion, we shall bless the bread and give it to the 12 and they to the multitude, after which we shall bless the wine and do likewise; while waiting ~~for the wine~~ I made the following remarks, that the time that we were required to tarry in Kirtland to be endued would be fulfilled in a few days, and then the Elders would go forth and each must stand for himself, that it was not necessary for them to be sent out two by two as in former times; but to go in all meekness in sobriety and preach Jesus Christ & him crucified not to contend with others on the account of their faith or systems of religion but pursue a steady course, this I delivered by way of commandment, and all that observe them not will pull down persecution upon ~~your~~ <their> heads, while those who do shall always be filled with the Holy Ghost. this I pronounced as a prophesy, sealed with a Hosanna & amen. Also that the seventies are not called to serve tables or preside over churches to settle difficulties, but to preach the gospel and build them up, and set others who do not belong to these quorums to preside over them who are high priests—the twelve also are not to serve tables, but to bear the keys of the kingdom to all nations, and unlock them and call upon the seventies to follow after them and assist them. The 12 are at liberty to go wheresoever they will [p. 188] and if one shall say, I wish to go to such a place let all the rest say Amen.

The seventies are at liberty to go to Zion if they please or go wheresoever they will and preach the gospel and let the redemtion of Zion be our object, and strive to affect it by sending up all the strength of the Lords house whereever we find them, and I want to enter into the following covenant, that if any more of our brethren are slain or driven from their lands in Missouri by the mob that we will give ourselves no rest until we are avenged of our enimies to the uttermost, this covenant was sealed unanimously by a hosanna and Amen.—I then observed to the quorums that I had now completed the organization of the church and we had passed through all the necessary ceremonies, that I had given them all the instruction they needed and that they now were at liberty after obtaining their lisences to go forth and build up the kingdom of God, and that it was expedient for me and the presidency to retire, having spent the night previous in waiting upon the Lord in his temple, and having to attend another dedication on the morrow, or conclude the one commenced on the last sabbath for the benifit of those of my brethren and sisters who could not get into the house on the former occasion but that it was expedient for the brethren to tarry all night and worship before the Lord in his house I left the meeting in the charge of the 12 and retired at about 9 o clock in the evening; the brethren continued exhorting, prophesying and speaking in tongues until 5 o clock in the morning—the Saviour made his appearance to some, while angels minestered unto others, and it was a penticost and enduement indeed, long to be remembered for the sound shall go forth from this place into all the [p. 189] world, and the occurrences of this day shall be hande[d] down upon the pages of sacred history to all generations, as the day of Pentecost, so shall this day be numbered and celebrated as a year of Jubilee and time of rejoicing to the saints of the most high God. . . .

Thursday morning 8 o clock March 31st [1836][55]

This day being set apart to perform again the ceremonies of the dedication for the benifit of those who could not get into the house on the preceeding sabbath I repaired to the temple at 8 o clock A.M. in company with the presidency, and arranged our door-keepers and stewards as on the former occasion, we then opened the doors and a large congregation entered the house and were comfortably seated, the authorities of the church were seated, in their respective order and the services of the day were commenced prosecuted and terminated in the same manner as at the former dedication and the spirit of God rested upon the congregation and great solemnity prevailed. . . .

[p. 191] Sabbath April 3^{d} [1836][56]

He attended meeting in the Lords House, assisted the other Presidents of the Church in seating the congregation and then became an attentive listener to the preaching from the Stand. T. B. Marsh & D. W. Patten spoke in the A.M. to an attentive audience of about 1000 persons. In the P.M. he assisted the other Presidents in distributing the elements of the Lords Supper to the church, receiving them from the ~~Hands~~ "Twelve" whose privilige it was to officiate in the sacred desk this day. After having performed this service to his brethren, he retired to the pulpit, the vails being dropped, [p. 192] and bowed, himself with O. Cowdery, in solemn, but silent prayer to the Most High. After rising from prayer the following vision was opened to both of them. [See D&C 110.]

Steven C. Harper is Assistant Professor of Church History and Doctrine at Brigham Young University.

The author first published the Benjamin Brown letter in BYU Studies *42, no. 2 (2003): 4–22.*

Notes

1. See Milton V. Backman Jr., *The Heavens Resound: A History of the Latter-day Saints in Ohio 1830–1838* (Salt Lake City: Deseret Book, 1983), 285–309; Karl Ricks Anderson, *Joseph Smith's Kirtland: Eyewitness Accounts* (Salt Lake City: Deseret Book, 1989), 169–91; Gregory Prince, *Power from on High: The Development of Mormon Priesthood* (Salt Lake City: Signature Books, 1995), 184–85, 160.

2. Dean C. Jessee, ed., *The Papers of Joseph Smith*, 2 vols. (Salt Lake City: Deseret Book, 1992), 2:77.

3. Lucius Pomeroy Parsons to Pamelia Parsons, April 10, 1836, Church Archives, The Church of Jesus Christ of Latter-day Saints, Salt Lake City. For Joseph Smith's explanation of the power the endowment would give to perform miracles, see Jessee, *Papers of Joseph Smith*, 2:77–78.

4. John Corrill, *A Brief History of the Church of Christ of Latter Day Saints (Commonly Called Mormons; Including an Account of Their Doctrine and Discipline; with the Reasons of the Author for Leaving the Church)* (St. Louis: By the author, 1839), 23. In Acts 2:13, mockers explained the spiritual manifestations simply: "These men are full of new wine." See William McLellin to M. H. Forscutt, October 1870, Library-Archives, Community of Christ, Independence, Missouri; William Harris, *Mormonism Portrayed* (Warsaw, Ill.: Sharp and Gamble, 1841), 136, for perpetuated rumors of similar drunkenness in the Kirtland Temple.

5. Richard L. Bushman, "The Visionary World of Joseph Smith," *BYU Studies* 37, no. 1 (1997–98): 183–204, outlines this culture and lists several primary documents that might comprise a genre with which the eyewitness accounts of the Kirtland experience share similarities. Similarly, see Larry C. Porter, "Solomon Chamberlin's Missing Pamphlet: Dreams, Visions, and Angelic Ministrants," *BYU Studies* 37, no. 2 (1997–98): 113–40; Ann Taves, *Fits, Trances, and Visions: Experiencing Religion and Explaining Experience from Wesley to James* (Princeton: Princeton University Press, 1999). See also Leigh Eric Schmidt, *Hearing Things: Religion, Illusion, and the American Enlightenment* (Cambridge, Mass.: Harvard University Press, 2000).

6. Benjamin Brown, *Testimonies for the Truth: A record of Manifestations of the Power of God, miraculous and providential, witnessed in the travels and experience of Benjamin Brown, high priest in the Church of Jesus Christ of Latter Day Saints, Pastor of the London, Reading, Kent, and Essex Conferences* (Liverpool: S. W. Richards, 1853), 5.

7. Brown, *Testimonies for the Truth*, 10–11. Joseph Smith's account of the events of March 27, 1836, which is reprinted later in this article, is in Jessee, *Papers of Joseph Smith*, 2:191–203.

8. Doctrine and Covenants 38:32; 88:67–76; 95:2–8.

9. Doctrine and Covenants 88:68–69; see also Joseph Smith to William Phelps, Kirtland, Ohio, January 11, 1833, in Dean C. Jessee, ed. and comp., *The Personal Writings of Joseph Smith*, rev. ed. (Salt Lake City: Deseret Book; Provo, Utah: Brigham Young University Press, 2002), 292–93.

10. William Phelps to Sally Phelps, January 1836, in Bruce A. Van Orden, ed., "Writing to Zion: The William W. Phelps Kirtland Letters (1835–1836)," *BYU Studies* 33, no. 3 (1993): 574.

11. Jessee, *Papers of Joseph Smith*, 2:77. Members of the School of the Prophets were "received by the ordinance of the washing of the feet" in January and February 1833 (D&C 88:139). That ordinance was next performed March 30, 1836, as the culminating ordinance of the Kirtland endowment. See Prince, *Power from on High*, 172–73.

12 Jessee, *Papers of Joseph Smith*, 207.

13. *The Latter-day Saints' Messenger and Advocate*, March 1836, 274–81.

14. Steven C. Harper, "Pentecost Continued: A Contemporaneous Account of the Kirtland Temple Dedication," *BYU Studies* 42, no. 2 (2003): 4–22.

15. Jessee, *Papers of Joseph Smith*, 2:191-210.

16. Brown, *Testimonies for the Truth*, 10–11.

17. This document was discovered by Mary Lee Burton in November 2002 among the papers of her recently deceased mother, a descendant of Benjamin Brown. Photographs of this document and an extended discussion of its historical context are in Harper, "Pentecost Continued," 4–22.

18. Mathias M. Bovee (1796–1846) lived in Chautaqua County, New York, as the Browns did, and may have carried this letter to Sarah Mumford Brown on Benjamin's behalf.

19. A reference to Philippians 4:7.

20. See Acts 2:1.

21. Besides the specific manifestations Brown goes on to document, other writers left accounts that confirm his general testimony of many visions and revelations. See, for example, Leonard J. Arrington, "Oliver Cowdery's Kirtland, Ohio, 'Sketch Book,'" *BYU Studies* 12, no. 4 (1972): 410–26; and Martha Sonntag Bradley and Mary Brown Firmage Woodward, "Spiritual Riches: The Huntington Sisters in Kirtland, 1836–38," *Four Zinas: A Story of Mothers and Daughters on the Mormon Frontier* (Salt Lake City: Signature Books, 2000), 51–76.

22. Joseph Smith Sr. (1771–1840) served the Church as Patriarch beginning in 1833 and in that capacity offered inspired blessings and personal prophecies including the one documented here by Benjamin Brown.

23. A Joseph Smith Sr. blessing given to James W. Angel (probably Angell, born in North Providence, Rhode Island, on October 15, 1776, father of Brigham's wife Mary Ann Angell Young and Church architect Truman O.

Angell), perhaps given early in 1836, includes a phrase that corresponds somewhat to the language of Brown's letter. It reads, "Thou shalt see many glorious scenes, the heavens shall be open unto thee and thou shalt say it is enough." The blessing is located in Church Archives.

24. Page 424 in the 1830 edition of the Book of Mormon, to which Brown refers here, is now Helaman 6, especially verses 21–27.

25. This was the evening of March 27, 1836.

26. Rules of order for the solemn assembly are in Joseph Smith's journal under January 14, 1836, and published in Jessee, *Papers of Joseph Smith*, 2:136–38. Eliza R. Snow independently confirmed this event. She adds that it was Joseph Smith Sr. to whom the unidentified woman came "in great distress, saying that she knew no one with whom she could leave her infant; and to be deprived of the privilege of attending the dedication seemed more than she could endure." Father Smith, the Church's Patriarch, "told her to take her child, at the same time giving the mother a promise that her babe should make no disturbance; and the promise was verified." Snow continues, noting as Brown does that the "babe joined in the shout" as the congregation offered hosannas. See Snow's account in Edward W. Tullidge, *The Women of Mormondom* (New York: Tullidge and Crandall, 1877), 94–95.

27. Most likely William Parks (1787–1856), who was living in Euclid, Cuyahoga County, Ohio, as of 1832.

28. Perhaps Abraham Stephens, about whom very little is known. Book of Patriarchal Blessings Index, 4:163, Church Archives.

29. Here, Brown initially writes April 29 instead of the correct date, March 29. See Joseph Smith's journal entry for March 29, below.

30. Oliver Cowdery, "Sketch Book," Church Archives, and published in Arrington, "Oliver Cowdery's Kirtland, Ohio, 'Sketch Book,'" 410–26.

31. That is, President of the High Priests.

32. Arrington, "Oliver Cowdery's Kirtland, Ohio, 'Sketch Book,'" 426.

33. This account was originally published in *Messenger and Advocate*, March 1836, 274–81. The words of the revealed prayer (now D&C 109) and the words of the hymns have been omitted here.

34. Scott H. Partridge, "Edward Partridge in Painesville, Ohio," *BYU Studies* 42, no. 1 (2003): 50–73.

35. Edward Partridge, Diaries, 1818 and 1835–1836, Church Archives.

36. The members of the First Presidency in 1836 were Joseph Smith, Sidney Rigdon, and Frederick G. Williams. Counselors to Bishop Edward Partridge were Isaac Morley and John Corrill, and counselors to Bishop Newel K. Whitney were Reynolds Cahoon and Vinson Knight.

37. Lorenzo Barnes wrote: "March the 30th attended the solom assembly and received the washing of feet by the hands of Zebedee Coultrin We had a

joyful time our meeting continued with out intermission from 9 in the morning until the dawn of the next day. There were between 250 & 300 Priests and Elders preasant & the servants of God spake with tongues & prophesied & the shout of Joy of a Hosanna to God & the Lamb resounded afar off." Lorenzo Barnes, Reminiscences and Diaries 1834–39, 43, Church Archives.

38. William Phelps to Sally Phelps, January 1836, in Van Orden, "Writing to Zion," 578.

39. William W. Phelps to Sally Phelps, April 1–6, 1836, William Wines Phelps Papers, L. Tom Perry Special Collections, Harold B. Lee Library, Brigham Young University, Provo, Utah. Jeanne A. Clawson and Stanley LeRoy Allen Jr., a great-great-grandson of Phelps, donated this to the Perry Special Collections in July 2002.

40. This is likely a reference to Bishop Edward Partridge and his counselors, John Corrill and Isaac Morley, the bishopric of the Church in Missouri.

41. Stephen Post, Papers, 1835–1921, Church Archives.

42. Max J. Evans, "The Stephen Post Collection," *BYU Studies* 14, no. 1 (1973): 100–103.

43. Jessee, *Papers of Joseph Smith*, 2:148–210.

44. Joseph Smith to William Phelps, Kirtland, January 11, 1833, in Jessee, *Personal Writings of Joseph Smith*, 293.

45. Joseph Smith to the Twelve Apostles, November 12, 1835, in Jessee, *Papers of Joseph Smith*, 2:76–77.

46. Warren Parrish was Joseph's scribe. Apparently Parrish joined the Church in 1833, marched with Zion's Camp the following year, and served a mission to Kentucky and Tennessee with Wilford Woodruff in 1835–36 as a member of the Quorum of Seventy. He clerked for Joseph Smith following his return to Kirtland in 1836. He was accused of embezzling from the Kirtland Safety Society, of which he was treasurer. In 1837 he resigned from the Church and led dissenters in opposition to Joseph Smith. He died in Kansas in 1887. See Jessee, *Papers of Joseph Smith*, 2:577–78.

47. Sylvester Smith was born in Connecticut in 1805 and converted to Mormonism in 1831. He marched with Zion's Camp in 1834 and was ordained one of the seven presidents of the Seventy in 1835. He served in that capacity until leaving the Church in 1837. See Jessee, *Papers of Joseph Smith*, 2:595.

48. This is the second consecutive p. 151.

49. The two hymns referred to are "Ere Long the Veil Will Rend in Twain," by Parley P. Pratt, and "O Happy Souls, Who Pray," by William W. Phelps.

50. "Adam-ondi-Ahman," by William W. Phelps. See *Hymns of the Church of Jesus Christ of Latter-day Saints* (Salt Lake City: The Church of Jesus Christ of Latter-day Saints, 1985), no. 49.

51. "How Pleased and Blessed Was I," by Isaac Watts.

52. "The Spirit of God," by William W. Phelps. *Hymns*, no. 2.

53. Jessee, *Papers of Joseph Smith*, 2:203–7.

54. Those in attendance included Joseph Smith Jr., Frederick G. Williams, and Sidney Rigdon along with Hyrum Smith and Oliver Cowdery. They were joined by the stake presidencies and bishoprics from Zion and Kirtland.

55. Jessee, *Papers of Joseph Smith*, 2:207–8.

56. Jessee, *Papers of Joseph Smith*, 2:209–210.

Library of Congress

Nauvoo, Illinois. Bird's-eye view from hill across the Mississippi River to Nauvoo. Steel engraving, ca. 1855, copyrighted by Herrmann J. Meyer.

The Mantle of the Prophet Joseph Passes to Brother Brigham: One Hundred Twenty-one Testimonies of a Collective Spiritual Witness

Lynne Watkins Jorgensen

On August 8, 1844, six weeks after the Prophet Joseph Smith's martyrdom, a meeting of the Saints was held in Nauvoo, Illinois. Brigham Young, President of the Quorum of the Twelve, and several other apostles had just returned from missions. The purpose of this meeting was to determine by vote who had the right and responsibility to lead the Church—Sidney Rigdon, first counselor in the First Presidency, or the Quorum of the Twelve with Brigham Young at their head.[1] In the course of the two meetings held that day, many in attendance received a divine witness that Brigham Young was to be the next leader: some Saints specifically state that Brigham Young assured the congregation that

> here is President Sidney Rigdon, who was counselor to Joseph. I ask, where are Joseph and Hyrum? They are gone beyond the veil; and if Elder Rigdon wants to act as his counselor, he must go beyond the veil where he [Joseph] is. . . . I say unto you that the quorum of the Twelve have the keys of the Kingdom of God in all the world.

During the meeting Brigham sounded and appeared remarkably like Joseph Smith; others simply say that the "mantle of Joseph" or the "mantle of the prophets" rested on Brigham Young; and others state that they were given a witness "by the spirit" that Brigham was to lead the Church.

This spiritual experience, which has come to be known as "the mantle of the Prophet falling on Brigham Young" or transfiguration,[2] served to unite and comfort the Saints as they mourned the death of their beloved prophet and to direct them when they voted to support Brigham and the Twelve as leaders of the Church. Some Saints who were not present at the August 8 meetings reported experiencing a similar "mantle" witness on later occasions. To date we are aware of 121 people who wrote or otherwise passed on their remembrances of this witness.

Most Mormon historians acknowledge the mantle story, agreeing that something important happened in August 1844. For example, Ronald K. Esplin states, "Though there is no contemporary diary account, the number of later retellings, many in remarkable detail, argues for the reality of some such experience."[3] Leonard J. Arrington and Davis Bitton acknowledge, "Many who were present at the August 8 meeting later remembered seeing in Brigham Young that day a new appearance and hearing from him a new voice—one that was very familiar, that of Joseph Smith. For them the 'Mantle of Joseph' was given directly, miraculously, to Young."[4] Arrington notes in another book that "the diaries, letters, and later recollections of many of those present testified to an experience that persuaded them that Brigham was the new Joseph." He acknowledges that an important event "took place" but observed that there may be psychological explanations for the phenomenon and reserves judgment regarding whether a miraculous transfiguration[5] occurred.[6] Others have concluded that it is unlikely that a miraculous spiritual manifestation took place. Richard S. Van Wagoner, for instance, writes, "When 8 August 1844 is stripped of emotional overlay, there is not a shred of irrefutable contemporary evidence to support the occurrence of a mystical event." Van Wagoner concludes that "a more likely scenario was that it was the force of Young's commanding presence, his well-timed arrival at the morning meeting, and perhaps a bit of theatrical mimicry that swayed the crowd."[7] Van Wagoner and others insist that transfiguration stories must appear on the day of occurrence or shortly thereafter to be acceptable.[8] However he has not presented documentation written on the day that refutes the fact that a transfiguration occurred. In fact, Van Wagoner eventually admits that as the August 8, 1844, afternoon meeting progressed, "the sentiment which had so recently changed in favor of the twelve became palpable."[9]

In order to enable readers to examine for themselves the evidence underlying these interpretations, numerous accounts of the mantle experience have been compiled in the document/testimony section of this article beginning on page 408. The evidence presented in these accounts demonstrates that many people testified powerfully that they had received a convincing sensory or spiritual witness of the mantle of the Prophet Joseph falling on Brigham Young. Brigham Young's remarks as recorded by Thomas Bullock at the August 8, 1844, morning meeting are found in the appendix to this article.

The Symbolic Mantle: Elijah and Elisha

The image of the mantle as a symbol of the passing of authority is at least as old as the well-known Old Testament story of the prophet Elijah and Elisha, his young follower.[10] The Lord told Elijah that he was to anoint Elisha "to be prophet in thy room." Elisha was plowing in the fields when Elijah walked past him and placed his rough mantle (cloak or cape) across the younger man's shoulders. Elisha left the fields to follow Elijah and to have Elijah minister to him (1 Kgs. 19:16–21).

As the story continues, the time came for Elijah to leave his earthly mission:

> And it came to pass, when they were gone over [the Jordan River], that Elijah said unto Elisha, Ask what I shall do for thee, before I be taken away from thee. And Elisha said, I pray thee, let a double portion of thy spirit be upon me. And he said, Thou hast asked a hard thing: nevertheless, if thou see me when I am taken from thee, it shall be so unto thee; but if not, it shall not be so. (2 Kgs. 2:9–10)

When the veil parted, there appeared a horse-drawn chariot of such brilliant glory it was called a "chariot of fire." This vehicle swept between Elijah and Elisha, and Elijah "went up by a whirlwind into heaven" (2 Kgs. 2:11).

> And Elisha saw it, and he cried, My father, my father, the chariot of Israel, and the horsemen thereof. And he saw him no more: and he took hold of his own clothes, and rent them in two pieces. He took up also the mantle of Elijah that fell from him, and went back, and stood by the bank of Jordan; And he took the mantle of Elijah that fell from him, and smote the waters, and said, Where is the Lord God of Elijah? and when he also had smitten the waters, they parted hither and thither: and Elisha went over. And when the sons of the prophets which were to view at Jericho saw him, they said, The spirit of Elijah doth rest on Elisha. And they came to meet him, and bowed themselves to the ground before him. (2 Kgs. 2:12–15)

Like the "sons of the prophets," many of the Saints in Nauvoo experienced a witness of the Lord's designation of the next prophet as they met in conference in Nauvoo on August 8, 1844. The mantle experience of 1844 has become a symbol of the transfer of prophetic authority in the Church. After the death of a prophet and the identification of his successor, members of the Church frequently say that "the mantle has fallen once again."[11]

Oral Tradition of Mantle Testimonies

Several years ago, on a warm Sunday morning on a houseboat at Lake Powell, my father, Victor Watkins, gathered his children and grandchildren together to share with them his testimony of the August 8, 1844, miracle.[12] He told them about his own grandfather William Lampard Watkins, who was seventeen at the time of Joseph Smith's martyrdom on June 27, 1844. When William heard the tragic news, he was in Kentucky campaigning for the Prophet, who was running for president of the United States.[13] William hurried back to Nauvoo to join other grieving and confused mourners. At this point in the story, my father pulled a wrinkled paper from his pocket and began to read directly from William's own words:

> A meeting was appointed for August 8th [1844] by which time Brigham Young and most of the other apostles had returned home.

> It was at this meeting Sidney Rigdon made a lengthy and tedious speech presenting his claims, telling the people what wonderful things he had planned for them.
>
> . . . The darkness was soon dispelled, for Brigham Young explained before the people on that day, the order of the Priesthood. He was filled with the power of the Holy Ghost. He stood before the people as the Prophet Joseph Smith often had done and we heard the voice of the true shepherd, for he spoke with the voice of Joseph. His manner and appearance were like unto Joseph's and it was manifested to all those present upon whom the responsibility rested to carry on the work of God and lead the Saints.[14]

Sharing an ancestor's testimony of seeing and/or hearing Brigham's transformation before the multitude of Saints is a tradition for many Latter-day Saint families whose forebears witnessed the event. Juanita Leavitt Brooks recalled that her grandfather Dudley Leavitt loved to retell the story as long as he lived.[15] John and Eliza Billington Welch "were both present at the meeting held August 8, 1844 where the mantle of the Prophet fell on Brigham Young . . . and these facts they related many, many times to their children and grandchildren, greatly strengthening and adding to the testimonies of those who listened."[16] Some descendants of Cynthia Harrington Durphy Bowen have for generations encouraged their children to memorize Cynthia's account of the event.[17] William Ervin Stoker, who was raised from the age of six by his grandfather William Stoker, stated with pride that his grandfather "knew the Prophet Joseph Smith personally and was present when the Mantle of Joseph fell upon Brigham Young, and received a personal testimony." He would add that he owed much to his grandfather for building up his faith by relating this story to him.[18]

While the faith of most Church members certainly is not dependent on testimonies of the mantle experience, clearly some members of the Church were strengthened by their faith in the validity of their own or a loved one's mantle experience. The purpose of this work is to present the written and oral narratives of the people in Nauvoo who firmly believed they had experienced a miracle and who left their testimonies as a witness.

The August 8 Conference

One session of the August 8, 1844, conference was held in the morning and another in the afternoon. Many historians of the transfiguration, including Leonard J. Arrington and Thomas G. Alexander, have concluded that the mantle event took place on the morning of August 8, 1844, after Rigdon's labored discourse offering to lead the Saints.[19] Others, including D. Michael Quinn, are convinced that "the available evidence also allows the setting to have been the afternoon meeting."[20] Often the actual witnesses do not record an exact date or time but merely call it "the meeting." However, a careful review of many of the available witness stories reveals that a series of at least three distinct manifestations actually occurred, in the same way spiritual experiences recur at successive temple dedications or general conference sessions.[21]

Records indicate that Sidney Rigdon addressed the congregation in the morning session.[22] After Rigdon's speech, Brigham Young suddenly stood up to call for an afternoon session and to make a few remarks. Brigham Young spoke again in the afternoon along with Parley P. Pratt, Amasa Lyman, and W. W. Phelps,[23] but apparently Sidney Rigdon did not accept the invitation to respond. The conference was of great interest to the membership of the Church, and estimates of the attendance at the meetings range from hundreds to thousands, including men, women, and children of all ages.[24] Whole families attended, all expecting an answer to the succession dilemma.

In the morning session, Sidney Rigdon outlined his claim to be guardian of the Church. Many accounts describe the mantle phenomenon coming at the end of the morning session after Rigdon completed his remarks. As Brigham rose to call for an afternoon session, the witnesses saw or heard Joseph, and some, startled, rose to their feet.[25] In the afternoon, Brigham Young actively defended the position of the Quorum of the Twelve. This was a more dignified, better organized meeting. Some attenders claim they witnessed the miracle during the second session of the conference, stating that many Saints saw or heard Joseph as Brigham delivered his message.

One of the most precise descriptions of the afternoon event was written by Judge William Hyde. Hyde described the Nauvoo events of 1844 in minute detail, specifically recording that the mantle experience took place in the afternoon. His account conforms closely to the official minute reports of the afternoon as found in *History of the Church* 7:231–43.[26]

Detail of Brigham Young from a steel engraving of the First Presidency and Twelve Apostles published by S. W. Richards and M. Cannon, January 1, 1853. Engraving by Frederick Piercy.

> In the afternoon President Brigham Young came to the stand and addressed the vast multitude of anxious listeners as follows: . . . The Church had had the privilege of coming to Joseph and of receiving, but now he has stepped to the other side of the veil. He loved the Church even unto death, and laid down his life for it. . . .
>
> President Young again arose and spoke concerning the endowments of the Elders. . . . On this day it was plainly manifest that the mantle of Joseph had rested upon President Young. The voice of the same spirit by which he, Joseph, spake was this day sounded in our ears, so much so that I once, unthoughtedly, raised my head to see if it was not actually Joseph addressing the assembly.[27]

In the course of the August 8 conference, a vote was taken, with the majority voting for Brigham Young's position that the Quorum of the Twelve should assume leadership of the Church.

Other Manifestations

The accounts of still others indicate that they witnessed a transformation not on August 8, but rather on a later date.[28] Church historian Leonard J. Arrington verified, "It was not uncommon for people to see Joseph speaking through Brigham many years after 'the mantle had fallen on him.'"[29] An example is the account of the apostle Orson Hyde, who did not arrive in Nauvoo until August 12, 1844. He twice testified publicly to his "mantle" experience, which he shared with his wife, Mary Anne Price Hyde.[30]

A number of witnesses do not specifically mention seeing or hearing a vision but testify in general terms that "the mantle" or "the spirit of Joseph" rested on Brigham;[31] others simply report that Brigham and/or they were touched by the Spirit.[32]

Traits of the Living Joseph

Of the witnesses to the transformation, a few provided specific details about the traits they recognized as Joseph's. Homer Duncan not only commented on the voice of Brigham sounding like that of Joseph's, but also referred to one of Joseph's mannerisms: "The very gestures of his right hand when he was saying anything very positive reminded me of Joseph. My decision was then made as to who should lead the Church of Jesus Christ of Latter Day Saints for surely the mantle of Joseph has fallen upon Brigham."[33] Mosiah Lyman Hancock commented, "I saw in him the look of Joseph, and the voice of Joseph; and it seemed to me that he was as tall as Joseph too."[34] Benjamin F. Johnson also observed Joseph's "tall, straight and portly [robust] form." He then added his famous comments about Joseph's speech and a missing tooth, remarking that he "heard the real and perfect voice of the Prophet, even to the whistle, as in years past caused by the loss of a tooth said to have been broken out by a mob at Hyrum [Ohio]."[35] George Morris also described Joseph's familiar speech patterns, noting:

> In the afternoon Presedent Young arose . . . when I was startled by Earing Josephs Voice—he had a way of Clearing his Throat before he began to speak—by a peculier Effort of His own—like Ah-hem—
>
> I raised my Head sudinly—and the first thing I saw was Joseph—as plain as I ever saw Him in my life. . . . That was Testemony anough to Convince me where the Proper athoraty rested.[36]

Did Brigham himself know that something miraculous had happened? His own account, dated August 8, 1844, simply states:

> I arose and spocke to the people. my hart was swolen with composion toards them and by the power of the Holy Gost even the spirit of the Prophets I was enabled to comfort the harts of the Saints. in the afternoon a corden to my request the people assembld by thousands[.] I lade before them the order of the church and the Power of the Preasthood. after a long and laboras talk of a bout two ours in the open air with the wind blowing, the church was of one hart and one mind[.] they wanted the twelve to lead the church as Br Joseph had dun in his day.[37]

Perhaps Brigham was alluding to the miracle in his reference to "the spirit of the Prophets." However, records do not indicate that he publicly acknowledged the manifestations at the time they occurred. Brigham Young was careful never to claim to take Joseph's place. As early as August 15, 1844, he wrote an epistle to the Saints that stated emphatically, "Let no man presume for a moment that his [Joseph's] place will be filled by another; for, *remember, he stands in his own place* and always will."[38] Later Brigham advised, "The spirit of Joseph which fell upon me is ready to fall upon somebody else when I am removed."[39]

Testimonies of the Mantle Experience of 1844

It is impossible to verify the number of those in attendance at the conference who saw a physical transformation or heard Joseph's voice. Currently known records establish 121 written testimonies of people who say a transformation or other spiritual manifestation occurred.[40] Of these, sixty-eight are firsthand documents: personal journals, personal narratives told to a scribe, or first-person testimonies published in Church magazine articles. Fifty-two are secondhand testimonies: accounts gleaned from biographies written by family members or from historical compilations.

The mantle testimonies come from people who eventually settled all over the Utah Territory—from northern Utah and Idaho to southern Utah and Arizona—and even in Tahiti. There is no pocket location of people who recorded this experience.

At least the earliest writers had no opportunity to read other detailed written accounts of the mantle experience before recording their own. Some testimonies[41] were written at least fifteen to twenty years before the publication of the most comprehensive, Church-sanctioned mantle testimony—George Q. Cannon's 1870 essay in the *Juvenile Instructor*.[42] Prior to the publication of Elder Cannon's essay, printed references to the "mantle of Joseph" falling on Brigham appeared in the *Millennial Star*[43] and in the *Times and Seasons*.[44] These two Church publications do not mention any visions among members of the congregation but simply focus on the point of ecclesiastical interest—that the mantle had fallen on Brigham Young or, more generally, the Twelve.

In an address given on July 19, 1857, Brigham Young referred to Albert Carrington's mantle experience, which occurred two months after the August 8 meeting: "He [Carrington] could not tell me from Joseph Smith, when I was speaking in the stand in Nauvoo during the October Conference of 1844. Somebody came along and passed a finger over his eyes and he could not see any one but Joseph speaking, until I got through addressing the congregation."[45] This talk was printed ten days later in the *Deseret News*[46] and may have inspired some Saints to write down their memories of the events of August 1844.

As stories about the mantle experience began to circulate in the 1850s, some writers may have responded by offering their own personalized or embellished accounts—such is human nature. However, most of the stories recorded after this point were not identical. It does not seem that the writers were relying on the same source for their versions of the event. In fact, the accounts contradict each other to some extent in their descriptions of the events of the day, suggesting that each person wrote his or her account as remembered, not as described by Church leaders years later.

George Romney vigorously defended the veracity of the mantle stories:

> I testify to you in all fervor, before God, that the mantle of Joseph Smith fell upon Brigham Young. It was Joseph's voice; absolutely Joseph's voice and manner, as Brigham Young addressed the people and told them who should be their leader. Now this is no fiction;

this is true as I stand here after so many years, passing from the year 1844 up to the present time.[47]

Testimony of the Succession of the Twelve

In 1844 the Twelve were beginning to understand their role in the Church. Joseph had carefully instructed them as to their responsibilities and had given them all the keys they would need to continue with the Lord's work,[48] but they did not always understand the significance of what they were taught. Brigham himself suggested that when he heard of Joseph's death he was at first overcome, fearing the keys of the priesthood were gone. Then, he said, "I felt it come like a flash of lightening to my mind, and I said 'the keys of the kingdom are here.'"[49] When he "came to Nauvoo," he knew "by visions of the Spirit" that from the Twelve would come a new First Presidency.[50] Several years passed, however, before all the Twelve agreed. Meanwhile, the support engendered by the events of the August 1844 conference gave him, as President of the Quorum of the Twelve, the authority he needed to guide the Church in the ensuing transitional period.

During the weeks following Joseph's death, the Saints had been obviously concerned about the succession of leadership. For the many who already believed that the Twelve held the keys and the authority to the leadership of the Church, the mantle experience was an additional testimony of the rightful succession of the Twelve; for others it might have been an answer to prayer. The powerful events of August 1844 finalized loyalties for many Nauvoo Saints and resolved the direction of their religious commitment. As Wilford Woodruff recalled, the mantle manifestation was the turning point. In 1872 he reminded Church members, "There was a reason for this [the mantle experience] in the mind of God: it convinced the people."[51] By 1846 most of the Saints who attended the meeting were ready to leave Nauvoo and follow Brigham Young and the Twelve west.

Edward Hunter and Talitha Cheney affirmed in their mantle testimonies that they had no doubt that Brigham Young should lead the Church.[52] Anson Call and William Allred concluded that they were "perfectly satisfied."[53] Homer Duncan pledged, "My decision was then made."[54] Mary Dunn, an eleven-year-old, soberly recalled her father's remarks as the family was returning home from the meeting: "They need not hunt any farther. Brigham Young is the man to lead us."[55]

For others, however, the way was not so clear. A few families were split in their loyalties. In the case of Albert and Ada Winchell Clements, the mantle episode led to a divorce. Albert was a missionary called to serve shortly before Joseph's death. On learning of the martyrdom, he started his journey back to Nauvoo. As he traveled home, he encountered his friend Sidney Rigdon. Sidney told him he was hurrying back to Nauvoo to take his place as guardian of the Church. Albert was satisfied with Rigdon's position.

Albert did not arrive home until August 15, 1844, when he learned of the August 8 meeting, which his wife, Ada, had attended. She happily described the mantle event, testifying that Brigham Young had actually looked and sounded like Joseph Smith. Albert inquired about Rigdon. Ada answered that he had spoken, but the Spirit was not with him. Albert still took the side of his friend Sidney Rigdon. Ada vowed she would continue with The Church of Jesus Christ of Latter-day Saints. She and the children left in the exodus to the Rocky Mountains; Albert stayed behind.[56]

Though Albert refused to accept Ada's testimony, other individuals bolstered their commitment to the Twelve through the witness of a close family member who had attended the August 1844 meeting. Sarah Studevant Leavitt accepted her husband's testimony without question:

> My husband, Jeremiah, was attending a meeting where this question was being discussed. Brigham Young was speaking when suddenly he seemed to be clothed with all the authority of Joseph Smith. Jeremiah said that he had the same appearance, the same voice, as the Prophet. If he had not known that Joseph Smith was dead, he would have thought that Brigham Young was Joseph Smith. Tears dampened many cheeks. Joy and gladness filled many hearts. The Lord had not forgotten his people. . . . After that there was no one to doubt that Brigham Young was to be our new leader and Prophet. If Brigham had any doubts, my husband Jeremiah did not.[57]

Aurelia Spencer Rogers acknowledged that the testimony of her sister Ellen Spencer Clawson was what "strengthened my faith in the truth of Mormonism." Aurelia wrote:

> [Ellen] was at a meeting of the Saints. . . . At this meeting, Brigham Young, who was President of the Quorum of Apostles, arose to speak, when "The Mantle of Joseph" fell upon him, and he was like one transformed; his countenance, voice and form were like those of the late Prophet. Many in the congregation, even children saw this miracle; it satisfied the people and decided the question who was to be the leader.[58]

George Armstrong Hicks struggled throughout his life with his own testimony, but he was adamant concerning the reality of his father's testimony concerning the mantle experience. He wrote in his journal:

> I have heard my father [George Barton Hicks] say that he was present at the time when it is said that the mantle of Joseph fell upon Brigham Young. I believe [his testimony], I believe the spirit of Joseph took possession of the body of Brigham and spoke to the people through him. Brigham was the man to take the lead.[59]

Even a twentieth-century prophet of The Church of Jesus Christ of Latter-day Saints responded with gratitude for the mantle testimony of his mother, Rachel Ridgeway Ivins Grant. In a letter to a friend he acknowledged, "I am grateful that my mother was present and had the same testimony which she often gave in public. . . . Sincerely your friend and brother, Heber J. Grant."[60]

Evidence of Contemporaneous Discussion of the Experience

In Nauvoo throughout the temple building period, people seem to have talked and written about the mantle experience and about Brigham Young's resemblance to Joseph Smith.[61] These very tentative discussions are a testimony for many scholars that the mantle experience was not orchestrated either as a public relations ploy or as a psychological phenomenon. The mantle references came forth slowly, almost reluctantly, as many participants were unwilling to publicly discuss spiritual events. Historian D. Michael Quinn writes this about the immediate response:

> There *were* contemporary references to Young's "transfiguration." The *Times and Seasons* reported that just before the sustaining vote at the afternoon session of the August meeting, "every Saint could see that Elijah's mantle had truly fallen upon the 'Twelve.'" Although the church newspaper did not refer to Young specifically for this "mantle" experience, on 15 November 1844 Henry and Catharine Brooke wrote from Nauvoo that Young "favours Br Joseph, both in person, manner of speaking more than any person ever you saw, looks like another." Five days later Arza Hinckley referred to "Brigham Young on [w]hom the mantle of the prophet Joseph has fallen."[62]

Some time after the August 8, 1844, meeting, Howard Egan wrote a letter to Jesse C. Little in the East that also attested to a transfiguration. On December 8, 1844, Brother Little quoted Egan's words in a letter to Brigham Young stating, "I recd a Letter from Bro Egan at the time of the Conference he said 'if a man had been blinded he would hardly have known if it were not Joseph.'" This account is one of the earliest acknowledgments of a transfiguration.[63]

Ezra T. Benson, who was present at the August 8 meeting, later recorded in his autobiography that "many said, when they heard Brigham talk, that it was not Brigham's voice, but the voice of Joseph." Benson made no claim to having seen the transfiguration himself but evidently heard others discussing their experience, which he seems to have accepted without question.[64]

The diary of William Burton, a missionary who returned to Nauvoo in spring 1845, may refer to residents talking about the mantle experience. In May 1845, he recorded events in his diary that had occurred during his absence from Nauvoo:

> [That which] had taken place during the time that I was out on my mission;-that grevious and hard to be borne. This was the Martyrdom of the Prophet and Seer, and Patriarch, whose voices I could not hear, declaring the truths of Heaven. But their [Joseph's and Hyrum's] places were filled by others much better than I once was supposed they could have been. The spirit of Joseph appeared to rest upon Brigham.[65]

Burton's use of the past tense—"the spirit of Joseph appeared to rest upon Brigham"—in the context of his discussion of events that had transpired in his absence is significant. If Burton was referring by these words to the mantle experience, he must have heard of the event from others who had been at the meetings. If this was the case, at that early date at least some Nauvoo residents were discussing the incident.

In a February 1845 letter, Wilford Woodruff shared the mantle news with fellow Saints in the British Isles by assuring them that

> on the second day after our arrival August 8th, 1844, we met in a special conference, all the quorums, authorities, and members of the Church that could assemble in Nauvoo. [We] were addressed by elder Brigham Young, the president of the quorum of the twelve. It was evident to the Saints that the mantle of Joseph had fallen upon him, the road that he pointed out could be seen so plainly.[66]

Recording the Experience

The spiritual witness received at the August conference was of such magnitude that believers were willing—even eager—to follow Brigham Young and the Twelve.[67] However, scholars continue to search for a witness account written on the same day as the mantle experience.[68] If the experience was so "intense and life-changing"[69] for followers of the Prophet Joseph, why were none of the accounts that record the miracle written on the day of the manifestation or shortly thereafter? It is a question that unfortunately cannot be answered definitively.

A partial explanation may be that life was chaotic and dangerous for Nauvoo citizens in 1844 and 1845. The citizens were stunned by events, and some did not have the luxury of good health, time, money, or even access to writing materials.[70] After the death of Joseph and the acceptance of the leadership of Brigham and the Twelve, the Saints' primary goals were to feed their families and to finish the Nauvoo Temple as quickly as possible[71]—a charge repeatedly given by Joseph Smith and then amplified by Brigham Young.[72] In fact, Judge William Hyde recorded that Brigham Young spoke in the afternoon session of the August 8 meeting concerning the need to finish the Nauvoo Temple.[73]

The urgency expressed by Young motivated the Nauvoo Saints to complete as much of the temple in the next eighteen months "as had been accomplished in the previous three years."[74] He organized the brethren into work crews and continued to commit the sisters to contribute a penny a week for glass and nails. Furthermore, Brigham "put the missionary work in order, studied Joseph Smith's plan for an expansion of gathering places, and vigorously pushed industrial development and construction." Numerous new frame and brick homes as well as the Seventies Hall were erected in the next year.[75]

Additionally, the Nauvoo Saints were threatened by mobs and other lawless citizens, and the stresses that led to the murders of Joseph and Hyrum immediately reappeared, leading to the abandonment of Nauvoo in 1846. Grief and depression followed the martyrdom, and recurring diseases such as malaria and cholera were both endemic and virulent in this river town even during the best of times, which deterred record keeping.

Some diarists who had been keeping fairly regular diaries stopped writing around the time of the martyrdom and did not resume until later. For example, Thomas Bullock's personal journal shows a gap from June 15 until October 8, 1844; Charles Coulson Rich made no entries from June 28, 1844, to January 1, 1845; and Eliza Roxcy Snow ceased writing in April 1844 and did not resume until February 1846.[76] Abraham O. Smoot stopped writing in his journal about the time he returned to Nauvoo (July 28, 1844) and picked up his narrative again on November 3, 1844.[77] Emmeline B. Wells, an important diarist of the Nauvoo period, did not begin her "Nauvoo Diary" until 1845.[78]

Bloody flux, summer sickness, typhoid, and tuberculosis are all named in the records of the city after Joseph's death, in addition to the normal childhood diseases of the nineteenth century that were often fatal.[79] Thirteen-year-old George Washington Bean summed up the years following the Prophet's death as being filled with hardships such as "scurvy and blackleg." He was forced to grow up fast: "During this season I managed most of the family business as most of my folks were ill."[80] Caroline Barnes Crosby verified that "persecution continued all around us. The brethren were obliged to be on guard all the time. The sickly season soon commenced. I was sick several weeks."[81] One of the brethren on guard was Appleton Milo Harmon, who wrote:

> They arose in mob and broke open the jail and killed Joseph and Hyrum and severely wounded Elder John Taylor, on the 27th day of June, 1844. During this time I was serving as policeman on almost constant duty night and day and in so doing exposed myself to wet and cold and soon after was taken sick with chills and fever and for three months was very sick, in fact the sickest I ever was in my life. My recovery was but slowly.[82]

Emily Smith Hoyt explained that she was often sick two or three months at a time and that her life was despaired of by her friends. Her husband was in even worse health.[83] In such an atmosphere, journal keeping was simply not a priority for people who were trying to survive and still accomplish the Lord's work. In his journal, Joseph Grafton Hovey recorded:

> The people said let the Lord God of Israel choose. Then the Twelve did explain the subject and made it as clear as the noon day sun of their power and authority given them by Joseph, have not time and space to write all the particulars. For I do work hard on the Temple of the Lord cutting and sawing stone and I do get so fatigued when I leave my labors that I have not much courage to write my life.[84]

Additionally, most of the ordinary folk did not keep records. Diary entries, if kept at all, were generally logs or daybooks. Most members, even those few who kept journals, were very circumspect and may have been uncomfortable with writing about sacred spiritual and emotional events, as many are today.[85] One early Saint recorded her feelings about a vision she had experienced years before:

> When a true spirit makes known anything to you, in the daytime, we call it a vision. If it is a true spirit it will never leave you, every particular will be as plain fifty years hence as now. I said to myself then, my [vision] I saw in Kentucky, when I thought I could almost see Zion, was a true vision, though I did not know what to call it and seldom ever spoke of it, for I thought it was given to me for my own benefit.[86]

Others may have not fully appreciated the pivotal importance of the meetings of that day and of the mantle experience until later in their lives. Because of the very personal nature of a spiritual experience, some Saints may have been reluctant to record their impressions. In a letter to Elder George S. Gibbs, Benjamin F. Johnson explains:

> So deeply was I impressed with what I saw and heard in the transfiguration, that for years I dared not tell what was given me of the Lord to see. But when in later years I did publicly bear this testimony, I found that others had testified to having seen and heard the same. But to what proportion of the congregation that were present, I could never know. But I do know that this, my testimony is true.[87]

By the time they recorded their experiences, the Church's progression under President Young's leadership and the accounts of others who had attended the meeting had helped to validate their experience and testifying to its reality had become an honorable activity.

Early Written Accounts—Two Women's Testimonies

It is not always possible to determine when each account was first recited or written. Two of the earliest known accounts of the mantle experience were recorded by Caroline Barnes Crosby and Emily Smith Hoyt, two formidable pioneer women who zealously recognized their mantle experience as an opportunity for them to place on record one of the few episodes where they were an equal witness to a miraculous vision. Crosby and Hoyt recorded their mantle testimonies when they finally found the essential element they needed—a solid block of time. At the end of 1850, after six hectic and life-threatening years, Caroline and Emily both found the time and solitude to begin journals of their experiences. Each woman felt that the mantle story was important enough to include at the beginning of her history.

Caroline Barnes Crosby was one of the first women to be called as a missionary for the Church, assigned to serve with her husband, Jonathan Crosby.[88] In 1846 the indefatigable Caroline left Nauvoo. In 1848 she helped lead her family from Council Bluffs, Iowa, to the Salt

Lake Valley.[89] Then in spring 1850, Jonathan and Caroline, along with Addison Pratt and Louisa Barnes Pratt (Caroline's sister), accepted a mission assignment to the Society Islands, a group of islands in the west part of French Polynesia. During fall 1850, Jonathan and Addison conducted business elsewhere, leaving Caroline and Louisa alone on the island of Tubuai Manu.[90] There, Caroline could finally settle down long enough to write her memoirs, including her account of the mantle experience. An educated witness, Caroline wrote:

> Sidney Rigdon came to the stand and tried to show to the people that he was the rightful successor of Joseph. And his arguments were so powerful that many were almost pursuaded to believe him such. But as soon as the twelve apostles with bro Brigham Young at their head took the stand it was shown conclusively where the power rested. It was the first time that I ever thought he [Brigham] resembled bro Joseph. But almost every one exclaimed that the mantle of Joseph had fallen on Brigham. For one I never had any doubts afterwards.[91]

Like Caroline, Emily Smith Hoyt, who arrived in the Utah Territory on October 30, 1851, wrote of her experience.[92] Emily was the Prophet's first cousin, the daughter of Joseph Smith's Uncle Asael, who had served briefly as Patriarch to the Church.[93] She found time to write her memoirs just before she left her home in Iowa to travel to the Utah Territory.[94]

In 1840, Emily and her husband, Samuel Pierce Hoyt, had purchased property just over the river from Nauvoo in Nashville (now Galland, Lee County, Iowa); erected a cabin; and then built a very substantial home with ten bedrooms and five fireplaces. Emily described her home as being just "four miles from a certain point in Nauvoo. . . . Eventually we could see the [Nauvoo] temple by standing in my front door."[95]

She and her family had supported Joseph Smith from the first moment they read the Book of Mormon in 1834. After learning of the murders of Emily's two cousins, the Hoyts traveled across the river to Nauvoo. Emily recalled, "We returned from that melancholy scene heart sick and sorrowful cast down but not in despair."[96] She continued, "We were summoned over the river again and went to hear what

21

The last one arose. It was the then, President of the twelve Brigham Young. He spoke to the people altogether in a different style from any of those who had preceded him. A cloud of witnesses arose after B. Y. had sat down and testified to the truth of what he had said. President B. Y. arose from his seat the second time and addressed the audience. I had been well acquainted with Joseph the latter part of his life. We had been at his home many times and Joseph Hiram and families felt at home with us. From a place of retreat before the Ill, mob Joseph sent to S. P. for money to aid him in escaping for a time from the grasp of his ungodly pursuers S. P. sent the money and they had the power in their own hands to go any place they might choose. They consulted and deliberated. Emma Joseph's wife wanted her husband and his brother Hiram to give themselves up, called them cowards etc. Joseph said if it would save the people he was willing to be sacrificed. After every thing was ready for them to get away. Joseph said he would go and give himself up to the State authorities. The Governor was pledged to protect them. Joseph said he felt that it might be, like a lamb going to the slaughter The result of his counsel is well known. They returned and were murdered. And the Latter day Saints apparently left without a leader. But the God of Heaven who had said it was his business to provide for his saints, sent President B. Young home just in time, and clothed him not with "the mantle of Elijah," but the spirit and power which had rested on Joseph I was an eye, and ear, witness. The manner of reasoning, the expression of the countenance, the sound of the voice thrilled my whole soul. My own eyes had beheld Joseph's murdered body. My own hands, had felt death's icy coldness, on his once noble forehead. I knew that Joseph was dead. And yet I often startled and involuntarily looked at the stand to see if it was not Joseph It was not, it was Brigham Young and if any one doubts the right of Brigham to manage affairs for the saints, all I have to say to them is this. Get the spirit of God and know for yourselves. The Lord will provide for his own. Has the word of the Lord ever failed. Br Young will not live forever clothed with mortality. But He who rules in heaven and on earth will control all things by the counsel of his own will. Saints will live

Courtesy Johnathan A. Dibble

Page from the Emily Smith Hoyt journal. In 1851, Emily recorded her experience at the August 8, 1844, meeting. "S. P." refers to her husband.

was wanted."[97] Thus Samuel and Emily were in Nauvoo for the meeting in the bowery on August 8, 1844, where they witnessed Brigham's transformation. For five long years, starting in 1846, Emily's home served as a way station for LDS refugees, a place where Saints could receive aid and nursing care before they followed the Twelve west.[98]

By 1851, Emily was determined to let the whole world know of her unflagging testimony concerning her cousin. Knowing that the Smith family was split in their loyalties to Brigham Young, Emily began her record with her mantle testimony and justified her choices in following the Saints west. Emphasizing that she and Joseph were about the same age and that Joseph had spent much time in her home, she explained that on August 8, 1844,

> President B. Y. [Brigham Young] arose from his seat . . . and addressed the audience. I had been well acquainted with Joseph the latter part of his life. We had been at his home many times and Joseph, Hiram and families felt at home with us. . . . But the God of Heaven who had said it was his business to provide for his saints, sent President B. Young home just in time, and clothed him not with "the mantle of Elijah," but the spirit and power which had rested on Joseph. I was an eye, and ear, witness. The manner of reasoning, the expression of the countenance, the sound of the voice thrilled my whole soul. . . . I knew that Joseph was dead. And yet I often startled and involuntarily looked at the stand to see if it was not Joseph. It was not, it was Brigham Young and if any one doubts the right of Brigham to manage affairs for the Saints, all I have to say to them is this. Get the spirit of God and know for yourselves. The Lord will provide for his own.[99]

Emily Smith Hoyt was an educated woman, a graduate of a teachers' academy. She had family ties to Joseph Smith and knew him well. She was certainly also acquainted with Brigham Young. It seems hard to imagine that she could have been duped by a "bit of theatrical mimicry."

"The Prophet Is Not Dead!"—Children's Testimonies

Adults were not the only witnesses of the mantle event. A number of those present at the meeting were children. William Van Orden

Carbine was only nine years old in 1844, but he was well acquainted with the Prophet Joseph. He remembered sitting in the meeting with his mother, Adelia Rider Carbine, and saying, "The Prophet [is] not dead, for I [see] him on the stand." William's experience became a favorite story of his mother, who retold it many times.[100]

James Madison Fisher, an eleven-year-old who had often played ball with the Prophet Joseph, also remembered the unexpected vision of his friend, "Rigdon spoke first it did not have the wright ring to it when he sat down brother Brigham got up, the mantle of Joseph fell upon him, he was the picture of the Prophet [Joseph] and he had the Prophet's voice it was a great surprise for the people, the saints was shown who was to be their leader."[101]

One of the children, eight-year-old Mary Field, specifically identified what she was doing at the time of the event. She recalled:

> Mother [Mary Harding Field] had the baby on her knee, who was playing with a tin cup. He dropped it, attracting our attention to the floor. Mother stooped over to pick it up, when we were startled by hearing the voice of Joseph. Looking up quickly we saw the form of the Prophet Joseph standing before us. Brother Brigham looked and talked so much like Joseph that for a minute we thought it was Joseph.[102]

The Mantle Testimonies Are Finally Published

Emily Smith Hoyt and Caroline Barnes Crosby wrote their memoirs a few years after the event, long before the first detailed accounts of the mantle experience were published. It was not until the 1870s that a mantle account relating in detail the miraculous vision of Joseph was finally published and made generally accessible to the members of the Church.[103]

Orson Hyde's remembrance of his mantle experience was delivered publicly in Salt Lake City on October 6, 1869, and published in the *Deseret News Semi-weekly* on November 16, 1869.[104] But it was George Q. Cannon's testimony that the congregation "both saw and heard [Joseph] with their natural eyes and ears," published in the *Juvenile Instructor* in 1870, that became the major source for "transfiguration" accounts by Mormon historians such as B. H. Roberts in *A Comprehensive History of The Church of Jesus Christ of Latter-day Saints.*[105] On April 8, 1872, Wilford Woodruff publicly bore his testimony concerning the mantle experience. This testimony was published in the *Deseret News Weekly* on May 22, 1872.[106] Cannon's and Woodruff's published testimonies were followed by other testimonies that were recorded in histories written by Edward W. Tullidge and Orson F. Whitney.[107] A mantle statement from William C. Staines was published in the *Contributor* in June 1891, ten years after his death.[108]

In 1905, the young women of the Church were also presented with the deeply personal testimonies of three redoubtable Mormon women who remembered August 8, 1844, as a day that changed their lives. Maria Wealthy Wilcox, Jane Snyder Richards, and Rachel Ridgeway Grant each wrote about their memories of Joseph the Prophet for the *Young Woman's Journal.*[109]

Like Wilcox, Richards, and Grant, many witnesses did not write about their experience until late in their lives. Perhaps the published accounts validated their own experience; perhaps they were pressured by their children to write the story they had told over the years. As death approached, they may have felt the need to leave their written testimonies for posterity, or they may have wanted to leave a document that would silence any doubters. Several of the accounts became grand, almost poetic proclamations of belief, as though the writers felt that the formal rhetoric would lend weight to their testimonies.

Mantle Testimonies into the Twentieth Century

Mantle testimonies recorded after 1900 begin to read very much alike, probably because the participants had read the published accounts. However, significant and unique renderings were still to come. On July 2, 1902, the first known legal document concerning the mantle event made its appearance in a statement that John Welch swore before the county clerk in Logan, Cache County, Utah.[110] Less than a year later, Robert Crookston wrote an affidavit affirming his witness of the mantle event.[111] In 1916, Eliza Ann Haven Westover recorded her testimony in a letter to her son.[112] The last documented and formally witnessed testimony of the mantle experience by a living participant appeared in 1925 by Jacob Jones.[113]

Bishop George Romney twice testified publicly seventy-five years after Joseph's death. Romney was only thirteen when he witnessed the mantle event. At age eighty-eight, he delivered his testimony in the Ensign Ward in Salt Lake City on June 22, 1919. The message was so powerful that a listener immediately recorded his words for posterity:

> I shall never forget in this world or in the world to come the scene as Brigham Young arose. . . . When Brigham got up the mantle of Joseph Smith fell upon him. It was Joseph's voice; it was Joseph's appearance, and I testify to you, if I never again do so on this earth, in the presence of God and angels, that this is verily the truth. This is true—that the mantle of Joseph did fall upon Brigham Young and the people knew it.[114]

With equal power, Bishop Romney also bore his testimony before the Swedish Saints in Salt Lake City on December 17, 1919. It was published for the missionaries of the Church in the *Liahona, the Elders' Journal* on April 13, 1920.[115]

Conclusion

At least ninety-five people have declared, through their own or others' records, that Brigham Young took on the appearance, voice, and/or mannerisms of the Prophet Joseph Smith. When we include the records that state without further explanation that "the mantle fell on Brigham," we can increase the number of these testimonies. These records are impressive evidence that must be weighed carefully. The introduction to the legal text *Eyewitness Testimony: Civil and Criminal* explains the value of eyewitness testimony: "Lawyers can neither afford to exclude eyewitness testimony legally nor ignore it. Sometimes it is the only evidence available, and *it is often correct*."[116]

In his book *In Search of Stones*, psychiatrist M. Scott Peck, states, "One of the tests of proof, of reality, is termed 'consensual validation,' . . . [that is,] whenever two or more very different people make exactly the same extraordinary assessment of a phenomenon, then . . . it needs to be taken seriously."[117]

To those who accept with little question the visions and spiritual experiences of the Prophet Joseph Smith and his associates, it is also plausible that a large body of Saints could witness a miraculous manifestation. At meetings of the School of the Prophets and gatherings at the time of the Kirtland Temple dedication, numbers of Saints experienced group manifestations.[118] Nancy Alexander Tracy reported that during the dedication of the Kirtland Temple in 1836, many witnessed the appearance of heavenly beings.[119] As with the mantle experience, not all the Saints present reported having seen these visions,[120] nor did everyone who was reported by others to have seen a vision actually record the experience themselves. Those to whom visions have been opened may well report seeing different things, as was the case with the personal descriptions of a manifestation shared in Hawaii by a group of Saints that included David O. McKay.[121]

In spite of the silence of some in regard to the events of August 8, the time lapse between the event and the written expression of others, and differences in detail or similarities in wording of the written accounts, the simple fact remains that many Saints who attended that conference in the grove behind the Nauvoo Temple, testified that they saw, heard, and/or felt a manifestation that helped determine or confirm the direction for the rest of their lives, and sustain a willingness to sacrifice everything.

In the afternoon session of the August 8 conference, Sidney Rigdon chose W. W. Phelps to speak for him. Phelps was an inadvisable choice, because he spoke supporting Brigham Young.[122] Phelps was obviously affected by the spirit of that session. Long before he died in 1878, Phelps penned in verse and music his witness of the mantle experience:

> Up, up! ye royal priesthood holders,
> Joseph's robe's on Brigham's shoulders,
> Clear the way; clear the way; clear the way,
> Israel reigns.[123]

Lynne Watkins Jorgensen is an Accredited Genealogist and has an M.A. in family and community history from BYU. She recently retired as a Consultant in the U.S./Canada Reference Department of the Family History Library of The Church of Jesus Christ of Latter-day Saints. She concurrently taught family history and genealogy classes for Brigham Young University.

I, the author, acknowledge the assistance of the BYU Studies *staff, who double-checked all sources. I would like to thank Barbara Bennett Roach, whose husband and father both served as directors of the Family History Library. Her father, Archibald Bennett, collected family names of ancestors who were at the mantle meeting, and she forwarded several additional names to me that I had not found. Thanks also to Myrtle Stevens Hyde who forwarded a detailed timeline and information concerning Mary Anne and Orson Hyde. Thanks also to my husband, Dr. Leland H. Jorgensen, for his wise counsel and encouragement. I would also like to acknowledge the help of others who, when learning of this research project, informed me about mantle accounts in their family records. Without such help I might not have located all those accounts. Testimonies appearing in this project were those I was able to document. Many descendants suggested ancestor names for this project, but my research discovered their testimonies were part of an oral family tradition and not formally recorded. I am grateful for all suggestions. Any readers aware of documented testimonies of the mantle experience that are not included in this collection are invited to contact BYU Studies by email at byu_studies@byu.edu.*

An earlier version of this article appeared in BYU Studies *36, no. 4 (1996–97): 125–204.*

Notes

1. The most complete text of the minutes of August 8, 1844, as gathered by early Church historians is found in Joseph Smith Jr., *History of The Church of Jesus Christ of Latter-day Saints*, ed. B. H. Roberts, 2d ed., rev., 7 vols. (Salt Lake City: Deseret Book, 1971), 7:231–43 (hereafter cited as *History of the Church*) For more on these events, see Ronald K. Esplin, "Joseph, Brigham and the Twelve:

A Succession of Continuity," *BYU Studies* 21, no. 3 (1981): 301–41; and Martin B. Hickman, "Succession in the Presidency," in *Encyclopedia of Mormonism*, ed. Daniel H. Ludlow, 4 vols. (New York: Macmillan, 1992), 3:1420–21.

2. *History of the Church*, 7:233.

3. Esplin, "Joseph, Brigham and the Twelve," 325n84.

4. Leonard J. Arrington and Davis Bitton, *The Mormon Experience: A History of the Latter-day Saints* (New York: Alfred A. Knopf, 1979), 84–85.

5. The term "transfiguration" was used by early LDS writers in reference to the specific meeting of August 8, 1844, when the mantle of the Prophet Joseph descended upon Brigham Young. Although not everyone witnessed a change in the voice and form of Brigham Young, many reported that they did; hence the use of the term. One meaning of transfiguration is "an act, process, or instance of changing or being changed in form or appearance." *Webster's New International Dictionary*, 3d ed., s.v. *transfiguration*. Compare Matthew 17:1–2.

6. Leonard J. Arrington, *Brigham Young: American Moses* (New York: Alfred A. Knopf, 1985), 114–15. Arrington acknowledges that it is possible to attribute the mantle experience to "the downcast spirits of the Saints, who had mourned Joseph's passing for forty days; their yearning to be comforted by their lost leader; their disappointment with Rigdon, whose ambition had diluted his sincerity; their surprise at the presence of 'Brother Brigham,' who was thought by many to be still on his way back from Boston, and Brigham's talent for mimicry." Most Mormon historians who have written about the mantle phenomenon matter-of-factly report that many Saints later testified that they had witnessed a miraculous transfiguration of Brigham Young. See Thomas G. Alexander, *Things of Heaven and Earth: The Life and Times of Wilford Woodruff, a Mormon Prophet* (Salt Lake City: Signature Books, 1991), 114; James B. Allen and Glen M. Leonard, *The Story of the Latter-day Saints*, 2d ed. (Salt Lake City: Deseret Book, 1992), 216; and D. Michael Quinn, *The Mormon Hierarchy: Origins of Power* (Salt Lake City: Signature Books, 1994), 166–67.

7. Richard S. Van Wagoner, "The Making of a Mormon Myth: The 1844 Transfiguration of Brigham Young," *Dialogue: A Journal of Mormon Thought* 28 (Winter 1995): 21.

8. Van Wagoner, "Making of a Mormon Myth," 22–23; see also Reid L. Harper, "The Mantle of Joseph: Creation of a Mormon Miracle," *Journal of Mormon History* 22 (Fall 1996): 35–71.

9. Van Wagoner, "The Making of a Mormon Myth," 11. See also Richard S. Van Wagoner, *Sidney Rigdon: A Portrait of Religious Excess* (Salt Lake City: Signature Books, 1994), 341.

10. Most converts learned to read from the Bible and were familiar with the term *mantle*. For more information on Elijah, Elisha, and prophetic succession, see Fred E. Woods, "Elisha and the Children: The Question of Accepting Prophetic Succession," *BYU Studies* 32, no. 3 (1992): 47–58.

11. It is important to understand the part that the vote of this conference played in establishing the succession of authority in The Church of Jesus Christ of Latter-day Saints. The authority of the Twelve as the governing body of the Church upon the death of a President was confirmed as the congregation chose to support Brigham Young in his calling as President of the Quorum of the Twelve. Each time a new President of the Church is sustained, this plan of priesthood leadership is followed. See Esplin, "Joseph, Brigham, and the Twelve," 301–40. See also Hickman, "Succession," and Ronald W. Walker, "Grant's Watershed: Succession in The Presidency, 1887–89," in *Qualities That Count: Heber J. Grant as Businessman, Missionary, and Apostle* (Provo, Utah: Brigham Young University Press, 2004), 195–229.

12. The story of the Lake Powell family reunion is found in Victor Watkins, Diary, June 19, 1977, in possession of the author.

13. *History of the Church*, 6:338.

14. See document/testimony 64. This narrative of the mantle experience is one of the more well-written accounts. Though a member of a working-class London family, William was one of six scholarship boys at Brewers School and received a classical education. Watkins became the executive secretary of the highly successful Brigham City Cooperative. Lynne Watkins Jorgensen, "The First London Mormons, 1840–45: 'What Am I and My Brethren Here For?'" (master's thesis, Brigham Young University, 1988), 69, 100.

15. See document 100.

16. See document 75; see also document 65. Eliza Billington and John Welch were married in Nauvoo on May 18, 1845.

17. While I was researching this paper, Katherine Adams Peterson, a Cynthia Bowen descendant, learned of my project. She immediately took a table napkin and on it wrote from memory Cynthia's account. See document 6.

18. See document 114.

19. Arrington, *Brigham Young*, 455n7, says, "There is some confusion in Latter-day Saint literature about the timing of the 'mantle of the Prophet' episode. Most published accounts have it occurring during the afternoon meeting, but my reading of Brigham Young's own diary, entry made on August 8, and the recollections of others who were there have persuaded me that it must have occurred when Brigham made his brief talk after Rigdon's speech in the morning"; Alexander, *Things in Heaven and Earth*, 371n106.

20. Quinn, *Mormon Hierarchy*, 393n111.

21. At the June 14, 1993, Mormon History Association conference, Ronald Esplin noted that he initially decided that the suggestion of three primary mantle events was almost too convenient as the answer to the various mantle discrepancies. Then the idea that it might have occurred that way seemed to fall into place based on careful research in pioneer diaries.

22. "Nauvoo, Hancock Co., Illinois," Andrew Jenson, ed., *Historical Record* 8, nos. 2 & 3 (March 1889): 789.

23. William Hyde, "The Private Journal of William Hyde, 1868," holograph, 64–67, Church Archives, The Church of Jesus Christ of Latter-day Saints, Salt Lake City (document 36).

24. For attendance estimates, see documents 68B, 104, 105. Brigham Young wrote, "The people assembled by thousands." Brigham Young, "Diary, 27 July 1837–1 April 1845," August 8, 1844, holograph, Brigham Young Collection, Church Archives. For testimonies that mention very young children, see documents 21, 111.

25. See documents 10, 26B, 29, 30, 38A, 38B, 48, 91A, 98, 111, 115.

26. See document 36 for a detailed account of the afternoon session.

27. Hyde, "Private Journal," 64–67.

28. See documents 12, 41, 79. Charles Wesley Hubbard's account (document 93) mentions a date of August 4, 1844, and then goes on to describe the meeting of August 8. This August 4 date is probably an error in memory or in transcription.

29. Arrington, *Brigham Young*, 115. For instance, John D. Lee who penned a powerful testimony concerning the mantle experience actually did not arrive in Nauvoo until August 20, 1844, according to his diary. He obviously had his mantle experience "after the fact," as did Orson Hyde, Mary Anne Price Hyde, Anson Call, Jacob Hamlin, Albert Carrington, and others. See also note 21 for Ronald Esplin's comment concerning multiple manifestations.

30. Orson Hyde, in *Journal of Discourses*, 26 vols. (Liverpool: F. D. Richards, 1855–86), 13:178–83, October 6, 1869. See also Orson Hyde, in *Journal of Discourses*, 19:58, April 5, 1877. Information and time line concerning Orson Hyde and Mary Anne Price Hyde sent to me by his biographer Myrtle Stevens Hyde. See also Myrtle Stevens Hyde, *Orson Hyde: The Olive Branch of Israel* (Salt Lake City: Agreka Books, 2000), 181–82.

31. See documents 2, 9, 11, 20, 24, 31, 49, 68A, 68B, 71, 75, 77, 110, 112, 113A, 113B, 114.

32. See documents 23, 44, 58. Joseph Fielding's journal entry regarding the conference does not mention a transfiguration but states simply that "I felt doubtful about it [Rigdon's authority] . . . partly because the Spirit did not bear witness to it." Fielding continues:

> A Meeting was called and Rigdon again addressed us but seemed to have no Liberty or Power after which Elder Brigham Young spoke to [the] People . . . he had much Liberty and the Power of the Spirit in speaking . . . and the Saints soon began to see how things were and that the 12 must now hold the Keys of Power and Authority according to the Revelation which says the 12 are equal with the first Presidency.

(Joseph Fielding, "'They Might Have Known That He Was Not a Fallen Prophet'—The Nauvoo Journal of Joseph Fielding," Andrew F. Ehat, ed., *BYU Studies* 19, no. 2 [1979]: 155, original in Church Archives; typescript in L. Tom Perry Special Collections, Harold B. Lee Library, Brigham Young University, Provo, Utah)

Lorenzo Hill Hatch was serving a mission in Vermont when he received word of the martyrdom; at the same time, he received a spiritual witness that Brigham should succeed Joseph:

> I received the sad news of this awful affair [the martyrdom] in the town of Bristol, Addison County, Vermont. While I yet had the letter in my hand this letter was written by my uncle who claimed that Sidney Rigdon was the man to lead the Church—a voice spoke to me and said, "Brigham Young is the successor of Joseph Smith." (Lorenzo Hill Hatch, Lorenzo Hill Hatch Journal [Provo, Utah: Mimeographed by BYU Adult Education and Extension Services, 1958], 282. This collection was originally copied by Ruth Savage Hilton from the original journals.)

33. See document 17.

34. See document 27. Joseph was well over six feet tall while Brigham was several inches shorter.

35. See documents 38A, 38B. Although Joseph's tooth had been repaired before his death, to Benjamin Johnson the whistle was proof that he had heard Joseph's voice.

36. See document 46.

37. Young, "Diary," August 8, 1844. This passage is in Brigham Young's handwriting with his spelling and punctuation. Dean C. Jessee identifies which diary passages are actually written by Brigham Young and which are written by scribes. See Dean C. Jessee, "The Writings of Brigham Young," *Western Historical Quarterly* 4 (July 1973): 284.

38. *History of the Church*, 7:250; italics in original.

39. Brigham Young, in *Journal of Discourses*, 5:57, July 19, 1857.

40. The testimonies included in this project were those I was able to document. It is possible to nearly double the number of mantle witnesses from the testimonies already included in this project. Many of the testimonies tell of spouses, parents, children, brothers, sisters, friends, and other individuals accompanying each participant. For example, see document 61. Mary Ann Stearns tells of attending the meeting with her little friend Julia Felshaw. They had to stand on benches to behold the wonderful transformation.

41. See documents 3, 16, 27, 32, 42.

42. See document 13.

43. See document 9; Thomas Bullock, *Millennial Star* 14 (July 13, 1852): 299.

44. "While the prophet lived, we all walked by 'sight'; he is taken from us and we must now walk by 'faith.' After he [Brigham] explained matters so satisfactorily that every saint could see that Elijah's mantle had truly fallen upon the 'Twelve.'" "Special Meeting," *Times and Seasons* 5 (September 2, 1844): 637.

45. See document 79.

46. Brigham Young, "Remarks," *Deseret News*, July 29, 1857, 164.

47. See documents 55A and 55B.

48. See Esplin, "Joseph, Brigham and the Twelve," 301–41.

49. Manuscript Minutes of Brigham Young Sermon, December 25, 1857, Brigham Young Collection, Church Archives.

50. Miscellaneous Minutes, February 12, 1849, Brigham Young Collection, Church Archives.

51. See document 68B.

52. See documents 80 and 94.

53. See documents 12 and 2.

54. See document 17.

55. See document 18.

56. See documents 83A and 83B. Some years later, Albert sent a letter with an elder asking his wife for a divorce, which she granted. Both partners remarried. After the death of both mates, Albert rejoined the Church, traveled to Utah, and he and Ada went with their son to the Endowment House, where they were remarried and sealed. "The Lonely Trail," in *Our Pioneer Heritage*, comp. Kate B. Carter, 20 vols. (Salt Lake City: Daughters of Utah Pioneers, 1958–77), 3:111–12.

57. See document 101.

58. See document 82.

59. See document 92.

60. See document 37A and 37B.

61. See Carol Cornwall Madsen, *In Their Own Words: Women and the Story of Nauvoo* (Salt Lake City: Deseret Book, 1994), 168, 185, 204, 235, 242, 255–56.

62. Quinn, *Mormon Hierarchy*, 166; first italics added.

63. Jesse C. Little to Brigham Young, December 8, 1844, filed December 30, 1844, Brigham Young Papers, Church Archives (document 19).

64. John Henry Evans and Minnie Egan Anderson, *Ezra T. Benson: Pioneer—Statesman—Saint* (Salt Lake City: Deseret News Press, 1947), 88–89.

65. See document 11.

66. See document 68A.

67. Brent L. Top and Lawrence R. Flake, "'The Kingdom of God Will Roll On': Succession in the Presidency," *Ensign* 26 (August 1996): 25.

68. A few Nauvoo Saints who kept daily records, personal or official, made entries on August 8, recording the results or proceedings of the meeting without mentioning a mantle experience at that time. (See document 33.) Wilford Woodruff, concerned with keeping an official record, made careful notes on the comments made by the speakers during the conference but makes no mention of a specific spiritual manifestation at the meeting. See Wilford Woodruff, *Wilford Woodruff's Journal, 1833–1898, Typescript,* ed. Scott G. Kenney, 9 vols. (Midvale, Utah: Signature Books, 1983–84), 2:434–40. In their personal journals, William Clayton and Heber C. Kimball both briefly mention only the results of the vote taken at the meeting. See George D. Smith, *An Intimate Chronicle: The Journals of William Clayton* (Salt Lake City: Signature Books, 1991), 142; and Heber C. Kimball, Journal, Church Archives.

Willard Richards's journal has a two-and-one-half page entry for August 7, a very brief entry for August 8 followed by a blank page, then another long entry for August 9. The entry marked August 8 is made up of a few short lines that simply state that Rigdon spoke in the morning and that the Twelve were voted by the Church to stand as the First Presidency. Then Richards writes, "See Times and Seasons." The first reference to the August 8 meeting in the *Times and Seasons* is in the issue dated September 2, 1844 (see note 44), indicating that Richards probably made the entry after August 8. Willard Richards, Journal, Church Archives.

Thomas Bullock's personal journal has no entries for August 8, 1844. However, he did attend the meeting and kept minutes. His notes for the afternoon meeting make no mention of a mantle experience. His minutes of the morning meeting, taken in his particular shorthand, are notes taken during Sidney's and Brigham's speeches, with no additional comments of any kind. Thomas Bullock, Minutes, Thomas Bullock Collection, Church Archives. See the appendix to this article, Bullock's recently transcribed minutes of Brigham Young's comments in the morning meeting.

69. Carol C. Madsen comments, "Some human experiences are so intense and life-changing that memory returns not only the event in its fullness, but also the emotions that surround it." Madsen, *In Their Own Words*, 158.

70. For a discussion concerning the lack of paper in Nauvoo in 1844, see George W. Givens, *In Old Nauvoo: Everyday Life in the City of Joseph* (Salt Lake City: Deseret Book, 1990), 266. On November 13, 1844, the *Nauvoo Neighbor* announced a lack of paper caused by the "bad state of navigation, &c."

71. After giving his testimony of the mantle falling on Brigham Young, Edmund Ellsworth explained that President Young told them that the temple must be built. He added, "We went to work as one in poverty." Edmund Ellsworth, Autobiography [ca. 1892], holograph, 4–5, Church Archives.

72. Esplin, "Joseph, Brigham and the Twelve," 330. The Saints did complete enough of the temple to enable many to receive their endowments before the exodus in 1846.

73. See document 36.

74. Arrington and Bitton, *Mormon Experience*, 85.

75. Allen and Leonard, *Story of the Latter-day Saints*, 202.

76. Davis Bitton, *Guide to Mormon Diaries and Autobiographies* (Provo, Utah: Brigham Young University Press, 1977), 47, 289, 331–32.

77. Abraham Owen Smoot, "Abraham Owen Smoot Journal, 1844–1845," Abraham Owen Smoot Papers, Perry Special Collections.

78. Emmeline B. Harris Wells, "My Testimony," in Preston Nibley, comp., *Faith Promoting Stories* (Salt Lake City: Deseret Book, 1943), 139; Madsen, *In Their Own Words*, 43–49. Madsen explains that Emmeline was sixteen, had just lost a baby, and had been deserted by her husband, James Harris, when she began to write her daily account. The early diary is typical of a heartbroken sixteen-year-old. She did not write of current events that surrounded her. She wrote of her adolescent pains and lost romance. Emmeline wrote about "the mantle" in her later years when she finally became aware of the significance of this event. See documents 91A and 91B.

79. Givens, "Sickness and Death," *In Old Nauvoo*, 112–30.

80. George Washington Bean, *George Washington Bean and His Family Records*, comp. Flora Diana Bean Horne (Salt Lake City: Utah Printing, 1945), 23, 31.

81. Caroline Barnes Crosby, "Memoirs Begun at Tubuai, Society Islands, 1851," holograph, unpaged, Church Archives.

82. Appleton Milo Harmon, "Appleton Milo Harmon's Early History and Journal for His Travels through the United States, England, and Scotland in 1850, 1851, and 1852," Perry Special Collections.

83. Emily Smith Hoyt, Reminiscences and Diaries, 1851–1893, microfilm of holograph, 19–20, Church Archives.

84. Joseph Grafton Hovey, "Biography of Joseph Grafton Hovey, Copied and Arranged from His Journal by His Grand Son, M. R. Hovey of Logan, Utah," typescript, Perry Special Collections. Hovey's use of the phrase "as clear as the noon day sun," sometimes associated with a visionary experience (Joseph Smith—History 1:16; D&C 110:3; Acts 9:3), may or may not have any special significance.

85. As a case in point, while teaching family history classes for the BYU Salt Lake Center, I asked my students how many of them had personally experienced a spiritual manifestation or knew of a spiritual experience of someone close to them. Nearly every hand went up. I then asked how many had written these experiences down. Nearly every hand went down. Only one or two of the

students had actually kept a journal account. When I asked why they had not recorded the experience, they answered that they were uncomfortable writing about sacred events.

86. Martha Pane Jones Thomas, Autobiography, in *Daniel Stillwell Thomas Family History* (Salt Lake City: Kate Woodhouse Kirkham, 1927), 30–31; spelling standardized.

87. See document 38A.

88. Carol Cornwall Madsen, "Mormon Missionary Wives in Nineteenth-Century Polynesia," *Journal of Mormon History* 13 (1986–87): 61.

89. Crosby, "Memoirs."

90. Crosby, "Memoirs."

91. See document 16.

92. Hoyt, Reminiscences and Diaries, 67.

93. Andrew Jenson, *Latter-day Saint Biographical Encyclopedia: A Compilation of Biographical Sketches of Prominent Men and Women in The Church of Jesus Christ of Latter-day Saints*, 4 vols. (Salt Lake City: Andrew Jenson History, 1901–36), 1:182.

94. Hoyt, Reminiscences and Diaries, 19–20.

95. Hoyt, Reminiscences and Diaries, 19.

96. Hoyt, Reminiscences and Diaries, 20.

97. Hoyt, Reminiscences and Diaries, 20.

98. Hoyt, Reminiscences and Diaries, 20–21.

99. See document 32; underlining in original.

100. See document 78A; see also document 78B.

101. See document 22.

102. See document 21.

103. As already noted, the only "official" mantle references that had been previously published were Brigham Young's reference in 1857 to Albert Carrington's experience and the statements in the *Times and Seasons* and the *Millennial Star*.

104. See document 35A. In this 1869 discourse, Orson Hyde speaks as if he had been present at the August 8 conference in Nauvoo. He mentions Rigdon's speech to the congregation as well as Brigham Young's. However, Wilford Woodruff's diary places Orson's arrival in Nauvoo on August 13.

105. See document 13. See also B. H. Roberts, *A Comprehensive History of The Church of Jesus Christ of Latter-day Saints, Century One*, 6 vols. (Provo, Utah: Corporation of the President, The Church of Jesus Christ of Latter-day Saints, 1965), 2:418; *History of the Church*, 7:236n. George Q. Cannon's account has become a widely quoted source for the mantle stories in major histories of the Nauvoo period. It is still accepted as a faithful version and reappears in contemporary Latter-day Saint historical and educational materials. Elder Cannon's

account was quoted most recently in the *Ensign*, along with Benjamin F. Johnson to Elder George S. Gibbs, 1903. See Top and Flake, "Kingdom of God Will Roll On," 25.

106. See document 68B.

107. See Edward W. Tullidge, *Life of Brigham Young; or, Utah and Her Founders* (New York: n.p., 1877); and Orson F. Whitney, *History of Utah* (Salt Lake City: Cannon and Sons, 1892–1904).

108. See document 60.

109. See documents 37A, 54B, 67.

110. See document 65.

111. See document 15.

112. See document 29.

113. See document 40.

114. See document 55B.

115. See document 55A.

116. Elizabeth F. Loftus and James M. Doyle, *Eyewitness Testimony: Civil and Criminal*, 2d ed. (Charlottesville, Va: Michie Company Law Publishers, 1992), 8; italics added.

117. M. Scott Peck, "Holiness," in *In Search of Stones: A Pilgrimage of Faith, Reason, and Discovery* (New York: Hyperion, 1995), 75.

118. Milton V. Backman Jr., *The Heavens Resound: A History of the Latter-day Saints in Ohio, 1830–1838* (Salt Lake City: Deseret Book, 1983), 264–68, 284–309. See also Karl Ricks Anderson, *Joseph Smith's Kirtland: Eyewitness Accounts* (Salt Lake City: Deseret Book, 1989), 169–91.

119. Backman, *Heavens Resound*, 300.

120. Ezra T. Benson makes no claim to having had a mantle vision personally but mentions and apparently accepts the experience of others (see note 62). A number of Saints, whose reminiscent accounts have been located, were careful to record that they were at the meeting on August 8 but make no specific reference to a transfiguration. See the following accounts: (1) Lucy Diantha Morley Allen, "Joseph Smith, the Prophet," *Young Woman's Journal* 17 (December 1906): 537; (2) Gilbert Belnap, Autobiography, typescript, 37, Perry Special Collections; and (3) David E. Fullmer, "A Brief Sketch of the Life of David E. Fullmer and His Father Peter Fullmer," holograph, 40, Church Archives.

121. Lavina Fielding Anderson, "Prayer under a Pepper Tree: Sixteen Accounts of a Spiritual Manifestation," *BYU Studies* 33, no. 1 (1993): 73–74.

122. See *History of the Church*, 7:237–38; Quinn, *Mormon Hierarchy*, 165; and Van Wagoner, "The Making of a Mormon Myth," 12.

123. W. W. Phelps, Letter to Brigham Young, January 1, 1862, holograph, Church Archives.

The Documents/Testimonies

The following are the known testimonies of persons who left a record of their mantle experience. These records were either written in the person's own hand or dictated by them to a scribe. Women are listed under the names they had in August 1844. This section includes sources and appropriate notes, as well as each person's name, birth and death dates, age in August 1844, and testimony. Underlining is reproduced from the original document. Editorial marks include brackets [ ] to indicate editorial comments.

Firsthand Accounts

1. William Adams

January 8, 1822–September 30, 1901, age 22

There was a great multitude attending the meeting, more than one half the crowd could not find seats, and stood on their feet. Never were so many at one meeting that I ever saw. I was sitting down and could not see the speakers on the stand. I was listening very attentively, so that I could hear every word.

I heard a voice speaking, I was surprised, and jumping to my feet, expecting Joseph the Prophet was speaking, having heard him often in public and private, so that I was quite acquainted with his voice. This was a strong testimony that the Twelve Apostles were the rightful leaders of the church and that the mouth of Joseph had fallen on Brigham Young.[1]

2. William Moore Allred

December 24, 1819–January 8, 1901, age 24

Sidney Rigdon one of Joseph's counselors had moved to Pittsburg, and when he heard of Joseph's death he came to Nauvoo claiming his right to lead the Church. At least he said the Church was 14 years old and had the right to choose a guardien, but Brigham Young, the President of the twelve Apostles and others of the twelve (that had been on a mission) just got home as the meeting was called for Rigdon to preach. And after he got through Brigham got up and spoke with such power that it convinced nearly all that were present that the Mantle of Joseph had fallen on him. I was perfectly satisfied.[2]

3. Benjamin Ashby

December 19, 1828–November 19, 1907, age 15

Soon the twelve Began to return, also Sidney Rigdon who endeavored to have himself elected as guardain of the Church and I was presant when he made his silly and boastful, speach about leading the Church back to Pittsburg and Twerling the nose of Queen Victoria &c. &c. Too foolish to be worth remembering I did not know Rigdon when he was in the Spirit of his Calling and cannot say what manner of Man he was. but when I knew him he had lost the favor of God and he was as dry as sticks in his preaching[.]

I was in the congregation when the Question of the succesion to the leadership of the Church was before the people and I solemly assert and testify that the last time I saw the Features. the Gestures and heard the sound of the voice of Joseph Smith: was when the form, voice, and countanance of Brigham Young was tranfiguard before the congregation so that he appeared like Joseph Smith in every particular. Thus the Lord showed the people that the Mantle of Joseph had been bestowed upon Brigham.[3]

4. Lewis Barney

September 8, 1808–November 5, 1894, age 35

The next day President Brigham Young arived in Nauvoo with some of the other apostles from a Mission to the Eastern States And Called a meeting and invited Sidney Rigdon to the Stand and in the presance of the assembled thousands of the Saints Said to Sidney Now if you have any thing to say you have the apertunity and you can take the stand[.] But Sidney declined and kept his seat. President young then arose and took the stand his face and Countinence having the apearanc[e] of Joseph his voice and words were the familiar voice and Words of our martered prophet so much so the Who[l]e Congregation was fully satisfied that the mantle of the Prophet Joseph had fallen on him and some of the saints realy Believed it was in reality the Prophet himself[.] Well do I remember the feelings that possesed my Breast at that time I knew it was Brigham Young and being familiar with the Countinance voice and the maner of the Speech of the Prophet Joseph Smith I also knew the mantle of the prophet had fallen on Brigham and it was marvelous and a mericle wrought by the Power of God in the Sight and hearing of the Whole multitude that they might never doubt that Brigham was the Chosen leader of the Church.[4]

5. Eunice Billings

January 3, 1830–November 25, 1914, age 14

There were so many opinions as who would be the leader of the Saints at that time. Sidney Rigdon was sure he was the man. He stood up and declared that he was the one, but he was called down and Brigham Young stood up and spoke with the power and voice of Joseph. He surely had the Prophet Joseph's mantle on. There seemed to be no doubt of Brigham Young being the one to lead the saints at that time.[5]

6. Cynthia Harrington Durphy/Durfey Bowen

November 30, 1811–November 1883, age 32

While at the prayer meeting that was called after hearing Sydney Rigdon speak an event that gave me great strength took place. Brigham Young stood before us & as I listened to him, his countenance changed & I saw the prophet Joseph Smith & heard his voice speaking as well & I knew who was to be the next prophet of the Lord & who was to lead the Saints.[6]

Catharine Brooke

[no available dates]

See Henry Brooke.

7. Henry Brooke

[no available dates]

The loss of Br. Joseph and Hyrum has been greatly felt but we have the twelve apostles to preside in their stead. Br. Brigham Young is president of the twelve and stands as prophet, seer, and revelator to the Church. He is an excellent man, and favours Br. Joseph, both in person, and manner of speaking, more than any person ever you saw looks like another.[7]

8. Henry Schuler Buckwalter

May 12, 1831–November 6, 1908, age 13

Was at the meeting when Sid[n]ey Rigdon tried to lay claim to the presidency of the Church And President Brigham Young told him different and his voice and looks was precisely like that of the Prophet Joseph.[8]

9. Thomas Bullock

December 23, 1816–February 10, 1885, age 27

They [Joseph and Hyrum] were two good men when living, and they died good men; they died martyrs for the truth, and they sealed their testimony with their blood; and their testimony is true. . . .

The mantle of Joseph fell on Brigham Young, the blood of the martyrs became as seed on the earth.[9]

10. Robert Taylor Burton

October 25, 1821–November 11, 1907, age 22

This morning, at the Presiding Bishop's Office, after reading what purported to be an appeal to the Latter-day Saints by Frederick J. Smith in regard to the successor of the Prophet Joseph Smith Jr., I had occasion, in conversation with Bishop O. P. Miller to refer to my experience in Nauvoo, Illinois some time after the martyrdom of Joseph and Hyrum Smith, and upon his request, I made the following statement:

> This to my mind was one of the most critical periods in the history of the Church. A number of persons claimed the legal succession, and to have this authority, among them Sidney Rigdon, James J. Strang, Aaron and Moses Smith and others. The occasion that I now refer to was a general meeting of the Latter-day Saints, soon after the return to Nauvoo of President Brigham Young and other members of the Quorum of Twelve Apostles, from their missions. The meeting had been called to order, and after the usual opening exercises President Brigham Young arose to address the assembly.

At that time I was not acquainted with President Young, but his voice, manner, expression, and in fact, his personal appearance was so strikingly that of the martyred Prophet, that I rose from my seat, as did hundreds of others, to look at the Prophet Joseph Smith Jr. The likeness was so marked that I could hardly make myself believe that the Prophet had not himself returned; not that there was a resemblance between the two men. I am not going to say why this was other than I received it, as an evidence to the people that God had chose Brigham Young as successor to the Prophet Joseph Smith Jr. There were dozens, even hundreds of others, who were impressed just the same as I was at that time, and I have heard many, many who are now gone make similar statements or expressions to that I am here making.

(signed) R. T. Burton[10]

11. William Burton

October 3, 1809–March 17, 1851, age 34

We arrived in Nauvoo in May. . . . [T]here was one change more that had taken place during the time that I was out on my mission; -that grevious and hard to be borne. This was the Martyrdom of the Prophet and Seer, and Patriarch, whose voices I could not hear, declaring the truths of Heaven. But their [Joseph's and Hyrum's] places were filled by others much better than I once was supposed they could have been. The spirit of Joseph appeared to rest upon Brigham. . . . Great and mysterious are the ways of God![11]

12. Anson Call

May 13, 1810–August 31, 1890, age 34

That week, Brigham Young and others of the 12 came to the city. On the Sunday following, Brigham and a portion of the Twelve presented themselves in our congregation. He said he had not come to electioneer, nor set up any particular claim, but to do his duty, and it was for the people to judge between truth and error. Before he [Brigham] had spoken many sentences, I discovered that it was the voice of Joseph, and had I have been where my eyes could not have beheld him, I should have believed that Joseph had been speaking. It was Joseph's voice and Joseph's gestures through the entire discourse, I became perfectly satisfied that it was the voice for me to follow in connection with the majority of the brethren.[12]

13. George Q. Cannon

January 11, 1827–April 12, 1901, age 17

It was the first sound of his voice [Brigham's] which the people had heard since he had gone east on his mission, and the effect upon them was most wonderful. Who that was present on that occasion can ever forget the impression it made upon them! If Joseph had risen from the dead and again spoken in their hearing, the effect could not have been more startling than it was to many present at that meeting. It was the voice of Joseph himself; and not only was it the voice of Joseph which was heard; but it seemed in the eyes of the people as though it was the very person of Joseph which stood before them. A more wonderful and miraculous event than was wrought that day in the presence of that congregation we never heard of. The Lord gave His people a testimony that left no room for doubt as to who was the man He had chosen to lead them. They both saw and heard with their natural eyes and ears, and then the words which were uttered came, accompanied by the convincing power of God, to their hearts, and they were filled with the Spirit and with great joy. There had been gloom, and, in some hearts probably, doubt and uncertainty; but now it was plain to all that here was the man upon whom the Lord had bestowed the necessary authority to act in their midst in Joseph's stead.[13]

14. Elias Cox

January 15, 1835–May 8, 1917, age 9

I heard Brother Brigham speak and that is the first time that I ever saw two men look and sound so much alike in all my life. And after he had sat down, I wondered where Joseph had gone.[14]

15. Robert Crookston

September 21, 1821–September 25, 1917, age 22

I attended the funeral of the Prophet Joseph and his brother Hyrum Smith. I was also present at the meeting held in the grove at Nauvoo August 8, 1844, when Sidney Rigdon made the claim that it was his right to assume the leadership and presidency of the church. I saw Brigham Young stand up and speak to the people, and he spoke with the voice of Joseph Smith. I further testify that I was well acquainted with the Prophet Joseph Smith and heard him speak many times. Among the many sermons I heard him preach was at the funeral of King Follett. I also heard him deliver his last adieu to the Nauvoo Legion. As to Brigham Young, I know of a surety that he spoke with the voice of Joseph Smith, and I was convinced then and never doubted during all the intervening years that passed that Brigham Young was chosen and ordained of God to lead the church.[15]

16. Caroline Barnes Crosby

January 5, 1807–February 16, 1884, age 37

Sidney Rigdon came to the stand and tried to show to the people that he was the rightful successor of Joseph. And his arguments were so powerful that many were almost pursuaded to believe him such. But as soon as the twelve apostles with bro Brigham Young at their head took the stand it was shown conclusively where the power rested. It was the first time that I ever thought he [Brigham] resembled bro Joseph. But almost every one exclaimed that the mantle of Joseph had fallen on Brigham. For one I never had any doubts afterwards. We all soon became comforted concerning our leaders, but persecution continued all around us. The brethren were obliged to be on guard all the time.[16]

17. Homer Duncan

January 19, 1815–March 23, 1906, age 29

I must make mention on one [more] manifestation of the Lord's goodness to me. At the special meeting held at Nauvoo after the Prophet Joseph Smith's death at the time that the mantle of the Prophet of the Lord fell upon Brigham Young. I sat listening to someone speaking with my head down, my face in the palms of my hands and my elbows on my knees. While in this position, Brigham Young came to the stand and commenced to speak with the voice of Joseph the Prophet. Being so well acquainted with the Prophet's voice, I nearly sprang from my seat through astonishment, but I sat and heard the Prophet's [Joseph's] voice as long as Brigham Young was speaking. Not only did the voice of Brigham [sound] like that of Joseph, but the very gestures of his right hand when he was saying anything very positive reminded me of Joseph. My decision was then made as to who should lead the Church of Jesus Christ of Latter Day Saints for surely the mantle of Joseph has fallen upon Brigham.[17]

18. Mary Dunn

November 2, 1833–November 7, ?, age 11

I well remember when the bodies of the martyrs were brought home and placed in the Mansion House and thousands came to view their remains. We wondered what would become of the Church and who would lead it. It seemed that everything was at a standstill but you all know the story of how the mantle of Joseph fell on Brigham Young. I was at the meeting. Father said on our way home, "They need not hunt any farther. Brigham Young is the man to lead us."[18]

19. Howard Egan

June 15, 1815–March 18, 1878, age 29

Jesse C. Little quoted Egan's words in his letter to Brigham Young dated December 30, 1844: "I rec[eive]d a Letter from Bro [Howard] Egan at the time of the Conference he said "if a man had been blinded he would hardly have known if it were not Joseph."[19]

20. Edmund Ellsworth

July 1, 1819–December 29, 1893, age 25

The Prophet concluded to run for the President of the United States. I was called to the State of New York on an electioneering mission to which place I immediately started where I labored untill the death of the Prophet when I received a letter from President Young calling the Elders home. I was present at the meeting which tried President Sydney Rigdon, where I plainly saw the Mantle of the Priesthood fall upon President Young with its power and spirit. The testimony of this was given to most of the congregation.[20]

21. Mary Field

February 1, 1836–July 20, 1943, age 8

After Joseph Smith's death there was some confusion as to who should be our leader. Sidney Rigdon claimed to have had a vision that he should be our head, but I, with my mother, was present at the meeting in the bowery when the mantle of Joseph fell upon Brigham Young while he was talking with the people. Mother had the baby on her knee, who was playing with a tin cup. He dropped it, attracting our attention to the floor. Mother stooped over to pick it up, when we startled by hearing the voice of Joseph. Looking up quickly we saw the form of the Prophet Joseph standing before us. Brother Brigham looked and talked so much like Joseph that for a minute we thought it was Joseph. There was no doubt in the hearts of the Saints from that moment on who was to be their inspired leader.

After Brigham Young was sustained as our prophet and leader, the Church was again restored to order under his guiding hand. The Saints were anxious to complete the Nauvoo Temple, as they had been commanded by the Prophet Joseph before his death. By hard work and determination the Saints completed the temple and large numbers received their endowments there.[21]

22. James Madison Fisher

July 22, 1833–January 1, 1907, age 11

The twelve apostles were all away from home, before they got back Sydney Rigdon wanted to call a meeting and have the people choose him for their leader the people said no wait untill the twelve comes home. Brigham Young was the first to arive after they all come home there was a meeting caled to choose a leader it was held in a grove where they held meetings in the summer time. I was there, Rigdon spoke first it did not have the wright ring to it when he sat down brother Brigham got up, the mantle of Joseph fell upon him, he was the picture of the Prophet [Joseph] and he had the Prophet's voice it was a great surprise for the people, the saints was shown who was to be their leader, Rigdon left the Church went to Penn. and started a Church of his own wich soon flatened out.[22]

Mary Field Garner

See Mary Field.

23. Jacob Gates

March 9, 1811–April 14, 1892, age 33

After the Death of Joseph and Hyrum the Excitement Seemed [?] to die away. Meantime Sidney Rigdon who was a Counsiller to Joseph arived and attempted to userpe arthority over the Church as the Succeser of Joseph but the Church was saved by the timely arival of the Twelve and the Spirit of God which always teaches right and the result was that Rigdon was cut of from the Church for his miss conduct and went up to Pittsburg followed by a few who were men as himself whose mouth was ful of cursing and bitterness. The Power of the Preasthood rested down upon the Twelve backed up by the Spirit of God which enabled them to give that instruction which [seemed] to unite the harts of the Saints together as the heart of one Man. They moved forward to build the Temple.[23]

24. James Harvey Glines

April 19, 1822–August 31, 1905, age 22

I arrived in time to hear Sidney Rigdon's last lectures before the Church. President Brigham Young and others of the twelve apostles now arrived and appointed a meeting in the grove at the stand east of the temple block. . . .

Sidney Rigdon stopped speaking. President Brigham Young stood up and commenced speaking, and all eyes were turned upon him for he seemed to have the voice of the prophet Joseph, as many testified at the time, for he spoke with great power and authority to the convincing of the Saints that the mantle had fallen from Joseph to Brigham.[24]

Rachel Ridgeway Ivins Grant

See Rachel Ridgeway Ivins.

Mary Clough/Cluff Greenhalgh

March 18, 1814–December 16, 1851, age 30

See William Greenhalgh.

25. William Greenhalgh

July 29, 1811–April 3, 1882, age 33

In a few days Sidney Rigdon came up to Nauvoo to see if the people would accept him as a guardian to act for Joseph. He told the people if they did not accept him, God would reject them as a people with their dead. He was to return to Pittsburg and God would raise up a people at Pittsburg for him. With uplifted hands he called on God and angels to bear him witness. He spoke next day to them and (to) see if the people would accept him.

Just at this time came home Brigham Young and Heber C. Kimball. The morning following Brigham Young ordered the people to bring a wagon to the south side of the congregation that the people could all hear what he had to say. Brigham rose and said, "I would to God, there was not such a hurried spirit here." He spoke with such power and the voice of Joseph sounded through him so plain that the people who could not see him, knew that it was the voice of Joseph speaking through Brigham Young. My wife Mary sitting close by me not able to turn her head asked me if that was Joseph. I told her no, but it was the voice of Joseph speaking through Brigham Young. This was a living testimony that the mantle had fallen from Joseph on to Brigham—and from this time many wanted to well off and part from the Saints—But Brigham forbid them and told them that the flock must not be scattered.[25]

26A and 26B. Jacob Hamblin

April 2, 1819–August 31, 1886, age 25

Come the 24th when I arived at Nauvoo I saw thare was a gertherin [gathering] of the Saints at the Stand as I drew nere I saw Mr. Sidney Rigdon [a]ddressing the Congregation I listened a few minits and Said in my hart it was not the vois of the trew Sepherd.[26]

At Nauvoo I found Sidney Rigdon busy among the Saints, trying to establish his claim to the presidency of the Church. He was first Counselor to the Prophet Joseph at the time of the latter's death. The Church was fourteen years old, and he claimed that it was its privilege and duty to appoint a guardian; and he wished the people to sanction his guardianship.

I was much dissatisfied with the course he was taking, and, as I could not sustain him, I felt to leave Nauvoo for a season. I went into the country, where I had left my wife and two children with my sister Melissa. . . .

On the 8th of August, 1844, I attended a general meeting of the Saints. Elder Rigdon was there, urging his claims to the presidency of the Church. His voice did not sound like the voice of the true shepherd. When he was about to call a vote of the congregation to sustain him as President of the Church, Elders Brigham Young, Parley P. Pratt and Heber C. Kimball stepped into the stand.

Brigham Young remarked to the congregation: "I will manage this voting for Elder Rigdon. He does not preside here. This child" (meaning himself) "will manage this flock for a season." The voice and the gestures of the man were those of the Prophet Joseph.

The people, with few exceptions, visibly saw that the mantle of the prophet Joseph had fallen upon Brigham Young. To some it seemed as though Joseph again stood before them.

I arose to my feet and said to a man sitting by me, "That is the voice of the true shepherd—the chief of the Apostles."[27]

27. Mosiah Lyman Hancock

April 9, 1834–January 14, 1907, age 10

Altho only a boy, I saw the mantle of the Prophet Joseph rest on Brigham Young; and he arose lion-like to the occasion, and lead the people forth. . . .

I remember Sidney Rigdon in his great desire to become Guardian of the Church. But I had seen the Prophet [Joseph] proclaim these words before the people, "I have carried Sidney Rigdon long enough—I now throw him from my shoulders. If my brother Hyrum wishes to pick him up and carry him, he may—I carry him no longer."

I saw Brother Brigham Young, of the Quorum of the Twelve, arise before the people—and I saw in him the look of Joseph, and the voice of Joseph; and it seemed to me that he was as tall as Joseph too. I knew that the mantle of Joseph had fallen on Brigham. I had heard the Prophet say from the frame that he threw the furtherence of this Church and Kingdom upon the shoulders of the Twelve; that they should bear and send this Gospel to every nation under heaven.[28]

28. John Nelson Harper

March 9, 1813–March 31, 1863, age 31

When the Twelve returned home the Saints was troubled to know who should lead the Church; Sidney Rigdon was there from Pittsburg and wanted to choose a guardian for the Church, but when Bro Brigham arose on the stand I received a testimony for myself, he appeared to me as if it was Bro Joseph and it was Joseph's voice and there the mantle of Joseph fell on Brigham. He [Brigham] said it was no enviable place to stand at the head of the people for at them the arrows of the enemy would be directed. But he was willing to stand where God placed him.[29]

29. Eliza Ann Haven

May 15, 1829–January 20, 1923, age 15

I was then 15 year[s] and I felt so sad I was to meeting when Sidney [or Sidny] Rigdon declared himself our true Prophet and leader very [or vey – 'ry's run together] few responded to the call, am happy to say none of my Fathers family f[el]t [rip] th[at] [rip] he was soon after Prest. Young came home from the east where he was on a mission I was to meeting when he said he was our Prophet & seer when he spoke it was Br Josephs voice I gave a jump of[f] my seat and said our Prophet [t looks like an n] Joseph has come to life we have our Prophet back I looked up and there stood Br. Joseph just as plain as I ever saw him when alive [page break] 3 for a minute I heard Br Joseph voice and saw his features then a mist seemed to pass from Brigham face and go up then there stood Br Brigham talki ng combined] to us. hundreds seen the same that I did but not all that were present.[30]

30. Drusilla Dorris Hendricks

February 8, 1810–May 20, 1881, age 34

It was not long before Sidney Rigdon called a meeting in order to present his claims to the presidency of the Church. Some of the Twelve had returned from their missions and the day the meeting was held and while it was in session, Brigham Young (President of the quorum of the Twelve Apostles) and others slipped up to the stand and said nothing until Sidney Rigdon was through, he was standing near the center of the audience in a wagon. As the meeting was in the Boury [Bowery]. Then Pres. Brigham Young began to speak. I jumped up to look and see if it was not Brother Joseph for surely it was his voice and gestures. Every Latter Day Saint could easily see upon whom the priesthood descended for Brigham Young held the keys. Sidney Rigdon led off a few, but where are they now. They have dwindled away in unbelief and have come to naught.[31]

31. Arza Erastus Hinckley

August 15, 1827–February 18, 1901, age 16

The entry after 20 November 1844 in the diary of Arza Hinckley at Brigham Young University states: ". . . and Brigham Young on hom the mantle of the prophet Joseph has falen is a men of god and he ceeps all things in good order."[32]

32. Emily Smith Hoyt

September 1, 1806–August 6, 1893, age 37

[After the martyrdom] we [Emily and Samuel] were summoned over the river again and went to hear what was wanted. Brigham Young then President of the twelve had returned home. The people were convened in the Old Bowry where Joseph had last spoken to the people. Sydney Rigdon made a speech and claimed to have authority to lead the Church others had similar claims. None appeared reasonable to me. The last one arose. It was the then, President of the twelve Brigham Young. He spoke to the people altogether in a different style from any of those, who had preceeded him. A crowd of witnessses arose after B. Y. had sat down and testified to the truth of what he had said. President B. Y. arose from his seat the second time and addressed the audience. I had been well acquainted with Joseph the latter part of his life. We had been at his home many times and Joseph, Hiram and families felt at home with us. [Emily writes of events leading to martyrdom of Joseph and Hyrum.] . . . But the God of Heaven who had said it was his business to provide for his saints, sent President B. Young home just in time, and clothed him not with "the mantle of Elijah," but the spirit and power which had rested on Joseph. I was an eye, and ear, witness. The manner of reasoning, the expression of the countenance, the sound of the voice thrilled my whole soul. My own eyes had beheld Joseph's murdered body. My own hands, had felt death's icy coldness on his once noble forehead. I knew that Joseph was dead. And yet I often startled and involuntarily looked at the stand to see if it was not Joseph. It was not, it was Brigham Young and if any one doubts the right of Brigham to manage affairs for the Saints, all I have to say to them is this. Get the spirit of God and know for yourselves. The Lord will provide for his own. Has the word of the Lord ever failed. Br Young will not live forever clothed with mortality. But He who rules in heaven and on earth will control all things by the counsel of his own will. Saints will live.[33]

33A and 33B. Zina Diantha Huntington

January 13, 1821–August 27, 1901, age 23

I went to meeting in the afternoon, Thanks be to Him who reigns on high, the majority of the Twelve are her[e]. Brigham Youngs spoke and the Church voted that the 12 should act in the office of there calling next to Joseph or the three first presidents.[34]

Never can it be told in words what the saints suffered in those days of trial; but the sweet spirit—the comforter—did not forsake them; and when the twelve returned, the mantle of Joseph fell upon Brigham.

When I approached the stand (on the occasion when Sidney Rigdon was striving for the guardianship of the Church), President Young was speaking. It was the voice of Joseph Smith—not that of Brigham Young. His very person was changed. The mantle was truly given to another. There was no doubting this in the minds of that vast assembly. All witnessed the transfiguration, and even to-day thousands bear testimony thereof. I closed my eyes. I could have exclaimed, I know that is Joseph Smith's voice! Yet I knew he had gone. But the same spirit was with the people; the comforter remained.[35]

34. Mary Anne [Price] Hyde

June 5, 1816–June 16, 1900, age 28

In listening to the remarks of President Young, it carried me back to the time when the spirit and mantle of Joseph fell upon him. I was there and witnessed that scene at the time it occurred. I looked, and it seemed as though it was Joseph himself. I said to those near me, "See there is Joseph," not even taking my eyes off for fear I should lose the sight of it. It was a testimony to me that he was the right man in the right place.[36]

35A and 35B. Orson Hyde

January 8, 1805–November 28, 1878, age 39

I will tell you that as long as God has a Church on the earth, He will govern it. Now I will tell you a little of my feelings in relation to it. I know that when President Young returned with the Twelve to Nauvoo, he gathered them around him, and said he: "I want you to disperse among the congregation and feel the pulse of the people while I go upon the stand and speak."

We went among the congregation and President Young went on the stand. Well, he spoke; and his words went through me like electricity. "Am I mistaken?" said I, "or is it really the voice of Joseph Smith?" This is my testimony, it was not only the voice of Joseph, but there were the features, the gestures and even the *stature* of Joseph there before us in the person of Brigham. And though it may be said that President Young is a complete *mimic*, and can mimic anybody, I would like to see the man who can mimic another *in stature* who was about *four or five inches higher than himself.*—every one who was inspired by the spirit of the Lord, felt it. They knew it. They realized it.

I sat myself down in the midst of the congregation, with my two wives, whom Joseph had given and sealed to me. When President Young began to speak, one of them said: "It is the voice of Joseph! It is Joseph Smith!" The exclamation of the other was,—"I do not see him, where is he?["] Well the thought occurred to my mind respecting the Scripture which President Young has just quoted:—"My sheep know my voice and follow me." Where is the one that recognized the voice of Joseph in President Young? Where is she? She is in the line of her duty. But where is the other? Gone where I wish she were not. The sheep of the good shepherd will follow the voice they know; but they will not follow the voice of a stranger.

Now, this was a manifestation of the power of the Almighty—it was the power of God resting on an individual in the eyes of all the people; not only in feature and voice, but actually in *stature*. This is my testimony. . . . Did it require proof that Joseph was there in the person of Brigham, speaking with an angel's voice? It required no argument; with those who feared God and loved truth, it required none.[37]

At the time our Prophet and Patriarch were killed, or at least soon afterwards, when the Twelve returned to Nauvoo, their immediate circumstances were not altogether agreeable and pleasant or profitable. But suffice it to say we had a meeting, a Conference, at which President Young was the centre of attraction. On his rising to speak, and as soon as he opened his mouth, I heard the voice of Joseph through him, and it was as familiar to me as the voice of my wife, the voice of my child, or the voice of my father. And not only the voice of Joseph did I distinctly and unmistakably hear, but I saw the very gestures of his person, the very features of his countenance, and if I mistake not, the very size of his person appeared on the stand. And it went through me with the thrill of conviction that Brigham was the man to lead this people. And from that day to the present there had not been a query or a doubt upon my mind with regard to the divinity of his appointment; I know that he was the man selected of God to fill the position he now holds.[38]

36. William Hyde

September 11, 1818–March 2, 1874, age 25

On Thursday, August the 8th, I attended a special conference in Nauvoo. Elder Rigdon addressed the assembly in the forenoon. Elder Rigdon sought, as he expressed it, the guardianship of the Church, but it was plainly manifest that the Spirit of the Lord had withdrawn from him, and that he sought that which did not belong to him. From the time the saints were driven from Missouri he had evidently been on the background, and had not walked up to his station, and on one occasion I heard Joseph Smith say that he had carried Elder Rigdon on his back long enough, and then turning to the Twelve said that if they did not help him at that time in shaking him off, the time would come when they would have to do, and that without his, Joseph's assistance. And on Thursday, the 8th of August, was this saying of the Prophet brought home with weight to my mind.

In the afternoon President Brigham Young came upon the stand and addressed the vast multitude of anxious listeners as follows: "For the first time the Twelve walk up to the stand in their place, we have walked by sight and not by faith. The Church had had the privilege of coming to Joseph and of receiving, but now he has stepped to the other side of the veil. He loved the Church even unto death, and laid down his life for it." President Young then asked the following questions: "Do you want to choose a person to lead you into the Kingdom, if so manifest it." All were silent. "If there is any person present that wishes to draw away [a] party after them let them rise." But no one rose. "I have wanted," said President Young, "to fast thirty days, and clothe my house in mourning, but it seems that the saints are determined to drive business. They are not willing to wait and let everything come in its place, but business must be driven, and as it falls to my lot to speak, I shall speak in plainess. Do you want President Rigdon to take Joseph's place, if so take him. Here are the Twelve. Have my knees ever faltered, have these hands ever slackened?" "No." and "No." said voices from all directions. "[T]he Twelve hold the keys and are in authority equal with the First President when the first is absent. Do you want to choose a trustee in trust to take Joseph's place, if so the Twelve must ordain him, for the power rests in them, and in them alone, the Church cannot do it. . . ."

And then he said that if Elder Rigdon wanted to be a spokesman for Joseph, let him go to the other side of the veil. "Who," said he, "ever heard of such a thing as a person on one side of the veil acting as a spokesman for a person on the other side." The President further stated that no person could stand between Joseph and the Twelve. And then turning to the people, said it was their place to rise up and help roll on the Kingdom. "But let us not undertake anything new, let us follow the law and not undertake to divide the Priesthood one hair."

Elders P. P. Pratt and Amasa Lyman made some very appropriate remarks, confirming what President Young had said. . . .

President Young again arose and spoke concerning the endowments of the Elders. Said that if they did not get them in the Temple, they should have them if they had to receive them in the wilderness, for the Devil could not cheat them out of them. He then called upon the saints to know if they would receive the Twelve and let them stand in their place as the First Presidency of the Church in the absense of Joseph. The vote was unanimous in the affirmative. On this day it was plainly manifest that the mantle of Joseph had rested upon President Young. The voice of the same spirit by which he, Joseph, spake was this day sounded in our ears, so much so that I once, unthoughtedly, raised my head to see if it was not actually Joseph addressing the assembly. The assembly was dismissed by President Young after being blessed in the name of the Lord.[39]

37A and 37B. Rachel Ridgeway Ivins

March 7, 1821–January 27, 1909, age 23

After the Prophet's death when Sidney Rigdon came to Nauvoo and spoke, he thought that it was his right and privilege to be President of the Church. President Young jumped right up on the seat and spoke. If you had had your eyes shut, you would have thought it was the Prophet [Joseph]. In fact he looked like him, his very countenance seemed to change, and he spoke like him.[40]

In a letter, President Heber J. Grant recorded the following about his mother's mantle testimony:

I read [Ezra Clark's] testimony of the transfiguration . . . of Brigham Young at the time that Sidney Rigdon tried to claim appointment as the guardian of the Church, representing the Prophet Joseph, and how Brigham Young spoke with the voice, and used the gestures, and had the personal appearance of Joseph Smith. I am grateful that my mother was present and had the same testimony which she often gave in public.[41]

38A and 38B. Benjamin Franklin Johnson

July 28, 1818–November 18, 1905, age 26

Of Brigham Young as President of the Church, I will again bear this as a faithful testimony that I do know and bear record that upon the head of Brigham Young as chief, with the Apostleship in full, was by the voice of the Prophet Joseph, in my hearing, laid the full responsibility of bearing of the Kingdom of God to all the world. And I do further bear this as a testimony, faithful and true, to the Church and to all the world that at a conference of the whole Church, at Nauvoo, subsequent to the Prophet's death and before the return of the absent Apostles, that I sat in the assembly near President Rigdon, closely attentive to his appeal to the conference to recognize and sustain his claim as "Guardian for the Church." And was, perhaps, to a degree, forgetful of what I knew to be the rights and duties of the apostleship, and as he closed his address and sat down, my back was partly turned to the seats occupied by Apostle Brigham Young and other Apostles, when suddenly, and as from Heaven, I heard the voice of the Prophet Joseph, that thrilled my whole being, and quickly turning around I saw in the transfiguration of Brigham Young, the tall, straight and portly form of the Prophet Joseph Smith, clothed in a sheen of light, covering him to his feet; and I heard the real and perfect voice of the Prophet, even to the whistle, as in years past caused by the loss of a tooth said to have been broken out by a mob at Hyrum. This vision, or view, although but for seconds, was to me a vivid and real as the glare of lightening or the voice of thunder from the heavens, and so deeply was I impressed with what I saw and heard in the transfiguration, that for years I dared not tell what was given me of the Lord to see. But when in later years I did publicly bear this testimony, I found that others had testified to having seen and heard the same. But to what proportion of the congregation that were present, I could never know. But I do know this, my testimony is true.

The Prophet's lost tooth, to which I allude, was, as generally understood, broken out by the mob at Hyrum while trying to pry open his mouth to strangle him with acid, from which time, until the tooth was replaced by a dentist neighbor, a year or two previous to his death, there had been a whistle-like sound accompanying all his public speaking which I again plainly heard at the time of which I write.

And while I do know that Brigham Young, as President of the Church, was the right man in the right place, and a great leader for Israel, I still know that he never claimed to be perfect in all his ways, but that, like his brethren, he at times was liable to mistakes.[42]

At the time of the martyrdom all the Quorum of the Twelve were absent except John Taylor and Dr. Richards, both of whom were with the Prophet in the Carthage jail, and Sidney Rigdon having retained a partial fellowship as one of Joseph's counselors, came forward claiming the right of Guardian of the Church. James J. Strang also claimed through a spurious revelation purporting to be through the Prophet that he should lead the Church. And so matters stood until the return of the Twelve, when a conference was assembled, and President Rigdon was called upon to put forth his claim before the people, which he did, and after closing his remarks, which were void of all power or influence, President Brigham Young arose and spoke. I saw him arise, but as soon as he spoke I jumped upon my feet, for in every possible degree it was Joseph's voice, and his person, in look, attitude, dress and appearance was Joseph himself, personified; and I knew in a moment the spirit and mantle of Joseph was upon him. Then I remembered his saying to the Council of which Sidney Rigdon was never a member, and I knew for myself who was now the leader of Israel.[43]

39. Dan Jones

August 4, 1811–January 3, 1862, age 33

They [the Apostles] returned to Nauvoo as soon as they heard; and on the 8th of August an assembly was held in Nauvoo to organize things for the future, and to bring into effect the measures arranged through Joseph Smith; but primarily for the apostles to stand in their proper place at the head of the church on earth, in the absence of their former leaders. There were between twelve and fifteen thousand Saints gathered there. . . . Brigham Young, Orson Hyde, P. P. Pratt, and others addressed the crowd warmly and effectively, so that everyone perceived that the mantle of the prophet had truly fallen on the apostles; and the whole crowd without exception manifested their approval of the apostles as leaders of the church by raising their right hand.[44]

40. Jacob Jones

April 26, 1835–March 17, 1926, age 9

Just before we had to leave Nauvoo, my father took me in to the Temple and I well remember almost everything about the Temple. I remember Sidney Rigdon, and I was present at the meeting when the mantle of the Prophet Joseph fell upon Brigham Young. When Brigham Young began to speak, we all felt that he was the chosen one to succeed the Prophet Joseph. You could just feel that he was the divinely appointed leader to lead this people.[45]

41. Zadoc Knapp Judd

October 15, 1827–January 28, 1909, age 16

Right here I might relate another circumstance that to me was a sufficient testimony of the truth of the Gospel. I had for years been more or less acquainted with the Prophet Joseph Smith. I had many many times heard him preach; had heard him talk with others in common conversation. I had known his voice as well as I do that of my most intimate friend. . . . [T]his circumstance I am going to relate happened late in the fall or early winter. The people had usually convened for meeting [in] a little grove near the temple. A bowery had been built, and seats arranged to accommodate all. . . . In the meantime the building of the temple had progressed; the roof was on, the windows were in, the floor was laid, but no seats arranged. It was very cold, wet Sunday and a drizzling rain. The meeting had been adjourned from the grove to the temple for there people could get shelter. While waiting for the people to gather and also for the hour of meeting, Brigham Young, Heber C. Kimball and some others of the quorum of the twelve had come to an upper room or kind of gallery and seemed to be passing and repassing an open door and window and from the position I had chosen, which was next to the wall and near the stand, I could see them very plainly, and although I knew Joseph was dead, I could scarcely make myself believe he was not there. His [Brigham's] look, his motion, his walk, were precisely like that of Joseph and yet it was Brigham Young, and when he came and commenced to speak to the people his voice was like that of Joseph's.

In the meantime people had gathered in and standing, huddled close together, made such an immense weight on the floor that the propping under the center gave way and let the floor settle a few inches, which caused a panic among the people and some tried to rush for the door, but the loud voice of the prophet Joseph soon restored quiet and only a few were hurt by being pushed down and stepped on. No damage was done, only a few broken windows.

The change of voice and appearance I could not account for only that the mantle of Joseph had fallen on Brigham Young.[46]

42. George Laub

October 5, 1814–November 14, 1877, age 29

Now after the death of Br. Joseph & Hyrum, Sidney Rigdon having A mision appointed him by Joseph to Pittsburg before his death. Now after his death Sidney came in all the hast[e] in him to Nauvoo from Pittsburg to claime the presidency of the church, him not knowing that Joseph Sent him out of the way to get r[i]d of him. Now when he returned to Nauvoo he called all the people to gether to choos them a guardian, as he Expressed himself. Now, Said he, the Church is 14 years old and it was the duty of the church to choose a guardien & preached there for Two days on that subject of guardinism & the Lords way was not as mans ways, But as the heavens are hier than the earth So are the Lords ways above mans ways, etc. Just about the time that the Vote was to be taken for him to be president & guardien, But as the Lord would have the Twelve to come home & I felt to praise God to See Bro Brigham Young walk upon the stand then. Thes[e] positive Revelations of Rigdon's ware only guess So, & he thinks So & hoap so, while the lord had told him how to proseed before according to his one [own] mouth & after wards ony Suposed them so.

Now when President Young arose to address the congregation his Voice was the Voice of Bro. Joseph and his face appeared as Joseph's face, & Should I not have seen his face but herd his Voice I Should have declared that it was Joseph.[47]

43. Wandle Mace

February 19, 1809–August 10, 1890, age 35

Upon arriving in Nauvoo he—Sidney—immediately appointed a meeting for the people to choose a Guardian for the church. Fortunately the Twelve with the President Brigham Young, arrived in time to attend this meeting.—Sidneys intentions was to hold this meeting before the Twelve arrived.—

The meeting was held according to appointment, Sidney Rigdon addressing us, giving his views upon our situation and called upon the people to choose a Guardian or trustee for the church, but there seemed to be no spirit of the Gospel in his remarks, and it was evident to all that he was not dictated by the Holy Ghost.

A Meeting was appointed or rather continued as a Special Conference and in the afternoon and President Brigham Young addressed the people. At this meeting the soieit [spirit] was truly manifest inasmuch it seemed that Joseph himself was addressing us, the voice, the countenance was Joseph. The mantle of Joseph had indeed fallen upon Brigham Young. There was no dubiaty now, if there had been any before, who held the power. All could see and bore testimony that the spirit had manifested to them that Brigham Young was the right man, and he was in the right place. Said Joseph with his hands upon the head of Brigham Young, in the house of John P. Green at quincy, "While you live no other man can occupy this place."

. . . President Brigham Young gave his views of the present situation of the church, now our Prophet and patriarch is taken from our midst. He said,

". . . While the Prophet lived, we walked by 'sight' he is taken from us, and we must now walk by 'faith.'" After he had explained matters so satisfactory that every Saint present could see that as aforetime the—mantle of Elijah fell upon Elisha—so also fell the mantle or the spirit and power which Joseph held in his life time had fallen upon Brigham Young as President of the Twelve, which was the hightest Quorum, and holding the highest—or first Presidency—of the Church of God upon the earth.[48]

44. Philemon Christopher Merrill

1820–1904, age 24

Sad was the day that the Saints met by a call of the Apostles in a Grove, east of our beloved Temple which was unfinished, to listen to what might be said. For where was the good Shepherd? We were left alone as we thought, with none to lead us. It was a gloomy time. Sidney Rigdon talked to us and said we were of age, choose our guardian and he offered himself as that one to lead the Church but it did not satisfy the people. But when President Brigham Young arose and said to the people, "Stand still and see the Salvation of the Lord," the Spirit of God rested upon me, and I received a testimony at that time that upon Brigham Young rested the Authority of the Holy Priesthood.[49]

45. Elmira Pond Miller

February 14, 1811–September 3, 1904, age 33

We [Elmira and her husband, Henry] were there [at home, four miles from Carthage] when Joseph and Hyrum were shot. Did not hear of it till next morning. I could not describe my feelings. It had not entered into my mind that our enemies would take the life of our Prophet. It seemed a dark day to be left without a leader; But when Brother Brigham returned and spoke to the Saints it was plainly manifest that the same spirit rested on him that was on Bro. Joseph.[50]

Henry William Miller

May 1, 1807–October 9, 1885, age 37

See Elmira Pond Miller.

46. George Morris

August 24, 1816–June 27, 1897, age 27

Sidney Rigdon set up his Clame as Guardain of the Church—Saying that it was not of Age to do Buisness for itself being Only about 14 years of Age—and as he was the next in athoraty to Joseph—it was his Duty to act as Guardain for it untill it was Old enough to do Business for itself—on the 5th [*sic*] of Augast 1844 a special meeting was apointed for the Church to come together to here what he had to say upon the subject—he ocupied the time in the forenoon.—in the afternoon Presedent Young arose to reply to what he had said—and when he arose to speak I was sitting right Before Him holding down my Head—reflecting about what Rigdon had said—when I was startled by Earing Josephs Voice—he had a way of Clearing his Throat before he began to speak—by a peculier Effort of His own—like Ah-hem—I raised my Head sudinly—and the first thing I saw was Joseph—as plain as I ever saw Him in my life—and the first words he uttered whare, Right here—is the Athoraty to Lead This Church—and at the same time srikeing his hand upon his Bosam and, after uttering another sentance or two—it was Brigham Young—That was Testemony anough to Convince me where the Proper athoraty rested.[51]

47. Joseph Stacy Murdock

June 26, 1822–February 15, 1899, age 22

I went with Brother Joseph Smith when he was on the way to Carthage Jail. I went in among the horses and held onto his pants and begged to go with him. . . . His remains were brought to Nauvoo and the people in sorrow witnessed the scene in mourning for the Prophet of the Lord. Times rolled on until Brother Brigham Young came forward and took the stand in Nauvoo. I seen Brigham transfigured into the image of Joseph Smith. The teeth out of his mouth, that the mob broke of Brother Joseph's when they undertook to turn [poison] down him, was a testimony to me that the Lord had placed the rolling on of the Great Latter-day work upon Brigham Young. I heard Brother Joseph Smith call the calling of this great Latter-day work upon the Twelve Apostles with Brigham Young at the head. From this time, Brother Brigham had control of the Latter-day Saints.[52]

48. William Bryam Pace

February 9, 1832–June 18, 1907, age 12

Sidney Rigdon spent, what seemed to me several hours, harrangueing the people on the importance of making him their Leader, after which, Brigham Young arose and said only a word, when it was observed by the whole congregation that the mantle of "Joseph" was upon him, in word, gesture and general appearance.

The people arose en-masse to their feet astonished, as it appeared that Joseph had returned and was speaking to the people.

I was small and got upon a bench that I might more fully witness the "Phenonomia."

There was no longer any question as to who was the Leader.[53]

49. George Patten

October 8, 1825, or October 26, 1828–February 16, 1914, age 15

I was acquainted with the Prophet Joseph Smith, and saw him in death, and one of the strongest testimonies I ever had of the truth of this Latter-day work was when President Young got up before the people and the spirit of the Prophet [Joseph] rested upon him, and his countenance resembled the Prophet, and his voice sounded like the Prophet's, so the Lord showed the people who and where the leader was for there were several clamoring as to their right to lead the church. "The mantle which our prophet wore was sought for by a half a score." But God knew the very man so therefore it fell upon Brigham Young, and with few exceptions, the people went to their homes rejoicing and contented.[54]

50. William Wines Phelps

February 17, 1792–March 6, 1878, age 52

"Israel Reigns" [verse two]—tune "Dixie"

We love the words of the prophet Joseph,
While the gentile only knows of
War and wo; war and wo; war and wo,
Israel reigns;

Up, up! ye royal priesthood holders,
Joseph's robe's on Brigham's shoulders,
Clear the way; clear the way; clear the way,
Israel reigns.[55]

51. Nathan Tanner Porter

July 10, 1820–April 9, 1897, age 24

It was now a matter of question with Some as to who Should lead the Church, which caused mutch comment in private circles, and many conjectures to arrise in the minds of the People, as to who was the Legitemate Successor in the Presidency of the Church. As Sidney Rigdon had preseeded the Twelve in his return from the East & claimed that it was his right, in deavering to get the People together for the purpose of rattifying his claims by their voice. But the Twelve having returned before this was accomplished Brigham Young Being the President of the Quorum appointed a special Conference of the whole Church, at which it was vissably made manifest to the most if not all present That he was chosen of God to stand in Josephs Stead in moving on the cause of Zion[.] For as he arose & began to speak to the People he was transfigured into Josephs likeness in looks appearance & the sound of his voice so that a low whisper ran through the vast Assembly—thats Joseph—thats Joseph while the eyes of the multitude became fastened upon him with wonder & astonishment. this prodused a firm conviction in the minds of the People beyond all doubt that he was the Man and thus he was incorporated by a unaminous voice of all present with Heber C Kimble & Willard Richards as his Councilloors[.] I being in attendence was also an eye witness to this marvelous manifestation.[56]

52. John Pulsipher

July 17, 1827–August 9, 1891, age 17

I have been with the Prophet Joseph and heard his instruction weekly and sometimes daily. The last time I heard him speak in public he spoke to the Legion. After telling over what he had passed thru and what he had suffered from men because he preached the Gospel of Jesus Christ, He says: from my boyhood up to the present time I have been hunted like a roe upon the mountains. I have never been allowed to live like other men. I have been driven, chased, stoned, whipped, robbed, mobbed, imprisoned, persecuted, accused falsely of everything bad. I have suffered till the Lord knows I have suffered enough.

After the death of Joseph, Sidney Rigdon came and sought to place himself at the head of the church. By his flattery he deceived many. Just before he called a vote of the public congregation, Brigham Young the president of the Twelve, arrived from his mission. This was a joyful meeting. The faithful knew not that Joseph had ordained Brother Brigham and the Twelve to lead the church but they knew that the Twel[v]e were the next quorum in authority. They that served the Lord faithful were not deceived. I went to [the] meeting where the church met in the grove east of the Temple where President Brigham Young arose and spoke and behold he spoke with the voice of Joseph. The very moment I heard him speak (august 8th) I thought of Joseph and from that time on his voice sounded like Joseph's and from that time the church generally were satisfied that the mantle of Joseph was on Brigham. Notwithstanding all this, Sidney Rigdon, James J. Strang, Lyman Wight, James Emmet and others led away many people from the church.[57]

53. Zerah Pulsipher

June 24, 1789–January 1, 1872, age 55

At this time the mob expected we should rise and give them battle; we thought best not to do it. We just kept still and continued our work on the Temple, finished it and got our End[owments]. But at that time most of the 12 were absent on missions. Sidney Rigdon, who aspired for the Presidency came and called the church together and presented his claim for the Presidency. But the 12 soon came home and appeared on the stand at the day appointed for choosing. Sidney made his plea. Brigham Young began to speak and at that time I sat with my back towards the stand as did many others. And when Brigham spoke he spoke with the voice of Joseph and we turned around to see Brigham speaking in Joseph's voice and behold Joseph's mantle had fallen on him. The people understood it in the same way. Brigham stood at the head of the Twelve therefore the church turned to him.[58]

54A and 54B. Jane Snyder Richards

January 31, 1823–November 17, 1912, age 21

Upon the return of the Apostles and Elders a meeting was called and by a unanimous vote Brigham Young was chosen President as he stood on the stand he said he felt as though he would rather sit in sack cloth and ashes for a month than appear before the people. But then loneliness seemed to require somebody to step forward and he felt constrained to do so. And we knew he was [to be president] because he had the voice and manner of Joseph at the time as hundreds can testify.[59]

After his [Joseph's] tragic death I attended the meeting at which President Brigham Young addressed the Saints, and saw his face illuminated and appear as the face of Joseph while the voice of Joseph seemed to address the people through the mouth of Brigham. I can never forget the divine thrill that passed through the audience on that occasion and the impression that the appearance and voice of Joseph produced upon his hearers.[60]

Maria Wealthy Wilcox Richards

See Maria Wealthy Wilcox.

55A and 55B. George Romney

August 14, 1831–February 1 or 2, 1920, age 12

Well, the time came when the Twelve returned to Nauvoo. They called a meeting in the Bowery, and Sidney Rigdon with all the eloquence possible for a man to have, spoke for one hour and a half, but when he sat down, Brigham Young got up, and I testify to you in all fervor, before God, that the mantle of Joseph Smith fell upon Brigham Young. It was Joseph's voice; absolutely Joseph's voice and manner, as Brigham Young addressed the people and told them who should be their leader. Now this is no fiction; this is true as I stand here after so many years, passing from the year 1844 up to the present time.[61]

They were children as it were; and when the man of God, as the people knew him, was taken away they did not know what would become of them. That was the condition we were in—sorrow and anguish for the loss of that man. I said the people were all children. But they knew the shepherd's voice. Sidney Rigdon and the others said, "I am the man, I am the man" but it did not take. The sheep knew better. And when the Twelve returned from the east, I shall never forget in this world or in the world to come the scene as Brigham Young arose after Sidney Rigdon had used up an hour and a half delivering an eloquent discourse. When Brigham got up the mantle of Joseph Smith fell upon him. It was Joseph's voice; it was Joseph's appearance, and I testify to you, if I never again do so on this earth, in the presence of God and angels, that this is verily the truth. This is true—that the mantle of Joseph did fall upon Brigham Young and the people knew it.[62]

56. Job Taylor Smith

December 2, 1828–January 3, 1913, age 15

Sometime during this week in August Sidney Rigdon returned and called the people together to listen to his oratory and special claims. I heard all his discourses and they were lengthy and to the point that the father of the church was dead and needed a guardian and that he was the man to fill that position.

But on the 8th of August the apostles appeared on the stand, having very recently returned from the east. And to me it was a sensation. President Brigham Young arose to speak and every eye was turned towards him, and as he spoke I fancied it was the prophet's voice speaking through him, I scarcely remember much that he said in the way of reasoning, but the ring of his voice will never cease from my memory as he uttered aloud the words, "If you wish to know who is the president of the church of Jesus Christ of Latter-Day Saints it is I." Historians have given his remarks in full, but I merely write from memory. I also remember his coupling with the motion to sustain the twelve apostles as the presiding authority of the church, the further carrying out of the measures of the prophet in finishing the building of the temple and giving the people their endowments. The votes for these measures were given heartily, for the sheep know the shepherd's voice, and a stranger, or one weakened in time of trouble they would not follow.[63]

57. Abraham Owen Smoot

February 17, 1815–March 5, 1895, age 29

I was present at the meeting held in Nauvoo on the occasion when President Young assumed leadership of the Church, and can testify with hundreds of others that he spoke by the power of God on that occasion and that he had the very voice and appearance of Joseph Smith.[64]

58. Margaret Thompson McMeans Adkinson Smoot

April 16, 1809–September 1, 1884, age 35

I was present upon the occasion when the Twelve Apostles with Pres Brigham Young at their head, took the presidency of the church by the unanimous vote of all Israel there assembled and personally witnessed the supernatural power shown through Brigham Young. And was firmly convinced that he was the legitimate successor to the Martered Prophet. And was as ready and willing from that moment to obey his council, and receive his Revelations, as I was those of Joseph Smith.[65]

Eunice Billings Warner Snow

See Eunice Billings.

59. Warren Stone Snow

June 15, 1818–September 19 or 20, 1896, age 26

For Sidney Rigdon rose up and asserted his right to be the guardian of the church. I was at the meeting when President Brigham Young stood up and I saw the mantle of Joseph rest upon him and I heard the voice of Joseph and had I not known that Joseph was dead I should say that was Joseph speaking and this convinced me that I was in the right channel for truth.[66]

60. William C. Staines

September 26, 1818–August 3, 1881, age 25

After this [a speech from Sidney Rigdon lasting about one and a half hours] President Young stated he had listened to all that had been said by the speaker. . . . But as the subject had been broached and the people would be anxious to know something about those who would lead, he said in a loud voice: "I will tell you who your leaders or guardians will be—The Twelve! I at their head!" This was with a voice like the voice of the Prophet Joseph. I thought it was his, and so did the thousands who heard it.[67]

61. Mary Ann Stearns

April 6, 1833–April 2, 1912, age 11

I was at the great meeting when the mantle of Brother Joseph rested upon Brigham Young until his whole being seemed changed and his voice was like that of the Prophet. The people around me, rising to their feet to get a better chance to hear and see, I and my little companion of the day, Julia Felshaw, being small of stature, stood upon the benches that we, too might behold the wonderful transformation, and I know that from that time on the power of that change remained with Brother Brigham Young as long as he lived on earth. The faithful and honest hearted were quick to discern the right and took up the armor of the Gospel anew, rallied round the faithful Brigham whose rightful leadership had been plainly shown to them.[68]

62. Catherine Thomas

March 17, 1834–September 15, 1927, age 10

The Saints were soon called to the Temple and the great question as to who should be their Leader was settled. Then Brigham Young was chosen to fill the vancancy of our beloved Prophet. I saw Brother Young rise to take his place as President of our Church and testify that he appeared to me and others to be Joseph the Prophet himself in person and voice, and I exclaimed "Oh, the Prophet Joseph is Resurrected." My sister Rachel said "No, that is Brother Brigham Young."[69]

63A and 63B. Nancy Naomi Alexander Tracy

1814–1902, age 30

We bore faithful testimony to our relatives and in the spring, bid our friends [in the East] farewell to return again to our home in Nauvoo. We landed at the City of the Saints about the middle of April, on Sunday morning. But oh, how lonely it seemed, our Prophet and Patriarch was not among the Saints in person, but that day his spirit rested upon Brigham Young, and as the mantle of Elijah fell upon Elisha, so the mantle of Joseph fell upon Brigham. It seemed that the voice and every gesture was like Joseph, and he was sustained as the prophet, seer and revelator by the voice of the people.[70]

As soon as we arrived, we went right home and prepared to go to meeting for that day was appointed for us to choose a first presidency to lead the Church. The saints convened in a grove. Sidney Rigdon and his followers were on hand to contest their right to be the leaders of the Saints. At one time he was one of Brother Josephs councilors, but he was not righteous, and Joseph shook him off saying that the [*sic*] had carried him long enough and he would carry him no longer. Therefore, it was out of the question to have such a man lead the people.

Brigham Young was the man chosen and sustained by unanimous vote to be the mouthpiece of God to the Saints. I can testify that the mantle of Joseph fell upon Brigham that day as that of Elijah did fall upon Elisha, for it seemed that his voice, his gestures, and all were Joseph. It seemed that we had him again with us. He was sustained by the voice of the people to be the prophet, seer, and revelator.[71]

64. William Lampard Watkins

February 7, 1827–September 18, 1911, age 17

A meeting was appointed for August 8th by which time Brigham Young and most of the other apostles had returned home. It was at this meeting Sidney Rigdon made a lengthy and tedious speech presenting his claims, telling the people what wonderful things he had planned for them.

It was a solemn time for he was a man who on account of his experience and talents had been sustained as Joseph's counselor by the people, although contrary to the Prophet's wish for some time past, but the darkness was soon dispelled, for Brigham Young explained before the people on that day, the order of the Priesthood. He was filled with the power of the Holy Ghost. He stood before the people as the Prophet Joseph Smith often had done and we heard the voice of the true shepherd, for he spoke with the voice of Joseph. His manner and appearance were like unto Joseph's and it was manifested to all those present upon whom the responsibility rested to carry on the work of God and lead the Saints.

I sat in that assembly and did not realize for a time but that I was still listening to the Prophet Joseph, so great and marvelous was the manner in which the manifestation before the entire congregation was made, that when the proposition was placed before the people to decide whom they would sustain as the leader of the church, the twelve apostles with Brigham Young as their President were almost unanamously sustained. This circumstance, although the Saints were in deep trouble and filled with sorrow for the condition in which they were placed brought a great relief and gave joy to the Saints for they realized that God was still mindful of them.[72]

65. John Welch

January 6, 1823–November 8, 1910, age 21

I, John Welch, being of mature years desire to leave to my friends and descendants the following statement:

. . . I was babtized into the Church of Jesus Christ of Latter-day Saints in the year 1841; emigrated to Nauvoo, Ill., in 1843 and to Salt Lake City in the year 1852. I was well acquainted with the Prophet Joseph Smith and heard him speak both in public and private many times. I was present at the meeting in the grove at Nauvoo August 8th, 1844, when Sidney Rigdon made the claim. . . . I saw Brigham Young, then President of the Twelve Apostles, stand up to speak to the people and he spoke with the voice of Joseph Smith; and I further declare and testify that he, Brigham Young, had the appearance of the Prophet Joseph Smith while he, Young, was talking; that I was convinced then, and have never doubted in all the intervening years from that time up to the present, that Brigham Young was the right man and the man chosen of God to lead the Church.

Signed, John Welch
Sworn before
A. L. Farrell,
County Clerke, Cache Co, Utah[73]

Eliza Ann Haven Westover

See Eliza Ann Haven.

66. Helen Mar Kimball Whitney

August 25, 1828–November 15, 1896, age 15

I can bear witness, with hundreds of others who stood that day under the sound of Brigham's voice, of the wonderful and startling effect that it had upon us. If Joseph had risen from the dead and stood before them, it could hardly have made a deeper or more lasting impression. It was the very voice of Joseph himself. This was repeatedly spoken of by the Latter-day Saints. And surely it was a most powerful and convincing testimony to them that he was the man, instead of Sidney Rigdon, that was destined to become the "great leader," and upon whose shoulders the mantle of Joseph had fallen.[74]

67. Maria Wealthy Wilcox

June 17, 1827–January 13, 1909, age 17

I well remember the Sunday morning when the sorrowing saints were gathered together, in the little grove where they were accustomed to meet. Sidney Rigdon presented his claim as successor to the Prophet Joseph, making quite an impression upon the people; but Brigham Young, President of the Apostles, had just returned to Nauvoo, from his mission, in time to attend the afternoon meeting, and in a voice not unlike the Prophet's, he told the people that although the Prophet Joseph was dead, Joseph had left behind the Keys of the Kingdom, and had conferred the same power, and authority that he himself possessed upon the Twelve Apostles, and that the Church would not be left without a leader and a guide. Truly the mantle of Joseph had fallen upon Brigham, and he spoke with power, even to the convincing of the saints, assuring them that they had nothing to fear, as all would yet be well, if they would harken to the Word of God, and to the counsel of his servants, and keep his commandments.[75]

Mary Ann Stearns Winters

See Mary Ann Stearns.

68A, 68B, and 68C. Wilford Woodruff

March 1, 1807–September 2, 1898, age 37

In an address published in February 1845, Wilford Woodruff shared the mantle news with "[Church] officers and members" in England by assuring them that

On the second day after our arrival August 8th, 1844, we met in a special conference, all the quorums, authorities, and members of the Church that could assemble in Nauvoo. They were addressed by elder Brigham Young, the president of the quorum of the twelve. It was evident to the Saints that the mantle of Joseph had fallen upon him, the road that he pointed out could be seen so plainly, that none need err therein; the spirit of wisdom and counsel attended all his teachings, he struck upon a chord, with which all hearts beat in unison.[76]

I know this work is of God. I know Joseph Smith was a prophet of God. I have heard two or three of the brethren testify about Brother Young in Nauvoo. Every man and every woman in that assembly, which perhaps might number thousands, could bear the same testimony. I was there, the Twelve were there, and a good many others, and all can bear the same testimony. The question might be asked why was the appearance of Joseph Smith given to Brigham Young? Because here was Sidney Rigdon and other men rising up and claiming to be the leaders of the Church; and men stood, as it were, on a pivot, not knowing which way to turn. But just as quick as Brigham Young rose in that assembly, his face was that of Joseph Smith—the mantle of Joseph had fallen upon him, the power of God that was upon Joseph Smith was upon him; he had the voice of Joseph, and it was the voice of the shepherd. There was not a person in that assembly, Rigdon, himself, not excepted, but was satisfied in his own mind that Brigham was the proper leader of the people, for he [Rigdon] would not have his name presented, by his own consent, after that sermon was delivered. There was a reason for this in the mind of God: it convinced the people. They saw and heard for themselves, and it was by the power of God.[77]

I do not know if there is any one present here tonight but myself who was there at that conference. There are but few living who were present on that occasion . . . and when Brigham arose and commenced speaking, as has been said, if my eyes had not been so I could see, if I had not seen him with my own eyes, there is no one that could have convinced me that it was not Joseph Smith.[78]

Secondhand Accounts

This section contains secondhand accounts of the mantle experience. These accounts concern people who reported a personal mantle experience but did not record their own story. Their oral testimonies were recorded later by others, usually family members. Other accounts in this section come from firsthand diaries that are unavailable to the author of this paper; in these cases, secondary sources have been cited. As with the firsthand accounts, these accounts list each person's name, birth and death dates, age in August 1844, and testimony, including sources, and appropriate notes. Women are listed under the name they had in August 1844.

69. Sally Adams

May 29, 1825–February 15, 1905, age 19

"I well remember that June day of 1844, when the announcement reached Nauvoo that the Prophet and Patriarch had been killed by a cruel mob. The news fell like a thunderbolt upon the Saints. Their grief was indescribable. Many thought he, like the Savior, would rise again to become their leader. . . . The memory of the occasion can never be erased. This sad occurrence marks the culmination of the devil inspired persecutions of two of God's greatest and truest noblemen."

Sally told of being at the meeting on August 8, 1844, when Brigham Young spoke in the voice of the martyred Prophet. He assumed the form and appearance of Joseph, so that the thousands at the meeting believed for the moment that President Smith actually stood before them.[79]

70. Abigail Jane Daley Andrus

January 26, 1815–October 27, 1894, age 29

Abigail and Milo pressed on in whatever was asked of them during that turbulent time. They were both present at the meeting where the transfiguration of Brigham Young occurred. Both saw and felt the miracle and Abigail was startled to hear Br. Brigham state that they would be leaving Nauvoo for the wilderness.[80]

Milo Andrus

March 6, 1814–June 19, 1893, age 30

See Abigail Jane Daley Andrus.

71. Truman Osborn Angell

June 5, 1810–October 16, 1887, age 34

Not only did Truman Angell neglect to record much about his personal and professional life during this period, but he also wrote little of the larger historical events occurring around him. He mentions only that he "suffered much—in common with the rest of my Brethern—during the persecutions in which the Prophet and Patriarch lost their lives." Angell's loyalty lay with the Apostles in the aftermath of this tragedy. "Although the Prophet Joseph and Hyrum Smith had lost their lives by mob violence," he writes, "the Twelve Apostles came forward, with Brigham Young at their head, and the mantle of Joseph was upon them in all that was done."[81]

72. Elizabeth Haven Barlow

December 28, 1811–December 25, 1892, age 32

When Brigham Young, the President of the Twelve, began speaking I saw a change come over him—saw him take on the form of Joseph Smith and heard his voice change to that of the Prophet's. Thousands in that assembly testified to the same thing. From that moment forward I knew whom the Lord had chosen. So did all the true Latter Day Saints. The crowd felt that the Lord had not forsaken them.[82]

73. Eli Bennett

November 26, 1831–October 14, 1906, age 13

Eli had been in Nauvoo at the time Joseph and Hyrum Smith had been murdered. He was at the meeting to decide who would be the next leader of the Church. He stated that when Brigham Young walked into the meeting "he walked like the Prophet; his voice and gestures were those of Joseph. . ." This manifestation of the mantle of the Prophet falling upon Brigham Young made a deep impression upon the mind of this boy, not yet 14.[83]

Eliza Ann Perry Benson

See Eliza Ann Perry.

74. Ezra T[aft] Benson

February 22, 1811–September 3, 1869, age 33

When Brother Brigham Young rose before the people and spoke . . . it was very easy to see who possessed the mantle of Joseph. Truly, as Jesus said, "My sheep know my voice, but a stranger they will not follow." For many said, when they heard Brigham talk, that it was not Brigham's voice, but the voice of Joseph.[84]

75. Eliza Billington

December 16, 1825–August 16, 1916, age 18

They [Eliza and her husband, John Welch] were both well acquainted with the Prophet Joseph Smith and his brother, Hyrum, in life and were permitted to view their remains after the martyrdom. John Welch was one of the guards over the bodies as they lay in state. They were both present at the meeting held August 8, 1844, where the mantle of the Prophet fell on Brigham Young, and they knew Brigham Young had been called by Divine Authority and power, and these facts they related many, many times to their children and grandchildren, greatly strengthening and adding to the testimonies of those who listened.[85]

76. William Snow Burgess

May 20, 1794–November 20, 1880, age 50

After the death of the Prophet Joseph Smith, the Church members met in the grove east of the Temple. There Brigham Young spoke, and while he was speaking the Mantle of Joseph Smith fell on him. . . . Even his features and voice were like the Prophet's. . . . So the Saints knew who was to be their leader.[86]

77. Ann Cannon

January 28, 1832–July 25, 1921, age 12

After the prophet's death, I was at the meeting where Sydney Rigdon, standing in a wagon box to make his speech, presented his claim to be guardian of the Church. When Brigham Young presented his claim, the mantle of the prophet rested on him and we knew he was to be the new leader.[87]

78A and 78B. William Van Orden Carbine

February 17, 1835–May 11, 1921, age 9

I was nine years old when the Prophet was martyred. I remember the excitement at that time. The people hardly knew what to do. The Prophet was gone and Sidney Rigdon wanted a guardian put in for the Church. Brother Thomas Grover, one of the High Council, spoke and told the people not to be in a hurry: the Twelve would be home soon and they would tell the people what to do. When Brigham Young came home he held a meeting at which time, the mantle of Joseph fell on him. It was a manifestation to let the people know who was to lead the Church. His looks and ways were like the Prophet. I, as a boy, was quite well accquainted with the Prophet. I was sitting with my mother in the meeting and I thought it was the Prophet and told my mother so. There are a good many who have heard my mother tell this.[88]

Though I was only a boy, I remember it quite distinctly. I told my mother [Adelia] that the Prophet was not dead, for I had seen him on the stand.[89]

79. Albert Carrington

January 8, 1813–September 19, 1889, age 31

In his conference address delivered in the Bowery in Salt Lake City on July 19, 1857, Brigham Young referred to Albert Carrington's mantle experience, which is reported to have taken place during the October conference of 1844:

Do people imagine that they can kill "Mormonism?" I may die for my religion, and who cares for that? Brother Carrington has told you that God can carry on his own work, and the spirit of Joseph which fell upon me [Brigham] is ready to fall upon somebody else when I am removed. . . .

. . . Brother Carrington's testimony proves to you that men's eyes are liable to be deceived. It may appear strange to some that he [Carrington] could not tell me from Joseph Smith, when I was speaking in the stand in Nauvoo during the October Conference of 1844. Somebody came along and passed a finger over his eyes and he could not see any one but Joseph speaking, until I got through addressing the congregation.[90]

80. Talitha Garlik Avery Cheney

September 22, 1824–April 17, 1902, age 19

I was in Nauvoo when Sidney Rigdon came from the east after Brother Joseph and Hyrum were killed to take lead of the church. There were none of the Twelve Apostles at home but Brother Taylor and Brother Richards. Brother Taylor had been badly wounded so Sidney Rigdon thought he would have things his own way, but he was mistaken; he called a meeting and said the church was old enough to choose a guardian for itself, it had been fourteen years since it was organized. But Brother Brigham and the rest of the Apostles got there in time to be at the meeting. After Rigdon sat down Brother Brigham got up and said, "All who want Brother Rigdon to lead them can have him, but I tell you the Keys of the Kingdom are in the hands of the Twelve Apostles. They are the ones to lead this people."

As soon as Brother Brigham got up to speak, I said to myself, "That is the man to take the lead of this people." He looked just like Brother Joseph and spoke like him, I said "Surely the mantle of the Prophet Joseph has fallen on Brother Brigham." I never had a doubt, I knew Brother Brigham was the man to fill the place of our beloved Prophet. I knew Joseph Smith was a true Prophet of God and was the mouthpiece of God to the people and that Brother Brigham was his lawful successor and a man of God.[91]

81. Ezra Thompson Clark

November 23, 1823–October 17, 1901, age 20

When a meeting of the Saints was called to consider leadership, Sidney Rigdon put in a plea for his promotion as president of the Church and gave a two-hour discourse. In the afternoon President Young gave a clarion call to which all hearts responded. In his "Attention All," as he addressed the Saints, he demonstrated his power, his authority, and his masterful leadership. The Saints no longer felt that they had no shepherd. So striking was

Brigham Young's commanding personality, manifesting as it did the same desire as Joseph's to serve the Saints, love them, and lead them to a triumphant accomplishment of the plan which the Lord had revealed for their salvation, that the Saints declared that it was almost as though the Prophet Joseph had returned.

Ezra and his wife were at this meeting. He often referred to the spirit of that gathering and said that it was a strong testimony to the divine calling of Brigham Young.[92]

82. Ellen Spencer Clawson

November 21, 1832–August 24, 1896, age 11

Aurelia Spencer Rogers writes the following concerning her sister Ellen:

My sister Ellen's testimony has also strengthened my faith in the truth of Mormonism, and it seems to me appropriate to give it here, as it may prove a help to others. She was at a meeting of the Saints, held in a grove west of the Temple in Nauvoo, soon after the death of the Prophet Joseph Smith. The question under consideration, who should take the Prophet's place in presiding over the Church. Sidney Rigdon, who had been one of Joseph's Counselors, claimed the right to the position; yet the spirit he manifested was not in accord with the spirit of the Gospel. At this meeting, Brigham Young, who was President of the Quorum of Apostles, arose to speak, when "The Mantle of Joseph" fell upon him, and he was like one transformed; his countenance, voice and form were like those of the late Prophet. Many in the congregation, even children saw this miracle; it satisfied the people and decided the question who was to be the leader. Sister Ellen occasionally referred to this circumstance, and said whenever she was tired, or felt to doubt any of the principles of the Gospel, this testimony came up before her.[93]

83A and 83B. Ada Winchell Clements

December 24, 1801–March 4, 1890, age 42

When Joseph and Hyrum Smith were martyred, Albert [Ada's husband] was away from home, working for the Church interests and also the support of his family. When he heard of the terrible news he immediately started for home. On the way his horse took sick and he stopped at a store to obtain medicine. Here he met his friend Sidney Rigdon. Sidney told Albert he was hurrying back to Nauvoo to be with the Saints during this time of sorrow, and to take his place as their leader. Albert was happy to learn of Mr. Rigdon's decision. On August 15, 1844, Albert arrived home, and Ada immediately told him all that had happened, including the meeting she had attended wherein the Saints had chosen Brigham Young as their leader.[94]

Ada related the events of this meeting. She told Albert how Elder Young had actually sounded and looked like Joseph Smith. Albert was surprised! He inquired about Sidney Rigdon. Ada said he had spoken, but the spirit was not with him. Albert took the side of his friend Sidney Rigdon. This was a sad day for the Clements family. Albert asked Ada if she were going to leave him and go west with Brigham Young? She said she would continue with the Church of Jesus Christ of Latter-Day Saints. However, she said she would always love him and pray for Albert to see the truth.[95]

84. Catherine Stephenson Coreless

December 13, 1807–September 27, 1902, age 36

[John Coreless, a son of Catherine and Edward] was with his parents at the meeting and John said he heard his mother and others say when Brigham Young arose and began to speak, "O! It's Joseph himself."[96]

85. Edward Corless

March 14, 1804–January 18, 1873, age 40

After the opening of this meeting President Brigham Young, President of the Twelve Apostles, spoke on the duties of the Twelve Apostles, and while he was speaking the Mantile of Joseph fell on President Young and he looked like Joseph and he spoke in Joseph's voice, and many thought it was Joseph himself.[97]

86. Sarah Louisa Norris Decker

about 1824–1914, age 20

Not satisfied yet those opposed to us began a series of persecutions; also a great apostacy took place and jealousy arose as to who should lead the Church. Sidney Rigdon, Lyman Wight and Strang had their followers but when a meeting was called and Brigham Young arose and spoke with power, it was as if the Prophet Joseph's very voice spoke through him. I heard my father and mother when they returned from meeting testify to this, and many others since then. I believe it was the largest attended meeting ever held in Nauvoo.[98]

87. Oliver De Mille

March 30, 1830–July 8, 1908, age 14

After talking about a minute, his voice changed to the voice of Joseph, his countenance and every appearance and motion was that of Joseph, and his language was so convincing and prophetic that it seemed to bring conviction to the hears [*sic*] of all who were present.

I was in the meeting and see with my own eyes and heard with my own ears all that was said and done and know for asurety whereof I speak and I lie not.[99]

88. Tamson Parshly Egan

July 27, 1824–March 31, 1905, age 20

After the martyrdom of the Prophet and Patriarch at the time of the return of the Twelve Apostles . . . Mother [Tamson Parshly Egan] saw Brigham Young look like Joseph and speak in his voice at a meeting held Aug. 8th, 1844 showing conclusively where the authority of leadership laid.[100]

Luvera Ellen Ensign

See Luvera Ellen Ensign Preece.

89. Evaline McLean Fisher

December 25, 1805–July 19, 1893, age 38

They [Evaline and her husband, Joseph] were in Nauvoo at the time of the martyrdom of the Prophet Joseph Smith and his brother Hyrum and supposedly was at the meeting when the mantle of the Prophet fell upon Brigham Young.[101]

Joseph Fisher

November 25, 1801–March 21, 1867, age 43

See Evaline McLean Fisher.

90. Mary Elizabeth Grover

April 13, 1833–September 28, 1921, age 11

She then related to me a story about a meeting she attended and tried to impress upon me its importance. In fact, after she told the story once, she repeated it. . . . I am grateful now that she did repeat it, because its importance to her has stayed with me all my life. I remember it as follows:

". . . the prophet was dead. I attended this meeting along with several others. Several men spoke. Brigham Young got up to speak and while he was talking, his voice began to sound like the Prophet Joseph's. His face looked like Joseph's and all who saw this knew that Brigham Young was God's choice to replace the Prophet Joseph as next President of the Church and none of the other men who had spoken. I saw and heard it!"

As she related this story, the tears ran down her wrinkled old face and I knew she spoke the truth.[102]

91A and 91B. Emmeline Blanche Woodward Harris

February 29, 1828–April 25, 1921, age 16

The people were gathered in the grove where there was a rude stand to speak from and very rude benches for the choir and others. The crowd extended through the grove and even outside the trees, many people standing in their wagon boxes, drawn up against the trees, to listen to what was going on. . . . But when Brigham Young rose in the midst of the people, most of them rose to their feet. . . . Well, we all stood on our feet, and as President Young spoke, everyone that had known the Prophet Joseph declared in a loud voice, as loud as they could, almost, that it was the Prophet Joseph himself risen again . . . that it was his voice, his manner, his clothing, himself, that stood there in the midst of the people. Of course this talking after a while subsided, and by and by most of them doubtless realized that it was Brigham Young. But it was a transfiguration real and convincing.[103]

I was standing in a wagon box on wheels, so I did not have to rise, but those who were seated arose and made the exclamation. I could see very well, and every one of them thought it was really the Prophet Joseph risen from the dead. But after Brigham Young had spoken a few words, the tumult subsided, and the people really knew that it was not the Prophet Joseph, but the President of the quorum of the Twelve Apostles. It was the most wonderful manifestation, I think, that I have known or seen, and I have seen a very great number.[104]

92. George Barton Hicks

December 15, 1803–April 2, 1885, age 41

In his journal, George Armstrong Hicks referred to his father's mantle experience:

I have heard my father [George Barton Hicks] say that he was present at the time when it is said that the mantle of Joseph fell upon Brigham Young. I believe it, I believe the spirit of Joseph took possession of the body of Brigham and spoke to the people through him. Brigham was the man to take the lead.[105]

93. Charles Wesley Hubbard

February 7, 1810–December 19, 1903, age 34

On the morning of 4 August 1844 [*sic*] when Rigdon was given the opportunity of laying his claim before the whole church, Brigham Young addressed the gathering in the afternoon. . . . Charles Hubbard later recorded that before his death in Willard, Utah, he walked two blocks to fast meeting and bore his testimony in a language and spirit that held the audience in silence and attention. One of the men present said: "There was not a sound in the room other that his [Charles's] voice; many were in tears, the spirit was so strong as he declared he knew that Joseph Smith was a true prophet of God and that Brigham Young was the rightful successor, for he was at the meeting when the mantle fell on Brigham Young. Brigham Young looked like the Prophet [Joseph] and no one who was present could ever doubt that Brigham Young was called of God."[106]

94. Edward Hunter

June 22, 1793–October 16, 1883, age 51

"I went to the meeting that had been called and listened thoughtfully to what was said and done. The longer I listened the more mystified I became. I bowed my head in my hands and prayed for God to give me understanding. While I was in this attitude, Brother Brigham rose to speak, I suppose. I heard a voice—the Prophet's [Joseph's] voice as natural and true as I ever heard it. I raised up quickly, fully expecting to see the Prophet [Joseph], and I did. There he stood and gradually changed to that of Brother Brigham, but the voice was not Brother Brigham's. It was still the Prophet's [Joseph's]. Then beside Brother Brigham I saw the Prophet [Joseph], who turned toward the speaker and smiled. My heart beat rapidly with joy and I know beyond the shadow of a doubt that Brother Brigham was called of God to lead the Church."

Others of the assembled Saints received the same remarkable manifestation; and when a vote was called for, the Council of the Twelve was unanimously sustained as the ruling body of the Church.[107]

95. Joseph Ellis Johnson

April 28, 1817–December 17, 1882, age 27

During the dismal days following the murders of Joseph and Hyrum, JEJ [Joseph Ellis Johnson] and others of the family lived through the grief, fears, uncertainties and confusion into which all had been plunged. They were present when Sidney Rigdon voiced his plea to be named Guardian of the Church, which fell on unresponsive ears. They also saw Brigham Young rise to begin his speech and they declared that they witnessed a miracle. As he began to speak his voice suddenly became that of the slain prophet, and they and the audience were electrified by the change in his appearance which became that of Joseph Smith. So lifelike was he that BFJ [Benjamin F. Johnson] said he jumped to his feet in amazement and awe. They with the others of the congregation, convinced that the mantle of the prophet had fallen upon Brigham, voted to sustain him as leader of the Church. Later the rejected Sidney Rigdon, who was really a brilliant man in many ways, apostatized and formed a small church organization in Pittsburg, Pa.[108]

96. Sophronia Eldridge Corbitt Stowell Kelley

July 22, 1825–January 24, 1907, age 19

Mother [Sophronia] was present when the cornerstone of the Nauvoo Temple was laid. She had seen the Prophet Joseph Smith and heard him talk many times. She was present when Brigham Young, as President of the Quorum of Twelve Apostles, assumed leadership of the Church. She has testified many times that he was transfigured and appeared both in voice and general appearance to be the Prophet Joseph himself.[109]

97. Martha McBride Knight

March 17, 1805–November 1, 1901, age 39

She [Martha] often told her grandchildren of the cruel martyrdom of the prophet, the sorrowing of the Saints and the solemn services; her witnesss-ing the form of Brigham Young change to the person of Joseph Smith, and Brigham's voice ringing out in the tone of Joseph's voice, declaring him the leader of the wondering Saints.[110]

98. Samuel Knight

October 14, 1832–February 11, 1910, age 12

Another incident I have heard him [Samuel Knight] narrate was when the succession to the presidency of the Church, after the martyrdom, was being discussed, and he was in attendance at the meeting. As a small boy, perhaps playing with his marbles or otherwise passing the time, he was surprised to hear what he thought was the voice of Joseph Smith. He [Samuel] arose in astonishment and beheld the transfiguration of Brigham Young as related in Church History.[111]

James Lake

October 17, 1788–October 7, 1874, age 55

See Philomela Smith Lake.

99. Philomela Smith Lake

April 13, 1794–March 20, 1873, age 50

After the awful scene at Nauvoo, when they saw the forms of the Prophets they had loved so well laid in the grave, they sought a testimony from God as to their future procedure, and this testimony they received at the great meeting held in the grove at Nauvoo, August 8, 1844, where they witnessed the sublime personality of Joseph Smith as it cast its mantle of splendor around the chosen form of Brigham Young, he being transformed before the eyes of the people, as a heavenly witness to them that God had caused the Majesty of His High Priesthood to fall upon "whom he would," that His work might continue. Father and Mother Lake received that testimony and took up their march again with the Saints.[112]

100. Dudley Leavitt

August 31, 1830–October 15, 1908, age 13

It was not until Brigham Young and a number of the Twelve had returned that a public meeting was held to determine the successor to Joseph Smith.

All the Leavitt family were present on that occasion, August 8, 1844, for, to them, this was a matter of great importance. [Nearly] Fourteen-year-old Dudley was with his friends near the back of the large audience which had gathered to hear the talks of the authorities. . . . Brigham Young arose to speak. . . .

On the edge of the crowd, Dudley whispered to some of his companions. Suddenly they all stopped and listened. It was their Prophet Joseph speaking! How well they knew his accents. They raised up and looked toward the stand. For a second, they thought it was the Prophet who stood there. But they knew it was not, and soon the vision passed. It was so real to Dudley that it made a lasting impression. For him, the mantle of Joseph had in reality fallen upon Brigham. As long as he lived he loved to re-tell the incident.[113]

101. Jeremiah Leavitt

May 30, 1796–August 20, 1846, age 48

Sarah Studevant Leavitt (September 5, 1799–April 5, 1878, age 45), Jeremiah's wife, wrote:

When the news came the whole city of Nauvoo was thunderstruck. Oh such mourning and lamentation. . . . There were many, myself among them, that would gladly give our lives in place of his, if his life could have been spared in so doing. I never had spoken to Joseph Smith in my life. My husband, Jeremiah, had, but I had heard him preach and I had seen him and knew that he was a Prophet of God. He had been sent here to set up his Kingdom upon the Earth. I knew that the God of Heaven was back of this latter day Kingdom, and I knew that it never could be thrown down by mortal man.

As I looked around me in despair, I wondered how that great work was to be accomplished. The answer was not long in coming. My husband, Jeremiah, was attending a meeting where this question was being discussed. Brigham Young was speaking when suddenly he seemed to be clothed with all the authority of Joseph Smith. Jeremiah said that he had the same appearance, the same voice, as the Prophet. If he had not known that Joseph Smith was dead, he would have thought that Brigham Young was Joseph Smith. Tears dampened many cheeks. Joy and gladness filled many hearts. The Lord had not forgotten his people. Brigham Young was absent in the east when Joseph and Hyrum Smith had been killed. Sidney Rigdon tried hard to take Joseph Smith's place and assume the Presidency of the Church, but his lies and deceit were proven by the Twelve Apostles, that returned about this time. And also by the incident I have just related. After that there was no one to doubt that Brigham Young was to be our new leader and Prophet. If Brigham had any doubts, my husband Jeremiah did not. From that moment on he was our Prophet and our leader.[114]

102. Esther Meleta Johnson LeBaron

January 12, 1828–March 15, 1874, age 16

Esther Meleta was at the meeting in August 1844, when Brigham Young was transfigured before the audience. She said Sidney Rigdon had spoke long and tried to convince the people that he was the rightful leader of the Church. When Brigham Young arose and began to speak, he was changed so that he looked like the Prophet Joseph Smith and his voice and manner of speech was the same so when the Saints saw this change there was no doubt as to who should lead the Church, the President of the Quorum of the Twelve Apostles with Brigham Young as the Prophet.[115]

103. John Doyle Lee

September 6, 1812–March 23, 1877, age 31

Time passed on until the whole twelve got in from their missions, and a conference was held, and the several claimants come forward with their claims. Sidney Rigdon was the first who appeared upon the stand. He had been considered rather in the back-ground for sometime previous to the death of the Prophet. He made but a weak claim. Strong (Strang) did not file any. Just them [*sic*] Brigham Young arose and roared like a young lion, imitating the style and voice of Joseph, the Prophet. Many of the brethren declared that they saw the mantle of Joseph fall upon him. I myself, at the time, imagined that I saw and heard a strong resemblance to the Prophet in him, and felt that he was the man to lead us until Joseph's legal successor should grow up to manhood, when he should surrender the Presidency to the man who held the birthright.[116]

104. Amasa Mason Lyman

March 30, 1813–February 4, 1877, age 31

He [Amasa Lyman] was not blinded with foolish ambition. He had recognized the true ring of authority in the voice of Brigham Young. . . .

"I do not rise to electioneer," he declared, wanting the Saints to know at once that he was making no claims to leadership. . . . "I have been at the back of Joseph Smith and I will be at the back of the Twelve forever, and then I will be saved."

. . . Being awake with "his lamp trimmed and burning" at the momentous occasion, he was able with thousands of Latter-day Saints to see the splendid and undisputed manifestation of the power of God in presenting Brigham Young before the Saints as the martyred Prophet, for Brigham spoke with the Prophet's voice and appeared so nearly like the martyred leader that many of the people thought it was really Joseph Smith, and in this way they were shown clearly that the Prophet's mantle had fallen on Brigham Young.[117]

105. Horace Murdock

December 24, 1824–May 1, 1915, age 19

After the martyrdom of the Prophet Joseph Smith, the presidency of the Church developed upon the quorum of the Apostles, and President Brigham Young stood at their head as captain and file leader, to carry out the plans that had been designated by the Prophet Joseph. There were many hundreds, perhaps thousands, present at the meeting held in the grove near the Temple at Nauvoo, in August, 1844, when President Young was recognized by miraculous manifestation as the leader of the Church, and they have testified it was evident that the mantle of Joseph the Prophet fell upon him. . . . I had a letter recently from Brothers Horace and John R. Murdoch of Beaver, who testify that they were eyewitness to the wonderful transformation and power manifested through President Brigham Young on that occasion [when the mantle of the Prophet Joseph fell upon him].[118]

106A and 106B. John Riggs Murdock

September 13, 1826–November 12, 1913, age 17

It was the greatest manifestation I ever beheld, for the voice, the gesture, the whole appearance of President Young was just exactly as if the Prophet Joseph stood there in person.[119]

I had a letter recently from Brothers Horace and John R. Murdoch of Beaver, who testify that they were eyewitness to the wonderful transformation and power manifested through President Brigham Young on that occasion [when the mantle of the Prophet Joseph fell upon him].[120]

107. James Clark Owens

July 7, 1832–February 1, 1901, age 12

With his parents he passed through the trials and drivings of the Saints, first in Missouri and afterwards in Illinois. . . . He attended the conference at Nauvoo, August 8, 1844, and remembered how Brigham Young was transformed in the eyes of the people.[121]

108. James Palmer

August 6, 1820–October 6, 1905, age 24

Brigham Young, the President of the Twelve Apostles, came to the front and stated in a public meeting that the Twelve in their organized capacity had the authority and the legal right to preside over the Church in all the world. As he was speaking in a public meeting, the mantle of Joseph fell upon Brigham and it was as if the Prophet were speaking. It was truly the voice of the Prophet, and it seemed to be the Prophet in person! It was a convincing and a remarkable demonstration of the power of God unto His people. In the minds of the faithful there was now no further question about who our rightful leader was, and this was acknowledged by the main body of the people. Those who did not accept this order of things went their own way.[122]

109. Eliza Ann Perry

March 20, 1828–May 13, 1913, age 16

After Eliza Ann Perry arrived in Nauvoo, she met the Prophet, Joseph Smith, and became well acquainted with him. Eliza Ann was a member of the Nauvoo Choir. She also contributed to the purchase of glass for the windows of the Nauvoo Temple. She was present at the meeting called by Sidney Rigdon to choose a guardian for the church. In her diary she said, and I quote, "Suddenly, Joseph came on the stand to all appearance. But, the mantle of Joseph fell upon Brigham Young, his voice, the color of his hair, his general appearance. People raised from their seats enmass and exclaimed, 'Joseph has come! He is here!' Then they knew that Brigham was the man to lead these people."[123]

110. Luvera Ellen Ensign Preece

June 24, 1826–June 14, 1898, age 18

[On] August 8, 1844, she [Luvera] was at the meeting called to appoint the new leader of the church and witnessed the mantle of Joseph Smith cover Brigham Young as he talked to the assembled Saints.[124]

111. Jane Wadley Smith

January 2, 1814–May 22, 1888, age 30

Mother and father were present at the meeting when the mantle of Joseph Smith fell on Brigham Young. She said Brigham Young was not present at the meeting when it started, but he had been called back from a mission because of the martydom of the Prophet Joseph and his brother, Hyrum. Brigham Young came up from the boat and took his place on the stand. Mother had leaned over her baby and just then Brigham Young started to speak. She said she raised up suddenly because she heard what she believed was the Prophet's [Joseph's] voice, although she knew he was dead. This thoroughly convinced them that he was the successor to Joseph Smith, chosen of God.[125]

112. John Sivel Smith

March 10, 1809–February 12, 1905, age 35

John was present when the Prophet Joseph Smith delivered his last address to the Nauvoo Legion, and he also attended the memorably [*sic*] meeting held at Navoo August 8, 1844, when the mantle of Joseph fell upon Brigham Young. He often testified that Brigham Young was the Lord's chosen prophet.[126]

113A and 113B. James Chauncey Snow

January 11, 1817–April 30, 1884, age 27

He [James C. Snow] was present at the meeting August 8, when Brigham Young spoke with great power, reminding the people that the Church was the Church of Jesus Christ. . . . All the powers of the Priesthood were vested in the Twelve until a new Presidency should be nominated by them through the spirit of revelation and sustained by the vote of the people. Both James and Warren [brothers] saw the mantle of Joseph fall upon Brigham Young as he spoke, an event of which they both often testified afterwards, and they were convinced that Brigham Young was to be their leader.[127]

Bro. Snow, together with other missionaries, was called home shortly after the martyrdom, and he was present at the meeting when the mantle of Joseph fell upon Brigham Young—an event of which he often testified afterwards.[128]

Sally Adams Snow

See Sally Adams.

114. William Stoker

March 26, 1819–May 19, 1892, age 25

From the age of six, he [Bishop W. E. Stoker] was raised by his grandfather [William Stoker], who knew the Prophet Joseph Smith personally and was present when the Mantle of Joseph fell upon Brigham Young, and received a personal testimony. Bishop Stoker felt he owed much to his grandfather for building up his faith through the relating of this Church experience.[129]

115. Pleasant Green Taylor

February 8, 1827–May 16, 1917, age 17

After the death of Joseph the question arose as to who should lead the church. The twelve apostles being away on missions. Sidney Rigdon claimed the right to lead the church though his claim was not looked on with favor by the majority of the Saints. He was present and saw Brigham Young come into the bowery where the Saints had assembled. He, as well as hundreds of others, arose to his feet and felt sure that Joseph had been resurrected. And even after Brigham began to speak he still thought it was the Prophet Joseph who was speaking to them.[130]

116. Martha Tuttle

1830–1922, age 14

I well remember the Sunday morning the sorrowing Saints were gathered together in the little Grove wher they were accustomed to meet. Sidney Rigdon presented his claim as successor to the Prophet Joseph making quite an impression upon the people. But Brigham Young, Pres. of the Quorum of the Twelve Apostles, had just arrived in Nauvoo from his mission in time to attend the afternoon meeting. In a voice not unlike that of the Prophet Joseph, [Brigham] told the people that although Joseph was dead, Joseph had left behind the keys of the Kingdom and had conferred the same power and authority that he himself possessed upon the Twelve Apostles and the church would not be left without a leader and a guide. Truly the mantle of Joseph had fallen upon Brigham and he spake with power even to the convincing of the Saints, assuring them they had nothing to worry about as all would be well if they would hearken to the word of God and The council of his servants and keep His Commandments.[131]

117. Peter Edmund Van Orden

January 27, 1830–September 25, 1911, age 14

Peter remembers that after the Prophet's funeral, Sidney Rigdon, came and claimed the right to rule the Church. He held a meeting and talked to the people about it, asking them to return later to make a decision. It was at this later meeting that Brigham Young spoke and the Mantle of the Prophet fell over his shoulders. The people knew this was their sign that Brigham was to be their leader. Peter witnessed this event and bore testimony of it until his dying day.[132]

118A and 118B. Henson Walker

March 13, 1820–January 24, 1904, age 24

At the death of Joseph Smith, Brigham Young who was President of the Quorum of the Twelve apostles, assumed the leadership of the Church. Sidney Rigdon, one of the counselors to Joseph in the Presidency, felt it was his right to take the place. Henson was present at the public meeting held in the bowery at which both Sidney and Brigham spoke. Sidney Rigdon made his claims first. Henson said that Brother Rigdon was an eloquent speaker and made a forceful appeal to the people. When he finished Brigham Young arose to speak. In the words of Henson, "The mantle of Joseph Smith fell upon Brigham Young and the congregation knew who their leader was. He looked like the Prophet Joseph and the tone of his voice was like his."[133]

Henson was present at the time that Sidney Rigdon set forth his claims to the presidency. He also witnessed the mantle of Joseph resting upon Brigham Young and was fully convinced that he was the future Prophet of God.[134]

119. Abraham Daniel Washburn

March 17, 1805–June 17, 1886, age 39

Abraham sometimes related incidents from the trying times when the people were overcome by persecution and grief at the time of the martyrdom of their beloved leader Joseph and his brother Hyrum. Abraham was at the meeting when the mantle of Joseph fell upon Brigham.[135]

Eliza Billington Welch

See Eliza Billington.

Emmeline Blanche Woodward Harris Whitney Wells

See Emmeline Blanche Woodward Harris.

120. William West Woodland

January 2, 1832–February 19, 1906, age 12

[William] accompanied his parents through all the drivings that took place in the early days of the Church and was exposed to the many spiritual manifestations that happened . . . even as a youth witness to the grand experience of the mantle of the Prophet Joseph falling upon Brigham Young after the death of the Prophet Joseph. This did more to influence him in future years than most any other experience.[136]

121. Samuel Amos Woolley

September 11, 1825–March 23, 1900, age 18

During the troublesome times of 1844 I served as a city guard in Nauvoo. After the martyrdom of Joseph and Hyrum Smith I was present at the important meeting where President Brigham Young first spoke to the Saints of Joseph's death, and I received a testimony that the mantle of Joseph had fallen upon Brigham Young's shoulder, for when he spoke it seemed as if Joseph himself were speaking, his voice and gestures being exactly like those of the martyred Prophet.[137]

Notes to the Documents/Testimonies

1. William Adams, "Autobiography of William Adams, 1822–1894," typescript, 14, L. Tom Perry Special Collections, Harold B. Lee Library, Brigham Young University, Provo, Utah; William Adams, "Autobiography 1894," typescript, 14, Church Archives, The Church of Jesus Christ of Latter-day Saints, Salt Lake City.

2. William Moore Allred, "Reminiscences and Diary, 1883," holograph, 11, Church Archives.

3. Benjamin Ashby, "Autobiography of Benjamin Ashby, 1828–1907," holograph, unpaged, microfilm, Family History Library, The Church of Jesus Christ of Latter-day Saints, Salt Lake City (hereafter cited as FHL Archives); Robert L. Ashby, ed., *Ashby Ancestry: Something of the Origin of the Name and Family* (Salt Lake City: Stringham Ashby Steven, 1941) unpaged; see also Armis J. Ashby, *The Robert L. Ashby and Hannah Cropper Family Book of Their Descendants and Ancestors* (Salt Lake City: Ashby-Cropper Family Organization, 1991), 16.

4. Lewis Barney, Reminiscences [1888], holograph, 15–16, microfilm, Church Archives.

5. "Eunice Billings Warner Snow Tells Her Own Story" [sent to Archibald Bennett], edited by Marva Peck Hale, Provo, Utah. Transcript copy, FHL Archives; "Writings of Eunice Billings Snow" written in 1910, edited by Marva Peck Hale.

6. Information presented personally to the author by a descendant, Katherine Adams Peterson, August 1996.

7. Henry and Catharine Brooke to Leonard Pickell, November 15, 1844, Yale University, copy at Church Archives, quoted in Glen M. Leonard, *Nauvoo: A Place of Peace, a People of Promise* (Salt Lake City: Deseret Book; Provo, Utah: Brigham Young University Press, 2002), 438. This handwritten note includes the signatures of both Henry and Catharine.

8. Henry Schuler Buckwalter, "Biographical Sketch of Henry Schuler Buckwalter," Miscellaneous Mormon Diaries, 11:3, typescript, Perry Special Collections.

9. Thomas Bullock to John O. Angus, Salt Lake City, December 18, 1851, in *Millennial Star* 14 (July 3, 1852): 299.

10. Robert Taylor Burton, "Statement Concerning the Transfiguration," July 28, 1905, typescript, two pages, Church Archives; see also Janet Burton Seegmiller, "Be Kind to the Poor: The Life Story of Robert Taylor Burton" (n.p.: Robert Taylor Burton Family Organization, 1988), 49.

11. William Burton, Journal, May 1845 [under entry of April 26, 1845], Perry Special Collections; William Burton, "William Burton Diaries, 1839–1851," May 1845, 2–8, Church Archives; see also Eugene England, *Brother Brigham*

(Salt Lake City: Bookcraft, 1980), 75; and D. Michael Quinn, "The Mormon Succession Crisis of 1844," *BYU Studies* 16, no. 2 (1976): 212. This is one of the earliest surviving contemporary accounts, written ten months after the event. Burton was not in Nauvoo in 1844. He was on a mission.

12. Anson Call, "The Life and Record of Anson Call: Commenced in 1839," holograph, 30, Church Archives. In a note at the end of Call's journal in the Church Archives, T. Edgar Lyon identifies Mary Flint Call as Anson's scribe. Anson Call, "The Journal of Anson Call" (n.p.: Ethan L. Call and Christine Shatter Call, 1986), 31–32. This journal began in 1839 and was dictated to or recopied by "various individuals, presumably his wives." Call, "Journal of Anson Call," publisher's note.

13. George Q. Cannon, *Juvenile Instructor* 5 (October 29, 1870): 174–75; see also Edward W. Tullidge, *Life of Brigham Young; or, Utah and Her Founders* (New York: n.p., 1877), 115; B. H. Roberts, *A Comprehensive History of The Church of Jesus Christ of Latter-day Saints, Century One*, 6 vols. (Provo, Utah: Corporation of the President, The Church of Jesus Christ of Latter-day Saints, 1965), 2:418; and Leonard Arrington, *Brigham Young: American Moses* (New York: Alfred A. Knopf, 1985), 115.

14. Elias Cox, "Joseph Smith, the Prophet," *Young Woman's Journal* 17 (December 1906): 544.

15. Robert Crookston, "Affidavit, February 3, 1903," copies in the possession of Gloria Hansen, a great-granddaughter of Robert Crookston, and Church Archives. The affidavit was written and sealed by Robert Crookston and witnessed by Lydia Owen and H. J. Mathews at Logan City, Cache County, Utah.

16. Caroline Barnes Crosby, "Memoirs Begun at Tubuai, Society Islands, 1851," holograph, unpaged, Church Archives; Caroline Barnes Crosby, "The Papers of Jonathan and Caroline Crosby," unpaged, microfilm, FHL Archives. The journal of Caroline Barnes Crosby began in 1851 in the Society Islands while the Crosbys were on a mission.

17. Homer Duncan, Autobiographical Sketch, holograph, 22–23, Church Archives.

18. Effie Ensign Merrill, essay for the Sea Gull Camp of the Daughters of Utah Pioneers, September 12, 1941, copy in possession of the author. This family history was shared with me by Colonel Amos Wright.

19. Jesse C. Little to Brigham Young, December 30, 1844, Brigham Young Papers, Church Archives, quoted in Leonard, *Nauvoo*, 438.

20. Edmund Ellsworth, Autobiography [ca. 1892], holograph, 4–5, Church Archives.

21. Mary Field Garner, Autobiographical Sketch, typescript, 6–7, Church Archives; Mary Field Garner, "Biography as-told-to Harold H. Jenson and

Mary's Granddaughter Annie Garner Barton," typescript, 6–7, Perry Special Collections, copy in possession of the author.

22. Typescript of journal of James Madison Fisher [1906] in Lucy Elizabeth Fisher Brown, comp., "History and Genealogy of Jesse, Joseph, and James Madison Fisher and Evaline McLean," typescript, 5–6, microfilm, FHL Archives.

23. Jacob Gates, Journals, 1836–1861, vol. 2, holograph, unpaged, Church Archives.

24. James Harvey Glines, "Reminiscences and Diary, March 1845–December 1899," holograph, 41, Church Archives.

25. William Greenhalgh, "The History of William Greenhalgh: As Written by Himself," typescript, 1–2, FHL Archives, copy in possession of the author. This typescript was written in the 1870s based on earlier diary accounts. This copy was given to the author and to the FHL Archives by William's great-grandson Glade Greenhalgh. The holographic original is owned by Jean Bluth of Colorado Springs, Colorado.

26. Jacob Hamblin, Journal 8, typescript, microfilm, Church Archives.

27. James A. Little, *Jacob Hamblin: A Narrative of His Personal Experience, as a Frontiersman, Missionary to the Indians and Explorer* (Salt Lake City: Juvenile Instructor Office, 1881), 19–20. Little writes in the preface that Jacob Hamblin "was induced to narrate, for Brother James A. Little's pen to record, the incidents herein published." See also Pearson H. Corbett, *Jacob Hamblin, the Peacemaker* (Salt Lake City: Deseret Book, 1952), 21–22.

28. Mosiah Lyman Hancock, "Autobiography of Mosiah Lyman Hancock," 1834–65, holograph, unpaged, Church Archives; Mosiah Lyman Hancock, "Mosiah Lyman Hancock," 23, 30, microfilm, FHL Archives; Mosiah Lyman Hancock, "Life Story of Mosiah Lyman Hancock," typescript, 16, 20, Perry Special Collections.

29. John Nelson Harper, Autobiography [ca. 1861], typescript, 10, typed by Jewel B. Furniss, Church Archives. "This book was copied from the old original that was written by John Harper" (title page).

30. Eliza Ann Haven Westover to Lew [Haven], July 2, 1916, copy in possession of Douglas M. Chabries; she wrote a similar account to another son two years later relating the same information, see Eliza Westover, "Letter to Son Written 1918," 4, Church Archives; Seegmiller, "Life Story of Robert Taylor Burton," 50; see also Ora Haven Barlow, *The Israel Barlow Story and Mormon Mores* (Salt Lake City: By the author, 1968), 205.

31. Drusilla Dorris Hendricks, "Historical Sketch of James Hendricks and Drusilla Dorris Hendricks," typescript, unpaged, microfilm, FHL Archives, dictated by Drusilla after the death of her husband in 1870; Drusilla Dorris Hendricks, "Historical Sketch of James Hendricks and Drusilla Dorris Hendricks,"

typescript, 18, microfilm, Church Archives; Marguerite H. Allen, comp., Henry Hendricks Genealogy (n.p.: Hendricks Family Organization, 1963), 26. See also Carol Cornwall Madsen, *In Their Own Words: Women and the Story of Nauvoo* (Salt Lake City: Deseret Book, 1994), 168.

32. Quinn, "Mormon Succession Crisis," 212n69.

33. Emily Smith Hoyt, Reminiscenses and Diaries 1851–1893, holograph, 20–21, microfilm, Church Archives, original diary in the possession of Jonathan A. Dibble, Salt Lake City.

34. Zina Diantha Huntington Young, Diaries 1844–1845, August 8, 1844, holograph, Church Archives, published in Maureen Ursenbach Beecher, "'All Things Move in Order in the City': The Nauvoo Diary of Zina Diantha Huntington Jacobs," *BYU Studies* 19, no. 3 (1979): 285–320.

35. Edward W. Tullidge, *The Women of Mormondom* (New York: Tullidge and Crandall, 1877), 326–27; see also Richard Neitzel Holzapfel and Jeni Broberg Holzapfel, *Women of Nauvoo* (Salt Lake City: Bookcraft, 1992), 134–35.

36. John M. Whittaker, "Memorial Anniversary," *Woman's Exponent* 17 (August 15, 1888): 460. The above quote was published in a report of a Relief Society meeting held in the Ogden Tabernacle, July 19, 1888, in commemoration of the last public visit and instructions of President Brigham Young eleven years previous, just prior to his death. Mary Anne Price Hyde, widow of Orson Hyde, was president of the Relief Society of the Sanpete Stake and spoke at that meeting. This was her testimony. See also Myrtle Stevens Hyde, *Orson Hyde: The Olive Branch of Israel* (Salt Lake City: Agreka Books, 2000), 181–82.

37. Orson Hyde, "Remarks," *Deseret News Semi-Weekly*, November 16, 1869 (discourse given October 6, 1869); see also Orson Hyde, in *Journal of Discourses*, 26 vols. (Liverpool: F. D. Richards, 1855–86), 13:181, October 6, 1869. A summary of Elder Hyde's discourse was also published in "Thirty-Ninth Semi-Annual Conference," *Deseret News*, October 13, 1869.

38. Hyde, in *Journal of Discourses*, 19:58, April 5, 1877.

39. William Hyde, "The Private Journal of William Hyde, 1868," holograph, 64–67, and typescript, 21–23, Church Archives; William Hyde, "The Private Journal of William Hyde," typescript, 13–15, microfilm, FHL Archives.

William was baptized in 1834 and kept a dated and detailed record of his Church activities. If this handwritten journal was not kept concurrently, it must have been based on copious and dated notes. He admitted that on occasion instructions were given "which he did not pen." Hyde, "Private Journal," 16, FHL Archives. This indicates that the information in his journal was generally written at the time of offering.

Elder George Albert Smith, a member of the Quorum of the Twelve Apostles, saw the original journal in the home of a granddaughter, Elizabeth Hyde Geary, and scanned its contents. Recognizing the wide sweep of Church history contained in this private journal, he immediately requested it for the Church Archives and had a typed copy made for Sister Geary. Introduction to Hyde Journal, Church Archives.

40. Rachel Ridgeway Grant, "Joseph Smith the Prophet," *Young Woman's Journal* 16 (December 1905): 551; see also Ronald W. Walker, "Rachel R. Grant: The Continuing Legacy of the Feminine Ideal," in *Supporting Saints: Life Stories of Nineteenth-Century Mormons*, ed. Donald Q. Cannon and David J. Whittaker (Provo, Utah: Religious Studies Center, Brigham Young University, 1985), 24.

41. Heber J. Grant to Edward B. Clark, reproduced in Annie Clark Tanner, *A Biography of Ezra Thompson Clark* (Salt Lake City: Tanner Trust Fund, University of Utah, 1931), xi.

42. "An Interesting Letter: From Patriarch Benjamin F. Johnson to Elder Geo. S. Gibbs," typescript, 15, Perry Special Collections; Benjamin F. Johnson to George S. Gibbs, 1903, Church Archives, cited in E. Dale LeBaron, "Benjamin Franklin Johnson: Colonizer, Public Servant, and Church Leader" (master's thesis, Brigham Young University, 1967), 343–44. This letter was written in the early part of 1903, when Johnson was about eighty-five years old ("Interesting Letter," i). See also Dean R. Zimmerman, *I Knew the Prophets: An Analysis of the Letter of Benjamin F. Johnson to George F. Gibbs, Reporting Doctrinal Views of Joseph Smith and Brigham Young* (Bountiful, Utah: Horizon, 1976), 65–67.

43. Benjamin F. Johnson, *My Life's Review* (n.d.; reprint, Mesa, Ariz.: Lofgreen Printing, 1979), 103–4; see also Arrington, *Brigham Young*, 114–15n8.

44. Dan Jones, *History of the Latter-day Saints*, trans. Ronald D. Dennis (1847; reprint, Provo, Utah: Brigham Young University Religious Studies Center, 2002), 92.

45. Helen D. O'Connor, "Jacob Jones—Biography of a Pioneer," Biographical Sketch Competition Entries, Church Archives. The excerpt from the affidavit of May 24, 1925, given at Sugar City, Idaho, and witnessed by Stake President Fred Schwendiman, is found on p. 3.

46. Zadoc Knapp Judd, "Autobiography of Zadoc Knapp Judd, 1827–1909," typescript, 17–19, Perry Special Collections; Zadoc Knapp Judd, "Autobiography," 1900, typescript, 17–19, Church Archives.

47. George Laub, "George Laub's Journal, 1845–46," holograph, 90–91, microfilm, Church Archives; Eugene England, ed., "George Laub's Nauvoo Journal," *BYU Studies* 18, no. 2 (1978): 166.

The above quotation has been challenged by Richard S. Van Wagoner in his book *Sidney Rigdon: A Portrait of Religious Excess* (Salt Lake City: Signature Books, 1994), 351n99. Van Wagoner states Laub's mantle account was not written until after he arrived in the Utah Territory in 1852. Van Wagoner's claim is that Laub's 1845–46 journal was actually copied from another Laub journal dated 1845–52 and that the transfiguration incident was then appropriately inserted. Both journals are currently stored in the Church Archives. Historian Michael Quinn explains:

> Eugene England edited "George Laub's Nauvoo Journal," *Brigham Young University Studies* 18 (Winter 1978): 166, which also gives an explicit description of Brigham Young's transfiguration. However, Van Wagoner, *Sidney Rigdon*, demonstrates that England had edited Laub's own revision (dated about 1852) of his original Nauvoo diary that was unavailable to England. Donated to LDS Archives after England's article, Laub's original diary made no reference to a mystical experience at the August 1844 meeting. (D. Michael Quinn, *The Mormon Hierarchy: Origins of Power* [Salt Lake City: Signature Books, 1994], 393n114)

The George Laub journal order, which Van Wagoner presents as proof that early Laub memoirs might be suspect, can only be accepted as his personal opinion according to the late Eugene England, who stated that Van Wagoner's conclusion cannot be proved one way or the other. In a personal interview with England in the summer of 1997, I found he angrily and firmly stood by the timeline of his article "George Laub's Nauvoo Journal."

If Van Wagoner is correct in redating to 1852 Laub's journal mentioning the mantle, this account is still one of the earliest renderings, written at least seventeen to eighteen years before the first complete published account of the mantle experience.

48. Wandle Mace, "The Diary of Wandle Mace" (Salt Lake City: Genealogical Society of Utah, 1964), 156–57, microfilm, FHL Archives; Wandle Mace, Autobiography [ca. 1890], holograph, 95–96, microfilm, Church Archives. See also Wandle Mace, Autobiography [ca. 1890], holograph [written in 1911], 113–14, Church Archives. Both of the autobiographies in the Church Archives were copied by his wife, Elizabeth Howell Mace.

49. Philemon Christopher Merrill, Autobiography [ca. 1890], typescript, 4, Church Archives. Transcription by Zola S. Hardy, the wife of a great-grandson of Philemon, from a six-page holograph.

50. Elmira Pond Miller, "A Biography of the Life of Elmira Pond Miller Written by Herself in 1890, Fourteen Years Before Her Death," typescript, 4, Daughters of Utah Pioneers Library and Archives, Salt Lake City. Submitted by Julia T. Bodily in 1964.

51. George Morris, "Life Story of George Morris of the Seventeenth Ward, Salt Lake," holograph, unpaged, microfilm, FHL Archives; see also George Morris, "Autobiography of George Morris," typescript, 27, Perry Special Collections. Morris's autobiography has been edited, but the editor is not given.

52. "Diary of Joseph Stacy Murdock," quoted in *History of Alphonso and Betsey Bonney (Murdock) Green* (n.p., 1993), 34. Diary excerpt also quoted in

George A. Thompson, *Advancing the Mormon Frontier: The Life and Times of Joseph Stacy Murdock*, 31, microfilm, FHL Archives. Joseph Murdock wrote the text to the Latter-day Saint hymn "Come, Listen to a Prophet's Voice."

53. William Bryam Pace, "Diary of William Bryam Pace and Biography of His Father, James Pace," typescript, 7, Perry Special Collections. This is a copy from an original in the possession of Sidney A. Pace, Orem, Utah.

54. George Patten, "Life Sketch," 1900, holograph, unpaged, Church Archives; George Patten, "A Short Sketch [ca. 1909]," typescript, 2, microfilm, Church Archives.

55. W. W. Phelps to Brigham Young, January 1, 1862, holograph, Church Archives. ("Israel Reigns" was a part of the collection "New Songs by W. W. Phelps," which was shared at a Mormon History Association conference, perhaps by Michael Hicks.) Concerning Phelps's participation in the August 8 meeting, Michael Quinn, *Mormon Hierarchy*, 165, notes that in the afternoon session, "[Sidney] Rigdon . . . asked William W. Phelps to speak in his behalf. He could not have chosen a worse advocate." Hyde, "Private Journal," 65, states that "Elder W. W. Phelps also made some very comforting remarks" after Brigham spoke in the afternoon session.

56. Nathan Tanner Porter, Reminiscences [ca. 1879], holograph, 131–33, microfilm, Church Archives. He has conflated the August 8, 1844, meeting with the meeting at Winter Quarters on December 5, 1847, when Brigham Young was sustained as president of the Church with Heber C. Kimball and Willard Richards as councilors.

57. John Pulsipher, "A Short Sketch of the History of John Pulsipher," typescript, 7–8, Church Archives; Linda King Newell and Valeen Tippetts Avery, *Mormon Enigma: Emma Hale Smith* (New York: Doubleday, 1984), 203.

58. Zerah Pulsipher, Autobiographical sketch, Church Archives; Nora Hall Lund and Terry Lund, comps., "Pulsipher Family History Book," 23, FHL Archives.

59. Jane Snyder Richards, "Papers 1869–," holograph, 13, Church Archives; Madsen, *In Their Own Words*, 174.

60. Jane Snyder Richards, "Joseph Smith, the Prophet," *Young Woman's Journal* 16 (December 1905): 550.

61. George Romney, "Joseph Smith Was the Chosen Prophet of God—His Mantle Fell upon Brigham Young," *Liahona, the Elders' Journal* 17 (April 13, 1920): 339; Caroline Eyring Miner, *Miles Romney and Elizabeth Gaskell Romney and Family* (Salt Lake City: Miles Romney Family Organization, 1978), 74. Romney's last public testimony was delivered at a meeting of the Swedish Saints in the Twelfth-Thirteenth Ward Chapel in Salt Lake City on December 17, 1919, seventy-five years after the August 1844 mantle phenomenon. A proud old man of eighty-eight, he bore a powerful testimony of the mantle miracle.

62. George Romney, typescript account of testimony, typed by Mary R. Ross, Church Archives; England, *Brother Brigham*, 75; Gustave Arnt Iverson, "The Mantle of the Prophet," typescript, Church Archives. Testimony of Bishop George Romney at a stake conference on June 22, 1919, in the Ensign Ward, Salt Lake City.

63. Job Taylor Smith, "Diary of Job Taylor Smith; a Pioneer of Nauvoo, Illinois and Utah [ca. 1902]," typescript, 8, Church Archives.

64. Abraham O. Smoot, "Early Experiences of A. O. Smoot," *Early Scenes in Church History: Eighth Book in the Faith-Promoting Series* (Salt Lake City: Juvenile Instructor's Office, 1882), 24; C. Elliott Berlin, "Abraham O. Smoot, Pioneer Mormon Leader" (master's thesis, Brigham Young University, 1955), 35–36.

65. Margaret T. Smoot to Mr. [H. H.] Bancroft, "Experiences of a Mormon Wife," September 2, 1880, Provo City, Utah, microfilm, Perry Special Collections; see also Berlin, "Abraham O. Smoot," 36.

66. "Biography of Warren Stone Snow," typescript, 1, Church Archives, prepared by Lund and Laura Johnson, and Merlene Tew Colarusso and Thomas G. Colarusso. See Archibald Bennett, Ella M. Bennett, and Barbara Bennett Roach, *Valiant in the Faith: Gardner and Sarah Snow and Their Family* (Murray, Utah: Roylance, 1990), 56, 384; and John A. Peterson, "Warren Stone Snow, A Man In Between: The Biography of a Mormon Defender" (master's thesis, Brigham Young University, 1985), 33.

67. William C. Staines, "Reminiscenses of William C. Staines," *Contributor* 12 (June 1891): 315; see also Staines, quoted in Roberts, *Comprehensive History*, 2:418n12.

68. Mary Ann Stearns Winters, "An Autobiographical Sketch of the Life of the Late Mary Ann Stearns Winters, daughter of Mary Ann Stearns Pratt," typescript, Church Archives.

69. Catherine Thomas Lieshman, Autobiographical sketch [May 1, 1914], typescript, 2–3, microfilm, Church Archives.

70. Nancy Naomi Alexander Tracy, "Autobiography," holograph, 5, microfilm, FHL Archives; Nancy Alexander Tracy, "A Short Sketch of the Life and Travels of Nancy N. Tracy," typescript (prepared by grandson David E. Ellingson), 19, Perry Special Collections. See also Madsen, *In Their Own Words*, 255–56. The account indicates that Nancy and her husband were in the East at the time of the August 8 meeting or that Nancy had confused the dates. Her story may have been secondhand or might be an account of something they experienced later.

71. Nancy N. Tracy, Autobiography, typescript, 31, Church Archives.

72. William Lampard Watkins, "A Brief History of William Lampard Watkins, from His Birth until His Arrival in Utah on September 12th, 1852," typescript, 2, Perry Special Collections; William Lampard Watkins, "Autobiography

of William Lampard Watkins, from His Birth until He Arrived in Utah on 12 September 1852," 4, Church History Library, The Church of Jesus Christ of Latter-day Saints, Salt Lake City; Marie M. Hayes, *That Others Might Know: A History of the Watkins and Lampard Families* (Seattle: By the author, 1979), 24.

73. John Welch, "Deposition, July 5, 1902," typescript, microfilm, Church Archives. This is a copy of a statement that John Welch made July 5, 1902, at Logan City, Cache County, Utah. It was signed, sealed, and sworn before A. L. Farrell, Cache County Clerk. Parts of the deposition are also included in Evaline Dunn Snow, "John and Eliza B. Welch Biographical Sketch," transcript, 2, microfilm, Church Archives.

74. Helen Mar Whitney, "Scenes in Nauvoo after the Martyrdom of the Prophet and Patriarch," *Woman's Exponent* 11 (February 1, 1883): 130; Stanley B. Kimball, "Heber C. Kimball and Family, the Nauvoo Years," *BYU Studies* 15, no. 4 (1975): 472.

75. Maria Wealthy Wilcox, "Joseph Smith, the Prophet," *Young Woman's Journal* 16 (December 1905): 553–54.

76. Wilford Woodruff, "To the Officers and Members of the Church of Jesus Christ of Latter-Day Saints in the British Islands," *Millennial Star* 5 (February 1845): 138.

77. Wilford Woodruff, "Remarks," *Deseret News*, May 22, 1872; see also Wilford Woodruff, in *Journal of Discourses*, 15:81, April 8, 1872.

78. Wilford Woodruff, "Priesthood and the Right of Succession," *Deseret Semi-weekly*, March 15, 1892, 3. This testimony was publicly delivered at a gathering of Young Men Mutual Improvement Association groups. Speaker B. H. Roberts was presenting a lecture on the succession in the presidency of The Church of Jesus Christ of Latter-day Saints. At Roberts's request, President Woodruff, who was present in the audience, was asked to present his testimony concerning the events of August 8, 1844, and the mantle experience. See also Arrington, *Brigham Young*, 115.

79. Celestia Snow Gardner, *History of the William Snow and Robert Gardner Families: Pioneers of 1847 and 1850* (Salt Lake City: Acorn Printing, 1942), 17–18. Sally married William Snow in January 1846 in the Nauvoo Temple (18).

80. Carla Spencer Anderson, "Brief Life Sketches of Our Pioneer Foremothers," in *Our Sister Saints: A Sesquicentennial Family Project to Commemorate the Arrival in the Salt Lake Valley of the Mormon Pioneers* (Soldotna, Alaska: n.p., 1997).

81. Truman O. Angell, "Biography of Truman Osborn Angell Sr.," typescript, 6, Church Archives, quoted in Paul L. Anderson, "Truman O. Angell: Architect and Saint," in *Supporting Saints: Life Stories of Nineteenth-Century Mormons*, ed. Donald Q. Cannon and David J. Whittaker (Provo, Utah: Religious Studies Center, Brigham Young University, 1985), 143.

82. Pamela Barlow Thompson, "Biography of Elizabeth Haven Barlow," 6, FHL Archives, quoted in Ora Haven Barlow, *The Israel Barlow Story and Mormon Mores* (Salt Lake City: By the author, 1968), 204–5.

83. William H. Bennett, "Life Story of William Alvin Bennett," in *Our Legacy from William and Elizabeth New*, comp. Archibald F. Bennett and Blanche Bennett Nordgren, 2 vols. (Provo, Utah: New Family Organization, 1984), 1:356. William H. Bennett was William Alvin Bennett's son, and assistant to the Quorum of the Twelve. William Alvin Bennett was the son of Eli Bennett. "[Eli] Bennett heard the Prophet Joseph Smith preach upon several occasions. . . . He was at the meeting in Nauvoo on Aug. 8, 184[4] when the mantle of Joseph Smith the prophet fell upon Brigham Young." "Obituary," *Deseret News*, October 19, 1906, 3.

84. John Henry Evans and Minnie Egan Anderson, *Ezra T. Benson: Pioneer—Statesman—Saint* (Salt Lake City: Deseret News Press, 1947), 88–89.

85. Evaline Dunn Snow, "John and Eliza B. Welch Biographical Sketch," typescript, 2, microfilm, Church Archives. Evaline is a granddaughter of John and Eliza.

86. "Sketch of the Life of William Burgess Sr., Pioneer," 5, by Jennie Caroline Burgess Miles, granddaughter, Daughters of Utah Pioneers Library and Archives, Salt Lake City (hereafter cited as DUP Archives). Sent to the County Historian of Washington County Chapter of DUP in 1937.

87. Beatrice Cannon Evans and Janath Russell Cannon, eds., *Cannon Family Historical Treasury* (Salt Lake City: George Cannon Family Association, 1967), 162–63; condensed from Angus M. Woodbury, arr. and ed., *Reminiscences of Ann Cannon Woodbury* (n.p., 1963). Grandson Angus M. Woodbury prepared Ann's journals for publication.

88. "In the Valley of the Saints," in *Our Pioneer Heritage*, comp. Kate B. Carter, 20 vols. (Salt Lake City: Daughters of Utah Pioneers, 1958–77), 6:204. The account was written by William Van Orden Carbine.

89. Andrew Jenson, *Latter-day Saint Biographical Encyclopedia: A Compilation of Biographical Sketches of Prominent Men and Women in The Church of Jesus Christ of Latter-day Saints*, 4 vols. (Salt Lake City: Andrew Jenson History, 1901–36), 3:41.

90. Brigham Young, in *Journal of Discourses*, 26 vols. (Liverpool: F. D. Richards, 1855–86), 5:57–58, July 19, 1857; see also Leonard Arrington, *Brigham Young: American Moses* (New York: Alfred A. Knopf, 1985), 115.

91. "The Unpublished Story," in Carter, *Our Pioneer Heritage*, 12:202.

92. Annie Clark Tanner, *A Biography of Ezra Thompson Clark* (Salt Lake City: Tanner Trust Fund, University of Utah Library, 1931), 8.

93. Aurelia Spencer Rogers, *Life Sketches of Orson Spencer and Others* (Salt Lake City: George Q. Cannon and Sons, 1898), 331–32.

94. Bertha M. Linebarger, "Ada Winchell Clements," in Carter, *Our Pioneer Heritage*, 3:111–12.

95. Charlotte Parker, "How Mormonism Affected the Lives of the Clements Family" (paper written for History 100, Brigham Young University, April 1982), 14; copy in the possession of author. Ada (Aidah) Clements evidently worked for Joseph and Emma Smith in the Mansion House. Linda King Newell and Valeen Tippetts Avery, *Mormon Enigma: Emma Hale Smith* (New York: Doubleday, 1984), 134.

96. William G. Hartley, *Kindred Saints: The Mormon Immigrant Heritage of Alvin and Kathryne Christenson* (Salt Lake City: Eden Hill, 1986), 25; see also Grace Wilson Norris, "Biography of John Corless," and "Catherine Stephenson Corless: A Pioneer of 1848," Christenson Family Archives, in the possession of Richard A. Christenson, Salt Lake City, copy given to the author by Pat Heilpren, a Corless descendant. Grace is a great-granddaughter of Edward and Catherine.

97. Grace Wilson Norris, "Edward Coreless: A Pioneer of 1848," 3, Christenson Family Archives, copy in the possession of author.

98. Louisa Decker, "Reminiscences of Nauvoo," *Woman's Exponent* 37 (March 1909): 41–42; Carol Cornwall Madsen, *In Their Own Words: Women and the Story of Nauvoo* (Salt Lake City: Deseret Book, 1994), 242–43.

99. William G. Hartley, *"They Are My Friends": A History of the Joseph Knight Family, 1825–1850* (Provo, Utah: Grandin Book, 1986), 154.

100. Quote by Howard Ransom Egan, in *Pioneering the West 1846 to 1878: Major Howard Egan's Diary*, ed. William M. Egan (Richmond, Utah: Howard R. Egan, 1917), 10–11. Major Howard Egan is the father of Howard Ransom Egan, who included his own autobiography in this book.

101. Lucy E. Fisher Brown, comp., "Genealogical and Historical Record of the Fisher Family," holograph, 3, microfilm, FHL Archives. Lucy is Evaline's granddaughter.

102. Sylvia Lola Read Thatcher, *Inspirational Experiences* (Hancock, New York: East Branch Family Press, 1989), 4.

103. "That They May Live Again," in Carter, *Our Pioneer Heritage*, 8:198.

104. Emmeline B. Wells, "My Testimony," in Preston Nibley, comp., *Faith Promoting Stories* (Salt Lake City: Deseret Book, 1943), 137. In his foreword, Nibley states, "The stories contained in this volume have been selected with care from books and periodicals on file in the Church Historians Library."

105. Davis Bitton, "'I'd Rather Have Some Roasting Ears': The Peregrinations of George Armstrong Hicks," *Utah Historical Quarterly* 68, no. 3 (2000): 201. This article is based on the history of George Armstrong Hicks written by him in 1878, which is still held in his family and which Bitton examined meticulously. George Armstrong Hicks, *Family Record and History of George Armstrong Hicks* (n.p.: Kerry J. Zabriskie, 1995), 11.

106. Ouida Blanthorn to author, October 21, 1995, quoting *A Record of Charles W. Hubbard and Descendants, 1810–1955* (privately printed, 1956), 13. Ouida is a great-granddaughter of Charles.

107. William E. Hunter, *Edward Hunter: Faithful Steward*, ed. Janath Russell Cannon (n.p.: Mrs. William E. Hunter, 1970), 79.

108. Rufus David Johnson, *J. E. J. [Joseph Ellis Johnson]: Trail to Sundown* ([Salt Lake City]: Deseret News Press, 1961), 90. Written from personal recollections. Rufus was the last of Joseph's twenty-nine children. See also "True to the Faith," in Carter, *Our Pioneer Heritage*, 15:230–31.

109. Martha S. Hill, "Immigrant Pioneer Women," in *An Enduring Legacy*, comp. Lesson Committee, 12 vols. (Salt Lake City: Daughters of Utah Pioneers, 1977–89), 9:86. Martha is Sophronia's daughter.

110. Florence R. Ellison, "Martha McBride Knight," in *Historical Pamphlet, 1942*, comp. Kate B. Carter (Salt Lake City: Daughters of Utah Pioneers, 1942), 242; see also Martha McBride Knight, in "Biographies of the Belnap and Knight Families," 18, Perry Special Collections, copy in the possession of Della Belnap of Ogden, Utah.

111. Arthur Knight Hafen, "History of Samuel Knight," 1960; copy in the possession of author. Arthur is a grandson of Samuel.

112. Jenson, *Biographical Encyclopedia*, 2:389. This narrative is related by Philomela's granddaughter Samantha T. B. Foley.

113. Juanita [Leavitt] Brooks, *Dudley Leavitt: Pioneer to Southern Utah* (n.p., 1942), 9. Juanita is a granddaughter of Dudley. In her foreword, Brooks writes, "In 1933 I began collecting the diaries and journals of pioneers of the southwest. In many of them I found references to Dudley Leavitt. These, with the material from the family records, have formed the basis of this work."

114. Sarah Studevant Leavitt, "Autobiography of Sarah Studevant Leavitt, April 19, 1875," rev. by Joseph Page Leavitt, April 12, 1978, typescript, 18–19, FHL Archives. Joseph is a grandson of Sarah. See also "Courageous Pioneers," in Carter, *Our Pioneer Heritage*, 7:246.

115. Dollene LeBaron Noson, "Esther Meleta Johnson LeBaron," essay for the Daughters of Utah Pioneers, DUP Archives, copy in possession of the author. Dollene is a granddaughter of Esther.

116. John Doyle Lee, *Mormonism Unveiled; or, The Life and Confessions of the Late Mormon Bishop, John D. Lee* (St. Louis: Bryan and Brand, 1877), 155; see also Juanita Brooks, *John Doyle Lee: Zealot, Pioneer Builder, Scapegoat* (Glendale, Calif.: Arthur H. Clark, 1962), 63. Historian D. Michael Quinn considers Lee's statement as an important witness that Lee had a mystical mantle experience. Quinn states, "John D. Lee's bitter rejection of Brigham Young in later life actually verified the honesty of Mormons who waited years before speaking and writing about Young's transfiguration." Quinn, *Mormon Hierarchy*, 167. When

considering the timing of the mantle experience, one should note that Lee did not arrive in Nauvoo until August 20, 1844, according to his diary. Because of controversy surrounding the publication of Lee's memoirs and because his original manuscript is not available, I have included this account with the secondhand testimonies.

117. Albert R. Lyman, *Amasa Mason Lyman: Trailblazer and Pioneer from the Atlantic to the Pacific*, ed. Melvin A. Lyman (Delta, Utah: Melvin A. Lyman, 1957), 119–20. Amasa Lyman became a counselor to Joseph Smith just before his death. Elder Lyman was asked by Brigham Young to present his case at the August 8 meeting to be considered as Joseph's successor. This rather florid account is based, according to the authors, on information from Amasa Lyman Journals, 23 vols., Church Archives. However, source checkers could find nothing in the journals other than the statement that Lyman spent the day with the brethren, so this account of the transfiguration may come from other family sources.

118. Seymour B. Young, in *Seventy-Sixth Annual Conference of The Church of Jesus Christ of Latter-day Saints* (Salt Lake City: The Church of Jesus Christ of Latter-day Saints, 1906), 12.

119. J. M. Tanner, *A Biographical Sketch of John Riggs Murdock* (Salt Lake City: Deseret News Press, 1909), 71. This biography was written in 1909 by Tanner, a friend of John Riggs Murdock for many years, and was read to Murdock for his approval. See also Barlow, *Israel Barlow Story*, 204.

120. Young, in *Seventy-Sixth Annual Conference*, 12.

121. Jenson, *Biographical Encyclopedia*, 3:191.

122. James Palmer, *James Palmer's Travels and Ministry in the Gospel*, ed. Fannie Palmer (n.p.: Mrs. Fannie Palmer Gleave, 1963), 61. Fannie is a daughter of James. In Palmer's holograph account, he is less specific: "Brigham Young, the President of the Twelve Apostles, came to the front and stated in a public meeting that the Twelve in their organized capacity had the authority and the legal right to preside over the Church in all the world and their rights were acknowledged by the main body of the people." James Palmer, "Journal: James Palmer's Travels and Ministry in the Gospel," holograph, 80, Church Archives.

123. Donald Benson Alder and Elsie L. Alder, comps., *The Benson Family: The Ancestory and Descendants of Ezra T. Benson* (Salt Lake City: Ezra T. Benson Genealogical Society, 1979), 151, which was written from diaries, records, letters, histories, and interviews from family members. This section is quoted from Eliza Perry's diary. Donald is a great-grandson of Eliza's husband Ezra T. Benson through a different wife.

124. Lucy Preece Stewart, "Biography Sketch of Luvera Ellen Ensign Preece," typescript, 2, Margaret Steed Hess Pioneer Histories Collection, Perry Special Collections. Lucy is a daughter of Luvera. Margaret Hess is noted as "Camp Historian."

125. Harriet Smith and Leona L. Adams, "History of Jane Wadley Smith," *John Sivel Smith Family Newsletter*, no. 1 (January 28, 1965): 4, microfiche, FHL Archives.

126. Jenson, *Biographical Encyclopedia*, 3:241–42; Mary Smith Steed Porter, "Brief History of John Sivel Smith," *John Sivel Smith Family Newsletter*, no. 1 (January 28, 1965): 3, microfiche, FHL Archives.

127. Archibald F. Bennett, Ella M. Bennett, and Barbara Bennett Roach, *Valiant in the Faith: Gardner and Sarah Snow and Their Family* (Murray, Utah: Roylance, 1990), 56; Jenson, *Biographical Encyclopedia*, 1:794–95.

128. Jenson, *Biographical Encyclopedia*, 1:794–95.

129. Ruth J. Martin, comp, "Biography of Bishop William Ervin Stoker," *Twentieth Ward History, 1856–1979*, 69, microfilm, FHL Archives.

130. Levi James Taylor, "Pleasant Green Taylor Family Records," typescript, 6, Church Archives. Levi is a son of Pleasant. See also Fred G. Taylor, "Pleasant Green Taylor," in *Outlines of Study, 1942–43*, comp. Kate B. Carter ([Salt Lake City]: Daughters of Utah Pioneers, n.d.), 255–56.

131. Martha Tuttle, quoted in Opal Jackman Harper, Notebook, in possession of Steven Harper, published in Steven C. Harper, ed., "A Testimony Written by Martha Tuttle Gardner," *Nauvoo Journal* 7, no. 2 (Fall 1995): 57–59.

132. "Peter Edmund Van Orden 1830–1911," 2, Van Orden Family Archives, in the possession of Bruce Van Orden, Springville, Utah. This was recorded by an unnamed grandchild of Peter after listening to many of Peter's accounts.

133. Jennie Walker Johnson, "Biography of Henson Walker Jr.," 48, microfilm, FHL Archives.

134. Jenson, *Biographical Encyclopedia*, 1:509.

135. Ella Larsen Turner, *The Ancestors and Descendants of Abraham Daniel Washburn and His Wife Flora Clarinda Gleason* (Provo, Utah: By the author, 1963), 21.

136. Mary W. Fox and Daniel P. Woodland, "Life of William West Woodland," typescript copy in the possession of John W. Welch. Daniel is a son of William.

137. Jenson, *Biographical Encyclopedia*, 1:781–82. See also Florence Woolley Russell, "History of Samuel Amos Woolley, Pioneer of 1848," 2, Church Archives. Florence is a daughter of Samuel.

Appendix

Minutes of Brigham Young's Remarks at the Morning Meeting, August 8, 1844

Skeptics have implied that Thomas Bullock's curious shorthand minutes from the meeting of August 8, 1844 have not been transcribed and made available to historians or general researchers because this text has material that would prove embarrassing to mantle advocates. The following minutes were transcribed in August 1997 at the request of BYU Studies editors and were provided by Church Archives.

Literal Transcription[1]

Pres Young: If I can make the people hear I want their attention a few minutes be perfectly still [--?] you can't hear in the first place I have not asked any man or woman for their following I feel much better than a shiprat and can refrain from weeping [three words crossed out: I have not] I rise to [said/set/st/sd] to this congregation about their support of being in a hurry to transact business here [where/we're/who] are [in/any] laboring under a mistake I am sorry that the [three letters written out: LLS/LDS?] should be in a hurry and as there has been a meeting called for this day to choose for themselves an agent not knowing what has been we have ------- a meeting for next [letter written out: T] I wanted to sit weep for 30 days before the priesthood to business but there is a spirit who shall be greatest in our midst and it will be foiled by that Jehovah and all things will be made right

we are surrounded by enemies come [tkr] this afternoon at 2 and there will be no meeting on [written out: T.] it is not the feelings of my brethren in the name of the people I say we will have a meeting [at two/here] show our hands my private feelings might always bend for the public good the [kmstrts] [west/would] be in that [letter/later/elder] for the general good of all and in regard to the question why [poor/brother] [written out: J.S.] [has been?] in a hurry I [now/no] know for myself and I wish I would hear from every [written out: E. H. O.] and all I want to know where every brother and sister were that [would/will] submit to the organization that is [b/p rt-- tl/tion] a plan the question is asked who will take [written out: J] place he keeps it himself let every man stand in his own place and all will [be peace and harmony] gather together all men and there we can transact business right and when we can get all things right we can [tell you about?] it I want to know what is in them I will [now?] want every man in his [trntl/trntion?] awake up at his post and all things will be right I will say to our brethren the [two letters written out: HC] take their seats by themselves [written out: PM] take his seat here in this seat it will be proper and right for every man be in his place [br.] [letter written out: R] come and take his seat at our right hand then other [letters written out: H.C. then the LB] the other persons in their place this will be the right way [words on fold of paper illegible] resolves and we can do the things [several words on fold of paper illegible] [--] as well as we are we are not going to act against every other and every man and woman will [written out: Amen] meeting to be [end of document]

Edited Transcription

Pres Young: If I can make the people hear, I want their attention a few minutes. Be perfectly still, or you can't hear.

In the first place, I have not asked any man or woman for their following. I feel [not] much better than a shiprat and can [hardly] refrain from weeping. I have not. I rise to [speak] to this congregation about their support.

Of being in a hurry to transact business here. Where are any laboring under a mistake. I am sorry that the LDS should be in a hurry as there has been a meeting called for this day to choose for themselves an agent not knowing what has been [scheduled]. We have a meeting [scheduled] for next T[uesday]. I wanted to sit [and] weep for 30 days before the priesthood [took up] business, but there is a spirit who shall be greatest in our midst and it will be foiled by that Jehovah and all things will be made right.

We are surrounded by enemies. Come [together] this afternoon at 2 and there will be no meeting on T[uesday]. It is not the feelings of my brethren. In the name of the people I say we will have a meeting at two. [We will] show our hands.

My private feelings might always bend for the public good. The [kmstrts] would be in that [leader] for the general good of all.

And in regard to the question why [brother] J.S. [has been?] in a hurry.

I now know for myself.

And I wish I would hear from every E. H. O. and all. I want to know where every brother and sister are that will submit to the organization that is [?] a plan.

The question is asked, Who will take J[oseph's] place? He keeps it himself.

Let every man stand in his own place and all will be [in] peace and harmony.

Gather together all men and there we can transact business right. And when we can get all things right, we can [tell you about?] it. I want to know what is in them. I will [now?] want every man in his [?] awake up at his post and all things will be right.

I will say to our brethren. The H[igh] C[ouncil] take their seats by themselves. PM take his seat here in this seat. It will be proper and right for every man [to] be in his place. Brother R[igdon] come and take his seat at our right hand. Then other H.C. then the L.B. The other persons in their place. This will be the right way.

resolves and we can do the things

as well as we are

we are not going to act against every other, and every man and woman will

Amen.

Meeting to be

Note

1. Transcription by LaJean Purcell Carruth in August 1997, provided by Church Archives, The Church of Jesus Christ of Latter-day Saints, Salt Lake City. Bullock's minutes were written in Taylor Shorthand, a very rudimentary shorthand developed by Samuel Taylor in 1786. This shorthand has no vowels, except a dot may be used to indicate a strong vowel at the beginning or end of a word; this, however, does not indicate which vowel is intended. Words where the transcription is uncertain are indicated by square brackets [ ]. At times the transcriber has included two or more possibilities when it is impossible to determine the most likely one. Taylor does not include any punctuation: the end of a sentence is shown only by a longer space between words, and is often difficult to determine. The transcriber has preserved these spaces. Many sentences are incomplete, some just fragmented phrases, as the recorder apparently struggled to keep up with the speaker.

Further Early Church Historical Documents Originally Published in *BYU Studies*

This bibliography contains a briefly annotated list of articles that have been published in *BYU Studies* relating to many important events in early Church history, generally events which occurred during Joseph Smith's lifetime. These articles contain at least portions of primary oral or written accounts that document additional key events or provide historical context for other divine manifestations in the Restoration. The articles are listed in approximate chronological order of those historical events. All these articles are available for download from http://byustudies.byu.edu.

The First Vision (1820)

Backman, Milton V., Jr. "Awakenings in the Burned-over District: New Light on the Historical Setting of the First Vision." *BYU Studies* 9, no. 3 (1969): 301–20. Study of the evidence of the revival atmosphere in and around Palmyra that led to Joseph's prayer and First Vision.

Anderson, Richard Lloyd. "Circumstantial Confirmation of the First Vision through Reminiscences." *BYU Studies* 9, no. 3 (1969): 373–404. Compares Cowdery's account and other contemporary (1830s) accounts.

The Coming Forth of the Book of Mormon (1823)

Walker, Kyle R. "Katharine Smith Salisbury's Recollections of Joseph's Meetings with Moroni." *BYU Studies* 41, no. 3 (2002): 4–17. Newspaper report of speech given by Joseph Smith's younger sister.

Kimball, Stanley B. "The Anthon Transcript: People, Primary Sources, and Problems." *BYU Studies* 10, no. 3 (1970): 325–52. Discussion of the transcript, as well as analysis of the people involved and the general history and spreading of the story.

Jessee, Dean C. "Joseph Knight's Recollection of Early Mormon History." *BYU Studies* 17, no. 1 (1976): 29–58. Knight's undated "Manuscript of the Early History of Joseph Smith," written sometime after Knight left Missouri in 1833, which treats subjects such as the translating and printing of the Book of Mormon and the organization of the Church.

Jessee, Dean C. "The Original Book of Mormon Manuscript." *BYU Studies* 10, no. 3 (1970): 259–78. History and handwriting analysis of the manuscript with a transcription of three pages.

Ashworth, Brent. "Martin Harris's 1873 Letter to Walter Conrad." *BYU Studies* 23, no. 1 (1983): 112–19. Letter reaffirming Harris's witness of the Book of Mormon.

Rich, Russell R. "The Dogberry Papers and the Book of Mormon." *BYU Studies* 10, no. 3 (1970): 315–20. Comments in the *Reflector* about the "gold bible" and the Book of Mormon.

Jenson, Janet. "Variations between Copies of the First Edition of the Book of Mormon." *BYU Studies* 13, no. 2 (1973): 214–22. Explains typesetting variations in copies of the 1830 edition.

Arrington, Leonard J. "James Gordon Bennett's 1831 Report on 'The Mormonites.'" *BYU Studies* 10, no. 3 (1970): 353–64. Two journal entries (August 7 and 8) and the resulting two-part newspaper article. Gives contemporary description of Hill Cumorah, recounts money-digging, Harris going to Anthon and Mitchill, publishing the Book of Mormon, and impressions of the new religion.

Backman, Milton V., Jr. "Truman Coe's 1836 Description of Mormonism." *BYU Studies* 17, no. 3 (1977): 347–54. An article in the Ohio Observer by a Presbyterian pastor giving a brief history of the

Church beginning with the visions of Moroni, as well as general impressions of the Saints in Kirtland and a few doctrines.

Porter, Larry C. "William E. McLellan's Testimony of the Book of Mormon." *BYU Studies* 10, no. 4 (1970): 485–87. Letter written to James T. Cobb in response to his inquiry trying to establish the falsity of the Book of Mormon.

The Restoration of the Priesthood (1829)

Garr, Arnold K. Review of *Having Authority: The Origins and Development of Priesthood during the Ministry of Joseph Smith* by Gregory A. Prince. *BYU Studies* 37, no. 1 (1997–98): 219–24. Discussion of the restoration and organization of the priesthood in the early days of the Church.

The Organization of the Church (1830)

Peterson, Paul H. Review of *Inventing Mormonism: Tradition and the Historical Record* by Wesley P. Walters and H. Michael Marquardt. *BYU Studies* 35, no. 4 (1996): 209–27. Extensive discussion of when the Smiths moved to Manchester and where the Church was organized on April 6, 1830.

Continuing Revelations from Heaven (1830–44)

Matthews, Robert J. "The New Translation of the Bible, 1830–1833: Doctrinal Development During the Kirtland Era." *BYU Studies* 11, no. 4 (1971): 400–422. Discusses many of the new doctrines received through revelation while Joseph Smith was translating the Bible.

Olson, Earl E. "The Chronology of the Ohio Revelations." *BYU Studies* 11, no. 4 (1971): 329–49. Analysis of the manuscripts, scribes, recording errors, and general history of the revelations received in Ohio.

Lund, Christopher C. "A Letter Regarding the Acquisition of the Book of Abraham." *BYU Studies* 20, no. 4 (1980): 402–3. An 1835 letter giving an account of the purchase of the Egyptian mummies.

Jessee, Dean C., and John W. Welch. "Revelations in Context: Joseph Smith's Letter from Liberty Jail, March 20, 1839." *BYU Studies* 39, no. 3 (2000): 125–45. Complete original text of the letter from which Doctrine and Covenants sections 121–23 are taken.

Larson, Stan. "The King Follett Discourse: A Newly Amalgamated Text." *BYU Studies* 18, no. 2 (1978): 193–208. Compilation from accounts of perhaps Joseph Smith's greatest sermon by Bullock, Clayton, Richards, and Woodruff that differs significantly from the Grimshaw amalgamation of 1855.

Cannon, Donald Q. "The King Follett Discourse: Joseph Smith's Greatest Sermon in Historical Perspective." *BYU Studies* 18, no. 2 (1978):179–92.

Matthews, Robert J. "A Study of the Text of Joseph Smith's Inspired Version of the Bible." *BYU Studies* 9, no. 1 (1968): 3–16. Comparison of the Bernheisel manuscript with the 1867 and 1944 RLDS publications.

Matthews, Robert J. "The Bernhisel Manuscript Copy of Joseph Smith's Inspired Version of the Bible." *BYU Studies* 11, no. 3 (1971): 253–74. Comparison of the original 1833 version with Bernhisel's copy, made in Nauvoo.

Missionary Work and Gathering the Saints (1830–44)

Flake, Lawrence R. "A Shaker View of a Mormon Mission." *BYU Studies* 20, no. 1 (1979): 94–99. Missionary efforts of Oliver Cowdery, Sidney Rigdon, Leman Copley, and Parley P. Pratt to the Shakers near Kirtland as a result of the revelation in D&C 49 and a conversation with Newel K. Knight Jr.

Backman, Milton V., Jr., editor. "A Non-Mormon View of the Birth of Mormonism in Ohio." *BYU Studies* 12, no. 3 (1972): 306–11. Newspaper article written by Josiah Jones of Kirtland, published June 1841 in *The Evangelist*, noting the missionary efforts and subsequent conversion of Sidney Rigdon and others.

Anderson, Richard Lloyd. "The Impact of the First Preaching in Ohio." *BYU Studies* 11, no. 4 (1971): 474–96. Includes a copy of the covenant among the first four missionaries.

Gentry, Leland H. "Light on the 'Mission to the Lamanites.'" *BYU Studies* 36, no. 2 (1996–97): 226–34. Missionary covenant of Oliver Cowdery and others, as well as a February 14, 1831, letter from Cowdery and a February 15, 1831, letter from Indian agent Richard W. Cummins. Both letters are written to the superintendent of Indian affairs requesting permission to establish a mission to the Native Americans.

Slover, Robert H., II. "A Newly Discovered 1838 Wilford Woodruff Letter." *BYU Studies* 15, no. 3 (1975): 349–61. Woodruff's testimony to his brother, including his conversion of his parents and their plans to move to Far West. Also lists the dates of his ordinations, and mentions his new calling to be an Apostle.

Barney, Ronald O. "Letters of a Missionary Apostle to His Wife: Brigham Young to Mary Ann Angell Young, 1839–1841." *BYU Studies* 38, no. 2 (1999): 156–201. Eight letters during the Twelve's mission to England, describing the journey, the conditions in England, some of Brigham's dreams about his family, plans for emigration, and the status of the Church in London.

Allen, James B., and Malcolm R. Thorp. "The Mission of the Twelve to England, 1840–41: Mormon Apostles and the Working Classes." *BYU Studies* 15, no. 4 (1975): 499–526. Recounts missionary experiences of the Twelve while introducing the gospel in England.

Allen, James B. "'We Had a Very Hard Voyage for the Season': John Moon's Account of the First Emigrant Company of British Saints." *BYU Studies* 17, no. 3 (1977): 339–41. Letter describing the emigration voyage of the first British Saints.

Walker, Ronald W. "The Willard Richards and Brigham Young 5 September 1840 Letter from England to Nauvoo." *BYU Studies* 18, no. 3 (1978): 466–75. Describes the social, economic, and religious atmosphere in England and asks about printing Church books.

Esplin, Ronald K. "Inside Brigham Young: Abrahamic Tests as Preparation for Leadership." *BYU Studies* 20, no. 3 (1980): 300–310. Letter of Brigham while on his mission with the Twelve to England and smaller excerpts of letters from shorter, later missions.

Leonard, Glen M. "Letters Home: The Immigrant View from Nauvoo." *BYU Studies* 31, no. 1 (1991): 89–100. Two letters, the first mentioning the Nauvoo Legion and building the Nauvoo House, the second mentioning temple sealing.

Pratt, David H. "Oh! Brother Joseph." *BYU Studies* 27, no. 1 (1987): 127–31. Letter of Parley P. Pratt to the Prophet describing conditions in England.

Walker, Ronald W., and David J. Whittaker. "The Historians' Corner: Brigham Young to Mary Ann Young: August 17, 1843, and Brigham Young to Hiram McKee: May 3, 1860." *BYU Studies* 32, no. 3 (1992): 87–100. Mentions raising money for buildings in Nauvoo and the brethren leaving for missions in England.

The Construction and Keys of the Temple (1832–45)

Erekson, Keith A., and Lloyd D. Newell. "The Conversion of Artemus Millet and His Call to Kirtland." *BYU Studies* 41, no. 2 (2002): 76–115. Documents story of Millet's conversion and subsequent contributions to building the Kirtland Temple.

Van Orden, Bruce A. "Writing to Zion: The William W. Phelps Kirtland Letters (1835–1836)." *BYU Studies* 33, no. 3 (1993): 542–93. Discusses numerous topics, including Joseph's sermons and the Kirtland Temple.

Arrington, Leonard J. "Oliver Cowdery's Kirtland, Ohio, 'Sketch Book.'" *BYU Studies* 12, no. 4 (1972): 410–26. Events leading up to the Kirtland Temple dedication.

Ricks, Stephen D. "The Appearance of Elijah and Moses in the Kirtland Temple and the Jewish Passover." *BYU Studies* 23, no. 4 (1983): 483–86. Meeting of Jewish expectation and Latter-day Saint tradition concerning the appearance of Elijah.

Jessee, Dean C. "The Kirtland Diary of Wilford Woodruff." *BYU Studies* 12, no. 4 (1972): 365–99. Discusses the Kirtland Temple, his marriage to Phebe, and their patriarchal blessings.

Ehat, Andrew F. "'They Might Have Known That He Was Not a Fallen Prophet'—The Nauvoo Journal of Joseph Fielding." *BYU Studies* 19, no. 2 (1979): 133–66. Describes the apostasy of some individuals, the Martyrdom, construction of the temple, the battle of and expulsion from Nauvoo, and the miracle of the quails.

Jessee, Dean C., editor. "The John Taylor Nauvoo Journal: January 1845–September 1845." *BYU Studies* 23, no. 3 (1983): 1–105. Includes the dedication of the Seventies Hall, construction of the temple, and increased mob violence, as well as copies of letters, public documents, and proclamations.

The Character of the Prophet (1820–46)

Anderson, Richard Lloyd. "Joseph Smith's New York Reputation Reappraised." *BYU Studies* 10, no. 3 (1970): 283–314. Comparison of collections of affidavits and interviews from 1834, 1867, 1881, and 1888.

Porter, Larry C. "Solomon Chamberlain—Early Missionary." *BYU Studies* 12, no. 3 (1972): 314–18. Account of Chamberlain meeting Joseph Smith, and of the "gold bible" and missionary work.

Cook, Lyndon W. "'Brother Joseph Is Truly a Wonderful Man, He Is All We Could Wish a Prophet to Be': Pre-1844 Letters of William Law." *BYU Studies* 20, no. 2 (1980): 207–18. Mentions the Prophet's visit to Upper Canada, troubles in Missouri, the return to fellowship of Orson Hyde, and the Kirtland bank.

Jessee, Dean C. "The Writing of Joseph Smith's History." *BYU Studies* 11, no. 4 (1971): 439–74. Analysis of the scribes and the methods of compilation.

Lyon, Thomas Edgar. "Recollections of 'Old Nauvooers': Memories from Oral History." *BYU Studies* 18, no. 2 (1978): 143–50. Nauvooers' memories and testimonies of Joseph Smith recalled from Lyon's youth.

Jessee, Dean C. "Howard Coray's Recollection of Joseph Smith." *BYU Studies* 17, no. 3 (1977): 341–47. Two undated autobiographical manuscripts showing Coray's close association with the Prophet—copying letters and writing the Church's history—and recollections of his words.

Allen, James B. "To the Saints in England: Impressions of a Mormon Immigrant." *BYU Studies* 18, no. 3 (1978): 475–80. Letter from

William Clayton describing his immigration and meeting Joseph Smith.

Clayton, William. "'A Letter to England, 1842.'" Edited by James B. Allen. *BYU Studies* 12, no. 1 (1971): 119–23. Clayton's immigration, feelings about the Church, and meeting Joseph Smith.

Cook, Lyndon W. "'A More Virtuous Man Never Existed on the Footstool of the Great Jehovah': George Miller on Joseph Smith." *BYU Studies* 19, no. 3 (1979): 402–7. Letter witnessing to the character and whereabouts of Joseph in the matter of the assassination attempt on Boggs.

Ashurst-McGee, Mark. "The Josiah Stowell Jr.–John S. Fullmer Correspondence." *BYU Studies* 38, no. 3 (1999): 108–17. Letter requesting and return letter witnessing to the character of Joseph Smith when he was about twenty.

Barney, Ronald O. "'A Man That You Could Not Help Likeing': Joseph Smith and Nauvoo Portrayed in a Letter by Susannah and George W. Taggert." *BYU Studies* 40, no. 2 (2001): 165–79. Description of Joseph and the conditions in Nauvoo.

Woodworth, Jed. "Josiah Quincy's 1844 Visit with Joseph Smith." *BYU Studies* 39, no. 4 (2000): 71–87. Letter from Quincy to his wife describing Nauvoo and his visit with the Prophet.

Cannon, Brian Q. "John C. Calhoun, Jr., Meets the Prophet Joseph Smith Shortly before the Departure for Carthage." *BYU Studies* 33, no. 4 (1993): 772–80. Letter from Calhoun to his brother mentioning his visit to Nauvoo on the day Governor Ford was sent to arrest the Prophet.

Walker, Ronald W. "Lucy Mack Smith Speaks to the Nauvoo Saints." *BYU Studies* 32, no. 1–2 (1992): 276–84. Includes a reprint of an 1845 Nauvoo general conference talk by Mother Smith addressing various subjects, including the early origins of the Church.

The Martyrdom of the Prophet (1844)

Shipps, Jan. "A Little Known Account of the Murders of Joseph and Hyrum Smith." *BYU Studies* 14, no. 3 (1974): 389–92. Letter by Mr. H. H. Bliss describing events leading up to the Martyrdom.

Jones, Dan. "'The Martyrdom of Joseph Smith and His Brother Hyrum.'" Trans. and introduced by Ronald D. Dennis. *BYU Studies* 24, no. 1 (1984): 78–109. Letter and an excerpt from a small book in Welsh detailing the events of the Martyrdom.

Esplin, Ronald K. "Life in Nauvoo, June 1844: Vilate Kimball's Martyrdom Letters." *BYU Studies* 19, no. 2 (1979): 231–40. Two letters describing the tenor of the city before and after the Martyrdom.

Kimball, Stanley B. "Thomas L. Barnes: Coroner of Carthage." *BYU Studies* 11, no. 2 (1971): 141–47. Letters giving an account of the Martyrdom, and a resolution by anti-Mormons in Carthage.

Van Wagoner, Richard, and Steven C. Walker. "The Joseph/Hyrum Smith Funeral Sermon." *BYU Studies* 23, no. 1 (1983): 3–18. Phelps's recollection of his speech.

Jennings, Warren A. "The Lynching of an American Prophet." *BYU Studies* 40, no. 1 (2001): 205–16. Three letters by David Wells Kilbourne in Fort Madison, Iowa, describing events surrounding and after the Martyrdom.

Ellsworth, Paul D. "Mobocracy and the Rule of Law: American Press Reaction to the Murder of Joseph Smith." *BYU Studies* 20, no. 1 (1979): 71–82. Accounts from newspapers across the country.

Succession in the Presidency (1844–46)

Beecher, Maureen Ursenbach. "'All Things Move in Order in the City': The Nauvoo Diary of Zina Diantha Huntington Jacobs." *BYU Studies* 19, no. 3 (1979): 285–320. Describes the events of the martyrdom, the succession of the Presidency, the trial of Joseph's murderers, the building of the temple, and increased persecution.

England, Eugene, editor. "George Laub's Nauvoo Journal." *BYU Studies* 18, no. 2 (1978): 151–78. Recounts sermons of Church leaders including the King Follett discourse. Also includes details of the Martyrdom, the succession and the mantle of Joseph falling on Brigham Young, and the exodus from Nauvoo.

The Exodus to the West

Knight, Gregory R., editor. "Journal of Thomas Bullock (1816–1885): 31 August 1845 to 5 July 1846." *BYU Studies* 31, no. 1 (1991): 5–75. Describes events during the last days of Nauvoo, including mob and state militia actions, temple work, and preparations for moving west.

Beecher, Maureen Ursenbach, editor. "The Iowa Journal of Lorenzo Snow." *BYU Studies* 24, no. 3 (1984): 261–73. Describes traveling from Sugar Creek and settling at Mt. Pisgah.

Dahl, Paul E. "'All Is Well . . .': The Story of 'the Hymn That Went around the World.'" *BYU Studies* 21, no. 4 (1981): 515–27. William Clayton's journal entry for the day he composed "Come, Come, Ye Saints" during the exodus from Nauvoo and a discussion of the tune and its subsequent history.

Cannon, Donald Q. "Thomas L. Kane Meets the Mormons." *BYU Studies* 18, no. 1 (1977): 126–28. Includes Kane's letter describing conditions in Council Bluffs, reasons the Saints would not be leaving for California until the next year, and gives first impressions of the Saints.

Pearson, Carol Lynn. "'Nine Children Were Born': A Historical Problem from the Sugar Creek Episode." *BYU Studies* 21, no. 4 (1981): 441–44. Statement by Jane Johnson gives the circumstances of the last stages of the exodus from Nauvoo.

Historical Name Index

H

I

J